Internet Communications and Management

Internet Communications and Management

Edited by **Grant Harper**

New York

Published by Willford Press,
118-35 Queens Blvd., Suite 400,
Forest Hills, NY 11375, USA
www.willfordpress.com

Internet Communications and Management
Edited by Grant Harper

International Standard Book Number: 978-1-68285-187-6 (Hardback)

Printed in the United States of America.

Contents

Permissions

List of Contributors

Preface

This book aims to highlight the current researches and provides a platform to further the scope of innovations in this area. This book is a product of the combined efforts of many researchers and scientists from different parts of the world. The objective of this book is to provide the readers with the latest information in the field.

The rapid progress in internet services and its applications have transformed the world into a digital book. This book is a compilation of chapters that discuss the most vital concepts and emerging trends in the field of internet communications. Some of the diverse topics covered in this book address the varied branches that fall under this category, such as networking protocols, web protocols, cloud computing, internet of things, networking architecture, etc. This book is meant for students who are looking for an elaborate reference text on internet communications. As this field is emerging at a rapid pace, the contents of this book will help the readers understand the modern concepts and applications of the subject.

I would like to express my sincere thanks to the authors for their dedicated efforts in the completion of this book. I acknowledge the efforts of the publisher for providing constant support. Lastly, I would like to thank my family for their support in all academic endeavors.

Editor

An efficient selection algorithm for building a super-peer overlay

Meirong Liu*, Erkki Harjula and Mika Ylianttila

Abstract

Super-peer overlay provides an efficient way to run applications by exploring the heterogeneity of nodes in a Peer-to-Peer overlay network. Identifying nodes with high capacity as super-peers plays an important role in improving the performance of P2P applications, such as live streaming. In this paper, we present a super-peer selection algorithm (SPS) to select super-peers for quickly building a super-peer overlay. In the SPS, each peer periodically builds its set of super-peer candidates through gossip communication with its neighbors, in order to select super-peers and client peers. Simulation results demonstrate that the SPS is efficient in selecting super-peers, and in quickly building a super-peer overlay. The proposed SPS also possesses good scalability and robustness to failure of super-peers.

Keywords: Peer-to-Peer, Super-peer, Overlay, Gossip

1. Introduction

Peer-to-Peer (P2P) overlay technologies have been widely applied for constructing large-scale network applications and services (*e.g.*, Skype [1], BitTorrent [2], Gnutella [3], and PPLive [4]) because of their inherent decentralization and redundant structures [5,6]. A lot of efforts have been made on P2P overlay construction (*e.g.*, [7-12]). Super-peer overlay (*e.g.*, Kazaa [13]) is an important type of P2P overlay. In a super-peer overlay, there are two types of peers: client peers and super-peers. Each client peer should connect to a super-peer in order to communicate with other peers in the overlay. A super-peer acts as the centralized server for its client peers and connects to other super-peers in the same way as in the pure P2P network [14]. Client peers with low capacity are shielded from massive query traffic by super-peers, which improves the scalability of the system and makes it feasible to connect *e.g.*, mobile devices to a P2P network. In the paper, the capacity of a peer refers to the combination of its available computational resource, network connections, and lifespan in the network.

Super-peer overlay enables applications to run more efficiently by exploring the heterogeneity of nodes in the

overlay network. For example, in file sharing applications (*e.g.*, Gnutella [3]), Skype voice streaming, and live video streaming applications [15], the performance of these applications is improved through assigning nodes with high network bandwidth, long on-line time, or high processing capability as super-peers. Thus, super-peer selection in a given overlay is an important issue when building a super-peer overlay. On the other hand, particularly in dynamic network environment, it is common that peers join or leave (*e.g.*, a failure of a super-peer) a super-peer overlay [9,16,17]. To achieve a robust overlay, it should also be taken into account how to handle the failure of peers in the super-peer overlay construction. Therefore, efficient super-peer selection method in order to quickly build a robust super-peer overlay is an important research issue.

Many studies have been undertaken on building a super-peer overlay [7,8,10,12,14,18-22]. The principles and guidance of designing a super-peer overlay were addressed by Kirk [3] and Yang *et al.* [14], but no experimental results were reported. Some efforts utilized network proximity for building a super-peer overlay, *e.g.*, [8,12,18,21]. Client peers are connected with super-peers based on their distances. However, these studies focused on reducing communication latency between nodes by exploring network proximity rather than the efficiency of quickly building a super-peer overlay by exploring the

* Correspondence: meirong.liu@ee.oulu.fi
Media Team Oulu research group, Department of Computer Science and Engineering, University of Oulu, Oulu, Finland

capacity of nodes. Super-peer selection has to make a trade-off between reducing communication latency and selecting powerful super-peers. Other studies investigated the semantic similarity of peers when building a super-peer overlay, e.g., [7,10,23]. Client peers that share the same interest are connected to same super-peers. However, these studies aimed to improve the search efficiency rather than the efficiency of quickly building a robust super-peer overlay. In addition, some super-peers could be overloaded because of popular content. The connections between super-peers and client peers in a super-peer overlay were also investigated [19,22,24,25]. However, these studies assumed that a super-peer overlay already exists and focused on managing an existing overlay instead of building an initial super-peer overlay. Wang et al. [15] presented a Labeled Tree to build a super-peer overlay. However, they aimed to achieve reliable high speed transmission in live stream rather than the efficiency of quickly building a super-peer overlay. In their study, super-peers are selected only based on the online-time, which did not take account of other information of nodes, e.g., processing capacity, bandwidth. Montresor [11] proposed a gossip based algorithm SG-1 for the efficiency of quickly building a super-peer overlay. In SG-1, peers decide whether they should take a role of a super-peer by comparing their capacities with a randomly sampled neighbor peer, which is simple but takes long time to select needed super-peers. A super-peer searches and adds client peers only among its one-hop neighbors. All the peers in the overlay take the role of a super-peer in the beginning of the overlay construction.

In this paper, we focus on studying the efficiency of quickly building a robust super-peer overlay by taking account of capacity of nodes. Only peers that have high capacity (compared to neighbor peers) are selected as super-peers. The reason for this is that peers with a high capacity can contribute more to applications and enable applications to run more efficiently [3,15]. To this end, we present an efficient super-peer selection algorithm (SPS) to select peers with high capacity as super-peers for quickly building a robust super-peer overlay.

In the SPS algorithm, each peer maintains a set of super-peer candidates. Peers disseminate the information of super-peer candidates through a gossip method Newscast [26], which is efficient in information dissemination and enables peers to capture the dynamicity of a P2P overlay as well. Each peer periodically rebuilds its set of super-peer candidates and decides whether it takes the role of a super-peer based on its set of super-peer candidates, which differs from the super-peer selection method presented in SG-1 [11]. After that, peers execute the corresponding operations according to their roles: joining a super-peer or recruiting client peers. In the SPS, all the peers act as a client peer in the beginning of the overlay construction.

Overall, the proposed SPS algorithm has the following contributions:

(1) The SPS algorithm introduces a set of super-peer candidates for each peer to select super-peers, which enables the algorithm to select peers with high capacity as super-peers and consequently reduces the time of super-peer selection.
(2) The SPS algorithm employs a conditional two-top search method for super-peers to find and add client peers, which reduces both the time for building an overlay and the communication overhead.
(3) The SPS algorithm achieves a comparable robustness, and better performance in terms of convergence time, scalability, compared to related work SG-1 [11].

This paper extends our previous work [20]. In this paper, we provide a more in-depth development and analysis of our SPS algorithm. We also carry out additional experiments to evaluate the performance of our SPS algorithm compared to related work SG-1 [11]. The remainder of the paper is organised as follows: in Section 2, we briefly explain a communication method, called Newscast, utilized by the SPS, and present the SPS algorithm. In Section 3, we evaluate performance of the SPS in terms of convergence time, communication overhead, scalability, and robustness. In Section 4, we conclude the paper with future directions.

2. The SPS algorithm

In this section, we first give the background of a gossip based communication method utilized in the SPS (called Newscast [26]), and then present the design rationale. After that, we provide the general idea of the SPS algorithm. Finally, we depict the details of the SPS algorithm for super-peer overlay construction. We consider a set of nodes connected through an existing network, and assume that each node stores identifiers of its neighbors. Each node can directly or indirectly communicate with other nodes via its neighbors. In this paper, we consider a dynamic network environment and nodes may join or leave the overlay network at anytime. A node's information, such as its identifier, available resources, current role (i.e., client peer or super-peer), neighbors, and lifespan are assumed to be disseminated through Newscast. A peer can capture the dynamicity of the network through message exchange of Newscast.

2.1. Background of a communication method utilized by the SPS algorithm

In our work, we use Newscast [26] (a gossip protocol that maintains a dynamic random topology) for information dissemination between peers. Newscast has been used for P2P applications, such as broadcast [24] and aggregation [26] for its effective information dissemination. Furthermore, Newscast is designed for dynamic environment and enables peers to capture the dynamicity of an overlay, e.g., joining of a new node or leaving of a node [26].

The general idea of Newscast is as follows: in Newscast, each node maintains a partial view that is constituted of a fixed-size set of peer descriptors. A peer descriptor is composed of the information of the address of a node, a timestamp identifying when the descriptor is created, and application specific information. Each node periodically exchanges and merges its partial view with a randomly selected node to get an up-to-date partial view and a better approximation of the target topology. More information can be found in Jelasity et al. [26].

2.2. Design rationale

We build a super-peer overlay as an additional overlay imposed on top of an existing connected topology (i.e., a random graph), which is maintained by Newscast. In a random graph, peers are randomly connected with each other. The neighborhood of a node in the SPS algorithm is set as follows: if a node is a super-peer, it connects to a random sample of other super-peers and to the set of client peers that are managed by this super-peer. If a node is a client peer, it connects to only one super-peer. The initial role of all the nodes is a client peer. The SPS uses a node's capacity as a criterion for selecting a super-peer candidate and a super-peer. The SPS selects as few super-peers as possible when building a super-peer overlay, which aims to maximize the contribution of nodes with high capacity. Inspired by the method called VoRonoi Regions for mobile network [27], the SPS selects super-peers first during the super-peer overlay construction. Note that the reason for building a super-peer overlay on top of a connected overlay is to avoid a danger of disconnection if a large number of super-peers are failed.

The SPS overlay interacts with the Newscast overlay (i.e., the connected overlay) to disseminate information of the set of super-peer candidates utilized by the SPS. Specifically, when a node disseminates the information of a set of super-peer candidates (which contains samples of super-peer candidates), this node needs to interact with Newscast overlay to get a random peer from the connected Newscast overlay. Then, this node sends its partial view to the randomly selected node to exchange and update their descriptors. Finally, the descriptor of this node contains not only an identifier, a time stamp, but also a set of super-peer candidates, which in its turn is used by the upper SPS overlay for selecting super-peers.

2.3. Overview of the SPS algorithm

The general idea of the SPS algorithm for selecting super-peers and client peers is as follows: all the nodes in the overlay periodically perform operations (1) and (2) described below until the super-peer overlay is built.

(1) A node n_i rebuilds its super-peer candidates CanSP (n_i) through communication with its neighbors for their super-peer candidates. Nodes with higher capacity (chosen from retrieved super-peer candidates) are promoted as super-peer candidates (i.e., added into CanSP(n_i)).

(2) By checking whether there is a change in the rebuilt CanSP(n_i) retrieved in (1) (i.e., whether new super-peer candidates are rebuilt into CanSP(n_i) or not), n_i will perform one of the operations (a) or (b) given below.

(a) If there are new super-peer candidates added in CanSP(n_i), n_i notifies its neighbors of the new super-peer candidates and has its role determined again. Specifically, if n_i is a client peer and belongs to CanSP(n_i), n_i changes its role to become a super-peer. If n_i is a super-peer but it does not belong to CanSP(n_i), n_i changes its role to become a client peer and transfers its client peers (if any) to other super-peers.

(b) If CanSP(n_i) is not changed, n_i proceeds as follows: if n_i is a super-peer, it searches and adds client peers until n_i is fully loaded or no more client peers can be found. If n_i is a client peer and belongs to CanSP(n_i), n_i changes its role to become a super-peer. If n_i is a client peer and does not belong to CanSP(n_i), and has not joined a super-peer, n_i searches and joins a super-peer.

Note that initially each node n_i takes the role of a client peer and sets its super-peer candidates CanSP(n_i) to be itself and its super-peer to be null. Then, each node starts to perform the SPS algorithm described above to build a super-peer overlay. The super-peer candidates of each node are rebuilt periodically and the role of each node could be changed dynamically during the super-peer overlay construction. When a new node n_i joins the overlay, it declares itself as a client peer, sets its super-peer candidates CanSP(n_i) to be itself and its super-peer to be null. Then, this node executes the SPS algorithm.

2.4. Detailed description of the SPS

Before presenting the details of the SPS algorithm, the notations used in the SPS are summarized as follows:

(1) n_i denotes a node in an N-node P2P overlay network. n_i has only one of the exclusive roles: client peer or super-peer. n_i has two optional states, i.e., State(n_i) = {normal, failed}. The former denotes that n_i is part of the overlay without suffering from a failure, and the latter denotes that n_i is failed. Each client peer maintains three sets of data: its neighbors, its super-peer, and a set of super-peer candidates. Each super-peer in its turn maintains the data of its neighbors, a set of super-peer candidates, and a set of client peers.

(2) SP(n_i) denotes the super-peer of node n_i.

(3) C(n_i) represents the capacity of node n_i. C(n_i) is the aggregation of three resource metrics: computational resource (CPU cycles, storage), network bandwidth, and lifespan. It is represented as follows:

$$C(n_i) = \sum_{k=1}^{3} w_k * v_k, \qquad (1)$$

where w_k is the weight of the kth resource metric, and v_k is the value of the kth resource metric. Each metric of C(n_i) has a different weight, which can be set according to specific applications. The value of C(n_i) is set in the beginning of building a super-peer overlay. For simplicity, we omit computation details of C(n_i) and assign the number of client peers that n_i can manage to C(n_i), which does not affect the presentation of the SPS.

(4) CanSP(n_i) denotes the set of super-peer candidates of n_i. It is used to judge the role of n_i. Nodes with high capacity are promoted as super-peer candidates. The number of super-peer candidates included in CanSP(n_i) is computed as: $\frac{overlay size}{super-peers' maximum capacity}$. Each node stores the overlay size and computes the number of super-peer candidates when building a super-peer overlay. It should be noted that in real life, the overlay size is retrieved by utilizing an underlying gossip aggregation protocol to compute the number of nodes in the overlay.

(5) Ld(n_i) denotes the workload of node n_i, which shows how many client peers is managed by n_i. If the workload Ld(n_i) is lower than C(n_i), n_i is set as under-loaded, otherwise n_i is set as full-loaded.

Figures 1 and 2 show the detailed actions of a client peer and a super-peer that are running the SPS algorithm for building a super-peer overlay. Table 1 summarizes all the basic operations used in Figures 1 and 2. According to Figure 1, a client peer n_i running the SPS algorithm acts as follows: (1) in the case when n_i has joined a super-peer SP(n_i): if SP(n_i) is failed, n_i calls a super-peer-failure handler, otherwise n_i does nothing. (2) In the case when n_i has not joined a super-peer, (2.1) n_i checks whether there is a message about a failed super-peer. If there is such a message, n_i removes the failed super-peer from CanSP(n_i). (2.2) n_i checks whether there is a message about a new set of super-peer candidates. If such a message exits, n_i updates its CanSP(n_i). (2.3) n_i checks whether the super-peer candidates of its neighbors have higher capacity than its CanSP(n_i). If the super-peer candidates of n_i's neighbors have higher capacity than CanSP(n_i), n_i retrieves a new CanSP(n_i) based on super-peer candidates of its neighbors and has its role judged again according to the new CanSP(n_i). Otherwise, n_i searches and joins a super-peer.

As shown in Figure 2, an under-loaded super-peer n_i running the SPS algorithm proceeds as follows: (1) similar to the operation of a client peer shown in Figure 1, super-peer n_i checks whether there is a message about a new set of super-peer candidates. If such a message exits, n_i updates its CanSP(n_i). (2) Similar to the operation of a client peer shown in Figure 1 again, super-peer n_i also checks whether super-peer candidates of its

---

Input: A client peer n_i
Operation:
if SP(n_i) ≠ null **then**
    if State(SP(n_i)) ==failed **then**
     SPFailureHandler(n_i).
    else Do nothing and return.
    end if
else
    RemoveFailedSPIfExist(n_i).
    if *UpdSP* = RetriveUpdateSPc(n_i) **then**
     UpdateSPCandidates(n_i , *UpdSP*).
    end if
    if ExistBiggerSPCandidate(n_i) ==true **then**
    CanSP(n_i) = RetrieveNewSPCandidates(n_i).
    NotifyNewSPcandidates(n_i).
     if $n_i \in$ CanSP(n_i) **then**
      ChangeRole(n_i).
     end if
    else
     if $n_i \notin$ CanSP(n_i) **then**
      Search&JoinUnderLoadedSP(n_i).
     else
      ChangeRole(n_i).
     end if
    end if
end if

Figure 1 The action of a client peer running the SPS.

Input: A super-peer n_i and n_i is under-loaded
Operation:
if $UpdSP$ = RetriveUpdateSPc(n_i) **then**

UpdateSPCandidates(n_i , $UpdSP$).

end if

if ExistBiggerSPCandidate(n_i) == true **then**

CanSP(n_i) = RetriveNewSPCandidates(n_i).

NotifyNewSPcandidates(n_i).

if $n_i \notin$ CanSP(n_i) **then**

TransferClients(n_i).

ChangeRole(n_i).

end if

else

AddClientnodes(n_i).

end if

Figure 2 The action of a super-peer running the SPS.

neighbors have higher capacity than its CanSP(n_i). If the super-peer candidates of n_i's neighbors have higher capacity than CanSP(n_i), n_i retrieves a new CanSP(n_i) and has its role determined based on the new CanSP(n_i). If n_i cannot keep the role of super-peer, n_i transfers its client peers (if any) to other super-peers and changes its role to be a client peer. In contrast, if super-peer candidates of n_i's neighbors do not havehigher capacity than CanSP(n_i), the role of n_i is not changed. Then, n_i searches and adds client peers until n_i is fully loaded or no more client peers can be found.

Note that the operation AddClientnodes(n_i) (shown in Figure 2) employs a conditional two-hop search method for a super-peer to find client peers. That is, n_i increases search step from one hop to two hops in the condition of a worst case. Herein, the worst case is that a super-peer n_i manages some client peers and n_i finds that all neighbors of n_i have joined super-peers after it searches its neighbors. The worst case would increase the convergence time of building a super-peer overlay dramatically if only one-hop search method is used.

In the face of the worst case described above, if n_i changes its role to be a client peer and searches a super-peer, both the convergence time of the SPS algorithm and the network traffic would increase. Specifically, on one hand, n_i needs to transfer its client peers to other super-peers, which would increase the network traffic. On the other hand, after n_i changes its role to be a client peer, n_i needs to perform the SPS algorithm to find a super-peer, which in its turn would increase the

Table 1 The primitive operations used in the SPS algorithm

Operation	Description
AddClientnodes(n_i)	Node n_i adds client nodes until n_i is full-loaded or no more client nodes can be found. Specifically, n_i first searches its neighbors to find and add nodes. After that, if n_i is still under-loaded, n_i searches its neighbors' neighbors to find and add client nodes.
ChangeRole(n_i)	Node n_i changes its role.
ExistBiggerSPCandidate(n_i)	n_i sends messages to its neighbors to check whether its neighbors' super-peer candidates have higher capacity than CanSP(n_i). If that is the case, true is returned. Otherwise, false is returned.
NotifyNewSPcandidates (n_i)	n_i notifies its neighbors to update their sets of super-peer candidates to be CanSP(n_i).
RetriveUpdateSPc(n_i)	Node n_i checks whether there is a message about new super-peer candidates $UpdSP$. If such a message exists, $UpdSP$ is returned. Otherwise, null is returned.
RetriveNewSPCandidates(n_i)	Node n_i computes its new set of super-peer candidates CanSP(n_i) according to its retrieved set of super-peer candidates through communication with its neighbors.
RemoveFailedSPIfExist(n_i).	Node n_i checks whether there is a message about super-peer failure. If such a message exists, the failed super-peer contained in the message is removed from the super-peer candidates of n_i.
Search&JoinUnderLoadedSP(n_i)	Node n_i sends query messages to super-peers contained in its super-peer candidates to check these nodes' workloads. If a super-peer that is under-loaded is found, n_i joins this super-peer.
SPFailureHander(n_i)	When the super-peer of n_i (i.e., SP(n_i)) fails, n_i removes SP(n_i) from its set of super-peer candidates and empties its super-peer. n_i also notifies its neighbors of the failure of SP(n_i).
TransferClients(n_i)	When a super-peer n_i has to change its role to be a client peer, n_i transfers its client peers (if any) to super-peers that are randomly selected from its set of CanSP(n_i).
UpdateSPCandidates(n_i,$UpdSP$)	Node n_i updates its set of super-peer candidates to be $UpdSP$, which is an ordinary set to store updated super-peer candidates.

convergence time of the SPS. In contrast, when n_i increases the search step conditionally to two hops, a faster convergence time at the expense of network traffic is achieved by the SPS. Specifically, n_i searches the neighbors of its neighbors to find more client nodes in the face of the worse case, which reduces the convergence time of building a super-peer overlay. On the other hand, only a little more communication overhead is generated when increasing the search step conditionally to two hops, because super-peers that perform the two-hop search take only a very small portion of the whole peers. More importantly, our work aims to quickly build a super-peer overlay. Thus, we employ a conditional two-hop search method for a super-peer to find client peers in AddClientnodes(n_i).

3. Performance evaluation

In this section, we describe simulations conducted for evaluating the feasibility and performance of the SPS algorithm. First, we introduce experimental settings. Then, we evaluate performance of the SPS from four aspects: convergence time, communication overhead, scalability, and robustness, respectively.

3.1. Experimental setup

We use PeerSim [28] to carry out simulations. In PeerSim, one simulation round means that all the nodes finish performing deployed protocols once. Four performance metrics are emphasized in the experiments: (1) convergence time of the SPS and the impact of parameters (e.g., the maximum capacity of super-peers) on the SPS's convergence time, compared to related work SG-1 [11]; (2) communication overhead compared to SG-1; (3) scalability in comparison to SG-1, and (4) the SPS's robustness to failure of super-peers compared to SG-1. The overlay size for simulations is set as 10^5 unless separately specified. All the peers take the role of client peer in the beginning of simulations. The initial overlay topology adopted in the simulation is a random graph, where all the peers are randomly connected with each other. The initial random graph topology provides a good chance to verify the efficiency of the SPS because the initial overlay is far from the converged super-peer overlay.

3.2. Evaluation of the convergence time

In this section, we evaluate how fast the SPS can converge, and how parameters affect the convergence time of the SPS. Two types of distributions for nodes' capacity are evaluated: the uniform distribution and the power-law distribution. Simulation results are depicted in Figures 3 and 4.

Figure 3 shows the convergence of the SPS, i.e., the variation of the number of client peers that have joined super-peers as the simulation goes on. It should be noted that simulations converge in the condition that

no more client peers will join a super-peer. Specifically, when the capacity of peers follows the uniform distribution, it takes about 7 simulation rounds for all the client peers to finish selecting and joining super-peers (i.e., building a super-peer overlay). When the capacity of peers follows the power-law distribution, it takes about 4 rounds. The results show that the SPS performs well when measured with the convergence time for building a super-peer overlay. At simulation round 4, client peers that have joined super-peer in uniform distribution are almost the same as those in power-law distribution. However, in uniform distribution, the SPS algorithm continues running until by simulation round 7 because there are still nodes that have not joined super-peers at simulation round 4. This result shows that different distributions of peers' capacity lead to different convergence times (i.e., different numbers of needed simulation rounds). In other words, distribution of peers has an impact on the convergence time (i.e., simulation rounds) of the SPS algorithm [29]. The number of selected super-peers in power-law distribution is 370 according to the SPS algorithm. In contrast, the number of selected super-peers in uniform distribution is only 201. The reason is that in power-law distribution, only a small portion of peers have a relatively high capacity, and more super-peers are selected for managing client-peers when building the super-peer overlay. The result shows that the number of selected super-peers is related to the distribution of peers' capacity.

Figure 4 shows the impact of super-peers' maximum capacity on the SPS's convergence time compared to SG-1 [11]. Figure 4a depicts the number of selected super-peers in the target super-peer overlay as maximum capacity of super-peers increases. Figure 4b illustrates the number of needed simulation rounds for convergence as maximum capacity of super-peers increases.

The result shown in Figure 4a is as expected: the larger the maximum capacity of super-peers (i.e., a super-peer can manage more client peers according to the capacity defined in Section 2.2), the fewer super-peers are selected in the converged super-peer overlay.

According to Figure 4b, when the maximum capacity of super-peers increases, more simulation rounds are needed for convergence. Specifically, the SPS takes a few more simulation rounds to converge (i.e., from 8 to 9 rounds), but SG-1 gains an obvious increase in simulation rounds for convergence (i.e., from 8 to 14 rounds). This result shows that the SPS is less affected by the variation of super-peers' maximum capacity compared to SG-1.

The reason for different convergence times between the SPS and SG-1 is that different super-peer selection and search methods are used in the SPS and SG-1.

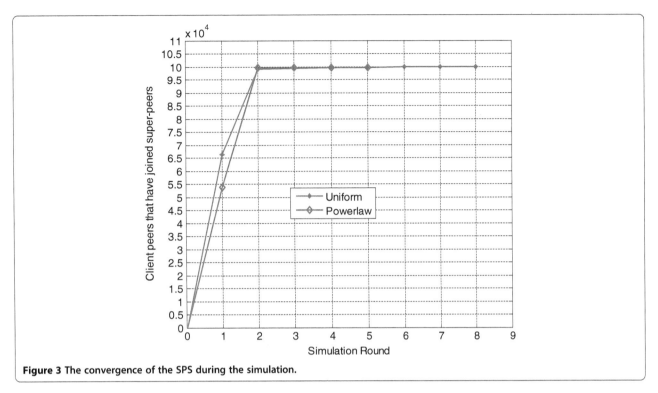

Figure 3 The convergence of the SPS during the simulation.

Specifically, when the maximum capacity of super-peers increases (*i.e.,* a super-peer can manage more client peers), the number of the required super-peers decreases. In the SPS, a set of super-peer candidates is built for selecting peers with very high capacity as super-peers, and a conditional two-hop search method is employed for super-peers to quickly find client peers. Even when the number of the required super-peers decreases, most of the super-peers can still be selected through super-peer candidates during the first few simulation rounds. As soon as super-peers are selected, client

peers can quickly join a super-peer and super-peers can quickly find and add client peers with a conditional two-hop search method (which makes the SPS converge even faster). However, for SG-1, when the number of the required super-peers decreases, more super-peers need to change their role to be client peers, since the initial role of all the peers is a super-peer. Moreover, super-peers only compare their capacities with one of their neighbors to determine their role and search client peers among its one-hop neighbors. Thus, it requires more simulation rounds of message exchanges to finish

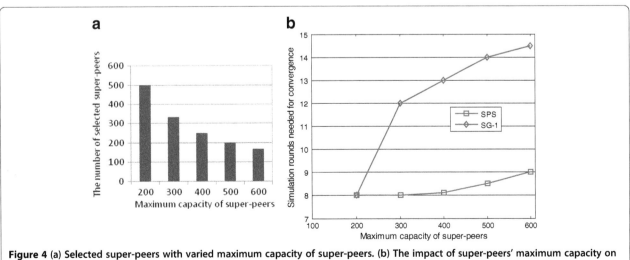

Figure 4 (a) Selected super-peers with varied maximum capacity of super-peers. (b) The impact of super-peers' maximum capacity on the convergence time.

selecting super- peers. Therefore, it takes longer for SG-1 to converge compared to the SPS when the maximum capacity of super-peers increases.

3.3. Evaluation of the communication overhead

In this section, we evaluate the communication overhead, *i.e.,* the number of messages that are transmitted between peers during a super-peer overlay construction. Three types of communication overhead are evaluated: (1) the total number of probes per node for query about the load of neighbor super-peers, (2) the number of gossip messages per node for building super-peer candidates, and (3) the number of client peer transfers per node. Herein, the term client peer transfer means that client peers are transferred to other super-peers when their super-peers change their roles to be a client peer. For simplicity, we use the average value of these three types of communication overhead for presenting results. Figure 5 shows the results and the comparison between the SPS and SG-1.

According to Figure 5, one can find out that: (1) for the SPS algorithm, the number of probes is independent from the overlay size and approximately one probe per node is sent for query about workload of super-peer (as shown in Figure 5a. (2) Taking account of the total communication overhead (*i.e.,* the sum of the three types of communication overhead), as shown in Figure 5a and b, the SPS is comparable to SG-1. Specifically, the number of communication messages generated in the SPS for building super-peer candidates per node is a little bit

large. However, the number of client peer transfers in the SPS (*i.e.,* 0.04 on average) is much smaller than that of SG-1 (*i.e.,* 9.5 on average). In other words, maintaining the set of super-peer candidates in the SPS generates more communication overhead; nevertheless it makes a significant positive effect on reducing the number of client peer transfers (as shown in Figure 5b).

The reason for the much lower number of client transfers in the SPS compared to SG-1 is as follows: the SPS selects peers with the highest capacity among its neighbors to be super-peer candidates and then picks up super-peers from the super-peer candidates. Thus, only a small portion of super-peers change their roles to be a client peer and the number of transferred client peers (because of role change of these super-peers) is low. However, in SG-1, one peer exchanges gossip messages with randomly selected neighbors to decide whether it keeps the role of super-peer or changes its role to be a client peer. Thus, one peer could frequently change its role when it compares its capacity with different neighbors. Consequently, client peers managed by these super-peers generate a large number of client peer transfers.

3.4. Evaluation of the scalability

In this section, we verify the scalability of the SPS in terms of convergence time. In other words, we examine the variation of the SPS's convergence time while the number of peers increases from 1,000 to 100,000. Two types of distributions for peers' capacity are examined:

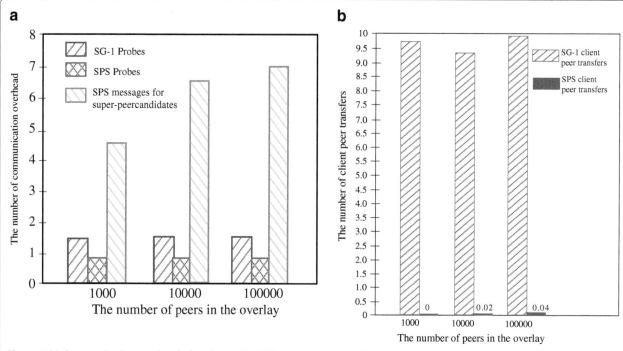

Figure 5 (a) Communication overhead of probes and building super-peer candidates. (b) Communication overhead of client peer transfers.

the power-law distribution and the uniform distribution. In addition, we compare the scalability of the SPS with that of SG-1. Figure 6 and Table 2 show the results and the comparison between SPS and SG-1.

According to Figure 6 and Table 2, one can find out that: (1) the SPS scales well and the number of needed simulation rounds for building a super-peer overlay grows gradually when the number of peers increases from 1,000 to 100,000. Specifically, the number of simulation rounds increases from 2.0 to 7.0 rounds for the uniform distribution, and from 3.0 to 12.0 rounds for the power-law distribution. (2) The deviation on the simulation rounds for convergence in the SPS is smaller than that in SG-1 when the total number of peers in the overlay increases (as shown in Table 2). For example, for the uniform distribution, the number of simulation rounds in the SPS increases from 2.0 to 7.0 rounds with a standard deviation of 2.5, and it increases from 7.0 to 19.0 rounds with a standard deviation of 6.0 in SG-1, as shown in Table 2. This result shows that the SPS has better scalability than SG-1.

The rationale behind result (1) mentioned above is that although there is a huge increase in the number of nodes in the overlay, most of the required super-peers can still be selected during the first few simulation rounds by all the peers executing the SPS algorithm. The rest of the required super-peers can be selected in the following simulation rounds. After that, client peers join super-peers, and super-peers search and add client peers using a conditional two-hop search (as explained in the end of Section 2). Therefore, the increase in the

overlay size has only a little impact on the needed simulation rounds for building a super-peer overlay.

The reason for result (2) mentioned above, is as follows: in the SPS, most of the required super-peers can be selected in the first few simulation rounds using the set of super-peer candidates. As soon as super-peers are identified, client peers can join super-peers and super-peers can search for client peers. However, for SG-1, when the overlay size increases, firstly, more super-peers need to change their roles to be client peers since the initial role of all the nodes is a client peer. Hence, more simulation rounds are inflicted on the convergence time. Secondly and more importantly, in SG-1, super-peers only compare their capacities with one of their neighbors to determine their role, which increases the time of selecting peers with high capacity as the target super-peers and the convergence time. In addition, in SG-1, a super-peer n_i only searches client peers among its one-hop neighbors. When n_i is still under-loaded after searching all its one-hop neighbors, n_i has to wait for client peers to join it. Thus, it takes longer for n_i to find client peers. As the overlay size increases, nodes like n_i increase and much more time is required for SG-1 to converge. Taking into account the three factors mentioned above, it takes longer for SG-1 to build a super-peer overlay when the overlay size increases.

3.5. Evaluation of the robustness
In this section, we verify the robustness of the SPS in the face of super-peers' failure and compare the result with that of SG-1. We examine three catastrophic

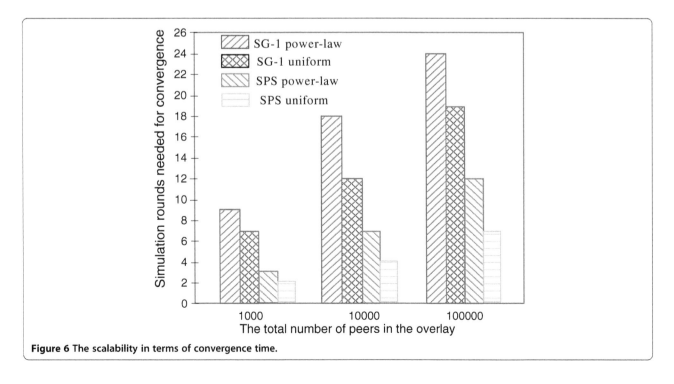

Figure 6 The scalability in terms of convergence time.

Table 2 Scalability of the SPS compared to SG-1

Algorithm	Capacity distribution	Simulation rounds needed with 1,000 peers	Simulation rounds needed with 10,000 peers	Simulation rounds needed with 10,0000 peers	Standard deviation of the simulation rounds needed as the overlay size increases
The SPS	Uniform	2.0	4.0	7.0	2.5
	Power-law	3.0	7.0	12.0	4.5
SG-1	Uniform	7.0	12.0	19.0	6,0
	Power-law	9.0	18.0	24.0	7.6

scenarios: (a) 10% of super-peers are removed at the sixth simulation round, (b) 20% of super-peers are removed at the sixth simulation round, and (c) 30% of super-peers are removed at the sixth simulation round. Results are shown in Figure 7 and Table 3.

According to Figure 7 and Table 3, one can find out that: the robustness of SPS is comparable to SG-1 in the face of super-peer failure when taking into account both the convergence time and the impact of super-peers' failure on client peers. For example, in the case of the

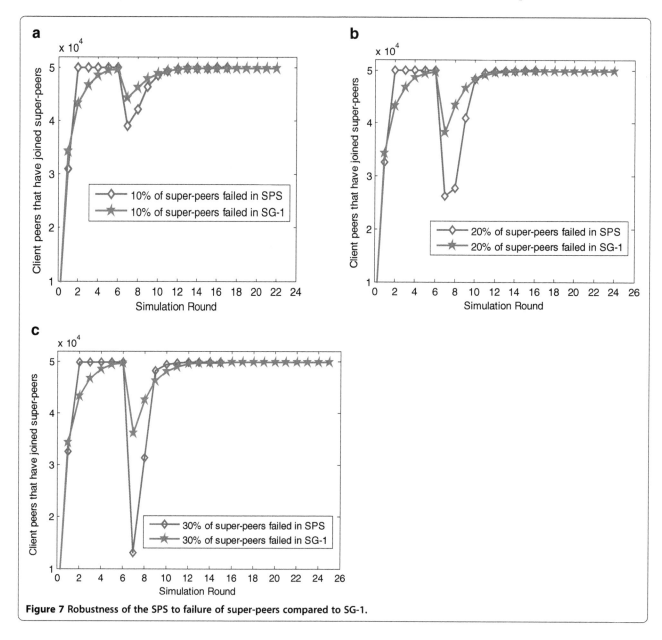

Figure 7 Robustness of the SPS to failure of super-peers compared to SG-1.

Table 3 Robustness of the SPS to failure of super-peers compared to SG-1

Algorithm	Simulation rounds needed when 10% of super-peers are failed	Simulation rounds needed when 20% of super-peers are failed	Simulation rounds needed when 30% of super-peers are failed	Standard deviation of the simulation rounds
The SPS	17.0	16.0	15.0	1.0
SG-1	22.0	24.0	25.0	1.5

failure of 30% super-peers as shown in Figure 7 (c), the number of client peers without a super-peer (because of super-peer failure) in SPS (around 3/5 of client peers) is larger than that of SG-1 (around 1/5 of client peers). That is, there is a sharp decrease in the number of client peers that have joined a super-peer in our SPS compared to a slight decrease in SG-1. In other words, the super-peer failure in SPS makes worse impact on client peers than that in SG-1. However, the needed simulation rounds for restoring stable state in our SPS (restored at round 10) are fewer than those in SG-1 (restored at round 12). In summary, our SPS takes fewer simulation rounds to restore in the face of larger number client peers without a super-peer (because of super-peer failure) compared to SG-1.

The rationale behind result (1) mentioned above is as follows: when some super-peers are failed at the sixth simulation round, they are removed from the overlay. On one hand, the client peers, whose super-peers have crashed, remove the failed super-peers from their sets of super-peer candidates and rebuild their sets of super-peer candidates by executing the SPS algorithm. Then, these client peers select and join new super-peers. On the other hand, most of the required super-peers can be selected during the first few simulation rounds. Thus, even more super-peers fail; there is only a little variation in the number of the required simulation rounds for the overlay to converge again. Based on the simulation results above, we can conclude that our SPS is robust to failure of super-peers and our SPS is efficient in re-organizing a super-peer overlay.

4. Conclusion and future work

In this paper, we have presented a gossip-based super-peer selection algorithm (SPS) for quickly building a super-peer overlay upon a connected overlay. In the SPS, each peer periodically rebuilds its set of super-peer candidates through gossip communication. Peers with high capacity are promoted to be super-peer candidates. The decision whether a peer takes the role of a super-peer is made based on its set of super-peer candidates. Once the roles of peers are determined, peers join a super-peer, or search and add client peers with a conditional two-hop search method according to their roles.

The conducted simulations show that the proposed SPS is efficient in both selecting super-peers and quick building a super-peer overlay. Furthermore, our SPS

achieves a comparable robustness and better performance in convergence time, scalability compared to SG-1 [11].

In the future work, we will reduce the communication overhead for building the set of super-peer candidates, and take account of the stability of a super-peer overlay using a local search method. Moreover, it would also be interesting to apply a greedy approach in selecting super-peers in our SPS algorithm in order to improve the performance of quickly building a super-peer overlay.

Competing interests
The authors declare that they have no competing interests.

Authors' contributions
ML had the initial idea of building a super-peer overlay (SPS), carried out simulations, and worked on formulating the paper. EH provided suggestions on the paper finalization and MY is the supervisor. All authors read and approved the final manuscript.

Acknowledgements
This work was supported by the ITEA2 Expeshare project, funded by the Finnish Funding Agency for Technology and Innovation (TEKES), the project of SOPSCC (Pervasive Service Computing: A Solution Based on Web Services), funded by the Academy of Finland, and the DECICOM project, funded by TEKES Ericsson, Nokia, and NetHawk. The authors would like to thank Dr. Vidyasagar Potdar from Curtin University in Australia and Dr. Jiehan Zhou for their valuable comments on improving the quality of the paper.

References
1. Baset S, Schulzrinne H (2004) An analysis of the Skype peer-to-peer internet telephony protocol. Technical Report CUCS-039-04. Columbia University, Department of Computer Science, New York
2. Cohen B BitTorrent, http://www.bittorrent.com/btusers/guides/bittorrent-user-manual/chapter-02-basic-guides/basics-bittorrent (last accessed 17-12-2009)
3. Kirk P RFC-Gnutella 0.6. http://rfc-gnutella.sourceforge.net/index.html (last accessed 17-12-2009)
4. PPLive, http://www.pplive.com, (last accessed 17-12-2009)
5. Milojicic DS, Kalogeraki V, Lukose R, Nagaraja K, Pruyne J, Richard B, Rollins S, Xu Z (2002) Peer-to-Peer Computing. Technical Report HPL-2002-57. HP Labs, Palo Alto
6. Oram A (ed) (2001) Peer-to-Peer: Harnessing the Power of Disruptive Technologies. O'Reilly & Associates, Inc, 101 Morris Street Sebastopol, CA 95472, USA
7. Garbacki P, Epema DHJ, Steen M (2010) The design and evaluation of a self-organizing superpeer network. IEEE Trans Comput 59(3):317–331
8. Jesi GP, Montresor A, Babaoglu O (2007) Proximity-aware superpeer overlay topologies. IEEE Trans Network Serv Manag 4(2):74–83
9. Lua K, Crowcroft J, Pias M, Sharma R, Lim S (2005) A survey and comparison of peer-to-peer overlay network schemes. IEEE Comm Surv Tutorials 7(2):72–93
10. Löser A, Naumann F, Siberski W, Nejdl W, Thaden U (2004) Semantic Overlay Clusters within Super-Peer Networks. In: Aberer K et al (eds) VLDB 2003 Ws DBISP2P, LNCS 2944. Springer, Berlin Heidelberg, Germany, pp 33–47

11. Montresor A (2004) A robust protocol for building super-peer overlay topologies. In: Proc. of International Conference on Peer-to-Peer Computing., pp 202–209

12. Yu J, Li M (2008) CBT: a proximity-aware peer clustering system in large scale BitTorrent-like Peer-to-Peer networks. Comput Comm 31(3):591–602

13. Kazaa, URL: http://www.kazaa.com/us/help/glossary/p2p-.htm (last accessed 17-12-2009)

14. Yang B, Garcia-Molina H (2003) Designing a super-peer network. Proc ICDE:49–60

15. Wang F, Liu J, Xiong Y (2008) Stable peers, existence, importance, and application in Peer-To-Peer live video streaming. Proc IEEE INFOCOM:1364–1372

16. Stutzbach D, Rejaie R (2005) Characterizing the two-tier Gnutella topology. Proc ACM SIGMETRICS:402–403

17. Voulgaris S, Gavidia D, Steen M (2005) YCLON, Inexpensive Membership Management for Unstructured P2P Overlays. J Netw Syst Manag 13(2):197–217

18. Jelasity M, Montresor A, Babaoglu O (2009) T-Man: gossip-based fast overlay topology construction. Comput Netw Elsevier 53(13):2321–2339

19. Li X, Zhuang Z, Liu Y (2005) Dynamic layer management in superpeer architectures. IEEE Trans Parallel Distr Syst 16(11):1078–1091

20. Liu M, Zhou J, Koskela T, Ylianttila M (2009) A robust algorithm for the membership management of super-peer overlay. Proc of 12th IFIP/IEEE International Conference on Management of Multimedia and Mobile Networks and Services:132–143

21. Lua EK, Zhou X, Crowcroft J, Mieghem PV (2008) Scalable multicasting with network-aware geometric overlay. J Comput Comm Elsevier 31(3):464–488

22. Sachez-Artigas M, Garcia-Lopez P, Skarmeta AFG (2008) On the Feasibility of Dynamic Super-peer Ratio Maintenance. In: Proc of International Conference on Peer-to-Peer Computing., pp 333–342

23. Nejdl W, Wolpers M, Siberski W, Schmitz C, Schlosser M, Brunkhorst I, Löser A (2004) Super-peer-based routing strategies for RDF-based peer-to-peer networks. J Web Semant: Sci Serv Agents World Wide Web 1(2):177–186

24. Ganesh AJ, Kermarrec AM, Massoulie L (2003) Peer-to-peer membership management for gossip-based protocols. IEEE Trans Comput 52(2):139–149

25. Min S, Holliday J, Cho DS (2006) Optimal Super-peer Selection for Large-scale P2P System. Proc Hybrid Inform Tech:588–593

26. Jelasity M, Kowalczyk W, Van Steen M (2003) Newscast Computing. Technical Report, IRCS-006. Dept. of Computer Science, Vrije Universiteit, Amsterdam

27. Yuan Q, Wu J (2008) DRIP: A Dynamic VoRonoi RegIons-Based Publish/Subscribe Protocol in Mobile Networks. In: proc. IEEE INFOCOM, pp 2110–2118

28. Jelasity M, Montresor A, Jesi GP, Voulgaris S (2009) PeerSim: P2P Simulator., http://peersim.sourceforge.net/

29. Laoutaris N, Smaragdakis G, Oikonomou K, Stavrakakis I, Bestavros (2007) A distributed placement of service facilities in large-scale networks. Proc IEEE INFOCOM:2144–2152

2

Heterogeneous resource federation with a centralized security model for information extraction

Milad Daivandy[1*], Denis Hünich[2], René Jäkel[2], Steffen Metzger[3], Ralph Müller-Pfefferkorn[2] and Bernd Schuller[1]

Abstract

With the continuous growth of data generated in various scientific and commercial endeavors and the rising need for interdisciplinary studies and applications in e-Science easy exchange of information and computation resources capable of processing large amounts of data to allow ad-hoc co-operation becomes ever more important. Unfortunately different communities often use incompatible resource management systems. In this work we try to alleviate the difficulties occurring on bridging the gap between different research eco-systems by federating resources and thus unifying resource access.

To this end, our solution presented in this paper outlines a secure, simple, yet highly interoperable and flexible architecture using RESTful Web services and WebDAV. While, first and foremost in the Grid computing domain, there are already standards and solutions in place addressing related problems, our solution differs from those approaches by allowing to federate data storage systems that are not aware of being federated. Access to these is enabled by our federation layer using storage system specific connectors. Hence, our federation approach is intended as an abstraction layer on top of existing storage or middleware solutions, allowing for a more uniform access mechanism. Additionally, our solution also allows for submission and management of computational jobs on said data, thereby federating not only data but also computational resources. Once resource access is unified, information from different data formats can be semantically unified by information extraction methods. It is our belief that the work in this paper can complement existing Grid computing efforts by facilitating access to data storage system not inherently available via commonly used Grid computing standards.

Keywords: Grid computing, Data federation, Metadata federation, Resource federation, webDAV, Single sign-On, Identity federation centralized security, Identity management, Trust delegation, Interoperability, Uniform access, Information extraction, Knowledge extraction

1 Introduction

In recent years the transparent and secure handling of large data sets has become increasingly important for a broad range of different scientific and commercial applications [1,2], in particular to handle huge amounts of scientific data for simulation or analysis in various research fields [3]. In the past years, Grid computing [4] has evolved for many different disciplines, ranging from solving computationally intensive tasks to the provision of services

for application steering, user management and the creation of complex workflows, but also of resources for data management [5]. A strong advantage of Grid computing is the ability to maintain distributed and heterogeneous resources using a middleware layer to distribute computational jobs or delegate user access to data storage space. The use of distributed computing resources becomes more and more important in many research fields using state-of-the-art information systems to even enable collaborative work over institutional boundaries. To some extent, Grid and, more recently, Cloud resources can be used for distributing computing tasks or providing access to distributed data resources. Since, generally speaking,

*Correspondence: j.daivandy@fz-juelich.de
[1] Jülich Supercomputing Centre, Forschungszentrum Jülich, 52428 Jülich, Germany
Full list of author information is available at the end of the article

the resource demand in scientific computing is continuously on the rise and the potential of interdisciplinary work is large, an easy and secure access to computing resources becomes even more important.

For large-scale projects usually including lots of partners from different organisations, the provision of relevant data can not be assured by a single organisation alone, but has to be organized among the partners across organisational boundaries. In the past, these efforts were often realized by nation-wide or even international cross-linking of computing centers providing a Grid of computing resources [4]. This has lead to rather large offers for the scientific community to access High Performance Computing (HPC) and High Throughput Computing (HTC) resources provided by large data centers, e.g. via XSede [6] in the U.S. or the EGI federation [7] supported by the EU. Other approaches such as the national German Grid Initiative D-Grid [8] emphasised and spread the idea of using Grid resources and methods of distributed computing in general in the their local scientific communities. In this context, we have examined capabilities for further decreasing hurdles typically faced by user-groups intending to adopt Grid computing to their daily work. The WisNetGrid [9] project of the aforementioned D-Grid initiative has investigated a more general approach for facilitating access to distributed storage solutions in general, ranging from traditional Grid middlewares over databases to Web-based resources.

By extending the range to additional data and information resources in general, the WisNetGrid project aims at furthering the potential for using data across different scientific disciplines and related fields, such as physics, biology, medicine, geographic information and humanities. Some of the aforementioned knowledge resources are publicly available via the Internet, others require authentication due to project-specific or commercial reasons. The common theme is that these resources, sometimes provided by governmental authorities [10,11], are often offered as databases or ontologies and thus might be of interest to interdisciplinary studies. However, these data are usually not accessible to Grid computing in a traditional and standardized manner. By having our access layer support a broader range of resource types and different underlying access control mechanisms, our solution is capable of providing uniform access to most distributed storage systems, both traditional Grid and Non-Grid.

In this paper, we introduce a system for federating multi-organizational and heterogeneous computer resources into a uniform namespace and making them accessible by way of a uniform interface using the widely supported WebDAV standard. We understand resource federation as logically joining resources, primarily data resources, from different distributed heterogeneous resources without moving or copying data from these resources to the resource access and federation system. Our resource access and federation system contrasts from related work in so far as the resources to be federated are not aware of being used in a federation context. This means, that a particular storage system is still being operated by the individual institutions or operators and that access modalities already in place are not modified. Our solution federates storage systems by way of storage system specific connectors (e.g. a MySQL connector for federating a MySQL database) running in the federation system backend and making use of our security model based on delegated authentication by way of supplied user credentials. Hence, it is safe to classify our approach as user-centric. See section 3 for more details regarding both the architecture and the realization of this federation mechanism.

Operators of our resource access and federation system do not necessarily have to own the distributed resources to be federated, but have to take care of two matters. First, they need negotiate and manage collaborative agreements for partners who wish to participate in the federation system. Second, they need to provide a connector element for each storage system to be federated. Although the main focus lies on the federation of data resources our system also supports submission and management of jobs operating on these data resources. Also, this work outlines how essential information contained in federated data can be further unified and leveraged by applying information extraction methods. While information extraction is computationally intensive, our architecture allows for parallelisable computational resources to be used.

To illustrate how higher-level applications can easily make use of uniform data access and to provide an example of data federation and information unification we discuss a use-case from the humanities. In this use-case the information extraction module is a higher-level application that benefits from uniform access to data resources provided by the system described in detail in section 3. This enables the extraction module to provide the user with a uniform representation of information found in source files of multiple origins without having to deal with the particular storage systems involved himself.

In particular, assume a humanities-oriented application scenario, where the research community is trying to link works of and about particular authors. Such works migh be available in digital form, but held by different legal entities. In adopting our solution, each group agreeing to share information only needs to integrate their data into the federation system, and all community members, who are granted the corresponding permissions, can access sources from all participating data providers via a uniform interface.

Additionally, the extraction system, acting on behalf of a particular user, can access all files the user holds access rights for. Thus, it can, for instance, lift entity mentions, i.e. mentions of persons, places etc. onto a semantically unambiguous level, linking e.g. different writings of a name or even different names for the same thing or person. This allows, for instance, to trace a particular semantic entity in different contexts without the need for expert users who know all possible ways the semantic entity could be addressed in these contexts. This also allows for interdisciplinary work, linking sources of different research communities. For instance, places or persons occurring in literary texts could be linked with information retrieved from historical or geological information sources. This use-case and the interaction between the high-level extraction services with the resource federation component is described in section 5.

In the following section 2 we discuss our approach regarding an infrastructural centric view of larger consortia and focusing on technical aspects of related solutions with similar approaches to realizing federated access to distributed storage systems. We intend for our data access system to strongly support the user with accessing the resources required for his use-case. To fulfill the aforementioned goals, developing a flexible and highly interoperable security solution was essential. Section 4 discusses how our solution is able to federate different distributed resources by accessing data from different resources while conforming to the different resource-specific authentication and authorization mechanisms.

2 Related work

In the Grid and, nowadays, the Cloud computing domains, middleware solutions are used as abstraction layers to facilitate access to and enable interoperability between (geographically) distributed computing infrastructures such as super computers, high-performance clusters and larger computing centers [12]. For accessing those computing resources, every middleware offers different services for job submission and management, data management on the application level, or user administration for Grid access and support.

Today, larger consortia have been established in order to focus efforts from individual data centers towards a more service-oriented approach for scientific communities to use larger computing resources, such as XSede [6] in the U.S. or data centers unified under the European Grid Infrastructure (EGI) [7]. Such a range of services is provided by a management layer to local data centers (service providers) running individual HPC or Grid resources. This typically does not mean that every provider offers the same services, either for accessing data storage space or for computing resources. Furthermore, services of different middleware solutions might not be compatible with each other.

The choice of selected middleware solutions at particular data centers might also represent a technical hurdle to be taken by new user groups, or by trying to combine existing technical solutions from different user groups to enable collaborative work between these groups. Typical hurdles are different security infrastructures (e.g. authentication via username/password or X.509 certificates [13]) or differing data representations (e.g. database or file systems), which are handled differently by various middlewares.

Within the context of our project, we have investigated a more generalized approach in order to be able to address a broad range of resources, not only Grid middlewares. Therefore, we do not compete with well-established Grid computing middlewares. Instead, we offer an additional way for accessing distributed resources by providing an additional access mechanism and do not intend to replace existing solutions.

A different, but interesting approach to distributed Grid resources is the access mechanism via science gateways, which also hides the technical details of the specific data access mechanism or its clients from user and provides a transparent interface. Several approaches are available to address Grid resources [14,15], but often with a strong focus on community-only requirements and services. Sharing data or services among different groups is still not the main focus of these developments.

Addressing the latter point, the data integration layer of three Grid projects from the German Grid initiative has been analyzed in terms of standardization [16] on the architectural level, but to our knowledge this work remains on the conceptual level. To tackle these interoperability concerns, the EMI project [17] aims at standardizing services of four different middleware solutions on a technical level. However, for the goals stated in this work, the scope of the EMI project shares related goals, albeit with a focus on Grid, since there are no non-Grid based data sources considered.

Using Grid computing, either for data or computing relevant concerns, also necessitates user authentication and authorization [18] mechanisms. To facilitate access and to increase usability of project-specific Grids, development of Web browser - based services, called Grid portals, was observed [19]. This combination of Web browser access and Grid computing requires passing user credentials throughout the federation system to transport user requests from the HTTP layer to the middleware execution layer. This concept of Single-Sign On was first adopted to the Grid computing domain by using proxy certificates [20,21]. In general, this concept is also integrated in science gateways as mentioned before, and realized in various community based projects, e.g. as described for PolarGrid [22] or other community based projects, such as MosGrid [23,24] (also a D-Grid project). Besides the authentication federation by OpenID [25], PolarGrid supports a more general non-OpenID based mechanism to also support further authentication services, albeit these are still in development [22]. Nonetheless, this marks an interesting approach to extend access and visibility of Grid computing systems to other access mechanisms like Social Networks.

A further solution to pass user credentials via Web Single Sign-On across organizational boundaries is Shibboleth [26]. It is based on SOAP Web services [27] and uses SAML 2.0 [28] to interact with arbitrary identity providers. Apart from authentication, SAML 2.0 also provides means for authorization and for user attributes (key-value pairs of arbitrary data). In use cases where components are not based on platforms SOAP Web services are easily available for or applicable to, the SOAP Web service dependency of SAML 2.0 can be a drawback, especially regarding our intention to provide a highly interoperable system. The GridShib [29,30] project combined Shibboleth and the Globus Toolkit to map SAML assertions to X.509 certificates [31]. However, the drawback is the restriction to the Globus Toolkit.

Concerning Web Single Sign-On in general, [32] outlines weaknesses of security protocols based on insecure properties of Public Key Infrastructure and the Domain Name System. Furthermore, a more secure cookie type is introduced and used as part of a proposal for a more secure Single Sign-On protocol. In contrast to usual cookies, it also contains a list of public keys denoting eligible target servers. During the SSL handshake between a Web browser with such a cookie and the target server, the target server needs to match one of the aforementioned public keys. A subsequent proof-of-concept with security evaluation regarding multiple attack types is given and shows that this concept secures against a malicious website impersonating a valid target server.

3 Resource federation

Accessing and manipulating data stored in different data storage systems such as databases, Grid data management or file systems within the context of a single use case can be difficult and time-consuming. First, there are many possible data representations (e.g. entries in a database or files), access and security protocols. Second, a use case requiring collecting and analyzing data from different data storage systems must know how to communicate with all of them and how to interpret the received data. Adding support for a new type of data storage system necessitates some sort of connector extension with regard to the required communication and security protocols, but also requires support for new data formats. This becomes increasingly inconvenient as more resources of different resource types need to be integrated.

In Grid environments, heterogeneous resources are mostly hidden from the user by a middleware layer which provides a uniform view on the resources. The middleware communicates with the underlying resources and is responsible for transforming client requests into formats consumable by the actual requested resources and vice versa. In our case, the aforementioned resources might be different data storage systems, as described in the beginning of this section.

3.1 Uniform access

The resource federation system described in this paper realizes such a middleware layer. It provides uniform access by using the WebDAV protocol,[a] which is an extension of the HTTP/1.1-protocol [33]. Although the HTTP/1.1 protocol already supports methods for reading (GET), writing (POST/PUT) and deleting (DELETE) resources, our resource federation system requires additional methods.

WebDAV provides further operations such as locking (LOCK/UNLOCK), copying (COPY) and moving (MOVE) resources on the respective data storage systems. Furthermore, methods for reading (PROPFIND) and updating (PROPPATCH) metadata of resources are supported which allows to represent resources and corresponding arbitrary metadata with one URI[b] even when they are stored at different locations. The increasing amount of data necessitates the use of data management systems with metadata management support. In the context of our work, we identified WebDAV as a suitable building block for our resource access and federation system, both regarding data and metadata management.

To provide the aforementioned uniform access our architecture consists of the following four components:

SSO Database Stores user information, authentication data and credentials

SSO Server Central access point of the security infrastructure

Credential Manager Graphical user interface for management of external credentials

Resource Federator Interface between the user and resources

Figure 1 shows how the four components interact with each other.

The SSO Database stores user information (e.g. name or e-mail address), the authentication data for accessing the SSO Server (username and password) and external credentials used by the Resource Federator for delegated user authentication on connected (i.e. federated) resources. The credential type depends on the underlying security model of the resource in question (e.g. a password for a MySQL database or a X.509 certificate for a Grid resource). Credentials are stored plain or encrypted with the public key provided by the server running the Resource Federator. The encryption allows the resource

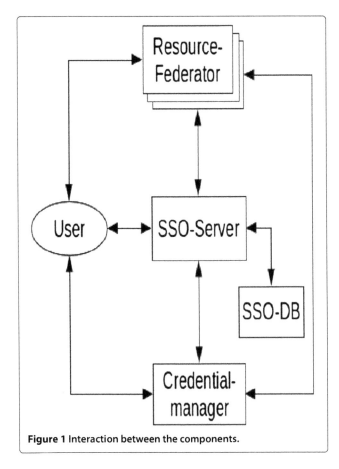

Figure 1 Interaction between the components.

MySQL input mask provides fields for username and password specification, whereas a UNICORE input mask provides a Java Applet (which, by default, runs locally on the user's computer) to issue a signed SAML 2.0 trust delegation token using the user's private key. Optionally, the user can encrypt his external credential with the public key of the corresponding Resource Federator instance. Subsection 4.1 sheds more light on this security model.

3.2 Resource federation

The aforementioned resource federation system is composed of three components:

- Web Server
- Routing Engine
- WebDAV Server

and is illustrated in Figure 2.

The *Web Server* interacts with the client according to the HTTP 1.1 protocol. Requests are forwarded to the *Routing Engine* and the system's response is sent back to the client. The *Routing Engine* allows to define routes and to process routed message using a set of intermediaries. The resource access and federation system defines a route by two endpoints (start and end points) and a certain number of intermediaries (elements for manipulating messages, from here on individually referred to as *Process*). The start point creates an exchange object (*Message*), stores the client request and an empty response in it and sends it to

providers to hide security relevant data from third party system.

The SSO Server is the only component, which is directly accessing the SSO Database and is the starting point for other components requiring security mechanisms. The SSO Server provides both a graphical user interface and a Web service interface. See subsection 4.2 for more details.

The federation of resources in our namespace is done by the Resource Federators instances. Each of those is able to integrate and process CRUD operations on resources (represented via URIs) depending on the user privileges and supported functions of the used Connectors (see section 3 for further details). The privileges required to use an integrated resource are composed of the authentication data (verified by the SSO Server) and the credentials (verified by the service provider of the resource).

The Credential Manager provides a graphical user interface to the external credential management part of the SSO Server Web service interface. Therefore, the Credential Manager is populated with URIs to all Resource Federator instances in the federation used to build an internal collection of all federated resources with corresponding types (e.g. MySQL, IRODS, UNICORE, local file system etc.). This information is used to generate corresponding input masks for external credential management. A

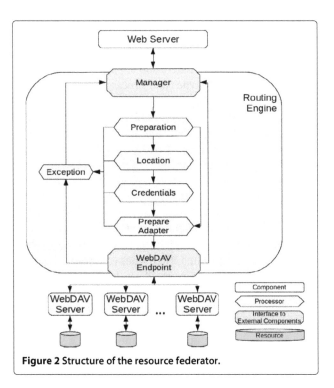

Figure 2 Structure of the resource federator.

the endpoint. Before the message reaches the endpoint it is processed by the following *Processes*:

Preparation Sets the name of the requested source and the relative path of the data

Location Loads information about the respective data storage system

Credential Connects to the Single Sign-On server to retrieve a user's external credentials (see section 4.1) for the data storage system hosting the requested resource

Connector Provides the interface between the WebDAV server and the specified data storage system

Exception Aborts the route and provides detailed error handling for the responses

Preparation scans the requested URI, takes the data storage system name and the relative path of the requested resource and stores both in *Message*. Using the data storage system name, *Location* loads information (defined in a configuration file) about this data storage system and adds this information to the *Message*. Then, the required external credential to access the requested resource on behalf of the user is retrieved from the Single Sign-On server and stored in *Message*. *Connector* loads the connector for the requested data storage system with the collected credential and location information and hands it over to *Message*. The connector provides methods to process data/metadata: it is specialized for a certain type of resource and acts as an interface between the resource and *WebDAV Server*. The endpoint of the route creates the *WebDAV Server* environment with the collected data in Message and starts it. *WebDAV Server* processes the request with the help of the connector and generates a response, which is sent to the Java Servlet in Web Server.

The generic resource federation supports the introduction of new connector types and *Process* implementations (e.g. a billing Process). Therefore, extensibility does not necessitate source code changes. Instead the Camel route, defined in the configuration file, must be changed. It is also possible to use other WebDAV server implementations or even a completely different protocol as endpoint. It is up to the specific user group which process has to be provided.

3.3 Submission and management of computational jobs

The architecture just described is not restricted to data access and manipulation. Other types of resources can be integrated as well. As a particularly important case, we have integrated data processing capabilities into our system. We chose to do this by implementing an connector which can submit jobs to the UNICORE Grid middleware. The user interacts with this job connector via a WebDAV directory. Job description documents can be uploaded (via HTTP POST) into this directory, while each submitted job

corresponds to a file in the directory. Viewing these job files in a browser or downloading them allows to check job status.

The security system described in section 4 is perfectly suited to integrate UNICORE resources, since UNICORE uses a trust delegation system based on signed SAML 2.0 assertions [34]. UNICORE jobs can participate in an active security session, and manipulate data through the WebDAV interface.

4 Security federation

As a multi-user distributed system comprised of multiple applications and potentially spanning multiple organizational boundaries, authentication (identity verification) and authorization (access control after successful authentication) are core requirements of the security infrastructure to apply.

Both for usability and administration considerations, a centralized Single Sign-On authentication approach is suitable for our resource federation system (see section 3). In this context, Single Sign-On is briefly described as follows: on accessing any given application within the resource federation system, a yet unauthenticated user is prompted to supply only one and the same valid security credential (a username and password combination) whereupon he is authenticated to the whole system. All applications thus protected form a shared Single Sign-On domain. Single Sign-Off specifies the reverse property where a user signing off at any given application within a Single Sign-On domain automatically terminates his access to all other applications within the same Single Sign-On domain.

Authorization comes into play after successful authentication: each subject has a set of roles that are used for access control.

In addition to this traditional sequence of authentication and authorization, we needed a trust delegation mechanism allowing our resource federation system to act on behalf of users to access federated external resources (see section 3 and Figure 3). To this end, our security model is required to allow a user to manage his respective resource credentials, giving him the means necessary to add, edit, configure and remove them. Also, our security model had to support users interacting with the system using both Web browsers and WebDAV clients, thereby necessitating two different security interfaces.

In addition to the aforementioned requirements, our security model had to accommodate the heterogeneous and distributed characteristics of the system described in chapter 3 and thus be interoperable. Finally, we intended our security solution to also be applicable to similar use cases aiming at heterogeneous resource federation, albeit without necessitating a complex security stack imposing too much of an interoperability overhead (e.g. SOAP-

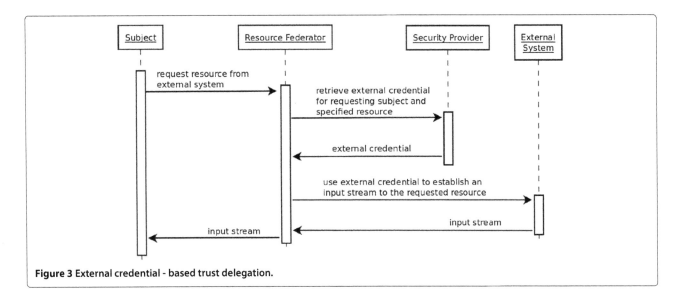

Figure 3 External credential - based trust delegation.

based, which is merited in SAML-based trust delegation scenarios, but not necessary for this scenario).

4.1 Security model

Our security model consists of four actors: the security provider, subject, service provider, and external system. Obviously, the security provider is the server-side part of our central security system we labeled 'Single Sign-On server'. Both terms are used interchangeably.

To define what a subject exactly encompasses, a definition is in order: in the course of this work, we regard any entity that can make requests to resources secured by the security provider as a subject. According to this, a subject can be a human, i.e. a user, or a non-human entity like a service, an application or, more generally, a computer system. A principal is an identifying attribute (or a set thereof) of an authenticated subject, such as a unique key or a user account. In our security model, it consists of a unique id, a password, roles, external credentials and further optional attributes, such as user details should the subject be a user.

A service provider is an application that delegates security to a Single Sign-On domain. Situated outside of a Single Sign-On domain are external systems containing resources a subject has access tokens to. This signifies use cases where a service provider acts as an intermediary between a subject and an external system containing resources requested by the subject. To fulfill this function, an intermediary service provider uses the corresponding external credential of the subject, thereby making it a necessity for the subject to trust the service provider with its extended credentials.

An external credential consists of a resource name denoting the external resource (e.g. a database), the subjects's id on that external system (if applicable) and the actual credential (e.g. a password). Since the latter is persisted in serialized form, its format can be arbitrary. It can be a plain text password, a X.509 certificate [13] or even a SAML assertion [28].

In this security model, the combination of subject id and password is used for authentication to the Single Sign-On domain. After successful authentication, the security provider can map the subject to its corresponding principal and thus provide respective service providers with its roles for access control and external credentials for trust delegation. Once authenticated, a subject is also identified by a unique session, itself consisting of a unique id and the aforementioned principal. Said unique session id is returned to a subject after successful authentication to be used as an identification token for subsequent requests. Its validity can be terminated on the client and server sides (see Section 4.2 of this chapter).

For trust delegation to work, a subject must provide external credentials for the external resources he intends to access. This needs to be done beforehand and only once, unless the actual access token is changed on the external system side. Optionally, the subject can opt to encrypt each external credential with the public key of a service provider, thereby restricting access to that service provider alone that can decrypt this credential using its private key.

4.2 Components and interaction

The Single Sign-On server was implemented with the Java programming language as was the Single Sign-On client library used by service providers. Furthermore, principals and corresponding authenticated sessions are persisted using an extensible persistence layer allowing for both local and remote databases and thereby implicitly supporting data replication depending on the specific persistence backend.

The Single Sign-On server offers Web browser and Web service [27] interfaces, both relying on Transport Layer Security for channel security. The former uses Simple Transport Layer Security, the latter requires mutual authentication using the client-authenticated extensions.

The Web browser interface is required for initial account registration and for account self-management. It also serves as the single point of Single Sign-On and Single Sign-Off for Web browser users and provides administrative functions, such as listing, locking, deleting user accounts and assigning user roles. The aforementioned unique session id used as an identification token is stored as a Cookie in the user's Web browser, thereby rendering that Cookie a client-side reference to the user's actual session in the Single Sign-On server. The Cookie is secured by both the 'Secure' and 'HttpOnly' options, together limiting Cookie communication to encrypted HTTP connections. Cookie validity is terminated by the Single Sign-On server after a session's idle time exceeds a customizable global session lifetime. Client-side Cookie termination is either directly performed by the user via the Web browser interface Single Sign-Off, thereby triggering the subsequent deletion of the corresponding session in the Single Sign-On server. This also leads to the Cookie being deleted in the user's Web browser. Closing the Web browser without performing Single Sign-Off will also delete the Cookie, but with the session still existing in the Single Sign-On server until it expires. For Web browser Single Sign-On to work, a user's Web browser needs to store one clone of the aforementioned Cookie for each service provider. Since Cookies are inherently bound to WWW domains, we implemented the cross-domain Cookie sharing algorithm outlined in [35].

For our Web service interface, we employed the Representational State Transfer (REST) [36] paradigm, since it uses HTTP methods, thereby only requiring a very basic and practically ubiquitous Internet protocol. This design choice was further influenced by the availability of opensource HTTP client libraries for a plethora of programming languages and systems, thereby strongly supporting our goal of providing a highly interoperable security solution for resource federation and similar use cases. One of those open-source HTTP client libraries [37] supports 42 programming and scripting languages.

The Web service interface also provides Single Sign-On (see Figure 4) and Single Sign-Off, but goes further by adding means for role and external credential retrieval. Also, external credentials can be added, updated and deleted. The aforementioned session id is supplied as part of the URI of the Web service request from a Single Sign-On client instance to the Single Sign-On server. In the same vein, we decided to use Javascript Object Notation [38] as data interchange format, a lightweight text-based open format that lends itself to data serialization and transmission over computer networks. This combination of HTTP-based Web service and text-based data interchange format makes the security provider highly interoperable.

Security delegation for service providers is facilitated by way of a high-level Java-based Single Sign-On client library abstracting from lower-level Web service data transformation and transmission mechanics. Thus, each service provider can use its Single Sign-On client to authenticate and authorize user requests without having to provide its own fully-fledged security system. Non-Java-based service providers need to provide Single Sign-On client implementations of their own, which in itself only constitutes a low barrier given the aforementioned highly interoperable nature of the Web service interface.

To reduce architectural complexity, we opted for delegating external credential management to a service provider of its own that makes use of the aforementioned Web service interface as opposed to integrate it within the Single Sign-On server. This service provider, labeled Credential Manager, is a small Java-based Web application using the aforementioned Single Sign-On client library to authenticate and authorize users. Once a user is authenticated, he can use the Credential Manager to create, modify and remove his external credentials.

4.3 Caching

Given the security validation necessary for every subject request (see Figure 2), it is easy to see why this interaction pattern constitutes a potential bottle neck, since a service provider needs to verify every request on secured resources with the security provider. At the very least, a service provider has to verify that a requesting subject is authenticated. It is safe to assume, that a service provider needs to verify a subject's roles for authorization purposes. If trust delegation is employed, a service provider also has to retrieve a subject's external credential(s) from the security provider. Thus, depending on the security verification pattern required by a service provider (see Figure 5), one subject request can necessitate three different request types with differently sized response data payloads to be made by a service provider to the security provider. In the context of a multi-user system where every user can make concurrent requests, it follows that the network connection between a service provider and the security provider constitutes a potential bottle neck. Hence, we decided on a client-side caching approach to reduce the amount of security verification requests

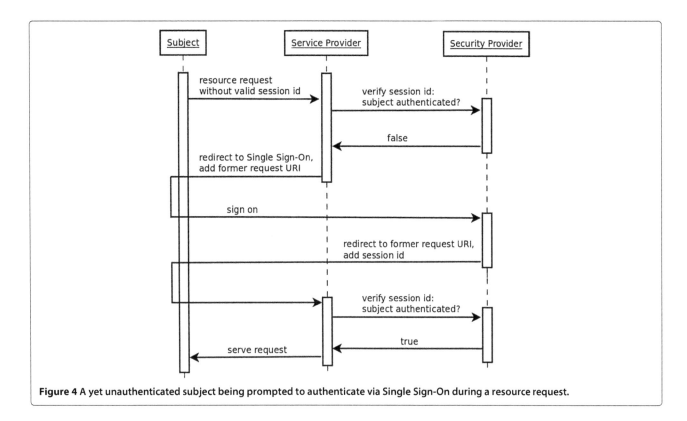

Figure 4 A yet unauthenticated subject being prompted to authenticate via Single Sign-On during a resource request.

necessary. To this end, each Single Sign-On client caches Client Session instances, a client-side representation of the session concept outlined in section 4.1 of this chapter. Whenever a user is signed on to the Single Sign-On domain via a Single Sign-On client, the Single Sign-On client creates a corresponding Client Session instance containing that subject's authentication state, roles and external credentials and puts it into the cache. This cache is periodically refreshed with fresh values from the Single Sign-On server. Also, each client session is only populated with external credentials the service provider currently requires to fulfill respective subject requests requiring

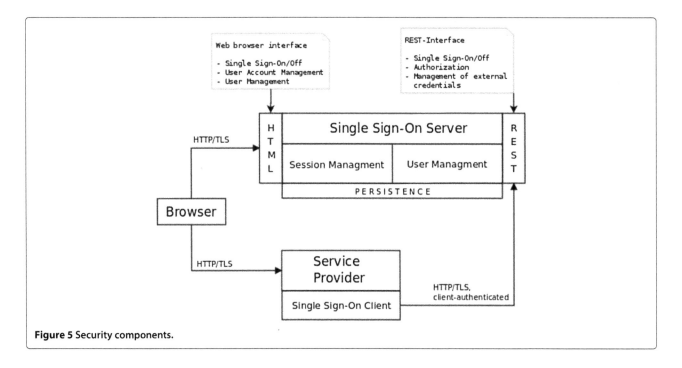

Figure 5 Security components.

trust delegation towards external systems. Additionally, invalid cached sessions are detected and disposed of. The client session refresh and the cache clean-up intervals can be customized by the service provider. While this approach reduces the time spent on security verification requests, there is a disconnect between cached security state on the service provider's side and actual security state on the security provider's side. Thus, it is the service provider's concern to choose respective values to strike a good balance between performance and security state consistency.

5 Interactive information extraction

In the past two sections we explained how the federation layer allows to access distributed data sources in a uniform way. In this section we illustrate how the federated data can also be semantically unified using an extraction framework that provides semi-supervised extraction methods. In addition, this serves as a use-case to illustrate how higher level services can make use of the federation layer to access large heterogeneously distributed data sets.

To explore the needs of users in real application scenarios, we work together with user groups from the humanities, for which large repositories of digitized textual data became available in recent years. In an example setting, we integrated their data into our federation layer and developed an interactive knowledge extraction system to help with the analysis of these large data sets. One goal in this domain is to cross-analyze the works of, or about particular figures, like famous authors. By identifying differently formulated references to semantically identical entities underlying semantic links between documents of different authorship can be discovered. For instance, when investigating the life, works and journeys of the famous writer Johann Wolfgang von Goethe in historical texts, references to the person Goethe may vary in different texts. In bibliographical texts he may be referenced by his full or partial name. In many letters, however, he is referred to as "Herr geheimer Rat", a reference to an official position he held. Similarly, names of cities and places can change over time and even the formulations used to express certain facts can differ depending on the author's writing style, the target audience of a text and the time of its creation.

Information extraction methods can link these variations by lifting entity references and statements indicating relations between such entities onto a semantically canonicalized level, where each entity as well as relations between entities are uniquely identifiable, i.e. it allows to represent knowledge expressed in texts in an ontological form.

This helps, for instance, to categorize and investigate large document collections and make them discoverable for non-experts, e.g. allowing to search or cluster documents by the referenced entities. It also allows to link information from different research areas, e.g. to enrich places mentioned by Goethe in his writings with geographical or historical information.

While information extraction on its own aims at semantic unification of varying textual representations, our federated framework allows for easier access to heterogeneously stored source data within a community as well as across different communities. By integration into the unified security and data access model, the extraction system needs not be aware of the concrete file system nor does it need to support different security methods. For instance, a user of one community may have access to files within its community stored on different grid systems, but also may cooperate with another community and thus have separate credentials to access some files of the other community. Since the federation level deals with all security issues, the extraction system only needs to know the single-sign-on (SSO) credentials to access files across both communities. This would, for instance, allow a researcher from the humanities to have access, and thus apply the extraction machinery, to works of or about Goethe held by different research groups or even data of other disciplines. Using the federation system he would only need his personal SSO account, given that the data owners granted access permissions and integrated their data with the federation system.

In the following we briefly discuss the extraction approach, what information it needs to function and how this information can be provided in an interactive way. Finally, we also discuss how the extraction components interact with the federation layer.

5.1 Knowledge extraction approach

The extraction framework we provide supports two levels of knowledge extraction.

The first level, commonly referred to as named entity recognition (NER), is usually understood as the problem to identify referenced entity types. For instance, occurrences of the strings "*London*" and "*Frankfurt*" in a text can be identified as references to locations and for occurrences like "*Einstein*" and "*Goethe*" the reference type could be person.

However, recent work in this field allows for uniquely identifying individual entities referenced in texts, given some background knowledge about the domain entities[39,40]. This allows for identifying the string "*Goethe*" as a reference to the particular historical person named *Johann Wolfgang von Goethe*, a famous German writer. The same holds for other references, e.g. to locations. For instance, if the string "*Frankfurt*" appears in the same text about that particular writer it is probably a reference to the city *Frankfurt on the Main*, where Goethe was born, and not to *Frankfurt on the Oder*. The problem to decide which concrete entity is meant by a reference is called *disambiguation*.

To semantically unify different references to an identical entity in such a way, there are several basic requirements. First the system needs to have basic knowledge about the unique entities of a domain, i.e. it needs to know the famous writer Goethe existed. Secondly, type information is of importance, i.e. knowing that Goethe was a human, a writer and so on. Thirdly, the system needs to know which 'names' can potentially refer to which unique entities, e.g. the string "Frankfurt" could refer to at least two different cities within Germany. And finally, any additional relational information, e.g. where Goethe was born or which plays he wrote, can help to solve the disambiguation problem.

Based on this first step relations connecting recognized entities can be extracted from texts as well. Such relations might, for instance, be the birthplace of persons, the books a writer authored, or the movies an actor participated in. While there are different approaches [41-43], we apply an iterative pattern-based approach based on [43,44] that aims at extracting instances of a fixed set of predefined binary relations.

A pattern in the most abstract sense is a recurring construct, e.g. a word phrasing or a tabular representation, expressing the abstract relations textually. For instance, consider the text "*Goethe, who was born in Frankfurt, is one of the most famous German writers*". It contains an instance of the textual pattern "*X, who was born in Y*". Assuming the system knows that all instances of this pattern express an abstract `bornIn` relation, it can derive a matching relation instance asserting that Goethe was born in Frankfurt. In learning relation instances and the links between patterns and relations the system follows an iterative approach. Using type information on relations and entities, the system learns from given example relation instances which patterns represent which of these relations by analyzing how well the instances of an observed textual pattern match the given instances of individual relations. Once a link between pattern and relation is established, these patterns can be applied to extract more relation instances, which provides the system with more examples to learn more patterns from and so on.

The approach has the advantage that the actual patterns and their meaning can be learned on the basis of examples. Thus a user needs no detailed understanding of the extraction process, he only needs to deal with ontological knowledge in which he is interested anyway. As discussed earlier, the system needs some domain knowledge to function, namely 1) the entities of the domain, 2) the names of the entities, 3) the types of the entities and relations, 4) example relation instances and 5) as much other relational information on entities as possible. While a user may provide all this information upfront, we find

that users are typically more motivated to provide this information in an interactive way, as they can observe the impact of their feedback efforts. This also ensures only information needed by the extraction system is provided. Thus, in the following section we shall briefly discuss the interaction between a user and the extraction system and especially which kind of information he can provide during the extraction process in the form of feedback.

5.2 Interface interaction

Some domain specific background knowledge needs to be provided beforehand, in particular the type hierarchy, the relations of interest (with their range and domain types), and at least a basic set of entities along with some of their reference names. Additionally, the more relation instances are provided the more efficient the system can work.

Once this basic domain knowledge is provided, an interactive workflow allows to grow the knowledge base in a semi-automatic fashion.

First a set of relevant files is selected. The automatic extraction system searches for relevant information in the selected text basis and afterwards the user can inspect the recognized entity and relation instance occurrences and directly provide feedback on these occurrences. In particular the user can:

- correct referenced entities
- correct relations expressed between two entities
- add new entity references
- add new relation instance occurrences

In each of the given cases, the system implicitly learns from these corrections, e.g. by adding new reference names for an entity when an entity is corrected or directly derive relation instances when they are added or corrected. The accumulated knowledge can be applied when the extraction is re-run on the same or on a different data set. Coming back to the above-mentioned example the user needs only to indicate once that "*Frankfurt*" in a text does indeed reference *Frankfurt on the Main*, and the engine will very likely get it right in the whole text.

5.3 Integration into the resource federation architecture

In sections 3 and 4 we explained how the federation layer allows to access distributed data sources. By invoking a Single Sign-On (SSO) client within software components, services can be realized that interact with the system in behalf of the user. We have realized the previously described interactive knowledge extraction service to extract knowledge from accessible federated data using this method. The interaction of the extraction system with the federation layer is illustrated in Figure 6. After the user has registered the relevant credentials for the data sources in the SSO infrastructure using a Web Browser interface,

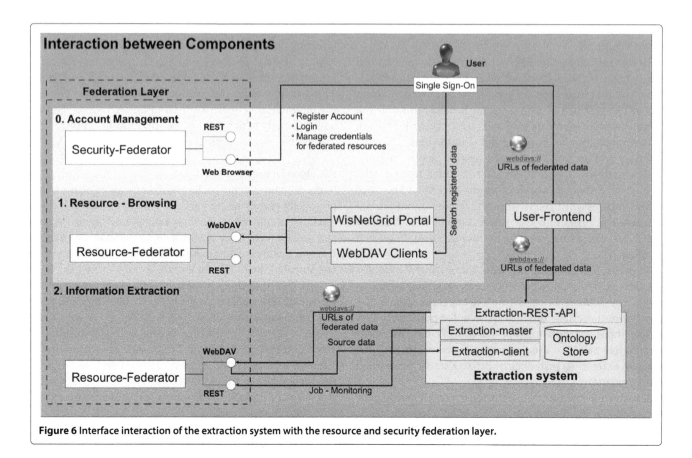

Figure 6 Interface interaction of the extraction system with the resource and security federation layer.

the extraction system can access data sources using the central authentication and authorization provided by the Single Sign-On REST interface. All the user needs to provide are his SSO credentials and WebDAV URLs in the uniform name-space of the federation layer.

The extraction system can also make use of available computation power to distribute the extraction process over the unified job submission interface. To this end the system is split up in two main components, a master and a client part. While the master unit controls the distribution, the clients are executed as distributed jobs to parse all documents. Both parts access a central ontology store that manages all knowledge be it extracted or provided by users. This requires that the client is installed on the grid nodes and the resource federation interface for job control is implemented for the particular grid engine. After each iteration the extraction master presents the results to the user, who can provide feedback and re-run the extraction machinery so it can take the new feedback into account.

For the interaction with the extraction system a simple web-based user interface is provided on top of a web-service API allowing the implementation of more sophisticated front-ends, e.g. enabling integration into a particular workflow environment of any community.

6 Conclusion

This paper describes an architecture providing a uniform access layer for different resources like Grid data management systems or databases. Therefore, a combination of Web server, routing engine and WebDAV environment generates a uniform namespace. The routing engine processes the client requests, forwarded by the Web server, in a defined route and directs them to the WebDAV environment. There, the requests are answered in a WebDAV-compliant response by interacting with a resource-dependent connector that mediates between the resource and the WebDAV server. This concept is not restricted to data management systems, but also supports computing resources. An example based on the UNICORE Grid computing middleware was described in section 3.3.

We achieved our goal to provide a scalable and highly interoperable security system for use cases related to our resource federation system. The security model, realized by the Single Sign-On server and client components outlined in section 4.2, can be used by any service provider to access federated resources in a Single Sign-On manner, allowing for both Web browser and RESTful Web service access. This flexibility increases usability and paves the way for running computational studies on large interdisciplinary data sets as intended in section 1.

From a security standpoint, future work should be invested in adopting the findings outlined in [32], most of all the channel binding proposed in RFC 5929 as well as cross-domain SLSOP authentication cookies.

Both the resource federation system and the underlying security model form the basis to enable cross-organizational information extraction among distributed resources, which also benefits from uniform access to available computation resources. In addition to the uniform access achieved by the federation layer, an extraction system can provide a unified view on documents of different times, writing styles and potentially also languages by providing semantic meta-information.

Also, overall scalability must be put to the test in future work to gather significant and reliable performance data.

Endnotes

[a]The specifications can be found online: http://webdav.org/specs/

[b]Unique Resource Identifier

Competing interest
The authors declare that they have no competing interests.

Authors' contributions
MD led architecture, design and implementation of the security system, communication and integration components, contributed to the original scenario integration and literature study, consulted on the resource federator architecture, authored sections 4 and 6, co-authored sections 1 and 2 and assumed proofreading responsibilities. DH led architecture, design and implementation of the resource federator, contributed to the original scenario integration and literature study, consulted on the security system architecture, authored section 3 and assumed proofreading responsibilities. RJ drafted the manuscript and original scenario integration plus literature study and contributed to the resource federation and extraction system. SM designed and implemented the extraction framework integration and contributed to the corresponding paper section. BS contributed to architecture, design and implementation of the resource federator and provided the UNICORE integration. RMP contributed to the architecture conception. All authors read and approved the final manuscript.

Acknowledgements
The architecture described in this work is being developed as part of the German D-Grid project WisNetGrid (http://wisnetgrid.org) and is funded by the German Federal Ministry of Education and Research (BMBF).

Author details
[1] Jülich Supercomputing Centre, Forschungszentrum Jülich, 52428 Jülich, Germany. [2]Center for Information Services and High Performance Computing (ZIH), 01062 Dresden, Germany. [3]Max-Planck-Institut for Informatics, 66123 Saarbrücken, Germany.

References
1. Cannataro M, Talia D, Srimani PK (2002) Parallel data intensive computing in scientific and commercial applications. Parallel Computing 28(5): 673–704. doi:10.1016/S0167-8191(02)00091-1
2. Kouzes R, Anderson G, Elbert S, Gorton I, Gracio D (2009) The changing paradigm of data-intensive computing. Computer 42(1): 26–34. doi:10.1109/MC.2009.26
3. Bryant R (2011) Data-intensive scalable computing for scientific applications. Computing in Science Engineering 13(6): 25–33. doi:10.1109/MCSE.2011.73
4. Foster I, Kesselman C (eds) (1999) The grid: blueprint for a new computing infrastructure. Morgan, Kaufmann Publishers Inc., San Francisco, CA, USA
5. Venugopal S, Buyya R, Ramamohanarao K (2006) A taxonomy of data grids for distributed data sharing, management, and processing. ACM Comput. Surv 38. http://doi.acm.org/10.1145/1132952.1132955
6. XSEDE: Extreme Science and Engineering Discovery Environment. https://www.xsede.org/home
7. EGI, European Grid Infrastructure. http://www.egi.eu/
8. D-Grid, The German Grid Initiative. http://www.d-grid-gmbh.de/index.php?id=1&L=1
9. WisNetGrid: WisNetGrid – Knowledge Networks for Grids. Grid Project within the German Grid Initiative (D-Grid). Jäkel R (ed) Technische Universität Dresden, 2009. Web. 04. http://wisnetgrid.org
10. PubMed: PubMed. National Institutes of Health, 1996. http://www.ncbi.nlm.nih.gov/pubmed/
11. United Nations Environment Programme: Environmental Data Explorer. The Environmental Database. N.p., n.d. Web. 04. http://geodata.grid.unep.ch/
12. Foster I, Zhao Y, Raicu I, Lu S (2008) Cloud computing and grid computing 360-degree compared. In: Grid Computing Environments Workshop, 2008. GCE '08. ACM, New York, pp 1–10. doi:10.1109/GCE.2008.4738445
13. Cooper D, Santesson S, Farrell S, Boeyen S, Housley R, Polk W (2008) Internet X.509 Public Key Infrastructure Certificate and Certificate Revocation List (CRL) Profile. D-Grid, The German Grid Initiative. http://tools.ietf.org/html/rfc5280
14. XSede: Science Gateways via User Portal. https://www.xsede.org/science-gateways
15. EGI, Science Gateways. http://www.egi.eu/services/support/science-gateways/
16. Plantikow S, Peter K, Hœgvist M, Grimme C, Papaspyrou A (2009) Generalizing the data management of three community grids. Future Generation Computer Systems 25(3): 281–289. doi:10.1016/j.future.2008.05.001
17. EMI, European Middleware Initiative. http://www.eu-emi.eu
18. Jie W, Arshad J, Sinnott R, Townend P, Lei Z (2011) A review of grid authentication and authorization technologies and support for federated access control. ACM Comput. Surv 43: 12:1–12:26. http://doi.acm.org/10.1145/1883612.1883619
19. Farkas Z, Kacsuk P (2011) P-grade portal: A generic workflow system to support user communities. Future Generation Computer Systems 27(5): 454–465. doi:10.1016/j.future.2010.12.001
20. Novotny J, Tuecke S, Welch V (2001) An online credential repository for the Grid: MyProxy. In: High Performance Distributed Computing, 2001. Proceedings. 10th IEEE International Symposium on, Internet2 Middleware Initiative, pp 104 –111. doi:10.1109/HPDC.2001.945181
21. Tuecke S, Engert D, Foster I, Welch V, Chicago U, Thompson M, Pearlman L, Kesselman C (2001) Internet X.509 Public Key Infrastructure Proxy Certificate Profile. Conference publication, Limerick, Revised July 2002
22. Guo Z, Singh R, Pierce M (2009) Building the PolarGrid portal using Web 2.0 and OpenSocial. In: Proceedings of the 5th Grid Computing Environments Workshop, GCE '09. ACM, New York, NY, USA, pp 5:1–5:8. doi:10.1145/1658260.1658267
23. MosGrid: Molecular Simulation Grid. https://mosgrid.de/portal
24. Gesing S, Grunzke R, Balaskó A, Birkenheuer G, Blunk D, Breuers S, Brinkmann A, Fels G, Herres-Pawlis S, Kacsuk P, Kozlovszky M, Krüger J, Packschies L, Schäfer P, Schuller B, Schuster J, Steinke T, Szikszay Fabri A, Wewior M, Müller-Pfefferkorn R, Kohlbacher O (2011) Granular security for a science gateway in structural bioinformatics. In: 3rd International Workshop on Science Gateways for Life Sciences (IWSG 2011), CEUR Workshop Proceedings, vol 819. Elsevier Science Publishers B. V., Amsterdam. http://ceur-ws.org/Vol-819/
25. Recordon, David and Fitzpatrick, Brad: OpenID Authentification 1.1 (2006). http://openid.net/specs/openid-authentication-1_1.html
26. Internet2 Middleware Initiative: Shibboleth. http://shibboleth.internet2.edu/
27. W3C Working Group: Web Services Architecture (2004). http://www.w3.org/TR/ws-arch/

28. OASIS Security Services TC: Security Assertion Markup Language (SAML) v2.0 (2005). http://www.oasis-open.org/standards#samlv2.0
29. NSF Middleware Initiative: GridShib. http://gridshib.globus.org
30. Barton T, Basney J, Freeman T, Scavo T, Siebenlist F, Welch V, Ananthakrishnan R, Baker B, Goode M, Keahey K (2006) Identity Federation and Attribute-based Authorization through the Globus Toolkit, Shibboleth, GridShib, and MyProxy. In: 5th Annual PKI R&D Workshop, IEEE Computer Society
31. NSF Middleware Initiative: GridShib SAML Tools (2008). http://gridshib. globus.org/docs/gridshib-saml-tools-0.5.0/readme.html
32. Schwenk J, Kohlar F, Amon M (2011) The power of recognition: secure single sign-on using TLS channel bindings. In: Proceedings of the 7th ACM workshop on Digital identity management, DIM '11. ACM, New York, NY, USA, pp 63–72. http://doi.acm.org/10.1145/2046642.2046656
33. Hypertext Transfer Protocol – HTTP/1.1. http://www.w3.org/Protocols/ rfc2616/rfc2616.html
34. Benedyczak K, Baa P, van den Berghe S, Menday R, Schuller B (2011) Key aspects of the unicore 6 security model. Future Generation Computer Systems 27(2): 195–201. doi:10.1016/j.future.2010.08.009
35. Berry W 15 seconds : Sharing cookies across domains. http://www. 15seconds.com/issue/971108.htm
36. Fielding R, Taylor R (2000) Principled design of the modern web architecture. In: Software Engineering, 2000. Proceedings of the 2000 International Conference on. Elsevier Science Publishers B. V., Amsterdam, pp 407–416. doi:10.1109/ICSE.2000.870431
37. W3C Working Group: libcurl - the multiprotocol file transfer library (2004). http://www.w3.org/TR/ws-arch/
38. Crockford D (2006) The application/json Media Type for JavaScript Object Notation (JSON). http://tools.ietf.org/html/rfc4627
39. Kulkarni S, Singh A, Ramakrishnan G, Chakrabarti S (2009) Collective annotation of Wikipedia entities in web text. In: Proceedings of the 15th ACM SIGKDD international conference on Knowledge discovery and data mining (KDD), University of Westminster, London. ACM, New York, pp 457–466. http://doi.acm.org/10.1145/1557019.1557073
40. Yosef MA, Hoffart J, Spaniol M, Weikum G (2011) Aida: An online tool for accurate disambiguation of named entities in text and tables. In: Jagadish HV, Blakeley J, Hellerstein JM, Koudas N, Lehner W, Sarawagi S, Röhm U (eds.) Proceedings of the 37th International Conference on Very Large Data Bases, Proceedings of the VLDB Endowment, vol 4. VLDB Endowment, Seattle, USA, pp 1450–1453
41. Auer S, Bizer C, Kobilarov G, Lehmann J, Ives Z (2007) DBpedia: A Nucleus for a Web of Open Data. In: Proceedings of 6th International Semantic Web Conference, 2nd Asian Semantic Web Conference (ISWC+ASWC 2007), Vol. 4825. Elsevier Science Publishers B. V., Amsterdam, pp 11–15
42. Brin S (1999) Extracting Patterns and Relations from the World Wide Web. In: Workshop on The World Wide Web and Databases (WebDB) at 6th International Conference on Extending Database Technology (EDBT). Springer-Verlag, Valencia, pp 172–183
43. Suchanek FM, Sozio M, Weikum G (2009) SOFIE: A Self-Organizing Framework for Information Extraction. In: WWW'09 : proceedings of the 18th International World Wide Web Conference. ACM, Madrid
44. Elbassuoni S, Hose K, Metzger S, Schenkel R (2010) Roxxi: Reviving witness dOcuments to eXplore eXtracted Information. In: Proceedings of the 36th International Conference on Very Large Data Bases, Proceedings of the VLDB Endowment, vol 3. ACM, Singapore, pp 1589–1592

3

Secure cross-domain cookies for HTTP

Paul Rabinovich

Abstract

Cookies represent an important element of HTTP providing state management to an otherwise stateless protocol. HTTP cookies currently in use are governed by the same origin policy that directs Web browsers to allow cookie sharing only between Web sites in the same DNS domain. As Web applications get richer, data sharing across domain boundaries becomes more important. While practical solutions to cross-domain data sharing exist, in many cases they increase complexity and cost. In this paper we propose a simple mechanism to share cookies using authorizations based on X.509 attribute and public key certificates. In addition to supporting secure cookie sharing between unrelated domains, it can be beneficial for hosts in the same domain when the currently used same origin policy is deemed too permissive, exposing cookies to leakage and spoofing.

Keywords: HTTP, Cross-domain cookie, Public key cryptography, Authorization model

1   Introduction

An HTTP cookie is a small file left in a Web browser by a Web server. Cookies were introduced by Netscape as a state management mechanism to the otherwise stateless HTTP protocol in 1994 [1]. The current implemented standard for HTTP cookies is RFC 2109 [2]; it defines the cookie format and the rules for proper handling of cookies by Web browsers, servers, and proxies. A newer standard, RFC 2965 [3], was never widely adopted[a]. A cookie carries a name/value pair (its useful payload) and a set of management attributes. The basic management attributes are shown in Table 1.

Cookies may be subdivided into *session cookies*, erased when the browser is closed, and *persistent cookies*, preserved across multiple browser sessions. Persistent cookies are frequently used as an inexpensive way to store users' preferences for a Web site. The advantage is that the Web site operator doesn't need to maintain an account for the user; all pertinent information is stored in the browser, and made available to the site when the user visits it. Cookies may also be used for tracking purposes: a cookie lets a Web site uniquely identify the user (on a given computer) and link to her all Web pages she visited on that site. Tracking is possible within a single Web site or across a group of cooperating Web sites.

A Web page is a hypertext document more often than not referencing other resources on the Web. Cookies received by the browser when accessing these resources are frequently called *third-party cookies*; those set by the main page are called *first-party cookies*. This distinction does not affect the HTTP protocol. It reflects the end users' perception of these artifacts and has important implications for user privacy since third-party cookies are frequently used for user tracking across multiple sites. See [5] for more details.

Browsers use the *same origin* policy to determine whether to send a cookie to a Web site: an HTTP request sent to a host will contain those and only those cookies whose Domain attribute identifies the host itself or the DNS domain to which the host belongs [2][b]. (The Path and Port attributes are also taken into account.) When setting a cookie, the Web server is allowed to omit the Domain attribute (then the browser sets this attribute to the server's host name) or to set it to the server's parent domain. For example, host x.domain1.com may set Domain to .domain1.com but not to .domain2.com. To set cookies Web servers use the Set-Cookie HTTP header; to relay cookies to Web servers browsers use the Cookie header[c].

One of the requirements of the same origin policy is that cookies be shared only between Web sites within the same *administrative* domain. Various heuristics were put in place to guess administrative domain boundaries using the hierarchical structure of DNS names [1,2,6]. For instance, servers cannot set the Domain attribute to one of the top level domains (TLD) since by definition each

Correspondence: paul.rabinovich@exostar.com
Security Software Development, Exostar, Herndon, USA

Table 1 HTTP cookie attributes [2]

Attribute	Description
Comment	Short description of the intended use of the cookie
Domain	DNS domain or IP address for which the cookie is valid
HttpOnly	If present, the cookie cannot be accessed by a client-side script (e.g., written in JavaScript). Although non-standard, this attribute is supported by most Web browsers [4]
Max-Age	Maximum period after which the cookie must be discarded
Path	Subset of URLs on qualifying hosts for which the cookie is valid
Port	List of TCP ports on qualifying hosts for which the cookie is valid
Secure	If present, the cookie may be transported only over a secure (e.g., SSL-protected) channel

TLD provides a common umbrella for a (large) set of completely unrelated domains.

The original Netscape proposal [7] never included provisions for cookie sharing between arbitrary Web sites. The subsequent standards [2,3] didn't change this basic assumption. In many cases, however, the same origin policy imposes unnecessary limitations on Web site developers and forces them to implement complex and expensive workarounds. They are also prone to failure. For example, sharing of state information can be accomplished by embedding data in URLs or posting them via HTML forms. But if the user clicks the Back button, the application's state will be rolled back rendering the user's experience inconsistent [1].

While the Web technology itself imposes limitations on state and context sharing across domain boundaries, the general trend in Web development is towards increased integration, regardless of such boundaries. Federated Web portals, Web mashups and composite applications provide a unified experience to end users, combining data, resources, and elements of the user interface from multiple sources [8-10]. Sharing of persistent data within these systems remains a challenge. As one example, in the world of identity federation it's often useful to automatically discover a user's identity provider, or IDP (an entity that holds her account and authenticates her) when she visits an affiliated Web site (a service provider, or SP). One way to accomplish this is for the identity provider to leave a cookie in the user's browser; subsequently the cookie can be read by service providers, and the browser can be automatically redirected to the IDP for authentication. Indeed, the SAML 2.0 Identity Provider Discovery Profile [11] uses this approach but necessarily assumes that the IDP and the SP(s) share a DNS domain. This model works well when used by a small number of closely related sites but is not practical for large-scale identity federations [12].

Recognizing stultifying effects of the same origin policy, manufacturers of Web client software (e.g., Adobe Flash, Microsoft Silverlight) added support for cross-domain communication (including cookie sharing) to their products, and recent analyses demonstrate that the use of this feature is on the rise [13,14]. However, there is no comparable *standards-based* mechanism for cross-domain cookie sharing.

The same origin policy for cookies as it is currently implemented may be too permissive in some cases. For example, some country-code top level domains have second level subdomains that act as generic, functional top level domains in their respective hierarchies. In many cases current domain name matching rules allow sharing of cookies with all sites in such domains [6,15]. Even in domains with more "administrative affinity" some hosts may want to interact via cookies without necessarily sharing information with, or receiving information from, other peer hosts. This unwanted sharing may result in cookie leakage (cookies are sent to unauthorized Web servers) or cookie spoofing (cookies are inadvertently or maliciously set by unauthorized Web servers) [1].

From these examples it should be clear that cookie sharing across domain boundaries is a desirable feature in Web applications and middleware. For such sharing to be secure an authorization mechanism needs to be developed granting access only to those hosts that require it. As our last example indicates, even hosts within a single domain may benefit from a more fine-grained access control model than the one currently in use. In this paper we propose such a model and introduce modifications to the HTTP protocol necessary to support it.

This paper is organized as follows. Section 2 provides a review of related work. Data structures required by our solution are described in Section 3. Section 4.3 explains how cross-domain cookies are set, and Section 4.4, how they are read. In Section 6 we discuss our proof of concept and evaluate communication overhead of the proposed solution. In Section 7 we analyze our proposal focusing especially on its security properties and implementability. Lastly, Section 8 summarizes the paper.

2 Related work

Many variants of the same folk protocol exist where one or more Web sites use another site as a cookie manager (CM): to set a cookie the Web sites redirect the browser to the manager passing the necessary data as a request parameter; the manager sets the cookie when redirecting back to the requesting page. (At this point the browser associates the cookie with the cookie manager's host or domain.) To receive a cookie, they do a redirect to the CM who receives the cookie from the browser and performs another redirect (back) passing the data, also as a request parameter. While this is a working solution, it requires multiple redirects (two per request) increasing communication overhead and design complexity. Our proposal, on the other hand, introduces native support for cross-domain cookies in HTTP and, thus, eliminates the need for redirects.

Callaghan et al. proposed a proxy-based solution that allows non-cooperating Web servers to communicate using standard HTTP cookies [16]. A forwarding proxy is configured to treat a group of Web sites as one; it captures cookies from passing HTTP traffic and makes them available to communicating browsers and servers by inserting `Cookie` and `Set-Cookie` HTTP headers as needed. In a more complex configuration, Callaghan et al. set up a "cookie manager" URL that the proxy itself responds to. Cross-site cookies are associated in the browser with that URL. When a browser sends a request to a participating server, the proxy initiates a cookie transfer from the "cookie manager" (CM) as follows:

1. Redirect to the CM keeping the target URL as a request parameter.
2. Intercept the request as the CM, receive all cookies, and redirect to the target URL encoding the cookies as request parameters.
3. Intercept the request again, convert the request parameters into cookies using the `Set-Cookie` header, and redirect to the target URL again.

After this the cookies will be associated with the target host as well as the CM itself. The drawback of this solution (in addition to multiple redirects) is that it tightly couples components in the user's domain (the forwarding proxy) and the application's domain (the Web servers). Such coupling may be achieved and maintained in a controlled environment, for example, within an enterprise, but cannot be easily replicated in other settings. Callaghan et al.'s approach was driven by constraints imposed by the same origin policy. Our solution does not adhere to this policy, cross-domain cookies are supported natively, and no additional components (such as proxies) are required. Since the proxy is not needed any longer, the tight coupling is eliminated, and the operational complexity of the system, reduced.

Guo and Zhou proposed a new type of cookie (called a *cross cookie*) geared towards Web mashups [17]. Their model consists of three tiers: content servers serving *gadgets*, aggregating servers that combine gadgets into mashups, and, finally, Web browsers rendering mashup pages. Cross cookies are exchanged between aggregating servers and browsers. A mashup can be represented as an HTML document object model (DOM) tree with subtrees containing gadgets from content servers. When an aggregating server receives a cookie with a gadget, it constructs a cross cookie capturing the name of the content server and the position of the gadget in the mashup DOM tree, and sends the cookie to the browser. Similarly, the browser sends cross cookies back to the aggregating server, and the latter converts them to traditional cookies when communicating with the content server-owner of the gadget. For example, if the same parameterized gadget is included k times in a mashup, the content server may send as many as k versions of the same cookie to the aggregating server; cross cookies will capture the cookie context (the position in the DOM tree) and provide enough information to the aggregator to return the correct version of the cookie on subsequent visits to the content server. Despite their name, cross cookies are not general purpose cross-domain cookies; they address a special need of Web mashup applications and work only between aggregating servers and browsers. By contrast, our proposal is general in nature and can be used in any HTTP-based communications.

The HTML 5 specification introduced *Web Storage*, a new state management mechanism for the Web [18]. The standard supports session storage and persistent storage, both indexed by origin. A storage object is a simple associative array. Although stored objects are governed by the same origin policy, they can participate in cross-domain data sharing through the use of another HTML 5 mechanism, *Web Messaging* [19]. Web Messaging is a JavaScript API for data exchange between browser windows. The communicating parties (scriptlets) may belong to different origins; they themselves make the decision whether to send (receive) a message based on the recipient's (sender's) origin. The significant advantage of the Web Storage/Web Messaging combination is its acceptance by the market. (Although [18,19] are only draft specifications, they have been implemented by all major browsers [6].) It requires careful client-side coding, however. Although both senders and recipients are encouraged to check each other's origins [20], in practice this is done inconsistently. For example, Hanna et al. [21] discovered that two of the most popular users of Web Messaging, Facebook Connect and Google Friend Connect, perform these checks only sporadically; the authors were able to compromise message integrity and confidentiality of both protocols. Our approach, on the other hand, does not require any coding; it abstracts security decisions into a small set of simple data structures (channel and authorization certificates) that lend themselves to efficient unified management by Web sites.

Another widely available cross-domain data sharing mechanism is *Cross-Origin Resource Sharing* (CORS) [22]. CORS allows a Web page associated with one origin to access resources associated with a different one. Based on the `Origin` header reported by the browser, the target Web site may choose to allow or deny access, or, more granularly, accept or expose certain HTTP headers (including `Cookie` and `Set-Cookie`). Like Web

Storage/Web Messaging, the CORS specification is supported by all major browser vendors. Its drawback is that it can only be used with AJAX (JavaScript) requests [23]. Our cross-domain cookies work like traditional cookies; they can be used with both browser-native and JavaScript-issued HTTP requests[d].

3 Channels, cookies and authorizations

3.1 Channels and channel names

To allow disparate domains to communicate using cookies we introduce the notion of a *cross-domain channel* (XDC). An XDC channel may be thought of as a folder in the browser to which writers write cookies and from which readers read them. Cross-domain channels have names. We propose a decentralized namespace where owners create and destroy channels as needed without coordinating it with anybody else. To avoid collisions we use channel names based on RSA keys. When creating an XDC channel, its owner generates a random RSA key pair (with a sufficiently long modulus), and computes a digest of the public key using a high quality hash algorithm. The computed digest is the channel name. This approach allows us (a) to generate names that are unique for all practical purposes, and (b) to use a simple scheme to prove one's ownership of a channel: just present the public key from which the channel name was derived and prove possession of the private key corresponding to it.

Channel owners issue *XDC channel certificates* to themselves and *XDC authorizations* to Web sites or DNS domains interested in using their channels. These data structures are covered in Section 3.3.

3.2 Secure channels

The owner may designate an XDC channel as secure. XDC cookies associated with a secure channel may be transmitted only over a secure (e.g., SSL-protected) connection. This is similar in spirit to the Secure attribute in traditional cookies [2]. Transmitting cookies only over a secure transport has several benefits. It enhances security and confidentiality of the cookies themselves. It also helps to mitigate against DNS spoofing: when a browser validates a server's certificate, it verifies that the host name in the certificate matches that of the host the browser is actually communicating with. To fool the browser the attacker would have to spoof the DNS and to gain access to the server's private key. In addition, in our scheme (Section 3.3) XDC authorizations for secure channels are bound to the holder's SSL certificate, providing an extra layer of protection against Web site impersonation.

Internet attribute certificates already have a provision for referencing the subject's identity certificate (specifically, its issuer name and serial number) [24]; we reuse this mechanism. When a Web browser receives a cookie, it finds the cookie's authorization; if it contains a reference

to the server's identity certificate and the cookie was received over an insecure channel, the cookie is ignored; if it's received over an SSL channel, the browser checks if the server's SSL certificate matches the reference in the XDC authorization: on match the cookie is accepted, on mismatch, discarded. XDC cookie delivery to Web servers works in a similar fashion. This is analogous to the approach proposed by Karlof et al. for traditional cookies [25].

3.3 Channel certificates and authorizations

The owner of an XDC issues authorizations to hosts that need to use it. The structure of an XDC authorization is shown in Figure 1. It consists of two components, an optional channel certificate and an authorization certificate granting access to the channel to a particular host or DNS domain.

The channel certificate is a self-signed X.509 public key certificate [26,27]. It contains a human-readable description of the channel, the channel name (along with the identifier of the hash algorithm used to compute it), and the secure flag. It is signed with the owner's private key. The channel certificate is optional in an authorization. If it is not included, the relying party (e.g., the browser) must be able to obtain it by other means. Our scheme provides a discovery mechanism for doing it.

The authorization certificate is also signed with the owner's private key. It is implemented as an Internet attribute certificate defined in RFC 3281 [24]. The authorization's subject's name is placed in the Holder field of the certificate. An authorization grants its holder a permission to read or to write (i.e., create, modify and delete) XDC cookies. In addition to the holder's name and permissions, the authorization certificate encodes the XDC channel name and a brief human-readable description of the channel or of the holder's use of the channel. For secure channels it also contains the ID of the holder's SSL certificate (the issuer name/serial number pair [24]). Like any attribute certificate, the authorization certificate has a validity period that must be checked every time the corresponding XDC cookie is used.

Internet attribute certificates support a revocation checking model based either on certificate revocation lists (CRL) or on the Online Certificate Status Protocol (OCSP). To simplify processing and minimize the overhead, however, we chose not to use revocation checking in our solution.

3.4 Cross-domain cookies

Cross-domain (or XDC) cookies have essentially the same structure as HTTP cookies currently in use. They still carry name/value pairs and additional management attributes (see Table 1). Instead of the Domain, Path and Port attributes, however, we introduce the XDC Name

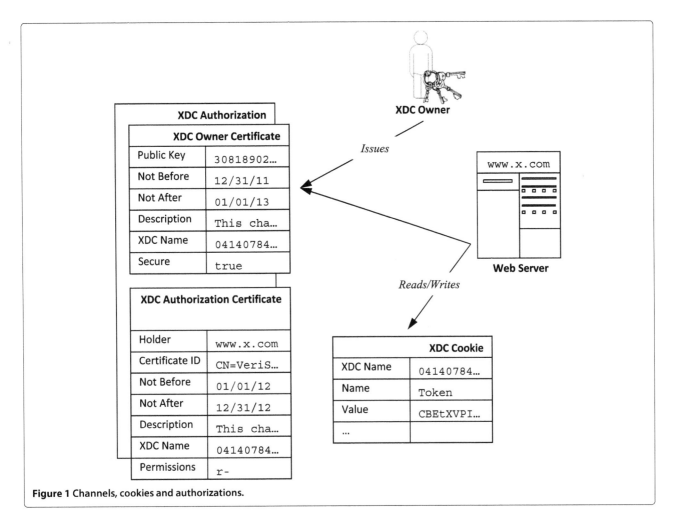

Figure 1 Channels, cookies and authorizations.

attribute; it contains the (properly encoded) name of the XDC channel to which the cookie belongs. XDC cookies do not allow access to scripts, so the HttpOnly attribute is not required, either. Finally, the Secure attribute is superseded by the (more resilient) secure flag in the XDC channel certificate.

4 The protocol

4.1 Data exchanges

When the browser makes a user-initiated request to Web server, it may have some XDC cookies to send to the server subject to the server's XDC authorizations. The browser may have some, all, or none of the authorizations issued to the server (or its parent DNS domain). Our proposal provides three mechanisms to discover all applicable authorizations:

- Send a *preflight request* to the server
- Send the user request, allow the server to provide any missing authorizations, and then resend the request again
- Perform a DNS lookup

We issue preflight requests for all user requests that use HTTP methods POST and PUT. Not doing so may result in the server activating the second discovery mechanism which, in turn, may lead to retransmission of large amounts of data in the request. Preflight information received from the server is cached (for the duration indicated by the server), so not all user requests require preflight authorization; only those with expired (or non-existent) cache entries do. Preflight information may include XDC channel certificates and XDC authorizations as well as the time to live for the information and additional options. The only option currently defined is a flag indicating whether the browser should use the DNS to look up additional authorizations for the server (or its parent DNS domain) and, if so, how often.

When the server receives an actual user request, it may discover that some XDC cookies it expects have not been included by the browser: the browser either doesn't have the cookies at all, or it has the cookies but doesn't have some authorizations for the server. To account for the latter case, the server may respond with missing authorizations, and request the browser to repeat the request, now with the missing cookies (presumably, covered by the just discovered authorizations).

A browser receiving XDC cookies from a server can use all previously cached authorizations or authorizations the server sends with the cookies themselves. Since the server can always bundle cookies and authorizations in a single response, no additional round trips are required to complete discovery.

The last source of XDC authorizations for a Web site is the DNS. To support out-of-band delivery, we propose to place XDC authorizations in TXT resource records[e] (RR) in the DNS [28], encoded to respect the rules of the DNS. Since TXT resource records may be used by many applications, there is a risk that a record received by the browser is not an XDC authorization. In our implementation the client just discarded the RR if it could not interpret it correctly; to minimize unnecessary traffic in the future an application-specific RR could be introduced or a general-purpose "kitchen sink RR" [29] reused if one is implemented.

A DNS lookup is performed on send when the browser finds an unresolved XDC cookie in the cookie "jar", and on receive when the server sends an XDC cookie that cannot be resolved by any other means (cached or in-band XDC authorizations). The DNS is not consulted unless the server indicates it in its response to a preflight request.

4.2 Preflight requests
A preflight request is an HTTP request; it uses the HTTP method OPTIONS and sets the request header `Xdc-Info-Request` to `true`. A preflight request is issued for the same URL as the original user request. A compliant server may return zero or more `Xdc-Channel` and `Xdc-Authorization` headers. It may also include the `Xdc-Max-Age` header indicating the maximum retention time of the information provided in the response. (If none is given, a protocol default will be used.) Finally, an `Xdc-Options` header may include additional XDC processing instructions; currently only

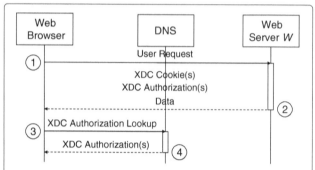

Figure 3 The sequence diagram for setting of XDC cookies. The browser sends the user's request and receives a response that may contain XDC cookies and authorizations. If any of the XDC cookies don't have a matching authorization, a DNS lookup is performed.

the `dns-max-age` option is defined; if set, it instructs the browser to look up missing XDC authorizations in the DNS and defines the maximum frequency of such lookups. A sample preflight request is shown in Figure 2.

4.3 Setting cross-domain cookies
Figure 3 shows the sequence diagram for an XDC cookie-setting server. The server uses the `Xdc-Authorization` (and possibly the `Xdc-Channel`) headers to convey its authorizations to the browser. The value of the header is an encoded XDC authorization. We use double encoding: first the value is base 64-encoded and then URL-encoded. To set cross-domain cookies our server uses the new `Xdc-Set-Cookie` header. Normally, the client would discard those cookies for which the server failed to provide an authorization. In our model, however, the client may contact the DNS to retrieve the missing authorizations. All XDC authorizations in hand, the client validates the cookies and stores them in the cookie "jar".

4.4 Reading cross-domain cookies
The sequence diagram for an XDC cookie-reading scenario is shown in Figure 4. Before sending XDC cookies

```
>> OPTIONS /xdc/read HTTP/1.1
>> Host: read.xdc.com:8080
>> Xdc-Info-Request: true
>> Connection: Keep-Alive
>> User-Agent: Mozilla/5.0 (Windows NT 6.1; WOW64; rv:7.0.1) Gecko/20100101 Firefox/7.0.12011-10-16 20:23:00

<< HTTP/1.1 200 OK
<< Server: Apache-Coyote/1.1
<< Transfer-Encoding: chunked
<< Content-Length: 0
<< Xdc-Channel: MIIB%2FzCCAWigAwIBAgIBATANBgkq...
<< Xdc-Authorization: MIIEB6CCAgMwggH%2FMIIBaKADAgEC...
<< Xdc-Max-Age: 36000
<< Xdc-Options: dns-max-age=1000
<< Date: Tue, 27 Dec 2011 19:15:01 GMT
```

Figure 2 A preflight request. >> marks headers sent to the server, **<<**, headers received from it.

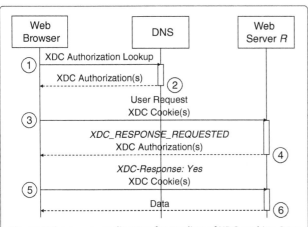

Figure 4 The sequence diagram for reading of XDC cookies. Prior to sending the user's request, the browser looks up missing authorizations (if any) in the DNS. Then the request is sent along with XDC cookies. The server may provide additional authorizations in order to receive XDC cookies it expected but did not receive (step 4). Having received an XDC response in step 5, the server responds with data. Steps 4 and 5 should not be needed for user requests requiring preflight authorizations.

expect additional XDC cookies that it doesn't receive with the request. Our Web server may respond with the missing `Xdc-Authorization` headers and set the HTTP status code to `XDC_RESPONSE_REQUESTED`, a value we introduced. This status code tells the browser that the sole purpose of the HTTP response is to provide the necessary XDC authorizations and that the browser must repeat the request including all valid XDC cookies. Since now two requests are treated as a single request, the server needs to remember that it already provided all XDC authorizations it has. To avoid the need to store the state of this two-step request on the server we propose a new header, `Xdc-Response` with values `true` and `false`. When a client repeats a request in response to the `XDC_RESPONSE_REQUESTED` status code, it sets this header to `true` and includes it in the request. Not sending the header is equivalent to sending `Xdc-Response: false`. The client repeats the operation by evaluating all XDC cookies it holds against the updated set of XDC authorizations for the target host.

Figure 5 shows the trace of a single request to an XDC cookie-reading server. Initially the browser doesn't have any authorizations for host `read.xdc.com`. The server responds with a set of four authorizations and sets the HTTP status code to `XDC_RESPONSE_REQUESTED` (399). The browser repeats the request setting the `Xdc-Response` header to `true` and including all eligible cookies. There are six valid cookies for the host spread over three cross-domain channels.

to the server the Web client needs to find all missing authorizations. It contacts the DNS and requests TXT resource records for the Web server's host. Having received and validated the authorizations, it sends the appropriate XDC cookies to the server using the new `Xdc-Cookie` header. As we mentioned, the server may

```
>> GET /xdc/read HTTP/1.1
>> Host: read.xdc.com:8080
>> Connection: Keep-Alive
>> User-Agent: Apache-HttpClient/4.1-alpha1 (java 1.5)

<< HTTP/1.1 399
<< Server: Apache-Coyote/1.1
<< Xdc-Authorization: MIIC2DCCAZkwggECoAMCAQICBEs%2B...
<< Xdc-Authorization: MIIC3DCCAZkwggECoAMCAQICBEtXVP...
<< Xdc-Authorization: MIIC4TCCAZkwggECoAMCAQICBEtXVP...
<< Xdc-Authorization: MIIC4TCCAZkwggECoAMCAQICBEtXVi...
<< Content-Length: 0
<< Date: Tue, 27 Dec 2011 18:28:43 GMT

>> GET /xdc/read HTTP/1.1
>> Xdc-Response: true
>> Xdc-Cookie: name=A3; value=Value3; channelName=axual9nhqawkv2ejkwwgzuig0q4xwtq%3d
>> Xdc-Cookie: name=B3; value=Value3; channelName=axual9nhqawkv2ejkwwgzuig0q4xwtq%3d
>> Xdc-Cookie: name=A1; value=Value1; channelName=axua9a7s5o87a7pasuu2xvbcyzsq1gc%3d
>> Xdc-Cookie: name=B1; value=Value1; channelName=axua9a7s5o87a7pasuu2xvbcyzsq1gc%3d
>> Xdc-Cookie: name=A2; value=Value2; channelName=axuafo%2bx2rcz4qke%2fkccqh8mustitos%3d
>> Xdc-Cookie: name=B2; value=Value2; channelName=axuafo%2bx2rcz4qke%2fkccqh8mustitos%3d
>> Host: read.xdc.com:8080
>> Connection: Keep-Alive
>> User-Agent: Apache-HttpClient/4.1-alpha1 (java 1.5)

<< HTTP/1.1 200 OK
<< Server: Apache-Coyote/1.1
<< Transfer-Encoding: chunked
<< Date: Tue, 27 Dec 2011 18:28:43 GMT
```

Figure 5 An HTTP request relaying XDC cookies to a server. >> marks headers sent to the server, <<, headers received from it.

4.5 Summary of changes to the HTTP protocol

In this section we summarize all additions to the HTTP protocol required to support our cross-domain cookies. Table 2 lists our proposed HTTP headers. Table 3 lists the single newly proposed HTTP status code.

5 Proof of concept

Our proof of concept consists of several components:

- Utilities to generate channel certificates, sign XDC authorizations, and save them in different formats
- An XDC cookie-reading application
- An XDC cookie-writing application
- An HTTP server capable of servicing XDC preflight requests
- A DNS server configured with XDC authorizations
- An XDC-capable client

The utilities and applications were written in Java. We used Bouncy Castle's cryptographic APIs [30] for all work with X.509 attribute and public key certificates. To host the applications, we used Apache Tomcat [31]. We enabled server-side support for preflight authorization by configuring our Apache HTTP proxy with two modules, mod_rewrite [32] and mod_headers [33]. The mod_rewrite configuration set an environment variable on HTTP OPTIONS requests that contained the header Xdc-Info-Request: true; the mod_headers configuration output XDC-specific HTTP headers if the environment variable was set. The DNS server hosted XDC authorizations. We used BIND 9.7.0 [34]. Our XDC-capable client was implemented as a Firefox browser extension. Firefox provides a pluggable framework for extending its functionality, and a cross-platform component object model, called XPCOM, for programming the extensions [35]. Multiple language bindings are supported for XPCOM; we implemented our extension in JavaScript. All source code and configuration instructions for our proof of concept are available from [36].

6 Evaluation

Our proposal adds communication overhead to normal browser/Web server interactions. Web sites not aware of our cross-domain cookies will incur minimal cost: the initial preflight request will either fail or return no information, and a protocol default (several days) will define the frequency of subsequent requests; DNS lookups will not be issued (no explicit instructions in the preflight response); and repeat requests will never be initiated. Overhead imposed by XDC-aware Web sites will depend on:

- The frequency of preflight requests
- The frequency of DNS lookups
- The frequency of repeat requests
- The number of channels with which the site interacts (i.e., reads or writes XDC cookies)
- The size of an individual XDC channel certificate and XDC authorization
- The number and size of XDC cookies set and received

Web sites can control the frequency of preflight requests by setting the header Xdc-Max-Age, and the frequency of DNS lookups by setting the header Xdc-Options (Section 4.2). Both settings are subject to tradeoff analysis

Table 2 HTTP headers

Name	Description	Request/response	When used
Xdc-Authorization	Contains a safely-encoded XDC authorization	Response	User, preflight requests
Xdc-Channel	Contains a safely-encoded XDC channel certificate	Response	User, preflight requests
Xdc-Cookie	The short representation of an XDC cookie (similar to the standard Cookie header [2]). May be replaced by the standard header if the Domain attribute can be overloaded with the XDC name and used included in requests (currently not supported)	Request	User, repeat requests
Xdc-Info-Request	Indicates a XDC preflight request. Always set to true	Request	Preflight requests
Xdc-Max-Age	Indicates the maximum retention period for preflight information	Response	Preflight requests
Xdc-Options	Provides additional instructions for XDC processing. Currently only the dns-max-age option is defined	Response	Preflight requests
Xdc-Response	Set to true to indicate a repeat request	Request	Repeat requests
Xdc-Set-Cookie	The long representation of an XDC cookie (similar to the standard Set-Cookie header [2]). May be replaced by the standard header if the Domain attribute can be overloaded with the XDC name	Response	User, repeat requests

Table 3 HTTP status codes

Mnemonic name	Description	Value	When used
XDC_RESPONSE_REQUESTED	Indicates that the Web server is expecting additional XDC cookies and, assuming the browser is missing XDC authorizations, for them sending some or all of them in the response	399	User requests (to initiate a repeat request)

(the number of unnecessary requests that discover no new information against the latency of discovering a change) but in most cases they can be set to days, weeks and even months.

It can be recalled from Section 4.4 that Web servers may initiate repeat requests only when XDC cookies they expect to receive are not provided by the browser. We expect that after several initial communications the browser will have all authorizations for a given Web server, and additional exchanges will not be required. Web servers catering to low bandwidth clients may elect to store all their XDC authorizations in the DNS; Web clients will only consult the DNS when an authorization for a particular cookie is missing.

Analysis by Tappenden and Miller [37] shows that the average number of cookies used by Web sites is 2.92, and the median number is 1.0; 75% of all sites use four or fewer cookies. This suggests that the number of cross-domain cookies used by a typical Web site should be small, and the number of channels with which they are associated, even smaller. About 278 kB of data are transferred in an average Web application session [38]. In our prototype fully-encoded XDC authorizations varied between 1,108 and 1,440 ASCII characters for 1024-bit RSA keys [f]. Even if preflight authorizations are not used, only a relatively small amount of data will be added to each session.

Our headers `Xdc-Cookie` and `Xdc-Set-Cookie` have the same basic structure as the corresponding headers for traditional cookies. As we explained in Table 2 the traditional headers can even be overloaded to support XDC functionality. Assuming that the payload size and the number of cross-domain cookies and of traditional cookies will not significantly differ, any additional overhead may come only from the XDC Name attribute. Based on the length of a raw XDC name (160 bits for SHA-1-generated names) and the fact that we use double encoding (base 64 and URL), it can be shown that the average length of an encoded XDC name is 31.6 characters. (In the interest of brevity we omit the calculation.) Comparing `Xdc-Set-Cookie` to `Set-Cookie` (which may carry a Domain attribute), and `Xdc-Cookie` and `Cookie` (which may not), we get the worst case average difference of 31.6 characters per cookie.

7 Discussion

7.1 General

The proposed scheme has several important properties. First, it allows us to generate unique channel names with negligible probability of collisions. Second, XDC authorizations provide a simple access control mechanism roughly equivalent to the one currently in use on the Web based on the domain matching rules and the same origin policy. Indeed, a traditional Web client looks at the Domain attribute in a cookie and decides if the communicating Web server's host name matches it; veracity of the host name is ascertained using the DNS. In our case, host name matching is based on direct comparison of the host name as reported by the DNS and the host name in the XDC authorization. Third, an XDC authorization is unforgeable (with current technologies); it cryptographically binds permissions to the cross-domain channel name which in turn is cryptographically bound to the owner of the channel: only the owner, possessor of the private key, could have signed the authorization. The binding between the owner's public key and the channel name relies on collision resistance properties of the hash function used to compute the name of the channel. In our experiments we used the SHA-1 algorithm [39].

7.2 Trust model for authorizations

As discussed in Section 3 our scheme does not support authorization revocation. Once granted, an XDC authorization remains valid until it expires, and cannot be withdrawn. In addition, if the XDC owner's private key is compromised, there is no remedial mechanism in place to migrate to the use of a new key (and a new XDC). We argue that this risk is acceptable. In the unlikely event that the key is compromised, the owner can generate a new key pair thus creating a new XDC, issue new XDC authorizations, and distribute them to all participating Web servers out-of-band. Servers that read XDC cookies can stop accepting the old cookies right away even if browsers continue to store them (and the old XDC authorizations) until expiration. Since anecdotal evidence suggests that revocations of SSL certificates due to key compromise are extremely rare, we expect that revocations of XDC keys will be infrequent as well. Building a complex infrastructure for such rare events, in our view, is not warranted.

Our use of the public key infrastructure in XDC authorizations is somewhat unconventional. The owner of a cross-domain channel acts as an application-specific certification authority (CA) whereas under normal circumstances CAs are application-independent, although they may issue end entity certificates suitable for a particular application. Using the traditional approach would have made our cookies less lightweight since (a) more information would need to be carried in XDC authorizations and (b) another trust infrastructure[g] would have to be tapped into to validate the application-specific certificates issued to XDC owners. As it is, our trust infrastructure is self-contained and doesn't have any external dependencies.

7.3   Threat model

A cookie can be viewed as a passive data element that interacts with the following actors: Web sites, the network, the browser, and the user. Traditional cookies are built on a *user-centric* threat model. The same origin policy assumes that the user is the ultimate owner of a cookie. If the browser and the network are honest, it protects against dishonest (or curious) Web servers that might want to gain unauthorized access to cookies. The cross-domain cookies we propose use the same basic threat model. In addition, secure XDC channels promote secure and confidential exchange of XDC cookies, mitigate against DNS spoofing attacks, and provide an extra layer of protection against Web site impersonation.

7.4   User control and privacy

Ultimately, the user must be in control of cookie sharing performed by his browser. The comment attributes in both XDC cookies and XDC authorizations should help him in making informed decisions about it.

In addition, the tracking protection framework ('Do Not Track', or *DNT*) nearing completion in the World Wide Web Consortium [5] can be adapted to cover XDC cookies as well. The DNT framework defines the users' rights vis-à-vis tracking by Web sites, the practices required of them to comply with the user preferences, and the technical means to express these preferences and compliance with them. We believe that cross-domain cookies proposed in this paper do not introduce any new concerns that don't already exist for traditional first-party and third-party cookies. To the degree that the DNT framework addresses those concerns, it should address them for XDC cookies as well. Specific compliance rules and technical mechanisms will need to be modified to incorporate a new scope, namely, an XDC channel. (At present, the DNT framework only considers sites and resources within those sites).

Even traditional cookies remain somewhat of a mystery to many end users, but at least they contain the Domain attribute that hints at the cookies' scope and applicability. Names of XDC cookies, on the other hand, are digests of public keys, and do not contain any information that may be recognized by the users. To mitigate this we suggest that browsers maintain a running log of recent use of all persistent XDC cookies capturing the channel name, the host name of the Web server reading or writing the cookie, the date and time of its last access, the type of access, and, possibly, the value set. This log can be used by administrators and advanced users to analyze XDC access patterns and modify their browsers' cookie acceptance rules if needed.

7.5   Compatibility with existing infrastructure

Although all functionality available through traditional cookies can be implemented with XDC cookies, we do not propose phasing them out, even in the long term. Traditional cookies enjoy widespread acceptance and have almost no operational and communication overhead. The two types of cookies should be able to coexist in the same protocol. Web browsers should treat these cookies as completely disjoint: a traditional cookie named X and an XDC cookie named X represent unrelated data even when they are received from (or need to be sent to) the same server. Such clean separation makes XDC cookies simpler to implement, and should ease their adoption by browser manufacturers.

Our proposal makes changes to the HTTP protocol. Any changes to HTTP must interoperate with the existing Web infrastructure. We need to evaluate how XDC-aware actors (i.e., servers, clients, and proxies) interact with those that are not XDC-aware. Three use cases may be considered:

- *XDC-aware client/unaware server.* This is the simplest case: the browser may issue XDC preflight requests, they will fail or return no information. The server will ignore any XDC cookies sent by the browser (if it manages to discover XDC authorizations for the server by other means).
- *XDC-aware server/unaware client.* The server's application must be coded defensively and have a backup implementation that doesn't rely on XDC cookies. The server may test the client by sending the status code `XDC_RESPONSE_REQUESTED` and checking if it receives a repeat request with an `Xdc-Response` header set to `true`.
- *XDC-unaware proxy.* Since preflight authorizations use the OPTIONS method (Section 4.2), and responses to OPTIONS requests are not cacheable [40], XDC-unaware proxies should not be disruptive for this part of our solution.

`XDC_RESPONSE_REQUESTED` responses which initiate repeat requests must set the `Cache-Control` header to `no-cache` to prevent their caching by any proxies. To forestall caching of XDC-specific headers responses to user requests must set the `Cache-Control` header to `no-cache= Xdc-Authorization; no-cache=Xdc-Channel` [40].

8 Conclusion

Cookies provide a simple state management mechanism for HTTP. As currently implemented, they can be shared only between hosts in the same DNS domain (with some limitations). In many cases, however, this is too restrictive, and the ability to share cookies across domains may be required. Although there are technical means to work around the current limitations, they are difficult to implement, costly and sometimes unsafe. Conversely, the same origin policy currently in use on the Web may be too permissive in some cases; it could benefit from a fine-grained access control mechanism if one was developed to support cookie sharing across domain boundaries.

In this paper we introduced a simple authorization model for sharing cookies between disparate DNS domains. Such cookies are written to or read from cross-domain channels (XDC). Both writers and readers are issued XDC authorizations granting appropriate permissions to their holders and binding these permissions cryptographically to the XDC channels' owners. XDC authorizations may be delivered in the HTTP stream that carries XDC cookies themselves, or looked up in the DNS. The binding of an XDC authorization to the host presenting it relies on the trustworthiness of the name resolution process and, therefore, may be vulnerable to pharming and other attacks against the DNS. Secure XDC channels allow their owners to indicate that cookies may be shared only across SSL connections; this mitigates against DNS spoofing and ensures security and confidentiality of the XDC cookies in transit.

Similar to CORS, the Cross-Origin Resource Sharing mechanism implemented in many browsers [22], our solution uses client-cacheable preflight authorizations which should minimize repeat requests and other XDC-related communication overhead. Preflight requests provide the browser with the Web sites' XDC authorizations, and also give additional instructions about XDC cookie handling (such as the frequency of DNS lookups). Since any given Web site is expected to use only a small number of cross-domain channels, XDC authorizations are fairly small (about 1.5 K), and XDC cookies themselves are only marginally bigger than traditional cookies, the overall solution is lightweight. At a modest cost our solution provides a simple and secure mechanism for cross-domain cookie sharing on the Web.

Endnotes

[a]Another HTTP state management standard has recently been proposed (RFC 6265) [41]. It obsoletes RFC 2965 and augments RFC 2109.

[b]In this paper we do not consider IP addresses used in HTTP URLs (and cookies' Domain attribute). Their direct use is generally discouraged [42].

[c]RFC 2965 also defines a new header, `Set-Cookie2` [3]. The differences with the older header are slight, and we will not discuss it further.

[d]Note that, like CORS, we make preflight requests to collect authorization information prior to fulfilling user requests.

[e]DNS resource records used to store arbitrary text [43]

[f]A newer version of our prototype can generate XDC authorizations using the ECDSA algorithm. With 192-bit elliptic curves, which provide security comparable to 1024-bit RSA keys [44], fully-encoded authorizations are about 200 bytes shorter.

[g]For example, the one used by the browsers' SSL/TLS implementations.

Competing interests

The author declares that he has no competing interests.

References

1. Kristol DM (2001) HTTP Cookies: Standards, privacy, and politics. ACM Trans Internet Technol 1(2): 151–198
2. Kristol D, Montulli L (1997) HTTP State Management Mechanism. IETF, RFC 2109
3. Kristol D, Montulli L (2000) HTTP state management mechanism. IETF, RFC 2965
4. HTTPOnly (2007) Open Web Application Security Project (OWASP)
5. Tracking Protection Working Group. (http://www.w3.org/2011/tracking-protection/). W3 Consortium (2012)
6. Zalewski M (2009) Browser security handbook. Google, Inc
7. Persistent Client State HTTP Cookies. Netscape communications corporation (undated)
8. How Businesses are Using Web 2.0: A McKinsey global survey. McKinsey and Company (2007)
9. O'Reilly T (2005) What Is Web 2.0: Design patterns and business models for the next generation of software. O'Reilly Network
10. Phifer G (2011) Hype cycle for web and user interaction technologies. Gartner, Inc
11. Hughes J, Cantor S, Hodges J, Hirsch F, Mishra P, Philpott R, Maler E (eds) (2005) Profiles for the OASIS Security Assertion Markup Language (SAML) V2.0
12. Lockhart H, Campbell B (eds) (2008) Identity provider discovery service protocol and profile
13. Jang D, Venkataraman A, Sawka GM, Shacham H (2011) Analyzing the crossdomain policies of flash applications. In: Proc. of the Web 2.0 Security and Privacy Workshop
14. Kontaxis G, Antoniades D, Polakis I, Markatos EP (2011) An Empirical study on the security of cross-domain policies in rich internet applications. In: Proc. of the 4th European Workshop on System Security
15. Pettersen Y (2008) HTTP state management mechanism v2. IETF. Internet Draft draft-pettersen-cookie-v2-05
16. Callaghan PJ, Howland MJ, Pritko SM (2008) Method, system and program products for sharing state information across Domains. U.S. Patent and Trademark Office. Patent Application Publication US 2008/0027824 A1

17. Guo R, Zhou B (2008) Cross Cookie: A cookie protocol for web mashups. In: Proc. of the 2008 International Symposium on Electronic Commerce and Security, 416–420
18. Hickson I (ed) (2011) Web Storage. W3 Consortium, W3C Candidate Recommendation 08/12/2011
19. Hickson I (ed) (2011) HTML5 Web Messaging. W3 Consortium, W3C Working Draft 10/20/2011
20. window.postMessage (https://developer.mozilla.org/en-US/docs/DOM/window.postMessage). Mozilla Developer Network (2012)
21. Hanna S, Shin R, Akhawe D, Boehm A, Saxena P, Song D (2010) The Emperor's New APIs: On the (In) secure usage of new client-side primitives. In: Proc. of the 4th Web 2.0 Security and Privacy Workshop
22. van Kesteren A (ed) (2010) Cross-origin resource sharing. World Wide Web Consortium, W3C Working Draft 07/27/2010
23. Zakas N (2010) Cross-domain Ajax with cross-origin resource sharing. NCZOnline, 2010
24. Farrell S, Housley R (2002) An internet attribute certificate profile for authorization. IETF, RFC 3281
25. Karlof CK, Shankar U, Tygar D, Wagner D (2007) Locked cookies: Web authentication security against Phishing, Pharming, and active attacks. University of California at Berkeley, Technical Report UCB/EECS-2007-25
26. Information Technology - Open Systems Interconnection - The Directory: Authentication Framework. ITU-T Recommendation X. 509 (1997)
27. Cooper D, Santesson S, Farrell S, Boeyen S, Housley R, Polk W (2008) Internet X.509 public key infrastructure certificate and Certificate Revocation List (CRL) profile. IETF, RFC 5280
28. Mockapetris P (1987) Domain names – Implementation and specification. IETF, RFC 1035
29. Eastlake DE (1999) The kitchen sink DNS resource record. IETF, Internet Draft draft-ietf-dnsind-kitchen-sink-02
30. The Legion of the Bouncy Castle: Welcome (http://www.bouncycastle.org/java.html). The Legion of the Bouncy Castle (2011)
31. Apache Tomcat, http://tomcat.apache.org/. Apache Software Foundation (2011)
32. Apache Module mod_rewrite http://httpd.apache.org/docs/current/mod/mod_rewrite.html. Apache Software Foundation (2011)
33. Apache Module mod_headers http://httpd.apache.org/docs/current/mod/mod_headers.html. Apache Software Foundation (2011)
34. ISC BIND Nameserver - Howtos, Links, Whitepapers. (http://www.bind9.net/). BIND9.NET/BIND9.ORG (2010)
35. Extensions https://developer.mozilla.org/en/Extensions. Mozilla developer network (2011)
36. Rabinovich P (2011) Cross-domain cookies, https://sourceforge.net/projects/xdccookies/. SourceForge.net
37. Tappenden AF, Miller J (2009) Cookies: A deployment study and the testing implications. ACM Trans Web 3(3): 1–49
38. Schneider F, Agarwal S, Alpcan T, Feldmann A (2008) The new web: characterizing AJAX traffic. In: Proc. of the 9th International Conference on Passive and Active Network Measurement, 31–40
39. Secure Hash Signature Standard. FIPS Publication 180-2 (2002)
40. Fielding R, Gettys J, Mogul J, Frystyk H, Masinter L, Leach P, Berners-Lee T (1999). Hypertext Transfer Protocol – HTTP/1.1. IETF, RFC 2616
41. Barth A (2011) HTTP state management mechanism. IETF, RFC 6265
42. A guide to building secure web applications and web services. Open Web Application Security Project (OWASP) (2005)
43. Rosenblum R (1987) Using the domain name system to store arbitrary string attributes. IETF, RFC 1464
44. Barker E, Barker W, Burr W, Polk W, Smid M (2012) Recommendation for key management – Part 1: General. NIST Special Publication Revision 3: 800–857

4

An approach to the correlation of security events based on machine learning techniques

Kleber Stroeh[1]*, Edmundo Roberto Mauro Madeira[2] and Siome Klein Goldenstein[2]

Abstract

Organizations face the ever growing challenge of providing security within their IT infrastructures. Static approaches to security, such as perimetral defense, have proven less than effective — and, therefore, more vulnerable — in a new scenario characterized by increasingly complex systems and by the evolution and automation of cyber attacks. Moreover, dynamic detection of attacks through *IDSs* (*Instrusion Detection Systems*) presents too many false positives to be effective. This work presents an approach on how to collect and normalize, as well as how to fuse and classify, security alerts. This approach involves collecting alerts from different sources and normalizes them according to standardized structures — IDMEF (*Intrusion Detection Message Exchange Format*). The normalized alerts are grouped into meta-alerts (fusion, or clustering), which are later classified using machine learning techniques into attacks or false alarms. We validate and report an implementation of this approach against the *DARPA Challenge* and the *Scan of the Month*, using three different classifications — SVMs, Bayesian Networks and Decision Trees — having achieved high levels of attack detection with little false positives. Our results also indicate that our approach outperforms other works when it comes to detecting new kinds of attacks, making it more suitable to a world of evolving attacks.

Keywords: IDS, Security, Correlation, Machine learning

1 Introduction

Protecting IT infrastructures against the attack of crackers is an increasing challenge in the present time, and promises to continue so in, at least, the near future. According to ISO/IEC 17799, there are a number of factors that augment this challenge: (1) IT infrastructures have become increasingly complex with the advent of new technologies (wireless and P2P networks, ever shrinking devices such as memory keys, cameras, etc); (2) Complex attacks have been productized and are available for download in the Internet; (3) Business challenges demand new services offered faster and on the net.

This trend is corroborated by Joosen at al [1] who state that the increasingly complexity and dynamicity of systems and applications is linked to the *Internet of Things*. Hale and Brusil [2] also raise the impact of virtualization and service-orientation on security management.

In this context, classic defense techniques, such as firewall-based architectures and stand-alone IDSs, are

no longer effective to protect the IT infrastructure, as noted by Ganame et al [3]. A more modern approach requires the cooperation of many IT security devices, with an emphasis on IDSs. Unfortunately, IDSs generate a high number of events (Perdisci et al [4]) and many false positives, making it difficult to determine which real attacks caused some subset of those events. Therefore, managing all the alerts generated by these devices overwhelms the security staff of most organizations, as observed by Ning et al [5], Boyer et al [6], Julisch [7] and Liu and Zang [8].

The difficulty imposed by IDSs generating a high number of alarms has been raised by many authors, such as Sabata and Orneds [9], Chyssler et al [10], among others. In this same line of research, Ohta et al [11] defend the necessity of decreasing false positives in order to reduce the cost of operation and increase the reliability of the system.

To tackle the excess of false positives, we propose a machine learning solution based upon two major concepts: (1) event fusion into meta-events: collecting, normalizing and fusing together events that are likely to be part of the same attack; (2) classification of meta-events:

*Correspondence: kleber.stroeh@icarotech.com
[1]Icaro Technologies, Campinas, SP, Brazil
Full list of author information is available at the end of the article

based upon the attributes of a meta-event, decide whether it represents an attack or a false alarm, using different machine learning techniques.

An implementation of this approach was tested against the DARPA Intrustion Detection Evaluation 1999 [12] and the Scan of the Month 34 from the Honeynet Project [13]. The results indicated that this approach can provide high levels of detection with lower levels of false positives. It also provides the ability to detect some new kinds of attacks (for which there was no previous information in the testing data), outperforming other works in this aspect. This is an important feature, as it makes our solution more flexible and suitable to an ever changing scenario of cyber attacks.

The contribution of the paper is proposing an approach to correlating security alerts based on machine learning techniques, a security event taxonomy and the fusion of different alerts into meta-alerts. We did experiments that verify how effective this approach is to detect real attacks while generating low levels of false positives, and how good it is in detecting new and stealthy attacks when compared to other works.

This work sets apart from most of the applied machine learning techniques on IDSs, once we do not analyze network traffic or series of system calls. Instead, we process alerts generated by sensors (IDSs such as Snort, applications, etc). By doing so, we work on a different level of abstraction, that carries more meaning to our machine learning approach, helping bridge the "semantic gap" (Paxson and Sommer [14]). We also apply specific security concepts to our fusing technique, which renders meta-alerts that are more relevant. These meta-alerts, appropriately filtered by machine learning algorithms, help reduce the "high cost of errors" [14] that overwhelm security groups nowadays.

This document is organized as follows: Section 2 presents related works in security alert correlation; Section 3 describes our approach to correlating alerts, including the layers of processing, a security alert taxonomy and an algorithm to fuse alerts into meta-alerts; Section 4 presents the experiments used to test our approach and the corresponding results; finally, Section 5 summarizes the conclusions derived from this work and indicates possible future works.

2 Related work

Ever since the Lincoln Laboratory at the Massachusetts Institute of Technology launched the DARPA Intrusion Detection Evaluation 1998 and 1999 [12], many teams around the globe have put efforts into the development of IDS technology. As a matter of fact, this very work (by the Lincoln Laboratory) became the main data set reference for intrusion detection systems testing ever since.

Some research groups focused on misuse detection systems. Bowen et al, for example, developed a domain-specific language, called BSML (behavioral monitoring specification language), to specify relevant properties for intrusion detection [15]. A similar approach is presented by the STAT Tool Suite, where a machine state-oriented language - STATL - is used to describe attack scenarios [16]. Systems based on misuse detection tend to be more precise in pinpointing specific attacks, generating less false-positives, while presenting more difficulty to detect previously unknown attack patterns.

On the other hand, other teams, like Lee et al, have used anomaly detection techniques for intrusion detection [17]. This particular team proposed the use of data-mining techniques and its concepts (accuracy, efficiency, usability, ROC, ensembles, among others) to the IDS challenge. Solutions based on anomaly detection present the ability to potentially detect new attack patterns at the cost of a higher false-positive detection rate.

Hybrid approaches, encompassing anomaly and misuse detection, have also been proposed, as in EMERALD [18], where a building-block architectural strategy hosts potentially different correlation, inference and reasoning systems, varying from signature engines to Bayesian analysis.

Interest in intrusion detection systems can also be perceived in Europe, where Safeguard (European project for information security in telecommunications and electricity networks) has fueled research in IDS technology. Chyssler et al propose a framework for SIEM (Security Information and Event Management), comparing the possible use of Neural Networks, K-Neighbours and Naive Bayes in detecting attacks [10]. Ganame et al [3] propose a distributed architecture named DSOC (Distributed Security Operation Center) to improve the detection of more complex attacks such as coordinated ones.

In a military and defense context, Grimaila et al [19] also propose a distributed approach to security event correlation in order to "identify potential threats in a timely manner". Rieke and Stoynova [20] present a blueprint of an archtitecture for predictive security analysis that uses process models in extension to security policies and models.

One of the most inspiring works in this area has been the probabilistic alert correlation presented by Valdes and Skinner [21]. This work, developed at SRI Internation, proposes a hierarchy of correlations. Security alerts - detected by sensors spread over a network - are fused into meta-alerts at three different processing levels: (1) intra-sensor or synthetic threads - alerts from a single sensor are fused together according to a high minimum expectation similarity on the sensor itself, the attack class, and source and target IPs; (2) security incidents - alerts that belong to the same class and target the same IP are fused together despite the expectation of similarity on the sensor identifier; (3) correlated attack reports: multistage attacks are possibly detected by relaxing the minimum expectation in similarity on the attack class.

Detecting multistage attacks is also handled by Ning et al, where prerequisites and consequences of attacks are represented as predicates of first order logic [5]. Alerts that represent different stages of a single attack are fused together into hyperalerts. This concept diminishes the number of alerts to be analysed by the security team.

Julisch proposes reducing the number of alerts by using clustering techniques [7]. He observes that a few dozens of rather persistent root causes generally account for over 90% of the alarms that an IDS triggers. He suggests the use of generalized attributes for an offline process of alarm clustering. This process indicates the root causes of alarm storms, enabling a security officer to tackle these causes and reduce the amount of alarms.

Asif-Iqbal et al [22] address the clustering of security logs by using data mining techniques, where the clustered logs are further filtered to remove unneeded entries. Corona et al [23] present a broad review on information fusion (clustering) for computer security.

Burroughs et al propose applying BMHT (Bayesian Multiple Hypothesis Tracking) onto fusing sensor process output in order to achieve situational awareness and allow security teams to respond to attacks more quickly [24]. Sabata, on the other hand, handles Bayesian Network fragments to correlate events and reduce the number of alerts analysed by security officers [9,25].

This work extends the concepts introduced by Julish [7] by having the algorithm run in real time instead of batch. It also does event correlation and fusion, like Valdes and Skinner [21], but it introduces hierarchies of event taxonomies to support the fusing process. This provides for a flexible, yet powerful, way of describing security events and meta-alerts. Deciding whether a meta-alert is an attack or not is implemented using machine learning techniques, similarly to Chyssler et al [10]; we, however, introduce more modern techniques such as SVMs and Bayesian Networks. Finally, not only do we compare our results to the ones of the DARPA challenge [12], but we also use real data from a honeynet to test our approach.

3 Proposed approach

Processing and correlating security events is key to an effective security management solution. Here, one seeks to achieve situational awareness, that is, the ability to analyze alerts in a broader and more holistic context.

Actually, a more precise and widely accepted definition of situational awareness is "the perception of elements in the environment within a volume of time and space, the comprehension of their meaning, and the projection of their status in the near future" [26].

Put in simple words, the more different the evidences that a security incident is taking place, the more likely it is true. Thus, we want to collect events from different sources and normalize them, so that they can be processed homogeneously.

The normalized events are fused (or clustered) into groups, or meta-events. Meta-events present a more complete description of a possible attack scenario than single events. They constitute a more refined expression of the underlying attack when compared to isolated alerts.

Grouping events into meta-events leads to better situational awareness, improving the classification between real attacks and false alarms; it also enhances the performance of the system, as the classification operates on meta-events rather than events (events typically outnumber meta-events by orders of magnitude).

Meta-events enable the contrast between new scenarios to previously learned attack scenarios. Machine learning techniques can be used to automate this process.

3.1 Hierarchical layers

Our approach encompasses three layers of processing stages: Collection (and Normalization), Fusion and Classification. Figure 1 shows the three layers.

Each stage provides a level of abstraction to the following one. Raw data are processed and transformed into standardized IDMEF [27] -like records by the Collection stage. The fusion stage takes these IDMEF-extended records and groups them into standardized meta-alerts. Finally, it is up to the Classification stage to take these meta-alerts and sort them into attacks and false alarms.

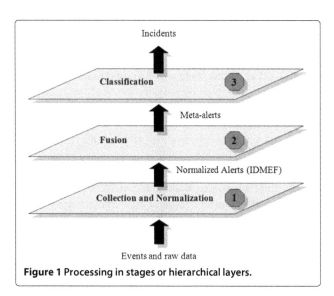

Figure 1 Processing in stages or hierarchical layers.

3.2 Collection and normalization

The Collection and Normalization layer is linked to the event sources: IDSs, firewalls, system logs, SNMP traps, and so on.

Collection elements are divided into two groups: passive and active. Passive elements gather alerts by the simple observation of evidences, events or element states. Examples of passive collection are the parsing of systems logs or the receival of SNMP traps. Active elements, on the other hand, interact with the managed objects in order to sinthetize alerts. Examples are ICMP probes or SNMP pollers.

Collection elements also differ on the cardinality of the generated alerts. In some scenarios, for each incoming event or element state (an SNMP trap, e.g.), there is an outgoing alert. In others, the collection element is responsible for filtering the incoming events, in order to generate fewer outgoing alerts. One typical example of the latter is the processing of operating system calls; only a subset of the logs of system calls correspond to potential threats.

Normalization guarantees that the outgoing alerts are represented in a standardized way. Our approach uses a linearized extension of the IDMEF standard. It corresponds to a string representation of the IDMEF record with minimum overhead. Overhead, here, meaning any character that does not relate to content data. Linearization provides for a better perfomance of the system when compared to the originally XML bus prescribed by the IDMEF standard, since the latter would be too heavy and resource consuming, as also noted by Ganame et al [3]. This is key, once it has to process millions of events a day in real time. Its extension regards the introduction of the new fields *ext_class*, *ext_src_node_addr_type*, *ext_tgt_node_addr_type*, *ext_priority* and *ext_taxonomy*. This scheme is similar to the one presented by Lan et al [28].

Field *ext_class* partitions the alert space into five groups: denial of service (DoS), probing (Probe), remote acess (R2L), superuser access (U2R) and data theft (Data). On the other hand, fields *ext_src_node_addr_type* and *ext_tgt_node_addr_type* classify, respectively, source and target nodes among: external, internal or pertaining to the Demilitarized Zone (DMZ).

Each alert is also given a priority in the *ext_priority* field. This attribute takes values from one (1) to three (3), where one is the highest priority, and three, the lowest; this scheme is analogous to the one employed by Snort [29]. Sensors usually fill this attribute with the information defined by its source. That is, whenever an alert source contains an attribute named severity or priority, their value is mapped onto the *ext_priority* field. There are, however, cases where the event source does not present its own view about

the priority of the alert. In these cases, the sensor will define the priority based on the type of the given alert. This implies that the sensor developer needs to have a good understanding of security alerts in order to consistently define this attribute. Also notice that priorities are pre-defined by sensors or alert sources, being, therefore, immutable regarding its operating environment.

Arguably the most important extension to the model is the introduction of the *ext_taxonomy* field. Taxonomy is the subject of research for many years, dating back to the work of Debar et al [27] . These works have resulted in the genesis of the IDMEF model. Despite its importance, the IDMEF model lacks a semantic description of the types of its events. Al-Fedaghi and Mahdi [30] have also observed the need for categorizing security log entries [30].

We need a simple way of identifying alerts that provides support to the fusion and classification processes. We want to identify each alert with a single value that depicts what that alert means. The naming space of *ext_taxonomy* needs to be finite, so that it can be further applied in some of the algorithms of the classification layer.

To achieve these two requirements (expressiveness and finitude) we derived a scheme based upon the observation of real-world alerts and its expression in natural language. This provides for a method of describing event types that is meaningful, yet well-structured.

By observing alerts coming from different sources (IDSs, system calls, web server access logs, Windows security events and firewall events), we have divided them into three main groups:

1. An action against an object (*<object>*:*<action>*).
2. A condition of an object (*<object>*:*<condition>*).
3. A suspicion of the state of an object (*<object>*:*<state>*).

Every group is, therefore, characterized by an *object* plus an *action*, a *condition* or a *state*. Objects are represented in a multilevel hierarchy. The most top level element of an object is a system, a network element, a protocol, a user, a file or security. Each of these elements is then subdivided into more granular concepts. Figure 2 describes an example of a hierarchy of objects as used in our experiments. This hierarchy may be extended to suite other managed elements and objects as necessary.

An *action* resembles a method to which an *object* is associated. Therefore, an alert about the shutdown of the operating system would be represented as *system.os:shutdown*. As with objects, actions are also represented in a multilevel hierarchy. The lower levels of the hierarchy qualify the upper ones. Qualifications may be adverbs associated with the action, the result of the

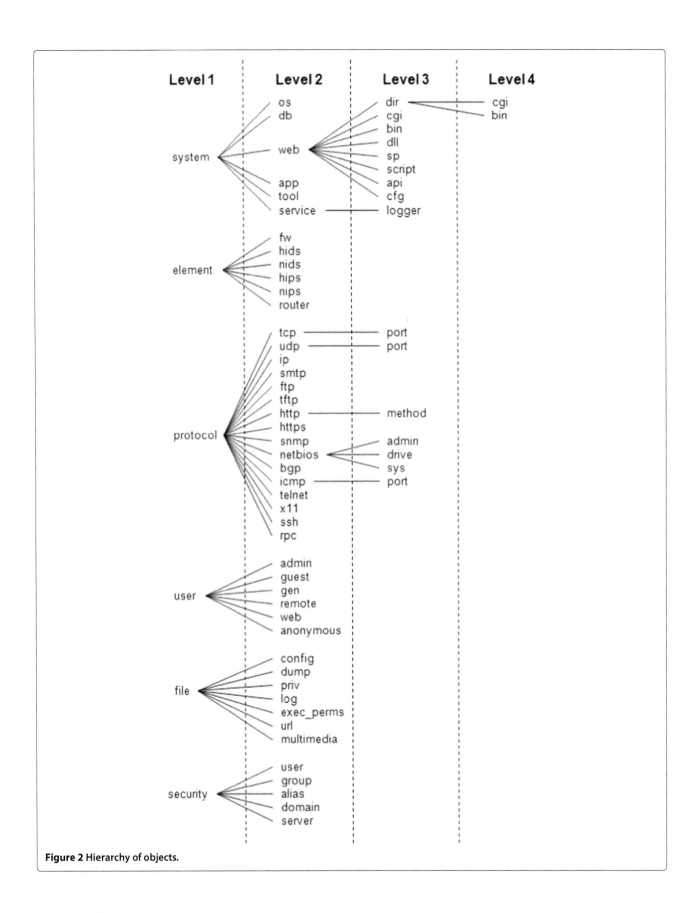

Figure 2 Hierarchy of objects.

action, or something similar. For example, a failure in the attempt to login as the administrator of a system — due to a wrong password — would be represented as *user.admin:login.fail.pwd.*

Actions are typically used to represent sentences of the following constructions:

- Subject + Intransitive Verb (+ Adverbial Clause);
- Transitive Verb + Direct Object (+ Adverbial 4 Clause).

The differentiation of both cases is dependent on the transitiveness of the verb. Nonetheless, this ambiguity does not present a practical impact in the use of the taxonomy. Solving this ambiguity would invariably make our notation more complex, without real gains to our approach.

Some alerts do not represent actions against objects, but states (or *conditions*) in which those objects are. These *conditions* are tipically represented by constructions like: Subject + Copulative Verb + Complement. For example, if one wants to represent that a TCP port is unaccessible, the taxonomy would render: *protocol.tcp.port: unreachable.*

Finally there is a category of alerts that represent suspicions towards a given activity or evidence. It differs from the previous cases in that it represents not a fact but deductions associated with facts. Given the inherent uncertainty, our taxonomy set *suspicions* apart from *actions* and *conditions*. An example would be the suspicion that there is an attempt to use a backdoor in a system. This would be described as: *system. os:malware.backdoor.attempt.*

Note that *objects*, *actions*, *conditions* and *suspicions* are all represented in multilevel hierachies. This allows correlations to operate on the level of granularity that is more convenient in each scenario. For example, if it is irrelevant to check if a login failure occurred due to an invalid user or an invalid password, than, the following taxonomies would be equivalent: *user.admin:login.fail,* *user.admin:login.fail.pwd,* and *user.admin:login.fail.user.* The use of hierarchical levels addresses this issue in an elegant manner, by making it possible to completely ignore the third level of the action hierarchy, reducing all the previous options simply to: *user.admin:login. fail.*

The result of this scheme is the ability to assign a single finite description to each security alert. This description is meaningful (is it was derived from real alerts), well-structured (use of hierarchy and natural language concepts) and finite.

Another advantage is that it establishes a new dictionary to be used when classifying alerts. Therefore, it does not matter whether the original source uses the term login, logon or begin_user_session; it does not matter if the original system classified the login as failed or denied; it also doesn't matter if the administration user is called root, superuser or administrator; in our taxonomy (and system), the fact that an administrator user tried to access a system and failed will always be described as *user.admin:login.fail.*

Therefore, our taxonomy provides the final tool to normalize events coming from different sources while still maintaining a proper, meaningful, description of the alert type.

Since our proposed taxonomy conforms to the structure we have outlined above (specially derived from natural language), developers can more easily associate an alert to an existing taxonomy entry or, better, create new entries to address new alert types that take place in his/her specific environment.

3.3 Fusion or clustering

This layer takes alerts provided by the collection and normalization layer and groups them into meta-alerts. This clustering process is an extension of the concepts introduced by Valdes and Skinner [31]. Its design fulfills the following requirements:

1. Efficience: operate under the shortest subset of alert attributes and limit searches to meta-alerts in time.
2. Intelligibility: the resulting meta-alerts must make sense to human beings.
3. Coherence: clustering mechanism must adhere to the types of attacks supported by the model.

We decided on using a deterministic, straightforward, algorithm to fusion. It enables the clustering of the alerts in real time as they are made available by the undelying layer. The resulting meta-alerts are simple and intelligible to human beings, as shown in Table 1.

Arguably, the most important field in the meta-alert structure is the *alert_taxonomy_set.* This is a bit array that represents each of the supported alert types of the taxonomy. If one (or more) alert(s) of a given type is (are) present in the meta-alert, its corresponding bit is set. Otherwise, it remains clear.

Think of this bit array as the set of all the possible clues in a crime scene. Potential attacks (or crimes), depicted by meta-alerts, present a subset of these clues. The more a set of clues resembles a previous known scenario, the more likely it is to be a real attack.

The use of an array bit provides support to internal product techniques that verify the similarity between two scenarios in the classification layer.

Filling in the meta-alert record is a natural result of the clustering algorithm below:

Require: $j\_cache > 0, j\_dos > 0, j\_probe > 0, j\_r2l > 0, j\_u2r > 0$
Require: $a \in Alertas$, M set of Meta-Alerts
Ensure: M updated with alert a

```
 1: f ← ∅
 2: for all m in M do
 3:     if a.ext_class ≠ m.ext_class then
 4:         nop
 5:     else if a.ext_class = DoS then
 6:         if (a.src_node_addr ∈ m.src_network_addr) and
            (a.tgt_node_addr ∈ m.tgt_node_addr_list) and
            (a.create_time ≤ (m.end_time + j_dos)) and
            (a.create_time ≥ (m.init_time − j_dos)) then
 7:             f ← m
 8:         end if
 9:     else if a.ext_class = Probe then
10:         if (a.src_node_addr ∈ m.src_node_addr_list) and
            (a.create_time ≤ (m.end_time + j_probe)) and
            (a.create_time ≥ (m.init_time − j_probe)) then
11:             f ← m
12:         end if
13:     else if a.ext_class = R2L then
14:         if (a.src_node_addr ∈ m.src_node_addr_list) and
            (a.tgt_node_addr ∈ m.tgt_node_addr_list) and
            (a.create_time ≤ (m.end_time + j_r2l)) and
            (a.create_time ≥ (m.init_time − j_r2l)) then
15:             f ← m
16:         end if
17:     else if a.ext_class = U2R then
18:         if (a.src_node_addr ∈ m.src_node_addr_list) and
            (a.tgt_node_addr ∈ m.tgt_node_addr_list) and
            (a.create_time ≤ (m.end_time + j_u2r)) and
            (a.create_time ≥ (m.init_time − j_u2r)) then
19:             f ← m
20:         end if
21:     end if
22: end for
23: if f = ∅ then
24:     n = new Meta-Alert
25:     init n with data from a
26:     a.meta_alert = n
27:     M = M ∪ {n}
28: else
29:     a.meta_alert = f
30:     Update f with data from a
31: end if
```

Alerts are grouped according to their timestamps and the time windows defined at the requirement lines. This defines sliding windows within which correlated alerts are fused.

Once an alert is received, the algorithm iterates over a cache of meta-alerts looking for potential candidates for fusion. Alerts are only fused together if they share the same alert class. Further requirements stand for each individual alert class. In the case of denial of services (DoS) attacks, the target address of the alerts must match in order for their alerts to be fused together. If it is a probing attack, then it is the source address that must remain unchanged.

Table 1 Meta-Alert record

Attribute	Type	Description
meta_alert_id	Integer	Unique identification of a meta-alert
analyzer_id_list	String	List of sensors that generated the alerts of this meta-alert
analyzer_count	Integer	Number of sensors that detected the alerts
init_time	Date	Timestamp of the oldest event in this meta-alert
end_time	Date	Timestamp of the most recent event in this meta-alert
time_window_len	Integer	Number of seconds between end_time e init_time
src_network_addr	String	Base address of the network that originatd the alerts
src_node_addr_list	LongText	List of the addresses that originated the alerts
src_node_count	Integer	Number of different addresses that originated the alerts
src_user_id_list	String	List of user identifications that originated the alerts
src_user_count	Integer	Number of users that originated the alerts
src_proc_id_list	String	List of process identifications that originated the alerts
src_proc_count	Integer	Number of processes that originated the alerts
tgt_node_addr_list	LongText	List of target addresses
tgt_node_count	Integer	Number of different target addresses
tgt_port_list	LongText	List of target ports
tgt_port_count	Integer	Number of different target ports
tgt_user_id_list	String	List of target user ids
tgt_user_count	Integer	Number of different target user ids
tgt_proc_id_list	String	List of target process ids
tgt_proc_count	Integer	Number of different target process ids
tgt_file_name_list	LongText	List of target file names
tgt_file_count	Integer	Number of different target file names
ext_class	String	Attack class of the meta-alert
ext_max_priority	Integer	Highest priority amongst the alerts in the meta-alert
alert_count	Integer	Number of alerts in the meta-alert
alert_taxonomy_set	BitArray	One bit set per alert type present in meta-alert

If a matching meta-alert is found, the alert is fused into it. Otherwise, a new meta-alert is synthetized with the information from this single alert.

This simple algorithm has presented excellent results in the Data to Information Ratio (DIR), and provides a good support to the classification layer, as we will show later.

There is a price to be paid for the simplicity, though. More refined attributes for fusion, such as sessions, users, process and files are left behind. The algorithm does not support the fusion of alerts pertaining to hybrid or multistage attacks, and we left these scenarios as future work.

3.4 Classification

Separating meta-alerts that represent attacks from false alarms is an ideal task for machine learning techniques. Here, we verify how modern techniques, such as SVMs and Bayesian Networks, behave within the classification layer.

Choosing the subset of the attributes of a meta-alert to be used by these techniques is key. One must avoid choosing too many attributes in order to avoid overfitting. From the list of attributes presented in Table 1, we have selected the following: *alert_count*, *ext_max_priority*, *tgt_node_count*, *tgt_port_count*, *analyzer_id_list*, *ext_class*, and *alert_type_set*.

Some attributes play important roles in the segregation between real attacks and false alarms. The number of alerts, nodes and port help detect DoS and Probe attacks. The list of sensors (*analyzer_id_list*) helps improve our situational awareness; the more sensors have detected traces of an attack, the more likely it is to be real.

However, it is the bit array representing entries of our taxonomy that plays the most central role in the

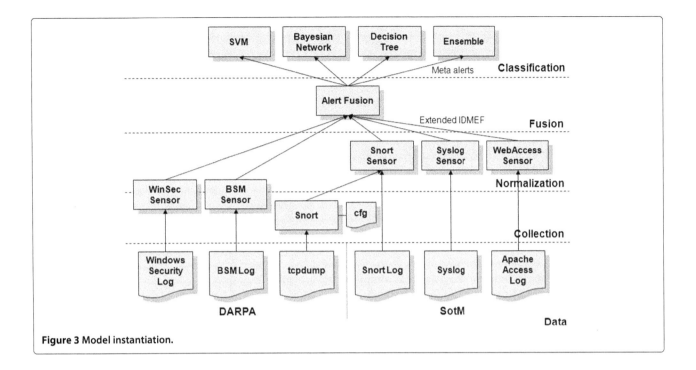

Figure 3 Model instantiation.

classification. This bit array is analogous to the *bag of words* technique used for comparing text documents. The internal product of two arrays represents the degree of similarity between two documents, or, in our case, two meta-alerts. This concept is very natural to SVMs, but has proven very succesful with Bayesian Networks and Decision Trees as well.

This approach was proven very flexible and resilient in the detection of new attacks. Naturally, the result is dependent upon the granularity of the taxonomy. If it is too specific, the learning algorithm might end up overfitting. If it is too generic, the classification is jeopardized by the lack of information in the decision making process.

4 Implementation and experiments

In order to test our approach, we had it implemented and tested against two major, publicly available, data sources: (a) the DARPA challenge [12], the *de facto* benchmark for IDS testing; and (b) the *Scan of the Month* (SotM) from the Honeynet Project [13]. These two sources have different and complementary characteristics.

The DARPA challenge was conceived by DARPA (Defense Advanced Research Project Agency) in association with MIT Lincoln Labs. It simulates an American Air Force base local network that has been attacked in very specific ways. Information about the traffic on the LAN and about the attacks is provided in the form of tcpdump files, BSM files, audit logs, Windows alerts and other

Table 2 DARPA event sources

		Analyzer			
		Int. Snort	Ext. Snort	BSM	Windows
Week 1	Records	142,674	143,098	2,063,809	581,192
	Alerts	142,674	143,098	846	2,953
Week 2	Records	47,405	47,826	2,151,011	3,650,045
	Alerts	47,405	47,826	728	405
Week 3	Records	18,742	21,687	2,147,384	3,574,791
	Alerts	18,742	21,687	10,752	419
Week 4	Records	17,169	23,032	1,841,269	2,292,926
	Alerts	17,169	23,032	701	643
Week 5	Records	34,652	53,612	2,949,363	2,476,508
	Alerts	34,652	53,612	912	852

sorts of audits. This set encompasses five weeks of activities, and has been used by many IDS research groups, such as: Ohta et al [11], Mahoney and Chan [32], Bowen et al [15], Mukkamala et al [33], Faraoun and Boukelif [34,35], Tandon and Chan [36], Lee et al [17], Mukkamala and Sung [37], Valdes and Skinner [31], and Sabata and Ornes [25].

There has been some controversy regarding the use of the DARPA dataset. Sommer and Paxson [14] state: "The two publicly available datasets that have provided something of a standardized setting in the past - DARPA ... KDD ... - are now a decade old...". On the other hand, Perdisci et al [4], states: "Even though the DARPA 1999 dataset has been largely critizicized, it is the reference dataset in the evaluation of IDS performance".

Our approach is less sensible to the age of the dataset, as it relies on alerts derived from the network traffic (by sensors such as Snort), instead of the network traffic itself. Therefore, the changes that have taken place in the characteristics of network traffic are masqueraded by our sensors and have a lesser impact on the effectiveness of our algorithms.

In order to further compensate for the limitations of the DARPA dataset, we decided to add a second dataset to our tests. The SotM data is provided by the *The Honeynet Project* [13] and provides information about real attacks that have been perpetrated against a honeynet controled by the project. This data set complements the first one, as it was originated in a real environment, and as it contains newer types of attacks. Forms of data include webserver logs, syslog, Snort logs and ipTables logs. Since they correspond to real attacks against honey pots, the noise ratio (data not related to attacks) is lower in these logs.

This is a newer dataset and a more real one (not synthesized). On the other hand, it is certainly a smaller one. As we will show later, our implementation has achieved even better results with this dataset.

4.1 Implementation

We implemented our model using Perl and three different machine learning techniques. The implementation handles the data sources of our test environments. Figure 3 shows a simplified view of the implementation.

Table 3 Event reduction in DARPA experiment

Entity	Quantity
Records	24,278,195
Alerts	569,108
Meta-alerts	19,550
Indicated attacks	268
Data to information ratio	2,124

Basically, for each data source there is one module for collection and normalization, namely: Windows Security Log, BSM Log, tcpdump and Snort Log, Syslog and Apache Access Log. These modules handle the specifics of the data source and generate alerts in extended IDMEF format.

The AlertFusion module clusters the normalized data using the algorithm described in Section 3.3, generating meta-alerts. The classification layer takes the resulting

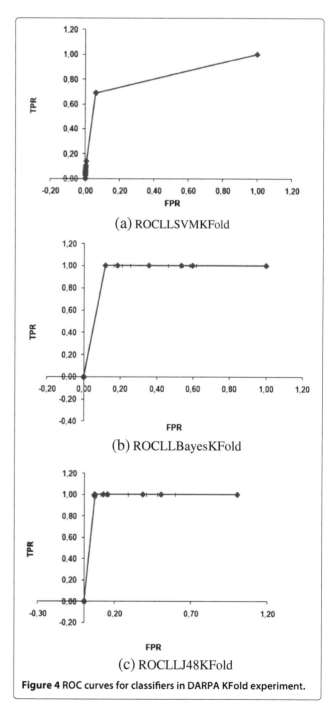

(a) ROCLLSVMKFold

(b) ROCLLBayesKFold

(c) ROCLLJ48KFold

Figure 4 ROC curves for classifiers in DARPA KFold experiment.

meta-alerts and processes them using three different machine learning algorithms: SVM, Bayesian Network and a Decision Tree.

For the SVM classifier we used the SVM implementation from libSVM [38]. We discretized attributes *alert_count*, *tgt_node_count* and *tgt_port_count* into four different values in order to reduce the sensitiveness of the algorithm to the learning data. Basically we do not want the algorithm to overlook a DoS attack composed of 200 alerts, just because it was previously trained with a scenario that contained 500 alerts. We also linearized attributes *ext_class* and *alert_type_set*; we mapped each possible value of the first and bit of the latter onto a different dimension (*dummy variables*). We optimized the resulting SVM using the guidelines proposed by Hsu et al [39]. Finally, we induced the learning process using different weights for false positives and false negatives; basically, a false negative had a higher cost than a false positive.

We implemented the Bayesian Network classifier and the Decision Tree using Weka [40]. We coded the first using *weka.classifiers.bayes.BayesNet*, while in the latter we used *weka.classifiers.trees.J48*, which implements algorithm C4.5. We also implemented the assimetry of costs described for the SVM classifier using *weka.classifiers.meta.CostSensitiveClassifier*.

4.2 Experiments

We have performed three experiments:

1. DARPA kFold: using the DARPA database, we tested the classifiers using a *5-fold cross validation*.
2. DARPA 3x2: using the DARPA database, we trained our classifiers with the three weeks of tagged attacks, and tested their performance against the remaining two weeks.
3. SotM kFold: using the SotM database, we tested the classifiers using a *5-fold cross validation*.

4.2.1 Experiment 1: DARPA kFold

Table 2 shows the result of the collection and normalization processes on the DARPA data.

The Snort Sensor is responsible for most of the collected alerts. In this sensor, every log entry corresponds to an alert. This is a passive sensor, with an 1x1 cardinality. For the BSM and Windows Sensors, we verify the results of the applied heuristics, where only a subset of the records is promoted to alerts. These sensors act as filters for the upper fusion layer.

As a consequence, from a domain of over 24 million records, sensors produce less than 570 thousand alerts.

Table 3 shows the performance of the Fusion layer applied to the DARPA database. As you can see, the implementation has reached a *Data to Information Ratio* of 2,124, a value higher than the ones obtained by Valdes and Skinner [21], and by Sabata and Ornes [25].

The classifiers were first tuned based upon cost assimetry, using different *weights* for false positives and false negatives. In average, we have found that an assimetry of 1:60 was the best solution for the classifers. These so-tuned classifiers returned the results summarized in the ROC curves depicted in Figure 4.

One can see that both the Bayesian and the Decision Tree classifiers have presented good results, giving rise to very steep inflexions in the graph. This translates into achieving high values in TPR for low values in FPR. That means more true positives and true negatives, for fewer false positives and false negatives.

This can also be observed in Figure 5. There one can see how the Bayesian Network classifier performs in detecting specific types of attacks as our sensitiveness variable is changed. High levels of detection have been achieved in all categories, with a special remark for DoS attacks. The detection of R2L attacks is the one that is more impacted by the change in the sensitiveness of the classifier.

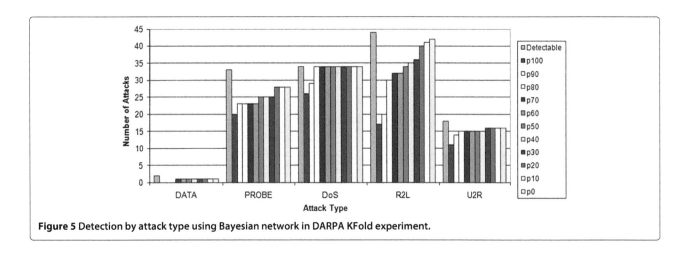

Figure 5 Detection by attack type using Bayesian network in DARPA KFold experiment.

4.2.2 Experiment 2: DARPA W3xW2

Performing the experiment against the two remaining weeks, we have achieved the results in Figure 6.

The conformance of the curves summarizes the good performance of the classifiers.

The combination of a generic taxonomy and the use of these classifiers have demonstrated the possibility of

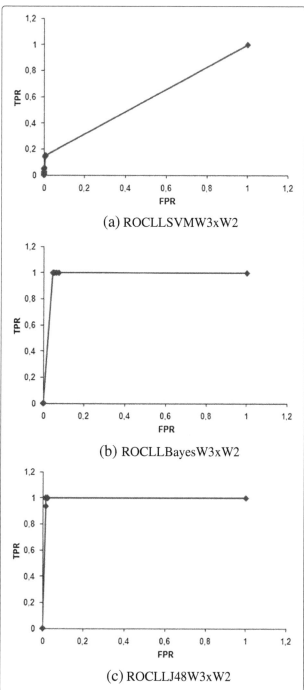

(a) ROCLLSVMW3xW2

(b) ROCLLBayesW3xW2

(c) ROCLLJ48W3xW2

Figure 6 ROC Curves for classifiers in DARPA W3xW2 experiment.

detecting new attacks, for which there had been no samples in the training data. This can also be seen in Figure 7.

The implementation managed to identify most of the detectable attacks in the data set provided by DARPA. We consider an attack detectable if some evidence of its existence could be tracked in the alerts provided to the Snort and other sensors used in our experiments.

Our implementation managed to detect attacks that were not detected by any of the contenders of the initial DARPA challenge, like *ipsweep, queso, snmpget* and *ntfsdos*. We also achieved a higher identification rate for *lsdomain, portsweep, ncftp* and *netbus*. Table 4 shows the results obtained for these attacks when compared to the results of the best system of the DARPA Challenge [12].

The results show that our approach improves the detection of new types of attacks, specially probe and R2L ones. We also improved the detection of Windows-related attacks.

4.2.3 Experiment 3: SotM kFold

To complement our study, we tested our implementation against a second data base: the *Scan of the Month 34* [13].

This database reflects real attacks performed by crackers against a honey net. Table 5 shows the sources used in the experiment and the results from the Collection and Normalization Layers.

Using the SotM database, we have achieved a lower, although good, Data to Information Ratio, as shown in Table 6. This reflects the fact that this database was collected at a honeynet, that typically presents less noise in the alerts.

The performance of the classifiers with this real-world attacks has been remarkable, as presented in Figure 8. Once again, high levels of true positives and true negatives have been achieved with low levels of false positives and false negatives.

These results derive from the good behaviour of the classifiers, specially the SVM and Decision Tree, in a more homogeneous attack environment. The DARPA data have been synthesized to emulate more complex attacks than the ones found on a daily basis in the real world. With the SotM, we have a data sample that is closer to the behaviour of an average cracker.

This scenario makes it easier for our machine learning techniques to learn patterns and apply them to the new attacks. Therefore, our results are even better in this more realistic scenario.

As shown in Figure 9, the Bayesian Network classifier was able to detect every single attack, with the exception of the *Probe* attack class.

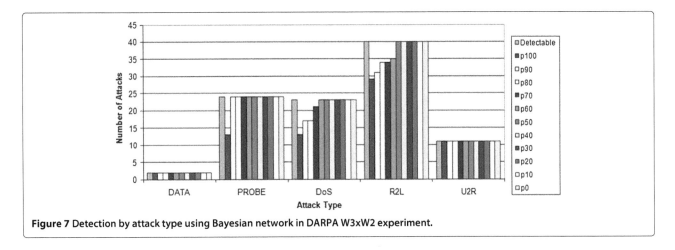

Figure 7 Detection by attack type using Bayesian network in DARPA W3xW2 experiment.

4.2.4 A comparative analysis

This work encomprises one of the largest testbeds in intrusion detection systems. We used two datasets (DARPA and SotM), several event sources and three different classification techniques.

Most of the published works in intrusion detection use only a subset of the event sources available in the DARPA challenge [12]. Others process only a portion of the data volume available: Faraoun and Boukelif use 10% of the DARPA dataset [34,35]; Mukkamala et al use 20% of the same dataset [33]. Our experiments made use of the five weeks of data from the DARPA challenge, spanning from the network data to the specific Solaris and Windows data sources.

Our results indicate higher levels of detection for new and stealthy attacks — *ipsweep, queso, snmpget, ntfsdos, lsdomain, portsweep, ncftp, netbus* — when compared to the contenders of the DARPA challenge, according to Lippmann et al [12], as depicted in Table 4. This is a consequence of the combined use of good classifiers (specially the Bayesian Network) and an effective taxonomy.

Detection rates were also better for the Probe attacks against Linux boxes, and for R2L attacks against Solaris servers. Our implementation also detected more R2L

and U2R attacks against Windows systems than the best implementation in the DARPA challenge [12]. This can verified in Table 7.

As noted by Kayacik and Zincir-Heywood, the number of false positives generated by a Snort IDS, using state of the art rules, is very high [41]. In all our experiments, this module was the one responsible for most of our alerts. Without the fusion and classification techniques we applied, it would be impossible for a security operations group to process the events generated by a Snort system in this busy network. This would also be the case in any real-world, enterprise-class, network.

Given the attacks for which there were evidences (detectable attacks), our approach achieved higher detection rates than the ones presented by Lippmann et al [12], even when the testing attacks did not match the ones used for training. Detection rates in this scenario approached 100% with a limited amount of false positives (Figure 6).

5 Conclusions

Information security remains an unsolved challenge for organizations. Old approaches, like perimeter defense, are no longer effective in a new scenario of ever growing threats and rapidly changing attack patterns.

Table 4 Detection of new and stealthy attacks

Attack name	Category	Details	Total instances	DARPA challenge	Bayesian classifier
ipsweep	Probe	Stealthy	4	0	4
lsdomain	Probe	Stealthy	2	1	2
portsweep	Probe	Stealthy	11	3	8
queso	Probe	New	4	0	4
ncftp	R2L	New	5	0	1
netbus	R2L	New-windows	3	1	3
snmpget	R2L	Old	4	0	4
ntfsdos	U2R	New-windows	3	1	3

Table 5 SotM event sources

Analyzer	Records	Alerts
Snort	69.039	69.039
Web logs	3.554	3.414
Syslog	1.158	953
Total	73.751	73.406

Facing this reality requires a more flexible and dynamic approach, that provides quick responses to incidents. Detecting incidents in real time is a challenge itself, once there are millions of events to be handled, and many of them correspond to false positives, that drain the energy and time of a security team.

This work holds the following contributions to this research area: (a) suggesting the use of a taxonomy to better classify security alerts - and providing one for the scope of our datasets; (b) applying a clustering mechanism to security alerts; (c) experimenting different machine learning techniques on top of these meta-alerts – the ones provided by the clustering mechanism–, specializing the classification module suggested by Perdisci et al [4].

Our work differs from most of the applied machine learning techniques on IDSs, as we do not analyze network traffic. Instead, we rely on alerts provided by sensors (IDSs such as Snort, logs, etc). Therefore, we work on a different level of abstraction, that carries more semantics to our machine learning approach. We believe this addresses part of the "semantic gap" raised by Sommer and Paxson [14]. It also seems to render us more independent on the "diversity of network traffic" (also criticized by Sommer and Paxson [14]) as it is no longer our subject of analysis. We also don't rely on "anomaly-detection", which is the technique that has been heavily criticized by Sommer and Paxson [14]. We chose to follow the classification path of machine learning, which seemed more natural and more semantically relevant. Finally, the fact that we provide meta-alerts composed of the underlying alerts also addresses the "high cost of errors" brought up by Sommer and Paxson [14], as we drastically reduce cardinality (1000x less meta-alerts than alerts to classify), properly classify them (low level

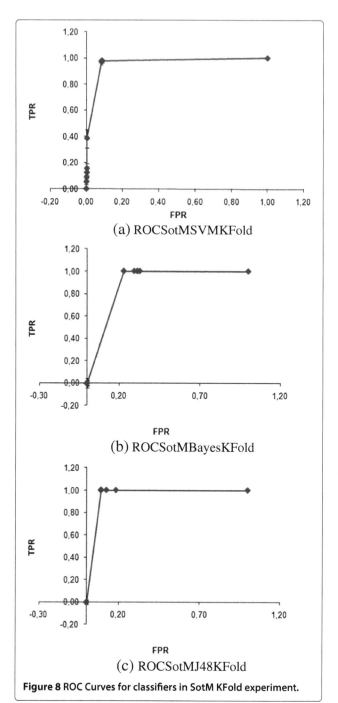

(a) ROCSotMSVMKFold

(b) ROCSotMBayesKFold

(c) ROCSotMJ48KFold

Figure 8 ROC Curves for classifiers in SotM KFold experiment.

Table 6 Event reduction in SotM experiment

Entity	Quantity
Records	73,751
Alerts	73,406
Meta-alerts	8,528
Indicated attacks	1,469
Data to information ratio	50

of false positives) and provide the underlying alerts of a meta-alert for faster analysis (more actionable piece of information).

We have been able to verify that the combination of a taxonomy and the fusing of alerts into meta-alerts provides a solid basis for the correlation of alerts. Using data mining techniques, specially Bayesian Networks, has also demonstrated to be a good approach to detecting new and stealthy attacks.

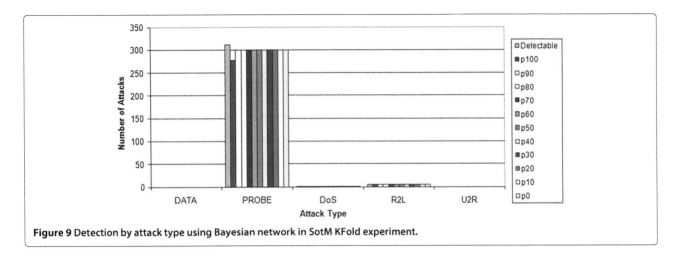

Figure 9 Detection by attack type using Bayesian network in SotM KFold experiment.

Our experiments have shown that it is possible to achieve high levels of Data to Information Ratio, and still be able to detect most of the attacks in our testing data. On top of that, new attacks — some that were not in our training datasets — have been detected by our combination of taxonomy–fusion–machine learning approach.

High detection rates have been achieved with low levels of false positives (lower than the thresholds suggested by the DARPA challenge [12]), making our approach a viable option for use in a scenario of intense, ever changing, attack types that constitute our reality and the near future.

This work can be extended in several dimensions; notably:

- Allow meta-alerts to be clustered into higher level meta-alerts, providing for the fusing of distinct attack types and multi-stage attacks;
- Research the use of *incremental clustering* as an alternative to the alert fusion algorithm;
- Analyze the possibility of using pre-defined topologies in the Bayesian Network classifier, in order to provide more deterministic and easier-to-understand classification criteria;
- Extend the taxonomy for different domains, including physical security;

Table 7 Comparison regarding the detection rate in different operating systems and attack types

OS	Attack type	Best in Darpa [12]	Bayesian classifier
Linux	Probe	60%	78%
Solaris	R2L	50%	67%
Windows	R2L	< 40%	78%
Windows	U2R	< 40%	50%

- Enhance the approach to integrate service level management practices, using CMDBs (*Configuration Management Data Base*) to analyse the impacts of security incidents.

Competing interests
The authors declare that they have no competing interests.

Authors' contributions
KS created and developed the approach. KS, ERMM and SKG participated in the experiments. KS, ERMM and SKG wrote the manuscript. All authors read and approved the final manuscript.

Acknowledgements
The authors would like to thank FAPESP and CNPq for the financial support.

Author details
[1] Icaro Technologies, Campinas, SP, Brazil. [2] IC - Institute of Computing UNICAMP, University of Campinas, Campinas, SP, Brazil.

References
1. Joosen W, Lagaisse B, Truyen E, Handekyn K (2012) Towards application driven security dashboards in future middleware. J Internet Serv Appl 3: 107–115. 10.1007/s13174-011-0047-6
2. Hale J, Brusil P (2007) Secur(e/ity) management: A continuing uphill climb. J Netw Syst Manage 15(4): 525–553
3. Ganame AK, Bourgeois J, Bidou R, Spies F (2008) A global security architecture for intrusion detection on computer networks. Elsevier Comput Secur 27: 30–47
4. Giacinto G, Perdisci R, Roli F (2005) Alarm clustering for intrusion detection systems in computer networks. In: Perner P, Imiya A (eds), vol 19. pp 429–438
5. Ning P, Cui Y, Reeves DS, Xu D (2004) Techniques and tools for analyzing intrusion alerts. ACM Trans Inf Syst Secur (TISSEC) 7: 274–318
6. Boyer S, Dain O, Cunningham R (2005) Stellar: A fusion system for scenario construction and security risk assessment. In: Proceedings of the Third IEEE International Workshop on Information Assurance. IEEE Computer Society, pp 105–116
7. Julisch K (2003) Clustering intrusion detection alarms to support root cause analysis. ACM Trans Inf Syst Security 6: 443–471
8. Liu P, Zang W, Yu M (2005) Incentive-based modeling and inference of attacker intent, objectives, and strategies. ACM Trans Inf Syst Secur (TISSEC) 8: 78–118
9. Sabata B (2005) Evidence aggregation in hierarchical evidential reasoning. In: UAI Applications Workshop, Uncertainty in AI 2005. Edinburgh, Scotland

10. Chyssler T, Burschka S, Semling M, Lingvall T, Burbeck K (2004) Alarm reduction and correlation in intrusion detection systems. In: Detection of Intrusions and Malware & Vulnerability Assessment workshop (DIMVA). Dortmund, Deutschland, pp 9–24

11. Ohta S, Kurebayashi R, Kobayashi K (2008) Minimizing false positives of a decision tree classifier for intrusion detection on the internet. J Netw Syst Manage 16: 399–419

12. Haines JW, Lippmann RP, Fried DJ, Tran E, Boswell S, Zissman MA (2000) The 1999 darpa off-line intrusion detection evaluation. Comput Netw. Int J Comput Telecommunications Netw 34: 579–595

13. Project TH (2004) Know Your Enemy : Learning about Security Threats (2nd Edition). Addison-Wesley Professional

14. Sommer R, Paxson V (2010) Outside the closed world: On using machine learning for network intrusion detection. In: Proceedings of the IEEE Symposium on Security and Privacy

15. Bowen T, Chee D, Segal M, Sekar R, Shanbhag T, Uppuluri P (2000) Building survivable systems: An integrated approach based on intrustion detection and damage containment. In: DARPA Information Survivability Conference (DISCEX)

16. Vigna G, Eckmann ST, Kemmerer RA (2000) The stat tool suite. In: Proceedings of DISCEX 2000. Hilton Head, IEEE Computer Society Press

17. Lee W, Stolfo SJ, Chan PK, Eskin E, Fan W, Miller M, Hershkop S, Zhang J (2001) Real time data mining-based intrusion detection. In: Proc. Second DARPA Information Survivability Conference and Exposition. Anaheim, USA, pp 85–100

18. Neumann PG, Porras PA (2005) Experience with EMERALD to date. In: Proceedings 1st USENIX Workshop on Intrusion Detection and Network Monitoring. Santa Clara, CA, USA, pp 73–80

19. Grimaila M, Myers J, Mills R, Peterson G (2011) Design and analysis of a dynamically configured log-based distributed security event detection methodology. J Defense Model Simul: Appl Methodolgy Tech: 1–23

20. Rieke R, Stoynova Z (2010) Predictive security analysis for eventdriven processes. In: MMM-ACNS'10 Proceedings of the 5th international conference on Mathematical methods, models and architectures for computer network security

21. Valdes A, Skinner K (2001) Probabilistic alert correlation. In: Proceedings of the 4th International Symposium on Recent Advances in Intrusion Detection (RAID 2001). Davis, CA, USA, pp 54–68

22. Asif-Iqbal H, Udzir NI, Mahmod R, Ghani AAA (2011) Filtering events using clustering in heterogeneous security logs. Inf Technol J 10: 798–806

23. Corona I, Giacinto G, Mazzariello C, Roli F, Sansone C (2011) Information fusion for computer security: State of the art and open issues. Inf Fusion 10: 274–284

24. Burroughs DJ, Wilson LF, Cybenko GV (2002) Analysis of distributed intrusion detection systems using bayesian methods. In: Proceedings of IEEE International Performance Computing and Communication Conference. Phoenix, AZ, USA, pp 329–334

25. Sabata B, Ornes C (2006) Multisource evidence fusion for cyber-situation assessment. In: Proc. SPIE Vol. 6242, 624201 (Apr. 18, 2006). Orlando, FL, USA

26. Endsley MR (1995) Toward a theory of situation awareness in dynamic systems. Human Factors: J Human Factor Ergon Soc 37: 32–64

27. Debar H, Curry D, Feinstein B (2007) The intrusion detection message exchange format (idmef). Internet experimental RFC 4765. Available at http://tools.ietf.org/html/rfc4765

28. Lan F, Chunlei W, Guoqing M (2010) A framework for network security situation awareness based on knowledge discovery. In: Computer Engineering and Technology (ICCET)

29. Cox K, Gerg C (2004) Managing security with snort and IDS tools. O'Reilly Media, Sebastopol

30. AlFedaghi S, Mahdi F (2010) Events classification in log audit. Int J Netw Secur Appl (IJNSA) 2: 58–73

31. Valdes A, Skinner K, International S (2000) Adaptive, model-based monitoring for cyber attack detection. In: Recent Advances in Intrusion Detection (RAID 2000). Springer-Verlag, pp 80–92

32. Mahoney MV, Chan PK (2002) Learning nonstationary models of normal network traffic for detecting novel attacks. In: Proceedings of the eighth ACM SIGKDD international conference on Knowledge discovery and data mining. ACM, pp 376–385

33. Mukkamala S, Sung AH, Abraham A (2003) Intrusion detection using ensemble of soft computing. In: Paradigms, Advances in Soft Computing. Springer Verlag, pp 239–248

34. Faraoun KM, Boukelif A (2006) Securing network traffic using genetically evolved transformations. Malays J Comput Sci 19(1): 9–28. (ISSN 0127-9084)

35. Faraoun KM, Boukelif A (2006) Neural networks learning improvement using the k-means clustering algorithm to detect network intrusions. Int J Comput Intell Appl 6(1): 77–99

36. Tandon G, Chan P (2003) Learning rules from system call arguments and sequences for anomaly detection. In: ICDM Workshop on Data Mining for Computer Security (DMSEC). Melbourne, FL, USA, pp 20–29

37. Mukkamala S, Sung AH (2002) Feature ranking and selection for intrusion detection systems using support vector machines. In: Proceedings of the Second Digital Forensic Research Workshop

38. Chang CC, Lin CJ (2001) LIBSVM: a library for support vector machines. Available at http://www.csie.ntu.edu.tw/~cjlin/libsvm

39. wei Hsu C, chung Chang C, jen Lin C (2007) A practical guide to support vector classification," tech. rep., Department of Computer Science, National Taiwan University. Available at http://www.csie.ntu.edu.tw/~cjlin

40. Witten IH, Frank E (2000) Data Mining: Practical Machine Learning Tools and Techniques (Second Edition). Morgan Kaufmann

41. Kayacik HG, Zincir-Heywood AN (2003) Using intrusion detection systems with a firewall: Evaluation on darpa 99 dataset. Tech. rep., NIMS Technical Report 062003

5

Catching modern botnets using active integrated evidential reasoning

Yongning Tang[1*], Guang Cheng[2,3], James T Yu[4] and Bin Zhang[4]

Abstract

Botnets are now recognized as one of the major security threats to start various security attacks (e.g., spamming, DDoS). Although substantial research has been done towards botnet detection, it is becoming much more difficult today, especially for highly polymorphic, intelligent and stealthy modern botnets. Traditional botnet detection (e.g., signature, anomaly or flow based) approaches cannot effectively detect modern botnets. In this paper, we propose a novel active integrated evidential reasoning approach called SeeBot to detect modern botnets. SeeBot can seamlessly and incrementally combine host and network level evidences and incorporate active actions into passive evidential reasoning process to improve the efficiency and accuracy of botnet detection. Our experiments show that both performance and accuracy of botnet detection can be greatly improved by the active evidential reasoning, especially when the evidence is weak, hidden or lost.

Keywords: Botnet detection; Evidential reasoning

1 Introduction

The total number of computers belonging to botnets increased from 3 millions in April-June 2009 to 6.5 millions during April-June 2010 [1]. Apparently, traditional botnet detection (e.g., signature, anomaly or flow based) approaches [2-6] cannot effectively detect and stop modern botnets. Based on a 2010 poll with chief information security officers and senior IT security directors at Fortune 500 corporations, all respondents stated that they considered malware and botnet to be a serious threat to their enterprise IT security.

Botnets are collections of infected computers that are controlled remotely by cyber-criminals. Originally botnets were created for a specific purpose such as sending spam, identity theft or DDoS (distributed denial-of-service) attacks. However, in 2010 bots that were designed to provide the cyber-criminal with the ability to build designer botnets (e.g., Zeus-based botnets) were rented out to other cyber-criminals for specific purposes (spam, identity theft, DDoS, etc). These criminal organizations invest significant building logical groupings of compromised systems that are organized around a sophisticated,

resilient Command-and-Control (C&C) infrastructure or even through social networks [7]. Such criminal networks are exceptionally stealthy and easily evade signature or behavior-based defenses. They can mimic normal application and traffic patterns, and can change their core software far faster than traditional security solutions can update their signature-based systems. We refer to such professionally designed and cyber-criminal oriented botnets as modern botnets, which have the following features:

- Highly polymorphic: The characteristics of botnets are varying even faster (e.g., via polymorphism or code obfuscation) than the signature update from security vendors. The prevalence of improved do-it-yourself (DIY) botnet construction kits and associated exploit packs make this feature much more evident in 2010 [8].
- Highly intelligent: The bots, used to be called zombies, are powered with much more intelligence now, such as Honeypot-aware botnets [9]. Modern botnets can run multiple simultaneous infection mechanisms, update the malware installed on their victims systems regularly, and optimize their serial variant malware production systems to release "personalized" and one-of-a-kind malware with each new victim infection.

*Correspondence: ytang@ilstu.edu
[1]School of Information Technology, Illinois State University, Normal, IL 61790, USA
Full list of author information is available at the end of the article

- Highly stealthy: Because of commerical motivation, modern botnets are designed to be more stealthy via many different mechanisms, such as randomly selected ports, traffic encryption and peer-to-peer based C&C.

Substantial research work has been done towards botnet detection. However, most botnet detection approaches attempted to follow and catch the trend of new botnet design, and then develop certain understanding or assumptions about the corresponding botnets. For example, (1) assuming certain botnet has a trackable payload pattern, payload signature based solutions [10] were developed; (2) assuming the existence of certain abnormal network activity or specific flow statistics, network anomaly detection based [6], flow feature [5] or communication pattern [4,11,12] detection based solutions were also developed; and (3) assuming the existence of similarities among bots, several behavior correlation based solutions have also been proposed [13,14]. In general, the more assumptions we make on botnets, the more restriction the corresponding botnet detection solutions suffer from, and accordingly, the easier being bypassed by modern botnets.

No matter how a botnet may change its behavior or appear differently, the motivation of botnets stays the same, which is to conduct certain profitable activities in underground market. Among all changeable appearances (e.g., spreading and control methods) of botnets, we classify them into three levels:

- Polymorphic appearance: Some features or characteristics of botnets are highly variable as designed. For example, the malware signatures. Various new system and network vulnerabilities will keep being discovered and exploited. The large number of software vendors and service providers will continue to contribute to this trend.
- Changeable appearance: C&C provides the channel between a botmaster and bots. Once certain C&C mechanism being well-studied and effective detection methods becoming available, new C&C mechanisms will show up soon. However, this type of changing is not as fast as we can find in polymorphic appearance of botnets. On the other hand, common infection and spreading methods may be more effective. Thus, for a certain time period, C&C can be still regarded as reliably recognizable appearance.
- Stable appearance: the final goal of a botnet is to perform certain profitable attack activities, such as spamming and DDoS attack. Even such behavior has become well-understood, botnets will not change it. New profitable activities may be discovered later. However, comparing to another two types of

appearance, Stable Appearance becomes the directly recognizable one.

In this paper, we advocate a rather different approach called SeeBot to show another niche in detecting modern botnets. SeeBot is built upon a new active evidential reasoning model, which integrates the advantage of both passive and active monitoring and detection into one framework. In this framework, SeeBot focuses on recognizing stable appearances, which are related to Infection and Attack actions (I&A), and Command and Control activities (C&C), as its initial detection targets (i.e., passive reasoning). In our approach, if the passive evidential reasoning is not sufficient to detect botnets, SeeBot automatically selects optimal verification actions to discover relevant symptoms that are important to collect the most critical evidences.

Our contribution in this work is twofold:

- We propose an active multi-layer causality model to seamlessly integrate active detection actions into passive evidential reasoning process, such that the robustness and resilience of a botnet detection system can be significantly increased, especially when initial symptoms are weak.
- We design an open and incremental evidential reasoning framework to be adaptive and extensible to a variety of different monitoring sources, such that the applicability and practicability of the system can be greatly improved, especially for detecting new botnets.

The rest of the paper is organized as the following. Section 2 discusses related work on botnet detection. Section 3 proposes an active evidential reasoning based botnet detection model. Section 4 evaluates SeeBot performance using simulations and controlled experiments with real traffic traces, and the conclusion is given in Section 5.

2 Related work

Sustantial research work has been done in botnet detection. In the following, we briefly discuss several related work.

Extensive studies have been conducted on understanding the characteristics and behaviors of various botnets. To collect and analyze bots, researchers widely utilize honeypot techniques [15-17]. Freiling et al. [16] used honeypots to track botnets in order to explore a root-cause methodology to prevent DoS attacks. Nepenthes [15] is a special honeypot tool for automatic malware sample collection. Rajab et al. [17] provided an in-depth measurement study of the current botnet activities by conducting a longitudinal multi-faceted approach to collect bots and track botnets. Cooke et al. [18] conducted several basic studies of botnet dynamics. In [19], Dagon et al. proposed to use DNS sinkholing technique for botnet study and pointed out the global diurnal behavior of botnets. Barford and Yegneswaran [20] provided a detailed study on the code base of several common bot families. Collins et al. [21] presented their observation of a relationship between botnets and scanning/spamming activities.

Several recent papers proposed different approaches to detect botnets. Ramachandran et al. [3] proposed using DNSBL (DNS blacklist) counter-intelligence to find botnet members that generate spams. This approach is useful for specific types of spam botnets. In [22], Reiter and Yen proposed a system TAMD to detect malware (including botnets) by aggregating traffic that shares the same external destination, similar payload, and that involves internal hosts with similar OS platforms. The corresponding aggregation method based on destination networks focuses on networks that experience an increase in traffic as compared to a historical baseline. Different from [14] that focuses on botnet detection. The scheme proposed in [22] aims to detect a broader range of malware.

Livadas et al. [4,11] proposed a machine learning based approach for botnet detection using some general network-level traffic features of chat-like protocols such as IRC. Karasaridis et al. [5] studied network flow level detection of IRC botnet controllers for backbone networks by matching a known IRC traffic profile. Rishi [10] is a signature-based IRC botnet detection system by matching known IRC bot nickname patterns. Binkley and Singh [6] proposed combining IRC statistics and TCP work weight for the detection of IRC-based botnets. Gu et al., 2007 [23] described BotHunter, which is a passive bot detection system that uses dialog correlation to associate IDS events to a user-defined bot infection dialog model. Different from BotHunter's dialog correlation or vertical correlation that mainly examines the behavior history associated with each distinct host, BotMiner utilizes a horizontal correlation approach that examines correlation across multiple hosts. BotSniffer [12] is an anomaly-based botnet C&C detection system that also utilizes horizontal correlation. However, it is used mainly for detecting centralized C&C activities (e.g., IRC and HTTP).

Many botnet detection solutions were designed based on certain assumptions on botnets with specific directly observable evidence (e.g., IRC botnet detection) or indirectly derivable evidence (e.g., correlation based botnet detection, a pattern of sequential observable network activities). Behavior similarity correlation based approach [13,14] cannot adapt to modern multi-function botnets with polymorphic behaviors.

More recently, p2p has been exploited as a new C&C mechanism in many modern botnets, which brings to a botnet detection system new challenges mainly on two aspects: (1) how to detect p2p traffic from background traffic; (2) how to distinguish C&C p2p traffic from legitimate p2p applications. Several solutions [24,25] have been proposed. Yen and Reiter, 2010 [24] showed that the different goals and circumstances, the features related to traffic volume, "churn" among peers, and differences between human-driven and machine-driven traffic make distinguishable behaviors in these p2p applications. Zhang et al., 2011 [25] proposed a novel botnet detection system based on statistical fingerprints to profile P2P traffic and identify stealthy P2P botnets.

In summary, we categorize those existing solutions designed based on certain pre-conditions (e.g., C&C mechanisms, sequential activities, behavior correlations) as condition-constrained botnet detection approach. All the solutions discussed here are in this category. To the best of our knowledge, SeeBot is the first active evidential reasoning framework for botnet detection that only assumes the intrinsic botnet activities. Many proposed solutions can work perfectly on detecting certain type of botnets as long as the expected pre-conditions are valid. The advantage of SeeBot lies in its high robustness, adaptability and applicability.

3 Active evidential reasoning

As discussed in Section 1, the three characteristics in modern botnet, namely highly polymorphic, intelligent and stealthy, make current botnet detection approaches miscellaneous and manifold. Botnet detection is essentially a process of detecting exposed botnet activities based on collected evidence.

An evidential reasoning approach usually uses a belief structure to model an assessment with uncertainty. In this section, we will formalize botnet detection as an evidential reasoning process. Accordingly, we will propose a new belief structure called Active Multi-layer Casuality Graph as shown in Figure 1, which seamlessly incorporate multiple components with different roles and levels, including Botnet, Evidence, Symptom and Actions, into the same active evidential reasoning framework.

In the following, we first introduce Active Multi-layer Casuality Graph, which is developed up the concept of casuality graph commonly used in evidential reasoning. Then we present the active evidential reasoning framework called SeeBot, and elaborate its functional modules.

3.1 Causality graph

A casualty graph [26] is a bipartite directed acylic graph to describe the Symptom-Cause correlation, which represents the causal relationship between each cause c_i and a set of observable symptoms S_{c_i} that may be triggered by c_i. Symptom-Cause causality graph provides a vector of correlation likelihood measure called likelihood indicator $I(s_j|c_i)$, to bind a root cause c_i to its relevant observable

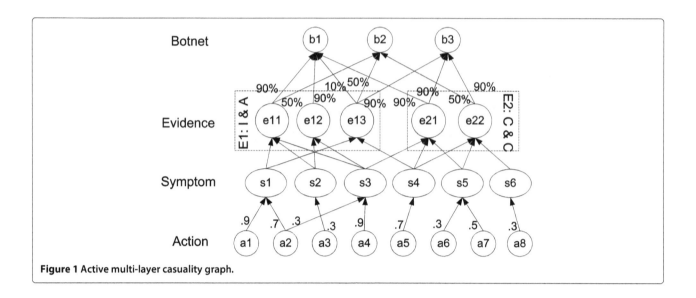

Figure 1 Active multi-layer casuality graph.

symptoms S_{c_i}. In a causality graph between root causes C and symptoms S, if $I(s_j|c_i) = 0$ or 1 for all (i, j), we call such causality model a deterministic model; otherwise, we call it a likelihood model.

However, a general casualty graph cannot satisfy the requirements in botnet detection, which can be mainly shown in the following two aspects.

First, the flat symptom structure in a casualty graph cannot completely represent the complicated relations among symptoms. A symptom may be the result from several other observed symptoms. For example, spamming, a symptom of common botnet attack, can be observed as the symptoms like (a) high volume of outbound TCP traffic with destination port TCP/25, and (b) multiple queries on different DNS MX records, etc. Accordingly, we break the original flat symptom structure into a two layer hierarchy between Symptom and Evidence to represent such complexity. Thus, a indirectly unobservable evidence can be jointly manifested by several directly observable symptoms. On the other hand, a symptom may contribute to believe the existence of different evidence.

Second, a general casualty graph can only represent a passive reasoning process. If any evidence is missing due to various reasons (e.g., packet loss), the passive reasoning result is commonly not satisfiable. Accordingly, in addition to the change made in the first step, we extend an action layer that is associated directly with the symptom layer to meet such requirement, which can selectively take actions to verify the most likely existed but lost evidence.

3.2 Active multi-layer causality graph
Active Multi-layer Causality Graph, denoted as AMCG and shown in Figure 1, consists of three bipartite directed acylic graphs hierarchically connected by different relationships. We use $B = \{b_1, b_2, \cdots, b_n\}$ to denote the cause

set representing different types of botnet (e.g., IRC or P2P botnet), $E = \{e_1, e_2, \cdots, e_m\}$ to denote the evidence set that can be jointly used to detect the occurrence of botnet (e.g., P2P traffic, spamming), $S = \{s_1, s_2, \cdots, s_k\}$ to denote the symptom set that can be directly observed, and used to determine the existence of evidences (e.g., high Max degree ratio [27], high volume of SMTP traffic), and $A = \{a_1, a_2, \cdots, a_q\}$ to denote the action set used to check the symptoms.

There are two casualty correlations between B and E denoted as $M_{B \times E}$, as well as between E and S denoted as $M_{E \times S}$. $M_{B \times E}$ is used to define causal certainty between various botnet b_i ($b_i \in B$) and evidence e_j ($e_i \in E$). $M_{E \times O}$ is used to define causal certainty between evidence e_j ($e_i \in E$) and symptom s_k ($s_k \in S$). Evidence-Botnet causality graph provides a vector of correlation likelihood measure denoted as indication measure $I(e_j|b_i)$ to bind a type of botnet b_i to a set of its evidences E_{b_i}. Similarly, Symptom-Evidence causality graph provides a vector of correlation likelihood measure denoted as indication measure $I(s_k|e_j)$ to bind an evidence e_j to a set of its symptom S_{e_j}.

We also use $A = \{a_1, a_2, \cdots, a_q\}$ to denote the list of actions that can be used to check symptoms. We describe the relation between actions and symptoms using Action Book represented as a bipartite graph as shown in Figure 1. For example, the symptom s_1 can be verified using action a_1 or a_2. The Action Book can be defined by network managers based on symptom type, the network topology, and the available symptom validation tools.

The active multi-layer hybrid causality graph Botnet-Evidence-Symptom-Action graph is viewed as a 6-tuple $(B; E; S; A; C_1; C_2; C_3)$, where botnet set B, evidence set E, symptom set S, and action set A are four independent vertex sets. Every correlation edge in C_1 connects a vertex in E and a vertex in B to indicate causality relationship between evidences and botnets. Every correlation edge in C_2 connects a vertex in O and a vertex in E to indicate causality relationship between symptoms and evidences. Every correlation edge in C_3 connects a vertex in A and a vertex in S to indicate verifiable relationship between actions and symptoms, referred as the Action Book.

3.3 Active evidential reasoning framework

SeeBot consists of four modules as shown in Figure 2, which are Evidence Mining (EM), Evidential Reasoning (ER), Plausible Reasoning (PR) and Action Selection (AS) modules. Evidence Mining module processes received symptoms from a passive network monitoring system and generate the corresponding evidences for all hosts in a monitored network based on Symptom-Evidence casuality relationship specified in AMCG. Evidential Reasoning module passively analyzes evidences, shows botnet likelihood evaluation for all hosts identified in from Evidence Mining module, and dynamically constructs a plausible graph presenting a plausible relationship between those hosts and each botnet category. Plausible Reasoning module identifies the smallest set of botnets to explain observed evidences for all related hosts, verifies if the confidence level of the reasoning result is satisfactory.

If the current related evidence is strong enough to explain the botnet hypothesis, then the reasoning process terminates. Otherwise, a list of most likely missing symptoms that can increase confidence on the botnet hypothesis is sent to Action Selection module. Selected actions are conducted to determine which unobserved symptoms have actually occurred and accordingly adjust

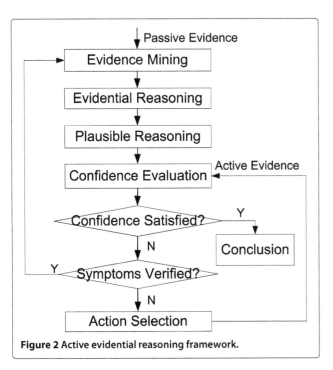

Figure 2 Active evidential reasoning framework.

hypothesis confidence level. If the new confidence level is satisfactory, then the reasoning process terminates; otherwise, the new symptom is fed into the fault reasoning module to create a new hypothesis. This process is recursively invoked until a highly credible hypothesis is found.

$$CF(b_i) = CF_1(b_i) \times CF_2(b_i)$$
$$= \prod_{t \in \{1,2\}} \left[1 - \prod_{e_j \in E_t} (1 - I(e_j)I(b_j|e_j)) \right] \quad (1)$$

$$CF^{n+1}(b_i|e) = \left[1 - (1 - CF_{T(e)})(1 - I(e)I(b_i|e)) \right] CF_{1-T(e)}$$
$$= I(e)I(b_i|e)CF_{1-T(e)} + (1 - I(e)I(b_i|e))CF^n \quad (2)$$

3.3.1 Evidence mining

In this paper, we characterize a botnet using two essential coexisted behavior or evidence categories, namely (1) Infection and Attack (I&A) evidence denoted as E_1 that reflect botnet motivation, and (2) coordinated command and control (C&C) evidence denoted as E_2 that show the fundamental difference of botnet from other malwares. For detecting a botnet, we should observe evidences from E_1 AND E_2.

We use Symptom-Evidence bipartite casuality graph, as discussed in Section 3.1, to represent the complex relationships among various observations from different network and security monitoring systems. For I&A evidence category, we choose 10 E_1 evidences in the current version of SeeBot, denoted as $E_1 = \{e_{11}, \cdots, e_{1A}\}$, including scanning activity, spamming, DDoS, portable executable (PE) binary downloading, etc. For C&C evidence category, we choose 4 E_2 evidences in the current version of SeeBot, denoted as $E_2 = \{e_{21}, \cdots, e_{24}\}$, including P2P, IRC, HTTP, DNS. We use a parameter Evidence Degree (or ED) to indicate the number of associated symptoms. For example, as shown in Table 1, $ED(e_{11}) = 2$ and $ED(e_{21}) = 3$. More specifically, if we have observed $\{s_1, s_6, s_7\}$, we strongly believe there is P2P communication among certain investigated hosts [27]. Please note that Table 1 just shows an example of Evidence-Symptom-Action Casuality graph. Our current implementation of SeeBot has the average evidence degree 23 among all defined evidences.

In our model as the example shown in Table 1, multiple symptoms are required to verify the existence of evidence, denoted as $e_{11} \Leftarrow \{s_1, s_2\}$; on the other hand, one symptom may also be used as supportive observation for different evidence, denoted as $s_1 \rightarrow \{e_{11}, e_{21}\}$. Furthermore, our Symptom-Evidence causality adopts a deterministic model, which implies $I(s_k|e_j) = 1$ if e_j exists $(\forall s_k \in S_{e_j})$. We believe such simplification via the deterministic model is a necessary and effective step to release many typical botnet detection solutions from the burden in keeping

Table 1 An example of evidence-symptom-action casuality

Category	Evidence	Symptom	Action
E_1 (I&A)	e_{11} (Scanning)	s_1(high TCP failure rate)	a_1 (snort)
		s_2(fast varying dest ports)	a_2 (argus)
	e_{12} (Spamming)	s_3(high volume TCP/25)	a_3 (NetFlow)
		s_4(multi DNS MX queries)	a_4 (DNS log)
		s_5(multi SMTP dest)	a_5 (snort)
E_2 (C&C)	e_{21} (P2P)	s_1 (high TCP failure rate)	a_1 (snort)
		s_6(high In-and-Out degree)	a_6 (Script 1)
		s_7(high Max Degree Ratio)	a_7 (Script 2)

track of the difference and details of various botnets. The input of this module is various tracking symptoms, and the output is all related evidences and their indication strength for each host relating to those symptoms.

3.3.2 Evidential reasoning

Evidence shows certain indication that leads to a decision with more or less uncertainty. The stronger indication an evidence shows, the less uncertainty a conclusion remains. Traditional uncertainty reasoning approaches based on Bayesian Network and Dempster-Shafer theory are inapplicable to intrusion detection due to lack of prior knowledge [28]. In our system, we adopt the scaling mechanism proposed in [28] to classify available evidence into three levels: strong (S), moderate (M), and weak (W) indications. Further, we evaluate a decision on botnet detection into three likelihood levels as well: strong, moderate and weak confidence. To facilitate the reasoning process and practical operation, we empirically quantify each evidence level with numerical values $S = 0.9, M = 0.5$ and $W = 0.1$ for strong, moderate, and weak likelihood levels.

In evidential reasoning, the confidence on botnet detection (CF), as shown in Eq. 1, depends on the confidence on the detection of I&A (CF_1) and C&C (CF_2). Furthermore, CF_1 and CF_2 rely on the joint events and their likelihood levels (i.e., S, M, W) from E_1 and E_2 respectively. In Eq. 1, $I(e_j) = \frac{|S_{e_j}^o|}{|S_{e_j}|}$, is denoted as evidence indication strength. If one type of evidence is completely missing, we use a null evidence (e_u) to represent, and $I(e_u) = 0$. In such a case, $CF = 0$.

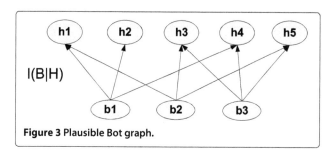

Figure 3 Plausible Bot graph.

Next, we present a method to incrementally update current confidence level denoted as CF^n to a new level CF^{n+1} when a new evidence e with $I(e) = x$ is observed. Here, we use a variable $T(e)$ ($T(e) \in \{0,1\}$) to represent the event category. If $T(e) = 0$, $e \in E_1$; otherwise, $e \in E_2$. Since $CF^n = CF_1 \times CF_2 = (1 - (1 - CF_1))(1 - (1 - CF_2))$, we derive the method as shown in Eq. 2 to incrementally update current confidence.

3.3.3 Plausible reasoning

After the process of Belief Reasoning, a *Plausible Bot Graph* as shown in Figure 3 is constructed as the following to represent the dynamic relationship between the potential faulty components and the evidence.

- For each botnet in B, to associate a botnet vertex b_i.
- For each investigated host component, to associate a host vertex h_j. with its total belief metric Ψ_c.
- For each investigated host component h_j, to associate a link to all its related botnets with the weight $I(b_i|h_j)$ (here, $I(b_i|h_j) = CF(b_i)$).

A *plausible botnet reasoning* problem is to find the minimal number of most likely botnets based on *Plausible Bot Graph* that explain all related evidences with investigated hosts.

Theorem 1. *A plausible botnet reasoning problem is NP-complete.*

Proof. A plausible botnet reasoning problem can be reduced to a Weighted Set Cover (WSC) problem as follows. For a set of investigated hosts $H = \{h_1, h_2, \cdots, h_n\}$, a cover is defined as a subset of hosts H_{b_i} that can be explained by one botnet b_i. Each cover H_{b_i} is assigned a weight as $W(H_{b_i}) = 1/\sum_{h_j \in H_{b_i}} I(b_i|h_j)$. Obviously, the less weight a cover is, it is more likely that the corresponding botnet is the cause. Thus, the plausible botnet reasoning is to find a collection of covers (i.e., botnets) such that $\bigcup_{b_i \in B} H_{b_i} = H$ with $min(\sum_{b_i \in B} W(H_{b_i}))$. This is a Weighted Set Cover problem that is NP-complete. $\square$

We adopt greedy heuristic algorithm [26] for the plausible botnet reasoning problem as shown in Algorithm 1, where B is a set of potentially botnets; H is a set of investigated hosts; R is a set of inferred botnets.

Algorithm 1 Plausible Botnet Reasoning Algorithm.

Step 1.　$R \leftarrow \emptyset$;

Step 2.　Find a botnet b_i ($b_i \in B$) with $min(W(H_{b_i}))$;

Step 3.　$R \leftarrow R \cup \{b_i\}$;

Step 4.　$H = H - H_{b_i}$;

Step 5.　Go to Step 2 until $H = \emptyset$.

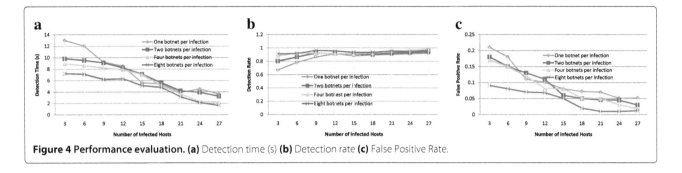

Figure 4 Performance evaluation. (a) Detection time (s) **(b)** Detection rate **(c)** False Positive Rate.

3.3.4 Action selection

Figure 1 presents the verification relationship between evidence $\{e_1, e_2, \cdots\}$ and actions $\{a_1, a_2, \cdots\}$. For example, Evidence e_1 can be verified by taking a combination of action a_1, a_2 and a_3, which can be denoted as a new virtual action vertex v_1 associated with a cost of the sum of $C(a_1), C(a_2)$ and $C(a_3)$. Action v_1 can verify all symptoms (s_1, s_2) that are verifiable by either a_1, a_2 or a_3. After converting joint actions to a virtual action, Symptom-Action correlation can be represented in a bipartite graph.

The goal of the Action Selection algorithm is to select the actions that cover all evidences E_{UO} with a minimal action cost. Based on Symptom-Action bipartite graph, we can model this problem as WSC problem to solve it [26].

4 Evaluation

In this section, we present our evaluation metrics, experiment methodology and experiment results.

4.1 Evaluation metrics

We evaluate SeeBot from the following three aspects: performance, accuracy and sensibility.

The performance of SeeBot is measured by botnet detection time τ, which is the time between receiving the first evidence (i.e., when malware becomes active) and identifying the actual botnets. The accuracy of SeeBot

depends on two factors: (1) the detection ratio (μ), which is the ratio of the number of true detected botnets (B_d is the total detected fault set) to the number of actual occurred botnets B_h, formally $\mu = \frac{|B_d \cap B_h|}{B_h}$; and (2) false positive ratio (v), which is the ratio of the number of false reported botnets to the total number of detected botnet, formally $v = \frac{|B_d - B_d \cap B_h|}{B_d}$. We have also analyzed system sensitivity showing the impact of the number of evidences and their evidence degrees on the system performance and accuracy.

4.2 Experiment methodology

One challenge in evaluating botnet detection solutions is the lack of group truth. The evaluation method adopted in our evaluation is called active evaluation, in which we execute real botnet binaries in a controlled network environment. By properly selecting different type of botnets, we can clearly demonstrate the applicability and robustness of SeeBot in detecting botnets.

Our controlled experiment environment has the following configuration: a Cisco ASA firewall with NetFlow enabled, a Cisco switch with SPAN port connecting a Snort IDS, and a event monitoring server with SeeBot installed for analyzing various symptoms, including Snort alerts, syslogs, DNS logs and host events (e.g., IRC activity log, HIDS events, AVG anti-virus application, malware alerts) from distributed systems. In our system, network

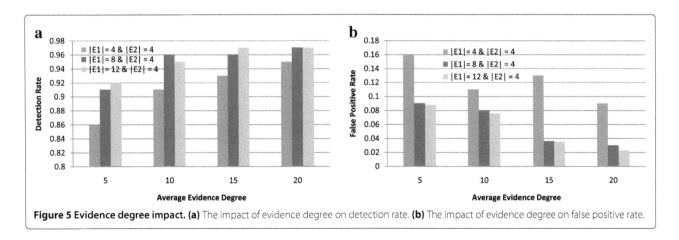

Figure 5 Evidence degree impact. (a) The impact of evidence degree on detection rate. **(b)** The impact of evidence degree on false positive rate.

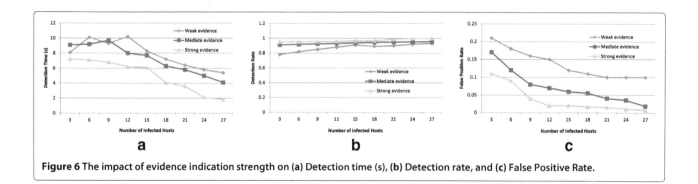

Figure 6 The impact of evidence indication strength on **(a)** Detection time (s), **(b)** Detection rate, and **(c)** False Positive Rate.

related evidence is adaptively combined with host related evidence. More specifically, network evidence will be initially analyzed at the first stage. The confidence evaluation on the generated detection hypotheses will be consistently conducted and incrementally updated with new evidence either passively input to actively collected from the monitored network system. Host based evidence such as security logs will be collected only when the passively input network related evidence is insufficient.

The testbed consists of eight physical workstations and 20 virtual machines, with Ubuntu and Windows XP installed. The system has been directly connected to th1e Internet for several months to record all traffic traces that will be used later as the background traffic when we disconnect the testbed from public network and run malicious software. More than 500 different type of botnet binaries have been collected over one year, and we selected 24 binaries among them, including 9 IRC botnet, 8 HTTP botnet, and 7 P2P botnets. In each test, the number of infected machines M increased from 3 to 27 at a speed 3 each time. For each test run, we randomly copied 1, 2, 4, 8 botnet binaries to the selected infection machines and execute them. In order to evaluate the impact of See-Bot parameters, we set up SeeBot with 3 different E_1/E_2 configurations as: 4/4, 8/4, and 12/4. For each event configuration (e.g., 4/4, standing for $4 E_1$ and $4 E_2$ events), the average event degrees (ED) are set to 5, 10, 15, and 20.

4.3 Experiment results

Figure 4 shows the performance evaluation results. Figure 4-(a) indicates SeeBot can detect botnets effectively (average in 5s), especially when more hosts infected. This is one obvious feature in an evidential reasoning system. Since SeeBot is not designed for any specific type of botnets, the evidence from multiple mixed botnets can jointly increase the detection performance, which is also clearly shown in Figure 4-(a). Figure 4-(b) shows the detection rate is above 90% on average with false positive rate less than 5% on average as shown in Figure 4-(c). In our framework, we identify the I&A and C&C related behaviors represent intrinsic botnet activities. If the evidence related to one of these two behaviors is significantly missing, SeeBot will not perform well initially. However, active reaction feature in SeeBot can effectively improve its detection rate by searching for missing evidence.

Figure 5 implies that with the increase of evidences and the corresponding associated symptoms, the overall performance of SeeBot is evidently increased. However, the improvement due to increasing evidences and symptoms becomes much slow after certain thresholds as the total evidences $|E_1| = 8$, $|E_2| = 4$ and the average evidence degree 15. Such an observation shows SeeBot can perform equivalently good as long as certain amount of evidence available to the system.

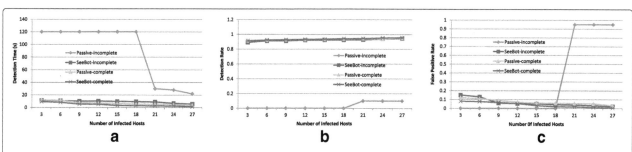

Figure 7 The performance comparison between SeeBot and the passive approach on **(a)** Detection time (s), **(b)** Detection rate, and **(c)** False Positive Rate.

As shown in Figure 5 and the following experiment results, the false positive rate sometime can be high. The main reason of causing false positive results is due to the multi-association (i.e., one symptom may associate to multiple evidence) between the elements in the evidence and symptom sets, especially when some symptoms are not detected or lost.

SeeBot provides an open framework such that different symptoms, evidences and botnets can be selected and associated together. Apparently, the evidence indication strength (as defined in Sec.3.3.2) between associated evidences and botnets can directly affect the system performance. Apparently, the general rule is to associate "Strong" evidences with botnets. However practically, the feasibility of constructing such a framework may depend on the configuration of a real network system. To clearly characterize the impact of the evidence indication strength on the performance of SeeBot, we have conducted experiments in three cases with all weak, all mediate and all strong evidences to validate the SeeBot performance. In our experiments, the different infection rates show the similar results. Thus, we only show the experiment results with two botnets per infection. As shown in Figure 6, the different evidence indication strength does cause some differences (10%–20% difference) on both detection time and detection rate, and makes significant difference on false positive rate (50%–500% difference). The time difference is caused by the consumed time in active reasoning process when SeeBot tries to increase the confidence level on the detection results. Even with weak evidence, SeeBot can still localize relevant botnets the same way as its receiving strong evidence. Thus, the difference on detection rate is not obvious. Since weak evidence is typically associated suspicious botnets, the false positive rate can be really high due to such ambiguity.

Many existing botnet detection tools were designed based on various assumptions, e.g., the existence of dialog model in BotHunter. The advantage of SeeBot lies in its reasoning capability in botnet detection, especially when available evidence is incomplete, which does not rely on certain botnet behavior to work. Since various botnets are used in our evaluation, for a fair comparison to the related work, we have implemented the essential passive reasoning system based on the proposed solution from [2,23,27]. To illustrate the difference in the passive approach and SeeBot, we further created two scenarios: (1) with incomplete evidence; (2) with complete evidence. As shown in Figure 7, when the observable evidence is complete, the difference between the two approaches are not obvious. However, when we only provided incomplete evidence to the two systems, the advantage of SeeBot over the passive approach is very significant. For instance, the passive approach cannot even start working (we set two minutes as a timeout threshold) when the evidence availability (i.e., 80% of evidence missing in our experiment) is low. Even when evidence availability rate increase to 50% such that the passive system started working, SeeBot is clearly superior to the passive approach as shown in Figure 7.

5 Conclusion and future work

In this paper, we advocate a rather different approach called SeeBot to show another niche in detecting modern botnets. SeeBot is built upon a new active evidential reasoning model, which integrates the advantage of both passive and active monitoring and detection into one framework. The experiments show that SeeBot can effectively detect modern botnets, especially when the initial evidence is not evident. Our future work includes the development of an uncertainty evaluation model to provide a confidence measurement on the detection results. We also feel it is important that SeeBot can detect hidden common characteristics embedded in collected evidences to characterize new botnets. The future version of SeeBot could be enhanced with certain effective learning mechanism such as reinforcement learning to achieve such a desirable feature.

Competing interests
The authors declare that they have no competing interests.

Authors' contributions
YT et al. proposed an active multi-layer causality model to seamlessly integrate active detection actions into passive evidential reasoning process. They designed an open and incremental evidential reasoning framework to be adaptive and extensible to a variety of different monitoring sources. All authors read and approved the final manuscript.

Author details
[1] School of Information Technology, Illinois State University, Normal, IL 61790, USA. [2] School of Computer Science and Engineering, Southeast University, Nanjing, P.R. China. [3] National Computer Network Key Laboratory, Southeast University, Nanjing, P.R. China. [4] School of Computing, DePaul University, Chicago, IL 60604, USA.

References
1. Microsoft's SIRv9 (2010) Security Intelligence Report volume 9. http://www.microsoft.com/security/sir
2. Shin S, Lin R, Gu G (2011) Cross-analysis of Botnet victims: new insights and implications. In: Proceedings of the 14th International Symposium on Recent Advances in Intrusion Detection (RAID 2011), Menlo Park, California, September 2011
3. Ramachandran A, Feamster N, Dagon D (2006) Revealing botnet membership using DNSBL counterintelligence. In: Proceedings of USENIX SRUTI'06
4. Strayer WT, Walsh R, Livadas C, Lapsley D (2006) Detecting botnets with tight command and control. In: Proceedings of the 31st IEEE Conference on Local Computer Networks (LCN'06)
5. Karasaridis A, Rexroad B, Hoeflin D (2007) Widescale botnet detection and characterization. In: Proceedings of USENIX HotBots'07
6. Binkley JR, Singh S (2006) An algorithm for anomaly-based botnet detection. In: Proceedings of USENIX SRUTI'06, July 2006, pp 43–48

7. Kartaltepe EJ, Morales JA, Xu S, Sandhu R (2010) Social network-based Botnet command-and-control: emerging threats and countermeasures. Applied Cryptography and Network Security. Lecture Notes in Computer Science Volume 6123, pp 511–528

8. Damballa Top 10 Botnet Threat Report 2010. http://www.damballa.com/downloads/r_pubs/Damballa_2010_Top_10_Botnets_Report.pdf

9. Zou CC, Cunningham R (2006) Honeypot-Aware Advanced Botnet Construction and Maintenance. In: the International Conference on Dependable Systems and Networks (DSN). June 25-28, p.199-208, Philadelphia

10. Goebel J, Holz T (2007) Rishi: Identify bot contaminated hosts by irc nickname evaluation. In: Proceedings of USENIX HotBots'07

11. Livadas C, Walsh R, Lapsley D, Strayer WT (2006) Using machine learning techniques to identify botnet traffic. In: Proceedings of the 2nd IEEE LCN Workshop on Network Security (WoNS'2006)

12. Gu G, Zhang J, Lee W (2008) BotSniffer: Detecting botnet command and control channels in network traffic. In: Proceedings of the 15th Annual Network and Distributed System Security Symposium (NDSS'08)

13. Zeng Y, Hu X, Shin KG (2010) Detection of Botnets Using Combined Host- and Network-Level Information. In: Proceedings of the 40th Annual IEEE/IFIP International Conference on Dependable Systems and Networks (DSN 2010), Chicago

14. Gu G, Perdisci R, Zhang J, Lee W (2008) BotMiner: clustering analysis of network traffic for protocol- and structure-independent botnet detection. In: Proceedings of the 17th USENIX Security Symposium (Security'08), San Jose, CA

15. Baecher P, Koetter M, Holz T, Dornseif M, Freiling F (2006) The nepenthes platform: an efficient approach to collect malware. In: Proceedings of International Symposium on Recent Advances in Intrusion Detection (RAID'06), Hamburg, September 2006

16. Freiling F, Holz T, Wicherski G (2005) Botnet tracking: exploring a root-cause methodology to prevent denial of service attacks. In: Proceedings of 10th European Symposium on Research in Computer Security (ESORICS'05)

17. Rajab M, Zarfoss J, Monrose F Terzis A (2006) A multi-faceted approach to understanding the botnet phenomenon. In: Proceedings of ACM SIGCOMM/USENIX Internet Measurement Conference (IMC'06), Brazil, October 2006

18. Cooke E, Jahanian F, McPherson D (2005) The zombie roundup: understanding, detecting, and disrupting botnets. In: Proceedings of USENIX SRUTI'05

19. Dagon D, Zou C, Lee W (2006) Modeling botnet propagation using timezones. In: Proceedings of the 13th Annual Network and Distributed System Security Symposium (NDSS'06), January 2006

20. Barford P, Yegneswaran V (2006) An inside look at Botnets. In: Special Workshop on Malware Detection, Advances in Information Security. Springer Verlag

21. Collins M, Shimeall T, Faber S, Janies J, Weaver R, Shon MD, Kadane J (2007) Using uncleanliness to predict future botnet addresses. In: Proceedings of ACM/USENIX Internet Measurement Conference (IMC'07)

22. Reiter MK, Yen T-F (2008) Traffic aggregation for malware detection. In: Proceedings of the Fifth GI International Conference on Detection of Intrusions and Malware, and Vulnerability Assessment (DIMVA'08)

23. Gu G, Porras P, Yegneswaran V, Fong M, Lee W (2007) Bothunter: detecting malware infection through ids-driven dialog correlation. In: 16th USENIX Security Symposium (Security'07)

24. Yen T-F, Reiter MK (2010) Are your hosts trading or plotting? Telling P2P file-sharing and Bots apart. In: The 2010 IEEE 30th International Conference on Distributed Computing Systems (ICDCS)

25. Zhang J, Perdisci R, Lee W, Sarfraz U, Luo X (2011) Detecting stealthy P2P Botnets using statistical traffic fingerprints. In: The 41th Annual IEEE/IFIP International Conference on Dependable Systems and Networks (DSN2011), Hong Kong, China

26. Tang Y, Al-Shaer E, Boutaba R (2008) Efficient fault diagnosis using incremental alarm correlation and active investigation for internet and overlay networks. IEEE Trans Netw Serv Manage 5(1):36–49

27. Iliofotou M, Pappu P, Faloutsos M, Mitzenmacher M, Varghese G, Kim H (2008) Graption: Automated detection of P2P applications using traffic dispersion graphs (TDGs). In: UC Riverside Technical Report, CS-2008-06080

28. Ou X, Raj Rajagopalan S, Sakthivelmurugan S (2009) An empirical approach to modeling uncertainty in intrusion analysis. In: Annual Computer Security Applications Conference (ACSAC), Honolulu, Hawaii, USA, Dec 2009

6

Internet-scale support for map-reduce processing

Fernando Costa*, Luís Veiga and Paulo Ferreira*

Abstract

Volunteer Computing systems (VC) harness computing resources of machines from around the world to perform distributed independent tasks. Existing infrastructures follow a master/worker model, with a centralized architecture. This limits the scalability of the solution due to its dependence on the server. Our goal is to create a fault-tolerant VC platform that supports complex applications, by using a distributed model which improves performance and reduces the burden on the server.

In this paper we present VMR, a VC system able to run MapReduce applications on top of volunteer resources, spread throughout the Internet. VMR leverages users' bandwidth through the use of inter-client communication, and uses a lightweight task validation mechanism. We describe VMR's architecture and evaluate its performance by executing several MapReduce applications on a wide area testbed.

Our results show that VMR successfully runs MapReduce tasks over the Internet. When compared to an unmodified VC system, VMR obtains a performance increase of over 60% in application turnaround time, while reducing server bandwidth use by two orders of magnitude and showing no discernible overhead.

1 Introduction

The use of volunteer PCs across the Internet to execute distributed applications has been increasing in popularity since its inception in the early 1990s, with the creation of projects such as Distributed.net [a], Seti@home [1] or Folding@home [2]. These Volunteer Computing (VC) systems harness computing resources from machines running commodity hardware and software, and perform highly parallel computations that do not require any interaction between network participants (also called bag-of-tasks).

Existing VC systems support over 60 scientific projects[b], and have over a million participants, rivaling supercomputers in computing power. The most popular middleware, BOINC [3], is currently being used by over 40 projects, from scientific fields ranging from climate prediction to protein folding. The amount of computational power available for large scale computing over the Internet can only keep increasing. On one hand, the number of Internet connected devices is expected to increase exponentially with the advent of mobile devices [4]. On the other hand, Moore's law continuous relevance shows that we can expect a sustained evolution of the hardware in the last mile of the Internet. This translates to an incredible amount of untapped computing and storage potential in machines spread throughout the world.

However, current VC systems have a centralized architecture that follows a master/worker model, as a small number of servers is responsible for task distribution and result validation. This limitation has prevented Volunteer Computing from reaching its true potential. In addition, the single point of failure inevitably creates a bottleneck, as projects expand and storage and network requirements become more demanding.

A Volunteer Computing system is sometimes described as a Desktop Grid (DG). However, in order to differentiate between both concepts we define DG as a Grid Computing cluster that uses idle desktop machines (PCs). A DG provides increased accountability, and typically offers better connectivity and availability than a typical VC environment, which spreads over the Internet. Desktop Grids may include enterprise environments, schools or scientific laboratories. This means that some Desktop Grids support more complex applications, such as MPI [5,6]. While a VC platform may be deployed on top of a desktop cluster, this is not the target environment intended for existing

*Correspondence: fcosta@gsd.inesc-id.pt; paulo.ferreira@inesc-id.pt
Distributed Systems Group, INESC-ID, Universidade de Lisboa, R. Alves Redol, 9, 1000-029 Lisboa, Portugal

systems. Therefore, throughout this document, whenever VC is mentioned we will be referring to large scale systems deployed over the Internet.

1.1 Goal and challenges

Our goal is to build a scalable, and fault-tolerant Volunteer Computing (VC) platform, which improves the performance of VC systems when running complex applications (e.g., MapReduce). This platform, called VMR (Volunteer MapReduce), must have minimal dependency on any central service, by decentralizing some of the mechanisms of existing systems that place an excessive burden on the central server.

As parallel and distributed computing becomes the answer for increased scalability for varied computational problems, several paradigms and solutions have been created during the last decade. Regarding the support for complex applications, among the potential candidates, we have chosen MapReduce [7] as the novel paradigm to support in VC for the following reasons: it is recent and widely adopted (e.g., Amazon's EC2^c); it is currently limited to clusters (Cloud Computing); many applications can be broken down into sequences of MapReduce jobs; it is a good example of data-intensive computing, requiring task coordination, and is heavily linked to distributed storage. MapReduce may also work as a stepping stone for other paradigms, such as scientific workflows, that could be adapted to a volunteer environment.

MapReduce leverages the concept of Map and Reduce commonly used in functional languages: a map task runs through each element of a list and produces a new list; reduce applies a new function to a list, reducing it to a single final value or output. In MapReduce, the user specifies a map function that processes tuples of key/values given as input, and generates a new intermediate list of key/value pairs. This map output is then used as input by a reduce function, also predefined by the user, that merges all intermediate values that belong to the same key. Therefore, all reduce inputs are outputs from the previous map task. Throughout the rest of the paper, we will be referring to them as map outputs. The adaptation of MapReduce to a volunteer environment is an interesting challenge because its current implementations are limited to cluster environments.

There are several challenges and requirements to consider, in order to achieve our objective.

First and foremost, our solution must be able to take advantage of the huge amount of VC resources that we previously mentioned. We must consider both the hardware capabilities of individual machines and the network bandwidth that is at our disposal, at the last mile of the Internet.

Our system must also be compatible with existing VC solutions (e.g. BOINC [3]), since developing a whole new platform from scratch would be of no practical use once the research was finished. Therefore, we must take into account existing systems and use their infrastructure to come up with a final prototype that can actually be used in the near future, in a real-world scenario. In fact, our solution would undoubtedly bring significant disadvantages if it required that only our system's clients were attached to a project.^{d} To avoid this situation we must guarantee compatibility with existing projects. Any client must be able to run any project application. On the other hand, our solution must support existing applications, and successfully schedule tasks on existing clients.

Additionally, the execution of our system on unreliable, non-dedicated resources requires fault tolerance mechanisms. This means it must account for unreachable clients, which have disconnected from the server, or are simply offline.

Another potential problem is caused by byzantine behavior [8]. Clients may maliciously return incorrect results, or inadvertently produce an incorrect output by encountering errors during the computation or data transfers.

Finally, our solution must be able to withstand transient server failures. This is particularly important in our case because we will be dealing with long running applications, with a potentially high level of server interactions. We need to prevent the execution on the clients to come to a halt, as they wait for the server to come back up.

1.2 Drawbacks of current solutions

Existing solutions do not fulfill the goal we described, and are inadequately prepared to meet the requirements mentioned above.

Most Volunteer Computing systems have a centralized architecture, with communication going through a single server. There are few exceptions and they were created with a smaller scope or environment in mind [9]. In BOINC [3], XtremWeb [10] and Folding@home [2], the server or coordinator must fulfill the role of job scheduler, by handling task distribution and result validation.

Current VC systems (not DG) are limited to bag-of-task applications since this architecture creates too much overhead on the server, when considering more complex data distribution or storage. Existing projects such as Climateprediction.net and MilkyWay@home have encountered problems when dealing with large files or having the same data shared by many clients [11]. Although some potential solutions have been proposed [12,13], they have not been deployed in the most widely used systems.

Fault tolerance is strictly confined to the client-side in current VC systems. Although some projects do have a set of mirrors that act as data repositories, all client requests and task scheduling goes through the central server. Therefore, any server fault that prevents it from communicating with clients has a very high probability of disrupting clients and stopping further task execution.

Finally, a considerable limitation of existing VC systems is their focus on bag-of-tasks applications, with little or no communication and without dependencies between the tasks. None of the current platforms support MapReduce, a widely used programming model that adapts well to a data-intensive class of applications. Supporting MapReduce requires fundamental changes on existing algorithms, and the introduction of on-the-fly task creation. This is currently not available on any present system.

In this paper we present VMR, a VC system that is able to execute MapReduce tasks over the large scale Internet, on top of volunteer resources. Our system is compatible with existing solutions (in particular BOINC). VMR is able to decentralize the existing architecture, by using client to client transfers, and minimizing the volume of data sent through the server. This also allows VMR to tolerate transient server failures, as the clients depend merely on other peers for data. It is also capable of tolerating VC clients' failure by using replication (i.e. running the same task on several VC machines). By increasing the replication factor, the probability of a failure of all clients running a certain task is lowered. Finally, byzantine behavior is controlled through the use of task validation in the server. By replicating each task at least twice, it is possible to compare the outcome and accept only the results in which a quorum has been reached.

This paper is organized as follows: VMR is presented in more detail in Section 2; Section 3 describes the most relevant implementation aspects, and presents experimental results, conducted with several different MapReduce applications, on a large scale testbed [14]; related work is discussed in Section 4; and Section 5 concludes.

2 VMR

VMR's architecture consists of a central server, and clients which can assume two different roles: mappers, which are responsible for bag-of-tasks in the map stage; and reducers, which perform the aggregation of all map output in the reduce step. VMR is compatible with BOINC (Berkeley Open Infrastructure for Network Computing), the most successful and popular volunteer computing middleware to date. Consequently, it is able to borrow its mechanisms and algorithms to deal with many of the challenges of Volunteer Computing systems.

However, BOINC suffers from the fundamental drawback of overloading the server because it follows a master/worker model, in which a central entity is responsible for scheduling and validating tasks. Although it is possible to use mirrors to hold data, many projects use a single machine for both data storage and scheduling.

Furthermore, these mirrors act as web servers, as all data is transferred through HTTP, making this impractical to implement on VC clients. Therefore, BOINC projects do not fully exploit users' increasing bandwidth, and deploy compute intensive applications. In data-intensive scenarios, BOINC is unable to quickly propagate input files that are shared by many clients, for example [12,13].

The parameters of the MapReduce job to run on top of VMR are defined by the user, and stored in the server. This includes the number of map and reduce tasks, the executable files used by map and reduce tasks, as well as their hardware and software requirements. Once all the MapReduce job characteristics have been defined, the VMR server creates the map tasks, and stores this information in its database — the VMR database is responsible for holding all persistent information on tasks, clients, and applications being run.

The overall VMR execution model is presented in Figure 1. A group of mappers first requests work from the VMR server's scheduler (1). The server follows a simple scheduling procedure when selecting which available task is assigned to each mapper or reducer; whenever it receives a work request, it matches each task's predefined hardware or software requirements to the client's machine characteristics. These requirements may include memory, disk space, CPU or Operating System specifications. If the client is suitable, the server assigns it a task and saves this information in its database. By taking advantage of the underlying middleware (i.e., BOINC), VMR is able to provide the same scheduling options. Therefore, it is possible to select scheduling techniques that are appropriate for the application. After selecting an appropriate map task for the requesting mapper, the scheduler sends back information on the task that the mapper must execute. This information includes the location of input and executable files, the deadline for task completion and the previously mentioned task requirements. The machines holding input and executable files are called data servers. Most VC projects store the data in a central server, represented in Figure 1 as VMR server, which also holds the remaining VC components (e.g., scheduler and database).

The mapper must then download the required data from the data server (2) before starting the computation (3). After the task execution is completed, the mapper creates an MD5 hash for each of the map output files. Therefore, at the end of the computation, each mapper is left with both the map output files and the same number of corresponding hashes. These hash sums are sent back to the server in place of the output files (4) (so it is compatible with current VC solutions, e.g. BOINC). This greatly reduces the upload volume from mappers to the VMR server (as discussed in Section 3).

The hashes are compared at the server in order to validate each corresponding task (5). If the result is valid, the

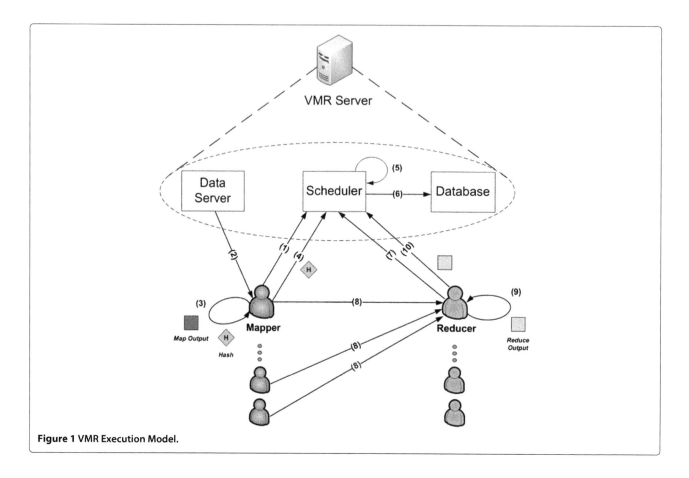

Figure 1 VMR Execution Model.

mapper's address is stored in VMR's database (6). Each time a map result is validated, the VMR server checks if all map tasks have been executed and validated. When this condition is met, the server creates the predefined number of reduce tasks. Existing MapReduce implementations typically allow for the reduce step to start as soon as a fraction of the map tasks are completed. The reducers can start downloading the required input files earlier, thus improving turnaround time. VMR is currently unable to provide this option, but it is considered as future work. We have postponed this improvement due to its complexity in terms of file transfer and data management. A reducer may then send a work request to the scheduler (7), in order to be assigned a reduce task. The VMR server follows the task scheduling procedure defined earlier and looks through the database to find a task that can be assigned to the reducer. If the reducer meets all the hardware and availability requirements, the scheduler replies with a reduce task that fits the request.

MapReduce jobs require communication between map and reduce stages since map outputs are used as input for reduce tasks. In the reduce step, each task performs join operations on the map outputs. Therefore, each reduce task must obtain all the map outputs that correspond to the key range it is responsible for. In order

to achieve good performance in MapReduce jobs, we leverage clients' resources by moving as much of the communication as possible to the client-side. This helps reduce the load on the central server, and creates a more suitable decentralized model for data-intensive scenarios, typical of MapReduce.

Note that, as previously stated, in current VC systems all data would have to be uploaded and downloaded from a central server. However, the VMR server stores the addresses of all mappers that returned valid map results. This information is included in the work request reply, and allows reducers to download the map output directly from the mappers, without having to go through the VMR server (8). Once the input files have been downloaded, the reduce task is executed (9) and the final result is returned to the server (10) for validation.

2.1 Byzantine behavior and fault tolerance

As we mentioned previously, dealing with distributed applications over unreliable resources requires mechanisms for byzantine tolerance. The results of a task cannot be blindly trusted as some node may have hardware problems, causing errors in the computation. Additionally, volunteers may intentionally return wrong results or sabotage the execution.

In VMR, byzantine behavior is handled through replication, and using majority voting. Each map and reduce task has at least 2 replicas, running on different clients. Upon receiving sufficient results (i.e., at least 2) for the same task, the server is able to consider it valid if a strict majority of clients return the same output. Unlike current VC systems, VMR uses hashes for task validation, which greatly reduces communication with the central server.

Task replication also helps guarantee fault tolerance against volunteers becoming unreachable or going offline. However, it does not help in case of a server failure. In order to achieve our goal of increasing the scalability of Volunteer Computing systems, VMR offers increased robustness, by being able to withstand transient server failures.

In our system, the VMR server is responsible for assigning tasks to clients for execution. Any fault or error that makes the server unreachable prevents new tasks from being scheduled. However, tasks that have already been scheduled can proceed with their execution if their required input files have been previously downloaded or if they are not stored in the server.

In existing VC systems, if the server becomes unavailable, the reducers are no longer able to obtain the map output files required for their task, preventing its execution. In VMR, however, all the reduce tasks that have been scheduled can proceed as normal, since map outputs are hosted at mappers (whose address is already known to reducers). The reducer's next communication with the server will only be used to report the task completion.

The scenario we have just described has a high probability of occurring because task scheduling is done in a short interval, immediately after the map stage is complete. In addition, the transfer of map outputs and corresponding execution of the reduce tasks takes up most of the MapReduce application turnaround time. Therefore, although VMR does not allow task scheduling if the server is offline, it is still able to keep MapReduce jobs executing if the failure occurs after the map stage. This is achieved due to VMR's use of inter-client transfers. In the case of a server failure during the reduce step, VMR reducers are unaffected.

2.2 Client to client transfer

As we stated previously, each mapper makes its map outputs available for download as soon as the task is finished. The map output files are available for download until a timeout is reached (set at several times the expected application runtime) or the MapReduce job is completed. A VMR mapper only accepts requests for the existing map output files, and discards messages that do not follow a predefined template.

Once the map task is completed and reported back to the server, each mapper's address is stored in the VMR server's database. After receiving a work request from a reducer, the VMR server includes the addresses of mappers that hold each of the map output files on the reply. Since map tasks are replicated, several mappers hold each map output file. Therefore, all reduce tasks sent to VMR reducers have the location of the required input data, as a list of IP addresses of mappers.

The list of mapper addresses is randomly ordered by the server. Upon receiving the reduce task information, the reducer goes through each mapper in the list returned by the VMR server in order. By having the mapper list randomly ordered, we implement a simple load balancing mechanism. This lowers the chance of having several reducers trying to download from the same mapper, and overloading it.

3 Implementation and evaluation

We evaluate VMR by running several tests over the Internet, in a scenario that resembles a typical VC environment. We run experiments with 4 different applications (word count, inverted index, N-Gram, and the NAS EP benchmark), in order to gauge our system's performance under different conditions. Apart from the NAS EP benchmark, used by NASA, the remaining applications are packaged by many MapReduce implementations as benchmarks. All of them have the characteristics expected of data-intensive jobs, and are described further ahead. This section presents the results of our experiments, describes the applications we use and reveals some implementation aspects.

It is part of our goal to improve the performance of VMR when running MapReduce applications. Therefore, we compare VMR with an existing VC system (BOINC). We use the VMR server in all our experiments, since current VC systems are unable to support MapReduce applications. As we previously mentioned, the VMR server is compatible with clients from existing VC solutions. Therefore, we are able to use VMR and unmodified BOINC clients in our experiments.

Throughout this section, we refer to the existing Volunteer Computing system we use for comparison as *VCS*. We run tests on two versions of our system: *VMR* corresponds to our system, as previously described; whereas *VMR-NH* is a VMR version that does not use hashes for map outputs. The VMR-NH client returns the map output files to the server, exactly as the VCS clients. However, both VMR-NH and VMR use inter-client transfers, while all communication goes through the server in VCS. VMR-NH allows us to assess the impact of using hashes (VMR), when compared to returning the output file back to the server but still using inter-client transfers (VMR-NH).

We measure application turnaround, while differentiating between map and reduce stages in order to pinpoint potential bottlenecks and areas that would benefit most from improvement. Additionally, we monitor network traffic on the server. This allows us to identify the benefits of reducing the dependence on the central server. Finally, we measure the overhead created by our system in terms of memory and CPU to compare the burden placed on the server.

We run our experiments on PlanetLab, a wide-area testbed that supports the development of distributed systems and networks services. We use 50 to 200 PlanetLab nodes that work as the clients. We initially deployed our server in a PlanetLab node, which imposed significant limitations (described ahead in 3.2.5) to our experiments. We then moved the server to a public machine of our local cluster, to run tests on a more controlled setting.

3.1 Implementation aspects

This section presents the most relevant implementation aspects of VMR. Instead of starting from scratch, and potentially creating a whole new platform that would be of no practical use once the research was finished, we extend BOINC, because of its popularity and for being open source. Therefore, we take advantage of its existing features and organization. In the server, a MySQL database is used, while backend components (e.g., file deleter) are daemons written in C or C++, or implemented in Python. VMR is designed on top of a BOINC client version 6.11.1, and server version 6.11.0. For the existing VC clients, we use BOINC's 6.13.0 version.

To support the execution of MapReduce jobs by BOINC clients, we modified the server. The VMR server, besides storing MapReduce job metadata, supports dynamic task creation: reduce work units are inserted into the database whenever all the map tasks have been finished. Furthermore, we have also changed the server to treat all map output data as input for the reduce work units. Therefore, when the reducers receive the reply to their work request, the locations of the input files are already updated and point to the server.

In our work, we try to stay faithful to existing communication and development procedures. Thus, we use (or modify) XML in messages between clients and the server. All data transfers between server and client are done through HTTP, while inter-client transfers are implemented through the use of a TCP connection. We have considered using UDP instead, but have kept TCP due to its inherent guarantees (e.g., message delivery).

In MapReduce, each mapper, with output available for reducers to download, stops accepting connections if one of the following situations occur: the client is shut down; the MapReduce job has completed successfully; or the mapper has reached a timeout in total hosting time.

VMR gives application developers the option to use hashes for validation or to use the traditional validation mechanism, which requires the transfer of output files from the clients. In the latter case, increasing the burden on the server can provide increased data availability. As an example, in MapReduce, reducers are able to download map output files from the server. This is used as a fall-back mechanism for failed inter-client transfers: after n failed attempts to download an output file directly from mappers, the reducer resorts to downloading all missing files from the server. In scenarios with low client availability or bandwidth, this prevents the execution from coming to a halt. However, our clients (i.e., reducers) always attempt to download from another client (i.e., mapper) before resorting to the server.

In that situation (unavailable mappers), the system reverts back to the original BOINC execution mode, in which all files are sent back to the server. In the worst-case scenario, in which all nodes are unavailable for uploading output files, the VMR server will simply work on the assumption that there are only original BOINC clients. Thus, even with client failures, the results would not be worse than the VCS scenario. Furthermore, the system can always resort to increasing the mapper replication until the required reliability is achieved.

3.2 Experimental setup

In order to coordinate the concurrent execution of clients in PlanetLab, we take advantage of Nebula and Plush[e], two PlanetLab tools that allow us to send commands to several nodes simultaneously. In order to evaluate our system, we create a VC project (following BOINC terminology) to run all the MapReduce applications. We describe each of them in turn.

3.2.1 Word count

The word count application is a widely accepted benchmark in MapReduce implementations. Each map task receives a file chunk as input, counts the number of words in it and outputs an intermediate file with "word n" pairs for each word found. The value n corresponds to the number of occurrences for each corresponding word. Typically, map tasks store the output immediately on the file system, so instead of having one line with "word 5", for example, the output file usually holds 5 lines with "word 1". This can be improved through the use of a local reducer, which aggregates identical results in memory before storing them in the file system. However, we decided to use the non-optimized version, and have our mappers always write "word 1" whenever a word is found. The reduce step collects all the map intermediate outputs and aggregates them into one final output.

3.2.2 Inverted index

This is another typical benchmark of MapReduce systems, in which the final output lists all the documents each word belongs to. The map task parses each chunk, and emits a sequence of "word document-ID" pairs. This means that for each word found, the map task identifies the document it belonged to through its ID. The reduce task merges all pairs for a given word, and emits a final "word list(document ID)" pair.

3.2.3 N-Gram

An N-Gram is a contiguous sequence of N items from a given input. The output from N-Gram applications can be used in various research areas, such as statistical machine translation or spell checking. In our case, it is useful to extract text patterns from large size text and give statistical information on patterns' frequency and length.

Each map task receives its corresponding file chunk as input, and counts all sequences of words of length 1 to N. In our case, we defined N as 2, for reasons explained in the next subsection. As in the previous applications, a map output produces a "sequence n" pair for each sequence with 1 or 2 words. Just as in the word count case, and following the typical execution model of MapReduce, n is always 1. Therefore, the map task produces an output file that dedicates a line for each sequence of words found in the text input file. The reduce step collects all the map intermediate outputs and aggregates all coinciding sequences into one final count, thus producing a pattern frequency result.

The map task from the two previous applications produces output files that are a little larger than the initial input. Therefore, the amount of data produced by mappers (and then sent to reducers) is similar to the volume received by mappers as input. On the other hand, for each 5 MB input, N-Gram's map task creates around *30 MB* of intermediate files which must be transferred to reducers. Therefore, N-Gram is helpful in assessing the performance of our system with applications with large intermediate files.

3.2.4 NAS EP Benchmark

The NASA Advanced Supercomputing (NAS) Division developed the NAS Parallel Benchmarks[f], which is a set of programs used to evaluate the performance of parallel supercomputers. This test suite includes 8 benchmarks, which have several implementations, and serve different purposes in evaluating system performance.

In our experiments, we use the NAS Embarrassingly Parallel Benchmark (referred to as NAS EP from here on), which generates complex pairs of uniform (0, 1) random numbers, using the Marsaglia polar method [15]. This application's main advantage is its simple adaptation to a MapReduce job: the map task works as a random number generator, while the reduce step gathers statistics on the results obtained.

Each map task receives a number range, and the seed for the random number generator as input, and outputs pairs of uniform random numbers, between 0 and 1. Each reduce task is responsible for gathering information on the numbers obtained for a set of seeds. This application provides a different challenge, when compared to the previous examples, since it has very small input and output files (unlike N-Gram), but creates a large amount of intermediate data.

We use an initial input text file of 1 GB, divided into 100 chunks (one 10 MB chunk per map task), in the word count and inverted index experiments. For the N-Gram application, we also split the input into 100 chunks, but each chunk is only 5 MB in size, due to the larger size of intermediate files. The NAS EP benchmark receives as input a small file with a number range and an initial seed (for a random number generator).

3.2.5 Limitations of PlanetLab

Each node in PlanetLab may be shared by multiple virtual machines (slivers) at any time. For obvious reasons, users do not have access to slivers they do not own, and cannot predict when they will be executed. As such, our experiments were occasionally influenced by other slivers running at the same time. This was especially notorious in the node acting as the server, as the network bandwidth could reduce suddenly and drastically. We were able to identify these incorrect experiments due to their unusually long execution time, and through the use of HTTP commands to occasionally download files from the server.

PlanetLab has another significant limitation: disk space. Each node running our virtual machine has access to 8 GB in disk, which is very limited for our purpose. This was especially true when running MapReduce jobs on unmodified VC clients (defined in the next section as VCS), since the server has to hold the initial map input, map output files and the final reduce output.

Therefore, we decided to move the server to a local, publicly accessible machine in our lab to overcome these constraints. All experiments involving more than 50 clients were performed with this scenario. This also allows us to correctly calculate the overhead of VMR.

3.3 Application turnaround

We begin by measuring application turnaround on all experiments. We measure the time it took each MapReduce job to finish, starting from the initial download of map input files from the VMR server, and ending with the upload of the last reduce output back to the server. We separate the map and reduce steps in order to identify their respective weight in regards to the overall application turnaround time. The map stage is considered to be finished once all its output has been validated in the VMR server. In our initial experiments, for the word count, inverted index and N-Gram applications, we use 50 clients, and the VMR server is deployed in PlanetLab. The experiments with 100 and 200 clients, for all applications, are discussed further ahead, still in this section.

We run the word count application with VMR, VMR-NH and VCS. The turnaround time of the word count application for the three alternatives is shown in Figure 2. For this application, the scenario with VMR clients has the lowest turnaround, followed by VMR-NH and then VCS. Both VMR and VMR-NH perform considerably better than VCS in the reduce step, taking only 40% of VCS's time. This speedup can be attributed to the inter-client transfers, which reduce the communication with the central server. On the map stage, VMR-NH and VCS have similar results, with VMR-NH performing marginally better. This was expected as both clients download map inputs and return its output files to the server. The use of hashes yields a considerable improvement on the map step, with VMR reducing its execution interval to 65% of VCS's value. When considering the full job turnaround, with map and reduce execution, VMR is able to cut the time required by existing VC systems in more than half.

The results obtained by VMR-NH in the remaining applications were very similar to the ones just described. VMR-NH is always slower than VMR in the map stage, but consistently faster than VCS in the reduce step. This means that VMR-NH always presents an application turnaround time below VCS, but larger than VMR. For that reason, for the remaining experiments we only show the results for VCS and VMR.

The results of the Inverted Index application support our previous findings, as we can see in Figure 3. VMR's map tasks finished almost twice as fast as VCS. The reduce step is also faster with VMR, with an overall speedup of 1.25.

In the N-Gram experiments the VMR server had to be deployed on a faster PlanetLab node in order to make sure the jobs finished. In fact, due to the large volume of map output data created, N-Gram creates a scenario in which the reduce task would take over 6 hours to complete, when

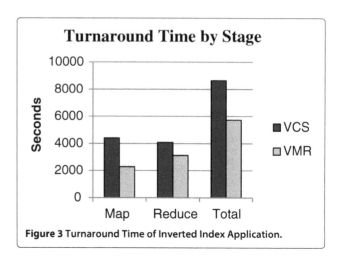

Figure 3 Turnaround Time of Inverted Index Application.

deploying the server on the previous node. The extended length of the experiment increased the probability of other virtual machines using the node, making it slow to a crawl in some cases, or even preventing the tests from finishing. Note that this excessive running time length was observed with the unmodified VC clients. When running our VMR clients, we were able to complete the execution of N-Gram jobs even with the server running on the slower node. This further proves that our approach allows slower machines to be used as server, as the burden is greatly reduced by leveraging VMR clients.

The results obtained with 50 nodes for N-Gram are shown in Figure 4. The first conclusion we can gather from a first look at the graph is that VMR is able to finish the MapReduce job in half the time of VCS. This is consistent with previous results from the word count application. However, in this experiment we can also observe that the reduce stage on VMR is only slightly faster than VCS. This can be explained by the better network connection of the node used as server specifically for this application. Despite its larger bandwidth, inter-client transfers still perform better than the centralized system. On the other

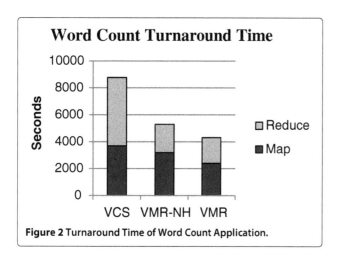

Figure 2 Turnaround Time of Word Count Application.

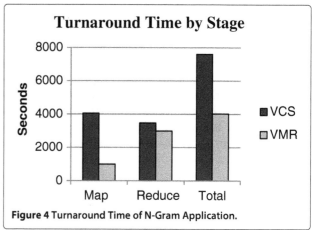

Figure 4 Turnaround Time of N-Gram Application.

hand, the differences in the map step are, as expected, much more significant. VMR is 4 times faster in executing the map stage, which translates to just a quarter of time needed by VCS to validate all its map tasks. This result shows us that VMR performs better with applications that create large intermediate files.

In the experiments presented so far (Figure 2 to Figure 4), we use a default replication factor of 2, for both the map and reduce tasks. This is the minimum required number of replicas, because a task is only considered valid if at least 2 replicas' results match. The use of inter-client transfers may suggest that a higher number of replicas increases data availability, and possibly improve the transfer speed. In order to test that hypothesis, we run further tests with VMR using the word count application, while varying the number of replicas of both map and reduce task.

When selecting the number of replicas to use, we took into consideration the values used in existing VC systems. In BOINC, for example, for each work unit (formal representation of a task, including its metadata), 3 replicated tasks are created and submitted to clients. This setup allows a VC platform to tolerate the failure of a single task. Furthermore, it reduces the impact of slower nodes since only the first two correct results returned are needed to validate a work unit. On the other hand, using more than 3 replicas creates unnecessary overhead, since many clients would be required to perform redundant computations. Thus, we decided to run tests with either 2 or 3 replicas for both the map and reduce tasks.

The results are shown in Figure 5. VMR is the baseline reference that uses 2 replicas for both map and reduce tasks. VMR-M3 creates 3 replicas for each map task while maintaining 2 reduce replicas. On the other hand, VMR-R3 replicates each reduce task three times, whereas each map task is only shared among 2 clients.

The results show that all three VMR versions have similar performance on the map stage. Curiously, VMR-M3, which uses 3 map replicas, has the worst results, which may suggest that the impact of slower nodes at this step was negligible. VMR and VMR-M3 present again close results in the reduce step. This means that, although there are more mappers to download from, there is not a visible gain from that larger pool. VMR-R3 has the worst results at this step, which can be explained by the additional data transfers between clients. Since each map output has to be uploaded to 3 reducers instead of 2, the mappers' upload bandwidth is the bottleneck. We conclude that having a larger pool of reducers does not translate to better performance, with a small number of nodes.

To investigate this issue further, we conduct experiments with both VCS and VMR clients, in larger scale settings, with 100 or 200 nodes. Throughout the remaining experiments on application turnaround, we use a simple notation to identify the number of replicas used in the reduce task: VMR-xRy. The x value corresponds to the number of unique reduce work units that have to be replicated, while y is the number of replicas created for each work unit. Therefore, VMR-15R2 corresponds to a VMR execution, with 15 reduce tasks, each with 2 replicas, while VCS-15R3 describes a VCS experiment, also with 15 reduce tasks, but with a replication factor of 3.

The results for the VMR version running the N-Gram application are shown in Figure 6. The VMR-15R2 version uses 100 nodes as clients, while 200 clients were deployed in all other executions. We only used 100 nodes in VMR-15R2 because after a certain threshold, there is no longer any difference by increasing the number of nodes, since there are only 15 reduce work units. This means that, with a replication factor of 2, there are only 30 reduce tasks being created (the remaining 70 nodes will be idle). Having 200 or 300 nodes does not improve performance since the map outputs are already spread throughout clients

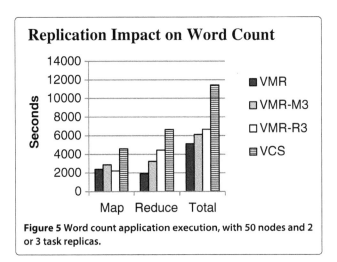

Figure 5 Word count application execution, with 50 nodes and 2 or 3 task replicas.

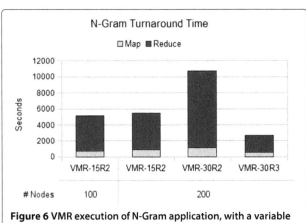

Figure 6 VMR execution of N-Gram application, with a variable number of nodes, reduce tasks, and replicas.

with 100 nodes. It is worth noting that despite the significant increase in clients, only the VMR-30R3 experiment showed improvement. This is explained by the fact that the execution of the reduce stage occupies the majority of the turnaround time.

The VMR-15R2 and VMR-30R2 scenarios have 15 and 30 reduce work units, respectively. However, both use only 2 replicas in the reduce step. With two replicas, each reduce task is indispensable for the MapReduce job to finish because a quorum of two identical results is required for validation. This means that, regardless of the number of clients reduce work units, a single reducer may delay the whole job.

The worst performance was obtained with VMR-30R2, when using more reduce work units, with a low replication factor. This is due to the increased probability of a slow or faulty node being assigned a reduce task. With 30 reduce work units, and a replication factor of 2, there are 60 tasks that may negatively impact the MapReduce job's turnaround time. On VMR-15R2 there are only 15 reduce work units, which translates to half the total number of tasks.

On the other hand, VMR-30R3 uses 3 replicas for each reduce task. In this case, only the first two returned results need to be validated (assuming they are both correct). This approach, despite creating overhead in data transfer and computation, allows the system to overcome lazy or slow workers, and offers a substantially improved performance.

We also performed the same tests in a scenario with VCS clients, because they allow us to better evaluate the impact of replication on the execution of MapReduce jobs. Figure 7 presents the results obtained when running the N-Gram application, which support our previous findings. The results of VMR-30R3 (the best performance settings for VMR) are also included, for comparison. Just as in the VMR example, merely increasing the number of nodes and reduce work units while maintaining two replicas (VCS-30R2) does not yield any benefits. However, a higher replication factor in the reduce step (VCS-30R3) improves the overall application turnaround time.

The results from the NAS EP application were similar, so we do not present them here. Application turnaround was decreased in 50%, mostly due to the reduce execution speedup. This is further discussed in the following section, on Network Traffic.

We conclude that, when using a larger number of nodes, it is worth providing a higher level of replication in the reduce stage, to account for stragglers and possible faulty behavior. Despite the obvious improvements, there were cases in which 2 out of the 3 replicas for a reduce work unit were executed by slow or faulty nodes. In this scenario, the validation of the whole MapReduce job was delayed due to this particular work unit. To overcome this shortcoming, we are considering introducing different scheduling and node selection algorithms in future work.

Finally, we have also evaluated our system's performance against Hadoop, an implementation of MapReduce tailored for clusters. VMR is designed for deployment over the Internet, and therefore cannot be expected to provide the same level of performance as Grid or Cloud Computing platform. However, it is interesting to find out VMR's overhead compared to a cluster execution of MapReduce. Thus, we ran Hadoop in our local cluster, which takes advantage of idle resources in computer labs. The cluster has access to 10 dedicated nodes, but it is able to use up to 90 nodes. For the comparison to be more precise, we ran a word count application, with varying input sizes. The results can be found in Table 1.

Unlike VMR, Hadoop does not replicate tasks, only data. This means that only one copy of the intermediate data (i.e., map outputs) is transferred from mappers to reducers. VMR, on the other hand, replicates the reduce task 3 times, which means that each map output is sent to 3 different hosts (reducers) in every execution. In the word count case, for each 1 GB input, 3 GB of intermediate data is transferred by VMR, while in Hadoop the same amount used as input (1 GB) is sent from mappers to reducers. Therefore, we include results for larger input data to compare scenarios with similar data profiles. The results show that Hadoop is around 5 times faster when

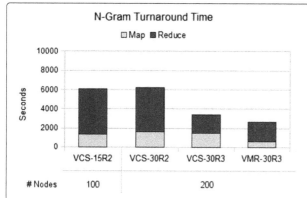

Figure 7 VCS and VMR execution of N-Gram application, with a variable number of nodes, reduce tasks, and replicas.

Table 1 VMR and Hadoop execution of Word Count application

Platform	Input (GB)	Intermediate (GB)	Turnaround Time (s)	Speedup
VMR	1	3	2475	1
Hadoop	1	1	508	4.87
	2	2	1079	2.3
	3	3	1485	1.67

executing the word count application on a cluster, when compared to an Internet deployment of VMR, for a 1 GB input. When the same total amount of data is handled by both systems (2 GB input for Hadoop), Hadoop is able to finish execution in around half the time of VMR. When it has to handle two thirds of the data (3 GB Hadoop input), VMR is able to perform only slightly worse than Hadoop.

It is worth noting that our system was not designed to perform better than data-intensive frameworks deployed in a high-bandwidth, low-latency environment. Our main contribution is a system that it is designed for the Internet, as a large-scale deployment, and that takes advantage of free volunteer resources. This creates many challenges and obstacles that are not found in cluster or data-center environments. The trade-off between execution speed and cost is advantageous for VMR whenever tight deadlines are not an issue, since VMR can obtain a similar performance for almost no cost. Clusters, on the other hand, have significant associated costs (i.e., maintenance, administration, and energy).

A summary of the turnaround time of the four applications running on PlanetLab is presented in Table 2. The Data Footprint corresponds to the size of input and intermediate data used by each application. This allows us to guarantee that all applications have to handle similar amounts of data. For each application, the total footprint is between 4 and 6 GB. We have also included the Hadoop results presented previously, to act as a baseline for comparison. The Hadoop implementation of word count is about 5 times faster than applications executed by VMR.

As we can see, the application with the largest footprint (NAS EP) still delivers a good level of performance when compared to the the remaining applications. This can be attributed to the fact that the intermediate files are much larger than the input and output data. By moving all data transfers to the client, VMR is able to better utilize bandwidth from volunteers (in this case, PlanetLab nodes), and achieve good turnaround time. The same can be observed in the N-Gram results.

We believe the results obtained with VMR can be translated to a real-world system, even considering the variable resources of hosts spread over the Internet. This is due to our system's ability to adapt to the available bandwidth between mappers and reducers. In cases where mappers have limited upload bandwidth, for example, we can simply increase the number of map tasks, by splitting map input into smaller chunks. It is also possible to further increase map task replication, thus making it more likely to have faster mappers upload their output to reducers. On the other hand, if the problem is in the reduce step, we can very easily increase the number of reduce tasks, by adapting the hashing algorithm that is used to divide map outputs into different key ranges (each reducer is responsible for a unique range). In our experiments, nodes have an average network download bandwidth of approximately 700 KB/s, while the nodes used as servers have around 10Mbit/s of upload bandwidth. These values are not too far from the average client and server bandwidths.

3.4 Network traffic

We measure upload and download traffic in the VMR server (see Figure 1), for VMR and VCS clients while running the applications. Monitoring the network traffic on the server provides a more accurate measure of its overhead. It also allows us to quantify the impact of our solution concerning the decentralization of the VC model. The server download traffic corresponds to the amount of data received by the server from the clients, while server upload traffic consists of the amount sent by the server to the clients. Note that, as mentioned in the previous section, VMR has a much lower application turnaround than VCS. This is why the VMR line in Figure 8 stops around second 4000 (the same happens in Figure 9), while VCS only finishes its execution much later. This can be observed in all experiments presented in this section.

The server upload traffic while running the word count application is presented in Figure 8. We can see that up until around second 2000, both the VCS and the VMR

Table 2 Turnaround time for all four applications running VMR

		Data Footprint	
Application	Turnaround time	Input	Intermediate
NAS EP	2569.5	400 KB	5.9 GB
Inverted Index	2547.7	1 GB	4.25 GB
N-Gram	2678.3	0.5 GB	4.15 GB
Word Count	2475.4	1 GB	3 GB
Word Count (Hadoop)	508.3	1 GB	1 GB

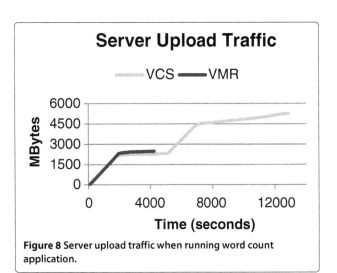

Figure 8 Server upload traffic when running word count application.

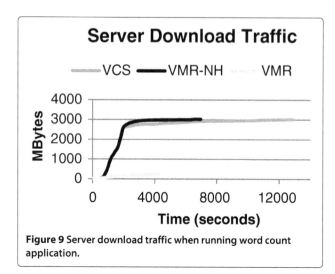

Figure 9 Server download traffic when running word count application.

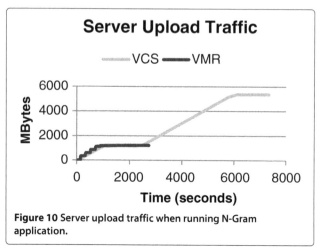

Figure 10 Server upload traffic when running N-Gram application.

server send the required map input files to the clients. However, once that step is completed, the VMR server is no longer responsible for uploading map outputs to reducers, unlike VCS which holds that responsibility. That explains the steep increase in the VCS line, around second 5000. Our server is required to upload 2,5 GB to clients, whereas VCS uploads more than double that amount.

Figure 9 shows the results on server download traffic. We include the results of VMR-NH to show the difference between returning hashes (VMR) or map outputs (VMR-NH). Since VMR-NH clients must return the map output back to the server, exactly as the regular VCS clients, the server receives the same amount of data from the clients in both cases. This is clearly shown in Figure 9, where we can see VMR-NH reaching the same value as VCS. VMR, on the other hand, through the use of hashes has almost completely eliminated data transfers from clients to the server. The VMR server receives a mere 250 MB from clients, a value 10 times smaller than VCS's 3 GB.

The inverted index application experiments yielded very similar results, so they are not shown here. VMR is able to reduce the amount of data sent to to clients from 6.5 GB to 2.3 GB and cut downloaded data by 96%.

N-Gram presents a different scenario from the two other applications, so it is worthwhile to analyze its results. The server upload traffic running N-Gram is shown in Figure 10. It is clear that there is a significant difference in the amount of data sent by the server to VMR and VCS clients. This is due to the large size of intermediate files, which causes the server in the VCS experiment to upload almost 5 times more data than the VMR scenario in the reduce step.

The server download traffic is exhibited in Figure 11. Here, we can see the benefits of using hashes for map task validation. Up until second 2000, the VMR server has received almost no data from the clients. At around that

time in the experiment, reducers that finished their task began sending their output back to the server. The VMR server downloads a total of 820 MB from the clients. On the other hand, the VCS server is responsible for downloading all map outputs from mappers, which corresponds to the steep increase up until second 4000. The VCS server is required to download 6 times more data than VMR.

Finally, the experiments with the NAS EP application are conducted with two different inputs. For the first set of tests, we use a smaller number range for input, which translates into a relatively small intermediate data file size: each map task creates around 15 MB of output data.

The upload traffic for a server running NAS EP with the small intermediate data is shown in Figure 12. The server starts by sending the input files and the map executable to VMR and VCS clients. The reduce executable is also sent to the clients in both scenarios. This corresponds to around 500 MB, reached around second 700 in VMR. However, the VCS server must also send the reduce inputs to the clients, unlike VMR. This accounts for the steep

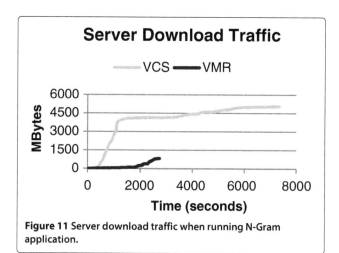

Figure 11 Server download traffic when running N-Gram application.

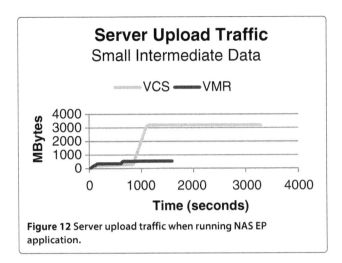

Figure 12 Server upload traffic when running NAS EP application.

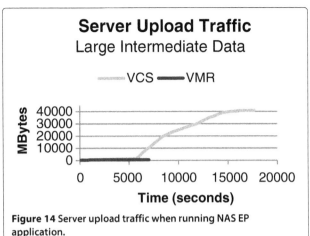

Figure 14 Server upload traffic when running NAS EP application.

increase around second 850. The VCS server is required to send over 3 GB of input data to clients.

However, the biggest difference in server load can be attributed to the download traffic, shown in Figure 13. As we mentioned previously, the NAS EP application produces very small reduce output files. Since VMR clients do not send the map output to the server, almost no data is received by the VMR server during the MapReduce job execution. The VCS version, on the other hand, receives over 3,7 GB of data.

For the final experiment, we increase the number range used as input for the NAS EP application. This in turn increases the intermediate data file size by an order of magnitude: each map task creates up to 300 MB of output data.

The upload traffic for a server running NAS EP with the large intermediate data is shown in Figure 14. As in the previous example, there is an initial upload of input files to clients, which is trivial when compared to the amount of data sent by the server to VCS clients. On the whole, the VCS server sends 40 GB of data to clients, which mostly

corresponds to the map output files. As in the smaller input range, the VMR server only has to send around 500 MB to clients.

Once again, the most noticeable reduction in server overhead is found in the data received by the server. As we can see in Figure 15, the VMR clients send a nominal amount of data to the server (a little over 60 MB). The centralized VCS scenario requires all map output files to go through the server. Thus, over 40 GB are sent to the server during the execution. This means that VMR is able to reduce server download traffic by two orders of magnitude, to a value that is more than 600 times lower.

As expected, VMR is naturally suited for applications with intermediate data that is much larger than their input and output. The centralized approach currently used by VC systems, exemplified by VCS, on the other hand creates numerous problems. The massive amount of data that goes through the server not only creates overhead on a single node, but it also creates significant strain on the network.[g]

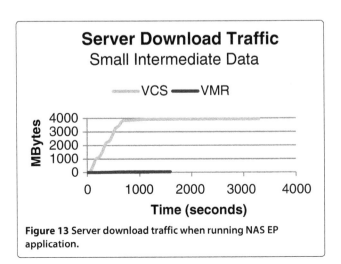

Figure 13 Server download traffic when running NAS EP application.

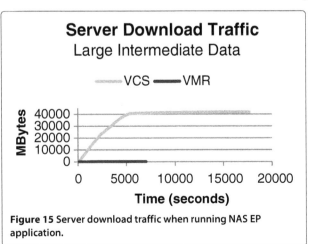

Figure 15 Server download traffic when running NAS EP application.

Therefore, we can conclude that VMR not only can perform better than VCS when running jobs with large intermediate files, but is also able to alleviate the server's network connection.

Performing a similar analysis on network traffic in clients (during the transition from map to reduce) may yield interesting results and help us better understand the performance of VMR. However, it is not easy (or sometimes even possible) to measure network traffic in clients, since they were deployed in PlanetLab nodes. Unlike our server, which is running in a dedicated machine of our lab, each client may be sharing resources with other virtual machines, at any time. This means that there is little to no control on the available bandwidth, and severely reduces the effectiveness of monitoring system resources in clients. Table 3 presents average network traffic and data transferred per client. We present the results obtained by reducers separately, due to the smaller number of nodes that are chosen for that role (90 reduce tasks). On the other hand, all 200 clients are usually mappers since there are 300 map tasks available.

For the inter-client network bandwidth experiment, 200 VMR clients executed the N-Gram application with 30 reduce work units, and a replication factor of 3. This means that out of the 200 hosts, 90 (30 workunits replicated three times) of them are chosen as reducers. The average download speed for the reducer is higher than the remaining nodes, since they are responsible for downloading all input data directly from mappers. These values correspond to the average obtained through system monitoring, during the entire duration of a MapReduce job execution, in which clients may often be either performing local I/O or CPU operations. Furthermore, as we mentioned previously, relying solely on system monitoring is not enough to provide a more accurate evaluation on client to client network traffic.

Therefore, we have instrumented the VMR client to measure the average speed when receiving files from other clients (i.e., acting as reducers). The average transfer speed for reducers downloading map outputs is around 1.1 MB/s. This considerably high download speed can be attributed to the map task replication and the random node selection mechanism when choosing which mapper to download from. By providing a large number of available mappers, the system is able to take advantage of clients' bandwidth. This resource is typically underutilized, as we can see from the average download and upload

speed for all clients. Due to the inherent overhead created by middleware instrumentation, VMR currently does not monitor the upload speed or the amount of data transferred by each client. We are considering extending the monitoring features provided, while keeping in mind that any changes must not impact the system's performance.

3.5 Overhead

To better evaluate the impact of our system, we measure both CPU and memory use on the server. The experiments ran with the server deployed on PlanetLab yielded inconclusive results, since during each execution the server node could be running tasks from other virtual machines. Therefore, we present the results from experiments running the N-Gram application that used a local machine as the server.

The CPU utilization measurements are shown in Table 4. VMR and VCS present similar average values. The low CPU utilization can be explained by the data-intensive characteristics of the applications. During most of the execution, the server would either be transferring data or awaiting client requests, instead of performing CPU intensive tasks (e.g., creating work units).

In the course of our experiments we also measure the memory usage. The values observed are shown in Table 5. As we can see from the average memory utilization, our system did not create any overhead during the VMR server execution. In fact, VMR's average values are lower than those of VCS. This can be attributed to the lower memory required to store the intermediate files that were returned by VCS clients, and validated at the server. In VMR only the hashes are returned and compared in order to reach a quorum. These results show that VMR does not impact the VC server in any way in terms of memory or CPU utilization.

4 Related work

Combining the concepts of Cloud and VC was proposed in [16], in which the authors studied the cost and benefits of using clouds as a substitute for volunteers or servers. This comparison was performed using information from the SETI@Home project, taking into consideration its I/O operations, storage and throughput requirements. To calculate the cloud's cost, the authors used Amazon's EC2. The authors conclude that it is only advantageous to deploy a VC server in the cloud for small projects, with at most around 1400 volunteers. Although this paper deals

Table 3 Client Network Bandwidth averages in VMR

VMR clients	Download speed (KB/s)	Upload speed (KB/s)	Data received (MB)	Data sent (MB)
All clients	84	48	243	167
Reducers	178	61	418	143

Table 4 Server CPU utilization

CPU Utilization	VCS (%)	VMR (%)
Average	3.13	0.6
Std. Deviation	6.5	1.31

with the same research areas, its application and goals are orthogonal to our work. It would be possible to use cloud resources as an alternative to volunteers, whenever harder deadlines were set or more resources were needed.

P2P-MapReduce [17] is a P2P model under the MapReduce framework. The system is tailored to a dynamic cloud environment, creating a cloud of clouds. P2P-MapReduce makes use of a general-purpose P2P library, JXTA [18], which organizes peers into groups based on their interests or services offered. This network dynamically assigns the MapReduce master role and manages master failures in a decentralized fashion. Ordinary nodes are "promoted" to masters whenever the percentage of masters in the system falls beneath a certain threshold. This means that the first node of the system will always be a master. This may be a problem, since there is a possibility that machines with lower availability will be given more responsibility, thus slowing down the system.

Although MapReduce was initially developed by Google [7], Apache's Hadoop[h] is the most widely used implementation[i]. Hadoop is open source, unlike Google's MapReduce implementation, thus facilitating its adoption by a larger number of institutions. MOON (MapReduce On opportunistic eNvironments) [19] is a Desktop Grid system that proposes an extension to Hadoop that implements adaptive task scheduling to account for node failure. MOON is tailored for a cluster environment, such as a research lab, in which nodes are trusted or even dedicated. It takes advantage of a two-layer node organization, in which a small set of reliable nodes are used to guarantee a certain level of availability. The remaining nodes are considered to be volatile, and are used as "cheap" resources, often unavailable, but easily replaced. The authors reach an interesting conclusion during their experiments: Hadoop is unable to finish MapReduce jobs whenever there are frequent node failures.

Table 5 Server memory utilization

Memory Utilization	VCS (MBytes)	VMR (MBytes)
Average	6186	4239
Std. Deviation	765	397

MapReduce was also adapted to desktop grids in [20]. The system was designed on top of BitDew [13], a middleware the handles data management through the use of various transfer protocols. The authors claim it is able to run MapReduce jobs on XtremWeb [10], over the Internet. However, their experiments were conducted in a cluster interconnected by Gigabit Ethernet. This environment more closely resembles the common scenario of XtremWeb, which consists of a federation of research labs. Nodes in this system are divided into 2 categories: stable, which are dedicated machines that act as the XtremWeb *master*, and handle the MapReduce and BitDew *services* (this role is typically fulfilled by a single node); and volatile, which correspond to the workers responsible for task execution. In MapReduce jobs, each reducer is sent all map output files for each replicated map task. Once it has obtained a required number of intermediate results, it is assumed that the result that appears most often is assumed to be correct.

Moca et al. [21] studied the effects of sabotage when running MapReduce jobs on the previously described system. The authors try to identify the impact that a faulty node may have on a MapReduce job correctness. The authors only propose and test using majority voting, through simulation, which is able to achieve an acceptable error rate with a replication factor of 3. They also conclude that a higher replication factor would create an unbearable communication overhead.

Having the reducers receive all map replicas completely removes the server from the intermediate validation process. While this eliminates client-server intermediate file transfers, it also creates 2 significant problems in communication overhead and Byzantine fault tolerance. First, this algorithm requires all map outputs to be sent to reducers. In the case of a higher error or fault rate, this would create a large volume of unnecessary data transfers, as many map outputs would be incorrect. Even in a typical scenario with lower error rates, all incorrect files would still have to be uploaded to reducers for them to be validated. Secondly, this creates a problem in identifying Byzantine behavior. Whenever an incorrect reduce result is obtained, the system has no way of knowing if there was an error in the map or reduce phase, since it did not have access to map outputs. This can be aggravated if a reducer is exhibiting Byzantine behavior, either by purposefully sabotaging the execution or by simply encountering bugs or hardware faults.

XtremWeb and MOON are Desktop Grid systems, meant for deployment on distributed clusters and data centers. VMR, on the other hand, is actually tailored for a truly volunteer environment over the Internet. By moving from benchmarks and proof-of-concepts to actual applications in a realistic testbed, we can state with more certainty what are the advantages and shortcomings of this paradigm on a volunteer computing environment.

5 Conclusion

We have presented VMR, a Volunteer Computing platform that leverages client resources in order to execute MapReduce applications over the Internet. Our system is able to tolerate volunteer faults, and transient server failures. Furthermore, it is compatible with existing VC systems (in particular BOINC). VMR significantly reduces the dependence on the central server, which is typically overburdened in current VC platforms, thus allowing it to obtain a better performance.

We evaluated VMR by measuring the application turnaround, server network traffic and overhead while running widely used MapReduce applications, which are representative of MapReduce jobs deployed in production environments. Our solution was able to improve the performance of all the MapReduce jobs we tested. The map stage was up to 4 times faster than in an existing VC system. The reduce step also showed an improvement, thus reducing each MapReduce job's execution time down to less than half.

Increasing task replication does not improve the system's performance with a smaller number of nodes. However, with 200 nodes, we were able to conclude that having a larger pool of clients does correspond directly to a performance boost. This was attributed to the lower impact of slow or faulty nodes on the job turnaround time.

Regarding the server's network traffic, VMR reduced server download traffic by an order of magnitude on the word count and inverted index applications. The N-Gram application provided a scenario with large intermediate data and large outputs. Therefore, we were able to witness a decrease in uploaded data to 20% of the existing VC system server's value. However, it was the NAS EP application that showed the biggest advantage of VMR on server traffic reduction. Due to its large intermediate files, and small output and input data, VMR was able to reduce network traffic consumption by two orders of magnitude. It reduced server download bandwidth more than 600-fold, when compared to VCS.

We were able to conclude that VMR not only can perform better than VCS when running jobs with large intermediate files, but is also able to significantly remove the burden on the server's network connection. It is important to note that the changes we introduced did not create any significant or visible overhead on the server side. Considering these results, and taking into consideration the typical compute-intensive nature of VC applications, we can determine that MapReduce jobs with large intermediate files are more suited (than others with smaller intermediate files) for VC. This can be explained by the reduced overhead on the server, since clients handle most of the

heavy data communication among themselves. Furthermore, small input and input data can reduce the influence of server-client transfers. There are quite a few examples of real-world applications with these characteristics, such as image rendering [22], market basket analysis, and N-Gram based functions (e.g., biological sequence analysis [23]).

Endnotes

[a]Distributed.net website. `http://www.distributed.net`

[b]List of active VC projects. `http://www.distributedcomputing.info/projects.html`

[c]Amazon EC2. `http://aws.amazon.com/ec2`

[d]A VC Project runs on top of existing middleware (e.g. BOINC) by developing an application and defining all parameters concerning its execution. The middleware takes care of all the mechanisms necessary for executing a distributed application over the Internet, making life easier for Project developers. They only have to make sure their tasks are properly configured and provide a publicly accessible machine to act as the VC server. Each volunteer chooses projects to attach its VC client to, based on the applications the user would like to run. A client may be attached to several projects at the same time, sharing the machine's resources in a round-robin fashion.

[e]Nebula and Plush. `http://plush.cs.williams.edu/nebula/`

[f]NAS Parallel Benchmarks. http://www.nas.nasa.gov/publications/npb.html

[g]This was very apparent during our experiments. In fact, it was so inconvenient that all HTTP traffic to our server was blocked by the network administrators during one of our runs.

[h]Apache Hadoop. `http://hadoop.apache.org/`

[i]List of institutions that are using Hadoop. `http://wiki.apache.org/hadoop/PoweredBy`

Competing interests
The authors declare that they have no competing interests.

Authors' contributions
All authors read and approved the final manuscript.

Acknowledgements
This work was partially supported by national funds through FCT – Fundação para a Ciência e Tecnologia, under projects PTDC/EIA-EIA/102250/2008, PTDC/EIA-EIA/113613/2009, PTDC/EIA-EIA/113993/2009 and PEst-OE/EEI/LA0021/2013.

References

1. Anderson DP, Cobb J, Korpela E, Lebofsky M, Werthimer D (2002) SETI@home: an experiment in public-resource computing. Commun ACM 45: 56–61

2. Beberg AL, Ensign DL, Jayachandran G, Khaliq S, Pande VS Folding@home: Lessons from eight years of volunteer distributed computing. In: Parallel & Distributed Processing, 2009. IPDPS 2009. IEEE International Symposium on, 23-29 May 2009, IEEE Computer Society, Washington, DC, USA, pp 1–8

3. Anderson DP (2004) BOINC: A system for public-resource computing and storage. In: Proceedings of the 5th IEEE/ACM International workshop on grid computing, GRID '04, IEEE Computer Society, Washington, DC, USA, pp 4–10

4. Cisco I (2012) Cisco visual networking index: forecast and methodology, 2011–2016. CISCO White Paper. http://www.cisco.com/en/US/solutions/collateral/ns341/ns525/ns537/ns705/ns827/white_paper_c11-481360_ns827_Networking_Solutions_White_Paper.html

5. Snir M, Otto SW, Walker DW, Dongarra J, Huss-Lederman S (1995) MPI: The Complete Reference. MIT Press, Cambridge, MA, USA

6. da Silva e Silva FJ, Kon F, Goldman A, Finger M, de Camargo RY, Filho FC, Costa FM (2010) Application execution management on the InteGrade opportunistic grid middleware. J Parallel Distributed Comput 70(5): 573–583

7. Dean J, Ghemawat S (2008) MapReduce: simplified data processing on large clusters. Commun. ACM 51: 107–113

8. Lamport L, Shostak R, Pease M (1982) The Byzantine generals problem. ACM Trans Program Lang Syst 4(3): 382–401

9. Cirne W, Brasileiro F, Andrade N, Costa L, Andrade A, Novaes R, Mowbray M (2006) Labs of the world, unite!!! J Grid Comput 4: 225–246

10. Cappello F, Djilali S, Fedak G, Herault T, Magniette F, Néri V, Lodygensky O (2005) Computing on large-scale distributed systems: XtremWeb architecture, programming models, security, tests and convergence with grid. Future Gener Comput Syst 21: 417–437

11. Costa F, Kelley I, Silva L, Fedak G (2008) Optimizing data distribution in desktop grid platforms. Parallel Process Lett (PPL) 18(3): 391–410

12. Costa F, Silva L, Fedak G, Kelley I (2008) Optimizing the data distribution layer of BOINC with BitTorrent. Parallel Distributed Process Symp Int 0: 1–8

13. Fedak G, He H, Cappello F (2008) BitDew: a programmable environment for large-scale data management and distribution. In: Proceedings of the 2008 ACM/IEEE conference on Supercomputing, SC '08, vol 1-45. IEEE Press, Piscataway, NJ, USA, p 12

14. Chun B, Culler D, Roscoe T, Bavier A, Peterson L, Wawrzoniak M, Bowman M (2003) PlanetLab: an overlay testbed for broad-coverage services. SIGCOMM Comput Commun Rev 33: 3–12

15. Marsaglia G, Bray TA (1964) A convenient method for generating normal variables. Siam Rev 6(3): 260–264

16. Kondo D, Javadi B, Malecot P, Cappello F, Anderson DP (2009) Cost-benefit analysis of Cloud Computing versus desktop grids. In: Proceedings of the 2009 IEEE International symposium on parallel& distributed processing, IPDPS '09, IEEE Computer Society, Washington, DC, USA, pp 1–12

17. Marozzo F, Talia D, Trunfio P (2012) P2P-MapReduce: Parallel data processing in dynamic Cloud environments. J Comput Syst Sci 78(5): 1382–1402

18. Gong L (2001) JXTA: A network programming environment. Internet Comput IEEE 5(3): 88–95

19. Lin H, Ma X, Archuleta J, Feng Wc, Gardner M, Zhang Z (2010) MOON: MapReduce On Opportunistic eNvironments. In: Proceedings of the 19th ACM International symposium on high performance distributed computing, HPDC '10, ACM, New York, NY, USA, pp 95–106

20. Tang B, Moca M, Chevalier S, He H, Fedak G (2010) Towards MapReduce for desktop grid computing. In: Proceedings of the 2010 International conference on P2P, parallel, grid, cloud and internet computing, 3PGCIC '10, IEEE Computer Society, Washington, DC, USA, pp 193–200

21. Moca M, Silaghi G, Fedak G (2011) Distributed results checking for MapReduce in volunteer computing. In: Parallel and distributed processing workshops and Phd Forum (IPDPSW), 2011 IEEE international symposium on, IEEE Computer Society, Washington, DC, USA, pp 1847–1854

22. Perry R (2009) High speed raster image streaming for digital presses using the Hadoop file system. HP Laboratories, HPL-2009-345, Technical Report. http://www.hpl.hp.com/techreports/2009/HPL-2009-345.html

23. Ganapathiraju M, Manoharan V, Klein-Seetharaman J (2004) BLMT. Appl Bioinformatics 3(2-3): 193–200

7

Incorporate intelligence into the differentiated services strategies of a Web server: an advanced feedback control approach

Malik Loudini[*], Sawsen Rezig and Yahia Salhi

Abstract

This paper presents an investigation into the application of advanced feedback control strategies to provide better web servers quality of service (QoS). Based on differentiated service strategies, fuzzy logic based control architectures are proposed to enhance the system capabilities. As a first control scheme, a Mamdani fuzzy logic controller (FLC) is adopted. Then, the Simulated Annealing (SA) algorithm (SAA) is used to optimize the FLC parameters with efficient tuning procedures. The SA optimized FLC (SAOFLC) is also implemented and applied to improve the system QoS. Simulation experiments are carried out to examine the performances of the proposed intelligent control strategies.

Keywords: Web server, Quality of service, DiffServ, Service delay guarantee, Absolute delay, Relative delay, Fuzzy logic controller, Simulated annealing

1 Background

With the tremendous growth of internet and its extraordinary success, the web servers become more and more numerous and diverse. They are, also, more and more exposed to high rates of incoming requests from users which are becoming increasingly reliant on these new sorts of modern service delivery. Providing high dynamic contents, integrating with huge databases and offering all sorts of complex and secure transactions, these internet applications are faced with growing difficulties to ensure adequate QoS [1].

Evaluation of web server QoS performance generally focuses on achievable delay of service or response time for a request-based type of workload as a function of a traffic load.

Adopting such metrics, many QoS performance enhancement architectures and mechanisms, particularly based on differentiation of service (DiffServ) [1-3], have been proposed by the community of researchers in this area. Among these, the feedback control (or closed-loop control) has been occupying a place of predilection.

Indeed, applying feedback control schemes to enhance the performance of software processes is becoming an attractive research area. The main advantage offered by this technique of automatic control is its robustness to modeling inaccuracies, system nonlinearities, and time variation of system parameters. These types of uncertainties are very common in unpredictable poorly modeled environments such as the Internet. For a literature review about the application of feedback control to computing systems, see [4-7].

Most of the feedback control techniques and algorithms are relying on the availability of formal parametric models of the controlled system and control theoretic tools. This is not always possible for software processes for which analytical models are not easily obtainable or the models themselves, if available, are too complex and nonlinear.

Furthermore, it is well known that web workloads are stochastic with significant parameter variations over time. So, a challenging problem is how to provide efficient performance control over a wide range of workload conditions knowing the highly nonlinear behavior of a web server in its response to the allocated resources.

It is precisely for processes and environments such these that we need judicious non-conventional control

* Correspondence: m_loudini@esi.dz
Ecole Nationale Supérieure d'Informatique (ESI), Laboratoire de Communication dans les Systèmes Informatiques (LCSI), B.P 68M, 16270 Oued Smar, El Harrach, Algiers, Algeria

algorithms that will be implemented without dependency on the availability of the above-mentioned requirements.

Computational intelligent approaches to handle the complexity and fuzziness present in such software systems surely have an essential role to play. We should therefore exploit their tolerance for imprecision and uncertainty to achieve tractability and robustness in control applications.

Feedback control schemes based on Fuzzy Logic Controllers (FLCs) are well known for their ability to adapt to dynamic imprecise and bursty environments such that of the web traffic.

It appears that this category of intelligent control structures should therefore be the most recommended.

In this paper, web server QoS enhancement solutions based on closed-loop intelligent control strategies, including fuzzy logic, are investigated.

As related works to our study context, examples of earlier relevant research investigations, using various control techniques, can be found in [8-23].

The remainder of this paper is organized as follows. In Sect. 2, we briefly describe how web servers operate, then we present some semantics of delays and service delay guarantees in web servers. We also briefly call back the main basics about fuzzy control. An introduction to the SA optimization method is given at the end of the section. In Sect. 3, the modeling of the web server system is described and different discrete models are given. In Sect. 4, we present the adopted feedback control strategy aimed to satisfy the desired performance of the web server. The implementation details and the simulation results are given in Sect. 5. Section 6 presents the related work. Finally, Sect. 7 concludes the paper.

2 Preliminaries

In this section, we briefly describe how web servers operate and then present some semantics about delays and service delay guarantees. We also briefly call back the main basics about fuzzy control and introduce the SA optimization method.

2.1 Web servers

Web servers are commonly defined as computers that deliver web pages. Having an IP address and generally a domain name, a web server is software responsible for accepting HTTP [24] requests from clients and offering them services as HTTP responses. HTTP lies behind every web transaction. An HTTP transaction consists of three steps: TCP [25] connection setup, HTTP layer processing and network processing. Once the connection has been established, the client sends a request for an object (HTML file, image file ...). The server handles the request and returns the object of this query [26].

It is well known that web servers adopt either a multi-threaded or a multi-process model to handle a large number of users simultaneously. Processes or threads can be either created on demand or maintained in a pre-existing pool that awaits incoming TCP connection requests to the server. In HTTP 1.0, each TCP connection carried a single web request. This resulted in an excessive number of concurrent TCP connections. To remedy this problem the new version of HTTP, called HTTP 1.1 [27], reduces the number of concurrent TCP connections with a mechanism called *persistent connections*, which allows multiple web requests to reuse the same connection [8].

As in [8,13], a multi-process model with a pool of processes is assumed, which is the model of the Apache server, the most commonly used web server today [28].

2.2 Differentiation of services

Differentiated Services (commonly known as DiffServ) has been proposed by the IETF Differentiated Services Working Group [2]. It is a computer networking protocol or architecture that allows different levels of services on a common network in order to provide a better QoS. In other words, it supports a manageable and scalable service differentiation for class-based aggregated traffic in IP networks. Two approaches exist in DiffServ architecture:

Absolute DiffServ: This model seeks to guarantee end-to-end QoS. In this architecture, the user receives an absolute service profile (e.g., end-to-end delay or bandwidth guarantee ...) and the network administrator attempts to maintain the absolute metric spacing between the users classes.

Relative DiffServ: This model seeks to provide relative or proportional services. In other words, it aims to guarantee to a higher priority class of users better (proportionally ratioed) service performances than those provided to a lower priority class.

2.3 Service delay guarantees: semantics, definitions and adopted Qos metrics

Our investigation being concerned with delays based QoS enhancement, we begin this paragraph by giving useful semantics and definitions relative to the service delay differentiation approach [13].

First, every HTTP request being supposed to belong to a class k ($0 \leq k < N$), two main delays are defined as:

Processing delay: It is the time interval between the arrival of an HTTP request to the process responsible for the corresponding connection and time the server completes transferring the response.

Connection delay: It is the time interval between the arrival of a TCP connection (establishment) request and the time where the connection is accepted (dequeued) by a server process. The connection delay includes the queuing delay. In other words, the connection delay of class k at the mth sampling instant, denoted by $C_k(m)$, is defined as the average connection delay of all established connections of class k within the time interval $[(m-1)$ $T_s, mT_s]$, where T_s is a constant sampling period.

The delay differentiation being applied to connection delays, the adopted QoS metrics in this work are the connection delay guarantees. Using, for simplicity, delay to refer to connection delay, they are defined as follows:

Relative delay guarantee: A desired relative delay (RD) W_k is assigned to each class k. A RD guarantee $\{W_k|\ 0 \le k < N\}$ requires that $C_j(m)/C_l(m) = W_j(m)/W_l(m)$ for classes j and l $(j \neq l)$.

Absolute Delay Guarantee: A desired absolute delay (AD) W_k is assigned to each class k. An AD guarantee $\{W_k|\ 0 \le k < N\}$ requires that $C_j(m) \le W_j(m)$ for any class j if there exists a lower priority class $l > j$ and $C_l(m) \le W_l$ (m) (a lower class number means a higher priority). Note that since system load can grow arbitrarily high in a web server, it is impossible to satisfy the desired delay of all service classes under overload conditions. The AD guarantee requires that all classes receive satisfactory delay if the server is not overloaded; otherwise desired delays are violated in the predefined priority order, i.e., low priority classes always suffer guarantee violation earlier than high priority classes.

2.4 Brief review of fuzzy control

The structure of a process controlled via a Mamdani type FLC [29,30] is shown in Figure 1.

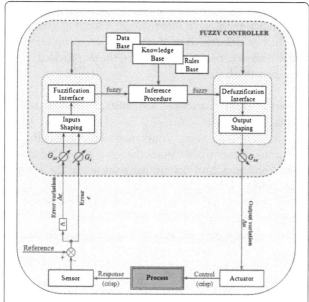

Figure 1 Basic structure of a process controlled via a Mamdani FLC.

The basic components of the considered FLC are briefly presented below:

- The *fuzzification interface* gets the values of input variables $(e, \Delta e)$, performs a scale mapping to transfer the range of their values into corresponding universes of discourse, and performs the function of fuzzification to convert input (crisp) data into linguistic values.
- The *knowledge base* comprises a rule base which characterizes the control policy and goals.
- The *data base* provides the necessary definitions about discretization and normalization of universes, fuzzy partition of input and output spaces, membership functions (MFs) definitions.
- The *inference procedure* process fuzzy input data and rules to infer fuzzy control actions employing fuzzy implication and the rules of inference in fuzzy logic.
- The *defuzzification interface* performs a scale mapping to convert the range of values of universes into corresponding output variables, and transformation of a fuzzy control action inferred into a nonfuzzy control action (Δu).
- G_e, $G_{\Delta e}$ are the inputs scaling factors and $G_{\Delta u}$ is the output scaling factor.

2.5 Simulated annealing

Inspired from nature, simulated annealing (SA) is a powerful stochastic local search algorithm first introduced by Metropolis et al. [31] as a modified Monte Carlo integration method and then proposed and made popular by Kirkpatrick et al. [32] to solve difficult combinatorial optimization problems. SA is based on the analogy between the annealing of solids and the solving of combinatorial optimization problems. Annealing is the process through which a solid material is initially heated over the melting point to be liquefied with randomly dispersed particles. Then the material is cooled slowly until it crystallizes into a state of perfect lattice according to a cooling scheduled.

3 Web server dynamic modeling

The systematic design of feedback systems requires an ability to quantify the effect of control inputs (e.g., buffer size) on measured outputs (e.g., response times), both of which may vary with time. Indeed, developing such models is at the heart of applying control theory in practice [5]. The models obtained are also used to make numerical simulations as needed in this work.

Our control investigation will be tested based on the dynamic models established in [13]. The approach employed, in deriving the mathematical models, is statistical (black-box method), a process that is referred to as system identification [33].

The system to be controlled is modeled as a difference equation with unknown parameters.

The web server is stimulated with pseudo-random digital white-noise input and a least squares estimator [33] is used to estimate the model parameters.

The details about the conducted experiments and the obtained results can be found in [13]. Lu et al. have established that, for both RD and AD control, the controlled system can be modeled as a second order difference equation with adequate accuracy for the purpose of control design. A brief presentation is given below.

The web server is modeled as a difference equation with unknown parameters, i.e., a n the order model can be described as follows:

$$V(m) = \sum_{j=1}^{n} a_j V(m-j) + \sum_{j=1}^{n} b_j U(m-j) \qquad (1)$$

In a n the order model, there are $2n$ parameters $\{a_j, b_j | 1 \le j < n\}$ that need to be decided by the least squares estimator.

The system identification results established that, the controlled system can be modeled by the following second order difference equation:

$$V(m) - a_1 V(m-1) - a_2 V(m-2) = b_1 U(m-1) + b_2 U(m-2) \qquad (2)$$

The system model defined by the difference equation (2) can be, easily, converted to a description by a discrete transfer function $G(z)$ from the control input $U(z)$ to the output $V(z)$ in the z-domain, given below:

$$G(z) = \frac{V(z)}{U(z)} = \frac{b_1 z + b_2}{z^2 - a_1 z - a_2} \qquad (3)$$

The stimulation of the web server being carried out based on SURGE [34] as the HTTP requests generator, two sets of experiments has been conducted, using three workloads with different user populations, for each of the two adopted approaches in service differentiation: the RD case and the AD case (see Table 1).

The variation of user populations (2 classes) is aimed to evaluate the sensitivity of the model parameters to workloads.

For each experience, a difference equation based dynamic model has been established. The resulting discrete transfer functions are given in Table 1.

4 Design of the FLC based feedback control system

In this section, we first present the global feedback control architecture for web server QoS, and then formally specify the proposed controllers.

4.1 Global feedback control architecture

The adopted feedback control architecture is illustrated in Figure 2.

In this architecture, the controlled system is the web server. The connection scheduler serves as an actuator transmitting, at each sampling instant m, the control input effort in terms of *process budgets* $\{B_k | 0 \le k < N\}$ (input U) computed and generated by the controller based on the errors provided by the feedback loops. These errors result from the comparisons between the desired relative or absolute delays $\{W_k | 0 \le k < N\}$ and the measured delays or the sampled connection delays $\{C_k | 0 \le k < N\}$ (output V) computed by the monitor at each sampling instant. For each of the AD and RD approaches, the control key variables are explicitly summarized in Table 2.

4.2 Derivation of the FLC

The FLC based web server process control strategy adopted in our work is illustrated in Figure 3.

This scheme, by its structure, is also called "Mamdani PI type FLC" where PI stands for Proportional-Integral.

The input variables of the FLC are the loop error e and its rate of change Δe which are defined as:

$$e(mT_s) = Ref(mT_s) - WSR(mT_s) \qquad (4)$$

where Ref is the reference input, WSR is the web server response, and mT^s is a sampling interval,

$$\Delta e(mT_s) = \frac{\{e(mT_s) - e[(m-1)T_s]\}}{T_s} \qquad (5)$$

Table 1 Experiments data and corresponding transfer functions

	RD case			AD case		
	Class 0	Class 1	Transfer function $G(z)$	Class 0	Class 1	Transfer function $G(z)$
Workload A	200	200	$\frac{0.95z - 0.12}{z^2 - 0.74z + 0.37}$	100	400	$\frac{-0.82z - 0.52}{z^2 + 0.13z + 0.03}$
Workload B	150	250	$\frac{2.28z + 0.08}{z^2 - 0.31z + 0.27}$	150	250	$\frac{-0.36z - 0.15}{z^2 - 0.14z + 0.05}$
Workload C	300	300	$\frac{0.47z + 0.21}{z^2 - 0.56z + 0.26}$	200	300	$\frac{-0.49z - 0.25}{z^2 - 0.25z + 0.03}$

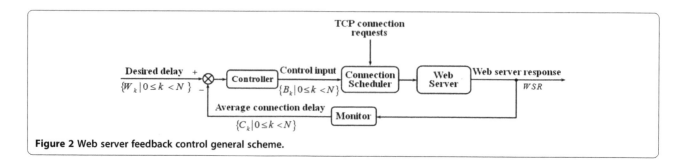

Figure 2 Web server feedback control general scheme.

The change in the control setting is denoted by $\Delta u(mT_s)$. G_e, $G_{\Delta e}$ are the inputs scaling factors and $G_{\Delta u}$ is the output scaling factor. Thus the PI type fuzzy logic command is given by

$$u(mT_s) = u[(m-1)T_s] + G_{\Delta u} * \Delta u(mT_s) \qquad (6)$$

2.3 Derivation of the SAOFLC

In order to try to improve the performances of the previous FLC designed based on observations and subjective choices, we apply the SA as an optimization algorithm to automatically adjust its design parameters:

- Number of MFs for each FLC variable
- MFs shapes for each FLC variable
- MFs distribution for each FLC variable
- Decision table rules
- Scaling factors.

The SAA tuning procedure is carried out according to the pseudo code provided in Figure 4.

4.3.1 Conception hypotheses and constraints

Certain assumptions and constraints about the decision table and the FLC variables MFs to be optimized are given here:

- The number of fuzzy sets (NFS) for each variable can take only one of the following possible values: 3, 5, 7 or 9.
- The fuzzy sets (FSs) will be symbolized (labeled) by the standard linguistic designation and indexed by an ascending order. If, for example, the number of FSs of a linguistic variable is equal to 5, the

corresponding FSs will be: NB, NM, ZE, PM, PB and indexed from 1 to 5. The FSs NB and NM are considered as the opposites to PB et PM respectively (symmetrically with respect to ZE).

- Note that the label ZE stands for linguistic (fuzzy) value zero, first letters N and P mean negative and positive and second letters B, M and S denote big, medium and small values respectively.
- All the FLC variables universes of discourse are normalized to lie between −1 and +1.
- The first and the last MFs have their apexes at −1 and +1 respectively.

4.3.2 Decision rules table deriving method

The adopted method for the decision rules table construction is inspired from the works developed in [35,36].

As a contribution, a new method of FSs assignment to each of the grid nodes in the special case of equality of distances between the points representing the candidate decision rules is proposed (see the decision rules table deriving method principle given below).

Note that this new procedure is adopted instead of the random assignment proposed in [36].

Principle of the method First, the grid is constructed using two spacing parameters PSG_e and $PSG_{\Delta e}$ relatively to the FLC two inputs e and Δe.

The first (resp. the second) spacing parameter $PSGe$ (resp. $PSG_{\Delta e}$) fix the grid nodes X-axis coordinates (resp. Y-axis coordinates) in the interval $[-1, +1]$ (universe of discourse (UD)) with a simple computing formula given in the next paragraph. Each abscissa (resp. ordinate) represents a fuzzy set (FS) of the variable e (resp. Δe). The number of the grid constitutive nodes is then equal to the product result between the two FLC input FSs

Table 2 Variables of the feedback control scheme

	AD	RD
Reference W_k	Desired delay of class k	Desired delay ratio between class k and k - 1
Output C_k (V)	Measured delay of class k	Measured delay ratio between class k and k - 1
Control input B_k (U)	Process budget of class k	Ratio between the process budgets of classes k and k

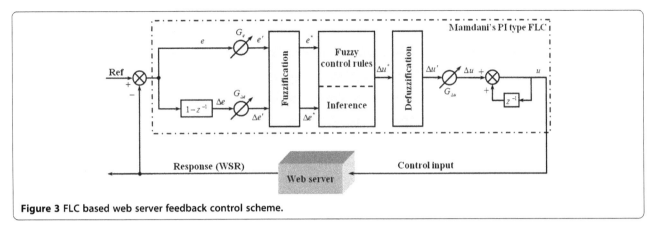

Figure 3 FLC based web server feedback control scheme.

numbers. Once, the nodes are fixed, we introduce the output points on a straight line corresponding to the FLC output variable Δu. Now, the points (output ones) represent the FSs and not their coordinates. The number of points is equal to the output variable FSs number.

A third spacing parameter $PSG_{\Delta u}$ fix the output points X-axis (Y-axis) coordinates similarly with the nodes fixing manner whereas the Y-axis (X-axis) coordinates are calculated by an angular parameter, noted *"Angle"*, which determine the slope of the straight line, supporting the output points, with respect to the horizontal. This angular parameter varies in the interval $[0, \pi/2]$ counterclockwise.

Each of the grid nodes represents a case of the decision table and each output point represents a FS of the control variable Δu.

Pseudo code of the SAA

Get an initial FLC FC_0 /*Initial solution*/

Let $FC = FC_0$

Let $Of = Of\ (FC)$ /*$Of\ ()$: Objective function*/

Set an initial temperature T and a final temperature T_{fin}

While $(T > T_{fin})$

  While $(Nit > 0)$ /*Nit : Number of iterations*/

    Generate the neighborhood $h\ (FC)$

    $FC_n \leftarrow FC_h$ /* FC_h is randomly selected in $h\ (FC)$ */

    If $Of\ (FC_n) - Of\ (FC) \leq 0$ **then** $FC \leftarrow FC_n$

    Else

    Generate a random number Rnb between 0 and 1

    If $Rnb < e^{[Of\ (FC_n) - Of(FC)]/T}$ **then** $FC \leftarrow FC_n$

    Endif

  End While

  Generate a random real α in [0,1] (Cooling Coefficient)

  $T \leftarrow T * \alpha$

End While

Figure 4 Pseudo code of the simulated annealing algorithm.

Once all the points coordinates (grid nodes and output points) are computed, we can proceed to the assignment by determining the minimal distance among all the distances separating each node of the grid from all the output points situated on the straight line. Then, we assign to each node of the grid the closest output point. Consequently, the decision table case corresponding to this node will contain the FS representing the selected output point. Nevertheless, an assignment conflict could arise in the case of equality between two minimal distances separating a node and two output points. We have proposed to select the output point which has the lower FS index if it is a case of the upper part with respect to the table diagonal or the output point which has the greater FS index if the case belongs to the lower part [37]. It should be noted that no more than two output points can be at the same distance from a given node of the grid since all the output points are on the same straight line.

Spacing parameter The grid spacing parameter PSG specifies how the positions C_1 of the intermediate points (between the center and the extreme of each graduated axis) are spaced out with respect to the central point.

This parameter offers flexibility in varying spacing. The more it is greater than 1, the more the points positions are closest to centre and vice versa. At the value 1, the positions are uniformly distributed in the UD interval $[-1, 1]$.

The number of positions C_1 and FSs being obviously the same, we have proposed a formulation of the spacing law in function of the spacing parameter PSG [37,38].

At a first stage, the positions C_i being equidistant are denoted by CEq_i and computed by:

$$CEq_i = 2\left(\frac{i-1}{NEF-1}\right) - 1, i = 1, \cdots NFS \quad (7)$$

The C_i values are, then, determined in terms of the spacing parameter PSG as follows:

$$C_i = sign(CEq_i) * |CEq_i|^{PSG} \tag{8}$$

with $sign(x) = \begin{cases} 1 & \text{if } x \geq 0 \\ -1 & \text{if } x < 0 \end{cases}$; $PSG = (PSG_1)^{PSG_2}$ with PSG_2 that can take the values +1 or –1.

Two illustrative examples of C_i computation are given in Table 3 for 7 FSs and 5 FSs, respectively, and for different values of the spacing parameter.

To understand the decision table deriving procedure, two detailed examples are given bellow. The constructing parameters are given in Table 4, then, the grids and their corresponding decision tables are shown in Figures 5 and 6 respectively.

Note that the nodes are represented by red stars and the output points by blue circles. The purple arrows are examples of minimal distances between the output points and the grid nodes describing the FSs assignment to the decision table.

It is interesting to note that the decision table obtained for $PSG_e = PSG_{\Delta e} = PSG_{\Delta u} = 1$ and $Angle = 45°$ is none other than the Mac Vicar-Whelan diagonal table [39].

4.3.3 Membership functions deriving method
Determination of the FLC MFs using the SAA takes place in three phases:

1. creation of primary MFs of the FLC input/output parameters,
2. parameterization,
3. adjustment of the MFs.

MFs shape and width optimization
Three types of MFs shapes are considered:

- triangular
- trapezoidal which include (generalize) the triangular one
- "two-sided" Gaussian with flattened summit

Table 3 C_i in function of *PSG* for 7 FSs

	PSG	Ci						
		C1	C2	C3	C4	C5	C6	C7
Example 1	0.25	−1	−0.90	−0.76	0	0.76	0.90	1
	0.5	−1	−0.81	−0.58	0	0.58	0.81	1
	1	−1	−0.67	−0.33	0	0.33	0.67	1
	2	−1	−0.44	−0.11	0	0.11	0.44	1
	4	−1	−0.20	−0.01	0	0.01	0.2	1
Example 2	0.25	−1	−0.84	0	0.84	1		
	0.5	−1	−0.70	0	0.70	1		
	1	−1	−0.50	0	0.50	1		
	2	−1	−0.25	0	0.25	1		
	4	−1	−0.06	0	0.06	1		

Table 4 Two illustrative examples

	NFS$_e$	NFS$_{\Delta e}$	NFS$_{\Delta u}$	PSG$_e$	PSG$_{\Delta e}$	PSG$_{\Delta u}$	Angle
Example 1	5	5	5	1	1	1	60°
Example 2	5	5	5	0.5	1	2	30°

The triangular shape is defined by three parameters $[P1 \quad P2 \quad P3]$ which represent respectively, the left abscissa of the triangle base, the peak abscissa, and the right abscissa of the triangle base.

Each triangle base begins at the precedent triangle peak abscissa and ends at that of the following one. The trapezoidal shape is defined by four parameters $[P1 \quad P2 \quad P3 \quad P4]$ representing, respectively, the base left abscissa, the summit left abscissa, the summit right abscissa, and the base right abscissa.

The trapezoidal shape is then framed by four points with the coordinates: $(P1, 0)$, $(P2, 1)$, $(P3, 1)$ and $(P4, 0)$. Note that if $P2 = P3$, we obtain a triangular shape (see Figure 7).

We also define the two-sided Gaussian shape by four parameters $[Sig1 \quad G1 \quad G2 \quad Sig2]$ (see Figure 8). The

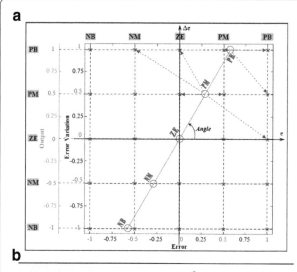

Figure 5 Example 1 grid and corresponding decision table: (a) Grid constitution; (b) Derived decision table.

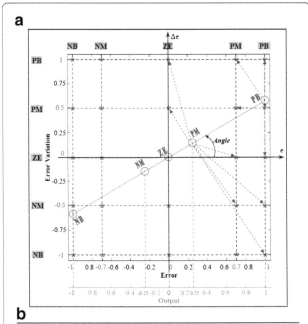

Figure 6 Example 2 grid and corresponding decision table: (a) Grid constitution; (b) Derived decision table.

Δu		e				
		NB	NM	ZE	PM	PB
	NB	NB	NB	NM	ZE	PM
	NM	NB	NB	NM	PM	PM
Δe	ZE	NB	NM	ZE	PM	PB
	PM	NM	NM	PM	PB	PB
	PB	NM	ZE	PM	PB	PB

left and right sides of the Gaussian are respectively defined by: $G(x) = e^{-\frac{(x-G1)^2}{2(Sig1)^2}}$ and $G(x) = e^{-\frac{(x-G2)^2}{2(Sig2)^2}}$.

To be able to use this two-sided Gaussian shape within the framework of our optimizing method, we must bound this shape by the same points used for the

trapezoidal shape (Figure 7). In other words, we must define the two-sides Gaussian shape in terms of the parameters $[P1\ \ P2\ \ P3\ \ P4]$ instead of $[Sig1\ \ G1\ \ G2\ \ Sig2]$. For that purpose, we adopted a very small positive real number ε ($\varepsilon = 0.01$ was quite suitable) such that:

- The Gaussian left curve includes the points *(P1,ε)* and *(P2,1)*.
- The Gaussian right curve includes the points *(P3,1)* and *(P4,ε)*.

This formulation leads to the establishing of the following two systems of equations:

$$\begin{cases} e^{-\frac{(P1-G1)^2}{2*(Sig1)^2}} = \varepsilon \\ e^{-\frac{(P2-G1)^2}{2*(Sig1)^2}} = 1 \end{cases} \tag{9}$$

$$\begin{cases} e^{-\frac{(P3-G2)^2}{2*(Sig2)^2}} = 1 \\ e^{-\frac{(P4-G2)^2}{2*(Sig2)^2}} = \varepsilon \end{cases} \tag{10}$$

The resolution of systems (9) and (10) gives:

$$G1 = P2; G2 = P3; Sig1 = \sqrt{-\frac{(P1-P2)^2}{2*\log\varepsilon}};$$

$$Sig2 = \sqrt{-\frac{(P4-P3)^2}{2*\log\varepsilon}}.$$

Note that ε has been used since the Gaussian two sides never pass by a null abscissa.

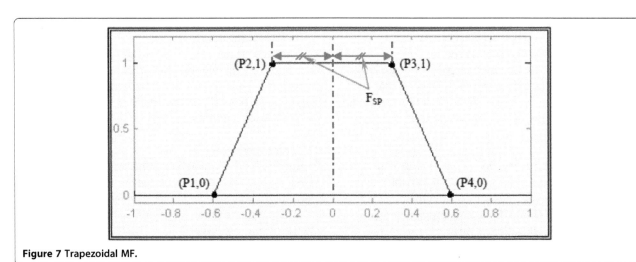

Figure 7 Trapezoidal MF.

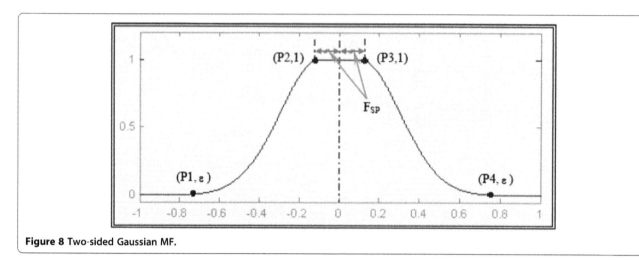

Figure 8 Two-sided Gaussian MF.

Width spacing parameter The summit abscissae of the different shapes are calculated with the same principle of parameter spacing used in the determination of the grid nodes and the points coordinates in the decision table derivation. The FLC input/output variables MFs spacing parameters are, respectively, denoted by PSF_e $PSF_{\Delta e}$ and $PSF_{\Delta u}$.

Shape optimizing parameter The MFs spacing method being inspired by the works of Park et al. [35], Foran [36], and Cheong and Lai [40], we propose a new technique for the MFs shape optimization [37] based on a design parameter called shape parameter (*SP*). This optimizing parameter gives possibilities of diversification (hybridization) of MFs shapes on the UD of each of the FLC input/output variables.

SP is considered as a real number belonging to the interval [0, 2[. Its integer part, denoted by I_{SP} will determine the shape of the MFs and its fractional one, denoted by F_{SP} will determine the spacing with respect to the center of the MF. The MF shape is specified by I_{SP} and F_{SP} as follows:

- I_{SP} = 0: trapezoidal or triangular shape
- I_{SP} = 1: two-sided Gaussian shape.
- F_{SP} determines the symmetric space with respect to the center of the MF as shown in Figure 7 and Figure 8. As we can see in Figure 7, if the spacing is equal to zero, the trapezoidal shape reduces to a triangular one.

Being optimized by the SAA, the number of MFs (*NFS*) for each of the FLC input/output variables, is not constant. Consequently, it is not feasible to assign a spacing parameter to each MF. So, we propose a solution, which consists in allocating a shaping parameter, denoted by SP_M, for the MF of the middle of the UD and another, denoted by SP_E, for the extreme MF.

The intermediate MFs shaping parameters, denoted by SP_I, are then deducted from SP_M and SP_E so that they will have equidistant intermediate values.

The ith shape parameter $SP_I(i)$ corresponding to the ith intermediate MF, is determined by:

$$SP_I(i) = SP_M + 2(i-1)\frac{SP_E - SP_M}{NFS - 1};\qquad(11)$$
$$i = 1, ..., \frac{NFS + 1}{2}$$

We can observe that $SP_I(1) = SP_M$ and $SP_I\left(\frac{NFS+1}{2}\right) = SP_E$. So, two parameters are enough for any number of FSs.

The previous MF shaping parameters are allocated to the FLC three variables e, Δe and Δu as follows:

- $SP_M e$, $SP_M \Delta e$ and $SP_M \Delta u$
- $SP_E e$, $SP_E \Delta e$ and $SP_E \Delta e$
- $SP_I e$, $SP_I \Delta e$ and $SP_I \Delta u$.

Note that if the medium and extreme MF shaping parameters are equal, all the UD MFs will have the same shape generated by the parameters value.

It is also important to prevent important overlapping between the generated MFs which is undesirable in fuzzy control (flattening phenomenon) [41]. For this purpose, we have fixed a maximum value to the space F_{SP} equal to the half of the minimal distance between the two nearby summits.

4.3.4 Parameter encoding

To run the SAA, suitable encoding for each of the optimizing parameters needs to be specified in terms of variation range, precision step and number of bits, since we use a binary encoding for a more thorough solution space exploration. Indeed, it is well known in control applications that it is recommended to use binary encoding to allow meticulous research by the metaheuristic algorithms. After many tests, we have adopted the data given in Table 5.

5 Simulation Study

In order to validate the proposed FLC based control schemes, digital simulations have been carried out on the basis of the adopted discrete-time process transfer functions.

The simulation study has been conducted according to the basic feedback control system architecture shown in Figure 9, with three different web server workloads (A, B, C) for a better effectiveness and robustness evaluation.

5.1 FLC application

After long series of trial/error tests, the following characteristics have been fixed for the two cases of FLC based web server control; i.e. absolute service delay and relative service delay guarantees:

- Five FSs have been chosen to describe the error, its rate of change and control variation amplitudes. As seen above, their linguistic formulation and symbols are defined in the usual fuzzy logic terminology by: Positive Big (PB), Positive Medium (PM), Zero (ZE), Negative Medium (NM), Negative Big (NB). The "meaning" of each linguistic value should be clear from its mnemonic.
- The set of decision rules forming the "rule base" which characterizes our strategy to control the studied dynamic process is organized in a matrix form (see Table 6) based on Mac Vicar-Whelan's diagonal decision table [39].
- The same triangular shapes have been assigned to the MFs of the FLC variables with a uniform distribution and a 50% overlap has been provided for the neighboring FSs (see Figure 10). Therefore, at any given point of the UD, no more than two FSs will have non-zero degree of membership.
- Often, for greater flexibility in FLC design and tuning, the universes of discourse for each process variable are "normalized" to the interval [−1,+1] by means of constant scaling factors.
- The scaling factors best values have been determined by a tedious trial-and-error process (see Table 7).

- The adopted inference method is based on the Mamdani's Implication mechanism. It is also called *SUPremum-MINimum composition principle* [35].
- To obtain crisp values of the inferred fuzzy control actions, we have selected the *Centre-Of-Gravity* defuzzification technique [42] which is the most commonly employed.

The obtained results are shown in Figure 11.

The FLC used to enforce the absolute and RD succeed to make the system output converge to the desired delay in an acceptable delay and maintain it at the vicinity of the reference before and after the two changes of workload occurring at 10 s and 20 s respectively. However, at these instants, inevitable but minor overshoots and undershoots occur due to the workload burst variations. Nevertheless, the FLC shows rather good robustness in the face of these situations.

To try to improve the obtained performances, we have applied the SAA as a tuning procedure in designing an optimized FLC. The SAOFLC application to the studied control system, in the same conditions, is presented in next subsection.

5.2 SAOFLC application

The SAOFLC based feedback control system architecture is shown in Figure 12.

As described above, the SAA optimization process starts with a first FLC FC_0 as an initial solution and begins the iterative evaluation of the generated new solutions by an objective (cost) function Of.

Of is chosen to maximize the inverse of the well known and the most adopted performance index: Integral of Time-weighted Absolute Error (ITAE) [43] abbreviated, here, by DITAE for its discrete form.

The mathematical expression of Of, minimized by the SAA, can be written as:

$$Of = \frac{1}{DITAE} = \frac{1}{\sum\limits_{m=m_0}^{m=m_f} [mT_s * |e(mT_s)|]}$$

where:

- m_0 and m_f are the initial and final discrete times of the evaluating period

Table 5 Encoding parameters

| Parameter | NFS | PSG$_1$ | PSG$_2$ | Angle | PSF$_1$ | PSF$_2$ | SP | G$_e$, G$_{\Delta e}$ | | G$_{\Delta u}$ |
								RD case	AD case	
Interval	[3,9]	[0.1,1]	[−1,1]	[0,π/2]	[0.1,1]	[−1,1]	[0,1.99]	[0.01,1]	[−1,−0.01] ∪ [0.01,1]	[0.1,1]
Precision	2	0.01	2	π/512	0.01	2	0.01	0.01	0.01	0.1
Number of encoding bits	2	7	1	9	7	1	8	7	8	4

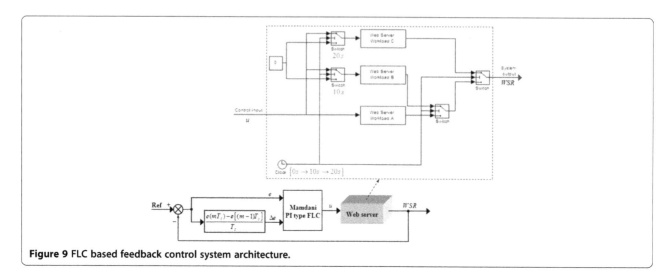

Figure 9 FLC based feedback control system architecture.

- T_s is the sampling period
- $e(mT_s) = W_k(mT_s) - C_k(mT_s)$ is the error, i.e., the difference, at a sampling instant, between the reference (set value) or the desired delay of class k (the desired delay ratio between class k and k-1) and the system response or the measured delay of class k (measured delay ratio between class k and k-1.

The algorithm for FLC optimal tuning based on the SA method is applied and the resulting controller parameters are set. As illustrated in Figure 12, red dashed lines are used to represent the representative signals of optimization.

During the search process, the SAA looks for the optimal setting of the FLC controller parameters which minimize the cost function Of. Solutions with low DITAE are considered as the fittest.

The SAA parameters chosen for the tuning purpose are shown in Table 8.

After the optimization process, the main characteristics (decision table, scaling factors and MFs) have been fixed for the two cases of FLC based web server control; i.e. absolute service delay and relative service delay guarantees as shown in Table 9, 10, Figures 13 and 14.

The digital simualtion results, illustrating the performances of the implemented SAOFLC applied to provide better QoS than those achieved by the classic Mamdani

FLC, in the two considered cases (AD control and RD control) are shown in Figure 15 (a) and Figure 15 (b) respectively.

As can be seen from these figures, the optimized controller exhibits rather better step response performance in terms of rise time, overshoot magnitude, oscillations around the reference (desired delay difference (ratio)) and response (settling) time. We can also see that the SAOFLC shows an improvement in terms of robustness when faced to the simulated sudden workload variations (very hard task for the controller), particularly for the RD case.

Under the SAOFLC strategy, the closed-loop controlled web server enforces, succesfully, the absolute (relative) delay guarantee by satisfying the required delay difference (delay ratio) for the high priority classes (class 0 and class 1) with an obvious superiority than the standard Mamdani type FLC.

Table 6 5X5 Mc Vicar-Whelan decision table

Δu				e		
		NB	NM	ZE	PM	PB
	NB	NB	NB	NB	NM	ZE
	NM	NB	NB	NM	ZE	PM
Δe	ZE	NB	NM	ZE	PM	PB
	PM	NM	ZE	PM	PB	PB
	PB	ZE	PM	PB	PB	PB

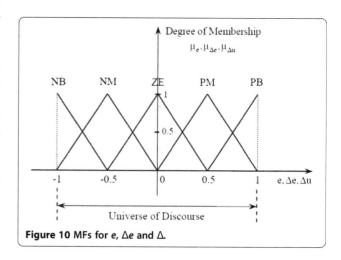

Figure 10 MFs for e, Δe and Δ.

Table 7 FLC scaling factors

	G_e	$G_{\Delta e}$	$G_{\Delta u}$
AD control	0.4	3	0.01
RD control	0.29	1	0.012

6 Related work

The problem of QoS performance enhancement for Web servers is an attractive research field. Even though several works have extensively investigated different QoS enhancing mechanisms supporting service differentiation, few research works addressing the application of feedback control methodologies are available.

We start our description on literature review of related works by pointing out some pertinent research works that have employed service delay differentiation approaches as mechanisms of QoS enhancement. We have found very interesting the investigations of Leung et al. [44], Tham and Subramaniam [45], Lee et al. [46], Li et al. [47], Rashid et al. [48], Wei et al. [49], Bourasa and Sevasti [50], Wu et al. [51], Garcia et al. [52],

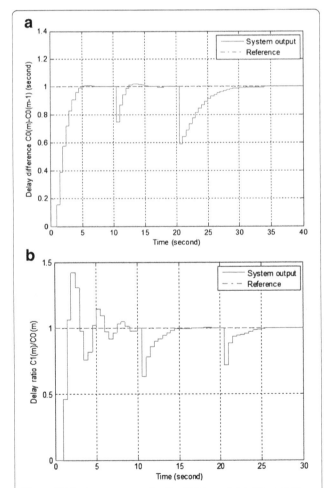

Figure 11 System response for the FLC based: (a) AD control (b) RD control for the three considered workloads.

Dimitriou and Tsaoussidis [53], Gao et al. [54], and Varela et al. [55].

The closest works to our investigation being those using feedback control techniques, we briefly present some relevant ones in a chronological order.

Andersson et al. [10] adopted a combination of queuing theory and control theory. The Apache web server has been modeled as a GI/G/1-system. Then, a standard PI-controller was employed as an admission control mechanism.

Henriksson et al. [56] presented a contribution as an extension of the classical combined feedforward/feedback control framework where the queuing theory is used for feedforward delay prediction. They replace the queuing model with a predictor that uses instantaneous measurements to predict future delays. The proposed strategy was evaluated in simulation and by experiments on an Apache web server.

Oottamakorn [57] proposed a resource management and scheduling algorithm to provide relative delays differentiated guarantees to classes of incoming requests at a QoS-aware web server. One of the key results of his work is the development of an efficient procedure for capturing the predictive traffic characteristics and performances by monitoring ongoing traffic arrivals. This allows the web server's resource management by determining sufficient server resource for each traffic class in order to meet its delay requirements. In order to achieve a self-stabilizing performance in delay QoS guarantees, he has implemented an adaptive feedback control mechanism.

The paper of Lu et al. [13] is the most important work upon which we have based our investigation. In this paper, the authors presented the design and implementation of an adaptive Web server architecture to provide relative and absolute connection delay guarantees for different service classes. Their first contribution is an adaptive architecture based on feedback control loops that enforce desired connection delays via dynamic connection scheduling and process reallocation. The second contribution is the use of control theoretic techniques (PI controllers based on the Root Locus method) to model and design the feedback loops with desired dynamic performance. Their adaptive architecture was implemented by modifying an Apache server.

Zhou et al. [15] investigated the problem of providing proportional QoS differentiation with respect to response time on Web servers. They first present a processing rate allocation scheme based on the foundations of queueing theory. They designed and implemented an adaptive process allocation approach, guided by the queueing-theoretical rate allocation scheme, on an Apache server. They established that this application-level implementation shows weak QoS predictability because

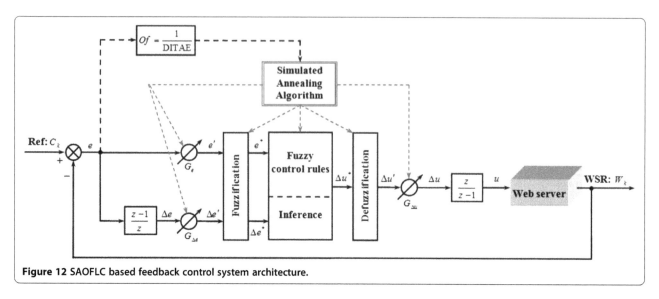

Figure 12 SAOFLC based feedback control system architecture.

it does not have fine-grained control over the consumption of resources that the kernel consumes and hence the processing rate is not strictly proportional to the number of processes allocated. They then designed a feedback controller and integrated it with the queueing-theoretical approach. The adopted feedback control strategy adjusts process allocations according to the difference between the target response time and the achieved response time using a Proportional-Integral -Derivative (PID) controller.

Qin and Wang [16] applied a control-theoretic approach to the performance management of Internet Web servers to meet service-level agreements. In particular, a CPU frequency management problem has been studied to provide response time guarantees with minimal energy cost. It was argued that linear time-invariant modeling and control may not be sufficient for the system to adapt to dynamically varying load conditions. Instead, they adopted a linear-parameter-varying (LPV) approach.

Kihl et al. [18] presented how admission control mechanisms can be designed with a combination of queuing theory and control theory. They modeled an Apache web server as a GI/G/1-system and validated their model as an accurate representation of the experimental system, in terms of average server utilization. Using simulations for discrete-event systems based on

queuing theory and with experiments on an Apache web server, they compared a PI controller and an RST-controller, both commonly used in automatic control, with a static controller and a step controller, both commonly used in telecommunication systems. Note that the controllers were implemented as modules inside the Apache source code. They have also performed a nonlinear stability analysis for the PI-controlled system.

In Yansu et al. [19], a self-tuning control framework to provide proportional delay differentiation guarantees on Web Server has been proposed. The approach updates the model and controller parameters based on the variations of object model to reduce system error and optimize the performances through an online identification.

In Lu et al. (Lu J, Dai G, Mu D, Yu J, Li H [58] QoS Guarantee in Tomcat Web Server: A Feedback Control Approach. In: Proceedings of the 2011), the authors considered providing two types of QoS guarantees, proportional delay differentiation and absolute delay guarantee, in the database connection pool in Tomcat Web server

Table 8 Simulated annealing algorithm parameters

SA property	Method/value
Neighborhood generation method	swap of two elements
Initial temperature (T)	85
Final temperature (T_{fin})	3
Maximum number of iterations	100
Neighbor list size	30

Table 9 Decision table of the SAOFLC for the two cases

Δu		e						
		NB	NM	NS	ZE	PS	PM	PB
Δe	NVB	NB	NB	NB	ZE	PB	PB	PB
	NB	NB	NB	NB	ZE	PB	PB	PB
	NM	NB	NB	NB	ZE	PB	PB	PB
	NS	NB	NB	NB	ZE	PB	PB	PB
	ZE	NB	NB	NB	ZE	PB	PB	PB
	PS	NB	NB	NB	ZE	PB	PB	PB
	PM	NB	NB	NB	ZE	PB	PB	PB
	PB	NB	NB	NB	ZE	PB	PB	PB
	PVB	NB	NB	NB	ZE	PB	PB	PB

Table 10 SAOFLC scaling factors

	G_e	$G_{\Delta e}$	$G_{\Delta u}$
AD control	0.7638	−0.0394	1
RD control	0.2381	0.6032	0.4286

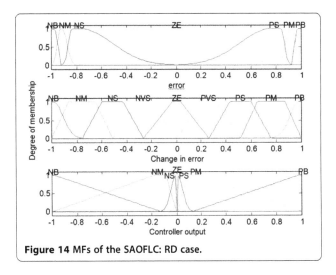

Figure 14 MFs of the SAOFLC: RD case.

application servers using the classical feedback control theory. To achieve these goals, they established approximate linear time-invariant models through system identification experimentally, and designed two PI controllers using the root locus method. These controllers are invoked periodically to calculate and adjust the probabilities for different classes of requests to use a limited number of database connections, according to the error between the measured QoS metric and the reference value.

In a recent work, Patikirikorala et al. [59] proposed a new approach for QoS performance management and resource provisioning by using an off-line identification of Hammerstein and Wiener nonlinear block structural model. Using the characteristic structure of the nonlinear model, a predictive feedback controller based on a gain schedule technique is incorporated in the design to achieve the performance objectives.

Examples of earlier research investigations using fuzzy logic based feedback control can be found in Diao et al. [9], Wei et al. [11], Chan and Chu [12], Wei et al. [14], Wei et al. [60], Tian et al. [20], Rao et al. [21].

In this paper, we have investigated the capabilities of two PI type Mamdani FLCs. The first has been obtained by trial-and-error process and the second synthesized by a SA based optimization.

Note that we have conducted performance evaluation of the proposed intelligent feedback control strategies based on validated mathematical models established by Lu et al. [13]. Our work focuses mainly on testing their robustness when faced with abrupt workload variations.

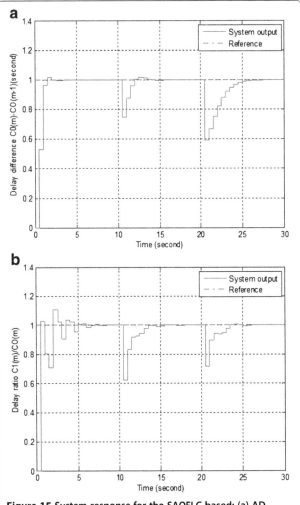

Figure 15 System response for the SAOFLC based: (a) AD control (b) RD control for the three considered workloads.

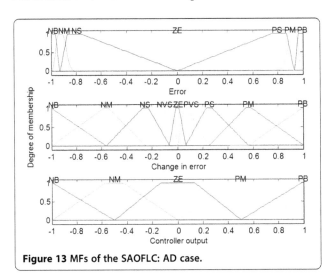

Figure 13 MFs of the SAOFLC: AD case.

7 Conclusion and further work

This paper has addressed the QoS feedback intelligent control of a web server by considering its two common models in service differentiation: the absolute delay and the relative delay guarantees.

The application of two fuzzy logic controllers has been investigated as robust solutions for enforcing desired service performances in face of unpredictable server workloads: a Mamdani type fuzzy logic controller (FLC) and a simulated annealing optimized FLC (SAOFLC).

The main contributions of the proposed optimizing approach have been revealed in the tuning procedures of all the FLC design parameters through the minimization of a performance index. Explicitly, the innovations concern:

- the technique of fuzzy sets assignment to each of the grid nodes in the special case of equality of minimal distances between the points representing the candidate decision rules
- the formulation of the spacing law in function of the spacing parameter in the decision rules table deriving method
- the formulations linking the trapezoidal and the two-sided Gaussian membership functions
- the optimization and the diversification of the membership functions shapes offering possibilities of hybridization on the universe of discourse of each of the FLC input/output variables
- a simple solution to prevent important overlapping between the generated membership functions.
- The digital simulations have allowed us to validate the effectiveness of the proposed structures of control. Indeed, both of the FLC and the SAOFLC capabilities have been evaluated when applied to guarantee desired dynamic performance of the web server delay services.

Both of the adopted intelligent control strategies have realized quite satisfactory results. But, it has been clearly noted that the optimized FLC achieves rather high control performances in comparison with those of the standard Mamdani FLC in terms of transition and steady-state response characteristics.

Further studies to improve the obtained performances by other feedback control schemes as well as the optimization by other techniques such as tabu search, genetic algorithm, ant colonies, swarm techniques, bio-inspired techniques ... will be conducted as well.

Competing interest
The authors declare that they have no competing interest.

Authors's contributions
ML and YS created and developed the proposed approaches. SR participated in the experiments. ML and SR wrote the manuscript. All authors read and approved the final manuscript.

Acknowledgements
This work was partially sponsored by MESRS/DGRSDT/CERIST/PNR8/E166/4884. We also would like to thank the anonymous reviewers who greatly contributed to the betterment of this work.

References
1. Wang Z (2001) Internet QoS. Architectures and mechanisms for quality of service. Morgan Kaufmann, San Fransisco, CA, USA
2. Blake S, Black D, Carlson M, Davies E, Wang Z, Weiss W (1998) An architecture for differentiated services. IETF. Request for Comments 2475
3. Kilkki K (1999) Differentiated services for the internet. Macmillan Technical Publishing, Indianapolis, IN, USA
4. Abdelzaher TF, Stankovic JA, Lu C, Zhang R, Lu Y (2003) Feedback performance control in software services. IEEE Control Syst 23(3):74–90
5. Hellerstein JL, Diao Y, Parekh S, Tilbury DM (2004) Feedback control of computing systems. IEEE Press-Wiley, Hoboken, NJ, USA
6. Abdelzaher TF, Diao Y, Hellerstein JL, Lu C, Zhu X (2008) Introduction to control theory and its application to computing systems. In: Liu Z, Xia CH (ed) Performance Modeling and Engineering. Springer, pp 185–215. Part II, Chapter 7
7. Parekh S (2010) Feedback control techniques for performance management, Ph.D Dissertation. University of Washington, Seattle, WA, USA
8. Lu C, Abdelzaher TF, Stancovic JA, Son SH (2001) A feedback control approach for guaranteeing relative delays in web servers. Proccedings of the Seventh IEEE Real-Time Technology and Applications Symposium, Taipei, Taiwan, pp 51–62
9. Diao Y, Hellerstein JL, Parekh S (2002) Optimizing quality of service using fuzzy contro. In: Feridun M, Kropf P, Babon G (ed) Management Technologies for E-commerce an E-Business Applications. Lecture Notes in Computer Science, 2506th edition. Springer, Berlin, pp 42–53
10. Andersson M, Kihl M, Robertsson A (2003) Modelling and Design of Admission Control Mechanisms for Web Servers using Non-linear Control Theory. In: Proceedings of the ITCom's Conference on Performance and Control of Next-Generation Communication Networks. SPIE proceedings series, 5244th edition. , Orlando, FL, USA, pp 53–64
11. Wei Y, Lin C, Chu X, Shan Z, Ren F (2005) Class-Based Latency Assurances for Web Servers. In: High Performance Computing and Communications. Lecture Notes in Computer Science, 3726th edition. Springer, Berlin, pp 388–394
12. Chan KH, Chu X (2006) Design of a fuzzy PI controller to guarantee proportional delay differentiation on web servers. Technical Report COMP-06-001. Department of Computer Science, Hong Kong Baptist University
13. Lu C, Abdelzaher TF, Stancovic JA, Son SH (2006) Feedback control architecture and design methodology for service delay guarantees in web servers. IEEE Trans on Parallel Distrib Syst 17(9):1014–1027
14. Wei Y, Xu C-Z, Zhou X, Li Q (2006) Fuzzy control for guaranteeing absolute delays in web servers. Int J High Performance Comput Netw 4(5–6):338–346
15. Zhou X, Cai Y, Chow E (2006) An integrated approach with feedback control for robust web QoS design. Comput Commun 29(16):3158–3169
16. Qin W, Wang Q (2007) Modeling and control design for performance management of web servers via an LPV approach. IEEE Trans Contr Syst Tech 15(2):259–275
17. Pan W, Mu D, Wu H, Yao L (2008) Feedback control-based QoS guarantees in web application servers. In: Proceedings of the IEEE International Conference on High Performance Computing and Communications, Dalian, China, pp 328–334
18. Kihl M, Robertsson A, Andersson M, Wittenmark B (2008) Control-theoretic Analysis of Admission Control Mechanisms for Web Server Systems. World Wide Web 11(1):193–116
19. Yansu H, Guanzhong D, Ang G, Wenping P (2009) A self-tuning control for web QoS. In: Proceedings of the International Conference on Information Engineering and Computer Science, Wuhan, China, pp 1–4

20. Tian F, Xu W, Sun J (2010) Web QoS control using fuzzy adaptive PI controller. Proceedings of the International Symposium on Distributed Computing and Applications to Business Engineering and Science, Hong Kong, pp 72–75

21. Rao J, Wei Y, Gong J, Xu C-Z (2011) DynaQoS: model-free self-tuning fuzzy control of virtualized resources for QoS provisioning. In: Proceedings of the 19th International Workshop on Quality of Service (IWQoS'11). IEEE Press, San Jose, CA, USA, pp 1–9

22. Venkatarama HS, Sekaran KC (2012) Autonomic Computing: A Fuzzy Control Approach towards Application Development. In: Cong-Vinh P (ed) Formal and Practical Aspects of Autonomic Computing and Networking: Specification, Development, and Verification. IGI Global, Hershey, PA, USA, pp 118–134. Chapter 5

23. Lama P, Zhou X (2012) Efficient Server Provisioning with Control for End-to-End Response Time Guarantee on Multitier. IEEE Trans on Parallel and Distributed Systems 23(1):78–86

24. Gourley D, Totty B, Sayer M, Aggarwal A, Reddy S (2002) HTTP: The Definitive Guide, O'Reilly Media

25. Kozierok CM (2005) The TCP/IP Guide: A Comprehensive. No Starch Press, Illustrated Internet Protocols Reference

26. Andersson M (2005) Introduction to Web Server Modeling and Control Research. Technical Report, Department of Communication Systems, Lund Institute of Technology

27. Fielding R, Gettys J, Mogul J, Frystyk H, Masinter L, Leach P, Berners-Lee T (1999) Hypertext Transfer Protocol-HTTP/1.1. IETF RFC 2616

28. http://news.netcraft.com/archives/2012/02/07/february-2012-web-server-survey.html

29. Lee CC (1990) Fuzzy logic in control systems: fuzzy logic controller- part I & part II. IEEE Trans on Systems Man and Cybernetics 20(2):404–435

30. Mamdani EH (1974) Applications of fuzzy algorithms for control of a simple dynamic plant. Proceedings of the IEE 121(12):1585–1588

31. Metropolis N, Rosenbluth AW, Rosenbluth MN, Teller AH, Teller E (1953) Equation of state calculations by fast computing machines. J Chem Phys 21:1087–1092

32. Kirkpatrick S, Gelatt CD, Vecchi MP (1983) Optimization by simulated annealing. Science 220:671–680

33. Ljung L (1999) System Identification - Theory For the User, 2nd edition. PTR Prentice Hall, Upper Saddle River, N.J., USA

34. Barford P, Crovella ME (1998) Generating Representative Web Workloads for Network and Server Performance Evaluation. Proceedings of the ACM SIGMETRICS Joint International Conference on Measurement and Modeling of Computer Systems, Madison, WI, USA, pp 151–160

35. Park YJ, Cho HS, Cha DH (1995) Genetic algorithm-based optimization of fuzzy logic controller using characteristic parameters. Proceedings of the IEEE International Conference on Evolutionary Computation, Perth, WA, Australia, pp 831–836

36. Foran J (2002) Optimisation of a fuzzy logic controller using genetic algorithms. Master of Engineering Project Report. Dublin City University, School of Electronic Engineering

37. Loudini M (2007) Contribution à la modélisation et à la commande intelligente d'un bras de robot manipulateur flexible. Ph.D. thesis, Electrical Engineering Dept., Ecole Nationale Polytechnique, Algiers, Algeria

38. Illoul R, Loudini M, Selatnia A (2011) Particle swarm optimization of a fuzzy regulator for an absorption packed column. Mediterranean Journal of Measurement and Control 7(1):174–182

39. Mac Vicar-Whelan PJ (1976) Fuzzy sets for man machine interactions. Int J of Man–machine Studies 8(6):687–697

40. Cheong F, Lai R (2000) Constraining the optimization of a fuzzy logic controller using an enhanced genetic algorithm. IEEE Trans Syst Man Cybern B Cybern 30(1):31–46

41. Bühler H (1994) Réglage par logique floue. Presses Polytechniques et Universitaires Romandes. Lausanne, Switzerland

42. Jager R, Verbruggen HB, Bruijn PM (1992) The role of defuzzification methods in the application of fuzzy control. Proceedings of the IFAC Symposium on Intelligent Components and Instuments for Control Applications, Malaga, Spain, pp 75–80

43. Graham D, Lathrop RC (1953) The synthesis of optimum transient response: Criteria and standard forms. Transacactions of the American Institute of Electrical Engineers, Applications and Industry 72:273–288

44. Leung MKH, Lui JCS, Yau DKY (2001) Adaptive proportional delay differentiated services: characterization and performance evaluation. IEEE/ACM Transactions on Networking 9(6):80–817

45. Tham C-K, Subramaniam VR (2002) Integrating web server and network QoS to provide end-to-end service differentiation. In: Proceedings of the 10th IEEE International Conference on Networks (ICON 2002). , Singapore, pp 389–394

46. Lee SCM, Lui JCS, Yau DKY (2004) A proportional-delay DiffServ-enabled Web server: admission control and dynamic adaptation. IEEE Trans Parallel Distrib Syst 15(5):385–400

47. Li ZG, Chen C, Soh YC (2004) Relative differentiated delay service: time varying deficit round robin. Proceedings of the Fifth World Congress on Intelligent Control and Automation, Hangzhou, China, pp 5608–5612

48. Rashid MM, Alfa AS, Hossain E, Maheswaran M (2005) An analytical approach to providing controllable differentiated quality of service in web servers. IEEE Trans Parallel Distrib Syst 16(11):1022–1033

49. Wei J, Xu C-Z, Zhou X, Li Q (2006) A robust packet scheduling algorithm for proportional delay differentiation services. Comput Commun 29(18):3679–3690

50. Bourasa C, Sevasti A (2007) An analytical QoS service model for delay-based differentiation. Computer Networks 51(12):3549–3563

51. Wu C-C, Wu H-M, Lin W (2008) High-performance packet scheduling to provide relative delay differentiation in future high-speed networks. Comput Commun 31(10):1865–1876

52. Garcia DF, Garcia J, Entrialgo J, Garcia M, Valledor P, Garcia R, Campos AM (2009) A QoS control mechanism to provide service differentiation and overload protection to internet scalable servers. IEEE Trans on Services Computing 2(1):3–16

53. Dimitriou S, Tsaoussidis V (2010) Promoting effective service differentiation with Size-oriented Queue Managemen. Computer Networks 54(18):3360–3372

54. Gao A, Mu D, Hu Y (2011) A QoS control approach in differentiated web cashing service. J of Networks 6(1):62–70

55. Varela A, Vazão T, Arroz G (2012) Providing service differentiation in pure IP-based networks. Comput Commun 35(1):33–46

56. Henriksson D, Lu Y, Abdelzaher T (2004) Improved prediction for web server delay control. In: Proceedings of the 16th Euromicro Conference on Real-Time Systems. IEEE Computer Press, Catania, Sicily, Italy, pp 61–68

57. Oottamakorn C (2005) Class-based guarantees of relative delay services in web servers. In: Proceedings of the IASTED International Conference on Parallel and Distributed Computing and Networks (PDCN 2005). part of the 23rd Multi-Conference on Applied Informatics, Innsbruck, Austria, pp 417–423

58. Lu J, Dai G, Mu D, Yu J, Li H (2011) QoS Guarantee in Tomcat Web Server: A Feedback Control Approach. In: Proceedings of the (2011) International Conference on Cyber-Enabled Distributed Computing and Knowledge Discovery. Beijing, China, pp 183–189

59. Patikirikorala T, Wang L, Colman A, Han J (2012) Hammerstein–Wiener nonlinear model based predictive control for relative QoS performance and resource management of software systems. Control Eng Pract 20(1):49–61

60. Wei J, Xu CZ (2007) Consistent proportional delay differentiation: A fuzzy control approach. Computer Networks 51(5–6):2015–2032

8

RRG: redundancy reduced gossip protocol for real-time N-to-N dynamic group communication

Vincent Wing-Hei Luk*, Albert Kai-Sun Wong, Chin-Tau Lea and Robin Wentao Ouyang

Abstract

Real-time group communication is an indispensable part of many interactive multimedia applications over the internet. In scenarios that involve large group sizes, sporadic sources, high user churns, and random network failures, gossip-based protocols can potentially provide advantages over structure-based group communication algorithms in ease of deployment, scalability, and resiliency against churns and failures. In this paper, we propose a novel protocol called Redundancy Reduced Gossip for real-time N-to-N group communication. We show that our proposed protocol can achieve a considerably lower traffic load than conventional push-based gossip protocols and conventional push-pull gossip protocols for the same probability of successful delivery, with higher performance gains in networks with smaller delays. We derive a mathematical model for estimating the frame non-delivery probability and the traffic load from overhead, and demonstrate the general correctness of the model by simulation. We implement a functioning prototype conferencing system using the proposed protocol, completed with functions including NTP synchronization, dynamic group size estimation, redundancy suppression, and other features needed for proper operation. We perform experiments over the campus network and PlanetLab, and the prototype system demonstrates the ability of our protocol to maintain robust performance in real-world network environments.

Keyword: Terms real-time distributed, Network protocols, Network communication, Multicast, Simulation, Verification, Reliability

I. Introduction

Real-time group communication is a fundamental part of many emerging interactive internet multimedia applications such as group chats [1,2], voice and video conferencing [1,3,4], telepresence [5,6], web-based classrooms [4,7], virtual reality [7], distributed collaborative environments [1,7-9], online multiplayer games [10,11], social networking applications [12,13] and social games [14,15], etc. Real-time group communication over the Internet presents the following requirements that must be considered:

1. The delay requirement of real-time communication is stringent - generally assumed to be comparable to what is required for conversational voice. The one-way delay should be kept below 400 msec [16].

Protocols for streaming are typically not designed with this stringent delay requirement in mind.

2. Communication among the group members is N-to-N in that a random number of active sources may generate voice, video, and control data information to be distributed to all other members at the same time. Protocols that consider individual sources in isolation may not be optimal in such a scenario.

3. The peers are sporadic meaning that each peer may switch between active and idle state rapidly.

4. There is a high degree of user churn meaning that users may join and leave the group dynamically at will.

There are three conventional approaches for real-time group communication. The first approach is network layer multicast [17], which means the use of IP multicast. The second approach is to use a centralized server (Figure 1a) for forwarding and mixing of multimedia streams. The third approach is to construct a fully

---
* Correspondence: vincentl@ece.ust.hk
Department of Electronic and Computer Engineering, Hong Kong University of Science and Technology, Hong Kong, Hong Kong

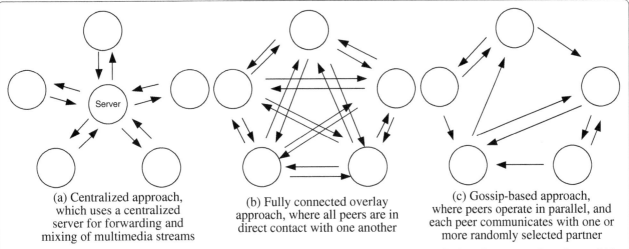

Figure 1 Illustration of three types of group communication topologies: (a) Centralized approach; (b) Fully connected overlay; and (c) Gossip-based approach.

connected peer-to-peer overlay network (Figure 1b) [18] that has all peers in direct contact with one another. The first approach enables server-free group communication, but currently IP multicast is not widely deployed, rendering this approach impractical over the general internet. The second approach requires a powerful central node with sufficient bandwidth, and faces problems of scalability and single point of failure. Skype, which can be considered a centralized-server approach [19,20] where the "centralized server" is also a peer node that is promoted by a peer election mechanism, for example, is not designed to support a large number of users or accommodate random user churns. The third approach requires that all users must have sufficient uplink bandwidth, which scales with the number of users, N, to broadcast their streams to other users. It also faces a serious problem with user churns because any potential source must quickly learn of all peers present.

In recent years, two leading approaches for supporting scalable real-time N-to-N communications have emerged: structure-based [21-42] and gossip-based [43,44].

Structure-based approaches require participating nodes to form a certain deterministic structure, often a tree constructed as a solution to a delay-constrained minimum Steiner tree problem by heuristics [25,26,29-34,36]. In such tree-based systems, bandwidth usage is very efficient as no duplicated messages are sent. The total bandwidth consumption can be further reduced by incorporating the mixing of audio streams within the structure [22-24,35], or by combining IP multicast in LAN [29]. In N-to-N group communication, multiple peers may generate information concurrently. Therefore, the authors in the papers [29,33,37] have argued that multiple source-specific multicast trees should be constructed instead of just one shared multicast tree. Other optimizations have also been

proposed, such as resources sharing among trees of different sessions [39], and the 2-hop delayed-bounded tree [40,41]. Examples of structure-based approaches that are not tree-based include chained-based overlay using layered coding [42] and snow-ball chunk [38].

Previous studies have shown that if the user churn is low so that the structure is stable, and if the network loss-rate is also low, then structure-based systems can perform very well. In the presence of user churn and network degradations, however, structure-based systems may become unreliable because the overhead for tree maintenance and message recovery may increase with a snowball effect, as pointed out in the papers [45-47]. Based on experience learned from the evolution of live streaming protocols, Zhang et al. [48] have also concluded that structure-based multicast protocols are impractical on the Internet because of user churn and network degradation dynamics. Note that churn-coping strategies for structured approaches were discussed in the papers [21,37]. But due to the fundamental limitation of structured approaches, the tolerated churn rate is very low. For example, a churn rate of 4/minute with a group size of 50–200 requires 2 seconds of recovery time [37]. Chu et al. have also acknowledged the poor transient performance in larger group sizes in their work [21]. A scheme using multiple distribution trees with Multiple Description Coding (MDC) is proposed as a churn coping measure in the paper [49], but this scheme can only be used for traffic types where MDC is applicable, i.e., video. MDC is not applicable to gaming control data and it is questionable whether it is applicable for voice.

Gossip-based protocols have been considered by many researchers to be reliable in a probabilistic sense as their randomized nature helps to "route around" peer churn and network degradation [50]. Gossip-based protocols have first been examined for information dissemination in what is known as randomized rumor spreading [51] or epidemic algorithm [52]. In a gossip-based protocol, each cycle of information spreading consists of multiple phases of gossip and in each phase, peers operate in parallel and each peer communicates with one or more randomly selected partners (Figure 1c). In synchronous gossip [51], a phase is launched simultaneously by all peers, and one phase is completed before the start of the next phase. Synchronous gossip assumes that the period of a phase is larger than the one-way delay between any pair of nodes, a condition that is unrealistic for real time communication. In asynchronous gossip [53], peers do not operate in synchronous phases but gossip asynchronously in response to messages received. In either synchronous or asynchronous gossip, the number of phases or the number of times a message is relayed in a cycle must be limited to a very small number independent of the population size for real-time communications because of the stringent delay requirement. This realtime requirement leads also to the use of push [54] rather than pull to reduce the amount of time needed for each phase. For example, Verma et al. [43] have proposed the use of an adaptive fanout to control an asynchronous infection pattern over a limited number of phases in a push manner, and Georgiou et al. [44] have derived the probability for successful rumor spreading in relation to the number of gossip targets under a given number of phases. To the best of our knowledge, all of the existing asynchronous gossip schemes for real time communication use one push or push-pull operation in one phase, and each gossip phase is independent of other phases. These push protocols usually produce a large number of duplicated messages and thus have a low bandwidth utilization efficiency.

In this paper, we propose a new asynchronous way of gossiping with limited delay. In our scheme, a peer establishes connectivity with multiple peers and uses a limited number of push-pull operations in each information spreading cycle. This repeated push-pulls between two peers during each cycle (details in Sec. III-A) results in a much smaller number of duplicated messages compared to conventional push-based gossip protocols and conventional push-pull gossip protocols for real-time applications [43,44]. Hence, we name our protocol Redundancy Reduced Gossip (RRG).

It is worth noting that some gossip protocols proposed for ad hoc networks also use fixed connectivity [55-57]. However, their connectivity is confined to near-neighbor links. In our scheme, the connectivity is randomly established among all participants. Melamed et al. in [47] also proposed the use of a gossip push to fixed downstream neighbors, but none of the

related works [47,55-57] uses multiple push-pulls in each cycle.

Results that are presented in this paper include:

1. A novel protocol, called Redundancy Reduced Gossip, for real-time N-to-N dynamic group communication is proposed. The protocol allows the distribution of information from an arbitrary number of random sources within a group, with low latency, minimal membership maintenance, and without assumption on the underlying network condition. The proposed protocol can achieve a given successful delivery probability with a considerably lower traffic load than conventional push gossip protocols and conventional push-pull gossip protocols for real time.
2. A mathematical model is developed and presented for analyzing the frame non-delivery probability and overhead of RRG. The model provides useful insights into the design of our protocol. It can also be used to evaluate the performance of other related protocols.
3. A Linux-based prototype system running the protocol is implemented and tested. Some details and challenges of the implementation are described. Experiment results of the system operating over a LAN as well as over the PlanetLab [58] are collected and analyzed. The prototype system demonstrates the ability of our protocol to maintain robust performance in real-world network environments.

The rest of the paper is organized as follows. Section II presents an overview of related works. Section III describes the RRG protocol. Section IV presents the performance evaluation results from a mathematical model and from the simulator. Section V presents the prototype design, challenges and network experiment results. Section VI concludes the paper.

II. Related works

Using gossip for real-time task execution systems has been proposed in the papers [59,60], but the research focuses and methods in these works are different from ours. Huang et al. [59] have proposed a gossip-based super-node architecture for query and routing in 1-to-1 information dissemination. Han et al. [60] have adopted the adaptive fanout gossip model proposed by [43] for peer discovery and applied the model to a real-time distributable thread scheduling problem.

Push-pull gossip has been studied in the papers [51,61,62]. For example, in the paper [61], one push-pull is used in one phase for the computation of aggregate information. Karp et al. [51] and Khambatti et al. [62] have proposed the use of push- followed by pull-gossip in two separate stages. They try to combine the expediency of push-gossip with the lower redundancy of pull-gossip. However, these two phase solutions [51,62] are not applicable to real-time communications.

Three-phase pull or lazy push gossip [63] is studied in the streaming papers [48,64-66]. It is important to note that streaming applications have a less stringent delay requirement (buffer built-out delays of 10 – 30 seconds are quoted in these papers). Each execution of the three-phase cycle of advertise-request-delivery is targeted to deliver information to only a single layer of peers. In RRG, each execution of the greeting-response-closure cycle is targeted to deliver information from all sources to all peers.

Using gossip to establish a random graph for information dissemination has been proposed in the papers [28,67,68]. Liang et al. have proposed the use of an on-demand tree for short-lived interactions [67]. However, the proposed scheme does not maintain the spanning tree for a prolonged period of time; hence, no repair mechanism to cope with failures is possible. Chunkyspread [28] uses a simple controlled flooding mechanism over a random graph maintained by Swaplinks [69] for trees construction. It also uses multiple trees to react quickly to membership changes. However, the tree heights are not bounded in the protocol. In contrast, the information dissemination of RRG is strictly bounded to around 3 hops to support the real-time communication delay constraint of 400 ms [16]. Carvalho et al. have proposed to probabilistically combine lazy push gossip and pure push gossip to obtain an emergent structure [68]. The use of lazy push gossip, however, hinders its applicability to real-time communications as we discussed above.

Asynchronous gossip has been studied for other purposes as well [70,71]. Boyd et al. have used asynchronous gossip to address the "averaging problem" in sensor networks [70]. Ram et al. have studied asynchronous gossip for summing the component functions in a distributed multi-agent system [71]. These protocols are not targeted for real-time N-to-N group communications.

Deb, Médard and Choute have studied N-to-N gossip with and without network coding in [72]. Their primary contribution is to quantify the gain of network coding in a multiple-source scenario. They assume synchronous gossiping with only one gossip target per peer per phase. Their study is not applicable to real-time group communications.

Several studies [46,47,50,63] have proposed the combining of the gossiping and structure-based approaches. These hybrid approaches combine the advantage of bandwidth efficiency in structure-based approaches with the churn-coping capability of gossiping approaches. Gossip is employed in the recovery of loss packets after the initial

delivery by a structure-based approach. Gupta et al. have used gossip in a sub-tree topology to reduce the traffic load [50]. Our RRG scheme can be extended to include these techniques.

Birman et al. [73], Gu et al. [24] and Lao et al. [32] have proposed the combining of the use of infrastructure and peer-to-peer approaches for real-time group communications. The objective of our paper is different from theirs. We focus on a pure peer-to-peer approach without any infrastructure support.

This paper is different from our original Globecom conference version of this paper [74] in three aspects. First, the protocol has been improved by the incorporation of a delayed response strategy. Second, additional performance evaluations are presented which include the traffic load performances under different scenarios and with user churn. Third, a prototype system running the protocol has been implemented and tested over the HKUST campus network and PlanetLab. In this paper, we identify the fact that the performance gain of our protocol is higher in networks with small delays.

III. Proposed N-to-N gossiping protocol
A. Protocol description
Our N-to-N gossiping protocol consists of n nodes, or peers, that operate in cycles. (The terms "peer" and "node" will be used interchangeably in this paper). Each cycle is initiated at fixed intervals and is identified by a global cycle ID. For simplicity, we assume that there is a global synchronization of the cycle ID and frame rate, and that this synchronization is achieved through the use of NTP. The use of a global cycle ID eliminates the need of a peer to manage the sequence numbering of sources individually and the need to transmit sequence numbers of individual chunks in a packet. Other mechanisms to achieve synchronization are possible but we assume that NTP is used so that we can focus on other aspects of our protocol. Each peer in a cycle can generate at most one information frame (e.g. a voice frame) to be distributed to the remaining $n-1$ peers through a multi-phase gossiping mechanism. The key to our protocol is the use of a synchronous global cycle ID and synchronous media generation. By "synchronous media generation" we mean that the packet generation rates are exactly the same for all active nodes. Most N-to-N real-time communication protocols in the literature have either assumed an asynchronous operation or have assumed a synchronous operation without addressing how this synchronicity is achieved. If using asynchronous operation, we would need to transmit and process individual sequence numbers as well as to perform frequency alignment across multiple streams. Also, the bundling of information from different sources into one transmitted packet cannot be done in as straightforward a manner -

in our protocol, we simply need to bundle information frames with the same cycle ID.

To meet the real-time requirement, we limit the number of phases to 3. In other words, in each cycle, each peer will be engaged in a 3-phase gossip with a random set of other peers, regardless of the number of frames to be distributed. Successive cycles can overlap each other in time. For ease of illustration, we first describe our protocol as if the launch of cycles and phases by different peers are synchronized. But in our protocol this is, in fact, not the case and more details will be added later on.

If a node is already in possession of an information frame to be spread in a specific cycle, the node is called an *infected node*.

Phase 1 (the greeting phase)

In this phase, each node randomly selects a small number of nodes and sends a **GREETING** message to each of them. If a node is already infected when it launches its greeting phase, its GREETING message will contain information frames that it has already received. The selected nodes are called the *"children"* of the selecting node, which is called the *"parent"* of its selected children.

During the greeting phase, connectivity is established for the entire network for the specific cycle. If some nodes are left out, then these nodes will surely not be able to receive the transmitted messages in that cycle. The degree of the established connectivity obviously depends on the number of peers that each node will select during the greeting phase. This number is called the *fanout* and is determined in our protocol using a dynamic group size estimation mechanism (discussed below). An illustration of our protocol operation in a group with 8 peers is shown in Figure 2a, where only one peer, *peer 1*, is a source in a cycle. The fanout is assumed to be 2 for all peers. Peers that are already infected at the

beginning of each phase are colored black, and peers to be infected by the end of the phase are colored grey in the figure. The information of *peer 1* is transmitted to *peer 4* and *peer 8* via the GREETING message. These two nodes, colored in grey, are infected at the end of this phase.

Phase 2 (the response phase)

During this phase, a node will send a **RESPONSE** message to all of its parents. If the child node is already infected at the beginning of this phase, the RESPONSE message contains all its received original frames (from different sources); if un-infected, the RESPONSE message contains no real data. In the example of Figure 2b, *peer 5* and *peer 1* are the parents of *peer 8*. Since *peer 8* is infected by *peer 1* during the greeting phase, *peer 8* will send the information frame from *peer 1* to *peer 5* during the response phase.

Phase 3 (the closure phase)

In this phase, only an infected parent node will send a **CLOSURE** message, containing all of its received original frames (i.e. from different sources) to its children. Un-infected nodes will not send out anything. In the example shown in Figure 2c, *peer 3* is a child of *peer 2* and *peer 8*. Thus both nodes will send a CLOSURE message to *peer 3*. Peer 6 remains un-connected after all phases.

B. More details
1) Cycle Launches through NTP
In the analysis, we assume that cycles and phases are launched simultaneously. In practice, timing information is acquired through NTP (Network Time Protocol). NTP can only correct the clock of a host to within a few tens of milliseconds [75]. Due to this inherent timing inaccuracy in NTP, cycles will be launched asynchronously among nodes. The interaction between the timing inaccuracy in NTP and the message network delay has

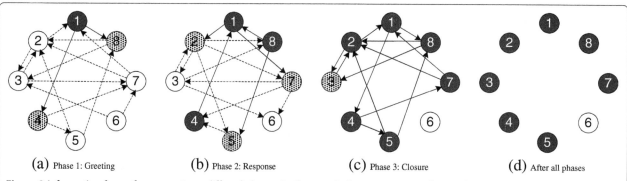

(a) Phase 1: Greeting   (b) Phase 2: Response   (c) Phase 3: Closure   (d) After all phases

Figure 2 Information frame from peer 1 are diffused via gossip that are 3-phase message exchanges in one cycle: (a) Phase 1: Greeting, (b) Phase 2: Response, (c) Phase 3: Closure, and (d) After all phases; Fanout=2; Peer(s) shaded black is infected at the beginning of the phase; Peer(s) shaded grey is infected at the end of the phase; Peers shaded white remain uninfected at the end of the phase; A solid line refers to a message containing a frame; A dotted line refers to an empty message.

some important implications for the real-world perform-ance of the protocol. Consider *peer 1* and *peer 2*, where *peer 1* is the parent of *peer 2*. Before *peer 2* sends back the RESPONSE message to *Peer 1*, ideally all GREETING messages should have arrived in *peer 2* so that the RESPONSE message will not be empty if any of its parents has sent a real message to *peer 2* during the GREETING phase. But this idealized situ-ation may not be achievable because of network de-lays and the inaccuracy in NTP. Hence, to increase the probability that a RESPONSE or CLOSURE mes-sage will contain useful information, we introduce what is called a delayed response mechanism where a peer will add a delay of d_s msec before sending out the RESPONSE and CLOSURE messages after receiving the GREETING and RESPONSE. This is illustrated in Figure 3. We have used a d_s of 50 msec based on the fact that the NTP in-accuracy and network message delays are typically in the range of a few tens of milliseconds and on the conside-ration that this delay should not be too large because of the delay requirement for real-time communications.

2) Redundancy suppression and active peer list

Each gossip message that a peer sends out contains an Active Peer List (APL) that lists the source of each infor-mation frame that it has already received for that cycle with the actual information frame attached if appro-priate. From the APL, the receiving peer extracts the in-formation frames that it needs, and also avoids sending back to the sender information frames that the sender already has - this mechanism is referred to as *redun-dancy suppression* and its purpose is to reduce the total amount of traffic. Thus, in the APL of a message, some listed entries will have an information frame attached and some entries will not.

APL contains the complete contact information of a peer in 6 bytes - 4 bytes for the IP address and 2 bytes for the port number. The APL is included in every mes-sage that a peer transmits. The length of the APL is vari-able as the number of peers may vary. Therefore, APL is

encoded in the Type-Length-Value (TLV) format, with 8-bit type and 16-bit length fields.

3) Bootstrapping

Any newly arrived peer is required to contact the boot-strapping point to acquire a list of peer contacts in the group, the current estimated community size (see Sec. III-B5 below) and the current cycle ID. The list of peer contacts does not need to be 100% correct because the new peer can learn the membership information from subsequent gossip, but it will impact the protocol per-formance. More details will be provided in Sec. IV-D. The newly arrived peer uses the current estimated size to determine its fanout value. Any peer in the group can be the bootstrapping point.

4) Dynamic group membership

A new peer joins the group through the bootstrapping point. Afterwards, its contact information is learned by other peers through the APL contained in the exchanged messages. Peers independently detect and remove a departed peer when that peer does not respond to a GREETING within a timeout.

5) Fanout estimation

In our protocol, each peer will independently decide how many peers to initiate gossip with based on its es-timate of the current group size, a target information non-delivery probability, and the estimated non-delivery probability from Eq. 6 we derive in Sec. VI. We adopt and extend the gossip-based size estimation algorithm proposed by M Jelasity et al. [76] to support asynchro-nous operation. The details of the algorithm are beyond the scope of this paper. Hence, we omit the details of this algorithm in this paper.

IV. Performance evaluation

In this section, we present the analytical model for a key performance measure in the proposed protocol: the frame non-delivery probability as a function of fanout. We also compare, through simulation, the performance of the proposed RRG with that of the conventional push gossip approach in [43,44] and the conventional push-pull gossip protocols in [54,61]. The evaluation metric is the ratio of the non-delivery rate versus the traffic load. The effectiveness of the redundancy suppression is presented. Lastly, the impact of churn is studied.

A. Analytical model for frame non-delivery probability in redundancy reduced gossip

In this section, an analytical model to study the non-delivery rate of information frames in the proposed N-to-N gossiping protocol is developed. The analysis is

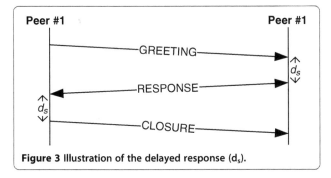

Figure 3 Illustration of the delayed response (d_s).

based on a perfectly-synchronized Redundancy Reduced Gossip protocol. Although a real implementation, as discussed in Sec. III above, has to be asynchronous, the synchronous assumption allows us to obtain a closed-form formula that provides some useful insights into the design tradeoffs of the protocol.

For source node s, its family tree (Figure 4) consists of the following members: parents, children, co-parents of parents of s, step children, grandchildren, and siblings. "*Parent*" and "*children*" were defined in Sec. III-A. The definitions of the other members of the family tree are given below.

"**Grandchild**": A child's child.
"**Sibling**": Two nodes having the same parent are called *siblings* of each other.
"**Co-parent**": A node and s are called *co-parents* of each other if they share any node as a common child.
"**Step Children**": If node A and B are co-parents of a node, A's children are called the "*step children*" of B and vice versa.

For a node to receive the broadcast message from source s in a cycle, the node must belong to the family tree of s. If not, the node will fail to receive the message. In the following we analyze the non-delivery probability p_l for a given node.

We first define the fanout as b. b is also the number of children of s.

Let's define the following random variables:

m_p the number of parents of s.
m_g the number of grandchildren of s.
m_{sb} the number of sibling of s.
m_c the number of co-parents with s.
m_s the number of step children of s.
We also define the following probabilities:
p_p the probability that a given node is a parent of s.
p_c the probability that a given node is a co-parent to s.
p_l the probability that the broadcast message of a cycle cannot be delivered to particular node.

First, consider m_p. p_p is the same as the probability that the given node selects s as a child. Hence $p_p=b/n\text{-}1$ and the expected number of parents of s is

$$E[m_p] = (n-1)p_p = b \tag{1}$$

Since each parent has b children, E(m_g), the expected total number of grandchildren m_g, has order $O(b^2)$. Likewise, E(m_{sb}), the expected total number of siblings m_{sb}, also has order $O(b^2)$.

Next, consider m_c. First, we observe that p_c is one minus the probability that a given node X selects all b children from the set of n-1-b (s has not selected X as child) or n-b (s has selected X as child) nodes not selected by s out of n-1 nodes:

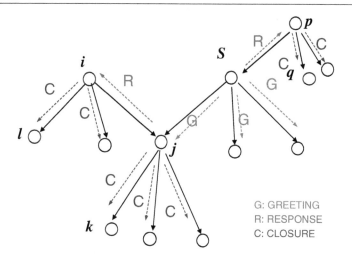

j: a child of s,
k: a child of j and thus a grandchild of s,
i: another parent of j and thus a co-parent with s,
l: a child of i and thus a step-child of s,
p: a parent of s,
q: a child of p and thus a sibling of s.

Figure 4 A family tree of the node s as source.

$$p_c = 1 - \left[\left(\frac{b}{n-1}\right) \frac{\binom{n-b}{b}}{\binom{n-1}{b}} + \left(1 - \frac{b}{n-1}\right) \frac{\binom{n-1-b}{b}}{\binom{n-1}{b}} \right]$$

(2)

An upper and lower bound can be written for p_c:

$$1 - \left(1 - \frac{b}{n-1}\right)^b < p_c < 1 - \left(1 - \frac{b}{n-b}\right)^b.$$

(3)

Since m_c follows a binomial distribution $B(n\text{-}1,\ p_c)$ with expected value $E[m_c] = (n\text{-}1)\ p_c$, the bound of Eq. 3 establishes that

$$E[m_c] \approx b^2$$

(4)

for a large n. Note that the ratio of the standard deviation to mean, $(np_c(1\text{-}p_c))^{0.5}/(n\text{-}1)\ p_c$, is very small and hence the probability mass will center on the mean. Since each co-parent can have b children, the expected total number of step children has order $O(b^3)$. Among the six members—children, grandchildren, parent, co-parent, step children, and sibling—of the family tree, the number of step children is one order higher (in b) than the rest. This means that the size of the family tree of s is determined by the number of step children, which has the order $O(b^3)$. Note that $O(b^3)$ must assume the same order as n (i.e. $O(n)$). If the order is higher, many received frames will be duplicates and

wasted; if lower, many nodes will not be part of the family tree and will not be able to receive the information frame from s. The above leads us to formulate b as $b = c\ n^{1/3}$, where c is a constant, and to focus on c in our analysis below.

The size of the family tree, as pointed out above, is determined by the number of step children when n is large and the probability mass for m_c is concentrated near its mean. Therefore, we can approximate the non-delivery probability p_l for a given source node as

$$p_l = \sum_{k=0}^{n-1} P[a \ node \ is \ not \ a \ step \ child | m_c = k] P[m_c = k]$$
$$\approx \left(1 - \frac{b}{n-1}\right)^{b^2}$$

(5)

Substitute $b = c\ n^{1/3}$ into the equation above, we obtain

$$p_l \approx \left(1 - \frac{b}{n-1}\right)^{b^2} = \left(1 - \frac{b}{n-1}\right)^{\frac{c^3 n}{b}} \approx e^{-c^3}$$

(6)

Figure 5 below plots the analytical and simulation results for the frame non-delivery probability. The simulation is done by repeatedly generating random graphs and collecting statistics of each graph. As shown in the figure below, the difference between (6) and the simulation result narrows as the value of n increases. If the value of c becomes too large, there are a large number of duplicated messages. A large number of peers may

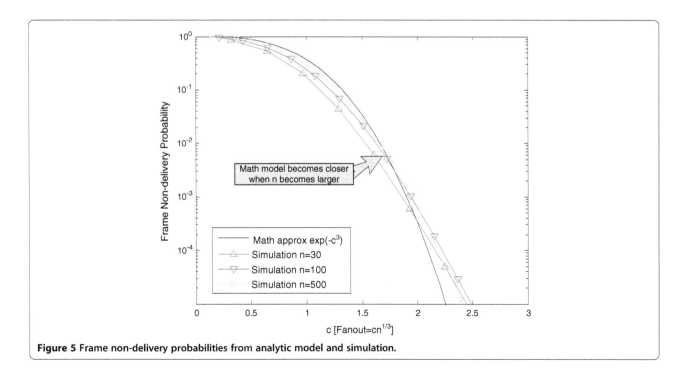

Figure 5 Frame non-delivery probabilities from analytic model and simulation.

also assume multiple roles in relation to s–they can be parents, children, etc., of s at the same time. This renders some of the approximations made in the approximate analysis inaccurate.

B. Frame non-delivery probability versus traffic load

Traffic load is another key performance metric in gossiping protocols. We define traffic load D as the actually measured average number of the same information frame that each peer receives. In other words, D is a measure of the redundancy or the bandwidth usage efficiency of the protocol. Without redundancy suppression, D should be in the order of c^3. With redundancy suppression, D is found to be smaller. By first focusing on the measured D, we are disregarding the protocol overhead, which we will come back to examine later.

In the following, we compare the frame non-delivery probability p_l as a function of traffic load D for the proposed gossip protocol and for the conventional push approach (used by most existing gossiping approaches [43,44]) and the conventional push-pull approach [54,61].

The model for the conventional push approach is as follows: a source node sends the information frame to b randomly selected nodes (phase 1), and each selected node will then push the frame to b other randomly selected nodes (phase 2), etc., with the selection of receiving nodes in each phase done independently. In addition, we include a buffer-map in the conventional approach to reduce redundancy [45-47]–a sending peer will avoid pushing to peers that are already marked in the buffer-map in messages that it has received, and will mark the buffer-map of peers that will receive the information frame in the outgoing message. Note that the buffer-map is more efficient than a list in this case because a list may contain almost all peers in the last phase of gossiping. We ignore the complexity involved in maintaining the mapping of buffer-map to peers in the presence of user churn.

The model for the conventional push-pull approach is as follows: each node randomly selects b nodes and initiates a two way push-pull with each selected node (phase 1 and 2). After that, unlike RRG, each node pushes all the possessed information frames to another b randomly selected nodes (phase 3). Phase 1 and 2 is independent of phase 3. The same buffer-map scheme is included as described in the conventional push approach above [45-47].

While closed-form formulae for the loss rate exist for many of the cases, a meaningful comparison of the loss rates requires that the comparison is done for the same traffic load. However, there is no closed-form formula to estimate the traffic load for protocols under various redundancy suppression schemes. Therefore, an event-driven simulation was developed for the comparison. The information frame is encoded at 8 kbps with a 20 ms

sampling interval, i.e. 20 bytes per cycle per peer. We simulate the message propagation, node and link failure, network topology and link delay. As in common practice in simulating peer-to-peer algorithms in existing works [38,46,53], we do not simulate the network-level packet details (such as specific queuing delays) in order to make the simulation scalable. The link delay x_{ij} from node i to node j is assumed to be a random variable, which is determined by a Weibull distribution $Weibull(a,b)$ (a is the scale parameter and $b=1.5$ is the shape parameter of a long tail delay). The average number of active peers is less than 3.

Another important simulation issue is related to the clock accuracy. The proposed protocol uses NTP to acquire time information. Due to the inherent timing inaccuracy in NTP, the cycle launch time at every node is not perfectly synchronized. As stated in RFC1305 [75], the timing accuracy of NTP is in the range of a few tens of milliseconds. The cycle launch time of peers is modeled to be uniformly distributed within 50 ms. As discussed earlier, d_s (the delay artificially added before sending out RESPONSE & CLOSURE) is set to 50 ms.

Figure 6 shows that RRG requires less traffic load than the conventional push gossip and the conventional push-pull to achieve the same non-delivery probability. For comparison, we also plot in Figure 6 the curve e^{-D}, which is the probability of zero arrival given that the arrival is Poisson with mean D. In a gossip algorithm that is completely random, the Poisson model could be a reasonable first order model for the arrival of information frames at a particular peer. Figure 6 shows that both RRG and the conventional push gossip perform better than e^{-D} and the conventional pull-push gossip perform slightly worse than e^{-D}. Finally, Figure 6 shows that the performance gain of RRG is higher in networks with smaller delays, such as metro area networks, for the reason illustrated in Figure 7. That is, in situations when the network delay, denoted by $T_{1,2}$, between *peer 1* and *peer 2* is smaller than the offset in *peer 2*'s cycle launch time compared to *peer 1*'s (denoted $O_{1,2}$), *peer 1*'s GREETING message, which contains real data, arrives before *peer 2* sends out its GREETING. As a result, *peer 2*'s GREETING can also contain real data even though *peer 2* is not a source. We call this situation a *bonus relay*.

Traffic load in Figure 6 is measured in terms of average number of copies of an information frame received by each peer. But each message contains protocol headers, and the resulting overheads for the two compared protocols are different. When $n=100$ and the average number of active peers is less than 3, with $c=2$, the overhead in RRG is around 20% of total traffic. Most of the overhead is contributed by the APL, where membership information is carried and requires 6 bytes per peer. In the same settings, the overhead of the conventional push

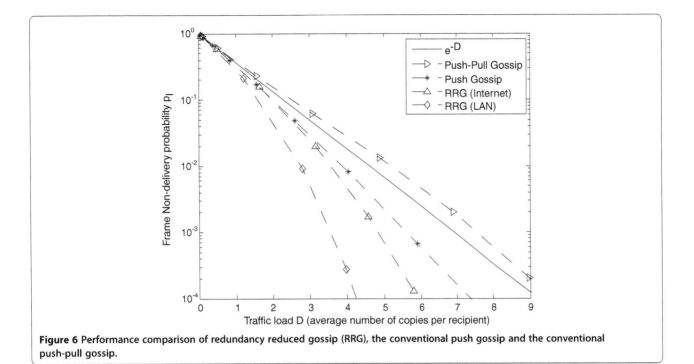

Figure 6 Performance comparison of redundancy reduced gossip (RRG), the conventional push gossip and the conventional push-pull gossip.

gossip and the conventional push-pull gossip are around 40% of total traffic. Most of the overhead is contributed by the buffer-map, which is at least 12 bytes per gossip message.

It is important to note that our protocol generates a smaller number of messages than the fully connected peer-to-peer overlay approach (Figure 1c) in N-to-N communication. The total number of messages in the fully connected overlay approach is $n(n-1)$ while that of our protocol is $3bn$. If $n=100$ with a target p_l of 10^{-2}, b is only 8 from Eq. 6. The number of messages of our protocol is only around 24% that of the fully connected overlay approach.

C. Effectiveness of redundancy suppression

Figure 8 shows the effectiveness of redundancy suppression by APL in RRG. We observe that this mechanism has reduced the traffic load by 35% at the non-delivery probability of 10^{-3}. As the connectivity between peers remains unchanged in each cycle, the average number of

copies of an information frame that a peer receives is bounded by the fanout, as validated in our result.

D. Impact of churn of the proposed protocol

We construct a dynamic scenario with sudden changes in group size over a simulation length of 6500 cycles (130 sec). The timeout detection threshold is set to 500 ms. The mean of the link latency is 50 ms. As shown in Figure 9, the changes of group size are in the range of +/−10%, +/−25%, +/−50% of the original group size. We observe that the non-delivery probability converges in less than 50 cycles (1 sec) in the event of a −50% sudden change. This means that it takes about 50 cycles for peers to detect and remove departed peers from their gossiping candidate set. In the event of new peers joining, their memberships are quickly recognized throughout the group through GREETINGS sent by the new peers and by the APL in the gossiping messages.

RRG has one advantage over hybrid protocols, which combine gossiping with a structure-based approach. [46,47,50,63], under user failures. Figure 10 shows a timing diagram comparing RRG and hybrid protocols under a user failure. We assume that the failure detection timeout is *500 ms* in both protocols and the cycle launch interval is *20 ms* in RRG. Note that any data recovery after the timeout *(500 ms)* is too late to be useful for real-time communication. Once RRG detects which peers have failed after the timeout, RRG will remove the failed peers from the gossip target set and recover from the failure immediately. However, hybrid protocols still need some time to heal the structure (e.g. tree) to resume data

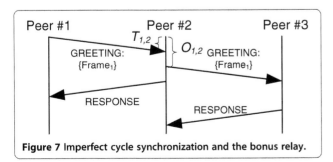

Figure 7 Imperfect cycle synchronization and the bonus relay.

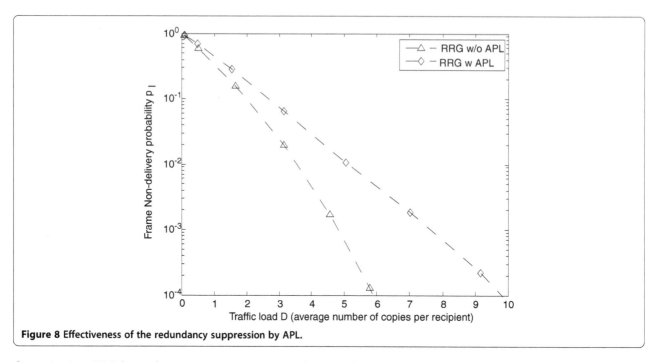

Figure 8 Effectiveness of the redundancy suppression by APL.

dissemination. RRG has a shorter convergence time under user failures. The cost for this shorter convergence time of RRG is the traffic load. RRG may have higher traffic load than hybrid protocols.

V. Prototype implementation and experimentation

The proposed protocol has been implemented in C on the Linux platform. An automated testing and measurement framework is also developed to support sound I/O from

audio script to enable large-scale unattended testing for statistical measurement and, in the future, sound quality measurements. The prototype has been deployed on the HKUST campus network and on the PlanetLab testbed. In the following, we discuss several important aspects of the implementation.

A. Design and architecture

The prototype takes a modularized approach and contains nine key modules (Figure 11), as described below:

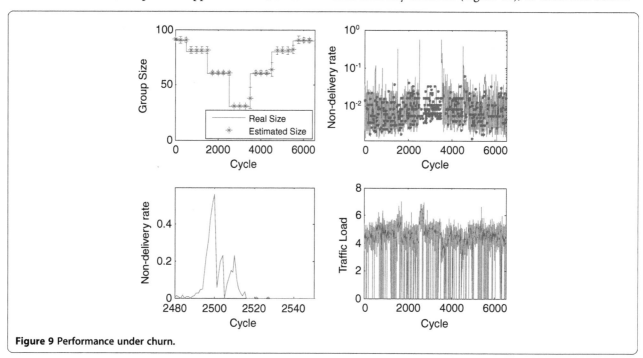

Figure 9 Performance under churn.

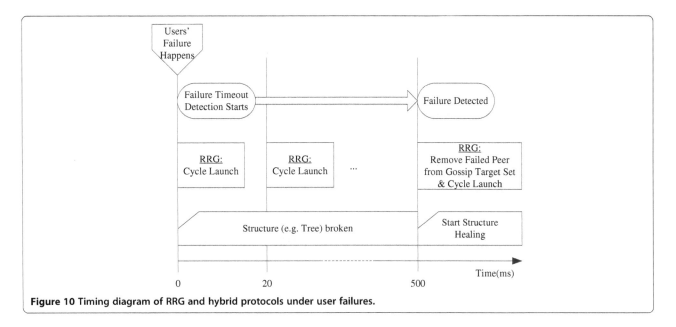

Figure 10 Timing diagram of RRG and hybrid protocols under user failures.

(1) ThreadNetIn: it receives packets from a network interface card (NIC);

(2) ThreadAudioInHW: it reads audio frames from a sound card buffer;

(3) ThreadAudioInFile: it reads audio frames from an audio script file;

(4) MainThread: it parses packets, implements voice activity detection and processes the gossiping logic;

(5) ThreadAudioOutJitterBuffer: it implements a jitter buffer and mixes audio frames from multiple remote parties;

(6) ThreadAudioOutHW: it writes frames to a sound card buffer;

(7) ThreadAudioOutFile: it writes frames to a file and records statistical information for performance evaluation;

(8) ThreadNetOut: it sends packets to the NIC;

(9) ThreadTimerService: it registers and invokes callback events after a specified elapsed time.

ThreadAudioInHW and ThreadAudioInFile are pluggable and interchangeable, and so are ThreadAudio OutHW and ThreadAudioOutFile. The design enables either human or machine based mouth-to-ear voice measurement or large scale remote unattended testing without actual sound I/O. All modules are connected by the producer-consumer design pattern [77]. Each consumer thread has a single work queue shared by possibly multiple producers.

The MainThread generates a GREETING, RESPONSE or CLOSURE according to the gossiping logic. The compiled GREETING, RESPONSE or CLOSURE encapsulated in UDP is sent to ThreadNetOut. Each frame is marked with a cycle ID, and each peer is synchronized using NTP [75].

B. Challenges

Our protocol is implemented on Linux platforms. As Linux is not a real-time operating system, this makes real-time scheduling difficult. To solve the problem, we implement a clock-driven event dispatching module to handle all time-related events, such as periodic sampling of sound cards, periodic cycle launch, de-jittering, playback, scheduling of next wake-up instances, etc. The clock-driven dispatching module invokes events according to a local clock in order to prevent the timing

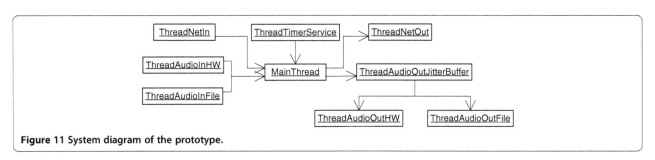

Figure 11 System diagram of the prototype.

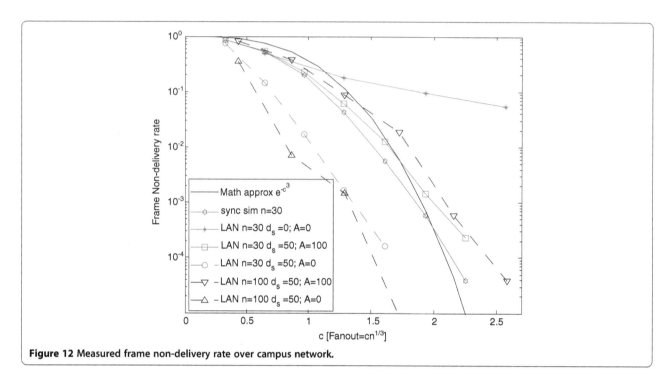

Figure 12 Measured frame non-delivery rate over campus network.

errors caused by factors such as system load, imperfect usleep() [78] and multi-threading switching, etc.

Another issue is that overloaded machines could cause inaccurate latency measurements, but finding idle machines as difficult in the PlanetLab. We observe that for a 30-party conferencing experiment, a maximum of 4 instances of our prototype peer may run on an idle Dual-core Pentium 4 3.2 GHz (Pentium D 940) concurrently. To tackle this problem, we use PlanetLab CoMon [79] to identify less loaded machines (which are quite rare) and then use Sirius Calendar Service [80] to reserve their CPU time [81].

C. Network experimentation results

We use our prototype system to measure the frame non-delivery probability p_l against c, where $c^3 = b^3/n$, to compare against the analytical result presented in Figure 5 in Sec. IV-A. We run two sets of experiments: one set over the HKUST campus LAN only and the second set over PlanetLab.

For experiments over the campus LAN, we deploy over 100 peers. Since all the machines are on the campus LAN, we add an artificial propagation delay of A in some of our experiments to better understand how the protocol would perform over a wide area. As shown in Figure 12, with $A=100$ and $d_s=50$ msec, the experimental results match the analytic model and the synchronous model simulation results in trend very well regardless of the number of peers n. Another observation is that in the LAN environment, with $A=0$ and $d_s=0$, the frame non-delivery probability remains high and becomes worse

than the analytic result when c is increased. This can be understood from Sec. III-B1 where the reason for introducing the delay response d_s is explained. But once a delayed response $d_s = 50$ *ms* is applied when $A=0$, the performance is greatly improved and is much better than what the analytical model predicts. This can be explained by the bonus relay effect - when the propagation delay is small, there is a larger probability for the GREETING message from a source that contains information frame to have arrived at a peer before that peer launches its GREETING messages, leading to additional chances for spreading of the information frame.

For experiments over PlanetLab, because of the overloading conditions of PlanetLab as discussed above, we can only conduct measurements with 19 peers: 9 machines in the US, each supporting one peer instance, and 5 machines on the HKUST campus, each supporting two peer instances, as shown in Table 1.

Table 1 List of the planet lamb machines in use

1	PLANET11.CSC.NCSU.EDU
2	PLANETLAB1.CSUOHIO.EDU
3	PLANETLAB-2.CALPOLY-NETLAB.NET
4	PLANETLAB2.CS.COLORADO.EDU
5	PLANETLAB2.CS.UML.EDU
6	PLANETLAB2.CSUOHIO.EDU
7	PLANETLAB-3.ICS.UCI.EDU
8	PLANETLAB6.CSEE.USF.EDU
9	PLGMU5.ITE.GMU.EDU

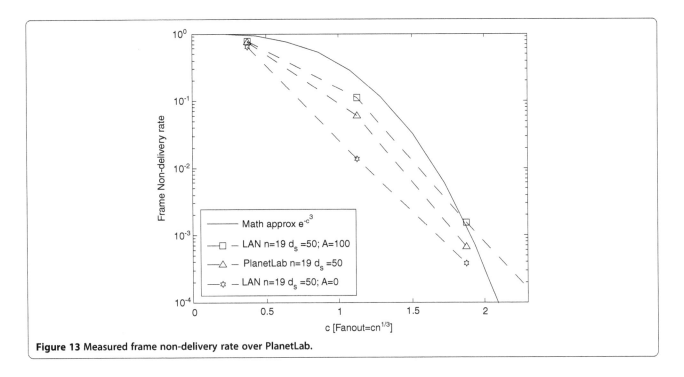

Figure 13 Measured frame non-delivery rate over PlanetLab.

For comparison, we also run experiments over the campus network with 19 peers. As shown in Figure 13, for $d_s=50$ and $n=19$, the performance of the PlanetLab falls between that of the campus network with $A=0$ and with $A=100$. This can be understood by the fact that some of the delays over the PlanetLab are larger than the offset in the cycle launch times of peers so that the chance of bonus relay is smaller over PlanetLab than over the campus network with no artificial delay. Therefore, the performance over PlanetLab is not as good as that over the campus network with no artificial delay.

Figure 14 plots p_l against the traffic load D, which is again the measured average number of the same frame received by each peer. As discussed before, D is an important measure that provides insight into the efficiency of the protocol. We observe in Figure 14 that when

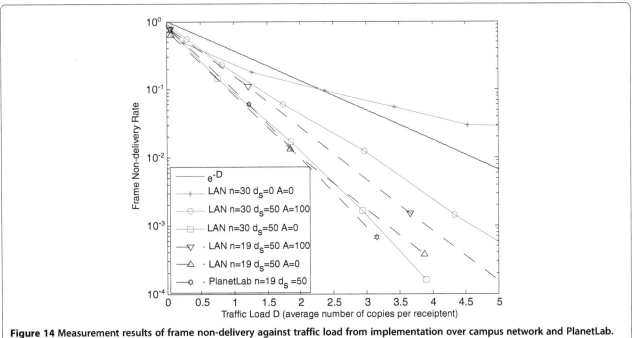

Figure 14 Measurement results of frame non-delivery against traffic load from implementation over campus network and PlanetLab.

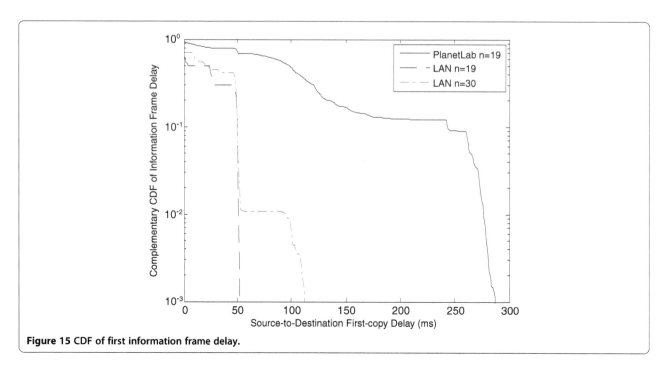

Figure 15 CDF of first information frame delay.

there is no delayed response ($d_s = 0$), the performance will not be as good as when d_s is set to 50 msec without a large artificial delay of $A=100$ inserted. We have conducted a larger scale experiment on the campus network with 100 peers and observed similar performances to that in the 30-peer case. In general, the results show that the protocol is capable of achieving a non-delivery probability of 10^{-2} to 10^{-3} with a traffic load of 2 to 3.

Those experimental scenarios with larger delays (e.g. LAN $A=100$ and PlanetLab) do not benefit much from

the bonus relay, as explained in Sec. IV-B and Figure 7. This explains why the results shown in Figures 12, 13 and 14 indicate that experimental scenarios with larger delay produce what are much closer to the analytical results than those with smaller delays.

Another important performance measure is the information delay of the protocol as the protocol is targeted for real-time communication. We define information delay as the difference between the first copy arrival time of an information frame at a receiving peer and the

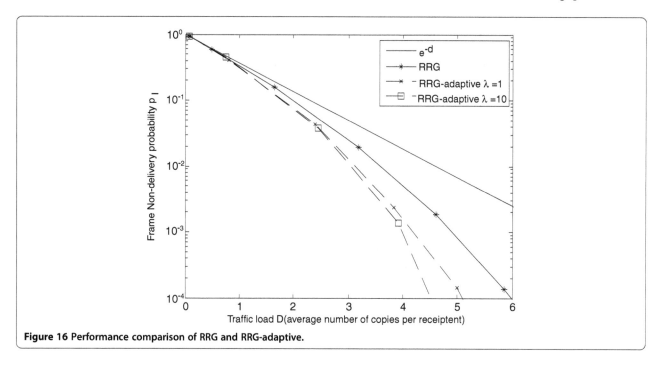

Figure 16 Performance comparison of RRG and RRG-adaptive.

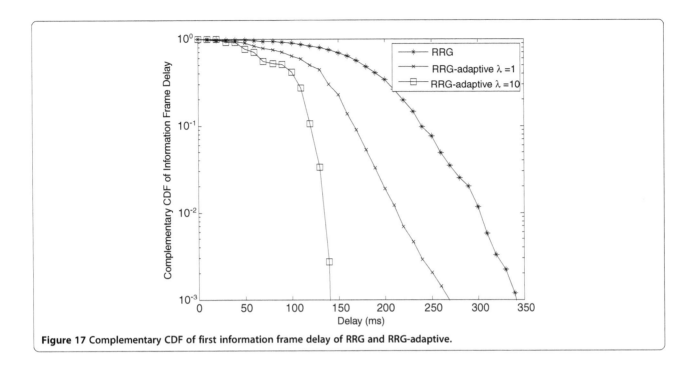

Figure 17 Complementary CDF of first information frame delay of RRG and RRG-adaptive.

generation time of the frame at the source. The clocks of all peers are synchronized using NTP throughout the experiment, and the clock drifts of the different machines are also examined to ensure that the end-to-end delay measurements are as accurate as possible. Figure 15 shows the CDF of the measured information delays with $d_s = 50$ ms. We observe that the 99.9-percentile of the first-copy delay is less than 120 ms over the campus LAN and less than 300 ms even over the cross-continent PlanetLab. Adding to this information delay a packetization and coding delay of, say, 50 ms the absolute one-way delay should be within the maximum limit of the 400ms for voice communications as specified in [16]; although, it will be quite a challenge to reduce the absolute delay to within 150 ms for transparent interactivity.

Finally, we use the prototype system to study the network behavior when the network experiences membership changes. In the case of a 30% decrease in group size, the non-delivery probability converges in less than 70 cycles (1.4 sec). In the case of a 30% sudden increase in group size, the convergence time is much shorter as new peers are quickly learned by other peers through their GREETINGS and subsequent gossip exchanges. Results are omitted here as they are similar to Figure 9 in Sec. IV-C.

VI. Future direction

There can be several directions for future improvements on the proposed RRG protocol. One is to make it adaptive to the traffic conditions. The RRG proposed so far changes its connectivity each cycle. But if some

links have low latency, we can give higher priority to those links when the topology is generated in the next cycle. This has been explored in other gossip-based protocols [28,63,68].

To see if the same idea can improve RRG, we have simulated an extension of RRG, named as RRG-adaptive, with some capabilities in being adaptive to traffic conditions. The simulation setup for the improved protocol is the same as in Sec. V-B. Peers use the latency information learned by past cycles and sort other peers into a descending order of latency as $p = [p_1, p_2, ..., p_{n-1}]$. The selections of new peers in the next cycle will follow the following PDF $f(p_i, \lambda) = \lambda e^{-\lambda p_i}$, where λ is the parameter tuning the degree of preference for choosing lower latency peers. Of course, other distributions can also be used as long as they prefer lower latency peers.

Figure 16 compares the non-delivery probability between the RRG and RRG-adaptive. We can observe that RRG-adaptive requires slightly less traffic load than RRG to achieve the same non-delivery probability. We can also see that the performance gain of RRG-adaptive is higher in larger λ. This can be expected because, as

Table 2 Recovery time of RRG/RRG-adaptive under user churn

	Recovery time (sec)
RRG	1.12
RRG-adaptive $\lambda = 1$	1.2
RRG-adaptive $\lambda = 10$	6.34

shown in Figure 7, the phenomenon of bonus relay (see Sec. V-B) occurs more frequently when round trip delay is lower. Figure 17 compares the delay performance. It shows how the delay is reduced as a function of λ. We observe that the 99-percentile of the information delay of RRG-adaptive with $\lambda = 10$ is only half of that of RRG.

The adaptive peer selection results in a longer recovery time of user churn. We define recovery time as the convergence time of non-delivery probability in an event of user churn. Table 2 shows the recovery time of RRG and RRG-adaptive schemes under –80% sudden change of the original group size. We can observe that RRG-adaptive takes a longer time for recovery than RRG. We can also see the longer recovery time in larger λ. The adaptive scheme reduces the randomness of gossip and weakens its churn coping capability. We plan to study this tradeoff thoroughly in the future. Past knowledge learnt apart from latency, such as network topology or heterogeneous peer capabilities, can be considered in a randomized choice [28,50,68,82].

Another area for further work is to consider ways for suppressing redundant information delivery to further improve bandwidth efficiency. There is also an increasing interest in allowing the sources to adjust their coding rates to match the network conditions and peer capabilities (e.g. multi-rate and adaptive coded video sources) [42,83]. The idea is also applicable to RRG.

VII. Conclusions

In this paper, we present a novel protocol, called Redundancy Reduced Gossip, for real-time N-to-N dynamic group communication. The protocol allows multiple sources to distribute information across a group with low latency, minimal membership maintenance, and without an assumption on the underlying network condition. We have shown that a considerably lower traffic load than conventional push gossip protocols and conventional push-pull gossip protocols can be achieved with the same probability of successful delivery. We have also shown that better performance can be achieved in networks with smaller delays and when a delay response strategy is added to RRG, which is an asynchronous gossip protocol. We have derived a mathematical model for the frame non-delivery probability and overhead of the protocol. This model provides important insights into the design of our protocol and has been used to evaluate the performance of other related protocols. A functional prototype system has been implemented in C on the Linux platform. Its design is described, and it has been used to evaluate the performance of our protocol over our campus network as well as over a less organized global network (PlanetLab). Our experiments demonstrate that our protocol can maintain a robust performance in real-world network environments.

Competing interest
The authors declare that they have no competing interest.

Authors' contribution
VWHL, AKSW & CTL designed, implemented and evaluated the protocol and wrote the manuscript. RWO participated in the performance evaluation. All authors read and approved the final manuscript.

Acknowledgement
This work was supported by Hong Kong Research Grant Council project 620410.

Reference
1. IBM (2010) IBM lotus sametime. [Online]. Available: http://www-01.ibm.com/software/lotus/sametime/
2. Google (2010) Google talk. [Online]. Available: http://www.google.com/talk/about.html
3. Skype Limited (2011) Skype video call. [Online]. Available: http://www.skype.com/intl/en-us/features/allfeatures/video-call/
4. Cisco (2010) WebEx solutions. [Online]. Available: http://www.webex.com/about-webex/index.html
5. Cisco (2010) Cisco TelePresense. [Online]. Available: www.cisco.com/web/go/telepresence
6. Polycom Inc (2010) Polycom telepresence solutions. [Online]. Available: http://www.polycom.com/products/telepresence_video/
7. Second Life (2010) Second life. [Online]. Available: http://secondlife.com/whatis/
8. Google (2012) Google hangouts. [Online]. Available: http://www.google.com/+/learnmore/hangouts/
9. EditGrid (2010) EditGrid. [Online]. Available: www.editgrid.com
10. Valve Corporation (2010) Counter-strike. [Online]. Available: http://www.valvesoftware.com/games/
11. Blizzard Entertainment (2010) World of warcraft. [Online]. Available: http://us.blizzard.com/en-us/games/wow/
12. Twitter (2010) Twitter. [Online]. Available: http://twitter.com/about
13. Facebook (2010) Facebook. [Online]. Available: http://www.facebook.com/
14. Five Minutes (2010) Happy farm. [Online]. Available: http://apps.facebook.com/happyfarmers
15. Zynga (2010) Café world. [Online]. Available: http://www.facebook.com/cafeworld?
16. ITU (1993) One-Way Transmission Time. In: ITU-T recommendation G.114. International Telecommunication Union, Geneva, Switzerland
17. Deering SE, Cheriton DR (1990) Multicast routing in datagram internetworks and extended LANs. ACM Trans Comput Syst 8:85–110
18. Lennox J, Schulzrinne H (2003) A protocol for reliable decentralized conferencing. In: NOSSDAV '03: Proceedings of the 13th International Workshop on Network and Operating Systems Support for Digital Audio and Video. , Monterey, CA, USA, pp 72–81
19. Kundan S, Gautam N, Henning S (2001) Centralized conferencing using SIP. In: Proc of the 2nd IP-Telephony Workshop. New York City, New York, USA
20. Baset SA, Schulzrinne H (2004) An analysis of the Skype peer-to-peer internet telephony protocol. In: Proceedings IEEE INFOCOM 2006 25TH IEEE International Conference on Computer Communications. IEEE Computer Society Press, Los Alamitos, CA, USA, pp 1–11
21. Yang-hua Chu SG, Rao S (2002) Seshan and Hui Zhang, A case for end system multicast, Selected Areas in Communications. IEEE Journal on 20:1456–1471
22. Li J, MutualCast (2005) MutualCast: A Serverless Peer-to-Peer Multiparty Real-Time Audio Conferencing System. Multimedia and Expo, 2005. ICME 2005. IEEE International Conference, pp 602–605
23. Irie M, Hyoudou K, Nakayama Y (2005) Tree-based Mixing: A New Communication Model for Voice-Over-IP Conferencing Systems. In: Proceedings of 2005 Internet and Multimedia Systems, and Applications, pp 353–358
24. Gu X, Wen Z, Yu PS, Shae ZY (2005) Supporting multi-party voice-over-IP services with peer-to-peer stream processing. In: Proceedings of the 13th Annual ACM International Conference on Multimedia, pp 303–306

25. Hosseini M, Georganas ND (2006) End System Multicast routing for multi-party videoconferencing applications. Comput Commun 29:2046–2065

26. Tseng S, Huang Y, Lin C (2006) Genetic algorithm for delay- and degree-constrained multimedia broadcasting on overlay networks. Comput Commun 29:3625–3632

27. Akkus IE, Civanlar MR, Ozkasap O (2006) Peer-to-peer multipoint video conferencing using layered video. Image Processing, 2006 IEEE International Conference, Antalya, pp 3053–3056

28. Venkataraman V, Yoshida K, Francis P (2006) Chunkyspread: Heterogeneous unstructured tree-based peer-to-peer multicast. Network Protocols, 2006. ICNP'06. Proceedings of the 2006 14th IEEE International Conference, Santa Barbara, CA, pp 2–11

29. Luo C, Wang W, Tang J, Sun J, Li J (2007) A Multiparty Videoconferencing System Over an Application-Level Multicast Protocol, *Multimedia*. IEEE Transactions on 9:1621–1632

30. Fahmy S, Minseok K (2007) Characterizing Overlay Multicast Networks and Their Costs,. Networking, IEEE/ACM Transactions on 15:373–386

31. Banik SM, Radhakrishnan S, Sekharan CN (2007) Multicast Routing with Delay and Delay Variation Constraints for Collaborative Applications on Overlay Networks, Parallel and Distributed Systems. IEEE Transactions on 18:421–431

32. Lao L, Cui J, Gerla M, Chen S (2007) A Scalable Overlay Multicast Architecture for Large-Scale Applications, Parallel and Distributed Systems. IEEE Transactions on 18:449–459

33. Tu W, Sreenan CJ, Jia W (2007) Worst-Case Delay Control in Multigroup Overlay Networks, Parallel and Distributed Systems. IEEE Transactions on 18:1407–1419

34. Tseng S, Lin C, Huang Y (2008) Ant colony-based algorithm for constructing broadcasting tree with degree and delay constraints. Expert Syst Appl 35:1473–1481

35. Zimmermann R, Liang K (2008) Spatialized audio streaming for networked virtual environments. In: Proceeding of the 16th ACM International Conference on Multimedia. Vancouver, British Columbia, Canada, pp 299–308

36. Nari S, Rabiee HR, Abedi A, Ghanbari M (2009) An efficient algorithm for overlay multicast routing in videoconferencing applications. Computer Communications and Networks, 2009. ICCCN 2009. Proceedings of 18th International Conference, San Francisco, CA, pp 1–6

37. Chia-Hui H, Kai-Wei K, Ho-Ting W (2009) An application layer multi-source multicast with proactive route maintenance. TENCON 2009–2009 IEEE Region 10 Conference, Singapore, pp 1–6

38. Liu Y (2010) Delay Bounds of Chunk-Based Peer-to-Peer Video Streaming, Networking. IEEE/ACM Transactions on 18:1195–1206

39. Liang C, Zhao M, Liu Y (2011) Optimal Bandwidth Sharing in Multiswarm Multiparty P2P Video-Conferencing Systems. Networking, IEEE/ACM Transactions on 19:1704–1716

40. Chen X, Chen M, Li B, Zhao Y, Wu Y, Li J (2011) Celerity: Towards low-delay multi-party conferencing over arbitrary network topologies. In: Proceedings of the 21th International Workshop on Network and Operating Systems Support for Digital Audio and Video (ACM NOSSDAV 2011), Vancouver, Canada

41. Chen X, Chen M, Li B, Zhao Y, Wu Y, Li J (2011) Celerity: A low-delay multi-party conferencing solution. In: Proceedings of the 19th ACM international conference on Multimedia. Scottsdale, Arizona

42. Akkus IE, Ozkasap O, Civanlar MR (2011) Peer-to-peer multipoint video conferencing with layered video. J Netw Comput Appl 34:137–150

43. Verma S, Wei Tsang O (2005) Controlling gossip protocol infection pattern using adaptive fanout. In: Distributed Computing Systems, 2005. ICDCS 2005. Proceedings. 25th IEEE International Conference, Columbus, OH, pp 665–674

44. Georgiou C, Gilbert S, Guerraoui R, Kowalski DR (2008) On the complexity of asynchronous gossip. Proceedings of the Twenty-Seventh ACM Symposium on Principles of Distributed Computing, Canada, Toronto, pp 135–144

45. Ozkasap O, Xiao Z, Birman KP (1999) Scalability of two reliable multicast protocols. Cornell University, Ithaca, NY

46. Tang C, Chang RN, Ward C (2005) GoCast: Gossip-enhanced overlay multicast for fast and dependable group communication. In: Dependable Systems and Networks, 2005. DSN 2005. Proceedings. International Conference, pp 140–149

47. Melamed R, Keidar I (2004) Araneola: A scalable reliable multicast system for dynamic environments,. Network Computing and Applications, 2004. (NCA

2004). Proceedings. Third IEEE International Symposium, Cambridge, MA, USA, pp 5–14

48. Zhang X, Liu J, Li B, Yum TSP (2005) CoolStreaming/DONet: A Data-driven Overlay Network for Peer-to-Peer Live Media Streaming, INFOCOM 2005. 24th Annual Joint Conference of the IEEE Computer and Communications Societies, vol 3. Proceedings IEEE, Miami, p 2102

49. Padmanabhan VN, Wang HJ, Chou PA, Sripanidkulchai K (2002) Distributing streaming media content using cooperative networking. In: Proceedings of the 12th International Workshop on Network and Operating Systems Support for Digital Audio and Video. ACM New York, NY, USA, pp 177–186

50. Gupta I, Kermarrec AM, Ganesh AJ (2006) Efficient and adaptive epidemic-style protocols for reliable and scalable multicast, Parallel and Distributed Systems. IEEE Transactions on 17:593–605

51. Karp R, Schindelhauer C, Shenker S, Vocking B (2000) Randomized rumor spreading. Foundations of Computer Science, 2000. Proceedings. 41st Annual Symposium, Redondo Beach, CA, pp 565–574

52. Eugster PT, Guerraoui R, Kermarrec A, Massoulié L (2004) From Epidemics to Distributed Computing. IEEE Computer 37:60–67

53. Kermarrec AM, Massoulie L, Ganesh AJ (2003) Probabilistic reliable dissemination in large-scale systems, Parallel and Distributed Systems. IEEE Transactions on 14:248–258

54. Demers A, Greene D, Hauser C, Irish W, Larson J, Shenker S, Sturgis H, Swinehart D, Terry D (1987) Epidemic algorithms for replicated database maintenance. In: Proceedings of the Sixth Annual ACM Symposium on Principles of Distributed Computing. ACM New York, NY, USA, pp 1–12

55. Chandra R, Ramasubramanian V, Birman K (2001) Anonymous gossip: Improving multicast reliability in mobile ad-hoc networks. Distributed Computing Systems, 2001. 21st International Conference, pp 275–283

56. Luo J, Eugster PT, Hubaux JP (2003) Route driven gossip: Probabilistic reliable multicast in ad hoc networks, INFOCOM 2003. Twenty-Second Annual Joint Conference of the IEEE Computer and Communications. IIEEE Societies 3:2229–2239. San Francisco, CA

57. Haas ZJ, Halpern JY, Li L (2006) Gossip-based ad hoc routing, Networking. IEEE/ACM Transactions on 14:479–491

58. Chun B, Culler D, Roscoe T, Bavier A, Peterson L, Wawrzoniak M, Bowman M (2003) PlanetLab: an overlay testbed for broad-coverage services. SIGCOMM Comput. Commun Rev 33:3–12

59. Fei H, Ravindran B, Jensen ED (2008) RT-P2P: A scalable real-time peer-to-peer system with probabilistic timing assurances,. Embedded and Ubiquitous Computing, 2008. EUC '08. IEEE/IFIP International Conference, Shanghai, China, pp 97–103

60. Kai H, Ravindran B, Jensen ED (2007) RTG-L: Dependably scheduling real-time distributable threads in large-scale, unreliable networks. Dependable Computing, 2007. PRDC 2007. 13th Pacific Rim International Symposium, Melbourne, Qld, pp 314–321

61. Kempe D, Dobra A, Gehrke J (2003) Gossip-based computation of aggregate information. Foundations of Computer Science, 2003. Proceedings. 44th Annual IEEE Symposium, Cambridge, MA, USA, pp 482–491

62. Mujtaba MK (2003) Push-pull gossiping for information sharing in peer-to-peer communities. In: Proc. International Conference on Parallel and Distributed Processing Techniques and Applications (PDPTA). Las Vegas, pp 1393–1399

63. Leitao J, Pereira J, Rodrigues L (2007) Epidemic broadcast trees. Reliable Distributed Systems, 2007. SRDS 2007. 26th IEEE International Symposium, Beijing, China, pp 301–310

64. Zhang X, Liu J (2004) Gossip based streaming. In: Proceedings of the 13th International World Wide Web Conference on Alternate Track Papers & Posters. ACM New York, NY, USA, pp 250–251

65. Li HC, Clement A, Wong EL, Napper J, Roy I, Alvisi L, Dahlin M (2006) BAR gossip. In: Proceedings of the 7th Symposium on Operating Systems Design and Implementation. USENIX Association, Berkeley, CA, pp 191–204

66. Frey D, Guerraoui R, Kermarrec AM, Monod M (2010) Boosting gossip for live streaming. Peer-to-Peer Computing (P2P), 2010 IEEE Tenth International Conference, Delft, pp 1–10

67. Liang J, Ko SY, Gupta I, Nahrstedt K (2005) MON: On-demand overlays for distributed system management. Proceedings of USENIX WORLDS, Edinburgh

68. Carvalho N, Pereira J, Oliveira R, Rodrigues L (2007) Emergent structure in unstructured epidemic multicast. Dependable Systems and Networks, 2007. DSN'07. 37th Annual IEEE/IFIP International Conference, pp 481–490

69. Vishnumurthy V, Francis P (2006) On overlay construction and random node selection in heterogeneous unstructured P2P networks. In: Proceedings of IEEE INFOCOM'06. , Barcelona, Spain

70. Boyd S, Ghosh A, Prabhakar B, Shah D (2006) Randomized gossip algorithms, Information Theory. IEEE Transactions on 52:2508–2530

71. Ram SS, Nedic A, Veeravalli VV (2009) Asynchronous gossip algorithms for stochastic optimization. Decision and Control, 2009 Held Jointly with the 2009 28th Chinese Control Conference. CDC/CCC 2009. Proceedings of the 48th IEEE Conference on, Shanghai, China, pp 3581–3586

72. Deb S, Medard M, Choute C (2006) Algebraic gossip: a network coding approach to optimal multiple rumor mongering, Information Theory. IEEE Transactions on 52:2486–2507

73. Birman KP, Hayden M, Ozkasap O, Xiao Z, Budiu M, Minsky Y (May, 1999) Bimodal multicast. ACM Trans Comput Syst 17:41–88

74. Luk VWH, Wong AKS, Ouyang RW, Lea CT (2008) Gossip-based delay-sensitive N-to-N information dissemination protocol. IEEE Global Communications Conference IEEE GLOBECOM 2008, pp 1–5

75. Mills D (1992) RFC1305. Internet Engineering Task Force

76. Jelasity M, Montresor A, Babaoglu O (2005) Gossip-based aggregation in large dynamic networks. ACM Trans Comput Syst 23:219–252

77. Wikipedia (2010) Producer consumer problem. [Online]. Available: http://en.wikipedia.org/wiki/Producer-consumer_problem

78. Jim M, Paul E (2010) Usleep(3) - linux man page. [Online]. Available: http://linux.die.net/man/3/usleep

79. Park K, Pai VS (2006) CoMon: a mostly-scalable monitoring system for PlanetLab. SIGOPS Oper Syst Rev 40:65–74

80. PlanetLab (2010) Sirius calendar service. [Online]. Available: https://www.planet-lab.org/db/sirius/index.php

81. PlanetLab (2010) Sirius upgrade. [Online]. Available: http://www.planet-lab.org/node/5

82. Liang C, Guo Y, Liu Y (2008) Is random scheduling sufficient in p2p video streaming?. Distributed Computing Systems, 2008. ICDCS'08. the 28th International Conference, Beijing, China, pp 53–60

83. Ponec M, Sengupta S, Chen M, Li J, Chou PA (2009) Multi-rate peer-to-peer video conferencing: A distributed approach using scalable coding. In: Multimedia and Expo, 2009. ICME 2009. IEEE International Conference on, pp 1406–1413

9

A survey on predicting the popularity of web content

Alexandru Tatar[1*], Marcelo Dias de Amorim[1], Serge Fdida[1] and Panayotis Antoniadis[2]

Abstract

Social media platforms have democratized the process of web content creation allowing mere consumers to become creators and distributors of content. But this has also contributed to an explosive growth of information and has intensified the online competition for users attention, since only a small number of items become popular while the rest remain unknown. Understanding what makes one item more popular than another, observing its popularity dynamics, and being able to predict its popularity has thus attracted a lot of interest in the past few years. Predicting the popularity of web content is useful in many areas such as network dimensioning (e.g., caching and replication), online marketing (e.g., recommendation systems and media advertising), or real-world outcome prediction (e.g., economical trends). In this survey, we review the current findings on web content popularity prediction. We describe the different popularity prediction models, present the features that have shown good predictive capabilities, and reveal factors known to influence web content popularity.

Keywords: Web content; Social media; Popularity; Prediction

1 Introduction

In the digital world, web content has become the main attraction. Whether it is useful information and entertainment to Internet users or a business opportunity for marketing companies and content providers, web content is a valuable asset on the Internet. At the same time, the growth in social media innovation, the ease of content creation and low publishing costs has created a world saturated with information. For example, every minute, users around the world send more than 300,000 tweets [1], share more than 680,000 pieces of content on Facebook [2], and upload 100 hours of video on YouTube [3]. Yet the online ecosystem adheres to a "winner-take-all" society: the attention is concentrated on only a few items. In this context, identifying the web content that will become popular becomes of utmost importance. Online users, flooded by information, can reduce the clutter and focus their attention – the most valuable resource in the online world – on the most relevant information for them. In a world where companies spend up to 30% of their budget on online marketing [4], early detection of the next rising

star of the Internet can maximize their revenues through better ad placement. Moreover, given the ever-growing consumer Internet traffic, content-distribution networks can rely on popularity prediction methods to proactively allocate resources according to the future users' demand.

But predicting the popularity of web content is a challenging task. First, different factors known to influence content popularity, such as the quality of the content or its relevance to users, are difficult to measure. Then, other factors, such as the relationship between events in the physical world and the content itself are hard to capture and included in a prediction model. Moreover, at a microscopic level, the evolution of content popularity may be described by complex online interactions and information cascades that are difficult to predict [5-7].

Predicting the popularity of web content has become an active area of research and, while still in an incipient phase, a large number of prediction methods for different types of web content have been proposed in the latest years. In this article we review the current state of research in this field, identify trends, and suggest domains that can benefit from these studies. To the best of our knowledge there has been no prior attempt to summarize this research area. The closest to our work is the

*Correspondence: tatar@npa.lip6.fr
[1] LIP6/CNRS – UPMC Sorbonne Universités, 4 Place Jussieu, 75005 Paris, France
Full list of author information is available at the end of the article

survey proposed by Yu and Kak, which describes the different real-life outcomes that can be predicted using social media (e.g., election results, box-office revenues, marketing impact) [8]. In our work we focus on a different prediction objective related to social media: predicting the amount of attention that web content will generate on the Internet.

The remainder of the paper is organized as follows. We narrow down the scope of this survey in Section 2 and briefly review the evolution of this research area in Section 3. We continue with a presentation of the most popular types of web content analyzed so far (Section 4) and describe the measures used to evaluate the prediction performance (Section 5). In order to structure the prediction methods, we propose a classification in Section 6 and describe the prediction methods based on this classification in Section 7. We present the factors known to influence content popularity (Section 8) and review the predictive features that have already been used in a prediction model in Section 9. Finally, we conclude with a presentation of some representative domains that could benefit from web content popularity prediction (Section 10) and look at potential future directions in Section 11.

2   Scope of the survey

Let us now define the scope of this survey. The term *web content* is effectively generic as it broadly defines any type of information on a web site. It can refer both to the subject of the information and the individual item used to deliver the information. In this survey we define web content as any individual item (in the form of text, image, audio, or video), publicly available on a web site, which contains a measure that reflects a certain level of interest showed by an online community.

On the Internet, the popularity of web content can have different connotations. If by content we refer to the subject of the content, such as a person or an organization, then popularity could be expressed by a greater web presence or activity. From a different perspective, one may see web content as an individual web link and define popularity as the popularity of the link (the quantity and quality of inbound links). For the scope of this survey, we consider popularity from the standpoint of the relationship between an individual item and the online users who consume it.

Seen from this perspective, there are different metrics used to quantitatively evaluate web content popularity. The classical way of doing this is to measure the number of views. However, this information is often hidden from the online users and crawling engines. For example, social networking sites, for various reasons, usually do not disclose this information to the online users [9].

But nowadays, with the growing prevalence of Web 2.0 platforms, there are new indicators – publicly available – that reflect users' interest. In response to the publication of a web content, users can now provide a direct feedback, through comments and ratings, or further share it in their online social circles (using, for example, Facebook, Twitter, or Digg). These metrics capture different levels of user engagement and provide valuable information, complementary to view counts: rating improves the quality of publications, comments increase the time spent on a web page, and sharing gives content a greater notoriety. In general, it has been observed that there is a moderate correlation between the different popularity metrics [9-13], as they probably capture different types of habits on the Internet (to observe, comment, rate, or share). In this context, studying these metrics individually or how they relate to each other [14,15] provides a wider and better perspective of what the popularity of a web content actually means.

3   A brief history of the evolution of popularity prediction methods

The beginning of this research area can be found in the early studies on users' web access patterns [16-19]. An important observation of these initial studies was that the distribution of users' requests for web pages is highly skewed and could be described by a Zipf's law [18]. Online videos, accounting for a significant amount of Internet traffic, have been one of the main attraction of these early measurements [20-27]. During this initial phase, researchers have looked at the degree of skewness in the popularity of videos [20,21,24,25] (to determine potential benefit of caching videos) and analyzed which probability distribution best describes the video access patterns (to understand the mechanism that explains users' consumption patterns [28]). These studies revealed that the interest generated by a web content is transient, heterogeneous, and often unpredictable [24,28].

After the properties of Web access patterns have been sufficiently well understood the challenge became to actually predict content popularity [29,30]. The first prediction methods were built on the observation that there is a strong positive correlation between the popularity of a web content at different stages during its lifetime [28,30]. As a result the first prediction methods consisted in linear regression functions that use the amount of attention that a web content generates early after publication to predict its popularity afterwards. The prevalence of Web 2.0 platforms, rich in metadata about how users interact with the web content and with peer online readers have further contributed to a fast evolution of this research area. Prediction methods based on the online social connections created between the users have been proposed, content published on various web sites has been analyzed, and different measures about web content popularity have been considered.

These initial prediction methods were simple but often inaccurate for web content that remains attractive for longer periods of time [30]. An important step forward has been made with the finding that the evolution of web content popularity over time can be described by a only small number of temporal patterns [31,32]. Thus, more accurate prediction methods that include information about the evolution patterns of content popularity, have been proposed [32-34]. But the content published on a web site is part of a global information ecosystem as it can spread on several web sites and reach consumers through different communication mediums. So, a further breakthrough in the design of more accurate prediction methods has been made with the development of algorithms that can extract and cross-correlate information from different web domains [14,35,36].

4 Types of web content

Users attention is spread across multiple web sites and various types of web content. Some of the most popular types of web content studied so far include: user-generated videos that account for a great percent of Internet traffic [37]; news articles, massively diffused through social networking sites [38] and heavily consumed on mobile devices [39]; stories published on social news aggregators that provide an even greater exposure to the most popular content on the Internet; and items (comments, photos, or videos) published on social networking sites, the most popular platforms to share information and encourage users' participation on a global scale.

Examples of the variety of web content, gathered from different web sites and used in the context of popularity prediction, are illustrated in Figure 1, together with information about the number of items and the time period covered by each data set.

Online videos. YouTube, the world's largest video sharing platform with 100 hours of upload per minute [3] and more than 1 trillion worldwide views per year [40], has been the main focus of the existing studies. The site's content, with more than 200 million unique videos, covers a broad range of topics and is sustained by a big and active online community [41]. Studying the popularity of YouTube content is challenging given the ever-growing number of videos, the many features that the platform provides (e.g., video recommendations, internal search, online social networking), and the limitations associated with the retrieval of a representative sample of videos [42].

The popularity of YouTube videos, commonly expressed by the number of views in research studies, follows a heavy-tailed distribution that, depending on the data set and the method used to fit the distribution, can be described by power-law with exponential cut-off [28], Weibull [41], log-normal [42], or Gamma distributions [43]. But the popularity of videos over time is highly non-stationary. From a high-level point of view, the popularity growth of videos over time can be represented by power-law or exponential distributions [44]. A more fine-grained analysis exhibits even more complex and diverse patterns. For instance, Crane and Sornette found that, while the activity around most YouTube videos can be described by a Poisson process, many videos reveal similar activity around the peak period that can be accurately described by three popularity evolution patterns [31]. Similar temporal evolution patterns have been observed by Figueiredo [45] and even more diverse shapes have been discovered by Gorsun et al. [32].

In addition to YouTube, the popularity of videos published on other platforms has been studied (e.g., Daum [28], Dutch TV [44], DailyMotion [46,47], Yahoo! video [47], Veoh [47], Metacafe [47], Vimeo [34]), but on a smaller scale, and no significant differences have been signaled in terms of popularity distributions.

Online news. The primary source of information in the digital world, news, are created in large numbers and massively diffused through online social networks [38]. Compared to videos that catch users' attention for a longer period of time, the interest in news articles fades quickly, within days after publication [14,48]. The popularity of online news, frequently expressed by the number of comments (the number of views are rarely disclosed by news platforms), is also highly skewed, and can be described by power-law [49,50] or log-normal [51] distributions.

Social bookmarking sites. The third major type of web content analyzed so far is represented by stories posted on social bookmarking sites such as Digg [30,52,53], Slashdot [29], or Reddit [53,54]. Content published on these sites experiences an even greater rate of change with stories reaching their attention peak in the first six hours after publication and being completely saturated within one day [30]. Prediction becomes even more difficult in this setting given the complex interactions between users [55,56] and the promotion algorithm based on the collective opinion of users [57,58]. The popularity of the content published on these sites is described by a heavy-tailed nature that is best represented by Weibull [53] or log-normal distributions [30,52,59].

Social networking services. Designed with the idea of facilitating interactions among people on the Internet,

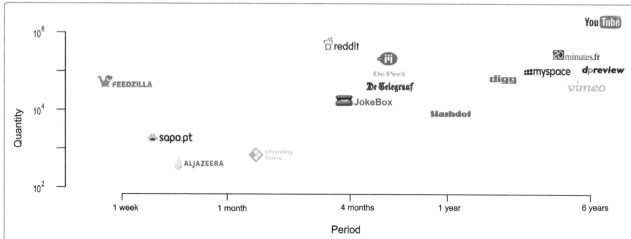

Figure 1 Data sets used as case studies to evaluate the performance of prediction methods. On a log-log scale we depict the total number of items and the cumulative time period covered by each data set.

these sites allow users to build and maintain online social relationships with people that share common interest, background, or real-life relationships. While there are different types of social networking services the most popular are the ones built on the idea of content sharing. Microblogs, such as Twitter and Weibo, are a specific type of social networking services that have been extensively studied. These platforms are probably the most dynamic representation of social media. Users create and share information in the form of short messages, known as tweets, containing up to 140 characters. When a user posts a (re)tweet it becomes visible to all its followers (i.e., members of the social group). Content can easily spread through the social connectivity graphs as followers can further share the content to their own list of followers. Two metrics have been used to measure the popularity of a tweet: the number of users that receive a message in their tweet feed [60], or most commonly, the number of retweets. The popularity of tweets is also highly skewed and can be described by a power-law distribution [61-63].

Tweets are probably one the most ephemeral type of web content as they become popular very fast and they quickly die out. For example, studies conducted on Tencent Weibo found out that an insignificant number of tweets get retweeted after one day [63]. Similarly, a study on Twitter revealed that most tweets receive half of their retweets within the first hour after publication [64]. Useful predictions thus need to be done in the order of minutes after the post of a tweet.

In addition to these main categories, content published on other web sites have been used for popularity prediction tasks such as threads published on discussion forums (DPReview, MySpace [65]) and movie ratings on

IMDb [36]. Due to the relevancy of the results we also include in our analysis the prediction results for the content published on two applications: an interactive video sharing application (Zync) [66] and a joke sharing application (JokeBox) [67].

5 Evaluating the prediction models

To provide a more explicit description of the prediction algorithms, let us introduce the terminology and the measures used to evaluate the efficiency of the prediction methods.

Terminology. Let $c \in C$ be an individual item from a set C observed during a period T. We use $t \in T$ to describe the age of an item (i.e., duration since the time it was published) and mark two important moments: indication time t_i, representing the time we perform the prediction and reference time t_r, the moment of time when we want to predict content popularity. Let $N_c(t_i)$ be the popularity of c from the time it was published until t_i and let $N_c(t_r)$ be the value that we want to predict, i.e., the popularity at a later time t_r. We define $\widehat{N}_c(t_i, t_r)$ the prediction outcome: the predicted popularity of c at t_r using the information available until t_i. Thus, the better the prediction, the closer $\widehat{N}_c(t_i, t_r)$ is to $N_c(t_r)$.

Evaluation. We distinguish two prediction goals: (i) Numerical prediction – predict the exact value of the popularity, (ii) Classification – predict the popularity range that an item is most likely to fall in.

5.1 Numerical prediction

There are different ways to assess the efficiency of a numerical prediction [68]. Mean Squared Error (MSE – Equation 1) is used to report the average of the squared errors. By taking the square root of MSE, one can express the error in the same dimension as the estimated value (RMSE – Equation 2). One important limitation of squared errors is that they put too much weight on the effect of outliers, and in this case reporting the absolute errors is a good alternative (MAE – Equation 3).

Absolute errors can be meaningfully interpreted if one knows the range of the actual popularity values. Otherwise, a good way of expressing the prediction performance is through relative errors such as the Mean Relative Error (MRE – Equation 4) and Mean Relative Squared Error (MRSE – Equation 5). Relative measures are also useful to compare the efficiency of prediction algorithm across studies, as in most cases the popularity values have widely different ranges (e.g., the number of views on YouTube is several orders of magnitude greater than the number of comments on a news web site). Special attention should be paid when using these error measures for zero-inflated variables as the relative error is undefined when the actual value is zero.

Another way of expressing the prediction error is through the Relative Squared Error (RSE – Equation 6), Root Relative Squared Error (RRSE – Equation 7), and Relative Absolute Error (RAE – Equation 8). The error in this case is expressed relative to the performance of a simple predictor, the average of the actual values (computed on the training data set).

The quality of a numerical prediction can also be reported using the correlation coefficient or the coefficient of determination (R^2). Compared to the previous measures, which show how the estimated values diverge from the actual ones, these evaluation criteria can only express the degree of linear association between the two variables (predicted and actual values).

$$\text{MSE} = \frac{1}{|C|} \sum_{c \in C} \left(\widehat{N}_c(t_i, t_r) - N_c(t_r) \right)^2.$$ (1)

$$\text{RMSE} = \sqrt{\frac{1}{|C|} \sum_{c \in C} \left(\widehat{N}_c(t_i, t_r) - N_c(t_r) \right)^2}.$$ (2)

$$\text{MAE} = \frac{1}{|C|} \sum_{c \in C} \left| \widehat{N}_c(t_i, t_r) - N_c(t_r) \right|.$$ (3)

$$\text{MRE} = \frac{1}{|C|} \sum_{c \in C} \left| \frac{\widehat{N}_c(t_i, t_r) - N_c(t_r)}{N_c(t_r)} \right|.$$ (4)

$$\text{MRSE} = \frac{1}{|C|} \sum_{c \in C} \left(\frac{\widehat{N}_c(t_i, t_r) - N_c(t_r)}{N_c(t_r)} \right)^2.$$ (5)

$$\text{RSE} = \frac{\sum_{c \in C} \left(\widehat{N}_c(t_i, t_r) - N_c(t_r) \right)^2}{\sum_{c \in C} \left(\widehat{N}_c(t_r - \overline{N}(t_r) \right)^2}.$$ (6)

$$\text{RRSE} = \sqrt{\frac{\sum_{c \in C} \left(\widehat{N}_c(t_i, t_r) - N_c(t_r) \right)^2}{\sum_{c \in C} \left(\widehat{N}_c(t_r - \overline{N}(t_r) \right)^2}}.$$ (7)

$$\text{RAE} = \frac{\sum_{c \in C} \left| \widehat{N}_c(t_i, t_r) - N_c(t_r) \right|}{\sum_{c \in C} \left| (\widehat{N}_c(t_r - \overline{N}(t_r) \right|}.$$ (8)

5.2 Classification

This prediction problem can also be addressed as a classification task, where, assuming that the popularity range is known, one can split this interval in k non-overlapping popularity ranges. Thus, given the k possible outcomes the prediction goal is to correctly predict the popularity class of a web content.

Various metrics are available to evaluate the quality of a classification method [68,69]. *Accuracy*, one of the most reported metric, is used to express the proportion of correctly classified instances. This measure is nevertheless inappropriate when dealing with highly imbalanced classes, which can often be the case when referring to web content popularity, characterized by a heavy-tail nature. For example, a possible experiment could be to learn a classifier that predicts which videos will get more that 10^6 views on YouTube - a "small" class (1%) according to a recent study [70]. A simple rule, that decides that all videos receive less than 10^6 views, will correctly predict 99% of the cases. Thus, a good level of accuracy is obtained without even learning any prediction rule on how to detect the popular items.

To measure the performance of the classifier on a "small" class, a good alternative is to use *precision, recall,* or *F-score* (the harmonic mean between *precision* and *recall*). But *F-score* measures the performance of a classifier for only one class. To report the aggregate performance over multiple classes, a good solution is to use the *macro-average* measure (average *F-score* over all k classes).

6 A classification of web content popularity prediction methods

To structure the prediction methods, we propose a classification that groups the methods according to the type

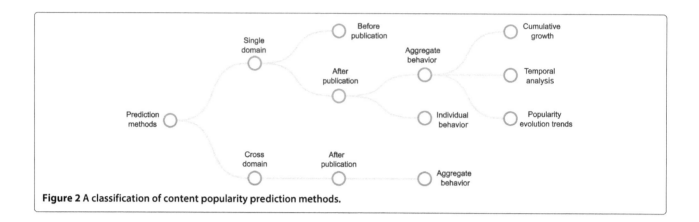

Figure 2 A classification of content popularity prediction methods.

and the granularity of information used in the prediction process (Figure 2).

6.1 Single domain

We define a domain as the web site where an individual item resides, regardless if it has been created or shared from an external source (e.g., news article shared on social bookmarking sites). Methods under this category are used to predict content popularity using only the information available on the web site.

6.1.1 Before publication

One of the most challenging objectives is to predict the popularity before the publication of a web content, relying only on content metadata or the online social connections of the publisher.

6.1.2 After publication

The alternative is to include in the prediction model data about the attention that one item receives after its publication.

Aggregate behavior. A common approach is to deduce future content popularity using the aggregate users' attention after the publication of a web content. This solution can further be separated in three main categories:

- Study the *cumulative growth* of attention, i.e., the amount of attention that one item receives from the moment it was published until the prediction moment.
- Perform a *temporal analysis* of how content popularity evolves over time until the prediction moment.
- Use clustering methods to find web items with similar *popularity evolution trends*.

Individual behavior. Instead of treating each user's action equally, one may further refine the prediction model by taking into account individual user behavior.

6.2 Cross domain

Explaining popularity from the perspective of single domain is limited due to the complex users' interactions across different platforms. Methods under this class draw conclusions by extracting and transferring information across web sites.

7 A survey on popularity prediction methods

Several popularity prediction methods have been proposed in the last decade, from simple linear regression functions to complex frameworks that cross-correlate information from different web sites. We describe these methods following the classification proposed in Section 6 and present their performance on predicting the popularity of different types of web content. A summary of these methods is also presented in Table 1.

7.1 Single domain

In the vast majority of cases, prediction methods rely entirely on the information available on the web site where content has been published.

7.1.1 Before publication

Predicting the popularity of an item before its publication is particularly useful for web content characterized by a short lifespan. News articles, which are time-sensitive by nature, fall under this category and have been analyzed in two studies [71,72].

Tsakias et al. address this prediction task as a two-steps classification problem: predict if news articles will receive comments and if they do, if the number of comments will be high or low [71]. The proposed prediction method is a random forest classifier trained on a large number of features (textual, semantic, and real-world). Using several Dutch online news sources the authors show that one can accurately predict which articles will receive comments and observe that the performance degrades significantly

Table 1 Summary of the popularity prediction methods presented in the survey

Class	Methods	Data sets	Benchmark model	Performance/Remarks
Before publication	SVM, Naive Bayes, Bagging, Decision Trees, Regression [72]	Feedzilla		Shows an accuracy of 84% in predicting the popularity range of a news article.
Before publication	Random Forests [71]	AD, De Pers, FD, NUjiji, Spits, Telegraaf, Trpuw, WMR		Good performance in identifying which articles will receive at least one comment.
Cumulative growth	Constant growth [29]	Slashdot		Good performance in predicting the number of comments one day after the publication of an article (MSE = 36%).
Cumulative growth	Constant scaling [30]	Digg, YouTube	Constant growth, Log-linear	Outperforms the constant growth and the log-linear models in terms of MRSE.
Cumulative growth	Log-linear [30]	Digg, YouTube	Constant growth, Constant scaling	Outperforms the constant growth and the constant scaling models in terms of MSE.
Cumulative growth	Survival analysis [65]	DPreview, MySpace		Using the information received in the first day after the publication it can detect with 80% accuracy which threads will receive more than 100 comments.
Cumulative growth	Logistic regression [61]	Twitter		The model can successfully identify which messages will not be retweeted (99% accuracy) and those that will be retweeted more than 10,000 times (98% accuracy).
Temporal analysis	Multivariate linear regression [33]	YouTube	Constant scaling	An average improvement of 15% in terms of MRSE compared to the constant scaling model.
Temporal analysis	Reservoir computing [77]	YouTube	Constant scaling	Minor improvement compared to the constant scaling model.
Temporal analysis	Time series prediction [32]	YouTube		Designed for frequently-accessed videos. Good performance in predicting the daily number of views.
Temporal analysis	kSAIT [63]	Twitter	Regression-based methods	Predict the number of tweets using information from the first hour after content publication. An improvement of up to 10% compared to regression-based methods.
Popularity evolution patterns	Hierarchical clustering [32]	YouTube		Designed for rarely-accessed videos. The model shows good performance for short-term predictions but significantly larger ones for long-term predictions.
Popularity evolution patterns	MRBF [33]	YouTube	Constant scaling, Multivariate linear regression	An average improvement of 5% in terms of MRSE compared to multivariate linear regression and 21% compared to constant scaling model.
Popularity evolution patterns	Temporal-evolution prediction [34]	YouTube, Vimeo, Digg	Log-linear	Significant improvement compared to the log-linear method. The model can be used to predict the temporal evolution of popularity.
Individual behavior	Social dynamics [81]	Digg	Log-linear	It incorporates information about the design of the web site. Shows an accuracy of 95% in identifying which articles will get on Digg's front page.
Individual behavior	Conformer Maverick [67]	JokeBox	Collaborative filtering solutions	Adequate for platforms that rank content based on user votes. Better performances than collaborative filtering solutions.
Individual behavior	Bayessian networks [64]	Twitter		MRE of 40% when predicting the total number of tweets using the information received in the first five minutes after publication.
Cross-domain	Linear regression [36]	IMDb, Twitter, YouTube		Designed to predict movie ratings using social media signals. The best performance was achieved when using textual features from Twitter and the fraction of likes over dislikes from YouTube.

Table 1 Summary of the popularity prediction methods presented in the survey *(Continued)*

Cross-domain	Linear regression [14]	Al Jazeera		Results show that a model based on social media reactions in the first ten minutes has the same performance as one based on the number of views received in the first three hours.
Cross-domain	Social transfer [35]	YouTube, Twitter	SVM basic	Shows a 70% accuracy in identifying which videos will receive sudden bursts of popularity (60% improvement over a model that uses only the information available on YouTube).

when trying to predict if the volume of comments will be high or low.

Bandari et al., using the number of tweets as an indicator of news popularity, formulate the prediction task both as a numerical and a classification problem [72]. The authors show that predicting the exact popularity of news articles is prone to large errors ($R^2 = 0.34$), but that predicting ranges of popularity is more effective, with an accuracy of 84% when identifying articles that would receive a small, medium, or large number of tweets.

7.1.2 After publication

Aggregate behavior The methods under this category have been used to predict web content popularity based on the aggregate users' attention received early after content publication.

Cumulative growth. One of the first solutions, used to predict the popularity of Slashdot stories, is proposed by Kaltenbrunner et al. [29]. The model, which we will refer to as `growth profile` (we adopt the terminology used in [30]), assumes that, depending on the time of the publication, news stories follow a constant growth that can be described by the following function:

$$\widehat{N}_c(t_i, t_r) = \frac{N_c(t_i)}{P(t_i, t_r)}, \tag{9}$$

where $P(t_i, t_r)$ is a rescaling parameter and represents the average growth of a story from t_i to t_r

$$P(t_i, t_r) = \frac{1}{|C|} \sum_{c \in C} \frac{N_c(t_i)}{N_c(t_r)}. \tag{10}$$

The effectiveness of this method was tested on a large corpus of Slashdot stories and shows a reasonable performance in predicting the popularity of stories using the aggregate users' reactions in the first day after news publication (average MRE of 36%).

Describing future popularity as a linear relationship of the popularity at earlier stages is also proposed by Szabo and Huberman under the `constant scaling` model [30]:

$$\widehat{N}_c(t_i, t_r) = \alpha_2(t_i, t_r) N_c(t_i). \tag{11}$$

Parameter α is computed in such a way that the model minimizes MRSE and is described by the following expression:

$$\alpha(t_i, t_r) = \frac{\sum_{c \in C} \frac{N_c(t_i)}{N_c(t_r)}}{\sum_{c \in C} \left[\frac{N_c(t_i)}{N_c(t_r)}\right]^2}. \tag{12}$$

Szabo and Huberman also observe a positive correlation between the popularity of an item early after its publication and its popularity at a later stage and propose a logarithmically transformed linear regression model (`log-linear`) expressed as

$$\widehat{N}_c(t_i, t_r) = \exp\left(\ln N_c(t_i) + \beta_0(t_i, t_r) + \frac{\sigma_0^2(t_i, t_r)}{2}\right). \tag{13}$$

For the coefficients of Equation 13, β_0 is computed on the training set using maximum likelihood parameter estimation on the regression function $\ln N_c(t_r) = \beta_0(t_i, t_r) + \ln N_c(t_i)$ and σ_0^2 is the estimate of the variance of the residuals on a logarithmic scale.

This method shows good predictive performance on several data sets: Digg stories [30], YouTube videos [30], articles published on a French news platform [73], and Dutch online news articles [51]. For example, Tsagkias et al. observe that, by using the number of comments received in the first ten hours after the publication of news articles, one can attain good performances in predicting the final number of comments (average MRSE of 20%) [51].

A different approach is proposed by Lee et al. [65]. Instead of predicting the exact amount of attention the authors study the possibility of predicting if a web content will continue to receive attention from online readers after a certain period of time. The prediction model proposed for this problem (Cox proportional-hazards regression) is a widely used method in `survival analysis` that allows one to model the time until an event occurs (a typical event is "death", from which the term survival analysis is derived). While the main utilization of this method could be to predict the lifetime of a web content, by changing the definition of an event, the method can also be used for popularity prediction tasks. The solution proposed by Lee et al. is to consider as event the time when a web content will reach a popularity value above a certain threshold. The performance of this method was tested on threads from two online discussion forums, DPreview and MySpace, with popularity expressed as the number of comments per thread. Using different statistics related to the users' comment arrival rate the authors show that, by observing user activity in the first day after publication, the method can detect with 80% accuracy the threads that will receive more than 100 comments.

Regression-based methods have been frequently used for this prediction task. Tatar et al. use a simple linear regression based on the early number of comments to predict the final number of comments for news articles [74]. The authors observe that there is no significant improvement when using specialized prediction models as a function of the category and the publication hour of an article. Marujo et al. study the problem of predicting the number of clicks that news stories will receive during one hour. Various prediction methods have been tested (multiple linear regression, regression-based trees, bagging, and additive regression) using different features extracted from the news web platform. The authors show that by combining different regression algorithms one can obtain fairly good results (MRE = 12%) in predicting the number of clicks received by news articles during one hour. Cho et al. use a linear model on a logarithmic scale to predict popularity ranges for political blog posts [75]. The authors show that, by looking at the number of page views in the first 30 minutes, one can classify articles in three classes of popularity with 86% accuracy. A different approach is proposed by Tatar et al. who study the performance of three popularity prediction methods (simple linear regression, linear-log, and constant scaling) to order news articles based on their future number of comments [50]. Using a data set of news articles and comments, the authors show that, out of the three methods, a simple linear regression is the most adequate for this prediction task, suggesting that a smaller least squares error does not imply a smaller ranking error.

Predicting the popularity of web content, based on the aggregate user behavior, has also been addressed as a classification problem. Jamali and Rangwala use the number of comments that Digg stories receive in the first ten hours to predict the final Digg score [56]. By training different classification methods the results indicate that it is possible to predict the popularity class of a Digg story with an accuracy of 80%, 64%, and 45% when separating stories in 2, 6, and 14 ranges of popularity. Hong et al. study the problem of predicting the number of retweets for Twitter posts [61]. The authors address this problem as a multiclass classification task, where, for a given tweet the goal is to predict the range of popularity and not the exact retweet count. Using a logistic regression classification function and various content, topological, and temporal features the authors show that they can successfully predict which messages will not be retweeted (99% accuracy) and those that will be retweeted more than 10,000 times (98% accuracy).

Temporal analysis. For web content that captures users' attention for longer periods of time (e.g., certain videos that are viewed during several months or even years) it has been observed that the aggregate-based prediction models are prone to large errors [30]. To improve the prediction effectiveness, one solution is to design models that can weight users' attention differently based on the recency of the information relative to the prediction moment. For this type of evaluation, the aggregate user behavior is sampled in equal-size intervals of duration δ where $x_c(i)$ is the popularity of an item c during the ith interval, and $X_c(t_i)$ is the vector of popularities for all intervals up to t_i: $X_c(t_i) = [x_c(1), x_c(2), x_c(3) \ldots, x_c(i)]^T$ $(N_c(t_i) = \sum_{j=1}^{i} x_c(t_j))$.

Pinto et al. rely on this approach to predict the popularity of YouTube videos [33]. Using a sampling rate of one day the authors use a `multivariate linear regression` expressed as

$$\widehat{N}_c(t_i, t_r) = \Theta(t_i, t_r) X_c(t_i). \tag{14}$$

The parameters of the model, $\Theta(t_i, t_r) = [\theta_1, \theta_2, .., \theta_i]$ are computed to minimize MRSE under the new definition of estimated popularity. Using a collection of YouTube videos this model shows a significant improvement compared to the `constant scaling` model. For instance, predicting the popularity of a video one-month after its publication using data from the first week shows an average improvement of 14% over the `constant scaling` model. The main drawback of this algorithm, as mentioned by the authors, is that in order for the prediction methods to be effective, additional exploration is needed to decide on the optimal history length and the sampling rate.

`Reservoir computing` [76], a novel paradigm in recurrent neural networks, is proposed as a model that could consider more complex interactions between early and late popularity values (between $X_c(t_i)$ and $N_c(t_r)$). More specifically, this technique is used to build a large recurrent neural network that allows one to create and evaluate nonlinear relationships between $X_c(t_i)$ and $N_c(t_r)$ [77]. On a small sample of YouTube videos this model shows a minor improvement over the `constant scaling` model in predicting the daily number of views based on the observations received in the previous ten days.

For videos that are popular over long periods of time (those that receive views during at least half a year), Gursun et al. [32] observe that the daily number of views can be modeled through a `time series prediction` model using Autoregressive Moving Average (ARMA). Thus, the popularity of a video at a given day n, $x_c(n)$, can be predicted using the following formula:

$$x_c(n) = \sum_{i=1}^{p} \alpha_i x_c(n-i) + \epsilon_n + \sum_{j=1}^{q} \theta_j \epsilon_{n-j}, \qquad (15)$$

where $\alpha_1, \ldots, \alpha_p$ are the parameters of the autoregressive model, $\theta_1, \ldots, \theta_q$ are the parameters of the moving average, and $\epsilon_n, \epsilon_{n-1}, \ldots$ are the white noise error terms.

The model shows good performance in predicting the number of daily views based on the viewership received in the previous week ($p = q = 7$), with an average MRE error of 15%. The main limitation of this method is that it has a very high computational cost as it requires one ARMA model for each video. To improve the scalability of the model the authors use principal component analysis (PCA) as follows: 1) use PCA to find the main principal components that can approximate the time series for the entire collection of videos and 2) apply ARMA modeling to the principal components instead of the individual time series. This solution significantly improves the scalability of the model (e.g., it requires 20 ARMA models to make predictions for the entire collection of videos) and shows a minor decrease in the prediction accuracy (MRE = 0.12 when using individual ARMA models compared to MRE = 0.14 when using principal component analysis).

Kong et al. propose `kSAIT` (top-k Similar Author-Identical historic Tweets), an algorithm that can predict the popularity of tweets one, two, or three days after publication based on the retweet information received in the first hour [63]. The underlying assumption of this algorithm is that, tweets are retweeted in a similar manner depending on the author of the tweet. The prediction algorithm is thus user-specific (there is one prediction function for each user) and uses as predictive features only users' retweeting behavior as it does not include any information about content itself or about users' centrality in the graph of social interactions. Each tweet is described by a set of features (e.g., retweet acceleration, retweet depth) derived from the time-series of the retweets published in the first hour after publication by the direct and n-level followers, the publication time of the tweet, and information about the users who retweeted the original tweet. When a new tweet is posted, the algorithm computes the similarity of the tweet and all other tweets published by the same user, selects the top-k most similar tweets, and estimates the popularity of the target tweet

as an average of the popularity of the top-k most similar tweets.

The performance of the algorithm was evaluated on a data set from Tencent Weibo and compared to several regression-based methods. The algorithm shows good prediction performance (an improvement of up to 10% in terms of MAE compared to regression-based methods), but training a personalized function for each user makes it difficult to be implemented in large-scale social networks. *Popularity evolution trends.* Several studies reveal that the evolution of content popularity over time can accurately be described by a small number of temporal patterns [31,32,45,78]. Crane and Sornette provide one of the first evidence of this fact while analyzing the popularity evolution of YouTube videos [31]. The authors observe that a Poisson process describes the attention around the majority of videos (90% of the videos) and the remaining ones follow three popularity evolution trends (illustrated in Figure 3). These trends are characterized by a single popularity peak but different patterns in which the popularity grows and declines. For more accurate predictions it is important to know that content exhibits well-known temporal dynamics, as the prediction function can be adapted to the specific shape of popularity evolution.

One of the first models that exploits the temporal evolution patterns is proposed by Gursun et al. [32]. While analyzing the viewership around YouTube videos the authors observe two overall categories of videos: those that are consistently popular over time and those that are viewed during a small period of time. The second category is characterized by short-time popularity bursts and can be described by a small number of temporal patterns. To reveal these patterns the authors use `hierarchical clustering` based on the time-series of videos popularity during 64 days centered on the peak. This strategy reveals that, for videos that are viewed during short periods of time, there are ten common shapes that describe the temporal evolution for most of the videos. Once these shapes are detected the prediction task consists in mapping videos to the clusters that best describe their evolution until the prediction moment (t_i) and in using the temporal evolution trends of the clusters to deduce future video popularity. On a sample of YouTube videos, this method shows good performance in making short-term predictions (predict the number of views in the next day) but significantly larger ones in making long-term predictions.

Pinto et al. put forward an improvement to the `multivariate linear regression` model by proposing a solution that captures the similarity between videos in terms of their temporal evolution patterns [33]. The model assumes that the temporal popularity evolution of a subset of videos is representative for the

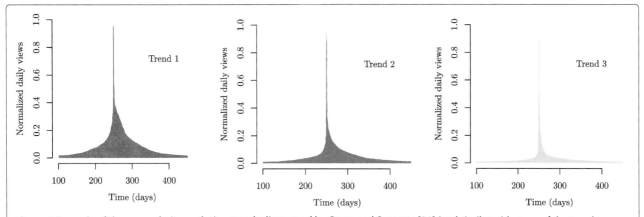

Figure 3 Example of three popularity evolution trends discovered by Crane and Sornette [31] (and similar with some of the trends presented by Figueiredo [45] and Gursun et al. [32]). The figure shows the average number of views over time normalized by the number of views during the peak day.

entire population and could be used to improve the prediction accuracy. More specifically, the prediction model, called `multivariate radial basis function` (MRBF), is described by the following relationship:

$$\widehat{N}_c(t_i, t_r) = \Theta(t_i, t_r) X_c(t_i) + \sum_{c_1 \in C_1} w_{c_1} \text{RBF}_{c_1}(c), \quad (16)$$

where $C_1 \in C$ is the representative subset of videos and w_{c_1} is the weight associated with each item. RBF stands for the Radial Basis Function with Gaussian kernel (chapter 6 [79]) and measures the similarity between the target video and each video in C_1. Training MRBF model involves finding the optimal parameters Θ and w_{c_1} to minimize MRSE, setting the optimal values of RBF kernel, and finding a representative set of videos. The performance of this model shows an average improvement of 5% over `multivariate linear regression` and 20% compared to the `constant scaling` model.

Ahmed et al. propose a model that uses a more granular description of the temporal evolution of content popularity [34]. Instead of using a set of representative items to describe the entire evolution of content popularity, this model selects representative members during regular intervals of duration δ and defines rules to model the transitions among subsequent intervals.

The representative members for each interval are computed using Affinity Propagation clustering algorithm [80]. To calculate the similarity between items, the authors derive two features from $X_c(t_i)$: one that compares if two items receive the same proportion of users' attention and another one that measures if the two items experience a similar popularity growth. Once the clusters of popularity are identified, they are grouped into a probabilistic framework used to describe the evolution of content popularity between clusters over time. Thus, by knowing to which cluster an individual item is most likely to belong at time t_i, one can predict its popularity at a future moment of time t_r.

The performance of the model was tested on three data sets (YouTube, Vimeo, and Digg) and shows a significant improvement over the `log-linear` model. For example, when using the observations received in the first 24 hours to predict the popularity four hours ahead, this model shows a MRSE error of 1% for Digg and 3.5% for Vimeo and YouTube; a significant improvement compared to the `log-linear` model that shows a performance of 17% for Digg, 24.2% for Vimeo, and 29.7% for YouTube.

Individual behavior Instead of treating each user's reaction equally in the prediction process, models under this category draw conclusions based on individual user behavior.

`Social dynamics`, the model proposed by Lerman and Hogg, describes the temporal evolution of web content popularity as a stochastic process of user behavior during a browsing session on a social media site [81]. In its original form, the model is designed according to the characteristics of the social bookmarking site Digg: stories can be found in three sections of the site (front, upcoming, and friend list pages), users can express their opinions through votes, and stories are arranged in pages or promoted to different sections of the site based on the dynamics of votes.

User behavior is modeled through a set of states that describe the possible actions that one can take on a site: browse through the different sections, read news stories, and cast votes to further recommend them to the Digg community. Browsing sessions are dynamic as stories circulate through the site (i.e., they may appear on different sections of the site or change position on the page) depending on the voting results. Individual user behavior is thus linked to the collective behavior, which in the end explains how stories receive votes over time. More specifically, the number of votes a story receives depends on its visibility and general interest. Visibility is expressed as the probability of finding a story in different sections of the site and interest is linked to the quality of the story estimated by the voting dynamics.

The authors validate the model on a small sample of Digg stories by studying user' reactions to the publication of stories and by taking into account the online connections created between Digg users. By using this algorithm, the authors reveal that they can predict in 95% of the cases which stories will become popular enough to reach Digg's front page.

For platforms that allow users to cast positive and negative votes on the content, Yin et al. propose `Conformer Maverick`, a model used to predict content popularity based on users' voting profiles [67]. The underlying assumption of the model is that, in the voting process, users can have two behaviors: obey the general users' opinion (the "conformers") or be against them (the "mavericks"). The profile of a user is in-between these two extremes but in general one trait prevails.

The first step is to build user profiles based on the voting history by comparing individual votes with the overall appreciation of the content, i.e., if the majority of votes is positive or negative. These profiles are later used to decide if an item will become popular by analyzing early user votes. Receiving positive votes from conformers and negative ones from mavericks is then considered as a good indication that an item will be appreciated by the majority. Using data from a joke sharing application the algorithm shows a better performance than a collaborative filtering solution.

Zaman et al. propose a probabilistic model based on Bayesian inference to predict the popularity of Twitter messages [64]. The predictive features are content-agnostic and based on retweets time-series and the social connectivity graph of the Twitter users. The model is based on the assumption that Twitter users have similar actions with regard to the post of a tweet that creates a pattern in the evolution of tweets popularity. In particular, the probability of a (re)tweet to be retweeted depends on the number of followers and the distance from the user that originally generated the tweet. Using a small data set of 52 tweets, the method shows a good performance (given the difficulty of the task), with an average MRE error of 40% using the retweeting information received in the first five minutes after the publication.

7.2   Cross domain

The second major category of methods is used to predict web content popularity using information from multiple web domains: extract data from one domain (e.g., social media) and transform it into knowledge to predict web content popularity in another domain (e.g., the site where content was published). Currently, only methods that predict content popularity *after publication* based on the *aggregate behavior* have been proposed.

Oghina et al. use data from Twitter and YouTube to predict movie ratings on IMDb [36]. By training a linear regression model on several textual features extracted from Twitter and various statistics from YouTube (likes, dislikes, and comments) the authors show that they can accurately predict movie ratings on IMDb. The authors indicate that the best performance is obtained by combining the ratio of likes over dislikes from YouTube activity with the subjective terms (positive and negative unigrams about the movies) extracted from Twitter.

The algorithm proposed by Roy et al., `Social Transfer`, extracts information from Twitter to detect videos that will experience sudden bursts of popularity on YouTube [35]. The model consists of the following steps: extract popular topics from Twitter, associate these topics to YouTube videos, and compare the popularity of videos on Twitter with their popularity on YouTube. A disproportionate share of attention on Twitter compared to YouTube is then used as strong evidence that a video will experience a sudden burst of popularity.

Topics are learned by analyzing Twitter stream, extracting topical words, and finding topics from words with semantic similarity. Each topic has a certain popularity on Twitter based on its prevalence in the Twitter stream and the time it first appeared. The algorithm uses the Social Transfer framework [82] to map videos – using only the textual information from the title and video description – to topics extracted from Twitter. The popularity of a video on Twitter, expressed by the popularity of its topic, is then compared to its popularity on YouTube (represented by number of views) and, if the difference is significant, the video is considered susceptible to receive a sudden burst of attention.

Using data from YouTube and Twitter, and by training a support vector machine classifier, the algorithm shows that it can predict with 70% accuracy which videos will experience a significant increase in popularity on a daily basis. This strategy shows an improvement of almost 60% compared to a model that uses only the information available on YouTube.

Castillo et al. propose a prediction method that collects information about the early attention that news articles receive on social networks to predict the total number of page views on a news site [14]. The statistical method used for this task is a `multiple linear regression` that uses as input the following variables: number of Facebook shares, number of tweets and retweets, entropy of tweet vocabulary, and the mean number of followers sharing the articles on Twitter. Using a collection of Al Jazeera news stories, the authors show that a model based on the social media signals received in the first ten minutes after publication achieves the same performance as one based on the number of page views received in the first three hours.

The effectiveness of cross-domain prediction methods indicate that, when information related to a web content is spread across multiple web sites, aggregating information from multiple sources can significantly improve the prediction accuracy. In particular, the information extracted from Twitter proved very useful in learning more accurate prediction models. The benefit of using social streams as an additional source of information can be explained by the fact that sharing is one of the most popular methods to reach information on the Internet. And, as sharing rarely happens inside the originating web domain, this information provides an additional – and more reactive – perspective about the actual popularity of a web content.

8 What makes web content popular?

The magic formula of what makes a web content popular is still unknown but some of the ingredients have been discovered. The content of a web item (e.g., the topic, message, or quality) plays a major role in its future success [83], but there are other elements (e.g., dissemination factors, promotion, or social influence) that have a significant contribution. Identifying the factors that impact content popularity is important in building more accurate prediction models by understanding which are the significant variables (i.e., variables that show a causal relationship) that should be used in a model or in finding alternative proxy variables when the original variable is difficult to measure. In this section we present the factors known to have a strong impact on web content popularity and we indicate in Section 9 which variables have already been used in a prediction model.

Content matters in the amount of attention that a web item will receive. Emotion is one of the most important drivers for online audience. Videos, evoking strong and mostly positive emotions, are more likely to be shared within online communities [84]. Similarly, content that generates high-arousal emotions (e.g., awe, anxiety) disseminates faster on the Internet and captures a larger amount of users' interest [85,86]. The quality of the content [87,88] and its geographic relevance [89,90] are also positively correlated with content popularity. The topic of the content is also important as content popularity is susceptible to bursts of attention in response to real-world events [91]. On the other hand, there are elements that have a negative impact on content popularity. One of them is the presence of multiple versions of the same content that tends to limit the popularity of each individual copy [28].

There are also several content-agnostic factors that have a strong impact on the popularity growth [92]. Popular Internet services, such as search tools, recommendation systems, and social sharing applications can extent web content visibility and increase its popularity. Taking the example of YouTube, the internal search engine accounts for most of the views, followed by the recommendation systems and the social sharing tools [12,92]. But the outcome of these services also play an important role in how popular a web content will become. For example, it has been observed that videos acquire a greater number of views if they are recommended in the related list of other popular videos [15,93] and the higher the position of a video in the list the greater the number of views [94]. The recommendation system thus creates a strong linked structure between similar videos, which influence each other in terms of popularity [95]. This information can be extremely valuable to newborn videos that can have a greater chance of becoming popular if they manage to create links – by choosing a relevant title, description, or keyword set – with similar popular videos.

Social sharing acts as an additional catalyst of user attention. Diffusing videos through social networks, blogs, or e-mail services generates peaks of attention during short periods of time [70]. Similarly, the social connections created within a site play an important role in how popular a web content will become. For example, it has been observed that in the early stages after the publication of a web content the greater the social network of the publisher the greater the increase in content popularity. Finally, social influence can have a non-negligible consequence on the popularity growth. A study conducted by Salganik et al. reveals that, when users are informed about the collective decisions of other individuals, the popularity of songs are driven by a "rich-get-richer" effect [87].

9 Predictive features

Accurate predictions depend on the predictive characteristics of the variables used in the model. While most prediction models proposed so far use the popularity at early moments as the only predictive variable there have been several attempts to include other features in a prediction model. We provide a brief summary of the various features used in the prediction models and report their predictive performance.

Characteristics of content creators. The online media ecosystem is populated by content creators (independent producers, professional bloggers, mainstream mass media, or news agencies) with different but relatively stable – and maybe predictable – audience. Including the identity of the content creator in a prediction model is exploited by Bandari et al. who notice that the publisher of a news article is one of the strongest predictor of the number of tweets that a news article will generate [72].

Textual features. Certain words or key phrases that probably refer to hot or controversial topics often produce a significant amount of attention. There have been two efforts to include textual features in a prediction model. Tsagkias et al. extract the top-100 most discriminative terms from various news sources and observe that these terms have a strong performance in predicting which articles will be highly commented [71]. Similarly, Marujo et al. show that popular key-phrases have a strong predictive power in predicting the number of views for news articles [96].

Content category. Designing specialized prediction models depending on the category of the content showed little benefit in predicting the popularity of videos [33] and new articles [72,96]. The only notable exceptions have been signaled for YouTube *Music* videos [33] and news articles related to *Technology* section [72]. The low predictive performance of using this information in a prediction model can be explained by the overlapping scope of categories, with content often belonging to multiple categories at once [28,72].

Named entity identification. Popular entities in the real world (people, locations, or organizations) can often be a catalyst of user attention in the online sphere. Tsagkias et al. observe a strong impact in including popular entities from Netherlands in a prediction model designed to spot news articles that will receive a high number of comments [71].

Sentiment analysis. The specific emotion triggered by a web content is highly correlated with its online popularity [86] but extracting the correct sentiment and learning how to use this information for popularity prediction is a difficult task. The subjectivity of the language has shown little predictive power in predicting the volume of tweets for online news stories [72]. However, it has been observed that articles that are written in a more positive or negative voice, associated with strong emotions (e.g., admiration or anger), are good indicators of how viral articles will become [85]. In addition, Oghina et al. observe that subjective terms from the discussions about movies on Twitter can successfully be used as a predictive variable in predicting movie ratings on IMDb [36].

Social media signals. As we saw in Section 7.2, social media conveys valuable information about web content popularity. Castillo et al. show that the attention that news articles generate across social networks (number of Facebook shares, number of tweets and retweets, the language of the Twitter messages) is effective in predicting the popularity of articles on a news site [14]. Oghina et al. successfully use information from Twitter and YouTube to predict movie ratings on IMDb. Another example of the predictive power of social media has been reported by Roy et al. who show that the popularity of a topic on Twitter provides a good indication that a YouTube video will experience a sudden burst in popularity [35].

Social sharing viewing behavior. Yahoo! Zync is an application that allows users to share and jointly manipulate video content in real time. Shamma et al. study how users' actions during a sharing session can be used to predict the popularity of YouTube videos and observe that these interactions are strong indicators of videos with a high number of views [66].

Real-world features. Content published in online media is strongly related to real-world events but transferring information from the physical to the online world is very challenging. An attempt to employ real-world information in the predictions process has been done by Tsagkias et al. who show that there is an insignificant benefit in using the weather conditions (average temperature in Netherlands) to predict the number of comments for news articles [71].

10 Shaping the future: Applications of web content popularity prediction

In the modern information age accurate popularity predictions can prove valuable to different actors: online users can filter more easily the huge amount of information; content producers and content providers can better organize their information and build more effective delivery platforms; and advertising networks can design more sophisticated and profitable advertising strategies. However, predicting the popularity of web content, as useful as it seems, has been employed in few real-world applications. We review the current practical uses of these methods and propose new applications that could benefit from this research area.

The capacity to predict the viewership or the engagement around web content can be used as a tool for content optimization. For example, news web sites select and organize articles from a highly dynamic content pool. Instead of relying on human editors (a practice that is still common nowadays), web sites can refine their decisions through automatic solutions using online content optimization methods [97]. Agarwal et al. show that they can significantly increase the number of clicks for Yahoo! news articles if, instead of using human editors to select and arrange the articles, one uses automatic selection algorithms that measure users' interest in news articles [97]. In this context, accurate popularity predictions, used to highlight and recommend articles, can improve user experience and boost the site's traffic. Moreover, by monitoring and reacting to social media signals, editors can increase the traffic through social media optimization solutions [11]. Currently, to the best of our knowledge, there have been no online evaluations of how the prediction methods described in this survey could be used to increase the traffic on a web site. In an offline setting Marujo et al. show good performance in predicting the number of clicks that news articles will receive during one hour [96]. Still in an offline evaluation mode, Tatar et al. explore the efficiency of two popularity prediction methods to rank news articles based on the future number of comments and show that the log-linear model could be an effective method for this ranking problem [73]. It is also important to understand how users react to information about the predicted popularity. Even if web content shows a mild resilience to self-fulfilling prophecies [98] the prediction outcome can become a strong form of social influence that inflates or dampens the success of a web item. One solution to this problem is to create a feedback loop to listen to users' reactions and adjust the decisions depending on how the audience is responding to the prediction outcome.

Information about the future amount of interest that web content will generate can also be valuable in online advertising as an alternative to existing contextual ad placement models [99]. The possibility to quickly spot the future popular items on the Internet creates the opportunity of additional profits for advertising agencies. Popularity prediction methods can also be used in the context of online marketing. For example, suppose that a company initiates a marketing campaign on social media with the goal of reaching a certain number of online users. To measure the success of a campaign one possible strategy is to wait until the interest in web content fades away. A more useful solution would be to monitor and predict in real-time the amount of interest that a certain post will generate and decide more quickly if additional publications would be needed [60].

Faced with an ever increasing traffic demand, content providers and content delivery networks set large-scale caching infrastructures to distribute copies of the web content across multiple locations. Optimal placement of replicas [100] – in terms of location and number of copies under bandwidth and storage constraints – depend on how accurate one can predict the future users' demand: which content will be popular [70], its geographic

locality of interest [89], and the amount of attention that it will generate.

Cache replacement policies (i.e., decide on which item to evict from a cache when there is no available space) remain an important issue for the performance of a proxy cache. Traditional cache replacement algorithms use the historical information about content requests to decide which item to keep in the cache to maximize a certain performance metric (e.g., hit rate, the amount of saved bandwidth) [101]. Two of the most used replacement policies, even nowadays, are LFU (prioritize the most requested item) and LRU (prioritize the most recently requested item). One way to improve the efficiency of cache replacement algorithms is to actually integrate popularity prediction methods in the cache replacement decision. Famaey et al. propose P-LFU, an adaptation of LFU that determines which content to evict from the cache based on the predicted future demand [102]. Four generic functions (linear, power-law, exponential, and Gaussian) have been used to predict future content demand with the exponential distribution showing the most accurate results. Using a workload trace from a Video-on-Demand service the authors show that popularity prediction methods can increase the cache hit-rate with up to 10% compared with LFU cache replacement strategy.

Another domain where popularity prediction can prove valuable is mobile data offloading. Under the increasing consumption of mobile data traffic, telecom operators look for new solutions to reduce the traffic from cellular networks. Opportunistic networks have recently been proposed as an appealing solution to offload content with non-real time constrains, where, instead of using the cellular network infrastructure, mobile users can retrieve content from collocated peers [103].

In this context, one possible strategy is to benefit from the spatio-temporal mobile users requests, proactively replicate (prefetch) popular web items into mobile users' cache according to the predicted future demand, and rely on device-to-device communications to treat future content requests. To increase the performance of this strategy, the decision of what content to replicate should reflect content popularity dynamics, i.e., to replicate web content according to the predicted demand. If popularity predictions are accurate enough, future content requests could be handled by collocated mobile users and thus bypass the communication with the infrastructure and reduce network traffic and battery consumption. If, however, predictions are inaccurate, this will lead to an inefficient use of mobile and network resources. In this scenario, the benefit of predictions could be even greater if, in addition to predicting the number of users interested in a web content, one could also predict which users will trigger the requests. Social networks have become an important mechanism for information spreading and by learning the social structures created by users one can understand the patterns of information diffusion [7,104] which further gives one the ability to predict when a user will be interested in a certain content. This type of approach has been proposed by Malandrino et al. that show that, by predicting information cascades, mobile users' requests can be treated in advance which can lead to a reduction of up to 50% of the cellular data traffic during periods of high data traffic loads [105].

Major Web search engines such as Google, Yahoo!, and Bing are always looking for new ranking factors to improve the relevancy of their search results. Over the years, search algorithms have become extremely sophisticated including hundreds of ranking factors based on the content of a web page or its importance in the Web graph. But even these complex algorithms may sometimes fail to retrieve the relevant information. For example, when searching for relevant information in the Blogosphere, Gonçalves et al. observe that commercial search engines (UOL, Yahoo!, and Google) failed to correctly retrieve an important percent of the relevant blogs on the first page of the results [106]. In the same study the authors show that the results of the query can significantly improve by including the popularity of the blog in the search algorithm. A search engine that includes the collective users' opinion about web content in its algorithm – if one has access to the different popularity statistics – is probably the future evolution of search engines [107,108]. Predicting web content popularity could fit well in this context as the outcome of a search query could prioritize future popular web content over expired one.

11   Summary and outlook

In this article we reviewed the current state-of-the-art on web content popularity prediction methods. We presented the different prediction methods, reported their performance, and suggested several applications that can benefit from these findings.

Even if research on predicting the popularity of web content has been an active area in the latest years there are many avenues that wait to be explored. We suggest some possible directions for the future work.

Predicting long-term popularity evolution. Most of the previous studies address the problem of predicting the exact amount of attention that a web content will receive up to a future moment in time. While this is useful for timely detections of popular items, a greater impact would come from a long-term evolution forecast [34,45] (i.e., to predict how content popularity evolves over time). Knowing this can reveal how content progresses through the different stages of popularity: initial growth, peak period, decline, and even popularity rebounds. This information can help online advertisers or content delivery networks in making more profitable decisions, focusing on a content during its popularity peak and wasting fewer resources on expired items.

Building richer models. In addition to early popularity measures, several studies analyzed the predictive power of various features. We believe that this direction has not been fully explored and further work is needed in finding more powerful predictive features. For example, except for Bandari et al. that use the identity of the publisher in the prediction model [72], to our knowledge no other work has studied the predictive power of a content publisher. Yet news columnists and video publishers attract a significant and maybe predictable audience on their own.

The topic of the web content plays an important role in its future popularity. The daily agenda of discussions on the Internet and mainstream media is centered on major topics with limited and different life cycles. Thus, capturing trending topics and learning how to include them in prediction models can lead to a major breakthrough in the prediction accuracy. Research in this field has made important advances in the recent years. Leskovec et al. show that the attention that online users pay to certain topics can accurately be described by six time-series shapes [109]. Similarly, Nikolov et al. propose an algorithm that can accurately predict the trending topics on Twitter earlier (with an average of 1.43 hours) than the internal algorithm used by Twitter [110].

For web content characterized by a very short lifecycle it has been observed that timely predictions present a real challenge. For example, news articles quickly become popular and "die-out" within hours. One way to improve the predictability of news would be to extract recurrent events over time, observe the level of interest that they generate, and predict when these future events will take place. Predicting global events in various fields (e.g., economy, seismology, society), as challenging as it may seem, is nevertheless plausible. Radinsky et al. propose two algorithms for this prediction task: PROFET, an algorithm that predicts the terms used in the future news stories based on the historical web query patterns [111]; and Pandit, a system that can predict future events given an existing news event [112].

Understanding and merging user activity stemming from different web channels is an important direction to follow. Up to now, Twitter feed has been used as the main source of information. But there are other potential directions to explore. For example, analyzing Web users' query behavior can unveil important insights about the popularity of certain topics and the ability to predict search queries, as showed by Radinsky et al. [113], could be incorporated in a popularity prediction model. Wikipedia is also a valuable source of information. Important real-life events are quickly recorded on Wikipedia and real-time monitoring of this channel can be transformed into valuable information in a prediction model. Wikipedia Live Monitor is a good example of automatic monitoring tool that detects breaking news events by studying simultaneous user activity for certain topics edited in different languages [114,115].

Beyond popularity predictions. Studying online content popularity should be used not only to better understand the dynamics of content consumption but also to improve various web services. For instance, by understanding which factors influence content popularity, content producers can design the genome of popular content. Although there are many factors that are difficult to control, creating content that is original (remember that multiple copies of the same content has a negative impact on popularity [28]), fresh (the advantage of the first-comer [92]), emotional (stronger emotions are correlated to content viralness [85]), and by tagging it with popular keywords (to appear in more popular recommendation lists [93]) can increase the likelihood of web content becoming popular. Then, online advertisers should try to figure out how to seize the opportunity of finding popular content in advance and design novel monetization strategies. Finally, there are few reports on how content popularity prediction can be used to design more effective networking solutions. Yet predicting web content popularity dynamics can be used to design more scalable content delivery solutions that proactively replicate content according to the future users' demand.

Competing interests
The authors declare that they have no competing interests.

Authors' contributions
AT, MDdA, SF, and PA summarized the papers covered in this article, classified the existing literature, and proposed future perspectives for this research area. All authors read and approved the final manuscript.

Acknowledgements
We are grateful to the anonymous reviewers for their valuable comments and suggestions. The work presented in this paper has been carried out at LINCS (www.lincs.fr) and was partially supported by EINS, the Network of Excellence in Internet Science, FP7 grant 28802.

Author details
[1] LIP6/CNRS – UPMC Sorbonne Universités, 4 Place Jussieu, 75005 Paris, France.
[2] Communication System Group – ETH Zurich, 35 Gloriastrasse, 8092 Zurich, Switzerland.

References
1. Telegraph (2013). http://www.telegraph.co.uk/technology/twitter/9945505/Twitter-in-numbers.html
2. Facebook statistics (2013). https://newsroom.fb.com/News
3. YouTube Statistics (2013). http://www.youtube.com/yt/press/statistics.html
4. Internet Advertising Bureau (2013). http://www.iabuk.net/about/press/archive/uk-digital-adspend-up-125-to-almost-55bn
5. Cha M, Mislove A, Adams B, Gummadi KP (2008) Characterizing social cascades in Flickr. In: Proceedings of the First Workshop on Online Social Networks. ACM, Seattle, Washington, USA, pp 13–18
6. Sadikov E, Medina M, Leskovec J, Garcia-Molina H (2011) Correcting for missing data in information cascades. In: Proceedings of the Fourth ACM International Conference on Web Search and Data Mining. ACM, Hong Kong, China, pp 55–64
7. Cheng J, Adamic L, Dow PA, Kleinberg JM, Leskovec J (2014) Can cascades be predicted? In: Proceedings of the 23rd International Conference on World Wide Web (WWW). ACM, Seoul, Republic of, Korea, pp 925–936
8. Yu S, Kak S (2012) A survey of prediction using social media. arXiv preprint arXiv:1203.1647
9. Bernstein MS, Bakshy E, Burke M, Karrer B (2013) Quantifying the invisible audience in social networks. In: Proceedings of the SIGCHI Conference on Human Factors in Computing Systems. ACM, Paris, France, pp 21–30
10. Agarwal D, Chen B-C, Wang X (2012) Multi-faceted ranking of news articles using post-read actions. In: Proceedings of the 21st International Conference on Information and Knowledge Management. CIKM '12. ACM, Maui, Hawaii, USA, pp 694–703
11. Lifshits Y (2010) Ediscope: Social analytics for online news. Technical Report YL-2010-008. Yahoo! Labs
12. Figueiredo F, Benevenuto F, Almeida JM (2011) The tube over time: characterizing popularity growth of youtube videos. In: Proceedings of the Fourth ACM International Conference on Web Search and Data Mining. ACM, Hong Kong, China, pp 745–754
13. Yao Y, Sun A (2013) Are most-viewed news articles most-shared? In: AIRS. Lecture Notes in Computer Science, vol. 8281. Springer, Singapore, pp 404–415
14. Castillo C, El-Haddad M, Pfeffer J, Stempeck M (2013) Characterizing the life cycle of online news stories using social media reactions. arXiv preprint arXiv:1304.3010
15. Chatzopoulou G, Sheng C, Faloutsos M (2010) A first step towards understanding popularity in youtube. In: INFOCOM IEEE Conference on Computer Communications Workshops. IEEE, San Diego, CA, pp 1–6
16. Cunha CR, Bestavros A, Crovella ME (1995) Characteristics of WWW client-based traces. Technical report, Computer Science Department, Boston University
17. Almeida V, Bestavros A, Crovella M, de Oliveira A (1996) Characterizing reference locality in the WWW. In: Parallel and Distributed Information Systems (PDIS). IEEE, Miami Beach, FL, pp 92–103
18. Breslau L, Cao P, Fan L, Phillips G, Shenker S (1999) Web caching and Zipf-like distributions: Evidence and implications. In: INFOCOM'99. Eighteenth Annual Joint Conference of the IEEE Computer and Communications Societies, vol. 1. IEEE, New York, NY, pp 126–134
19. Barford P, Bestavros A, Bradley A, Crovella M (1999) Changes in web client access patterns: Characteristics and caching implications. World Wide Web 2(1-2):15–28
20. Chesire M, Wolman A, Voelker GM, Levy HM (2001) Measurement and analysis of a streaming media workload. In: Proceedings of the 3rd Conference on USENIX Symposium on Internet Technologies and Systems, vol. 3. USENIX Association, San Francisco, California
21. Almeida JM, Krueger J, Eager DL, Vernon MK (2001) Analysis of educational media server workloads. In: Proceedings of the 11th International Workshop on Network and Operating Systems Support for Digital Audio and Video. ACM, Port Jefferson, New York, USA, pp 21–30
22. Sripanidkulchai K, Maggs B, Zhang H (2004) An analysis of live streaming workloads on the internet. In: Proceedings of the 4th ACM SIGCOMM Conference on Internet Measurement. ACM, Taormina, Sicily, Italy, pp 41–54
23. Yu H, Zheng D, Zhao BY, Zheng W (2006) Understanding user behavior in large-scale video-on-demand systems. In: ACM SIGOPS Operating Systems Review, vol. 40. ACM, Leuven, Belgium, pp 333–344

24.	Cherkasova L, Gupta M (2004) Analysis of enterprise media server workloads: access patterns, locality, content evolution, and rates of change. IEEE/ACM Trans Netw 12(5)781–794

25.	Gill P, Arlitt M, Li Z, Mahanti A (2007) Youtube traffic characterization: a view from the edge. In: Proceedings of the 7th ACM SIGCOMM Conference on Internet Measurement. ACM, San Diego, California, USA, pp 15–28

26.	Cha M, Kwak H, Rodriguez P, Ahn Y-Y, Moon S (2007) I tube, you tube, everybody tubes: analyzing the world's largest user generated content video system. In: Proceedings of the 7th ACM SIGCOMM Conference on Internet Measurement. ACM, San Diego, California, USA, pp 1–14

27.	Zink M, Suh K, Gu Y, Kurose J (2009) Characteristics of youtube network traffic at a campus network - measurements, models, and implications. Comput Netw 53(4)501–514

28.	Cha M, Kwak H, Rodriguez P, Ahn Y-Y, Moon S (2009) Analyzing the video popularity characteristics of large-scale user generated content systems. IEEE/ACM Trans Netw. (TON) 17(5)1357–1370

29.	Kaltenbrunner A, Gomez V, Lopez V (2007) Description and prediction of slashdot activity In: Web Conference, 2007. LA-WEB 2007. Latin American. IEEE, Santiago, Chile, pp 57–66

30.	Szabo G, Huberman BA (2010) Predicting the popularity of online content. Commun ACM 53(8)80–88

31.	Crane R, Sornette D (2008) Robust dynamic classes revealed by measuring the response function of a social system. Proc Nat Acad Sci 105(41)15649–15653

32.	Gursun G, Crovella M, Matta I (2011) Describing and forecasting video access patterns. In: INFOCOM, 2011 Proceedings IEEE. IEEE, Shanghai, pp 16–20

33.	Pinto H, Almeida JM, Gonçalves MA (2013) Using early view patterns to predict the popularity of youtube videos. In: Proceedings of the Sixth ACM International Conference on Web Search and Data Mining. WSDM '13. ACM, Rome, Italy, pp 365–374

34.	Ahmed M, Spagna S, Huici F, Niccolini S (2013) A peek into the future: predicting the evolution of popularity in user generated content. In: Proceedings of the Sixth ACM International Conference on Web Search and Data Mining. WSDM '13. ACM, Rome, Italy, pp 607–616

35.	Roy SD, Mei T, Zeng W, Li S (2013) Towards cross-domain learning for social video popularity prediction. IEEE Trans Multimedia 15(1255-1267)

36.	Oghina A, Breuss M, Tsagkias M, de Rijke M (2012) Predicting IMDb movie ratings using social media In: Proceedings of the 34th European Conference on Advances in Information Retrieval. ECIR'12. Springer, Barcelona, Spain, pp 503–507

37.	Cisco Visual Networking Index: Forecast and Methodology (2014). http://www.cisco.com/c/en/us/solutions/collateral/service-provider/ip-ngn-ip-next-generationnetwork/white_paper_c11-481360.html

38.	Kwak H, Lee C, Park H, Moon S (2010) What is twitter, a social network or a news media? In: Proceedings of the 19th International Conference on World Wide Web. ACM, Raleigh, North Carolina, USA, pp 591–600

39.	Reynolds Journalism Institute: News consumption on mobile media (2008). http://www.rjionline.org/research/rji-dpa-mobile-media-project/2013-q1-research-report-1

40.	Mashable (2013). http://mashable.com/2011/12/31/youtube-in-2011

41.	Cheng X, Dale C, Liu J (2008) Statistics and social network of youtube videos. In: 16th International Workshop on Quality of Service. IWQoS. IEEE, Enschede, pp 229–238

42.	Borghol Y, Mitra S, Ardon S, Carlsson N, Eager D, Mahanti A (2011) Characterizing and modelling popularity of user-generated videos. Perform Eval 68(11)1037–1055

43.	Cheng X, Dale C, Liu J (2007) Understanding the characteristics of internet short video sharing: Youtube as a case study. arXiv preprint arXiv:0707.3670

44.	Avramova Z, Wittevrongel S, Bruneel H, De Vleeschauwer D (2009) Analysis and modeling of video popularity evolution in various online video content systems: power-law versus exponential decay. In: First International Conference on Evolving Internet (INTERNET'09). IEEE, Cannes/La Bocca, pp 95–100

45.	Figueiredo F (2013) On the prediction of popularity of trends and hits for user generated videos. In: Proceedings of the Sixth ACM International Conference on Web Search and Data Mining. WSDM '13. ACM, Rome, Italy, pp 741–746

46.	Carlinet L, Huynh T, Kauffmann B, Mathieu F, Noirie L, Tixeuil S (2012) Four months in daily motion: Dissecting user video requests. In: Wireless Communications and Mobile Computing Conference (IWCMC). IEEE, Limassol, Cyprus, pp 613–618

47.	Mitra S, Agrawal M, Yadav A, Carlsson N, Eager D, Mahanti A (2011) Characterizing web-based video sharing workloads. ACM Trans Web (TWEB) 5(2)8

48.	Dezsö Z, Almaas E, Lukács A, Rácz B, Szakadát I, Barabási A-L (2006) Dynamics of information access on the web. Phys Rev E 73(6)066132

49.	Mishne G, Glance N (2006) Leave a reply: An analysis of weblog comments. In: Third Annual Workshop on the Weblogging Ecosystem. Edinburgh, UK

50.	Tatar A, Antoniadis P, de Amorim MD, Fdida S (2012) Ranking news articles based on popularity prediction. In: Proceedings of the 2012 International Conference on Advances in Social Networks Analysis and Mining (ASONAM 2012). IEEE, Istanbul, pp 106–110

51.	Tsagkias M, Weerkamp W, De Rijke M (2010) News comments: Exploring, modeling, and online prediction. In: Proceedings of the 32Nd European Conference on Advances in Information Retrieval. ECIR'2010. Springer, Milton Keynes, UK, pp 191–203

52.	Lerman K, Ghosh R (2010) Information contagion: An empirical study of the spread of news on Digg and Twitter social networks. In: ICWSM, vol. 10. The AAAI Press, Washington, DC, USA, pp 90–97

53.	Wang C, Ye M, Huberman BA (2012) From user comments to on-line conversations. In: Proceedings of the 18th ACM SIGKDD International Conference on Knowledge Discovery and Data Mining. KDD '12. ACM, Beijing, China, pp 244–252

54.	Wallenta C, Ahmed M, Brown I, Hailes S, Huici F (2008) Analysing and modelling traffic of systems with highly dynamic user generated content. University College London, Tech. Rep. RN/08/10

55.	Gómez V, Kaltenbrunner A, López V (2008) Statistical analysis of the social network and discussion threads in Slashdot. In: Proceedings of the 17th International Conference on World Wide Web. ACM, Beijing, China, pp 645–654

56.	Jamali S, Rangwala H (2009) Digging digg: Comment mining, popularity prediction, and social network analysis. In: International Conference on Web Information Systems and Mining (WISM). IEEE, Shanghai, China, pp 32–38

57.	Lerman K, Galstyan A (2008) Analysis of social voting patterns on digg. In: Proceedings of the First Workshop on Online Social Networks. ACM, Seattle, WA, USA, pp 7–12

58.	Tang S, Blenn N, Doerr C, Van Mieghem P (2011) Digging in the digg social news website. IEEE Trans Multimedia 13(5)1163–1175

59.	Van Mieghem P, Blenn N, Doerr C (2011) Lognormal distribution in the digg online social network. Eur Phys J B 83(2)251–261

60.	Kupavskii A, Umnov A, Gusev G, Serdyukov P (2013) Predicting the audience size of a tweet. In: ICWSM. Cambridge, Massachusetts, USA, The AAAI Press

61.	Hong L, Dan O, Davison BD (2011) Predicting popular messages in Twitter. In: Proceedings of the 20th International Conference Companion on World Wide Web. ACM, Hyderabad, India, pp 57–58

62.	Ma H, Qian W, Xia F, He X, Xu J, Zhou A (2013) Towards modeling popularity of microblogs. Front Comput Sci 7(2)171–184

63.	Kong S, Ye F, Feng L (2014) Predicting future retweet counts in a microblog. J Comput Inform Syst 10(4)1393–1404

64.	Zaman T, Fox EB, Bradlow ET (2013) A bayesian approach for predicting the popularity of tweets. arXiv preprint arXiv:1304.6777

65.	Lee JG, Moon S, Salamatian K (2012) Modeling and predicting the popularity of online contents with Cox proportional hazard regression model. Neurocomputing 76(1)134–145

66.	Shamma DA, Yew J, Kennedy L, Churchill EF (2011) Viral actions: Predicting video view counts using synchronous sharing behaviors. ICWSM, Barcelona, Spain

67.	Yin P, Luo P, Wang M, Lee W-C (2012) A straw shows which way the wind blows: ranking potentially popular items from early votes. In: Proceedings of the Fifth ACM International Conference on Web Search and Data Mining. ACM, Seattle, Washington, USA, pp 623–632

68.	Witten IH, Frank E (2005) Data Mining: Practical Machine Learning Tools and Techniques. Morgan Kaufmann, Burlington, Massachusetts, USA

69.	Manning CD, Raghavan P, Schütze H (2008) Introduction to Information Retrieval vol. 1. Cambridge University Press, Cambridge, NY

70.	Broxton T, Interian Y, Vaver J, Wattenhofer M (2010) Catching a viral video In: International Conference on Data Mining Workshops (ICDMW). IEEE, Sydney, NSW, pp 296–304

71. Tsagkias M, Weerkamp W, De Rijke M (2009) Predicting the volume of comments on online news stories. In: Proceedings of the 18th ACM Conference on Information and Knowledge Management. ACM, Hong Kong, China, pp 1765–1768

72. Bandari R, Asur S, Huberman BA (2012) The pulse of news in social media: Forecasting popularity. In: ICWSM. The AAAI Press, Dublin, Ireland

73. Tatar A, Antoniadis P, de Amorim MD, Fdida S (2014) From popularity prediction to ranking online news. Soc Netw Anal Min 4(174)

74. Tatar A, Leguay J, Antoniadis P, Limbourg A, de Amorim MD, Fdida S (2011) Predicting the popularity of online articles based on user comments. In: Proceedings of the International Conference on Web Intelligence, Mining and Semantics. ACM, Sogndal, Norway

75. Kim S-D, Kim S-H, Cho H-G (2011) Predicting the virtual temperature of web-blog articles as a measurement tool for online popularity. In: 11th International Conference on Computer and Information Technology (CIT). IEEE, Pafos, Cyprus, pp 449–454

76. Maass W, Natschläger T, Markram H (2002) Real-time computing without stable states: A new framework for neural computation based on perturbations. Neural Comput 14(11)2531–2560

77. Wu T, Timmers M, Vleeschauwer DD, Leekwijck WV (2010) On the use of reservoir computing in popularity prediction. In: Proceedings of the 2010 2nd International Conference on Evolving Internet. INTERNET '10. IEEE, Valencia, Spain, pp 19–24

78. Yang J, Leskovec J (2011) Patterns of temporal variation in online media. In: Proceedings of the Fourth ACM International Conference on Web Search and Data Mining. ACM, Hong Kong, China, pp 177–186

79. Hastie T, Tibshirani R, Friedman J, Franklin J (2009) The Elements of Statistical Learning: Data Mining, Inference and Prediction. 2nd edn. Springer, NY

80. Frey BJ, Dueck D (2007) Clustering by passing messages between data points. Science 315(5814)972–976

81. Lerman K, Hogg T (2010) Using a model of social dynamics to predict popularity of news. In: Proceedings of the 19th International Conference on World Wide Web. ACM, Raleigh, North Carolina, USA, pp 621–630

82. Roy SD, Mei T, Zeng W, Li S (2012) Socialtransfer: cross-domain transfer learning from social streams for media applications. In: Proceedings of the 20th ACM International Conference on Multimedia. ACM, Nara, Japan, pp 649–658

83. Figueiredo F, Almeida JM, Benevenuto F, Gummadi KP (2014) Does content determine information popularity in social media?: a case study of youtube videos' content and their popularity. In: Proceedings of the 32Nd Annual ACM Conference on Human Factors in Computing Systems. CHI '14. ACM, Toronto, ON, Canada, pp 979–982

84. Guadagno RE, Rempala DM, Murphy S, Okdie BM (2013) What makes a video go viral? An analysis of emotional contagion and internet memes. Comput Hum Behav 29(6)2312–2319

85. Berger JA, Milkman KL (2012) What makes online content viral? J Market Res 49(2)192–205

86. Berger J (2011) Arousal increases social transmission of information. Psychol Sci 22(7)891–893

87. Salganik MJ, Dodds PS, Watts DJ (2006) Experimental study of inequality and unpredictability in an artificial cultural market. Science 311(5762):854–856

88. Hogg T, Szabo G (2009) Diversity of user activity and content quality in online communities. In: Proceedings of 3rd International Conference on Weblogs and Social Media (ICWSM). The AAAI Press, San Jose, California, USA

89. Brodersen A, Scellato S, Wattenhofer M (2012) Youtube around the world: geographic popularity of videos. In: Proceedings of the 21st International Conference on World Wide Web. ACM, Lyon, France, pp 241–250

90. Huguenin K, Kermarrec A-M, Kloudas K, Taïani F (2012) Content and geographical locality in user-generated content sharing systems. In: Proceedings of the 22nd International Workshop on Network and Operating System Support for Digital Audio and Video. ACM, Toronto, Ontario, Canada, pp 77–82

91. Ratkiewicz J, Flammini A, Menczer F (2010) Traffic in social media I: paths through information networks. In: IEEE Second International Conference on Social Computing (SocialCom). IEEE, Minneapolis, MN, USA, pp 452–458

92. Borghol Y, Ardon S, Carlsson N, Eager D, Mahanti A (2012) The untold story of the clones: content-agnostic factors that impact youtube video popularity. In: Proceedings of the 18th ACM SIGKDD International Conference on Knowledge Discovery and Data Mining. ACM, Beijing, China, pp 1186–1194

93. Davidson J, Liebald B, Liu J, Nandy P, Van Vleet T, Gargi U, Gupta S, He Y, Lambert M, Livingston B, Sampath D (2010) The YouTube video recommendation system. In: Proceedings of the Fourth ACM Conference on Recommender Systems. ACM, Barcelona, Spain, pp 293–296

94. Zhou R, Khemmarat S, Gao L (2010) The impact of YouTube recommendation system on video views. In: Proceedings of the 10th ACM SIGCOMM Conference on Internet Measurement. IMC '10. ACM, Melbourne, Australia, pp 404–410

95. Zhou R, Khemmarat S, Gao L, Wang H (2011) Boosting video popularity through recommendation systems. In: Databases and Social Networks. ACM, Athens, Greece, pp 13–18

96. Marujo L, Bugalho M, Neto JPDS, Gershman A, Carbonell J (2013) Hourly traffic prediction of news stories. arXiv preprint arXiv:1306.4608

97. Agarwal D, Chen B-C, Elango P, Motgi N, Park S-T, Ramakrishnan R, Roy S, Zachariah J (2008) Online models for content optimization. In: Advances in Neural Information Processing Systems. MIT Press, Cambridge, MA, pp 17–24

98. Salganik MJ, Watts DJ (2008) Leading the herd astray: An experimental study of self-fulfilling prophecies in an artificial cultural market. Soc Psychol Q 71(4)338–355

99. Ghose A, Yang S (2009) An empirical analysis of search engine advertising: Sponsored search in electronic markets. Manag Sci 55(10)1605–1622

100. Applegate D, Archer A, Gopalakrishnan V, Lee S, Ramakrishnan KK (2010) Optimal content placement for a large-scale VoD system. In: CoNEXT. ACM, Philadelphia, Pennsylvania, USA

101. Podlipnig S, Böszörmenyi L (2003) A survey of web cache replacement strategies. ACM Computing Surveys (CSUR) 35(4)374–398

102. Famaey J, Iterbeke F, Wauters T, DeTurck F (2013) Towards a predictive cache replacement strategy for multimedia content. J Netw Comput Appl 36(1)219–227

103. Han B, Hui P, Kumar V, Marathe M, Shao J, Srinivasan A (2012) Mobile Data Offloading Through Opportunistic Communications and Social Participation. IEEE Transactions on Mobile Computing 11(5)821–834

104. Galuba W, Aberer K, Chakraborty D, Despotovic Z, Kellerer W (2010) Outtweeting the twitterers-predicting information cascades in microblogs. In: Proceedings of the 3rd Conference on Online Social Networks. USENIX Association, Boston, MA, pp 3–3

105. Malandrino F, Kurant M, Markopoulou A, Westphal C, Kozat UC (2012) Proactive seeding for information cascades in cellular networks. In: INFOCOM IEEE Conference on Computer Communications Workshops. IEEE, Orlando, FL, USA, pp 1719–1727

106. Gonçalves MA, Almeida JM, dos Santos LG, Laender AH, Almeida V (2010) On popularity in the blogosphere. Internet Comput IEEE 14(3)42–49

107. Bao S, Xue G, Wu X, Yu Y, Fei B, Su Z (2007) Optimizing web search using social annotations. In: Proceedings of the 16th International Conference on World Wide Web. ACM, Banff, Alberta, Canada, pp 501–510

108. Facebook search engine (2012). http://www.searchenginejournal.com/facebook-seo-beastrank-ranking-factors-facebook-search-engine/49696/

109. Leskovec J, Backstrom L, Kleinberg J (2009) Meme-tracking and the dynamics of the news cycle. In: Proceedings of the 15th ACM SIGKDD International Conference on Knowledge Discovery and Data Mining. KDD '09. ACM, Paris, France, pp 497–506

110. Nikolov S (2012) Trend or no trend: a novel nonparametric method for classifying time series. Master's thesis, Massachusetts Institute of Technology, Cambridge, MA, USA

111. Radinsky K, Davidovich S, Markovitch S (2008) Predicting the news of tomorrow using patterns in web search queries. In: Proceedings of the 2008 IEEE/WIC/ACM International Conference on Web Intelligence and Intelligent Agent Technology-Volume 01. IEEE Computer Society, Washington, DC,USA, pp 363–367

112. Radinsky K, Davidovich S, Markovitch S (2012) Learning causality for news events prediction. In: Proceedings of the 21st International Conference on World Wide Web. ACM, Lyon, France, pp 909–918

113. Radinsky K, Svore K, Dumais S, Teevan J, Bocharov A, Horvitz E (2012) Modeling and predicting behavioral dynamics on the web. In: Proceedings of the 21st International Conference on World Wide Web. ACM, Lyon, France, pp 599–608

114. Steiner T, van Hooland S, Summers E (2013) MJ no more: using
      concurrent Wikipedia edit spikes with social network plausibility checks
      for breaking news detection. In: Proceedings of the 22nd International
      Conference on World Wide Web Companion. International World Wide
      Web Conferences Steering Committee, Rio de Janeiro, Brazil, pp 791–794
115. Steiner T (2014) Telling breaking news stories from Wikipedia with social
      multimedia: A case study of the 2014 winter olympics. arXiv preprint
      arXiv:1403.4289

10

Service selection in web service compositions optimizing energy consumption and service response time

Yanik Ngoko[1*], Alfredo Goldman[2] and Dejan Milojicic[3]

Abstract

A challenging task in Web service composition is the runtime binding of a set of interconnected abstract services to concrete ones. This question, formulated as the service selection problem, has been studied in the area of service compositions implementing business processes. Despite the abundance of work on this topic, few of them match some practical needs that we are interested in. Indeed, while considering the business process implemented by service compositions, we can distinguish between two classes: compositions that correspond to single business process and those implementing multiple communicating processes. While most of the prior work focuses only on the first case, it is the latter that interests us in this paper. This paper contributes to the service selection by proposing a new algorithm that, in polynomial time, generates a mixed linear integer program for optimizing service compositions based on the service response time and the energy consumption. The novelty in this work is our focus on multi-process composition and energy consumption. The paper also proposes a new analysis of the service selection and an evaluation of the proposed algorithm.

Keywords: Web service composition; Service selection problem; Business Process Modeling Notation (BPMN)

1 Introduction

The prevalent techniques for building Web service compositions (WSCs) in middleware distinguish between two levels of service manipulation [1,2]. At the upper level, the middleware manipulates abstract services, defined through an interface of operations and a behavioral specification. This one might be expressed by using for instance OWL-S [3], WSDL-S [4] or DAML-S [5]. At this abstract level, we also have WSCs, here defined as a set of Web-based interactions over services operations. Underneath, there is a concrete level made of published Web services (WSs). In order to run the WSC, the middleware must at runtime associate each abstract operation with a concrete one. Our paper focuses on this aspect.

The automation of runtime binding in service composition has been addressed in previous work. The viewpoint that we adopt for its implementation is inspired by the work of Lee [2] and Ben Mokhtar et al. [1]. There are two successive tasks to be done for runtime binding. The first is the determination of the functional bindings of each abstract operation. This is done by comparing the specification defined for these operations, with published information, available on concrete WSs. For each abstract operation, the execution of this task returns a set of concrete operations that meets its specification. If this set is empty for an abstract operation, then the service composition is not realizable. Assuming that we have a realizable composition, the second task consists of finding the functional bindings that can result in an optimal composition, with respect to some QoS parameters (e.g. availability, service response time, price, energy consumption). Usually, we may have several abstract operations to bind, implying a combinatorial problem.

The work described in this paper is part of a middleware project [6] that aims at implementing both of these tasks (determining functional bindings and optimal binding choice) on ultra large scale compositions of WSs. Our study however only focuses on the second binding challenge. More precisely, given a realizable WSC, we seek the optimal concrete services for running it in order

*Correspondence: yanik.ngoko@lipn.univ-paris13.fr
[1] Laboratoire d'Informatique de Paris Nord, Villetaneuse, France
Full list of author information is available at the end of the article

to optimize the QoS of the composition. We focus, in this paper, on service response time (SRT) and energy consumption (EC).

The question of optimal binding regarding QoS has been addressed in previous studies under the service selection problem. In most of these work, the problem modeling considers two perspectives. From the middleware perspective, there is a global penalty function that on each WSC returns the QoS aggregate of its services constituents. The binding to find must minimize this function. From the perspective of the user, for each QoS dimension, a minimal performance must be guaranteed. This reduces the set of feasible solutions accepted for the problem. Both perspectives have a practical justification. While indeed the middleware optimizes its global performance, users set Service Level Agreement (SLA) for the minimal performance to be met. There are various studies for the service selection addressing SLAs [7-12]. However, few of them match our needs. This is made clear when considering the business process viewpoint of WSCs. Here, compositions belong to two classes: those that correspond to a single enterprise business process and those corresponding to multiple communicating enterprise processes [13]. While previous work on service selection addressed the first case, we are interested in the multi-process case.

In Figure 1, we illustrate a single and a multi-process. As stated by Goldman et al. [14], the multi-process case introduces other challenges such as the cost of inter-process communication (communication between E and F in Figure 1) and the distribution of the service composition graph. In addition, our work differs from existing ones in finding the optimal binding in regard to both SRT

and the EC. While the SRT is a common QoS parameter used in service selection, it is not the case with EC.

In this paper, we consider the optimal binding between abstract and concrete operations in a WSC corresponding to multiple communicating business processes. The binding must be optimized for the SRT and EC. We address this problem by extending the linear programming-based solution introduced by Goldman et al. [14] to EC prediction. Given a service composition, our global contribution is a polynomial time algorithm for generating a Mixed Linear Integer Program (MILP) whose execution will return the optimal binding for the composition. In a detailed viewpoint, we contribute by: (1) extending our prior model [14] to service selection related to SRT and EC; (2) analyzing the complexity and the feasibility of our modeling; (3) providing an analysis of the service selection problem; (4) proposing an evaluation of our solution.

The remainder of this paper is organized as follows. In Section 2, we present existing work on service selection. In Section 3 we describe our modeling of the service selection problem. The solution that we propose for its resolution is given in Section 4, an application case is studied in Section 5 and we conclude in Section 6.

2 Related work

We considered two separate tasks to perform for binding an abstract WSC to concrete services. The first task consists of finding adequate concrete operations for abstract ones. Our paper does not focus on it. However, interesting work on the topic have been proposed by Lee [2] and Burstein et al. [5].

Given a realizable WSC, we are interested in finding an optimal binding in order to optimize the global service

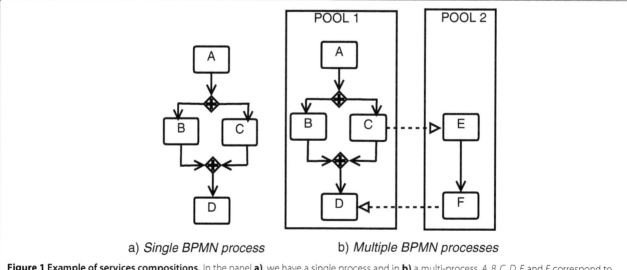

a) *Single BPMN process*   b) *Multiple BPMN processes*

Figure 1 Example of services compositions. In the panel **a)**, we have a single process and in **b)** a multi-process. *A, B, C, D, E* and *F* correspond to WSs operations. The notations are based on the BPMN collaboration diagram.

composition. This problem has been addressed in various work with ILP.

One of the precursor works based on ILP was done by Lee [2]. This work innovated by showing that even with just two QoS parameters (price, SRT), the service selection problem can be reduced to the multi-choice Knapsack problem that is NP-hard. Consequently, polynomial time algorithms should not be expected for this problem, unless P = NP. In considering a more general setting, with a finite number of QoS factors that can be aggregated linearly, an extended formulation of the Lee model was proposed by Yu et al. [11]. Their work also showed that the service selection problem can be reduced to the multidimensional multi-choice Knapsack problem. Let us recall that this confirms the NP-completeness of the problem. Zeng et al. [12], proposed an ILP for service selection on: price, duration, reputation, reliability and availability. The main interest of this work is to state how to linearize constraints related to availability, expressed in an exponential form in aggregation rules. A similar ILP was proposed by Ardagna et al. [15]. Moreover, the authors noticed that the global model was not always feasible. They then proposed a global negotiation algorithm for having a feasible service selection solution. Our work will highlight the benefit of such an algorithm.

ILPs provide an exact solution; but, they are not always efficient when dealing with large problem sizes. This motivated the study of the service selection problem with heuristics.

Zeng et al. [12] proposed an algorithm that, for each service, locally performs service selection optimized for the penalty. As they pointed out, this solution can be suboptimal; however it is a good option for obtaining fast results for the service selection problem. Yu et al. [11] showed how to use the relaxation of their ILP for building a branch and bound algorithm on service selection. The runtime of the resulting algorithm however can be exponential. A similar but faster algorithm was described by Alrifai et al. [7]. Ben Mokhtar et al. [1] proposed a two-phases heuristic for service selection. In the first phase, the heuristic classifies the concrete services regarding their local penalty. The classification is then used for guiding the selection process in the second phase. The advantage of this approach is to propose near-exact solutions for the service selection problem. Finally, genetic programming approaches were also used for solving the service selection problem [8,10,16]. Let us remark that from the service selection problem we can easily derive the gene representation that consists of a string where each character is a service operation. One downside of genetic algorithms is that additional parameters such as the population size need to be tuned.

At this point, it is clear that there are works on service selection. However, as already said in the introduction, our work considers a specific case of WSCs based on multiple collaborating processes. Moreover, we focus on SRT and EC as QoS dimensions. To the best of our knowledge, there is no previous work in this context. In the CHOReOS project we are involved with, near-exact heuristics and genetic programming are desirable for the service selection in order to deal with ultra-large WSCs. In this work however, we propose to use MILP as a preliminary solution. MILP are adequate for having an exact bound that can further be used for assessing the quality of future heuristics proposed on the question.

The next section is devoted to the description of the computational setting in which we study the service selection.

3 Model

For modeling WSCs, we use the hierarchical service graph (HSG) model proposed by Goldman et al. [14].

As shown in Figure 2, an HSG is a graph with three layers, each encapsulating a particular abstraction of a service composition; these are the business processes, the WSs and the machines layers.

The business processes layer, which we will also refer to as the **operations graph**, presents the logic of the service composition in the form of several communicating business processes. We specify this layer by the means of the BPMN graph for collaboration processes. As illustrated by Figure 2b, an operations graph is made of operations (as e.g. $A-D$ in Figure 2b), interconnected within business process (we will also use the term pool) by the means of BPMN connectors (e.g. AND split connector in Figure 2b); between the pools, there are messages exchanges (e.g, between C and E).

At the upper layer of an HSG, there are interactions between abstract operations; the behavior of these operations is implemented in the WSs of the second layer. In the general case, any abstract operation can be implemented within various WSs; moreover, each WS can exist in multiple instances, deployed on various machines [17]. In our study however, we will assume that any WS only exist in one instance, deployed on a single machine.

The connectivity of an HSG is mainly captured by the operations graph (a subgraph of the HSG). In a formal manner, we describe it as a tuple $G_o = (P, O, C, E_{ocp}, E_{oc}, E_{oo})$ where: $P = \{P_1, \ldots, P_h\}$ is the set of pools (business processes of the HSG), O the set of WSs operations, and C the set of BPMN connectors (we consider the AND, XOR and OR connectors).

Here, E_{oc} describes precedence constraints between operations and connectors; E_{ocp} states for each operation and connector its pool and E_{oo} describes messages connections between operations of separated pools.

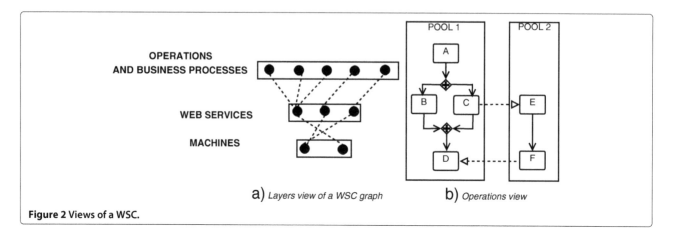

a) *Layers view of a WSC graph*   b) *Operations view*

Figure 2 Views of a WSC.

Given an HSG, we will refer to the part of the operations graph that is contained in a pool as a pool operations graph. Any operation that can send data will be referred to as a sending operation; those that can receive will be referred to as receiving ones.

As stated above, the HSG upper layer is made of multiple communicating business processes. Since the BPMN language is vast, there are multiple possible structures for the operations graph. For the sake of simplicity, we will reduce the potential pool operations graph to the ones derived by composing the patterns of Figure 3. Let us notice that many related works did similar considerations [12,15]. In these patterns, each G_i refers either to a subgraph built from a composition of the patterns, or to a single operation. $G_1*, \ldots G_n*$ refer to subgraphs of G_o, having a unique node without predecessors and a unique one without successors. Finally, let us remark that in the proposed patterns, for each subgraph having a split

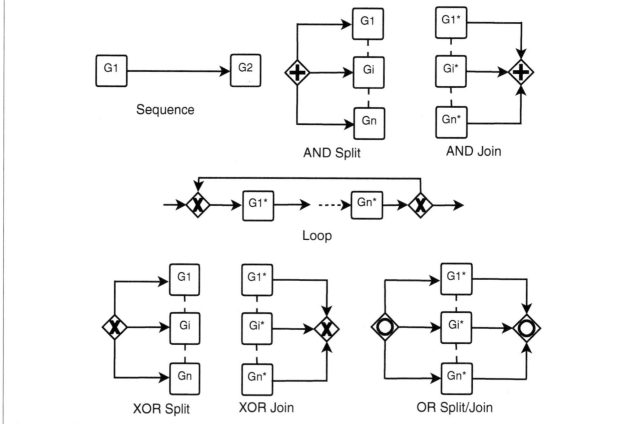

Figure 3 Set of generic subgraph patterns in the operations layer of an HSG. Each G_i is again a subgraph obtained from these patterns or an operation.

OR connector, there must be a corresponding join OR connector.

We described the HSG model that we will use for WSC representation. In the next section, we present our modeling of the service selection problem.

3.1 The service selection problem with HSG

In HSGs, abstract operations of the upper layer are associated with WSs implementations. We will use the term concrete operations for referring to these implementations. In the service selection problem the objective is to look for the best binding to operate between abstract and concrete operations in order to optimize the quality of the service composition. Below, we provide a formal description of the problem.

3.1.1 Problem inputs

Given an HSG, we have the set O of its operations. For each operation $u \in O$, there is a set of concrete implementations $Co(u) = \{u_1, \ldots u_{m_u}\}$. For each concrete implementation u_v, we have the mean SRT $S(u_v)$ and the energy consumption $E(u_v)$. Finally, we have two positive upper bounds $MaxS$ and $MaxE$ on the service response time and a weighted value $w \in [0, 1]$ tuned in the middleware for giving more priority to the SRT or the EC in the problem optimization goal.

3.1.2 Problem objective

We are looking for an assignment of concrete operations for O that fulfills the following constraints:

C_1: each operation must be associated with a unique concrete implementation;

C_2: the QoS of the resulting composition must not exceed $MaxS$ on SRT and $MaxE$ on EC;

C_3: if S is the SRT of the resulting composition and E its energy consumption, then the assignment must minimize the global penalty $w.S + (1 - w)E$.

This formulation is a classical one on service selection [1,2]. The constraint C_2 is used to include SLAs defined by the user on SRT and EC. C_3 defines the global penalty function to be optimized in the middleware perspective.

In our problem formulation, we assume that if we bind each operation with a concrete implementation, then we can compute the mean SRT and EC of the resulting WSC. In the following, we explain how we intend to compute these means by providing an execution semantics for HSGs.

3.2 Execution semantics of HSG

Our execution semantics is based on the idea that it is possible to have a good approximation of the mean value capturing the SRT and EC led by computations and communication on concrete operations. These estimates are then used throughout aggregation rules to infer the SRT and EC of WSCs. This section has two parts. In the first, we present the aggregation rules that we use. In the second, we discuss the computation of a good approximation for the mean SRT and EC.

3.2.1 Aggregation rules for SRT and EC in a pool

The objective of these rules is to state how to infer the SRT and the EC from the generic subgraphs of Figure 3. For the SRT, we will use the aggregation rules proposed in our previous work [14,17]. In our context, we did not find a previous work on aggregation rules for EC. However, we propose to deduce them (as previously done for SRT) from a mean analysis of the possible routing occurrences, in an HSG where the upper layer is reduced to a subgraph pattern. In applying this analysis for energy consumption, we obtain the aggregation rules of Table 1. Here, $E(G_i)$ denotes the SRT that can be expected from a subgraph G_i. On a generic XOR split graph, we assume a probability p_i for a request to be routed towards one subgraph $G_1, \ldots, G_n$. For a loop subgraph, we assume that there is a maximal number of loops n_l and a probability p_{li} to loop i times. Finally, for an OR split/join, we assume for simplification that the request can only be routed to the subgraph G_1, G_2 or simultaneously, to both. Each routing occurrence, has a known probability p_{or1}, p_{or2} and $p_{or\|}$.

The probability values that we consider are the same as the ones used for SRT aggregation as stated in our previous work [14]. For computing these values a training stage where the composition behavior is observed on multiple requests might be necessary. This is not however within the scope of our paper. Aggregation rules for EC differ from the SRT cases on AND and OR subgraphs. Indeed, the SRT for a request that traverses an AND subgraph is the maximal one obtained from the execution of all branches. However since all branches participate in the computation, the EC is obtained by accumulating the local consumptions.

The given rules state how to aggregate SRT and EC in a pool operations graph. For a complete aggregation, communication must be included. This is done in the following.

Table 1 Energy consumption aggregation on subgraphs patterns

Sequence	AND split	AND Join
$E(G_1) + E(G_2)$	$E(G_1) + \cdots + E(G_n)$	$E(G_1^*) + \cdots + E(G_n^*)$

XOR Split	XOR Join	LOOP
$\sum_{i=1}^{n} p_i.E(G_i)$	$\sum_{i=1}^{n} p_i.E(G_i^*)$	$\sum_{i=1}^{n_l} p_{li}.\sum E(G_j^*)$

OR Split/Join		
$p_{or1}.E(G_1) + p_{or2}.E(G_2) + p_{or\|}.(E(G_1) + E(G_2))$		

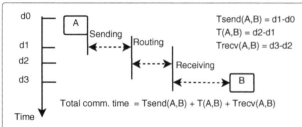

Figure 4 Exchange of information between *A* and *B*, starting at the date d_0 and ending at d_3.

3.2.2 SRT and EC aggregation for communication

For communication, we propose to decompose any data transfer between two operations *A* and *B* in three parts: a sending part where the sending operation is busy, a transit part where the data are routed and a receiving part, where the receiving operation is busy. Figure 4 presents this decomposition. For each of these parts, we have a mean duration time.

This decomposition is the one used in the port model [18]. Since this model has been proved efficient in many practical settings, our assumption on mean SRT for communication holds.

Finally, for estimating the EC for data transport, we refer to the work by Baliga et al. [19]. In their study, they estimate the EC required for sending a bit from a computer to a private or public data center. Their modeling does not contradict the port model. The main idea behind is that the resulting energy can be deduced by aggregating the power consumption of the switches that are part of the communication. Based on this result, we can assume that for any sending between *A* and *B*, we have an estimation of the resulting EC: $E_{A,B}$.

The aggregations rules can be used for computing the SRT and EC of a composition only if it is reasonable to expect a mean SRT and EC at the operation level. This assumption will be discussed in what follows.

3.2.3 Estimates of SRT and EC for computation

The SRT of a concrete operation is the mean time for which it returns a result. For computation we believe that such an estimation is possible if: (1) there is a low variation on the number of FLOPS performed in concrete operation runs; (2) there is a low variation on the mean frequency at which the computer performing the operation runs. With these two assumptions, a good approximation of the SRT can be computed from the mean number of operations performed by each machine in a time unit.

We would like to stress that for a precise estimation, it might be preferable to consider that the runtime of concrete operations are input sensitive. This has implications on modeling the mean time of a concrete operation as a function of the input data size that it processes. However, we did not make these considerations here for the sake

of simplicity. Other works also use similar SRT modeling [12,17,20].

For the EC of a WS operation, we adopt the definition of Bartalos et al. [21]. The EC of an operation is the total power consumed by hardware resources. We formalize this definition as follows. In our HSG model, *u* is executed on a unique machine $m(u)$. If at each time instant *t* during this run, a power $P_{m(u),u}(t)$ is consumed, then the energy consumption of this operation is $E_u(t) = \int_t^{t+t_u} P_{m(u),u}(t).dt$. In the same vein of our assumption (for the SRT case) of a low variation on machine frequency and number of FLOPS, we also consider that we have a low variation on the power $P_{m(u),u}(t)$ between distinct time instants. Therefore, the EC caused by o_u will be $E_u = P_{m(u),u}(0).t_u$. Here, t_u is the mean response time of the operation o_u.

At this stage, the service selection problem that we are addressing is clarified. In the next section, we will analyze this further.

3.3 Analysis of the service selection problem

Lee [2] established the NP-hardness of the service selection problem. The NP-hardness proof considers the service selection problem on a sequence of operations. However, we believe that by relaxing some constraints, the problem could be simpler. The aim of this section is to propose an analysis of the service selection in the specific case where $MaxS = MaxE = +\infty$. We will refer to this relaxed version as the SLAs free service selection problem. The SLA free problem has a practical implication on the negotiation stage when building a service composition. At the beginning, a user who wants to compose services might not have an idea of the SRT and EC that he expects. In such a context, we can globally minimize the penalty by deferring to the middleware to choose the best service composition. Now we present some results for the SLA free problem.

Property 1. In the case where we have (1) a sequence of operations; (2) an XOR split tree whose branches comprise sequence of operations; (3) a loop on a sequence of operations; the optimal solution for the SLA free problem can be obtained in polynomial time in the maximal number of abstract and concrete operations.

Proof. Let us consider indeed a sequence of *l* abstract operations $o^1, \ldots o^l$. If for any operation o^i, we chose a concrete one o_{is}^i then the total sequence penalty is $\sum_{i=1}^l [w.S(o_{is}^i) + (1-w).E(o_{is}^i)]$. This is the sum of the penalties of chosen operations. Therefore, the SLA free problem here consists of choosing a set of services such as to minimize the sum of their penalties. Since the penalty is always positive, we can then obtain an optimal solution by local optimization of the penalty. The same construction can be applied in the case of XOR trees and loops made of sequences. Finally if m is the maximal number of concrete services for each $o^i, i \in \{1, \ldots, l\}$, then the described process can be performed in $O(m.l)$. □

An interesting question then is whether or not the local optimization approach used in the previous proof gives an optimal solution on any type of process graphs. The answer is no.

Property 2. If the SRT and EC values can be drawn from any arbitrary distribution, then the local optimization approach on the SLA free problem is not always optimal if we have AND split patterns.

For instance, let us consider an AND split tree with two branches. The first tree branch has an operation u and the second an operation v. Here, $w = 0.1$ and each operation can be associated to two concrete ones according to the SRT and EC given in Table 2.

While local optimization will bind u with u_1 and v with v_1 (resulting penalty: $(0.1 * \max\{5, 8\} + (12 + 12.6) * 0.9 = 22.94$), the best solution consists of binding u with u_2 and v with v_1 (resulting penalty: $0.1 * \max\{8, 8\} + (11.8 + 12.6) * 0.9 = 22.76$).

Our proposed counter-example exploits the fact that it is only after choosing an assignment on all branches that we can deduce the final resulting SRT. Implicitly, this suggests that an exploration of possible solutions that consider all possible SRT values might give optimal results. Let us for example consider the specific case of a sequence of *elementary* Fork/Join. Each fork here comprises at most D branches made of one operation. Let us assume that the operations SRT are all positive integers and that each operation can be associated with at most m concrete ones. Let us also assume that $S^+ = \sum_{u \in O} \max_{x \in Co(u)} S(x)$. We have the following result.

Theorem 1. *Given an elementary Fork/join sequence. If D is the maximal number of branches to which a Fork can*

lead to, then the optimal solution for the SLA free problem can be computed in $O(h.D.(S^+)^2.(m \log m))$ where h is the depth of the sequence.

Proof. For elementary Fork/join sequences, we propose to make a bi-dimensional exploration on SRT and depth. Our exploration is also based on dynamic programming and work by exploring first the SRT dimension. Any point (e, f) is a partial assignment made for all services that are under the depth e and that leads to a global SRT equal to f. We associate each point (e, f) with an EC denoted $d(e, f)$. $d(e, f)$ is the minimal EC that can be obtained from any assignment for operations at depths $1, \ldots e - 1$ and whose SRT is f.

The computation of this weight obeys to a sub-optimality rule. Let $Z(e', f')$ be the minimal cumulated EC obtained from an assignment made on abstract operations of the depth v' and whose maximal SRT is e'. Then, we have the following equation:

$$d(e, f) = \min_{f' \in \{0, \ldots f-1\}} \{d(e - 1, f') + Z(e, f - f')\}.$$

The computation of $Z(e', f')$ can be done as follows. The operations whose SRT exceeds f' are firstly eliminated from all set of concrete services at the depth e'. If this leads to an empty set or if there is not an operation with SRT equal to f' then we return $Z(e', f') = +\infty$. Otherwise, we sort each set $Co(u)$ on the EC and we return for each operation, the minimal EC while ensuring that at least one operation of a branch has an SRT equal to f'. The sum of these minimal ECs is returned in $Z(e', f')$. Naturally, at each point (e, f), we have two cases: either an assignment is possible and then we keep the one leading to the minimization of $d(e, f)$ at depth f, or there is not a possible assignment (we only have infinite values when running Z). Then, there will not be any assignment associated with this point.

When we end the computations of values $d(h, f), f = 0, \ldots, S^+$, we then compute the possible penalty costs at height h. These can be obtained from the following relation: $u(h, f) = a.f + (1 - a).d(h, f)$. We return as optimal solution the one that leads to the minimal penalty at depth h.

The proposed Bellman equation assumes that we can decompose the optimal solution on a Fork/Join sequence into a set of solutions optimized for EC for any pair $(SRT, depth)$. Such a characterization holds on Fork/Join sequences. □

This dynamic programming can be used with local optimization to obtain an optimal solution on other cases such as an elementary AND split combined with a sequence, nested AND tree etc.

Table 2 Counter-example on the optimality of local optimization

(a) Costs on u			
SRT	EC	Penalty	Concrete operation
5	12	11.3	u_1
8	11.8	11.42	u_2

(b) Costs on v			
SRT	EC	Penalty	Concrete operation
8	12.6	12.14	v_1
9	12.7	12.33	v_2

We showed that fast solutions can be obtained on some cases of the SLA free problem. If however we include SLAs, even on sequence case, we already have an NP-hard problem to solve. Next, we will consider a more general approach for the resolution of the service selection problem in HSGs.

4 Solving the service selection problem

Our resolution of the service selection problem uses our prior algorithm proposed for QoS prediction [14]. Let us refer to it as **SRT_LP_gen**. Given an operations graph $G_o = (P, O, C, E_{ocp}, E_{oc}, E_{oo})$ where we already have a concrete service associated with each abstract one, **SRT_LP_gen** states how to generate a linear program that when solved will return the SRT of the resulting WSC. For solving the selection problem, we propose to modify **SRT_LP_gen** in order to: (1) introduce the choice of concrete services; (2) compute the EC of the composition; (3) introduce constraints related to SLAs and penalty. In doing so, instead of a Linear Program, we will obtain an MILP. Below, we give a description of these different stages.

4.1 Introducing a choice among concrete operations

For each operation $u \in O$, we associate a bi-dimensional $0 - 1$ variable $y_{u,j}$ such that

$$y_{u,j} = \begin{cases} 1 & \text{if the concrete service } u_j \in Co(u) \text{ is bound with } u \\ 0 & \text{otherwise.} \end{cases}$$

In **SRT_LP_gen**, any operation u has an SRT value defined as a constant $T(u)$. For the binding purpose, we

will change it into a variable. We also introduce a variable $D(u)$ giving the EC of the operation u. On these variables, we propose to generate the following equations:

$$T(u) = \sum_{j=1}^{|Co(u)|} y_{u,j}.S(u_j) \qquad \forall u \qquad (1)$$

$$D(u) = \sum_{j=1}^{|Co(u)|} y_{u,j}.E(u_j) \qquad \forall u \qquad (2)$$

$$y_{u,j} \in \{0, 1\} \qquad \forall u, j \qquad (3)$$

$$\sum_{j=1}^{|Co(u)|} y_{u,j} = 1 \qquad \forall u \qquad (4)$$

Let us remark that in defining $T(u)$ as variables, we still keep linear equations on SRT constraints. For each abstract operation u, the equations $1 - 4$ set in the variables $T(u)$ and $D(u)$, the SRT and EC that they will have, depending on the concrete service to which they are bound (the service u_j for which $y_{u,j} = 1$).

4.2 Computing the EC of a composition

We associate each operation $x \in O$ with a real variable e_x. **SRT_LP_gen** successively explores the sets E_{oc}, and E_{oo}. During this exploration, multiple interpretations are associated with every arc in order to generate the mean SRT. These interpretations will lead to the generation of an equation that we denote Eq. Our goal is to extend **SRT_LP_gen** to generate EC constraints. For this, we revisit the different arc interpretations in

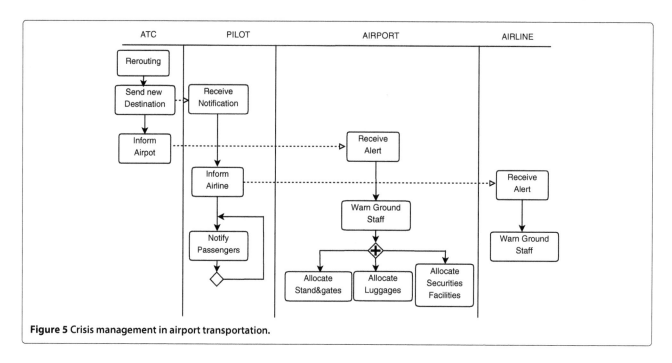

Figure 5 Crisis management in airport transportation.

SRT_LP_gen and include equations related to the EC. For any arc $(u, v) \in E_{oc}$ during the exploration, we thus have the following additional equations that we generate:

C_1: [u does not have a predecessor]: $Eq \longleftarrow e_u \geq D(u)$;

C_2: [$u, v \in O$] : $Eq \longleftarrow e_v \geq e_u + p_a[(u, v)].D(v)$;
$\quad$ [$u \in O \cup C, v \in C$]

C_3: If v is an XOR join that closes a loop (there is $(v, s) \in E_{oc}$ and a path $(s, y_1), \ldots, (y_n, u)$ of E_{oc}), then
$\quad Eq \longleftarrow e_v \geq \sum_{i=1}^{nl[v]} p_{li}(e_u - e_s) + e_s$;
$\quad$ Here, $nl[v]$ is the maximal index of looping stage;

C_4: If v is a split connector then $Eq \longleftarrow e_v \geq e_u$;
$\quad$ [$u \in C, v \in O \cup C$]

C_5: If u is a join connector then $Eq \longleftarrow e_v \geq e_u$;

C_6: If u is a split then $Eq \longleftarrow e_v \geq p_r[(u, v)].e_u$
$\quad + p_a[(u, v)].D(v)$; [v is a join connector whose predecessors are $u_1, \ldots, u_n$]

C_7: If v is an AND JOIN then $Eq \longleftarrow e_v \geq \sum_{i=1}^{n} e_{u_i}$;

C_8: If v is an XOR JOIN but does not close a loop then
$\quad Eq \longleftarrow e_v \geq \sum_{i=1}^{n} e_{u_i}$;

C_9: If v is a OR JOIN then $Eq \longleftarrow e_v \geq \sum_{i=1}^{2} e_{u_i} + p_{or||}$
$\quad (v).em(u_1, u_2)$ and $Eq \longleftarrow em(u_1, u_2) \geq \frac{e_{u_1}}{p_r[(u_1,v)]} +$
$\quad \frac{e_{u_1}}{p_r[(u_1,v)]}$;

$pr_a[(u, v)]$ and $p_a[(u, v)]$ are conditional and reachability probabilities. They are defined by Goldman et al. [14]. These constraints differ from the SRT ones in the interpretation of parallelism. While for SRT, we must take the SRT of the longest path, for EC, we must take the sum from all paths. Using the same philosophy for interpreting parallelism, we can easily extend on EC the constraints on SRT defined in **SRT_LP_gen** for aggregating EC in the resulting WSC.

4.3 SLAs and penalty constraints
With the proposed modifications, this stage we will have at two variables: ZS that comprises the SRT of the service composition and ZE that comprises its EC. We then add the following equations for computing SLAs and penalty:

$$ZS \leq MaxS \qquad (5)$$

$$ZE \leq MaxE \qquad (6)$$

$$Z = w.ZS + (1 - w).ZE \qquad (7)$$

Finally, we set that the objective function of the MILP is the minimization of the variable Z.

4.4 Analysis
It might seem that our algorithm generates too many variables or constraints. However, this number is polynomial as stated by the following result.

Theorem 2. *Given a graph* $G_0 = (P, O, C, E_{ocp}, E_{oc}, E_{oo})$, *the generated MILP has at most* $O(n.m)$ *variables and* $O(n.m)$ *equations where* $n = |O \cup C|$ *and* $m = \max_{u \in O} |Co(u)|$.

Proof. The execution of **SRT_LP_gen** in our approach will generate at most $O(n)$ variables and $O(n)$ equations [14]. By adding equations related to EC, we keep the same order of complexity. However, variables and constraints related to the choice of a concrete service will lead to $O(n.m)$ and equations. $\square$

Given the value *MaxS* and *MaxE*, the MILP might not find any solution because the problem is infeasible. In that case, it might be interesting to assist the user in the generation of a good compromise. We propose to approximate the intervals of SRT and EC values with which the problem is feasible.

For determining the interval $[S_{min}, \ldots, S_{max}]$ *of feasible values* for MaxS, we use two policies: the *SRT_Min_First* policy and the *SRT_Max_First*. In *SRT_Min_First*, we run the MILP with the variables $y_{u,j}$ tuned as follows:

$$y_{u,j} = \begin{cases} 1 \text{ if the concrete operation } u_j \text{ has the minimal SRT on } u \\ 0 \text{ otherwise} \end{cases}$$

The result that contains ZS after this run is S_{min}. In the *SRT_Max_First*, we proceed in the same way; however, we choose the concrete operations with a maximal SRT preference. At the end, we have an approximation of S_{max}. In the same way, we can develop *EC_Min_First* and *EC_Max_First* policies for computing the interval of possible EC values.

Finally, a user might want to know what is the minimal EC that he can expect given a maximal SRT value. In such cases, we propose to remove the equation $ZE \leq MaxE$ in the MILP, to set $w = 0$ and then run the MILP. ZE will return the minimal EC that can be expected for this SRT value. A similar transformation can be applied for

Table 3 Experimental settings

#Series	1	2	3	4	5	6	7	8	9	10
MaxE	1600	1600	1700	1700	1800	1800	1900	1900	2000	2000
MaxS	1600	1650	1650	1700	1700	1750	1750	1800	1800	1850

Given a series (e.g. 1) and a maximal number of concrete services (e.g. 20), we performed 100 experiments. We did not change the value of w in the experiments. We always have $w = 0.5$.

choosing the minimal SRT that can be expected given a maximal EC.

5 Application

The CHOReOS project is interested in optimizing the interactions among various processes collaborating on airport transportation. A collaboration use case is the crisis management when facing bad weather condition during a flight. This use case involves an air traffic control (ATC), a pilot (more precisely an internal plane system), an airport and an airline. We can describe the collaboration as follows. Due to bad weather conditions, the ATC decides to cancel all flights. It checks for scheduled flights, reroutes them and notifies all concerned pilots. The pilots inform their airlines and passengers. The ATC also informs the airport at which the flight is rerouted about its decision. This airport then prepares its ground staff for the new situation.

A complete description of the use case has been done by Chatel et al. [22]. In our work, we consider only the sub-view presented in Figure 5.

There are multiple possible Web implementations of the process given in Figure 5. In particular, we can either use a sub-composition for implementing an activity or a WS operation. In our experiment we will consider the latter option for all activities.

5.1 Experimental setting

For the crisis management example, we performed 10 series of 1000 experiments. These experiments had two objectives: the first was to show that the proposed MILP approach has a real qualitative advantage over local optimization. The second was to show that although we use MILP, reasonable time can be expected in practice.

Each series is determined by the parameters $MaxE$ and $MaxS$ used for SLAs. The ones that we used are set in

Table 3. For each experiment, we created multiple concrete operations to be associated with abstract ones. The number of concrete operations belongs to the set {10, 20, 30, 40, 50, 60, 70, 80, 90, 100}. For any experiment, we always chose the same number of concrete services for all abstract operations. This means that in any experiment, we have $\max_{u \in O} |Co(u)| = \min_{u \in O} |Co(u)|, \forall u$.

The concrete operations SRT values are drawn from the uniform distribution within $[100, 1000]$ (in ms). Assuming that an operation has an SRT equal to S and leads to a mean power consumption equal to P during its execution, we used the formula $E = P.S$ for computing its EC. We draw P (in watt) from the uniform distribution in the interval $[100, 200]$. Finally, we chose the number of loops for passenger notification from the uniform distribution between 1 and 10, the communication times between 10 and 40 (ms) and we normalized E in order to have a metric in watt-second.

We performed our experiments on an Intel Core i7 processor, 2.7 Ghz, 8 GB. The implementations were done in C language with the GLPK solver [23].

5.2 Experimental results

In Figure 6, we show the mean aggregated penalties obtained from our experiments with our MILP approach and the *EC_Min_First* and *SRT_Min_First* policies. The aggregates are made on the number of concrete operations used in the experiment. These results are the optimal ones that the GLPK solver computed in each case. The results describe an increase of the penalty on the maximal number of concrete operations. This is due to the fact that in increasing the number of concrete services, we increase the diversity (or the standard deviation) in SRT and EC per operations. We also did a comparison of the penalties between the local optimization policies and MILP. The results are reported in Table 4 and confirm the

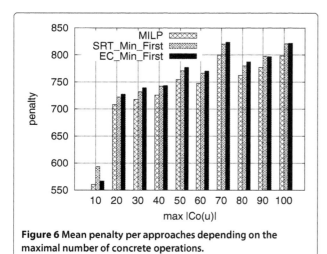

Figure 6 Mean penalty per approaches depending on the maximal number of concrete operations.

Table 4 Ratio of mean aggregated penalties between the local approaches and the MILP

$\max_{u \in O} |Co(u)|$	SRT_Min_First	EC_Min_First
10	1.059	1.011
20	1.020	1.027
30	1.022	1.030
40	1.021	1.024
50	1.025	1.029
60	1.025	1.030
70	1.022	1.029
80	1.026	1.032
90	1.027	1.025
100	1.028	1.029

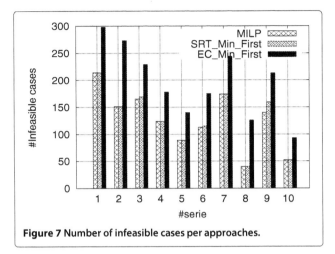

Figure 7 Number of infeasible cases per approaches.

Table 6 MILP Runtime (in 10^{-2} seconds)

#Series	1	2	3	4	5	6	7	8	9	10
Runtime	5.0	5.2	6.3	6.8	6.7	8.0	10.5	8.6	9.1	8.9

the NP-hardness of the service selection problem, we can expect to solve it in a reasonable runtime even with more than 1300 concrete operations. Let us however notice that we do not expect such results if we increase both the number of abstract and concrete services.

6 Conclusion

In this paper, we proposed new solutions for optimizing the selection of services on service response time and energy consumption on Web service compositions. We proposed two cases in the optimization: the SLAs free case where there is no constraint on the maximal service response time and energy consumption and the general case where such constraints are included. In the SLA free case, we showed that in some settings, the problem can be solved by the means of local optimization and dynamic programming. In the general case, we proposed an algorithm that generates an MILP solving the problem. We tested our solutions with multiple simulations that have globally shown that our MILP gives better results than local optimization.

We have multiple opportunities for continuing this work. The first is to extend the MILP generation on other QoS parameters such as the availability and the reputation. The main challenge will consist of translating the aggregation rules into adequate equations. Our second opportunity is to develop a global solution including negotiation for the SLAs. As our experiments showed, indeed there are many cases where we have infeasible problems. A negotiation stage might also be considered for another feature that we did not include: it is possible to re-select services in the case where our estimates of the service response time and energy consumption are wrong. Our third opportunity is to reconsider the modeling of the penalty function. One weak point of our formulation is that we aggregate values of different units (for instance ms and watt). An investigation of the best formulation to adopt certainly promising.

Finally, let us remark that for cloud architectures, we need to take into account virtualization. This implies modifications of the notion of HSG in other to add a virtualization layer. An immediate consequence of this modeling is that we must include potential QoS fluctuation due to the migration of virtual machines. For this, we envision two tasks to perform. One is to make a sensitivity analysis of our proposal. The other is to extend our approach to include this dynamicity in the modeling of SRT and EC.

superiority of MILP over local optimization as suggested by our previous analysis.

For the sake of fairness, we aggregated the penalties values in the experiments only when there were no approaches leading to an infeasible solution. In many cases indeed, the problem was infeasible. For each approach, Figure 7 reports the number of infeasible solutions that were detected. These results globally confirm the need to establish a negotiation procedure with the users for preventing infeasible problems. As shown by the results, it does not suffice to increase the maximal service response time or the energy consumption to have less infeasible cases. This number depends on the combination of these two parameters but also on the QoS of the concrete services. To conclude on infeasibility, we compared MILP and local optimization. The results presented in the Table 5 state that in all cases where a solution was found by local optimization, we found one with the MILP.

Finally in Table 6, we present the MILP runtime. The results are encouraging they show that despite

Table 5 Ratio of the number of infeasible cases between the local approaches and the MILP

#series	SRT_Min_First	EC_Min_First
1	1.000	1.392
2	1.000	1.807
3	1.024	1.387
4	1.000	1.435
5	1.000	1.573
6	1.017	1.548
7	1.000	1.402
8	1.000	3.15
9	1.136	1.521
10	1.000	1.788

Competing interests
The authors declare that they have no competing interests.

Authors' contributions
YN, AG and DM proposed an MILP-based algorithm for the service selection problem in web services compositions, implementing multiple business processes. All authors read and approved the final manuscript.

Acknowledgements
This research was funded by HP Brasil under the Baile Project and from the European Community's Seventh Framework Programme FP7/2007-2013 under grant agreement number 257178 (project CHOReOS-Large Scale Choreographies for the Future Internet). Yanik Ngoko was partially supported by the FAPESP foundation of the State of São Paulo.

Author details
[1] Laboratoire d'Informatique de Paris Nord, Villetaneuse, France. [2] IME-USP, São Paulo, Brasil. [3] HP Labs, Palo Alto, USA.

References
1. Ben Mokhtar S, Kaul A, Georgantas N, Issarny V (2006) Efficient semantic service discovery in pervasive computing environments In: Proceedings of the ACM/IFIP/USENIX 2006 international conference on Middleware, Middleware '06. Springer-Verlag New York, Inc., Melbourne, pp 240–259
2. Lee J (2003) Matching algorithms for composing business process solutions with web services. In: Bauknecht K, Tjoa AM, Quirchmayr G (eds) Proceedings of the 4th international conference on E-Commerce and web technologies, Lecture Notes in Computer Science. Springer, Prague, pp 393–402
3. OWL-S: Semantic Markup for Web Services. www.w3.org/Submission/OWL-S
4. Web Service Semantics – WSDL-S, Technical Note. lsdis.cs.uga.edu/projects/meteor-s/wsdl-s
5. Burstein MH, Hobbs JR, Lassila O, Martin D, McDermott DV, McIlraith SA, Narayanan S, Paolucci M, Payne TR, Sycara KP (2002) Daml-s: Web service description for the semantic web In: Proceedings of the first international semantic web conference on the semantic web, ISWC '02. Springer-Verlag, London, pp 348–363
6. The choreos project. www.choreos.eu
7. Alrifai M, Risse T, Dolog P, Nejdl W (2009) A scalable approach for qos-based web service selection. In: Feuerlicht G, Lamersdorf W (eds) Service-oriented computing — ICSOC 2008 workshops. Springer-Verlag, Berlin, Heidelberg, pp 190–199
8. Canfora G, Di Penta M, Esposito R, Villani ML (2005) An approach for qos-aware service composition based on genetic algorithms In: Proceedings of the 2005 conference on genetic and evolutionary computation, GECCO '05. ACM, Washington DC, pp 1069–1075
9. Issarny V, Georgantas N, Hachem S, Zarras A, Vassiliadis P, Autili M, Gerosa MA, Hamida AB (2011) Service-oriented middleware for the future internet: state of the art and research directions. J Internet Serv Appl 2(1): 23–45
10. Jaeger M, Rojec-Goldmann G, Muhl G (2004) Qos aggregation for web service composition using workflow patterns In: Proceeding EDOC '04 Proceedings of the Enterprise Distributed Object Computing Conference, Eighth IEEE International. IEEE Computer Society, Washington, DC, USA, pp 149–159
11. Yu T, Zhang Y, Lin KJ (2007) Efficient algorithms for web services selection with end-to-end qos constraints. ACM Trans. Web 1(1). doi:10.1145/1232722.1232728
12. Zeng L, Benatallah B, Ngu AHH, Dumas M, Kalagnanam J, Chang H (2004) Qos-aware middleware for web services composition. IEEE Trans. Softw. Eng. 30(5): 311–327
13. Weske M (2007) Business process management: concepts, languages, architectures. Springer
14. Goldman A, Ngoko Y, Milojicic D (2012) An analytical approach for predicting qos of web services choreographies In: Proceedings of the 10th international workshop on Middleware for grids, clouds and e-Science, MGC '12. ACM, Montreal, Canada, pp 4:1–4:6
15. Ardagna D, Pernici B (2007) Adaptive service composition in flexible processes. IEEE Trans Softw Eng 33(6): 369–384
16. Cao L, Li M, Cao J (2007) Using genetic algorithm to implement cost-driven web service selection. Multiagent Grid Syst 3(1): 9–17
17. Goldman A, Ngoko Y (2012) On graph reduction for qos prediction of very large web service compositions In: International conference on service oriented computing (SCC). IEEE Press, Hawai, pp 258–265
18. Banikazemi M, Sampathkumar J, Prabhu S, Panda DK, Sadayappan P (1999) Communication modeling of heterogeneous networks of workstations for performance characterization of collective operations In: Proceedings of the eighth Heterogeneous Computing Workshop, HCW '99. IEEE Computer Society, Washington, DC, pp 125–133
19. Baliga J, Ayre R, Hinton K, Tucker RS (2011) Green cloud computing: balancing energy in processing, storage, and transport. Proc IEEE 99(1): 149–167
20. Cardoso J, Miller J, Sheth A, Arnold J (2002) Modeling quality of service for workflows and web service processes. J Web Semantics 1: 281–308
21. Bartalos P, Blake MB (2012) Green Web Services: Modeling and Estimating Power Consumption of Web Services In: International Conference on Web Services. IEEE Computer Society, Honolulu, USA, pp 178–185
22. Châtel P, Léger A, Lockerbie J (2011) Choreos requirements and scenarios for the "passenger-friendly airport" (d6.1). http://hal.inria.fr/hal-00664313. Hal_id = hal-00664313
23. The GNU Linear Programming Kit. http://www.gnu.org/software/glpk/

11

Adoption of security as a service

Christian Senk

Abstract

Security as a Service systems enable new opportunities to compose security infrastructures for information systems. However, to date there are no holistic insights about their adoption and relevant predictors. Based on existing technology acceptance models we developed an extended application-specific research model including formative and reflective measures. The model was estimated applying the *Partial Least Squares* technique to address the prediction-oriented nature of the study. A subsequent online survey revealed that a large number of industries shows significant and steadily growing interest in *Security as a Service*. Adoption drivers were investigated systematically.

Keywords: Cloud computing, Partial least squares, Security as a service

1 Introduction

Companies face an increasing threat regarding the security and safety of their information systems due to the opening of security domains for web-based access in the course of current technological developments such as *Federated Identity Management* [1] and *Cloud Computing* [2,3]. In this regard, *Cloud Computing* is a model "for enabling convenient, on-demand network access to a shared pool of configurable computing resources [. . .]" [4]. These resources are referred to as *Cloud services* and can logically be assigned to the infrastructure, (*Infrastructure as a Service*, IaaS), middleware (*Platform as a Service*, PaaS) or application software layer (*Software as a Service*, SaaS) [5,6]. The *Cloud Computing* model itself not only induces certain security-related risks, it also opens up new opportunities to obtain innovative security solutions in a technically and economically flexible way in order to cope with rising security demands [7]. The outsourcing of security according to SaaS principles is referred to as *Security as a Service* (SECaaS) [3,8]. Such systems are considered to be the next step in the evolution of *Managed Security Services* (MSS) and differ clearly from traditional outsourcing models or on-premises deployments [3,8,9]. According to GARTNER RESEARCH, the demand for SECaaS will grow significantly and might substantially change existing IT security infrastructure landscapes [10]. However, no deep insights about the current adoption and future developments exist. In this regard, based on an expert-group discussion[a]

we defined that the answers to the following research questions (RQ) are important to predict the future of SECaaS:

- **RQ1:** Is there a market for SECaaS enterprise applications in general and for specific application types in particular?
- **RQ2:** Which are the key drivers and inhibitors for the adoption of SECaaS?
- **RQ3:** Which benefits are perceived to be relevant by potential adopters of SECaaS?
- **RQ4:** Which risks are perceived to be relevant by potential adopters of SECaaS?
- **RQ5:** Which organization-specific factors (e.g. company size) affect the acceptance of SECaaS?

The main objective of this paper is to answer these research questions through empirical research in order to gain insights valuable for both potential consumers and providers of SECaaS. The remainder of this paper is structured as follows: Section 2 defines SECaaS and overviews related work regarding the adoption of similar technologies. In Section 3 the research concept is specified and justified. Section 4 gives an overview of the results of the estimation of the research model and the related hypotheses. Afterward, the findings are discussed respecting the specified research questions. Section 5 concludes the paper.

Correspondence: christian.senk@wiwi.uni-regensburg.de
University of Regensburg, Regensburg, Germany

2 Theoretical background

This chapter provides the theoretical background for the context of the study. This includes the object of adoption (SECaaS), which is defined in Subsection 2.1. Subsequently, an overview of related work regarding the adoption of similar technological innovations is provided in Subsection 2.2 in order to identify adequate research approaches.

2.1 Security as a service

SECaaS is a service-oriented approach to IT security architecture and thus a consequent evolution of traditional security landscapes [8,9]. It is defined as a model for the delivery of standardized and comprehensive security functionality in accordance with the SaaS model [8,11]. It thus follows the *Cloud Computing* model. Hence, SECaaS systems are delivered in form of Cloud services complying with related principles. This excludes built-in security controls of existing Cloud services [11]. Key attributes of Cloud services contain the following [5,6,12]:

- Application and underlying infrastructure are abstracted and offered through service interfaces;

- Standardized network access by any device;

- Scalability and flexibility of the underlying infrastructure;

- Shared and multi-tenant resources;

- On-demand self-service provisioning and near real-time deployment;

- Flexible and fine grained pricing without up-front commitments.

Based on the market-oriented taxonomy of KARK for outsourced security services [13] and the adaption of SENK AND HOLZAPFEL [14] we classify SECaaS systems as depicted in Table 1. This classification scheme was recently validated by a survey of existing SECaaS offerings [14]. According to that survey, the majority of existing SECaaS products cover *Endpoint Security* or *Content Security* applications [14]. The authors further outline existing systems' deficient compliance with Cloud and SaaS design principles. Especially inflexible pricing models often restrict the potential value of existent SECaaS systems [14]. It has to be noted that the granularity of SECaaS offerings can vary from fine-grained basic services addressing highly specific security needs (e.g. biometric user authentication) to coarse-grained solutions covering a broad set of security functionalities.

The delivery of security services according to the SECaaS model differs clearly from traditional MSS provisioning and on-premises deployments (see Figure 1). *On-premises security systems* are deployed, operated, and maintained on the client's side [11]. This requires the allocation of dedicated IT and human resource capacities. Service costs do not scale up or down with the actual degree of capacity utilization. None of the identified Cloud principles apply [14]. *Managed Security Services* are characterized in that a dedicated security service instance is set up for a client organization by an external service provider. This involves the prior negotiation of individual *Service Level Agreements* (SLA) [11]. In this regard, the provider is responsible for the operation and maintenance of the system [15-17]. Such security services do not provide for native multi-tenancy. Hence, the instant service use is not feasible and economies of scale are not exhausted [18]. Additionally, service usage may involve the deployment of dedicated software and hardware components and due to the initial effort required clients are often bound to providers by fixed-term licenses and up-front commitments [19]. Traditional managed service provisioning thus follows the *Application Service Providing* (ASP) model [12,14,20]. In contrast, *Security as a Service* solutions are fully operated and maintained by the service provider with no dedicated client-sided hardware or software necessary [11,14]. Full virtualization of the security service ensures the highest degree of capacity utilization. This makes the service usage highly cost-effective to the customer and enables fine-grained pay-per-use models. A virtualized multi-tenancy architecture not only enables the instant start of service use but also leverages inherent data aggregation benefits for service providers [14]. Moreover, operational and organizational flexibility is improved [11].

2.2 Adoption of related technologies

The term *Adoption* can be traced back to ROGERS' (1962) diffusion of innovations theory and is defined as a consumer's positive decision to accept and use an innovation, which ultimately leads to a positive investment decision and actual use [21]. Adopters can be individuals or organizations [22].

There are only a few current insights regarding the adoption of the outsourcing of IT security. GARTNER and FORRESTER RESEARCH conducted analyses of the MSS market and forecasted a steady and significant growth [7,13]. Moreover, FORRESTER RESEARCH surveyed IT security decision makers and identified major benefits of MSS [13]: Quality improvements, 24×7 support, cost reduction, and decrease of the complexity of security infrastructures. However, the study is not suitable regarding the research questions identified in this paper since the adoption was not investigated holistically and not focused on Cloud systems.

Benlian et al. conducted a meta-survey of the adoption of SaaS systems and applied different research theories [23]. They concluded that behavioral theories reveal more consistent results regarding the adoption of SaaS systems

Table 1 Classification of SECaaS applications

Application type	Description
Application security	Secure operation of software applications (e.g. application firewalls, code analyzers)
Compliance & IT Security management (ITSM)	Support of the client organization's compliance and IT security management (e.g. automatic compliance checks, benchmarking)
Content security	Protection of content data from intended attacks and undesired events (e.g. e-mail encryption, filtering of network traffic)
Endpoint security	Protection of servers or client computers in networks (e.g. malware protection, host-based intrusion detection)
Identity & access management	Identification of users, provisioning of user identity attributes and assignment of necessary privileges (e.g. single sign-on, multi-factor authentication)
Devices management	Remote management of client-sided security systems (e.g. intrusion detection and prevention systems)
Security information & event management (SIEM)	Specific security-related functions for monitoring complex IT systems (e.g. archiving and analysis of log-data, forensic analysis)
Vulnerability & threat management (VTM)	Detection of threats apart of eminent internal security incidents (e.g. patch management, notifications on current attacks)

than economic or strategic research theories [23]. Behavioral theories include the *Technology Acceptance Model* (TAM) [24], the *Theory of the Diffusion of Innovation* [21], and the *Unified Theory of Acceptance and Use of Technology* (UTAUT) [22]. The results indicate that the adoption of SaaS technologies is mainly influenced by [23]:

- Social influences,
- Attitude toward the technology,
- Uncertainty of adoption,
- Strategic value of respective resources.

However, due to the underlying research design, these results do not provide for causality [23]. BENLIAN ET

AL. also concluded that both the adoption and adoption drivers differ across application types, which should be considered in future research [23]. Previous research indicates a higher susceptibility to SaaS adoption for smaller and medium-sized companies [23] and a different perception of risks and potential benefits by large-scale organizations [25], although no correlation was discovered between company size and adoption [23]. Udoh applied a combined model including elements of UTAUT and TAM and observed that the adoption of grid, Cloud and related technologies can be causally explained by four predictors [26]:

- Effort expectations (Perceived ease of use),

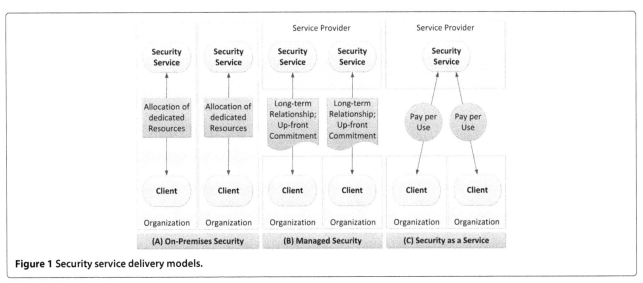

Figure 1 Security service delivery models.

- Risk expectations (Trust),
- Performance expectations (Perceived usefulness),
- Individual attitude.

Udoh's model provides a very high level of explanation which indicates a high aptitude for its application in similar technology acceptance studies [26]. Furthermore, its generic constructs can be itemized according to the specifics of subsequent research.

3 Research design

Based on related studies [23,26], this paper applies the *Structural Equations Modeling* methodology. For the model estimation involved, the *Partial Least Squares* technique is used. The methodology is introduced and justified in Subsection 3.1. Subsequently, in Subsection 3.2, a system of hypotheses -the research model- is developed. In Subsection 3.3, the measurement model is derived from this research model.

3.1 Methodology

Common technology acceptance theories like TAM or UTAUT are based on the development and testing of hypotheses regarding the influences of theoretical constructs on each other [22]. A system of hypotheses can be modeled as a system of equations [27]. A common approach to solving such systems is *Structural Equations Modeling* (SEM) [27]. SEM is defined as "a comprehensive statistical approach to testing hypotheses about relations among observed and latent variables" [27]. Besides the structural model, which primarily prescribes hypothetical relations between latent variables, a measurement model is required to quantize thes variables [27].

The measurement model prescribes not directly observed (latent) variables of the structural model by a set of measurable indicators [27]. Measurement models can be reflective or formative. Reflective measurement models assume empirically measurable variables. In this regard, the latent variable causes a set of reflective measurement indicators which correlate highly among each other [28]. In contrast, formative measurement models estimate a latent variable, applying a set of indicators, which are assumed to cause the construct [29]. This facilitates the differentiated analysis of the relevance and strength of certain influences on a theoretical construct [28]. Formative measures are mainly intended to explain the composition of a construct, whereas reflective measures only indicate a construct's outcome [28]. Therefore, on the one hand, formative measures lead to deeper practical insights than reflective ones and are more suitable for practical research applications [28]. On the other hand, such measurement models are restricted regarding the application of quality indicators [28]. To avoid this disadvantage, formative and reflective measures can be combined to form *Multiple Indicators, Multiple Causes* (MIMIC) models [28].

To estimate the comprehensive model either covariance-based approaches (CB-SEM) or the variance-based *Partial Least Squares* (PLS-SEM) technique can be applied [30]. Both approaches provide different benefits and drawbacks that imply their qualification for specific applications in research [28,30]. The PLS-SEM technique is more suitable for the research for this study due to four reasons: (1) the prediction-oriented research goal to explain the adoption of SECaaS (dependent variable) as comprehensively as possible; (2) the formative measurement of perceived overall risks and benefits which is required to get a deep and differentiated understanding of the composition of relevant adoption drivers; (3) the small sample size expected relative to the high complexity of the research model implied by the high number of hypothesized influences; (4) the possibility of applying fewer than four indicators for latent variables which is necessary to keep the study's questionnaire as purposive as possible [28].

The model estimation was performed using the software *SmartPLS* developed by Ringle et al. [31]. The tool facilitates the building of both structural and measurement models and was successfully applied in similar studies [32]. Further quality metrics were calculated using the statistics software *SPSS PASW Statistics*[b].

3.2 Research model

In SEM, hypotheses are relationships between latent variables which are represented by the structural model [27,28]. The system of hypotheses must be theoretically well-grounded [28]. This was assured since its development was based on related literature in the fields of *Cloud Computing*, SaaS and MSS, and continuously validated by an expert group[c] (Below, this expert group is referred to as the *Expert Panel*) using a dedicated online discussion platform (*PBworks*[d]). The labels used for the study's constructs represent the essence of the construct and are assumed to be independent regarding their theorized content. Constructs and hypothesized influences are described and justified below.

3.2.1 Adoption

The endogenous variable Adoption depicts the degree to which a certain entity intends to use SECaaS. This includes both the plan for future deployment [22,26] and the present adoption by an organization [22]. In this regard, the behavioral intention to use a system and actual use can be modeled either separately or using a single construct [33]. We chose the second option to keep the model purposive. The measurement of this variable allows implications about the current state and future development of the SECaaS market. Thus, we utilize Adoption to cope with RQ1. The variable was hypothesized to be driven by the general determinants for grid and Cloud adoption identified [26]. These address RQ2 and represent the first four hypotheses (H) of this study as depicted in Figure 2: `Adoption` is significantly influenced by `Perceived Ease of Use` (H1), `Perceived Usefulness` (H2), `Trust` (H3), and `Attitude` (H4).

3.2.2 Perceived ease of use

This variable is defined as the degree to which the adopter believes that applying SECaaS is effortless [22,26,34,35]. From a client organization's point of view this involves the integration in the IT security infrastructure [11,15] as well as the actual use of the system [36]. Cloud-based security systems promise high ease of use since service interfaces are based on standardized internet technologies and can be accessed ubiquitously via thin clients (e.g. web browsers) [14]. It is questionable whether this fact affects the adoption and whether it is reflected by the perception of the adopters.

3.2.3 Perceived usefulness

`Perceived Usefulness` is defined as the degree to which an organizational adopter believes that the application of SECaaS increases the performance of the organization [22,26,34,35]. Performance expectation is a key driver for adoption [22,34]. Based on related literature Benlian et al. identified five specific benefit dimensions for SaaS service consumers which are hypothesized for SECaaS according to RQ3 [25]:

- *Perceived Flexibility Benefits:* The SaaS model implies a low organizational dependence of service consumers on service providers. Therefore, switching barriers are low and strategic flexibility regarding IT and IT security architectures is increased [11,25]. Furthermore, service use can be adapted flexibly to actual quantitative and qualitative needs [25].
- *Improved Resource Access:* Low entry barriers enable easy access to specific resources, skills and technologies of the external service providers [15,25].

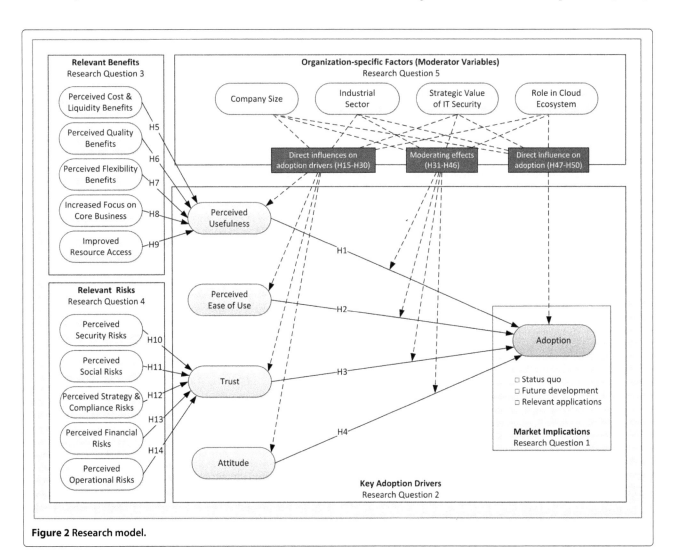

Figure 2 Research model.

Particularly mid-sized or smaller organizations might derive advantages from that when they cannot afford the time and effort involved in roviding sophisticated IT security resources on their own [11].

- *Perceived Cost & Liquidity Benefits:* Multi-tenancy architectures leverage economies of scale at the service providers' site. At the same time, service consumers' assumed low switching barriers induce a pricing pressure, forcing service providers to share respective savings. This ultimately leads to lower costs of operation and maintenance for service consumers [13,15,25]. Hence, on-demand pricing models enable decreased capital commitment [11,25]. Furthermore, the outsourcing model facilitates the transfer of financial risks of security incidents and thus the reduction of recovery costs [37].

- *Perceived Quality Benefits:* Security service providers use to be highly specialized, which implies their ability to provide a higher quality of service [11,13,15,16]. In addition, due to low switching barriers, service providers are forced to provide permanent high service quality [25]. Moreover, multi-tenancy architectures enable cross-client data aggregation and the application of business intelligence techniques [14]. Identified patterns can be used to improve quality of service, such as the performance of anti-virus applications, for instance. Lastly, SECaaS services are permanently up-to-date without the necessity of time-delayed updates at the client's site [11].

- *Improved Focus on Core Business:* The outsourcing of certain systems according to SaaS (or SECaaS) de-allocates internal resources [11,25]. These resources can be (re-)allocated to an organization's core business, which might increase overall performance [15,25] - assuming that IT security is not the core competency. Hence, this is also one of the major drivers for IT security outsourcing in general [38].

Many IT outsourcing programs do not yield expected performance outcomes [39,40]. Reasons include exaggerated expectations, poorly developed business cases, deficient change management, non-transparency of vendor performance, and lock-in effects [40]. This so-called "IT outsourcing paradox" [40] might affect the expected usefulness of SECaaS and its influence on the adoption.

3.2.4   Trust
The adoption of grid and Cloud systems is highly influenced by perceived risks [18,23,26,41,42]. This influence is represented by the variable `Trust`, which is interpreted as a semantic inversion of perceived risk. BENLIAN ET AL. identified SaaS-specific risk dimensions which are

hypothesized in analogy to `Perceived Usefulness` addressing RQ4 [25]:

- *Perceived Security Risks:* The outsourcing of systems according to SaaS implies the loss of control over the processed data and requires the client organization to interface with the external service. This causes risks regarding the enterprise data and affected processes [11,15,25,42]. In this regard, Cloud-specific security risks focus on resource protection, communication and storage security, and authentication and authorization [2].

- *Perceived Social Risks:* The outsourcing of applications induces social risks including internal resistance or negative influences on the organization's image [25].

- *Perceived Strategy & Compliance Risks:* The outsourcing of certain systems might involve the loss of critical capabilities [25] and, in turn, the risk of an increased dependency on the service provider [15,37]. Furthermore, the service consumers might lose the control to ensure the compliance with legal and regulative requirements [15].

- *Perceived Financial Risks:* The deployment of SaaS services might involve unanticipated costs [25]. This includes the organization's own security infrastructure and service customization [11,15].

- *Perceived Operational Risks:* Since service operation is fully controlled externally there is the risk of the service provider not complying with existing SLAs. This might affect service quality, performance, and availability [15,25,42].

3.2.5   Attitude
The `Attitude` construct represents an adopter's individual positive or negative behavior toward an innovation and is considered to be independent from the othervariables [22,26,43]. It can be prescribed by individual preferences or perceived relative advantage to related technologies [22,26]. Its relevance for SaaS adoption is indicated by previous research [23].

3.2.6   Moderator variables
The validity of PLS-SEM results can be compromised by heterogeneous and conflicting data [30]. Potential sources for heterogeneity can be modeled and tested by means of moderator analyses [30]. Venkatesh et al. propose the use of moderators in addition to key determinants to account for dynamic influences and thus to improve the quality of adoption research models [22]. Moderators are variables that influence the relation between two constructs positively or negatively [22,28]. Moderators at the individual level include demographic characteristics and organizational context (e.g. gender, age) [22]. Since our

Table 2 Metrically measured indicators

Construct	Indicator(s)	Reference(s)
Adoption (refl.)	Actual use	[22,23,26]
	Use intent short-term (next 3 years)	
	Use intent mid-term (4–7 years)	
	Use intent long-term (≥ 7 years)	
Adoption (form.)	Actual use/intent of Endpoint Security applications	[13,14,23]
	Actual use/intent of content security applications (appl.)	
	Actual use/intent of application security applications	
	Actual use/intent of compliance & IT security management appl.	
	Actual use/intent identity & access management appl.	
	Actual use/intent of managed devices applications	
	Actual use/intent of security information & event management appl.	
	Actual use/intent of threat & vulnerability management appl.	
Perceived ease of use (refl.)	General ease of use	[26,34]
	Ease of learning	
	Ease of target achievement	
Perceived ease of use (form.)	Ease of initial integration/deployment of the service	[13-15,36]
	Usability of the service	
	Ease of customizing the service	
	Comprehensive support by service provider	
Perceived usefulness (refl.)	Increase in performance	[26,34]
	General usefulness	
	Increase in effectiveness	
Perceived cost & liquidity benefits (form.)	Reduction in costs of operation and maintenance	[11,13-15,25,37]
	Variabilization of IT security costs	
	Reduction in recovery costs	
Perceived quality benefits (form.)	Transparency & control of security department	[11,13-16,25]
	Increase in organizational level of security	
	Improvement of legal and regulative compliance	
Perceived flexibility benefits (form.)	Flexibility of IT and security processes	[11,13,14,25]
	Flexibility of business processes	
	Reactivity regarding security-related problems	
Increased focus on core business (form.)	Decrease in employee errors	[11,13-15,25,37,38]
	Time savings in security management	
Improved resource access (form.)	Enablement of access to new technologies	[11,15,25]
	Access to external know-how	
	Independence from dedicated systems	
Trust (refl.)	Overall trust in adoption	[22,23,26]
	Trust in certified service providers	
	Hesitation due to uncertainty	
Perceived security risks (form.)	Vulnerability to unauthorized service access	[2,11,14]
	Deficient data mitigation and security	
	Vulnerability regarding network-based attacks	
	Deficient service continuity	

Table 2 Metrically measured indicators *(Continued)*

Perceived strategy & compliance risks (form.)	Dependence on service providers	[14,15,25,37]
	Inability to comply with obligations to produce supporting documents	
	Non-compliance with data protection regulations	
Perceived social risks (form.)	Internal resistance	[23,25]
	Loss of image	
Perceived financial & operational risks (form.)	Unexpected costs of integration	[11,15,25,42,45]
	Deficient provider's compliance with SLAs	
Attitude (refl.)	General attitude toward cloud technologies	[22,23,26]
	Relative advantage over managed security	
	Relative advantage over on-premises systems	
Strategic value of IT security (refl.)	Criticality of IT security for business	[23]

research focuses on adoption by organizational entities, we hypothesized new moderators to address RQ5. As part of the aforementioned expert workshop in the course of a session of the "IT security solutions" working group of the German Federal Association for Information Technology, Telecommunications and New Media, and based on related literature, we identified four relevant factors: Company size, industrial sector, a company's role in the Cloud ecosystem, and the strategic value of IT security. Moreover, we considered the respondent's job function and the division in which he or she works as potential sources for heterogeneity and modeled respective moderator variables.

3.3 Measures

Based on the constructs of the specified structural model a measurement model was developed. Therefore, an initial literature review was conducted in order to identify and classify the major related indicators which semantically describe the structural model's constructs. These indicators were presented to the *Expert Panel* via the aforementioned collaboration system *PBworks*. The experts actively discussed and supplemented the indicator set which was subsequently revised by the authors of this paper and transformed to the study's online questionnaire. Finally, the *Expert Panel* approved[e] the measurement model (including the online questionnaire).

The measurement model includes both formative and reflective elements to account for the methodological problems mentioned in Subsection 3.1. We developed two-construct MIMIC models separating formative and reflective indicators for the major latent variables `Perceived Ease of Use`, `Perceived Usefulness`, `Trust`, and `Adoption`. Within the structural equations model the latent variable is represented by a reflective construct; one or more formative constructs model the composition of the variable [44]. For the reflective (refl.) constructs, existing published

measures were applied. Formative (form.) constructs and indicators were based on related work and both specified and validated by the *Expert Panel*. The MIMIC models for `Perceived Usefulness` and `Trust` each consist of one reflective and several formative elements representing the respective benefit and risk dimensions as depicted in Figure 2. In this regard, operational and financial risks were merged to one variable. The remaining two variables were measured linking only one formative element. Table 2 provides an overview of all indicators of the study's primary variables and the variable `Strategic Value of IT Security`. The `Company Size` was determined by means of the company turnover and headcount. The remaining organization-specific factors were each measured by one global indicator with nominal scale.

All indicators were transformed into questionnaire items in German following general construction guidelines [28,46]. As mentioned in the beginning of this section, the supporting expert group validated the wording and soundness of all items as well as the structure of the entire questionnaire from a semantic point of view as suggested by CHURCHILL [47]. SEM requires metrically-scaled data for further analysis [28]. Thus, we applied a systematically constructed seven-point Likert scale, which produces data that can be interpreted metrically for SEM model estimations [28,46].

4 Findings

This section presents the empirical investigation of the research model. In Subsection 4.1, the sample and the process of data collection are described. In Subsection 4.2, implications regarding the market for SECaaS applications are deduced from descriptive data analysis. In Subsection 4.3, the model estimation including quality and hypotheses testing is laid out. Finally, in Subsection 4.4, the results are discussed respecting the research questions of the study.

Table 3 Participants by industrial sector

Class	Percentage	Number
Information technology	44.4%	71
Industry	16.9%	27
Other services	13.1%	21
Public services	10.6%	17
Financial services	8.8%	14
Retail	6.3%	10

Table 5 Participants by role in cloud ecosystem

Class	Percentage	Number
Cloud service Consumer (exclusively)	53.8%	86
Cloud service Provider (exclusively)	23.1%	37
Cloud service provider and consumer	23.1%	37

4.1 Data collection and sample

To carry out the data collection, the measurement model was implemented in an online survey tool and validated by a pre-test with 12 voluntary experts of the *Expert Panel*. In the period from 16 February to 15 April 2011 the survey was accessible via a dedicated Internet address. This address was distributed using the network of the German Federal Association for Information Technology, Telecommunications and New Media. The target population for this study was IT and business professionals who would be involved in their organization's decision-making process regarding the investment in SECaaS. The sample included key informants of provider and consumer organizations of IT solutions in Germany, Austria, and Switzerland and is considered to be representative for potential adopters of SECaaS technologies in the German-speaking area. The survey was preceded by a brief registration. The verified e-mail addresses were stored separately from the survey data in order to guarantee anonymity. The survey (see Additional file 1) began with a landing page including a brief definition of SECaaS, the purpose of the study and its target population, the estimated time expenditure, information about incentives, the privacy policy, and contacts. The questionnaire was divided into six sections.

The survey yielded 202 returns. The data was processed and cleaned as suggested by WEIBER AND MÜHLHAUS [28]. Accordingly, incomplete records were excluded. For the remaining records the squared *Mahalanobis* distances were calculated in order to identify those deviating markedly from the centroid; three outliers were identified and excluded. This left 160 records for further analysis.

The composition of the sample is depicted in Tables 3, 4, 5, 6 and 7 by means of the measured non-metrically scaled organization-specific factors. Of the participating companies, 44.4% originate from the IT sector, which indicates its relatively higher affinity toward SECaaS compared to other industrial sectors (see Table 3). Almost half of the sample (48.1%) consists of large-scale organizations. Medium-sized and smaller organizations each represent about a quarter (see Table 4). Regarding a company's primary role in the Cloud ecosystem, most respondents (53.8%) evaluate their organization to act as exclusive potential consumer of SECaaS. Further 23.1% see their organization in a hybrid role, potentially doing both consuming and providing SECaaS. Only 23.1% do not consider to consume SECaaS at all (see Table 5). Table 6 shows the composition of the sample grouped by the respondents' job function. The majority (37.5%) has an executive position. Also in this regard, most respondents originate from their organization's IT department. Other divisions are under-represented (see Table 7). The variable `Strategic Value of IT Security` was measured by one reflective item on a seven-point *Likert* scale (Mean: 6.244, standard deviation: 1.080). We assume the sample to be compliant with the study's target population and thus representative for the adoption of SECaaS.

4.2 Market implications

The measurement of the study's dependent variable `Adoption` reveals several implications about the market for SECaaS (RQ1). It was measured by two constructs: a reflective element covering the actual use and use intent of SECaaS in regard to the planning horizon, and a formative one containing different security application types. 18.1% of the respondents indicate that their organization is currently using SECaaS. The data further indicates a steadily rising adoption rate. In the long term, over 30% of the surveyed organizations clearly intend to use SECaaS.

Table 4 Participants by company size[f]

Class	Percentage	Number
Small & micro organization	24.4%	39
Medium-sized organization	27.5%	44
Large-scale organization	48.1%	77

Table 6 Participants by job function

Class	Percentage	Number
Manager	37.5%	60
Employee	21.9%	35
IT security officer	13.8%	22
Other	26.9%	43

Table 7 Participants by division

Class	Percentage	Number
Steering committee	10.6%	17
Management and support	17.5%	28
Research & development	5.0%	8
Production	2.5%	4
Information technology	50.6%	81
Sales & marketing	12.5%	20
Other	1.3%	2

Only 16% exclude the possibility of its use entirely. The positive development of the adoption of SECaaS in regard to the organizations' planning horizon is shown in Table 8.

Respondents were asked whether their organization uses or intends to use certain SECaaS application types. *Content Security*, *Endpoint Security*, and *Vulnerability & Threat Management* solutions exhibit especially high adoption rates. Whereas the market is already dominated by the first two application types, the diffusion of Cloud-based *Vulnerability & Threat Management* services is relatively low [14]. This indicates a high level of future adoption, especially for this type of application. Hence, the data indicate a very weak current and future interest in *Compliance & IT Security Management* products. Other types of application are middle-ranking. The overall results and detailed findings specific to industrial sector and company size are summarized in Table 9.

4.3 Model estimation

No adequate global indicators for goodness of model fit exist for PLS-SEM [30,48]. Instead, the measurement model should be estimated first, the structural model afterward [30,49].

4.3.1 Evaluation of the measurement model

The assessment of reflective measurement models includes their reliability and validity [28,30]. An indicator's reliability can be assumed for a minimal factor loading of 0.7 [30,50]. For values between 0.4 and 0.7 indicators

Table 8 Development of Adoption[f]

Planning horizon	Percentage with strong positive indication for adoption[a]	Standard deviation	Mean
Currently	18.1%	2.800	2.220
Short-term	24.4%	3.444	2.214
Mid-term	26.3%	3.988	1.939
Long-term	31.3%	4.269	1.856

[a]"strong positive indication" means the selection of 6 or 7 at the 7-point *Likert* scale where 7 represents the strongest intention.

should only be eliminated if this increases the construct's *Average Variance Extracted* (AVE) value [30]. Indicators with lower factor loadings indicate deficient reliability and should be removed [30]. According to these requirements, all reflective indicators featured reliability. The reliability of a construct is routinely estimated by means of its *Composite Reliability* (CR) indicating its internal consistency [30]. CR values should be 0.7 or higher [30,49]. This requirement is met for all latent variables. The assessment of the validity of the measurement model includes discriminant validity[g] and convergent validity[h] [30]. Discriminant validity was verified by calculating cross loadings [30]. All indicators have a higher correlation with the appertaining latent variable than with others and thus provide for discriminant validity. Furthermore, for each variable the AVE exceeds the minimal value of 0.5, which indicates the convergent validity of the entire measurement model [30,51]. Table 10 summarizes key metrics of the study's major latent variables including CR and AVE values. For Attitude no AVE value was calculated since no formative measures were applied.

The evaluation of formative indicators aims to support their relevance for the measured construct [30]. This includes the strength and the significance of its influence [28]. The significance can be determined by means of the bootstrap procedure calculating t-values [30]. A formative indicator's influence is assumed to be significant for a t-value = 1.646 (level of significance α = 10%, degrees of freedom df = 1,000). Weights should be 0.1 or higher. Though the results quantitatively indicate the minor relevance of four formative indicators they did not have to be excluded since the *Expert Panel* strongly supported their inclusion from a qualitative point of view [28,30]. Table 11 summarizes weights and significances of the formative indicators for Perceived Usefulness grouped by the corresponding benefit dimension. Additionally, the significance of the influence of the respective dimension on the core construct Perceived Usefulness (refl.) is shown. In analogy, Table 12 describes the MIMIC measurement model for Trust. The measurement model does not contain any redundant formative indicators: the *Variance Inflation Factor* (VIF) indicating multi-colinearity was calculated for all indices. All values (range [1.3; 4.2]) are smaller than the critical value of 5.0; thus, no indicators had to be reconsidered [30,44].

Since the measurement model meets existing requirements entirely, valid estimations of the study's latent variables can be assumed. This is requisite for the subsequent evaluation of the structural model [28,30].

4.3.2 Evaluation of the Structural Model

The evaluation of the structural model includes the degree of determination of the model's latent variables and the

Table 9 Application-specific adoption

Application type	IT	Public services	Financial services	Industry	Other services	Retail	Large-scale organizations	Mid-sized organizations	Small & micro org.	Overall
Content security	●	●	●	●	◕	●	●	◕	●	●
Endpoint security	●	◕	●	◕	◕	◐	●	◕	◕	◕
Vuln. & threat management	●	◕	◐	◕	◐	○	◕	◕	◐	◕
Application security	◕	◕	◐	◕	◕	◐	◐	◐	◐	◐
Identity & access mgmt.	◕	◕	◐	◐	◐	◐	◕	◐	◐	◐
Security info. & event mgmt.	◕	◐	◐	◐	○	◐	●	◐	◑	◐
Managed devices	◐	◑	◐	◐	◐	◐	◐	◑	◑	◐
Compliance & ITSM	◐	◐	◑	◑	◐	○	◑	◑	◑	◑
			Industrial sector					Org. size		

Very low (0%, ○), low (25%, ◔), medium (50%, ◑), high (75%, ◕), and very high (100%, ●) adoption rate. The range of mean values (range = [1.857; 4.364]) was linearly grouped into five equal classes.

Table 10 Latent variables

Variable	Mean	Standard deviation	R^2	AVE	CR
Adoption	3.444	4.733	.710	.729	.915
Perceived usefulness	4.476	2.983	.663	.849	.944
Perceived ease of use	4.151	2.212	.737	.829	.936
Trust	3.910	3.109	.512	.590	.805
Attitude	3.788	3.053	.587	n.a.	.810

evaluation of the hypothesized relations between them [30]. All independent latent variables meet the required minimal coefficient of determination (R^2) value of 0.3 and are thus sufficiently explained [49] (see Table 10). Due to the study's predictive research goal the R^2 of the dependent variable is of special importance [30]. CHIN suggests a critical value of 0.67 for substantial predictions [49]. This requirement is met for the study's dependent variable Adoption (R^2 = 0.71). We additionally proved the model's capacity to predict the dependent variable by means of the *Stone-Geisser* test (cross-validated redundancy Q^2 = 0.489 > 0) [30]. Thus, we consider the adoption of SECaaS to be explained comprehensively by this study's proposed model. To test the significances of the model's hypothesized relations, the bootstrap method (df = 1,000) was applied and t-values were calculated [31,52]. In regard to the study's non-directional hypotheses, the influence of one variable on another is considered to be significant when α = 10% [28,30]. Thus, a hypothesis is supported when the corresponding t-value $\geq$ 1.646 and the respective null hypothesis is falsified [28]. To get a deeper understanding of the relations we tested three levels of significance: α = 10% (*, t-value = 1.646); α = 5% (**, t-value = 1.962); α = 1% (***, t-value = 2.581). Moreover, corresponding path coefficients were calculated indicating both strength and direction of a variable's influence [28]. According

to Lohmoeller path coefficients $\geq$ 0.1 indicate relevance [53].

All in all 10 of the original 50 hypotheses were supported. Of the hypothesized key determinants only Attitude does not have a significant influence on Adoption. This might be caused by the consideration of the individual organization-specific factors; however, we did not find any relations between these variables and Attitude. The investigation of the MIMIC measurement models of Perceived Usefulness and Trust revealed that the respective constructs are determined by very few factors. Only quality, and cost and liquidity benefits matter significantly for Perceived Usefulness. Ex post we identified the significant influence of Trust and Perceived Ease of Use on the variable Perceived Usefulness. Trust is negatively correlated with security risks, social risks, and strategy and compliance risks. Financial and operational risks do not matter. Investigating the organization-specific factors we identified a moderating effect of Role in Cloud Ecosystem on the relationship between Perceived Usefulness and Adoption, and a direct (positive) influence of the Strategic Value of IT Security on Perceived Usefulness. Company Size and Industrial Sector do have neither a direct nor indirect influence on the adoption of SECaaS. However, in the course of a more detailed analysis we

Table 11 Formative measurement model for P. usefulness

Formative construct	Indicator weights	Indicator significances (t-Values)	Significance of construct (t-Value)
Cost & liquidity	.270	2.052	2.319**
Benefits	-.631	-4.576	
Quality	.290	2.420	3.632***
Benefits	-.537	-5.138	
Flexibility	.276	1.957	0.754
Benefits	-.613	-5.717	
Focus on	.492	3.044	0.225
Core business	-.601	-3.690	
Improved	.164	1.830	0.700
Resource access	-.635	-5.055	

Table 12 Formative measurement model for trust

Formative construct	Indicator weights	Indicator significances (t-Values)	Significance of construct (t-Value)
Security	.182	1.658	4.450***
Risks	-.453	-3.723	
Social	.278	1.660	1.984***
Risks	-.851	-7.291	
Strategy &	.288	1.706	1.742*
compl. risks	-.524	-4.057	
Financial &	.474	3.375	0.841
op. risks	-.755	-6.918	

found that financial risks matter more for bigger organizations, while social, operational, and strategy and compliance risks are more important to smaller organizations. Figure 3 depicts the reduced model including supported hypotheses. The path coefficients and significances of the hypothesized key drivers are summarized in Table 13.

4.4 Discussion

Below, the findings are discussed in regard to the research questions considering related findings.

4.4.1 RQ1: Is there a market for SECaaS enterprise applications in general and for specific application types in particular?

The market for SECaaS applications is still emerging. The study indicates an already significant and steadily growing acceptance by enterprise consumers. The adoption varies across different security service application types, which supports previous findings about SaaS [23]. The market's focus is on applications for *Content Security*, *Endpoint Security*, and *Vulnerability & Threat Management*.

4.4.2 RQ2: Which are the key drivers and inhibitors for the adoption of SECaaS?

Key drivers for the adoption of SECaaS are effort expectancies, perceived usefulness, and trust regarding the adoption of respective applications. These results basically confirm UDOH's findings regarding the adoption of grid and Cloud technologies [26]. Only the influence of the adopter's individual attitude toward the technology [23,26] was not supported for this research context. Hence, the influence of perceived risks and thus the

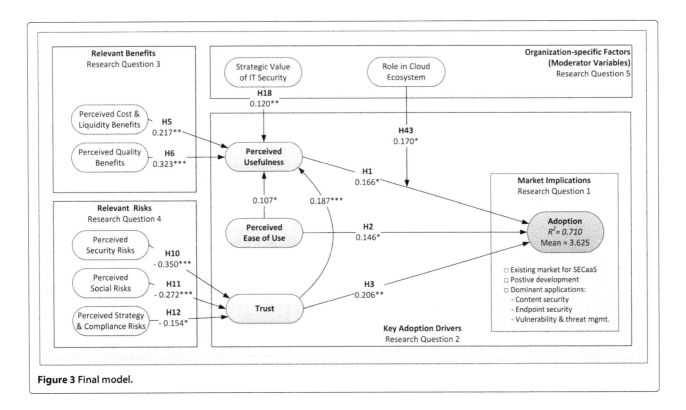

Figure 3 Final model.

Table 13 Estimation of hypothesized key drivers

Hypo-thesis	Relation	Path coefficient	Significance (t-Value)
H1	Perceived useful-ness ⇒ adoption	.168	1.912*
H2	Perceived ease of use ⇒ adoption	.146	1.818*
H3	Trust ⇒ adoption	.207	2.333**
H4	Attitude ⇒ adoption	.121	1.453

uncertainty of SECaaS adoption is more significant than the influence of the other drivers, including perceived usefulness. This supports the findings of BENLIAN ET AL. regarding SaaS adoption [23].

4.4.3 RQ3: Which benefits are perceived to be relevant by potential adopters of SECaaS?

The perceived usefulness of SECaaS is forged by quality as well as cost and liquidity benefits. Quality benefits mainly reflect the expected return in terms of an increased level of security and regulative compliance. Cost and liquidity benefits include the reduction of direct security expenditures and recovery costs. Thus, according to the adopter's perception, SECaaS potentially increases return on security investments [54]. Hence, the expected performance of SECaaS systems is positively correlated with effort expectancies and trust, which supports previous empirical findings [22,55,56].

4.4.4 RQ4: Which risks are perceived to be relevant by potential adopters of SECaaS?

Major barriers to SECaaS adoption are perceived security, social, strategy and compliance risks. Perceived social risks are mainly driven by expected internal resistance. In this context, an inherent problem is the possible fear of the direct loss of competencies in the course of outsourcing certain security systems. The significance of social influences regarding SaaS adoption was already identified by BENLIAN ET AL. [23]. To increase trust and thus future adoption the effectiveness of technical and organizational controls securing Cloud-based security services must be conveyed transparently to potential SECaaS consumers. Specific certification programs for service providers might support this, for example.

4.4.5 RQ5: Which organization-specific factors affect the acceptance of SECaaS?

The individual strategic value of IT security for an organization's business directly influences the perceived usefulness of SECaaS. The expected performance is thus higher for organizations with higher demands on IT security from a business point of view. This coherence was already laid out by BENLIAN ET AL. regarding SaaS [23]. Moreover, for the organization's role in

the Cloud ecosystem a moderating effect on the relation between the variables Perceived Usefulness and Adoption was identified. This means that perceived benefits matter less for the actual adoption of SECaaS technologies when the organization itself provides Cloud services for external customers, acting in the role of a *Value Added Reseller* [57]. On the contrary, general organization-specific factors like company size or industrial sector do not have any significant effects on the adoption. This, on the one hand, conflicts with the general rationale that SECaaS is particularly relevant for companies with limited capacities regarding IT security; on the other hand, however, it confirms previous findings regarding the adoption of SaaS [23].

4.4.6 Limitations

The applied methodology (PLS-SEM) is often criticized because calculations tend to be less precise compared to alternative CB-SEM techniques. However, PLS-SEM is more qualified for the application in this study as already laid out in Subsection 3.1. Considering the complexity of this study's research model and the achievable sample size, the application of CB-SEM would not have revealed valid results (compare e.g. [27,28,30]), which supports the authors' research design decision. The sample was selected among organizations with an existing affinity toward IT. Therefore we assume the sample to be representative for potential SECaaS adopters but not for all organizations. The survey explicitly addressed companies in the German-speaking area. Even though it is assumed to provide general insights about the adoption of SECaaS, observations might vary among different markets, for instance due to location-specific data protection regulations. Furthermore, the adoption of SECaaS by private consumers has not been considered and thus remains open for future research.

5 Conclusion

This paper systematically investigates the adoption of SECaaS. An application-specific research model was developed based on existing technology acceptance models. The model was estimated applying the *Partial Least Squares* technique to address the prediction-oriented nature of the study. Based on 160 valid responses from companies in the German-speaking area, we investigated the market potential for SECaaS, key adoption drivers, the relevance of certain risks and benefits, and the influence of organization-specific factors like company size or industrial sector.

The results make valuable contributions for both practice and research. They provide a benchmark for potential adopters of SECaaS. Moreover, the findings support the understanding of the adoption behavior of enterprise consumers. Service providers can use this understanding to direct research, development and marketing programs by considering the significance of perceived security-related risks, for instance. Therefore, this study contributes to driving the future adoption of SECaaS, addressing existing threats to the security of enterprise information systems. Moreover, the developed research model including its measures was validated and can be applied for related future studies.

Future research should reflect the adoption of Cloud-based security services in other markets, survey specific security application types, investigate most relevant application fields and success drivers.

Endnotes

[a]Session of the "IT security solutions" working group of the German Federal Association for Information Technology, Telecommunications and New Media (BITKOM e.V., see: http://www.bitkom.de last access: 01 August 2012).

[b]http://www.spss.com.hk/statistics/ (last access: 29 September 2012).

[c]16 selected IT and IT security professionals of the German Federal Association for Information Technology, Telecommunications and New Media (BITKOM e.V.).

[d]http://pbworks.com (last access: 01 August 2012).

[e]Therefore, a simple online poll with the options "I do not approve", "I am ok" and "I fully approve" was conducted. Four experts responded "I am ok" and eight fully approved.

[f]According to the European Commission, the number of a company's employees and its turnover (alternatively: balance sheet total) indicate its size. Companies are categorized as follows: "micro", when number of employees < 10 and turnover ≤ € 2,000,000; "small", when number of employees < 50 and turnover ≤ € 10,000,000; "medium-sized", when number of employees < 250 and turnover ≤ € 50,000,000. Larger organizations are labelled as "large-scale". See: http://ec.europa.eu/enterprise/policies/sme/facts-figures-analysis/sme-definition (last access: 01 August 2012).

[g]Discriminant validity is provided for when an indicator's loading with the assigned construct is higher than with remaining constructs. An indicator's loading with non-assigned constructs is referred to as cross loading.

[h]Convergent validity expresses the degree to which a latent variable explains the variance of assigned indicators.

Additional file

Additional file 1: Appendix: Online Questionnaire.

Competing interests
The author declare that they have no competing interests.

References

1. Hommel W (2007) Architektur- und Werkzeugkonzepte für föderiertes Identitäts-Management. Dr. Hut, München
2. Brock M, Goscinski A (2010) Toward a framework for cloud security. In: Hsu CH, Yang L, Park J, Yeo SS (eds) Algorithms and architectures for parallel processing, Lecture Notes in Computer Science, vol. 6082. Springer, Berlin/Heidelberg, pp 254–263
3. Rittinghouse J, Ransome J (2010) Cloud computing: implementation, management, and security. CRC, Boca Raton
4. Mell P, Grance T (2009) The nist definition of cloud computing. Natl Ins Stand Technol 53 (6): 50. [http://csrc.nist.gov/publications/nistpubs/800-145/SP800-145.pdf]
5. Furth B (2010) Cloud computing fundamentals. In: Furth B, Escalante A (eds) Handbook of Cloud Computing. Springer, US, Boston, pp 3–20
6. Höfer C, Karagiannis G (2011) Cloud computing services: taxonomy and comparison. J Internet Serv Appl 2(2): 1–14
7. Gartner Gartner says security delivered as a cloud-based service will more than triple in many segments by 2013 (2008). [www.gartner.com/it/page.jsp?id=722307]
8. Hafner M, Mukhtiar M, Breu R (2009) Seaas - a reference architecture for security services in soa. JUCS 15(15): 2916–2936
9. Peterson G (2009) Service-oriented security indications for use. Comput Sci Eng 7: 91–93
10. Smith DM (2010) Hype cycle for cloud computing 2010. [http://www.gartner.com/DisplayDocument?doc_cd=201557]
11. Staudenrauss P (2011) Untersuchung und Bewertung von Security-as-a-Service-Diensten. In: Helmbrecht U, Kretzschmar M, Eiseler V (eds) Seminar IT-Sicherheit - Sicherheit und Vertrauen in Cloud Computing. Institut füur Technische Informatik, München, pp 49–74
12. Mather T, Kumaraswamy S, Latif S (2009) Cloud security and privacy: an enterprise perspective on risks and compliance. O'Reilly Media Inc, Sebastopol
13. Kark K, Penn J, Whiteley R, Coit L (2010) Market overview: Managed security services. http://www.forrester.com/Market+Overview+Managed+Security+Services/fulltext/-/E-RES56068?objectid=RES56068
14. Senk C, Holzapfel A (2011) Market overview of security as a service systems. In: Pohlmann N, Reimer H, Schneider W (eds) ISSE 2011 Securing Electronic Business Processes
15. Allen J, Gabbard D, May C (2003) Outsourcing Managed Security Services. Carnegie Mellon University Software Engineering Institute. [http://books.google.de/books?id=CFGnNwAACAAJ]
16. Deshpande D (2005) Managed security services: an emerging solution to security In: Proceedings of the 2nd annual conference on Information security curriculum development, InfoSecCD '05. ACM, New York, pp 107–111
17. Keuper F, Wagner B, Wysuwa H (2009) Managed services: IT-Sourcing der nächsten Generation. Gabler. [http://books.google.de/books?id=5J7Qbx2GIYIC]
18. Martens B, Teuteberg F (2011) Decision-making in cloud computing environments: A cost and risk based approach. Inf Syst Front 14(4): 1–23
19. Huber M (2002) IT-security in global corporate networks. Center for Digital Technology and Management, München
20. Karyda M, Mitrou E, Quirchmayr G (2006) A framework for outsourcing is/it security services. Inf Manag Comput Secur 14(5): 402–415
21. Rogers E (2003) Diffusion of Innovations. 5th Edition. Simon & Schuster, New York
22. Venkatesh V, Morris MG, Davis GB, Davis FD (2003) User acceptance of information technology: Toward a unified view. MIS Q 27(3): 425–478
23. Benlian A, Hess T, Buxmann P (2009) Drivers of saas-adoption – an empirical study of different application types. Business Inf Syst Eng 1: 357–369
24. Davis FD, Bagozzi RP, Warshaw PR (1989) User acceptance of computer technology: A comparison of two theoretical models. Manage Sci 35(8): 982–1003
25. Benlian A, Hess T, Buxmann P (2010) Software-as-a-Service: Anbieterstrategien, Kundenbedürfnisse und Wertschöpfungsstrukturen. Gabler, Betriebswirt.-Vlg

26. Udoh E (2010). VDM Verlag Dr. Müller e.K., Saarbrücken

27. Hoyle R (1995) Structural equation modeling: concepts, issues and applications. Sage Publications, New York

28. Weiber R, Mühlhaus D (2010) Strukturgleichungsmodellierung: Eine anwendungsorientierte Einführung in die Kausalanalyse mit Hilfe von AMOS, SmartPLS und SPSS. Springer, Berlin, Heidelberg

29. Edwards JR, Bagozzi RP (2000) On the nature and direction of relationships between constructs and measures. Psychol Methods 5(2): 155–174

30. Hair J, Ringle CM (2011) PLS-SEM: Indeed a silver bullet. J Mark Theory Pract 19(2): 139–151

31. Ringle CM, Wende S, Will A (2005) Smartpls 2.0. http://www.smartpls.de

32. Bliemel F (2005) Handbuch PLS-Pfadmodellierung: Methoden, Anwendung, Praxisbeispiele. Schäffer-Poeschel, Stuttgart, Germany

33. Hamre LJ (2008) Exploring the use of social capital to support technology adoption and implementation. Ph.D. thesis, University of Bath

34. Davis FD (1989) Perceived usefulness, perceived ease of use, and user acceptance of information technology. MIS Q 13(3): 319–340

35. Thompson RL, Higgins CA, Howell JM (1991) Personal computing: Toward a conceptual model of utilization. MIS Q 15(1): 125–143

36. Cranor L, Garfinkel S (2005) Security and Usability. O'Reilly Media, Inc, Sebastopol

37. Böhme R (2010) Security metrics and security investment models In: Echizen I, Kunihiro N, Sasaki R(eds) Advances in Information and Computer Security, *Lecture Notes in Computer Science*, vol. 6434. Springer, Berlin / Heidelberg, pp 10–24

38. Schwarze L, Müller, PP (2005) IT-outsourcing - Erfahrungen, status und zukünftige herausforderungen. HMD-Praxis der Wirtschaftsinformatik. http://ephorie.de/pdfs/Schwarze_IT-Outsourcing-Erfahrungen_Status_und_zukuenftige_Herausforderungen.pdf

39. Aubert BA, Patry M, Rivard S (1998) Assessing the risk of IT outsourcing In: Proceedings of the Thirty-First Hawaii International Conference on System Sciences, Volume VI. Organizational Systems and Technology. IEEE Computer Society, Washington, U.S.A., pp 685–693

40. Rouse AC (2009) Is there an "Information technology outsourcing Paradox"? In: Hirschheim R, Heinzl A, Dibbern J (eds) Information systems outsourcing. Springer, Berlin Heidelberg, pp 129–146

41. Duisberg A (2011) Gelöste und ungelöste Rechtsfragen im IT-Outsourcing und Cloud Computing In: Picot A, Götz T, Hertz U (eds) Trust in IT. Springer, Berlin Heidelberg, pp 49–70

42. Subashini S, Kavitha V (2011) A survey on security issues in service delivery models of cloud computing. J Netw Comput Appl 34(1): 1–11

43. Fishbein M, Ajzen I (1975) Belief, attitude. Addison-Wesley, Reading

44. Diamantopoulos A, Winklhofer HM (2001) Index construction with formative indicators: An alternative to scale development. J Mark Res 38(2): 269–277

45. Senk C (2010) Securing inter-organizational workflows in highly flexible environments through biometrics In: Proc. of E C I S Pretoria

46. Bortz J, Döring N (2006) Forschungsmethoden und Evaluation für Human- und Sozialwissenschaftler Springer-Lehrbuch. Springer

47. Churchill GA (1979) A paradigm for developing better measures of marketing constructs. J Mark Res 16(1): 64–73

48. Hulland J (1999) Use of partial least squares (pls) in strategic management research: a review of four recent studies. Strateg Manage J 20(2): 195–204

49. Chin WW (1998) The partial least squares approach to structural equation modeling. Modern Methods Business Res 295: 336

50. Johnson MD, Herrmann A, Huber F (2006) The evolution of loyalty intentions. J Mark 70(2): 122–132

51. Fornell C, Bookstein FL (1982) Two structural equation models: Lisrel and pls applied to consumer exit-voice theory. J Mark Res 19(4): 440–452

52. Nevitt J, Hancock GR (2001) Performance of bootstrapping approaches to model test statistics and parameter standard error estimation in structural equation modeling. Struct Equation Model Multidisciplinary J 8(3): 353–377

53. Lohmoeller JB (1989) Latent variable path modeling with partial least squares. Physica, Heidelberg

54. Sonnenreich W, Albanese J, Stout B (2005) Return On Security Investment (ROSI) In: A practical quantitative model Journal of research and practice in information technology. INSTICC Press, Setubal, pp 239–252

55. Lee D, Park J, Ahn J (2001) Proceedings of the International Conference of Information Systems 2001 In: On the explanation of factors affecting E-commerce adoption, pp 109–120

56. Venkatesh V, Bala H (2008) Technology acceptance model 3 and a research agenda on interventions. Decis Sci 2: 273–315. 39

57. Baun C, Kunze M, Nimis J (2010) Cloud computing Web-basierte dynamische IT-services. Springer-Verlag, Berlin and Heidelberg

12

Access control as a service for the Cloud

Nikos Fotiou[*], Apostolis Machas, George C Polyzos and George Xylomenos

Abstract

Cloud computing has become the focus of attention in the computing industry. However, security concerns still impede the widespread adoption of this technology. Most enterprises are particularly worried about the lack of control over their outsourced data, since the authentication and authorization systems of Cloud providers are generic and they cannot be easily adapted to the requirements of each individual enterprise. An adaptation process requires the creation of complex protocols, often leading to security problems and "lock-in" conditions. In this paper we present the design of a lightweight access control solution that overcomes these problems. With our solution access control is offered as a service by a third trusted party, the Access Control Provider. Access control as a service enhances end-user privacy, eliminates the need for developing complex adaptation protocols, and offers data owners flexibility to switch among Cloud providers, or to use multiple, different Cloud providers concurrently. As a proof of concept, we have implemented and incorporated our solution in the popular open-source Cloud stack OpenStack. Moreover, we have designed and implemented a Web application that enables the incorporation of our solution into Google Drive.

Keywords: Authorization; Authentication; Delegation; Security; Policies

1 Introduction

Cloud computing is a technology that offers a cost-effective way for outsourcing data storage and computation. Nevertheless, despite its intriguing properties, enterprises are reluctant to fully adopt it, since they are concerned–among other things–about *losing the governance* of their outsourced assets, i.e., losing the ability to enforce their own, enterprise-specific, security policies. According to PwC's Global State of Information Security Survey 2012 [1], the largest perceived Cloud security risk is the "uncertain ability to enforce provider security policies," whereas according to the survey of Subashini and Kavitha [2] one of the biggest security challenges for providing Cloud-based services is the "adherence of the Cloud provider to the security policies of its clients," as well as "the administration of user authorization systems". This mismatch between provider-enterprise security policies severely impedes Cloud adoption and further research on effective solutions for this problem is required. Indeed, "effective models for managing and enforcing data access policies, regardless of whether the data is stored in the Cloud or cached locally on client

devices" was identified back in 2010 as a top research priority, by the European Network and Information Security Agency (ENISA) [3].

One question that may arise is how likely *loss of governance* of the outsourced data is, and what is its impact. According to ENISA's Cloud Computing Security Risk Assessment report [4], the loss of governance is a risk with *very high* probability and *very high* impact. The same report states that two of the vulnerabilities that may expose an enterprise to that risk are "unclear roles and responsibilities" and "poor enforcement of role definition." This outcome comes as no surprise, since the organizational structure and the security policies of an individual enterprise cannot be easily captured by a Cloud provider. Moreover, the interoperability between an enterprise and a Cloud provider requires the development of complex communication protocols; this, however, increases the chances of a security breach due to implementation errors, according to the Cloud Security Alliance [5]. Armando et al. [6] exploited such implementation errors in order to bypass the SAML-based[a] single sign-on system of Google apps. Similarly, Somorovsky et al. [7] gained access to multiple SAML-based systems by exploiting implementation bugs. Nevertheless, even if the developed protocol is implemented correctly, it will be Cloud provider specific, thus hindering the migration

*Correspondence: fotiou@aueb.gr

Mobile Multimedia Laboratory, Department of Informatics, School of Information Sciences and Technology, Athens University of Economics and Business, Evelpidon 47A, 113 62 Athens, Greece of an enterprise to another Cloud provider; this condition is known as *lock-in*, and has been identified as a *high* probability risk by ENISA [4].

In this paper, we propose a novel solution that enables a trusted entity to store enterprise-specific security policies and take access control decisions on behalf of a Cloud provider: the Cloud provider then has only to respect the access control decision. This trusted entity, which is referred to as the *Access Control Provider* (ACP), may as well be provided by the enterprise itself, for example, by leveraging its user management system, or by a third party. Compared to existing systems, our solution offers better end-user privacy and requires a much simpler communication protocol.

This paper extends our previous work presented in [8], with a more detailed system description, an additional proof of concept implementation, more extensive overhead evaluation, and further comparison with existing systems. The paper is organized as follows. In Section 2 we discuss related work in this area. In Section 3 we detail our scheme. In Section 4 we present our prototype that implements a secure private Cloud file storage service using OpenStack, an open source Cloud stack, as well as a Web application that enables the incorporation of our solution in Google Drive. In Section 5 we evaluate the security properties of our solution and analyze its performance. Finally, in Section 6 we discuss further extensions to our solution and we conclude in Section 7.

2 Related work

Many legacy systems rely on *Role Based Access Control* (RBAC) for controlling access to resources stored by 3rd parties (e.g., Cloud providers, web servers). These systems (e.g., [9-12]) usually adopt one of the following approaches for enforcing access control policies: (a) they either employ an existing language (such as XACML [13]) or define their own to specify the access control policy, which is then interpreted and enforced by the Cloud, or (b) they use cryptographic solutions (such as attribute based encryption [14]) to encrypt data in such a way that only authorized users can decrypt them. RBAC has a role that is orthogonal to our system: RBAC policy definition languages and roles can be used by the ACPs, whereas data stored in the cloud can be encrypted based on roles. Our system is concerned with access control delegation, rather than access control enforcement, where an RBAC solution may be used.

Single Sign-On (SSO) systems–such as Kerberos and, more recently, OpenID 2.0 [15] and OAuth 2.0 [16]– have similar goals with our scheme. Kerberos has been widely used for controlling access to network resources. In a Kerberos system a *Ticket Granting Service* (TGS) provides a "ticket" to an authenticated user that enables her to use a resource. The TGS and the resource, however,

have to belong to the same administration domain or they should be pre-configured with a shared secret. Our system requires neither common administrative domains nor pre-shared secrets.

OpenID is an identity management system that allows identity management delegation to a third trusted party, known as the *Identity Provider* (IdP). IdPs authenticate users and provide them with an "authentication token", which they can use to access a resource. OpenID has been studied in the context of Cloud computing. Nunez et al. [17] used OpenID in conjunction with proxy re-encryption in order to provide Cloud based identity management services. Similarly, Khan et al. [18] have implemented OpenID based authentication mechanisms for the OpenStack platform. OpenID provides only user authentication, therefore, in an OpenID-based access control system, the Cloud provider is responsible for evaluating the access control policies. Moreover, the authentication token is unique per user, therefore user activity can be tracked. In our system access control policies are evaluated by ACPs and not by the Cloud providers. In addition, in our system tokens are ephemeral, therefore they cannot be used to track the long term activity of a specific user.

OAuth 2.0 is an IETF standard for authorizing access to resources over HTTP. OAuth 2.0 requires the resource owner to be online during the user authorization procedure (Section 1.2 of [16]), and requires implicitly the development of a communication protocol between the resource server and the authorization server in order to be able to exchange an *access token* whose form–as mentioned in Section 1.4 of [16]–is not specified. This vagueness impedes implementations of systems where the resource server and the authorization server belong to different administrative domains. An approach for implementing access control using OAuth 2.0 is the following: an access control policy based on *attributes* that can be provided by an authorization server (e.g., user age, as provided by a social network) is defined and stored in the Cloud, the Cloud provider accesses the required attributes using OAuth 2.0 and uses them to evaluate the access control policy. In this scenario, the Cloud provider not only learns some information about the user (in this example his age), but it is also able to interpret them. In our system, Cloud providers neither learn anything about users nor do they have to understand any enterprise-specific semantics.

Policy Based Admission Control [19] is a framework that allows a *Policy Enforcement Point* (PEP) to delegate access control policy decisions to a *Policy Decision Point* (PDP). Each Cloud provider can operate a PEP, whereas PDPs can be implemented by third trusted parties, or even the enterprises themselves. A PEP is responsible for collecting all the information required by a PDP, which includes information about the user that requests access.

Moreover, a PEP and a PDP should agree on a, usually complex, communication protocol (e.g., COPS [20]). With our solution, Cloud providers are completely oblivious about access control policies. Moreover, Cloud providers neither collect nor learn any information about users. Finally, our communication protocol is much simpler, therefore less prone to implementation errors.

The Security Assertion Markup Language (SAML) is an XML-based security assertion language [21], used for exchanging authentication and authorization statements about *subjects*. Being a *language* and not a system, SAML is orthogonal to our work. As a matter of fact, messages in our scheme can be exchanged via SAML, using the Authentication Request Protocol (Section 3.4 of [21]).

3 System design

3.1 Overview

Our scheme is composed of the following entities: the *data owner (owner)*, the *data consumer (consumer)*, the *Cloud provider (CP)*, and the *access control provider (ACP)*. The goal of an owner is to store some data in a CP and allow *authorized* consumers to perform operations over this data. Each operation is protected by an *access control policy*. An access control policy is stored in an ACP and maps the *identity* of a consumer to a boolean output (true, false). When the output of an access control policy is true, the consumer that provided the identification data is considered authorized.

In our scheme, the following trust relationships are considered: owners trust ACPs to authorize consumers, and

owners and consumers trust CPs to respect the decisions of ACPs. The first type of trust relationship can be trivially established if the ACP is implemented by the owner (e.g., the ACP leverages the enterprise's user management system). The second type of trust relationship is a relaxed form of the trust relationship that currently exists between an owner and a Cloud provider: in a contemporary Cloud system where access control is implemented in the Cloud, an owner trusts a Cloud provider to (i) securely store some enterprise-specific security policies (ii) to use these policies correctly, i.e., understand their semantics, and (iii) to enforce the outcome of the access control decision.

As illustrated in Figure 1 a typical transaction in our system takes place as follows. Initially, an owner stores an access control policy in an ACP (step 1) and obtains a *URI* for that policy (step 2). As a next step, she implements an operation over some data in a CP and stores the URI of the policy that protects this operation (step 3). When a consumer tries to perform a protected operation for the first time (step 4), she receives in response the URI of the access control policy that protects the operation and a unique token (step 5). Then, the consumer authenticates herself to a suitable ACP by providing some form of identification data and requests authorization for the access control policy specified in the obtained URI (step 6). If the consumer "satisfies" the access control policy, the ACP *signs* the token and sends it back to the consumer (step 7). The consumer repeats her request to the CP including this time the signed token (step 8). The CP checks the validity

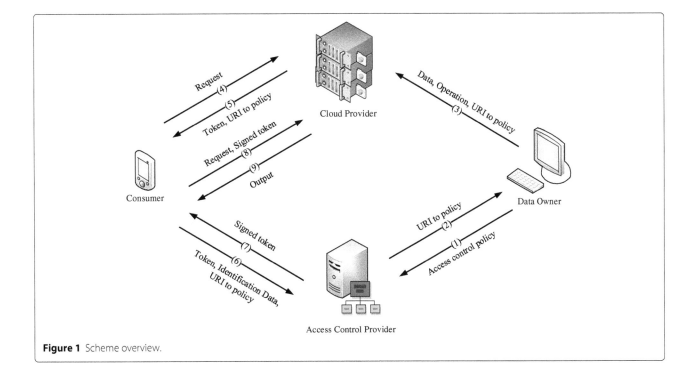

Figure 1 Scheme overview.

of the token and if the token is valid it executes the desired operation and returns its output (step 9).

3.2 Goals

Our goal is to build a system in which the following properties hold:

- *The system is secure:* Provided that all system entities respect the trust relationships described previously, it shall not be possible for an unauthorized user to perform a protected operation.
- *Consumer privacy is preserved:* A CP shall gain minimal information about the identity of a consumer. Ideally it will only learn that a consumer can be authorized by a specific ACP. Moreover an ACP should not be able to tell the operation a consumer wants to perform or the data she accesses.
- *Data can be easily migrated among different Cloud providers:* The only entities that should be aware of an access control policy and its implementation details are the ACP and the owner. CPs shall be oblivious about the access control policy implementation details. Therefore, if two CPs

implement our solution, moving data from one CP to another shall be almost as trivial as copy-pasting it.

- *An access control policy does not reveal anything about the data and the operations it protects:* Access control policies should be decoupled from the data and the operations they protect. An access control policy should be defined taking into account solely consumer attributes.
- *Access control policies are re-usable:* An access control policy should not be bound to a particular operation. It should be possible to protect many and diverse data items, stored in multiple CPs.
- *An access control policy can be easily modified:* The modification of an access control policy shall not involve CPs: the only entity involved in the modification of an access control policy should be the ACP where the policy is stored.

3.3 Detailed system description

We now detail our system design (Figure 2). We have made the following assumptions: (i) ACPs and CPs have a public-private key pair, (ii) ACP's and CP's public keys are known to the consumers and (iii) all messages are exchanged over a secure channel. Throughout this section the notation of Table 1 is used.

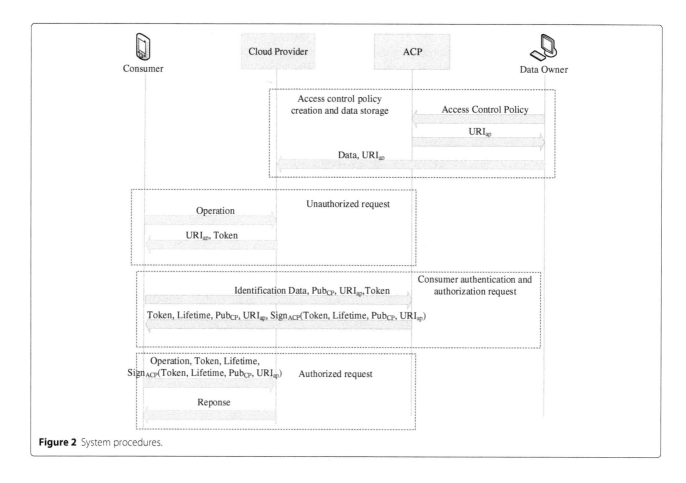

Figure 2 System procedures.

Table 1 Notation

Pub_{CP}	The public key of a CP
Pub_{ACP}	The public key of an ACP
URI_{ap}	The URI of an access control policy
$Sign_{ACP}(Y)$	The digital signature of plaintext Y generated using the private key of an ACP

Our system consists of the following procedures:

3.3.1 Access control policy creation and data storage

With this procedure an owner creates and stores an access control policy in an ACP. The ACP in return provides a URI_{ap}. For each protected operation implemented in a CP, the owner defines the URI_{ap} of the policy that protects it and the Pub_{ACP} of the ACP where the policy is stored. This information is maintained in the CP's *Access Table* that contains tuples of the form:

$$[\,operation, URI_{ap}, Pub_{ACP}]$$

A URI_{ap} is re-usable, i.e., it can be used for protecting multiple operations stored in various *CPs*. The mechanisms for creating an access control policy and for updating an Access Table are ACP specific and CP specific, respectively.

3.3.2 Unauthorized request

This procedure is executed by a consumer in order to perform an operation for the first time. The consumer sends an operation request message to the CP. Upon receiving the request the CP creates a unique *token* (i.e., an adequately large random number) and sends it back to the consumer, along with the corresponding URI_{ap}. Therefore, the following exchange of messages takes place:

(1) : $Consumer \rightarrow CP : operation\ request$
(2) : $CP \rightarrow Consumer : URI_{ap}, Token$

In order to keep track of the generated tokens, a CP maintains a *Token Table* that contains entries of the form:

$$[\,Token, authenticated, expires, URI_{ap}]$$

When a new token is generated, a new entry is added to this table. The value of the *authenticated* field of this entry is set to *false* and the value of the *expires* field to the generation time plus a very small amount of time, sufficient to obtain an authorization.

3.3.3 Consumer authentication and authorization request

This procedure is executed by a consumer upon receiving a response to an unauthorized request. Firstly, the consumer sends her identification data, Pub_{CP}, URI_{ap} and the token to an *ACP* responsible for evaluating the access control policy identified by URI_{ap}. If the consumer satisfies URI_{ap}, the ACP creates an *authorization* message

that contains the token, the amount of time that the token should be valid (i.e., its lifetime), URI_{ap}, and Pub_{CP}. Then it signs this message and sends it back to the consumer. Therefore, the following messages are exchanged:

(3) : $Consumer \rightarrow ACP : ID, Pub_{CP}, URI_{ap}, Token$
(4) : $ACP \rightarrow Consumer : auth, Sign_{ACP}(auth)$

where:

$$auth = Token, Lifetime, URI_{ap}, Pub_{CP}$$

3.3.4 Authorized request

This procedure is executed by an ACP authorized consumer in order to perform an operation. The consumer sends a message that includes the operation request, the token, the token's lifetime and the signature of the authorization message (i.e., message (4)). Therefore the following message is sent:

(5) : $Consumer \rightarrow CP :$
$\quad operation\ request, Token, Lifetime, Sign_{ACP}(Auth)$

Upon receiving this message, a CP should decide if the consumer is allowed to perform the requested operation. Therefore, it executes the following algorithm (Figure 3):

1. Retrieve the entry of the Token Table that contains the token and check if the token has expired. If it has expired, return an error
2. If the *authenticated* field of the corresponding record in the Token Table is *false* then

    (a) Retrieve the Pub_{ACP} that corresponds to the operation from the Access Table
    (b) Retrieve the URI_{ap} that corresponds to the token from the Token Table
    (c) Reconstruct the authorization message
    (d) Verify $Sign_{ACP}(auth)$, using Pub_{ACP}
    (e) If the signature verification succeeds, update the *Token Table* entry as follows: set the *expires* field equal to the *LifeTime* field of the authorization message and set the *authenticated* field to *true*. Proceed to Step 3a below.
    (f) If the signature verification fails, return an error

3. If the *authenticated* field of the corresponding record in the Token Table is *true* then

    (a) Find the URI_{ap} that corresponds to the token from the *Token Table*
    (b) Find the URI_{ap} of the requested operation from the *Access Table*
    (c) Check if the retrieved values match. If they match return, else return an error

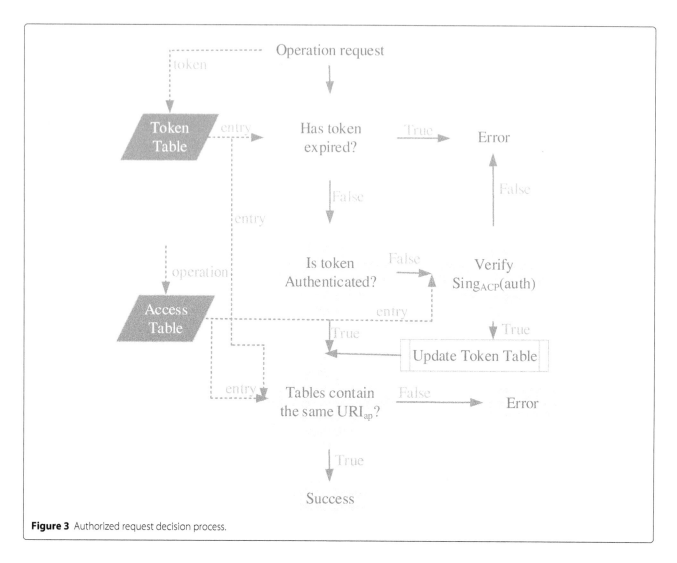

Figure 3 Authorized request decision process.

If this procedure is successful then any subsequent *authorized request* may include only the token. Moreover, the same token can be used multiple times, even for invoking different operations protected by the same URI_{ap}.

3.4 Use case

Let us now illustrate our scheme through a use case. Enterprise A has outsourced sales records storage and analysis to Cloud provider CP_A. The operations implemented in CP_A are: *update sales records, calculate statistics,* and *view statistics.* Enterprise A has the following access control policies:

- Policy 1: All sales department employees can update sales records
- Policy 2: Only the sales department director can calculate statistics
- Policy 3: All shareholders can view the statistics

Enterprise A implements the above access control policies in an ACP owned by itself. The public key of this

ACP is denoted by Pub_{ACP}. For each policy the ACP generates a URI, i.e., *entA.com/Policy1, entA.com/Policy2* and *entA.com/Policy3. CP_A's* Access Table is updated as shown in Table 2.

The sales department director issues an unauthorized request for the *calculate statistics* operation. CP_A generates a token, namely $Token_1$, and responds by sending the following message (entA.com/Policy2, $Token_1$). CP's Token Table is then updated with the entry shown in Table 3.

As a next step, the sales department director authenticates himself to the ACP, which responds with

Table 2 CP_A access table new entries

Operation	URI_{ap}	ACP public key
Update records	*entA.com/Policy1*	Pub_{ACP}
Calculate statistics	*entA.com/Policy2*	Pub_{ACP}
View statistics	*entA.com/Policy3*	Pub_{ACP}

Table 3 CP_A **token table new entries**

Token	Authenticated	Expires	URI_{ap}
$Token_1$	false	timestamp1	entA.com/Policy2

the following, digitally signed, authorization message: ($Token_1$, timestamp2, entA.com/Policy2, Pub_{CP_A}). Then, the sales department director issues the following authorized request: ("calculate statistics", $Token_1$, timestamp2, $Sign_{ACP}(auth)$). CP_A checks if $Token_1$ has expired. Then, it reconstructs the authorization message by retrieving the URI_{ap} associated with the *calculate statistics* operation (i.e., entA.com/Policy2) from the Access Table and verifies $Sign_{ACP}(auth)$ using Pub_{ACP} (also found in the Access Table). Finally, CP_A checks if the URI_{ap} found in the Access Table matches the URI_{ap} included in the entry for $Token_1$ in the Token Table. If all these steps are successful, CP_A executes the *calculate statistics* operation and modifies the entry for $Token_1$ in the Token Table as shown in Table 4.

Since $Token_1$ is now marked as *authenticated*, the sales department director can use it in all subsequent requests, until it expires. Moreover, as long as $Token_1$ remains valid, $Sign_{ACP}(auth)$ does not have to be included in subsequent requests.

3.5 The "level" extension

In the above use case, it can be observed that if the sales department director wishes to invoke the *update records* operation, he has to re-authenticate himself, since this operation is protected by a different URI_{ap}. The *level* extension mitigates this shortcoming by adding a new field to an Access Table: the consumer level. The consumer level is a number that denotes the *minimum* level that a consumer should have in order to invoke an operation. Using this extension, the Access Table of the Cloud provider considered in the use case of Section 3.4 can be modified as shown in Table 5.

With this extension, an ACP has to include the consumer level in the authorization messages. Moreover, a CP now takes part in the access control decision, since it has to check if the level included in the authorization message is greater or equal to the level included in the Access Table. Finally, if the level extension is used, Token Tables should, additionally, include the level that corresponds to a token.

Suppose that the level of the sales department director in the previous use case is 200. Then, he would be able to successfully invoke the *update records* operation, using $Token_1$, without re-authenticating himself.

Table 4 CP_A **token table modified entry**

Token	Authenticated	Expires	URI_{ap}
$Token_1$	true	timestamp2	entA.com/Policy2

Table 5 CP_A **access table using level extension**

Operation	URI_{ap}	Level
Update records	entA.com/Policy2	100
Calculate statistics	entA.com/Policy2	200
View statistics	entA.com/Policy3	100

The ACP public key column is not shown.

4 Implementation

As a proof of concept we implemented a secure file storage service using a popular open source Cloud stack, the OpenStack [22], as well as a Web application that allows the incorporation of our solution in Google Drive [23]. The ACP and the consumer software used in both implementations are the same. Our implementation supports the level extension. As a public-key encryption system we use RSA. Public keys are encoded in JSON format using the keyCzar [24] python library. The keyCzar library is also used for generating digital signatures.

4.1 ACP and consumer software

The ACP of our proof of concept is implemented as a PHP application hosted in an Apache web server. An SQLite database is used for storing username-password pairs, as well as username to URI_{ap}-level mappings. Usernames are unique and a username can be mapped to many URI_{ap}-level pairs (e.g., Table 6). The consumer software implements the *authentication and authorization request*, by encoding the username, the password and the request parameters in a JSON object and by POSTing this object to a particular URL, using HTTPS. The response to this request is again encoded in a JSON object. The consumer software has been pre-configured with the public keys of the *CP* and the *ACP* components.

Table 6 An instance of the user managements system

Username	Password
fotiou	12345
machas	12345
polyzos	12345
xylomenos	12345

Username	URI_{ap}	Level
fotiou	mmlab/Policy1	100
fotiou	mmlab/Policy2	200
machas	mmlab/Policy1	200
machas	mmlab/Policy3	300
polyzos	mmlab/Policy3	100
polyzos	mmlab/Policy4	200
xylomenos	mmlab/Policy3	100
xylomenos	mmlab/Policy4	200

4.2 OpenStack-based implementation

For our OpenStack-based CP (Figure 4), we leveraged the functionality of the OpenStack component *Swift*, which is used for building object storage systems. A Swift-based object storage system is composed of two networks: the internal (private) network that consists of *storage nodes*, and the external (public) network that consists of a *proxy* server and (optionally) an *authentication* server. The proxy server accepts HTTP(S) requests and processes them using a Web Server Gateway Interface. The parameters used in each request are encoded in HTTP headers. Each request is pipelined through a number of add-ons, each of which may transform it, forward it, or respond on behalf of the system to the user.

Objects stored in a Swift-based system are organized in a three level hierarchy. The topmost level of this hierarchy is the *accounts* level, followed by the *containers* level (second level) and the *objects* level (third level). The accounts level contains user accounts. Each user account is associated with many containers from the containers level. A container is used for organizing objects, therefore a container is associated with many objects from the objects level. An object may be a file or a folder (that contains other objects). Every object within a container is identified by a container-unique name. Each request for an operation over an object contains a URI that denotes the account, the container and the name of the object in question, i.e., it is of the form "https://CPHostName/accountname/containername/objectname".

We implemented our system as a Swift add-on added in the pipeline of the add-ons that process incoming requests. This add-on replaces Keystone; the default OpenStack component that handles user authentication. Our implementation allows file storage and retrieval, as well as the following operations over the stored files: organizing files in containers, listing the files of a container, copying a file, moving a file and deleting a file. Token and Access Tables are implemented as SQLite tables. An owner hard codes in the Access Table records of the form: [path,URI_{ap},level,Pub_{ACP}]. A path may be account-wide, container-wide, or object-wide.

Initially, the consumer software sends an unauthorized GET/POST request over HTTPS. The desired operation is specified in a HTTP header and the URL of the request denotes the object (or the container, or the account) that will be used as input to the operation. When an unauthorized request is pipelined through our add-on, the add-on checks if a URI_{ap} exists in the Access Table for the URL specified in the request: if such a URI_{ap} exists, the add-on generates a new token, using the token generation mechanism provided by Swift, and creates a response (as described in Section 3.3); each part of the response is encoded in a HTTP header. The add-on then creates a new entry in the Token Table. The initial expiration time of a token is set equal to the current time plus 10 sec. Upon receiving the response, the consumer software initiates the authentication and the authorization process described in Section 4.1. As a next step, the consumer software sends an authorized request, encoding all request parameters in HTTP headers. The add-on executes the authorized request decision algorithm and produces the appropriate output.

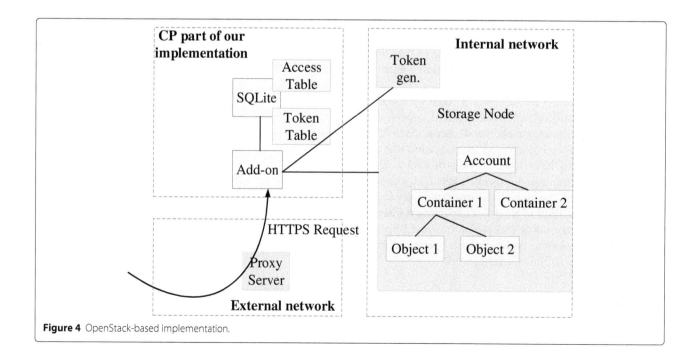

Figure 4 OpenStack-based implementation.

4.3 Google drive-based web application

Google Drive is a popular Cloud based storage service. Google Drive provides a rich API that can be used for building applications that interact with the service over HTTPS. In our implementation we used this API and built a Web application that extends (part of) the Google Drive API, thus providing support for our protocol (Figure 5). Our application is built using the Google App Engine [25] and the Python language. Access Tables and Token Tables have been implemented using the Google App Engine Datastore. Currently, our application supports operations for uploading and downloading files. Each operation can be invoked by making an HTTPS call to the operation-specific URL. All call parameters are encoded in HTTP headers.

Our application has been configured with a Google Drive account which is kept secret. Instead of interacting with the "drive" directly, the consumer software interacts with the application, which acts as a middleware, ensuring that only an authorized consumer can perform the implemented operations. The consumer learns no information about the Google Drive account.

The owner hard codes in the web application a URI_{ap} that controls who can invoke the *upload file* operation. A consumer initially performs an unauthorized request for uploading a file (the file is not included in this request). The web application generates a token using the UUID Python function, it responds to the consumer by encoding the token in an HTTP header and updates the Token Table. The consumer software initiates the authentication and the authorization process described in Section 4.1. Then, it issues an authorized request, by encoding the request parameters in HTTP headers and the file as raw POST data. The web application executes the authorized request decision algorithm and if the consumer is allowed to upload the file, it stores it in the Google Drive. When uploading files, consumers are able to specify a URI_{ap} that controls who can invoke the *download file* operation for that specific file.

5 Evaluation

5.1 Security evaluation

It can be easily observed that our system enhances *consumer* privacy. The only information that a CP learns about a consumer is his trust relationship with a particular ACP; if the level extension is used, the CP also learns his level. Of course, the latter can be encoded in a way that reveals no meaningful information. Any other sensitive information is stored in a (trusted) ACP. Moreover, regardless of the lifetime of a token, a consumer may drop it and request a new one in order to avoid CP *profiling*. Finally, an ACP gains no information about the operations a consumer invokes and the data he accesses: the only information that an ACP learns is the public key of the CP with which the consumer interacts.

Another security feature of our system is that access control policies can be easily modified. Access control policies are stored in a single point (i.e., the ACP) and all CPs have *pointers* to policies. Therefore, the modification of an access control policy does not involve communication with any CP. When an access control policy is modified, all new consumers will be authorized using the new policy, whereas all already authorized consumers will be re-authorized with the new policy when their token expires.

We now proceed to the security analysis of our system using the threat model proposed by Wang at al. [26], adapted to our system. In our analysis we consider

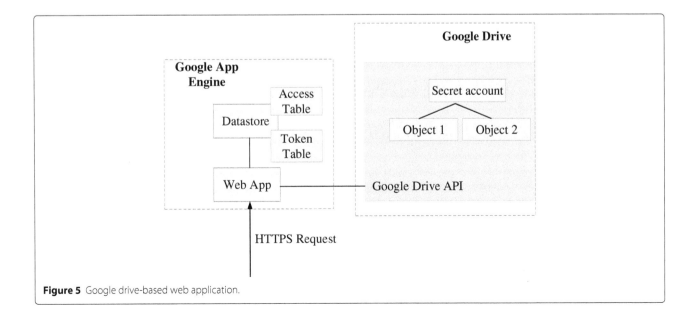

Figure 5 Google drive-based web application.

three different attack scenarios. In all scenarios we assume that messages are exchanged over a secure channel and communication endpoints cannot lie about their identity. We do not consider the case in which a malicious entity acts as an ACP and steals the credentials of a consumer, since this attack is out of the scope of our system.

5.1.1 Malicious entity acting as a consumer

In this attack scenario a malicious entity, Con_M, tries to perform an operation protected by an access control policy URI_{leg} stored in ACP_A. Con_M can only be authorized for the access control policy URI_{mal}, also stored in ACP_A. Con_M's goal is to obtain an authorization message of the form ($Token, Level, Lifetime,$ **URI$_{leg}$**$, Pub_{CP}$). By following our protocol Con_M will receive an authorization message of the form ($Token, Level, Lifetime,$ **URI$_{mal}$**$, Pub_{CP}$). If Con_M includes the signature of this message in his *authenticated request*, the *authorized request decision* algorithm will result in an error, since the CP will generate a different authorization message for which this signature is not valid (Figure 6). The only way for Con_M to obtain a valid signature is to include URI_{leg} in the *authentication and authorization request*, i.e., Con_M should send to ACP_A an authentication and authorization request of the following form: ($ID, Pub_{CP}, URI_{leg}, Token$). However, since Con_M does not abide by URI_{leg} this message will result in an error.

5.1.2 Malicious entity acting as a CP

In this attack scenario the attacker's goal is to perform an operation in CP_A, protected by an access control policy URI_A stored in ACP_A. The attacker is able to pretend to be a Cloud provider, CP_{mal}, as well as to lure a consumer Con_L that can be authorized for URI_A, to perform this operation. Therefore, this is a man-in-the-middle type of attack.

The attacker initially sends an unauthorized request to CP_A and receives $Token_A$ and URI_A. In order for this attack to be successful the attacker has to obtain an authorization message of the form (**Token$_A$**, $Level, Lifetime, URI_A,$ **Pub$_{CP_A}$**). Con_L is lured to send an unauthorized request to CP_{mal} (i.e., to the attacker), which responds with a message of the form: ($URI_A,$ **Token$_A$**). Subsequently, Con_L sends an authentication and authorization request to ACP_A of the following form: ($ID, Pub_{CP_{mal}}, URI_A,$ **Token$_A$**), and receives the following authorization message (**Token$_A$**, $Level, Lifetime, URI_A,$ **Pub$_{CP_{mal}}$**). If the attacker sends an authorized request using the signature of the previous message the *authorized request decision* algorithm will result in an error, since CP_A will generate an authorization message that includes Pub_{CP_A} and not $Pub_{CP_{mal}}$ (Figure 7).

5.1.3 Malicious entity co-located with a consumer

This attack scenario is applicable when a CP maintains a user management system and associates operations over

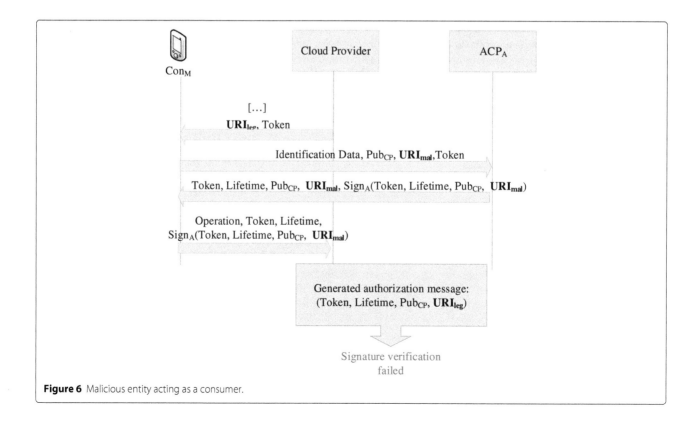

Figure 6 Malicious entity acting as a consumer.

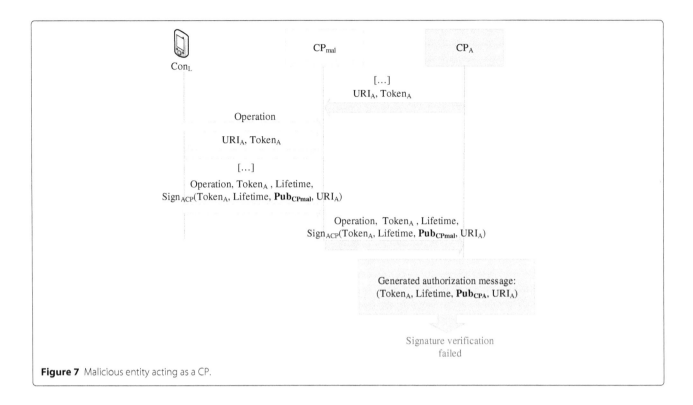

Figure 7 Malicious entity acting as a CP.

protected data with particular users (e.g., for charging reasons). In tis scenario a CP also maintains in its Token Table the *identifier* of the (CP) user for whom the token has been generated. The goal of an attacker in this scenario is to make a CP believe that a consumer Con_L wants to perform a protected operation. In this scenario the attacker is a valid CP user and he is eligible to perform the same operations as Con_L. Moreover, the attacker is able to inject messages on behalf of Con_L.

In this attack scenario, the attacker requests to perform an operation OP_A and proceeds through all steps until he receives the authorization message. At this point, instead of sending an authorized request on behalf of himself, he sends it on behalf of Con_L. It can be easily observed that this attack is trivially mitigated since the CP also maintains the identifiers of the users that correspond to each token, therefore this message will be rejected (Figure 8). It should be noted, however, that this is possible due to our design choice to have the CP generating the tokens, which is not always the case in other similar systems. This attack, for example, was successfully exploited by Wang at al. [26] against three popular websites that were using Facebook Connect and Twitter OAuth for associating their user accounts with their corresponding Facebook and Twitter profiles.

5.2 Overhead

In our implementation, HTTP methods are used for invoking the desired operation. As a public-key

encryption system we use RSA. The size of an RSA public key is 2048 bits, whereas the size of a JSON encoded public key is 400 bytes. Tokens are encoded in 32 byte hex-strings, digital signatures in 512 byte hex-strings and token lifetimes in 8 byte hex-strings. Finally, a single byte is used for representing access levels. When a consumer wants to invoke an operation in a *CP*, protected by a URI_{ap}, a number of messages has to be exchanged. If an ACP has already generated for the consumer an authorization message for URI_{ap} and the corresponding token has not expired, then a single message from the consumer to the CP has to be sent. In any other case five messages have to be exchanged: three between the consumer and the CP, and two between the consumer and the ACP.

It can therefore be observed that an ACP and a consumer have a strong motive to use long-lasting tokens[b]: the longer the duration of a token, the less the communication overhead for an ACP and a consumer. On the other hand, long-lasting tokens increase the state that a CP has to maintain in its Token Table. In order to illustrate this tradeoff, we simulate the following scenario: we consider a CP that hosts files of 100 different enterprises. Each enterprise has defined a single protected operation. Moreover, each enterprise has 100 employees who invoke the operation stored in the CP following a Poisson process with rate 0.1/min. We simulate a usage period of 8 hours and every 5 min we measure the average network load of each enterprise (caused by the messages exchanged with the ACP), as well as the size of the CP's Token Table (the measured

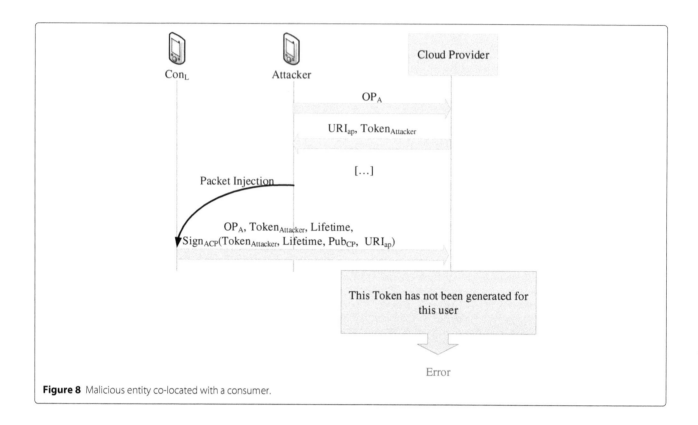

Figure 8 Malicious entity co-located with a consumer.

size is the average value of all the sizes the Token Table had within the 5 min measurement period). We consider two types of tokens: a token with short lifetime (20 min) and a token with long lifetime (2 hours). Figure 9 illustrates the average Token Table size of the CP throughout the simulation period, whereas Figure 10 illustrates the average number of messages transmitted inside each enterprise's network, throughout the simulation period.

5.3 Comparison with existing systems
We now compare our solution with two popular related systems: Google Drive and Amazon S3.

5.3.1 Google drive
The Google Drive Cloud-based storage service, enables users to access, share, and organize their files in the Cloud. The Google Drive API provides a limited set of policies,

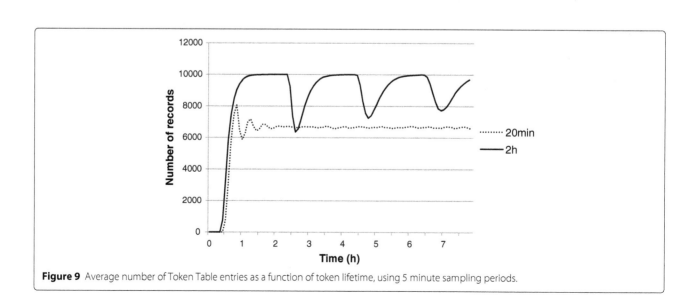

Figure 9 Average number of Token Table entries as a function of token lifetime, using 5 minute sampling periods.

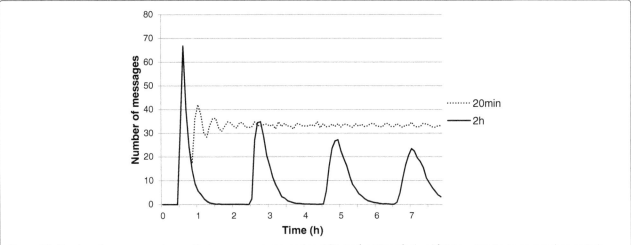

Figure 10 Number of messages exchanged between a consumer and an ACP as a function of token lifetime, using 5 minute sampling periods. During the lifetime of a token, no messages are exchanged.

namely, "full access", "read only access", "metadata only access", and "specific file access". These policies are not applied per stored item, instead they are granted in the form of "permissions" to applications that want to access a specific drive. Before using a "drive", an application requests from the drive owner one of the aforementioned permission types; the drive owner authenticates himself using a Google account and grants permissions using OAuth2.0. In most cases, the user that executes the application that requests permissions and the owner of the drive are the same entity. Permissions are granted in the form of a token that never expires: in order for a drive owner to remove permissions for a specific application, she has to revoke the token manually. Google Drive does not support integration with enterprise specific authentication and authorization systems[c].

In order for an application to perform an operation the following messages have to be exchanged (here we consider that the user executing the application is the drive owner, referred to as the consumer):

1. *Consumer → Google Auth*: Request permission
2. *Consumer → Google Auth*: Authenticate
3. *Consumer → Google Auth*: Grant permission
4. *Google Auth → Consumer*: Token
5. *Consumer → Google Drive*: Operation, Token

Compared to our system the same number of messages is required. Nevertheless, messages 1 to 4 are usually sent once, since tokens never expire. It should be also noted that the entity that performs the authorization is the drive owner herself (the consumer), therefore authorization is a manual process.

5.3.2 Amazon S3

Amazon Simple Storage Service, or S3 for short, is a well-known Cloud-based file storage service. S3 provides Web services that allow users to store and organize their files in the Cloud. Files are organized in "buckets". A user may set *Access Control Lists* (ACLs) that define the permissions that a user or a group of users have over a specific bucket, or over a specific file. ACLs are encoded in XML and the permissions that can be granted are "read", "write", "read ACL", "modify ACL", "full control". For more fine grained access control, S3 provides an "access control policy language", that allows users to create bucket-specific policies. These policies can control the access to a bucket, and its objects, based on user identities, source IP addresses, time and date, and some other parameters.

S3 provides an API that allows users (consumers) to be authenticated using their own (enterprise specific) *identity provider*. In order for an operation to be performed the following messages have to be exchanged:

1. *Consumer → Identity Provider*: Authenticate
2. *Identity Provider → Amazon Token Service*: Request Token
3. *Amazon Token Service → Identity Provider*: Token
4. *Identity Provider → Consumer*: Token
5. *Consumer → Amazon S3*: Operation, Token

It can be seen that the same number of messages is required, as in our system. Nevertheless, in the S3 system the authorization is performed by Amazon and not by the identity provider, therefore access control policies have to be stored in an Amazon server. This, combined with the fact that policies are defined using Amazon's specific policy definition language, creates a "lock-in" risk.

Moreover, all the users who are identified by their own identity provider are considered to have the same role (i.e., "federated users"), limiting the flexibility of the access control policies. Finally, a secret has to be shared between the identity provider of the user and Amazon's token service, in order for steps 2 and 3 to take place successfully.

6 Discussion

So far we have explored the possibilities that our solution offers in a "traditional" usage model: an enterprise that uses Cloud computing for outsourcing data storage and computations. However, the introduction of a new role, that of the ACP, and the decoupling of the data storage and access control assessment functions creates many new business opportunities.

One area that can benefit from our solution is that of B2B applications. Suppose that enterprise A wants to offer access to some of its (Cloud-based) services to a department of enterprise B. Enterprise B can expose a URI_{ap} that authenticates and authorizes the users of that particular department. Enterprise A can use this URI_{ap} in order to protect the shared services. With this, enterprise A can perform access control without learning anything about the internal user management system of enterprise B. Enterprise A may also offer services for the customers of enterprise B using a similar approach.

Our solution also creates a new business opportunity. We envision that a new market can arise due to our solution, that of the access control providers. In addition to the enterprise specific ACPs there can be independent ACPs that offer security services to end-users. Existing security companies can utilize their expertise to offer cutting edge access control services without investing in the Cloud market. Moreover, existing social networks may leverage their services and act as ACPs. To this end, future work for our scheme includes support for ACP federations and support for multiple URI_{ACP} definitions per single data item.

7 Conclusions

In this paper we proposed a solution to a thorny problem that prevents Cloud technology adoption: that of access control. The proposed solution enables data owners to outsource data storage and computation, without losing governance of their assets. In our solution access control is provided as a service by a new entity, the Access Control Provider (ACP). Access control as a service relieves Cloud providers from the burden of implementing complex security solutions and enables enterprises to deploy their own specific access control mechanisms. We demonstrated the feasibility of our scheme through proof of concept implementations. In particular, we implemented our system as an add-on for the open source Cloud stack OpenStack and we developed a Web application that allows the incorporation of our system in Google Drive. We show that our scheme is secure and has significant privacy properties. The proposed system adds minimal overhead, does not require any particular Cloud implementation or ACP structure and, therefore, it constitutes a realistic solution to the problem. Finally, we believe that the proposed solution can open the floor for new exciting applications and business opportunities.

Endnotes

[a]SAML is a generic XML language used for security assessments between different entities.

[b]Provided that this does not jeopardize the security of the scheme.

[c]Google provides a SAML based SSO system that can be used to integrate enterprise specific authentication systems, but only in Web applications.

Competing interests
The authors declare that they have no competing interests.

Authors' contributions
NF, AM, GCP and GX have made substantial contributions to the conception and design of the access control as a service architecture, and reviewed the final manuscript version. All authors read and approved the final manuscript.

Acknowledgment
This research was supported in part by a grant from the Greek General Secretariat for Research and Technology, financially managed by the Research Center of AUEB.

References
1. PwC: Global State of Information Security Survey (2012)
2. Subashini S, Kavitha V (2011) A survey on security issues in service delivery models of cloud computing. J Netw Comput Appl 34(1):1–11
3. Gorniak S (ed) (2010) Priorities for research on current and emerging network trends. ENISA. https://www.enisa.europa.eu/activities/identity-and-trust/library/deliverables/procent
4. Catteddu D, Hogben G (eds) (2009) Cloud Computing Benefits, risks and recommendations for information security. ENISA. https://downloads.cloudsecurityalliance.org/initiatives/top_threats/The_Notorious_Nine_Cloud_Computing_Top_Threats_in_2013.pdf
5. Cloud Security Alliance (2013) The Notorious Nine Cloud Computing Top Threats in 2013. https://cloudsecurityalliance.org/
6. Armando A, Carbone R, Compagna L, Cuellar J, Tobarra L (2008) Formal analysis of SAML 2.0 web browser single sign-on: breaking the SAML-based single sign-on for google apps. In: Proc. of the 6th ACM Workshop on Formal Methods in Security Engineering. ACM, New York, NY. pp 1–10
7. Somorovsky J, Mayer A, Schwenk J, Kampmann M, Jensen M (2012) On breaking SAML: Be whoever you want to be. In: Proc. of the 21st USENIX Security Symposium. USENIX Association, Berkeley, CA Vol. 12. pp 21–21
8. Fotiou N, Machas A, Polyzos GC, Xylomenos G (2014) Access control delegation for the cloud. In: Computer Communications Workshops (INFOCOM WKSHPS), 2014 IEEE Conference On. IEEE, Canada. pp 13–18
9. Wang G, Liu Q, Wu J (2010) Hierarchical attribute-based encryption for fine-grained access control in cloud storage services. In: Proceedings of the 17th ACM Conference on Computer and Communications Security. CCS '10. ACM, New York, NY, USA. pp 735–737
10. Zhou L, Varadharajan V, Hitchens M (2011) Enforcing role-based access control for secure data storage in the cloud. Comput J. doi:10.1093/comjnl/bxr080, http://comjnl.oxfordjournals.org/content/early/2011/09/02/comjnl.bxr080.abstract

11. Li J, Zhao G, Chen X, Xie D, Rong C, Li W, Tang L, Tang Y (2010)
     Fine-grained data access control systems with user accountability in
     cloud computing. In: Cloud Computing Technology and Science
     (CloudCom), 2010 IEEE Second International Conference On. IEEE
     Computer Society, Washington, DC. pp 89–96

12. Yu S, Wang C, Ren K, Lou W (2010) Achieving secure, scalable, and
     fine-grained data access control in cloud computing. In: INFOCOM, 2010
     Proceedings IEEE. IEEE Press, Piscataway, NJ. pp 1–9

13. OASIS (2013) eXtensible Access Control Markup Language (XACML)
     Version 3.0.22. http://docs.oasis-open.org/xacml/3.0/xacml-3.0-core-
     spec-en.html

14. Goyal V, Pandey O, Sahai A, Waters B (2006) Attribute-based encryption
     for fine-grained access control of encrypted data. In: Proceedings of the
     13th ACM Conference on Computer and Communications Security. CCS
     '06. ACM, New York, NY, USA. pp 89–98

15. Recordon D, Reed D (2006) OpenID 2.0: a platform for user-centric
     identity management. In: Proc. of the 2nd ACM Workshop on Digital
     Identity Management. ACM, New York, NY. pp 11–16

16. Hardt D (ed) (2012) The OAuth 2.0 authorization framework. RFC 6749.
     https://tools.ietf.org/html/rfc6749

17. Nunez D, Agudo I, Lopez J (2012) Integrating OpenID with proxy
     re-encryption to enhance privacy in cloud-based identity services. In: Proc
     of the IEEE 4th International Conference on Cloud Computing
     Technology and Science. IEEE Computer Society, Washington, DC, USA

18. Khan RH, Ylitalo J, Ahmed AS (2011) OpenID authentication as a service in
     OpenStack. In: Proc. of the 7th International Conference on Information
     Assurance and Security. IEEE. pp 372–377. (doi://10.1109/ISIAS.2011.
     6122782)

19. Yavatkar R, Pendarakis D, Guerin R (2000) A framework for policy-based
     admission control. RFC 2753. https://tools.ietf.org/html/rfc2753

20. Durham D (ed) (2000) The COPS (Common Open Policy Service) Protocol.
     RFC 2748. https://tools.ietf.org/html/rfc2748

21. Cantor S, Kemp J, Philpott R, Maler E (eds) (2005) Assertions and protocols
     for the OASIS Security Assertion Markup Language (SAML) v2.0. OASIS.
     https://docs.oasis-open.org/security/saml/v2.0/saml-core-2.0-os.pdf

22. Openstack homepage. http://www.openstack.org/, last accessed 27 Apr.
     2015

23. Google Drive homepage. https://drive.google.com, last accessed 27 Apr.
     2015

24. Google Keyczar homepage. https://github.com/google/keyczar, last
     accessed 27 Apr. 2015

25. Google App Engine homepage. https://developers.google.com/
     appengine/, last accessed 27 Apr. 2015

26. Wang R, Chen S, Wang X (2012) Signing me onto your accounts through
     facebook and google: A traffic-guided security study of commercially
     deployed single-sign-on web services. In: Proc. of the IEEE Symposium on
     Security and Privacy. IEEE Computer Society, Washington, DC, USA.
     pp 365–379

13

An adaptive semantics-aware replacement algorithm for web caching

André Pessoa Negrão[1,2]*, Carlos Roque[1,2], Paulo Ferreira[1,2] and Luís Veiga[1,2]

Abstract

As the web expands its overwhelming presence in our daily lives, the pressure to improve the performance of web servers increases. An essential optimization technique that enables Internet-scale web servers to service clients more efficiently and with lower resource demands consists in caching requested web objects on intermediate cache servers. At the core of the cache server operation is the replacement algorithm, which is in charge of selecting, according to a cache replacement policy, the cached pages that should be removed in order to make space for new pages. Traditional replacement policies used in practice take advantage of temporal reference locality by removing the least recently/frequently requested pages from the cache. In this paper we propose a new solution that adds a spatial dimension to the cache replacement process. Our solution is motivated by the observation that users typically browse the Web by successively following the links on the web pages they visit. Our system, called SACS, measures the distance between objects in terms of the number of links necessary to navigate from one object to another. Then, when replacement takes place, objects that are distant from the most recently accessed pages are candidates for removal; the closest an object is to a recently accessed page, the less likely it is to be evicted. We have implemented a cache server using SACS and evaluated our solution against other cache replacement strategies. In this paper we present the details of the design and implementation of SACS and discuss the evaluation results obtained.

Keywords: WWW; Web performance; Web caching; Replacement algorithms; Semantic awareness

1 Introduction

Two decades after its inception, the World Wide Web continues to be among the most popular Internet services [1,2]. Everyday, an extensive number of users from all over the world accesses the Web to read online newspapers, get in touch with their friends on Social Networks, share their ideas on blogs or even play on video game websites. Information that used to be difficult to obtain is now one click away from us, on our laptops, tablets or even smart phones.

While the ubiquity of the Internet is desired by both users and content providers, the resulting high number of user requests is a challenge to the performance and scalability of Web servers and Internet Service Providers (ISPs) alike [3]. This challenge takes the form of, for example, increased computational load and bandwidth requirements due to the necessity of processing requests from (and delivering responses to) an increasingly larger number of users. This may, in turn, lead to increased latency, which results in user perceived delays [4].

In order to continue satisfying users' demands and, at the same time, reduce the network and computational strain imposed on content providers, several optimization techniques have been proposed over the years [5]. One of the most successful of such techniques is Web caching [6]. Web caching consists in storing copies of the pages requested by users to a web server on intermediary machines that can service future requests to those pages on behalf of the actual web server. Web caches optimize the operation of a web system by 1) reducing the load and network bandwidth at the origin Web servers by minimizing the number of accesses to the actual website and 2) minimizing access latency by placing data closer to the users [7]. For these reasons, web caches have become an ubiquitous background presence on the web and can be found at different layers of the Internet hierarchy [8].

Due to their limited sizes, caches cannot store every web page/object indefinitely. When the cache becomes full, the

*Correspondence: andre.pessoa@ist.utl.pt
[1]Instituto Superior Técnico, Universidade de Lisboa, Rua Alves Redol 9, Lisboa, Portugal
[2]Distributed Systems Group, INESC-ID, Rua Alves Redol 9, Lisboa, Portugal

cache server must choose one or more objects to remove in order to make space for new objects. This decision is the responsibility of the cache replacement algorithm [9], one of the most critical components of a web cache system.

Among the most well known and highly used replacement algorithms are *Least Recently Used* (LRU) and *Least Frequently Used* (LFU), which remove the least recently or least frequently used object from the cache, respectively [10]. At the other end of the spectrum, more complex solutions based on machine learning try to predict which pages are going to be more frequently accessed by users based on past behavior [11-13]. In between, several other cache replacement algorithms have been proposed [14-21].

The most common approaches used in practice base their object replacement decisions on temporal locality information. In this paper, we propose adding a spatial dimension to the cache replacement problem. We propose a novel cache replacement algorithm, called SACS (from *Semantics Aware Caching System*), that takes into account semantic information about the cached web objects in order to decide which should be removed from the cache. More specifically, we propose looking into the structure of web pages, in particular the links between them, in order to try to predict which pages will be accessed in the near future. Our solution is based on the intuitive notion that an object that is linked by a recently accessed page has a higher probability of being accessed in the near future and, as such, should also be kept in the cache. Our system materializes this observation by assigning priorities to cached objects based on their link navigation information. This assignment is made in such a way that objects whose *distance* to recently accessed pages (measured as the length of the shortest path of links between them) is high have higher probability of being removed, while pages closer to recently accessed pages are kept cached. In addition, pages with the same distance factor are ordered according to their frequency information.

The main strength of our cache replacement algorithm is that it combines recency and frequency information with object access prediction based on the link relations between the different web pages/objects. By taking link information into account, SACS has additional information that allows it to reason in a more semantic way about future requests to the web cache server. This is in contrast with existing algorithms, which base their decision on syntactic information. In addition, by combining recency and frequency, our system is able to obtain the good results of these solutions in the scenarios in which they perform well, while, at the same time, being able to avoid their main shortcomings (e.g., cache pollution in LFU and eviction of popular pages that have not been recently requested in LRU).

The rest of this document is structured as follows. In Section 2 we describe the architecture of SACS and the design of the algorithm. In Section 3 we provide information about the implementation of our system. In Section 4 we present and discuss the results obtained in the evaluation of SACS. In Section 5 we discuss related work. Finally, in Section 6 we conclude the paper.

2 Architecture

SACS follows the execution loop of traditional cache management systems. When the cache receives a request for an object, it first verifies whether the object is already cached. If there is a version of the object available in the cache, that version is sent to the user. Otherwise, it is necessary to fetch the object from the origin web server and forward it to the user. In addition, the newly fetched document is placed in the cache. Doing so might require removing one or more objects from the cache, in case the available free space is not sufficient to hold the new object. The decision of which pages should be removed is made by the system's cache replacement algorithm.

In the next sections we present the design of SACS in detail. We start by introducing the main building blocks of our system in Section 2.1. Then, we describe SACS's cache replacement algorithm in Section 2.2.

2.1 Overview

Our system builds upon three main metrics: distance, recency and frequency. The *recency* metric tracks the last time an object was requested while in cache; it is the same metric used by the LRU replacement strategy. The *frequency* metric tracks the number of times an object was requested while in cache and is the metric used by the LFU replacement strategy.

The *distance* metric is a novel element introduced by our approach. It measures the distance between two objects in terms of the minimum number of links that need to be followed in order to navigate from one object to the other. In other words, given the web objects graph $G = (V, E)$, where V is the set of cached pages and E is the set of links between them, distance broadly corresponds to the length of the shortest navigation path between pages x_i and x_j. Implicitly, this metric is related with the probability that a user who requested object x_i will visit another object x_j to which there may be a navigation path rooted in x_i.

We denote the distance between two web objects x_i and x_j as d_{x_i, x_j}. Note that despite the notation implying otherwise, d_{x_i, x_j} refers to the distance of the navigation path from x_j to x_i; it means the *distance to get to x_i from x_j*. Due to the nature of the web, the distance function is not symmetric, which means that the distance between x_i and x_j might not be the same as the distance between x_j and x_i. In reality, it is clear that even if a page x_i is accessible from

x_j, the reverse might not be true, since there might not be a navigation path between x_j and x_i. It should also be clear that distance applies only when the root of the navigation path in consideration is an HTML page; the destination, on the other hand, can be any type of web object.

The distance between two objects depends not only on the number of links existing in the navigation path between the pages, but also on the type of HTML constructs (i.e., tags) that make up the links. We distinguish tags that must be explicitly clicked by the user (*explicit links*) from tags that refer to objects that are automatically loaded when the requested page is parsed (*implicit links*). Regarding explicit links, our system considers only the *a* HTML tag. A link in the navigation path referring to this tag is assigned a distance of 1, since traversing this link requires the user to follow the link, which is not guaranteed to happen.

As for implicit links, we consider tags *img*, *link*, and *frame*. Other tags, such as *script*, *audio*, *video* and similar ones, may also be considered, depending on the types of objects that the cache administrators consider to be cacheable. Implicit links, unlike explicit ones, are assigned a distance of 0, since they are aggregated with the object that is at the origin of the link and are meant to be loaded simultaneously. Figure 1 shows a simple example of a web site and the corresponding distances between its pages. In this example, we have $d_{menu.html,index.html} = 1$, while $d_{about.html,index.html} = 2$.

Consider the set V of direct links between cached pages. Further consider function τ that, given two objects, returns the type (implicit or explicit) of the link between the two. The following equation formalizes the definition of *link distance*:

$$d_{x_i,x_j} = \begin{cases} 0 & \text{iff } (x_i, x_j) \in V \ \wedge \ \tau(x_i, x_j) = \text{implicit} \\ 1 & \text{iff } (x_i, x_j) \in V \ \wedge \ \tau(x_i, x_j) = \text{explicit} \\ \infty & \text{iff } (x_i, x_j) \notin V \end{cases}$$

(1)

The following section explains how our system measures the distance metric and how it is used, along with the other metrics, by our cache replacement algorithm.

2.2 Cache replacement

At any moment, SACS keeps track of a set of pages that have a special interest to our replacement algorithm. We refer to these special pages as *pivots* and denote the pivot list as P. The importance of pivots stems from the fact that it is with relation to them that the distance assigned to each cached page is determined. More specifically, the distance assigned to a page x_i corresponds to its distance to the closest pivot:

$$d_{x_i} = min\left(d_{x_i,p_1}, \ldots, d_{x_i,p_n}\right), \forall p_i \in P \qquad (2)$$

If the object in question is directly linked by a pivot (i.e., $\exists p_i \in P : (x_i, p_i) \in V$) or if it is not linked by any other page (i.e., $\neg \exists x_j : (x_i, x_j) \in V$), then its distance is given by Equation 1. Otherwise, if the object has links to it, but none is a pivot, its distance is defined recursively as follows:

$$d_{x_i,p_i} = d_{x_i,x_j} + d_{x_j,p_i}, \forall x_j \in Parents(x_i) \qquad (3)$$

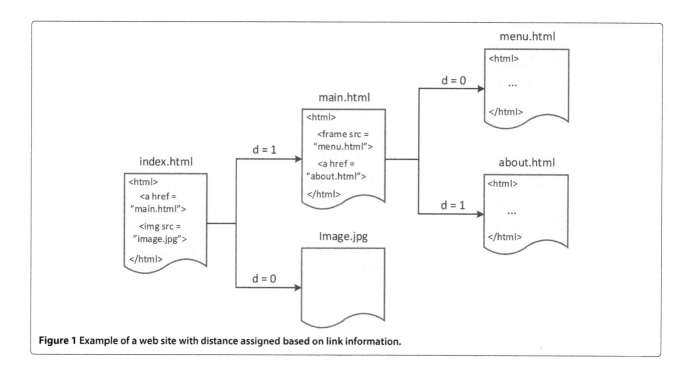

Figure 1 Example of a web site with distance assigned based on link information.

In our system, pivots correspond to the most recently accessed cached pages; it is this feature that allows us to prioritize caching the most recently accessed pages, similarly to LRU. More specifically, pivots correspond to the cached objects that have been requested in the last α seconds, where α is a parameter set by cache administrators. Consider that t is the current time and t_{x_i} is the timestamp of the latest request to object x_i. Further consider that R is the list of past requests submitted to the cache. The definition of *pivot* is formalized in the following formula:

$$x_i \in P \iff x_i \in R \wedge t - t_{x_i} < \alpha \qquad (4)$$

Algorithm 1 Processing received requests

```
 1: function RECEIVEREQUEST(URL, requestCount)
 2:    if URL ∈ cache then
 3:        obj ← cache[URL]
 4:        obj_timestamp ← requestCount
 5:        obj_count ← obj_count + 1
 6:        pivots ← pivots ∪ URL
 7:        response ← msg(obj_data)
 8:    else
 9:        obj ← GET_DATA_FROM_ORIGIN(URL)
10:        if obj is cacheable then
11:            if obj_size ≤ cache_maxSize − cache_size then
12:                cache[URL] ← obj
13:            else
14:                EVICT_AND_REPLACE(obj)
15:            end if
16:        end if
17:        response ← msg(obj_data)
18:    end if
19:    return response
20: end function
```

Our algorithm comprises two main phases: monitoring and eviction. In the monitoring phase (see Algorithm 1), the cache collects information about access to pages and user requests. The algorithm keeps, for each cached page, the page's hit count while cached (*frequency*) and the timestamp of the latest access to the page (*recency*). On a cache hit, the frequency and recency information of the requested object is updated and its cached version is returned to the user. If, on the other hand, the requested object is not cached, the system gets it from the origin server before returning it to the requesting user. In addition, a cache miss triggers the eviction phase of the algorithm if the requested object does not fit in the available free space.

The eviction phase (Algorithm 2) is triggered when the free space available in the cache is not sufficient to accommodate new pages. At that moment, the algorithm

chooses one or more pages to remove until a predefined *target cache size* threshold is reached. Since there may be different layers of storage within the server (e.g., memory and disk), each area has its own set of thresholds for the maximum and target cache size, so that they can be customized and controlled independently by the cache server administrator. The threshold values are specified in bytes and respect the property *TargetCacheSize < MaxCacheSize*.

To choose which page(s) to evict, our algorithm sorts the candidates for replacement according to our replacement policy. For performance reasons, the candidates for eviction consist of a randomly selected sample of size β of the cached objects. β can be freely set by the deployers of the cache according to their needs. We analyze the impact of this parameter in the performance of SACS in Section 4.3.3.

Our eviction algorithm requires obtaining the distance of each eviction candidate. Because computing this distance requires executing a search algorithm, it is not feasible nor scalable to execute this algorithm on the fly for every candidate object every time eviction is issued. Instead, our system continuously executes the distance computation function in the background. As a consequence, every object has its distance refreshed periodically. Our distance computation algorithm executes a Breadth First Search with bounded depth over the page graph. We bound the maximum depth of the search not only for performance reasons, but also because after a certain distance, the probability of a page being visited by following the links in a path decreases sharply. The search returns the depth of the first pivot encountered or *maxDepth*, if it reaches the maximum depth without finding a pivot.

Algorithm 2 Eviction phase

```
 1: function EVICTANDREPLACE(obj)
 2:    if obj_type is HTML then
 3:        CRAWLER.PARSE(obj_data)
 4:    end if
 5:    sample ← PICK_RANDOM_SAMPLE(β)
 6:    for c ∈ sample do
 7:        if c ∈ pivots then
 8:            c_distance ← 0
 9:        end if
10:    end for
11:    i ← 0
12:    SORT(sample)
13:    while cache_size ≥ cache_targetSize do
14:        cache.REMOVE(sample[i])
15:        i ← i + 1
16:    end while
17: end function
```

With the distance computation running in the background, during the eviction phase our system simply retrieves the distance information from the metadata of each candidate page. We perform one additional step that verifies, for each candidate, if it hasn't become a pivot since its distance was last refreshed by the distance computation function. After the distance information is obtained, the eviction candidates are ordered by their distance, with objects with higher distance being ordered before objects with lower distance. Then, the ordering of objects with the same distance depends on the frequency information of the pages, such that objects less frequently accessed are ordered before pages more frequently accessed. Objects are then removed in order until the target cache size threshold is reached.

Finally, when the new object is added to the cache, SACS parses it in the background to extract its link information and updates the link information in the page graph. As for the pages that are evicted, the cache does not remove their information from the graph immediately, as it may still be useful to compute another page's distance. Instead, this information is garbage collected either when no other cached page links to the removed page, or when memory becomes scarce.

3 Implementation

We implemented a prototype of a web cache server that uses SACS as its cache management system. Our implementation was written in Java and is built on top of the *Ehcache* [22] open-source cache software. Ehcache is a general-purpose caching library that implements a generic object cache that can be used to implement different types of caching systems. Ehcache implements both memory and disk caching, coupled with a simple API for managing interaction between the different caching layers. It comes preloaded with three cache replacement algorithms for the in-memory cache (LRU, LFU and FIFO), but allows custom made replacement policies to be plugged into the system. For the disk cache, however, only the LFU replacement strategy is available.

Ehcache stores cached data as generic *Element* objects. An element contains a key, a value and a set of useful metadata, such as the element's hit count and the timestamp of its last access. To add our own functionality, we created a *SACS Element* extending the original Element class with additional metadata required by our replacement algorithm.

Plugging our cache replacement algorithm into Ehcache required us to implement a *SACS Policy* class extending Ehcache's *Policy* interface. The Policy interface exports only three methods, which are necessary for deciding which element to evict from the cache. The most relevant of these is method *selectedBasedOnPolicy*, which receives a list of candidate elements from which the element to

remove is selected. However, when called by Ehcache, this method receives only a small sample of the cached elements, which limits the control of our system over the eviction process. As such, in order to grant our replacement algorithm access to the full element list, we had to make a few modifications to the source code of Ehcache. Further modifications to the source code of Ehcache had to be made in order to allow our system to control the value of the target cache size, which is not exported by Ehcache's configuration tools.

Besides Ehcache, our implementation uses two additional external libraries: *Netty*, and *htmlparser*. *htmlparser* [23] is a Java based html parsing library we use to parse HTML pages and extract link information from them. Netty [24] is a network I/O framework that abstracts different network protocols into a high level API, easing the effort of implementing network applications. We used it to handle several lower level aspects of the network communication part of the system, such as receiving and sending messages and managing user and server connections. We also used its HTTP parsing API to extract information from HTTP messages.

We keep a graph with the link information in store, indexed by a hash table, for direct access to the nodes in the graph. The graph is constructed iteratively, as new pages are added to the cache, and periodically by crawling the cached contents in the background. Crawling is necessary because parsing a page only obtains the links that originate in it, not the ones that point to it.

In our current implementation, we set the sample size to 10%, for performance and scalability reasons. To identify if an object is a pivot, we apply Equation 4. In other words, we verify if the timestamp of the last access to the object is within an interval of α seconds. In our current implementation, $\alpha = 120$.

4 Evaluation

We have conducted a series of trace-driven experiments with the goal of analyzing the performance of SACS regarding a number of metrics and execution scenarios. In this section, we provide detailed information about the evaluation process and the results obtained.

4.1 Dataset

Our evaluation was performed using the access logs of the FIFA World Cup 1998 web site [25]. The logs contain information about approximately 1.35 billion user requests made over a period of around 3 months, starting one month before the beginning of the world cup and finishing a few weeks after the conclusion of this event. Each log entry contains information about a single user request, including the identification of the user that made the request (abstracted as a unique numeric identifier for privacy reasons), the id of the requested object (also a unique identifier), the timestamp of the request, the number of bytes of the requested object and the HTTP code of the response sent to the user.

The main reason for choosing the FIFA logs is the fact that it provides us, directly or indirectly, with all the information required to evaluate our algorithm: 1) it directly provides us with user driven access patterns that represent the real way users have requested pages from the site; 2) it provides us with sufficient information to obtain the actual site, through which we can obtain crucial information about pages and links; and 3) it is readily available from the Internet with a manageable size. Other traces found online or used in literature often omit important information (such as the requested URLs) by anonymizing the traces or are no longer available.

Although the dataset does not include an actual copy of the web site, the logs come with a file that maps the unique identifiers of the web objects to their respective URLs. Since our solution requires that we have access to the link information (which is only available within the web pages), we used the Internet Archive [26] to download the web site. However, the Internet Archive does not possess a full copy of the web site. As a result, we were only able to obtain approximately 70% of the html pages of the website. Instead of discarding the remaining pages from the experiments, we created stub replacements for them containing no links to other pages. This allowed us to simulate a more realistic scenario, since in a real world setting, not every page in the cache will have links to other cached pages.

For most of the evaluation scenarios, we focused on an eleven day period from June 24 (day 60) to July 4 (day 70). This period contains the busiest days in the logs, with an average of 40 million requests per day, with the highest daily request count peaking at 80 million on July 1 (day 67). In total, this interval includes close to 450 million request, one third of the total number of requests in the logs.

4.2 Simulation environment

The main performance metrics considered in this evaluation were *hit rate* and *byte hit rate*. Hit rate measures the percentage of requests that are serviced from the cache (i.e., requests for pages that are cached). Byte hit rate measures the amount of data (in bytes) served from the cache as a percentage of the total amount of bytes requested. These metrics are among the most commonly used to evaluate caching systems [9,11-13,27], and allow us to analyze the ability of our caching system in caching the pages that are most likely to be requested in the near future.

We compared the results obtained by our solution with LRU and LFU. Our implementation of LRU evicts from the cache the pages with the oldest request number, while LFU evicts the ones with the lowest hit count. LRU is a good overall algorithm that is commonly used in practice

(for example, in Squid [28]). LFU is also a popular replacement algorithm that works well when the set of the most popular pages is mostly stable or changes slowly. However, it is subject to cache pollution when popularity changes more dynamically, as it tends to maintain in the cache objects that have been popular, but no longer are. Since the traces used in our experiments do not display this pattern of changes in popularity (object popularity in the logs is mostly stable), it does not allow us to clearly analyze how SACS compares with LFU. For this reason, we designed a synthetic scenario in which before running the simulation, we populate a percentage of the cache with pages that are not frequently requested in the logs. In addition, we set the initial hit count of those pages to a higher value than they would naturally have. In the evaluation, for each algorithm considered, we present the results obtained with this *biased* scenario against the *regular* scenario that starts with a clean cache.

In our simulation, uncacheable and invalid requests, which would have resulted in cache misses, are discarded and are not accounted for in the statistics. As a consequence, the values for both hit rate and byte hit rate obtained and presented here are higher than they would be in reality and can, thus, be regarded as an upper bound of the real values. However, since these requests would have been discarded by all algorithms, they only have a numeric impact on the results; they have no effect on the relative results of the algorithms evaluated and, as such, do not affect the reliability of the results obtained.

To analyze the performance of the system under different cache sizes, we executed each simulation with a cache size of 4MB and repeated it with an 8MB cache size. Although these values are small in absolute terms, they correspond, respectively, to 5% and 10% of the total size of the cacheable contents of the FIFA98 website.

Our experiences consisted in sequentially reading entries from a set of log files and feeding them directly to our cache server. As a result of this approach, issues related to concurrency are not considered, except later in Section 4.3.4. For each experiment we executed multiple simulations, logging the values obtained in each individual simulation and computing the corresponding averages. The values presented in this section correspond to the averages obtained. The experiments were executed on a single machine equipped with an Intel Core i7 870 2.93GHz CPU (4 cores) and 12GB of RAM running Ubuntu Linux.

4.3 Results

In this section we present the results obtained during the evaluation of our system. First, we present the results of our comparative analysis of SACS against LRU and LFU regarding hit and byte hit rate. We then compare the performance of SACS in terms of memory usage and

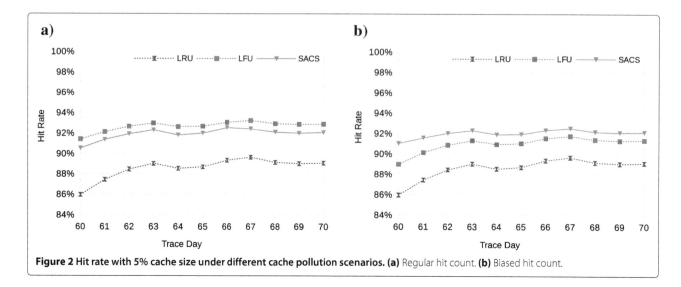

Figure 2 Hit rate with 5% cache size under different cache pollution scenarios. **(a)** Regular hit count. **(b)** Biased hit count.

throughput against the two competing algorithms. We follow this by analyzing the behavior of our system with different sample sizes. Finally, we evaluate the impact of network delays and concurrency on SACS.

4.3.1 Hit rate and byte hit rate

The first set of figures presented in this section compares the results obtained by the three systems under evaluation regarding hit rate. In the results presented in this section, we configured the sample size of all the algorithms to be the full cache (i.e., sample size = 100%). This allows us to compare the algorithms without perturbations from the inherent non determinism of the sampling process.

Figures 2 and 3 show the average hit rates obtained while executing several simulations with a cache size of 5% and 10%, respectively. Figure 2(a) shows the hit rate values obtained with a 5% cache size in the regular scenario (i.e.,

the cache starts empty). The results show that SACS is able to match the performance of LFU, falling just short of 0.5% of its performance, at most, while outperforming LRU by over 5%. LRU has a worst performance because frequently requested objects are not given higher priority over more recently accessed objects that are requested infrequently. This way, a popular object that, by chance, has not been accessed for some time may be removed by LRU instead of an object that, while recently requested, ends up being only accessed once. LFU, on the other hand, avoids this problem by keeping the most frequently accessed objects in the cache, regardless of the time of access. In the same way, SACS is also able to tackle this issue by weighing distance/recency with frequency. In particular, recently accessed objects that are no longer pivots, which with LRU would likely be kept, are only kept by SACS if their distance to a pivot and their frequency so determines.

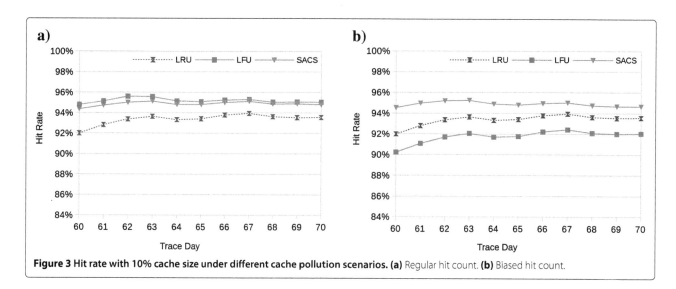

Figure 3 Hit rate with 10% cache size under different cache pollution scenarios. **(a)** Regular hit count. **(b)** Biased hit count.

Although LFU performs better than LRU in the previously analyzed data, the reason for its good performance is due to the characteristics of the data access patterns of the FIFA98 logs. Specifically, it is due to the fact that in these logs, the set of the most popular pages is stable and mostly fixed over time. However, it is well known that page popularity in the Internet varies dynamically and unpredictably. Thus, in order to analyze the performance of the algorithms under a more dynamic setting, we ran our biased scenario, which pre-populates the cache with a set of infrequently accessed pages. The results obtained in this scenario are shown in Figure 2(b).

As expected, the performance of LFU in the biased scenario is lower than in the regular scenario. This performance decay is due to the presence of objects that have high hit counts, but that are no longer frequently accessed. As the figure shows, this performance reduction is higher at the start of the simulation, which is when cache pollution is at its highest level. As the simulation moves forward, LFU's performance steadily increases. Once again, this steady improvement is a result of the characteristics of the FIFA98 logs, which generate a very low and unnoticeable rate of cache pollution.

SACS and LRU, on the other hand are less, if at all, affected by the cache pollution scenario, because both take recency in consideration. For LRU, frequency is completely ignored, which means that the polluting objects are readily removed from the cache and have a low impact on cache performance. And while SACS has frequency in consideration, even the pages with the highest hit count can become valid candidates for eviction if they are not close to a pivot. Hence, distance is able to filter frequently used pages that *are* relevant from frequently used pages that *have been* relevant, but no longer are.

The results presented thus far are further confirmed by Figure 3, which refers to the same scenarios analyzed

before, but this time regarding a 10% cache size. As before, and for the same reasons, LFU and SACS obtain similar results in the regular scenario, and outperform LRU. The biased scenario also follows the same pattern, with SACS and LRU not being affected by the cache pollution, unlike LFU. The main differences between Figures 2 and 3 are 1) the hit rate values, which are, as expected, higher with the largest cache, and 2) the magnitude of the performance decay of LFU, which in the case of the 10% cache size falls below the performance of LRU.

Byte hit rates (shown in Figures 4 and 5) follow the same pattern as the hit rate, both for the different hit count scenarios and the different cache sizes. However, the exact values for byte hit rate are about 10% lower than hit rates. The reason for this discrepancy is that while every hit/miss has the same weight (1) regarding hit rate, they have have different weights regarding byte rates, which depend on the sizes of the objects to which the hit/miss refers. Because in the FIFA logs some of the least frequently used objects are among the largest ones, byte hit rate is lower, since these large objects have a higher weight and often lead to misses.

4.3.2 System performance

We now take a look at the behavior of SACS from the perspective of system performance, when compared with LRU and LFU, still considering full cache sampling. We focused on two main system performance metrics: memory consumption and throughput (in number of requests serviced per second). We gathered memory usage information from within the simulation code by accessing the \proc virtual filesystem of Linux. Throughput information was collected by dividing the total number of requests received at the server by the total execution time of the simulation (considering the simulation starts when the first request is received). Note that the values

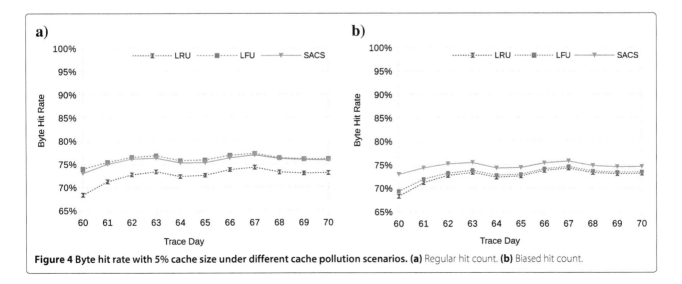

Figure 4 Byte hit rate with 5% cache size under different cache pollution scenarios. (a) Regular hit count. **(b)** Biased hit count.

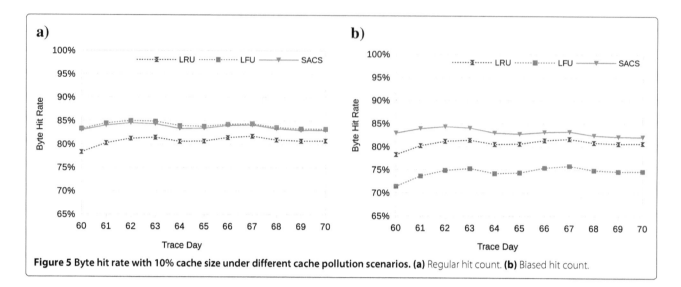

Figure 5 Byte hit rate with 10% cache size under different cache pollution scenarios. **(a)** Regular hit count. **(b)** Biased hit count.

obtained reflect only the processing time at the cache server, since no network communication occurs during the simulation.

Table 1 presents the memory usage results. The values presented correspond to the maximum amount of memory used by each strategy, excluding the memory reserved for the actual cache contents. This means that these results reflect only the additional data that each algorithm needs to maintain. For this same reason, the values measured were identical for both cache sizes used in the simulation.

As expected, the results show that our solution uses more memory than the competing strategies. This extra memory corresponds to the additional information and data structures used by SACS (in particular, the link/page graph) which are absent from LRU and LFU. Despite the overhead, the actual difference is only of 3MB, with an average of 700 graph nodes at any one time during the simulations. For comparison, column *SACS Max* shows the maximum possible amount of memory that would be used by SACS if the page graph contained information about every object (cached or not) seen by the cache server during the simulation.

Figure 6 presents the throughput achieved by the different algorithms with 5% and 10% cache size. Unlike memory usage, throughput varies with cache size, with larger caches delivering higher throughput because object

Table 1 Total memory used

Replacement strategy	RAM used
LRU	8MB
LFU	8MB
SACS	11MB
SACS Max	20MB

replacement is issued less frequently. Similarly to memory usage, the figure indicates that SACS has a slight computational overhead when compared to the two alternatives. The reduced throughput obtained is a result of the more complex computations required to select the most appropriate object in SACS. The main reason for this overhead is, as expected, the distance computation function, which continuously executes in the background.

It should be noted, however, that due to the characteristics of the simulation, the delays associated with responding back to users and requesting missing pages from the origin server are not reflected in the results. We argue that if these delays are taken into account the throughput of our system would be competitive with that of LRU and LFU, for the following reasons. First, the overhead due to the background distance computation process, would be masked by the network delays of fetching the missing pages, which are an order of magnitude larger than computational delays. Second, because our solution is able to obtain an overall higher hit rate, it would issue requests for missing pages less often, which would, in practice, lead to a higher responsiveness of the caching system. We further analyze this claim later in Section 4.3.4.

4.3.3 Cache sampling

So far, we have analyzed the performance of the systems under evaluation in a stable, concurrency free environment that favors hit rates, but exposes computational overheads more clearly. The overheads identified so far are, for the most part, due to the fact that the simulations have been conducted using full cache sampling. This means that every cached object has been considered as a candidate for eviction, which requires the algorithms to have to analyze and evaluate every object in the cache before one or more of them is selected for removal.

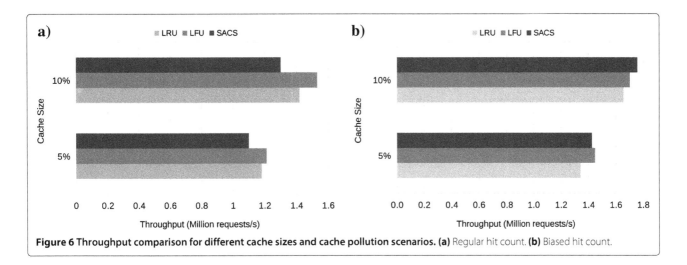

Figure 6 Throughput comparison for different cache sizes and cache pollution scenarios. **(a)** Regular hit count. **(b)** Biased hit count.

However, while this solution is able to maximize hit rate, it clearly is not scalable to larger caches in which the number of objects to analyze would be prohibitively high. The consequence is the reduction of throughput, which can lead to higher response times.

A strategy frequently used by commercial web caches (such as Squid) to circumvent this scalability limitation is to randomly select a sample of the cached objects as candidates for eviction, instead of the full cache. In this section, we analyze the impact of sampling in the performance of SACS. Based on Squid and Ehcache policies, we start by analyzing the performance of SACS with a sample size of 10% of the total cache size and compare it against LRU and LFU with the same sample size. After that, we analyze the performance of SACS alone with different sample sizes.

Figure 7 shows the results obtained by the three algorithms with a 10% sample size. Figure 7(a) presents the hit rates obtained with a 5% cache size, while Figure 7(b) presents throughput results for both 5% and 10% cache sizes. Both plots show the averages of the results obtained over a series of simulations of the *regular* (non biased) scenario. Unlike the previous figures (which showed results only for the interval between days 60 and 70), the results presented in Figure 7 are from a series of simulations spanning the full extent of the logs, starting in day 5 (the first with access information) until the last day.

The hit rates obtained during the simulations (byte hit rates, which we omit due to space limitations, follow an identical pattern, but with lower scores) show that SACS outperforms both LRU and LFU with a 10% sample. SACS tops the two competing algorithms in every day of the simulation with an average of 1.5% over LFU and 1.75% over LRU (with a maximum daily difference of 3.2% and 3.6%, respectively). Similar results were obtained with a 10% cache size, but with slightly higher overall hit rates

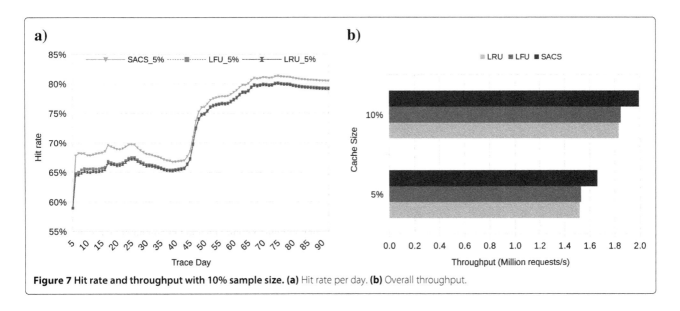

Figure 7 Hit rate and throughput with 10% sample size. **(a)** Hit rate per day. **(b)** Overall throughput.

for all the algorithms. The results confirm the ability of SACS to adapt to different situations and to obtain the most out of the information available to make replacement decisions. Overall, hit rates are 10% lower than the ones obtained with a 100% sample size, because sampling does not allow the algorithms to make a fully informed decision.

Contrary to hit rates, however, throughput is higher with smaller sample sizes. SACS, in particular, obtains a significant boost over the other two algorithms. This increase in throughput is a direct consequence of the lower complexity of the eviction algorithm, which now has to process a much more compact candidate list. As a consequence of the increased throughput, the cache will be able to respond more quickly to requests for cached objects. In contrast, a higher number of requests are not serviced from the cache, which means that the average response time may increase.

The results presented so far indicate the complex relation between hit rate and throughput, in particular regarding their combined effect on response times. On the one hand, higher hit rates inherently results in higher throughput, because more objects are serviced from the cache, bypassing the need to obtain the object from the origin web server. On the other hand, using larger samples to obtain higher hit rates results in lower throughput, due to the additional computational overhead of the eviction algorithm. To further illustrate this tradeoff between hit rate and throughput, we executed a series of simulations with SACS using different sample sizes and logged the average throughput and hit rates obtained over the various executions. The results are presented in Figures 8(a) and 8(b). The plots show the results obtained by SACS with a 20% and 30% sample size, accompanied,

for comparison, by the results of the full (100%) and 10% samples already presented before.

The tradeoff between throughput and cache accuracy/performance is particularly evident if we compare the throughput and hit rate obtained by the SACS_100% and SACS_10% configurations. For these configurations, the results show, on the one hand, that SACS_100% obtains the highest hit rate, while SACS_10% obtains the lowest hit rates, with a difference of approximately 10% between the two. On the other hand, the throughput of SACS_100% is the lowest of all configurations, by a clear margin, with a 26% difference to SACS_10%. Reducing the sample size from 100% to 30% results in a 6% reduction in hit rate, but in over 15% increase in throughput; reducing to 20% (from 100%) results in a 8% loss in hit rate and a throughput increase of 23%.

4.3.4 Network simulation

We finalize our evaluation by analyzing our previous claim (last paragraph of Section 4.3.2.) that in a real setting with concurrent accesses to the cache and network delays, the overhead caused by SACS's background tasks would be less significant. To this end, we modified our simulator so that requests would be issued by multiple threads rather than sequentially by a single process. Requests from each individual user, however, are still issued sequentially, although concurrently with other users.

In addition to issuing requests concurrently, we introduced artificial delays on cache misses to simulate the process of fetching pages not present in the cache from their origin web server. The delays were based on offline measurements we conducted by issuing requests to web servers placed on different locations. Similarly to the previously described experiments, we executed several

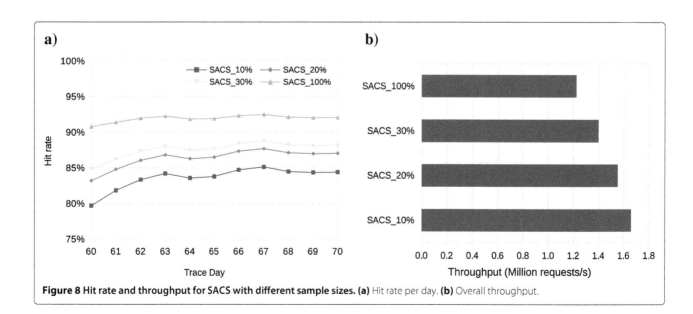

Figure 8 Hit rate and throughput for SACS with different sample sizes. **(a)** Hit rate per day. **(b)** Overall throughput.

simulations and computed the averages of the values obtained. In particular, we measured the hit rates and throughput obtained by the different systems over the interval between days 60 and 70 with a non biased 5% cache and full cache sampling. The results are shown in Figure 9.

The figures show that SACS is able to outperform LRU and LFU regarding both hit rates and throughput. SACS tops LFU by, on average, 1%, and LRU by over 10%. Throughput follows a similar pattern, with SACS obtaining a small margin over LFU, and a larger margin over LRU. Overall, throughput values are over three times lower than the ones obtained with the sequential simulations, due to the overhead of concurrency control and network delays. These factors end up diluting the computational tradeoff between throughput and hit rate. In this case, throughput is proportional to hit rate, because the higher the hit rate, the more concurrent requests the cache is able to serve, whereas in the sequential execution of the simulations, throughput was dependent on the algorithmic overhead of the replacement strategy.

5 Related work

Due to the importance of the replacement algorithm for the caching system, a large body of work in the area of cache replacement can be found in literature. According to a survey by Podlipnig and Böszörmenyi [9], these algorithms can be grouped into five different categories. The first category consists of *recency based algorithms* [16,17,29], which use the time elapsed since the last request to a cached page as the main factor in their replacement decisions. LRU is the most representative of such algorithms and other algorithms are usually extensions of standard LRU. For example, *LRU-min* [16] tries to minimize the number of removed pages by applying LRU to a candidate list composed solely of pages that are larger than the most recently requested page. The main drawback of these algorithms is, as mentioned throughout the paper, the fact that they are oblivious to page popularity.

Frequency based algorithms [14,17] use request frequency as their main criteria. LFU is an example of this group of algorithms and serves as the model for other algorithms in the class. Because LFU is prone to cache pollution, several other algorithms employ aging techniques that aim at minimizing the frequency count of some or all of the pages, either periodically or at some specific event. However, it is questionable if aging techniques are better than recency based strategies [9]. SACS, on the other hand, by combining distance with recency and frequency, is able to handle cache pollution efficiently, without compromising the performance of the cache during standard (non polluted) operation.

Similarly to SACS, *recency-frequency based algorithms* [18,30,31] combine recency with frequency (and, possibly, other factors). SACS sets itself apart from the algorithms in this group by emphasizing distance over recency or frequency, which allows it to base its predictions of future accesses not only on past behaviour, but also on semantic knowledge.

Function based algorithms [15,32,33] use potentially general utility functions to evaluate the eviction potential of pages. Several such algorithms exist, with the common aspect that all use multiple weighted factors to score a page. Function based algorithms provide an elegant solution that has the potential to seamlessly adapt to

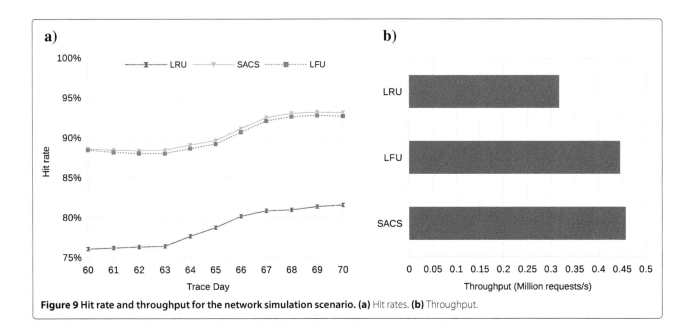

Figure 9 Hit rate and throughput for the network simulation scenario. (a) Hit rates. **(b)** Throughput.

different request patterns and workload dynamics. However, its main shortcoming lies in the difficulty of appropriately setting and tuning the parameters and weights of the utility function.

The final group of the taxonomy of Podlipnig and Böszörmenyi comprises algorithms which base their decisions on randomized choices [19,34,35], typically combined with other factors. *Randomized algorithms* were proposed to reduce the need for the complex data structures that are required by some of the traditional replacement algorithms. However, due to their intrinsic non-determinism, it is difficult to assert if their performance is consistent over time and under different request patterns and workloads.

In addition to the the groups identified by Podlipnig and Böszörmenyi, other authors have proposed replacement algorithms that employ machine learning techniques [11-13]. These algorithms include an offline learning phase in which the algorithm is trained with information from past requests (e.g., logs of a web server/cache). Then, the knowledge acquired in the learning phase is applied, at runtime, to choose the candidates for eviction. Unlike traditional cache replacement, machine learning algorithms are equipped with the mechanisms to predict future requests, rather than basing their decision only on past behaviour. However, their performance is tightly related with the data used during the training phase, which is itself solely based on past behaviour. SACS, on the other hand, looks into more immediate and contextual information which, as our evaluation results indicate, may prove useful in identifying future requests.

To the best of our knowledge, ours is the first work to look into the links inside web pages as a factor for replacement decisions in the context of web caching. By doing so, we base our predictions of future requests not only on past behaviour (by incorporating traditional techniques such as LRU and LFU), but also on semantic and contextual information. In addition, while in this paper we combine distance with standard LRU and LFU, our algorithm can easily be modified to have distance combined with other factors used in existing algorithms, including complex utility functions or randomized techniques.

Our solution is also related with the area of interest awareness in multiplayer games [36,37] and cooperative work [38,39]. Interest awareness systems manage the consistency of each user's view of the objects of a distributed application according to their distance to some special object(s). In multiplayer games, the consistency of game objects is stronger closer to each player's avatar and becomes weaker as the distance (within the virtual world) increases. In cooperative work applications, such as cooperative text editing and distributed software development, instead of metric distance, a *semantic distance* that measures the strength of the relations between different elements of a text document/software project is used. Similarly, our algorithm also assigns priorities according to distance, in an inversely proportional manner. However, in SACS, we do it to evaluate the eviction potential of web pages, rather than to determine the consistency requirements of distributed objects.

6 Conclusion

Caching of web pages is an optimization strategy that has been around since the early days of the web. Web caching improves server performance and response times by providing more than one source for each data item and/or placing contents closer to users. In this context, choosing which pages to keep in the cache and which to evict has a great impact on the performance of cache servers and, consequently, on the web as a whole. Traditional strategies used in practice base their decisions on static information and are, thus, vulnerable to the dynamism and unpredictability of user access patterns.

In this paper, we proposed SACS, a novel cache replacement algorithm that decides on which objects to remove based on the link navigation information of the cached pages. The design of SACS is inspired by the observation that the links contained in recently accessed pages are good indicators of future requests. SACS builds on this observation by assigning priorities to cached objects in such a way that objects whose distance to recently accessed pages (measured as the length of the shortest path of links between them) is high have higher probability of being removed, while pages closer to recently accessed pages are kept cached. Our solution additionally takes frequency into account, weighing it with distance when deciding on the eviction priority of each object. The evaluation results obtained and presented in this paper show that our solution is able to either match or even surpass the performance of existing algorithms in the scenarios in which they are better, while preventing their shortcomings in the scenario in which their performance falls short.

Competing interests

The authors declare that they have no competing interests.

Authors' contributions

AN designed and implemented the proposed system, conceived and carried out the evaluation and wrote the manuscript. CR implemented a preliminary version of the proposed system. LV and PF participated in the design of the system and revised the manuscript. All authors read and approved the final manuscript.

Acknowledgements

This work was supported by national funds through Fundação para a Ciência e Tecnologia (FCT) with reference UID/CEC/50021/2013.

References

1. Erman J, Gerber A, Hajiaghayi MT, Pei D, Spatscheck O (2009) Network-aware forward caching. In: Proceedings of the 18th International Conference on World Wide Web. WWW '09. ACM, New York, NY, USA. pp 291–300
2. Labovitz C, Iekel-Johnson S, McPherson D, Oberheide J, Jahanian F (2010) Internet inter-domain traffic. SIGCOMM Comput Commun Rev 40(4):75–86
3. Cardellini V, Casalicchio E, Colajanni M, Yu PS (2002) The state of the art in locally distributed web-server systems. ACM Comput Surv 34(2):263–311
4. Kanodia V, Knightly EW (2003) Ensuring latency targets in multiclass web servers. Parallel Distributed Syst IEEE Trans 14(1):84–93
5. Zhang Y, Ansari N, Wu M, Yu H (2012) On wide area network optimization. Commun Surv Tutor IEEE 14(4):1090–1113
6. Rabinovich M, Spatscheck O (2002) Web Caching and Replication. Addison-Wesley Longman Publishing Co., Inc, Boston, MA, USA
7. Davison BD (2001) A web caching primer. IEEE Internet Comput 5(4):38–45
8. Wang J (1999) A survey of web caching schemes for the internet. ACM SIGCOMM Comput Commun Rev 29(5):36–46
9. Podlipnig S, Böszörmenyi L (2003) A survey of web cache replacement strategies. ACM Comput Surv (CSUR) 35(4):374–398
10. Romano S, ElAarag H (2008) A quantitative study of recency and frequency based web cache replacement strategies. In: Proceedings of the 11th Communications and Networking Simulation Symposium. CNS '08. ACM, New York, NY, USA. pp 70–78
11. Ali W, Shamsuddin SM, Ismail AS (2012) Intelligent web proxy caching approaches based on machine learning techniques. Decis Support Syst 53(3):565–579
12. Cobb J, ElAarag H (2008) Web proxy cache replacement scheme based on back-propagation neural network. J Syst Softw 81(9):1539–1558
13. Koskela T, Heikkonen J, Kaski K (2003) Web cache optimization with nonlinear model using object features. Comput Netw 43(6):805–817
14. Arlitt M, Cherkasova L, Dilley J, Friedrich R, Jin T (2000) Evaluating content management techniques for web proxy caches. ACM SIGMETRICS Perform Eval Rev 27(4):3–11
15. Cao P, Irani S (1997) Cost-aware WWW proxy caching algorithms. In: 1st USENIX Symposium on Internet Technologies and Systems, USITS'97, Monterey, California, USA, December 8-11, 1997. USENIX Association, Berkley, California, USA
16. Abrams M, Standridge C. R, Abdulla G, Williams S, Fox EA (1995) Caching proxies: Limitations and potentials. In: Proceedings of the 4th International Conference on World Wide Web. WWW '95, Boston, Massachusetts, USA
17. Zhang J, Izmailov R, Reininger D, Ott M, A NUS (1999) Web caching framework: Analytical models and beyond. In: Proceedings of the 1999 IEEE Workshop on Internet Applications. WIAPP '99. IEEE Computer Society, Washington, DC, USA. p 132
18. Cheng K, Kambayashi Y (2000) Lru-sp: A size-adjusted and popularity-aware lru replacement algorithm for web caching. In: 24th International Computer Software and Applications Conference. COMPSAC '00. IEEE Computer Society, Washington, DC, USA. pp 48–53
19. Starobinski D, Tse D (2001) Probabilistic methods for web caching. Perform Eval 46(2-3):125–137
20. Bahn H, Koh K, Noh SH, Lyul SM (2002) Efficient replacement of nonuniform objects in web caches. Computer 35(6):65–73
21. Scheuermann P, Shim J, Vingralek R (1997) A case for delay-conscious caching of web documents. In: Proceedings of the Sixth International World Wide Web Conference, Santa Clara, California USA
22. Ehcache - Performance at any scale. http://ehcache.org/
23. HTML Parser. http://htmlparser.sourceforge.net/
24. Netty project. http://netty.io/
25. Arlitt M, Jin T 1998 World Cup Web Site Access Logs. http://www.acm.org/sigcomm/ITA/
26. Internet Archive. https://archive.org/
27. Wong K-Y (2006) Web cache replacement policies: a pragmatic approach. IEEE Network 20(1):28–34
28. Squid: Optimising Web Delivery. www.squid-cache.org
29. Aggarwal C, Wolf JL, Yu PS (1999) Caching on the world wide web. IEEE Trans Knowl Data Eng 11(1):94–107
30. Menaud J-M, Issarny V, Banâtre M (1999) Improving the effectiveness of web caching. In: Advances in Distributed Systems, Advanced Distributed Computing: From Algorithms to Systems. Springer, London, UK, UK. pp 375–401
31. Osawa N, Yuba T, Hakozaki K (1997) Generational replacement schemes for a www caching proxy server. In: Proceedings of the International Conference and Exhibition on High-Performance Computing and Networking. HPCN Europe '97. Springer, London, UK, UK. pp 940–949
32. Cohen E, Krishnamurthy B, Rexford J (1998) Evaluating server-assisted cache replacement in the web. In: Proceedings of the 6th Annual European Symposium on Algorithms. ESA '98. Springer, London, UK, UK. pp 307–319
33. Jin S, Bestavros A (2001) Greedydual* web caching algorithm: Exploiting the two sources of temporal locality in web request streams. Comput Commun 24(2):174–183
34. Hosseini-Khayat S (1998) Replacement algorithms for object caching. In: Proceedings of the 1998 ACM Symposium on Applied Computing. SAC '98. ACM, New York, NY, USA. pp 90–97
35. Psounis K, Prabhakar B (2002) Efficient randomized web-cache replacement schemes using samples from past eviction times. IEEE/ACM Trans Netw 10(4):441–455
36. Bezerra CE, Cecin FR, Geyer CFR (2008) A3: A novel interest management algorithm for distributed simulations of mmogs. In: Proceedings of the 2008 12th IEEE/ACM International Symposium on Distributed Simulation and Real-Time Applications. DS-RT '08. IEEE Computer Society, Washington, DC, USA. pp 35–42
37. Veiga L, Negrão A, Santos N, Ferreira P (2010) Unifying divergence bounding and locality awareness in replicated systems with vector-field consistency. J Int Serv Appl 1(2):95–115
38. Negrão AP, Costa J, Ferreira P, Veiga L (2014) Interest aware consistency for cooperative editing in heterogeneous environments. Int J Cooperative Inform Syst 23(1):42–75
39. Negrão A, Mateus M, Ferreira P, Veiga L (2013) Adaptive consistency and awareness support for distributed software development. In: 21st International Conference on Cooperative Information Systems (CoopIS 2013) – On the Move to Meaningful Internet Systems: OTM 2013 Conferences. Lecture Notes in Computer Science, Graz, Austria Vol. 8185. pp 259–266

14

Decentralized group formation

Anna Chmielowiec, Spyros Voulgaris and Maarten van Steen[*]

Abstract

Imagine a network of entities, being it replica servers aiming to minimize the probability of data loss, players of online team-based games and tournaments, or companies that look into co-branding opportunities. The objective of each entity in any of these scenarios is to find a few suitable partners to help them achieve a shared goal: replication of the data for fault tolerance, winning the game, successful marketing campaign. All information attainable by the entities is limited to the profiles of other entities that can be used to assess the pairwise fitness. How can they create teams without help of any centralized component and without going into each other's way? We propose a decentralized algorithm that helps nodes in the network to form groups of a specific size. The protocol works by finding an approximation of a weighted k-clique matching of the underlying graph of assessments. We discuss the basic version of the protocol, and explain how dissemination via gossiping helps in improving its scalability. We evaluate its performance through extensive simulations.

Keywords: Web service composition; Distributed clique formation

1 Introduction

Ever since the Internet substantially facilitated the sharing of distant resources, researchers have been pondering on how to effectively and efficiently exploit the immense collection of these resources. A well-known example are Web pages as resources, which are crawled and copied to centralized databases so that they can be used for searching information. Likewise, with the advent of Web services it became much easier to realize large and heterogeneous infrastructures for large-scale computing, eventually leading to the OGSA architecture for grid computing [1]. These two examples illustrate two radically different approaches for structuring the use of resources. Conceptually, when crawling the Web, resources are copied and pulled into a centralized shared database for further processing. In contrast, for grid computing, resources stay in place (and often cannot even be moved), resulting in a decentralized solution for their usage.

In this paper, we concentrate on organizing resources under the assumption that they are dispersed across the Internet, yet it is impossible, or undesirable, to copy or move them to a centralized location. The specific organization that we are seeking is dividing a potentially very large group of resources into nonoverlapping subsets of the same size, also known as the k-clique matching problem.

As an example, consider the case where a resource is a replica server operating in the cloud, and we are seeking to partition a dataset and replicate its parts for fault tolerance. In practice, a high degree of fault tolerance can be achieved if a data item is replicated across three servers, provided that failures of those servers are mutually independent. This means that a data item should not be replicated in the same data center, but be spread across three different ones. We can model this problem by organizing the servers into an overlay network, and representing that network as an undirected graph. The weight of an edge represents the quality of the associated communication link, along with the level of failure independence of its end nodes. We then compute a weight of a 3-clique as the arithmetic (or sometimes the geometric) mean of its edges. Obviously, the higher this weight, the better. By finding a maximal 3-clique matching, we have essentially partitioned the set of N replica servers into roughly $N/3$ highly reliable (distributed) virtual servers, each of which can now be used to store one or several data items. Note that our partitioning should be optimal: ideally, there is no partitioning that will lead to a better set of more reliable virtual servers.

*Correspondence: m.r.van.steen@vu.nl
Department of Computer Sciences and The Network Institute, VU University, De Boelelaan 1081A, 1081HV Amsterdam, The Netherlands

As a completely different example, consider a multiplayer online game in which teams of k members each compete in a tournament. Forming teams such that we get the most challenging tournament again boils down to finding a maximal k-clique matching in a set of N players, where each of the roughly N/k cliques forms a team. A weight between two players reflects how appropriate it is to put them in the same team. So, typically, if two players indicate their preference to play the role of a goalkeeper in an online soccer competition, then typically the weight between the two should be very low.

In a previous version of this paper [2], we showed how a solution to the k-clique matching problem could be used for optimal *co-branding* across the Web. Another application is the optimal construction of composite Internet services, services which are now often available only as part of a package provided by ISPs [3].

As said, we assume in this paper that resources cannot be copied or moved to a central location, or that it is undesirable to do so, for example, because there is a shared distrust in the integrity of the computations performed by a third party. This implies that we need to solve the k-clique matching problem in a decentralized manner. Our main contribution is a fully decentralized algorithm for solving this problem. The algorithm has been partly described and evaluated in [2]. In this paper, we describe important improvements that speed up the convergence of the algorithm, allow us to handle cases where the set of resources is subject to churn, and help in overcoming the communication overhead of the protocol in its basic version. In particular, we introduce the following modification to our k-clique matching protocol: random-subset heuristic, pruning, partial views, and gossiping of clique weights.

The remainder of the paper begins with an overview of related work in Section 2. Following is Section 3 in which the system model for decentralized k-clique matching of resources is further detailed and the problem of finding $k - 1$ partnering resources is formalized. The core of the paper is formed by the self-stabilizing distributed algorithm, which is described in Section 4. In Section 5, we present the optimizations that are useful in case of a large dynamically changing set of resources. Section 6 presents results of our extensive simulations followed by conclusions in Section 7.

2 Related work

Decentralized clustering based on weights between nodes has been studied in the context of self-organization for overlay construction in peer-to-peer (P2P) networks. Protocols such as T-Man [4] and Vicinity [5] assume weights between nodes. Nodes have a fixed outdegree of k neighbors, and periodically gossip with (some of) them to encounter new potential neighbors and replace ones with lower weight by ones having higher weight. When converged, each node has links to its k highest weight neighbors out of the whole network.

Although both this type of clustering and k-clique matching result in optimal weight links prevailing over suboptimal ones, they bear a fundamental difference. In the former, a node can serve as a preferred neighbor for *any* number of other nodes and formed links are not required to be reciprocated; in the latter each node can participate in exclusively *one* clique and all nodes must agree on participation in the same clique (symmetry constraint).

For $k = 2$ the k-clique matching problem reduces to the well-known and extensively studied problem of matching in graphs; a matching in a graph is defined as any subset of *nonadjacent* edges, which basically are cliques of size 2. In unweighted graphs, matching problems concentrate on finding a *maximum* matching (a matching with the largest number of edges). For this problem, sequential polynomial-time algorithms exist; for example, a maximum matching can be found in $O(\sqrt{|V|}|E|)$ time using one of the algorithms by Micali and Vazirani [6], Blum [7], or Gabow and Tarjan [8]. In our paper we focus solely on weighted graphs. In such graphs, for each matching its weight can be computed by summing the weights of the edges comprising the matching, and the standard matching problem is of finding a matching that is the *heaviest*, referred to as *maximum weighted matching*. Generalizations exist. One of them is the problem of finding in a graph the largest (the heaviest) subset of nonadjacent subgraphs, each of which is isomorphic to some given graph H. This type of problem is commonly referred to as an *H-packing* [9-11], an *H-matching* [12,13] or an *H-partition* [14]. In the special case when graph H is a clique of size k, we obtain a k-clique matching[a] problem that we address in this paper.

Whereas finding a maximum weighted matching can be done in polynomial time using, for instance, the algorithm by Gabow [15] that runs in $O(|V|(|E| + |V|log|V|))$ time, finding a maximum weighted k-clique matching for $k \geq 3$ becomes an NP-hard problem. This follows directly from work of Kirkpatrick and Hell in [14] which proves that finding a perfect H-partition of graph G is NP-complete if H contains a connected component with at least 3 vertices.

Moreover, when distributed algorithms are considered, there does not exist any algorithm that finds a maximum weighted matching. Yet, a few distributed approximation algorithms have been proposed, including the 1/2-approximation algorithm by Hoepman [16], the $O(log|V|)$-time $(1/2 - \epsilon)$-approximation algorithm by Lotker at al. [17], and a $(1 - \epsilon)$-approximation algorithm by Nieberg [18]. From our perspective, the most interesting are self-stabilizing algorithms for weighted matchings, such as a 1/2-approximation algorithm by Manne and Mjelde [19], which we extend in this paper to solve the more general problem of weighted k-clique matching. Whether other distributed approximation algorithms for weighted matching can also be extended to solve weighted k-clique matching remains an open question.

The research on distributed algorithms for H-packing is even more scarce. For unweighted graphs, there exist a few approximation algorithms for solving packing problems, for example, distributed H-packing algorithms for unit-disk graphs by Czygrinow and Hańćkowiak [10] and planar graphs by Czygrinow et al. [11]. Yet, to our best knowledge, there is no work on distributed algorithms for packing in *weighted* graphs. There is also little work on sequential approximation algorithms for weighted packing problems; a few algorithms that exist deal with randomized finding of a triangle packing in weighted complete graphs [20,21] and do not appear to be easily converted into a distributed algorithm or adapted to finding k-clique packings for any $k \geq 3$. With respect to available research, our work is unique in attempting to tackle the weighted k-clique matching problem in a distributed fashion.

Table 1 summarizes the presented research on matching problem and its generalizations.

3   The k-clique matching problem

We consider a set of N *entities*, be they commercial brands, players in a multiplayer game, servers in a decentralized pool of computers, or generally any type of resources that we may want to group together. Each pair of entities is marked with a *weight*, indicating the benefit of combining these two entities.

Regarding weights, we make the following three assumptions. First, they are nonnegative real numbers. Second, they are a global function, in the sense that any

entity can assess the weight between any two entities in the network. Third, weights are *symmetric*: the benefit perceived by entity A in being combined with entity B is the same as the one perceived by B in being combined with A. Satisfying these assumptions is not difficult. For example, in a co-branding case, each entity holds a profile that describes customer attitudes towards a given brand. The weight of the edge between any two entities can then be computed based on a symmetric function generally known by all entities.

The target is to group entities in cliques of k members in such a way that the aggregate clique weights are maximized. This problem can be formalized using terms from graph theory. We consider a graph $G = (V, E)$. Each entity corresponds to a single vertex in the graph. The edges connect only those vertices whose corresponding entities can be combined together. The weight of each edge tells how good this combination is.

In such a graph, we are mostly interested in *which k-cliques* can be created. A k-clique is a subgraph induced by k vertices in which an edge exists between every two vertices. Given the weights of the edges, it is possible to assess the weight of a k-clique. Some of the popular metrics include: sum of the edges, arithmetic or geometric mean, and the weight of the heaviest/lightest edge. We interpret the weight of the k-clique as an overall evaluation of suitability of the k entities for forming a k-group.

Each entity would like to be part of exactly one such group. Therefore, we want to partition the graph into disjoint k-cliques.

Definition 1. *(Weighted k-Clique Matching): Given a graph $G = (V, E)$ with nonnegative edge weights, a k-clique matching is a subgraph of G whose components are cliques of size k. The weight of the k-clique matching is defined as the sum of the weights of all its k-cliques.*

Table 1 Research on the matching problem and its generalizations

Problem	Sequential algorithms exact	Approximation	Distributed approximation algorithms
(2-clique) matching	unweighted: $O(\sqrt{V}E)$ [6-8], weighted: $O(V(E + V\log V))$ [8]	$O(E)$ 1/2-approx. [22], $O(E\log V)$ 1/2-approx. [23]	1/2-approx. [16,17,19], $(1 - \epsilon)$-approx. [18]
k-clique matching	NP-hard [14]	randomized in complete graphs for $k = 3$ [20,21]	1/k-approx. in our previous paper [2]
H-matching	NP-hard [14] max snp-complete [12]	—	unweighted: - in unit-disk graphs [10], - in planar graphs [11]

The mentioned algorithms are for the *weighted* version of the problem unless stated otherwise.

For $k = 2$, the problem of finding a 2-clique matching in the graph is equivalent to finding a traditional matching (a set of independent edges) in a graph. Its weighted version (when the total weight of the 2-cliques is to be maximized) is solvable in polynomial time: $O(|V|(|E| + |V| log |V|))$ [15]. Yet for any $k \geq 3$, a weighted k-clique matching problem becomes NP-hard (see [14]).

Luckily, finding an optimal solution for the weighted k-clique matching problem might not be always necessary, or even desirable; finding an approximation might be completely satisfactory. We can argue, for example, that in the case of k-replication, each server is concerned only with the quality of the cluster it is going to be part of and has no interest in optimizing the quality of other clusters. Thus, entities can be seen as being egocentric, preoccupied only with their own welfare. Based on this observation, we devise a distributed algorithm for finding an approximation of the optimal k-clique matching.

4   The k-clique matching protocol

4.1   2-clique matching

Our protocol for creating a k-clique matching overlay is inspired by the self-stabilizing algorithm by Manne and Mjelde [19], which finds a matching which is a 1/2-approximation of the optimal solution for the maximum weighted matching problem — the total weight of the matching found by this algorithm is at least 1/2 of the optimal matching weight. In this algorithm, each node v uses two variables: the first, m_v, to store the id of the node it would like to be matched with, the second, $\mathbf{w}_v$, to store the weight of the edge connecting it to that node. Every node tries to find the heaviest incident edge (by pointing with m_v to the other end of that edge), and the only rule that nodes have to obey is that a node v cannot link to a neighbor u if the value of $\mathbf{w}_u$ is higher than the weight of the edge joining v and u. This rule is meant to prevent nodes from bound-to-fail attempts to match with neighbors that have found heavier edges for matching. The final matching M is composed of those edges whose ends point to each other ($m_v = u$ and $m_u = v$) and is achieved in at most $2|M| + 1$ rounds under a fair scheduler, where each node has a chance to execute its step at least once per round.

In this section, we show that the algorithm from [19] can be easily generalized to find a weighted k-clique matching (for any $k \geq 2$) that is at most a factor k off from the maximum. Before we provide pseudo-code for this algorithm, we first present a sequential algorithm by Preis [22] that computes a 1/2-approximation of the weighted matching. A high-level explanation of this algorithm will help us gain intuition about how the self-stabilizing algorithms for weighted matching and weighted k-clique matching work.

Preis's sequential greedy algorithm is based on the observation that selecting locally heaviest edges produces the aforementioned approximation within a factor 1/2. Its running time is $O(|E|)$, which is faster than the running time of another sequential algorithm which creates a matching by adding the remaining globally heaviest edge (described in [23], with $O(|E| \cdot log |V|)$ running time). The locally heaviest edge is defined as an edge whose weight is at least as high as the weight of any incident edge. The matching is constructed by iteratively adding to the matching some locally heaviest edge from all the edges remaining in E and removing this edge and all edges incident to it from E until E becomes empty (see Figure 1).

Hoepman [16] describes how Preis's algorithm can be distributed deterministically. But we can also look at the algorithm from [19] as a self-stabilizing variant of Preis's algorithm. Some node v, by choosing one of its neighbors, u, and setting the weight of the edge $\langle v, u \rangle$ to variable $\mathbf{w}_v$, eliminates from the matching all other edges that have v as one of the ends and a weight smaller than $\mathbf{w}_v$. As a result other neighbors of v are forced to look for a matching node among their set of neighbors that does not include v. If an edge is locally the heaviest, i.e., there is no available edge of higher weight incident to it, then the nodes at the ends of this edge would point to each other and as a consequence this edge will become a part of the matching.

We can use the same reasoning to compute a weighted k-clique matching by selecting locally heaviest k-cliques and achieving an approximation factor of k.

4.2 k-clique matching

We denote by $N(v)$ the set of all neighbors of v and by $w(U)$ the weight of the subgraph induced by the nodes in U for any subset of nodes $U \subseteq V$; in particular, $w(\{v, u\})$ denotes the weight of an edge between two adjacent nodes u and v.

To accommodate the algorithm from [19] for solving the weighted k-clique matching problem, we start by changing the variables stored by each node. Instead of variable m_v, which kept track of the single neighbor's id that node v would like to be matched with, each node v will now store in $\mathbf{C}_v$ a set of $k-1$ ids of those neighbors with which v wants to create a k-clique. Therefore, node v will now store in variable $\mathbf{w}_v$ the weight of the clique composed of v and its $k - 1$ neighbors from $\mathbf{C}_v$. This modification has an obvious effect on which cliques we regard as

---

```
1:  M ← ∅
2:  while E ≠ ∅ do
3:     e ← locally heaviest edge from E
4:     M ← M + {e}
5:     E ← E − {e} − {e′ ∈ E : e′ is incident to e}
6:  end while
```

Figure 1 Sequential greedy algorithm for weighted matching.

matched: a clique induced by nodes $v_1, v_2, \ldots, v_k$ is considered as *matched* only if for each v_i ($1 \le i \le k$) variable $\mathbf{C}_{v_i}$ contains ids of the $k-1$ remaining nodes, i.e. $\mathbf{C}_{v_i} = \{v_1, v_2, \ldots, v_k\} - \{v_i\}$. Thus, in a stable state each node v that is part of some clique should have all other nodes from that clique stored in its set $\mathbf{C}_v$. Moreover, if in a stable state there is some node u that is not part of any clique, its set $\mathbf{C}_u$ should be empty.

Because the algorithm differentiates between cliques based solely on their weights, we need to guarantee that the weight of each k-clique in the graph is unique and that a total ordering of clique weights can be imposed. Otherwise, the protocol may be unable to converge to a correct k-clique matching due to some nodes becoming stuck in livelock or deadlock situations, such as shown in Figure 2. Here we have two adjacent 3-cliques $\triangle v_1, v_2, v_3$ and $\triangle v_1, v_3, v_4$ of equal weight. For nodes v_1 and v_3 either of these cliques is equally attractive, while nodes v_2 and v_4 can be part of only one clique each, $\triangle v_1, v_2, v_3$ or $\triangle v_1, v_3, v_4$ respectively. This leads to four possible configurations generated by choices made by v_1 and v_3: (a) both v_1 and v_3 choose $\triangle v_1, v_2, v_3$, (b) both v_1 and v_3 choose $\triangle v_1, v_3, v_4$, (c) v_1 chooses $\triangle v_1, v_2, v_3$, while v_3 chooses $\triangle v_1, v_3, v_4$, and (d) v_1 chooses $\triangle v_1, v_3, v_4$, while v_3 chooses $\triangle v_1, v_2, v_3$. Moreover, they can keep changing their decision, as either choice is equally good. None of the nodes in the graph can determine in which configuration the system is at the moment based solely on the weights of the cliques chosen by nodes. Thus, v_2 and v_4 are stuck in their choice of v_1 and v_3 for their clique partners, and at least one of them is not in the correctly matched clique according to our definition from the previous paragraph. As a result, none of these configurations leads to a correct 3-clique matching.

To avoid such problems, we assume that each node v has a unique identifier (without the loss of coherence we denote v's identifier simply as v) and that a total ordering is imposed on these identifiers. With that assumption, realization of uniqueness and total ordering of clique weights is straightforward: the weight of each clique is

extended with a sorted tuple of the ids of its nodes and a lexicographical ordering is applied to these new weights.

Moreover, we assume that each node has readily available information on the weights of any edge between itself and its neighbor and also between any pair of its neighbors. This information is necessary but also sufficient in order for a node to compute the weights of any cliques it can be part of. We abstract here from how the weights of these edges are obtained by each node. One feasible solution, is that the weights can be computed from the information a node has about its neighbors. The effects of using different weights, but also different weight distributions, is discussed in [24].

The pseudo-code of our weighted k-clique matching protocol is presented in Figure 3. In an infinite loop each node in the network looks for the most attractive k-clique that it can become part of (we will formalize attractiveness shortly). In order to discover such a clique, node v considers all $\binom{|N(v)|}{k-1}$ subsets of $k-1$ neighboring nodes (line 3) and keeps the most attractive one.

To assess the attractiveness $attr_v(U)$ of a clique formed with nodes from set U, node v has to ensure that none of these nodes is currently involved in a heavier clique, because such a node would not be interested in joining a clique of a smaller weight. To this end, we call a set $U = \{u_1, \ldots, u_{k-1}\}$ of $k-1$ neighbors *proper* if and only if for each neighbor u_i this set is heavier than any clique found by that neighbor so far, i.e.,

$$\forall u_i \in U : w(\{v, u_1, \ldots, u_{k-1}\}) \ge \mathbf{w}_{u_i}$$

We denote the fact that U is proper through the predicate $proper(v, U)$. Only cliques constructed with proper combinations of neighbors can be considered as admissible.

Subsequently, to compare any two sets of $k-1$ neighbors, nodes follow two straightforward rules. From the perspective of node v, subset C' is better than subset C if:

- C' is *proper* and C is not, **or**
- both C' and C are *proper* and $w(\{v\}+C') > w(\{v\}+C)$.

We can express it in a more concise way by, firstly, defining the function $attr_v()$:

$$attr_v(C) = \begin{cases} w(\{v\} + C) & \text{if } proper(v, C) \\ 0 & \text{otherwise} \end{cases}$$

In other words, the *attractiveness* of a set C for node v is expressed as the weight of C after adding v, provided C is indeed admissible, otherwise C should be ignored. We can now check whether C' is better than C by evaluating the expression $attr_v(C') > attr_v(C)$. By executing lines 3–7, node v chooses the most attractive clique, setting $\mathbf{C}_v$ and $\mathbf{w}_v$ accordingly.

Finally, node v sends the new value of $\mathbf{w}_v$ to all of its neighbors (line 10), allowing each neighbor to update

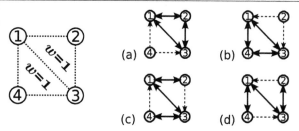

Figure 2 Two adjacent 3-cliques of equal weight impeding the correct convergence of the protocol and 4 possible configurations (a)–(d) that do not create a correct 3-clique matching: the contents of $\mathbf{C}_v$'s are visualized by outgoing arrows.

```
                    Variables:
                    Cᵥ    set of k − 1 neighbors with which v wants to create a clique
                    wᵥ    the weight w({v} + Cᵥ)

      1: loop
      2:     C ← {}
      3:     for all U ≡ {u₁, . . . , u_{k−1}} ⊆ N(v) do
      4:         if attr_v(U) > attr_v(C) then
      5:             C ← U
      6:         end if
      7:     end for
      8:     Cᵥ ← C
      9:     wᵥ ← w({v} + Cᵥ)
     10:     send wᵥ to all u ∈ N(v)
     11: end loop
```

Figure 3 Self-stabilizing weighted k-clique matching protocol (executed by node v).

information on the clique it was (hoping to) participate in. We need not assume that communication is reliable: message loss will merely slow down the algorithm, but does not affect its correctness.

To sum up, what every node is doing in each round boils down to solving a version of the heaviest k-subgraph problem in a graph induced by the node itself and all its neighbors. What is different from the classical k-subgraph problem is that: (a) we are interested only in k-subgraphs that are cliques, (b) one of the nodes from the resulting k-clique is fixed — the node itself must be a part of the solution, (c) each of the neighbors imposes a constraint on the minimum weight of a clique it can be part of.

5 Optimizations

In some applications of the algorithm it may happen that the average size of a node's neighborhood is relatively high, for example, it is restricted only by the size of the network, meaning that any k nodes in the network can, in principle, create a clique. This may lead to problems of applying the algorithm in its current form for several reasons.

High computational complexity of a single round. In each round every node has to examine $\binom{|N(v)|}{k-1}$ combinations of $k - 1$ neighbors with which it could potentially create a k-clique. If the number of neighbors is substantial then the cost of executing the protocol from Figure 3 may be prohibitively high even for small values of k.

Difficulty for a node to keep track of all other nodes in the network. In the case of a dynamic network, in which nodes may join and leave at any point in time, each node needs to be aware of all these changes. Failing to do so may prevent nodes from finding the best possible

cliques. For example, if nodes u, v, and w are the best candidates to form a 3-clique but each of them is unaware of the existence of at least one of the other two nodes, they would never be able to form a clique together and would be forced to settle down for lesser options.

Messaging overload. For the protocol to converge in a timely manner and even to work correctly, it is necessary that all nodes have constantly updated information about the clique weights pursued by their neighbors. Therefore, in each round every node v sends out to all its neighbors its current value of $\mathbf{w}_v$, which translates to broadcasting to each node in each round the number of messages relative to the size of the network.

5.1 Heuristics for finding the heaviest k-clique

To circumvent consideration of all possible $k − 1$ neighbor combinations, and thus, to reduce the high computational complexity of a single round, a node can use a heuristic to find its most attractive k-clique. The obvious candidates for heuristics to be used are the heuristics that perform well when trying to solve the heaviest k-subgraph problem, as that is in principle what each node is doing in every round. The choice of the heuristic requires careful consideration, as a wrong decision may result in suboptimal solutions.

For example, consider a simple greedy heuristic that constructs the k-clique for node v in the following manner. First, node v becomes the first node of a new clique: $U \leftarrow \{v\}$. Then $k − 1$ times, node u from $N(v) − U$ is chosen such that the sum of weights of edges between u and nodes from U is maximal, and added to the new clique. The $(k − 1)$-th node is chosen from $N(v) − U$ with the additional condition that $U − \{v\}$ is proper. The biggest disadvantage of using this heuristic is that it is simply too deterministic: the first $k − 2$ neighbors are always fixed (due to fixed edge weights), and in the choice of the $(k-1)$-th neighbor lies the node's only chance to find a promising clique. The portion of the explored solution space is therefore hugely restricted for the node; part of it will never be explored, and this can lead to nodes settling on suboptimal cliques or even not being able to find any clique to be part of. As is so often the case, it is much better to explicitly randomize how nodes select candidate nodes to team up with.

When incorporating a heuristic into the protocol, the biggest challenge is not to lose the convergence along the way. If the chosen heuristic was simply used to replace the lines 3–7 in the algorithm from Figure 3, in each round a node would most probably arrive at a different combination of neighbors to be set as $\mathbf{C}_v$, quite often this new combination would be also worse than the one from the previous round. This was not the case in the original protocol from Figure 3, in which we had the guarantee that in each round a subset of neighbors chosen by a node for a clique would be reconsidered, simply because all of the possible combinations are evaluated anew in every single round. Therefore, to avoid discarding a good clique candidate found in the previous round when a heuristic is used, in the modified protocol (see Figure 4) this clique is re-evaluated (lines 3–5). If this clique is still proper, it will be kept if no better clique is found.

Another modification is that nodes send out not only the information about the weight of their currently pursued clique but include in their message also the ids of the nodes from this clique (line 18). This information is mostly

beneficial to the nodes that are the owners of the aforementioned ids. These nodes are now able to improve their own clique choice (lines 6–10). What happens here can be interpreted as a parallelization of the heuristic computation, which greatly improves the convergence speed.

Lastly, in line 11, the heuristic algorithm is executed. As a starting point for its execution, the value of C computed in lines 3–10 may be utilized; or a randomly generated value can be used. The best solution found is saved in $\mathbf{C}_v$ and its weight in $\mathbf{w}_v$. The value of $\mathbf{w}_v$ is then sent to all the neighbors of node v. Moreover, nodes from $\mathbf{C}_v$ receive also the information about the contents of $\mathbf{C}_v$. Afterwards, a new execution of the loop begins.

The fact that in each round a node repeats the heuristic search, results in our protocol being transformed into a multi-start version of the chosen heuristic. Each round means the re-execution of the heuristic procedure with a new (randomly generated) solution as a starting point. When choosing a heuristic it is worth to take into account this multi-start property together with the implicit parallelization achieved by collaboration of nodes towards finding the best clique, mentioned in the previous paragraph.

5.1.1 VNS heuristic

We tested the modified protocol using variable neighborhood search (VNS) as a heuristic. The choice of this particular heuristic for our protocol is motivated by the work of Brimberg et al. who report in [25] that VNS consistently achieved the best results in solving the heaviest k-subgraph problem. The heuristics against which Brimberg et al. tested VNS include [26]: multi-start local search, tabu search, and scatter search. Each of these heuristics could also be applied to or adopted by our protocol, but investigating the differences of the protocol's performance under different heuristics falls out of scope of this paper.

VNS is a meta-heuristic that found its application in a vast range of combinatorial and global optimization problems [27] including various graph problems, knapsack and packing problems, scheduling problems, and data-mining problems. Its name stems from the term used to describe the subset of the solution space that, according to some predefined metric, is close to a particular point of this solution space. In our problem the solution space consists of all possible $(k-1)$-element combinations of a node's neighbors:

$$S_v = \{C | C \subseteq N(v) \text{ with } |C| = k-1\}.$$

A natural metric that can be imposed on this solution space defines the distance between two combinations as the number of nodes by which they differ, i.e.:

$$\delta(C, C') = |C - C'|.$$

```
 1:  loop
 2:      C ← {}
 3:      if proper(v, C_v) then
 4:          C ← C_v
 5:      end if
 6:      for all u ∈ N(v) do
 7:          if v ∈ C_u and
               attr_v(C_u + {u} − {v}) > attr_v(C) then
 8:              C ← C_u + {u} − {v}
 9:          end if
10:      end for
11:      C′ ← HEURISTIC(v, C)
12:      if attr_v(C′) > attr_v(C) then
13:          C ← C′
14:      end if
15:      C_v ← C
16:      w_v ← w({v} + C_v)
17:      send w_v to all u ∈ N(v)
18:      send C_v to all u ∈ C_v
19:  end loop
```

Figure 4 k-Clique matching protocol with a heuristic.

Then the d-th *neighborhood structure* of a certain combination C would consist of all combinations that differ by at most d nodes from C:

$$NS_d(C) = \{C' | C' \in S_v \text{ with } \delta(C, C') \le d\}.$$

Note that the neighborhood structure is not identical with the neighborhood of node v. v's neighborhood consists of all other nodes that are adjacent to the node by some edge, while the neighborhood structure consists of $(k-1)$-node subsets from v's neighborhood.

The VNS algorithm is composed of two functions which are executed in turns. First, the *shake* function modifies the current solution C by randomly changing a few nodes such that a new solution C' belongs to the d-th neighborhood structure of C. The goal of this step is to avoid getting stuck in a local optimum. Second, the *local search function* improves the new solution by trying to find a better one in the 1st neighborhood structure of C' (differing by a single node). This function can either return the first improvement found over C' or the best improvement (in our simulations the first improvement node was used). In case no improvement is found d is increased, otherwise it is set to some default value. The VNS algorithm executes until a certain halting condition is reached, for example, when the execution time exceeds some limit. For more details on how the VNS was adopted to our protocol, we refer to [2].

Applying the VNS heuristic proved to speed up the convergence of the protocol. This can be accounted to the fact that nodes inform each other not only about the weight of the clique they are trying to create but also about which nodes they are trying to create a clique with. This way nodes can learn quickly about good cliques without the need to search the entire solution space themselves. Yet, the assumption that each node has full (up-to-date) knowledge about the entire network (especially if the network is large, changes in time, nodes come and go, etc) is unrealistic. In Section 5.3 we present how this assumption can be dropped.

5.1.2 Random subset heuristic
Another heuristic is based on a simple trick: if considering all possible combinations of neighbors is computationally too expensive, a node can evaluate only a subset of neighbors in each round. The size of this subset can be set in such a way that for the given value of k, a node has enough resources to fully explore all $k-1$ combinations of nodes from the subset. To construct a subset, node v can simply pick randomly the necessary number of neighbors. Moreover, v can supplement the subset by adding $k-1$ neighbors that are in its current clique $\mathbf{C}_v$. Once the subset is created, the node executes the for-loop from the basic protocol (see Figure 3 lines 3–7) and returns the most attractive clique found.

The big advantage of this heuristic is that it is possible to implement the construction of the subsets in a completely distributed fashion, which eliminates the necessity of knowing all the nodes in the network by every node. We expand on this matter in Section 5.3.

5.2 Pruning
Completely independently from the heuristics, nodes can try to exploit their knowledge about the possible values of edge weights. For example, if the weights of the edges are bounded, node v can judge whether neighbor u has any chances to become a clique partner prior to considering any possible cliques this neighbor can be part of. To do that, v computes the best possible weight of the clique that it can create with u using the weight of the edge $\{v, u\}$ and the maximum possible value for the weights of remaining edges w_{max}. Thus, when the weight of a clique is computed as an arithmetic mean of the respective edges, the best possible weight of the clique with nodes v and u is:

$$w' = \frac{w\{v, u\} + \left(\binom{k}{2} - 1\right) w_{max}}{\binom{k}{2}}$$

If w' is smaller than either $\mathbf{w}_v$ or $\mathbf{w}_u$, node v can safely ignore this neighbor for two reasons. First, when $w' < \mathbf{w}_v$, node v has already found a better clique than any possible clique with u could be. Second, if $w' < \mathbf{w}_u$, node v has no chances in creating a clique with u since u has a better clique. Of course, because cliques pursued by nodes can change, in each round a node has to re-evaluate which nodes can be pruned. Nonetheless, once the set of neighbors is pruned, node v can apply any heuristic to this reduced set, which can greatly improve the convergence speed. Yet, one has to keep in mind that with the increase of k the impact of a single edge on the total weight of the cliques diminishes. A single edge weight contributes on average only $2/k(k-1)$ of the total clique's weight. As a consequence, pruning will bring the best results for small values of k.

5.3 Partial views with pruning
When any two nodes in the network can be each other's neighbors, then a list of any node's neighbors is limited only by the size of the network. In large dynamic networks maintaining such hefty lists by each node might be an expensive task. This is due not only to the sheer size of these neighbor lists but also to their volatility. Our goal is to remove the necessity of each node having complete information about the entire network, keeping a node's chances high of finding the best clique.

To this end, we allow nodes to maintain fixed-sized lists that contain only a relatively small number of all neighbors. We refer to such a list as a partial view of a node. Nodes present in the partial view of node v would be the only ones among which v would be able to look for the most promising clique in each round. Thus, we could look at this type of the protocol as a variation of the random subset heuristic for finding the best k-clique — in each round a node has a small subset of all neighbors available, in this subset v must find $k - 1$ neighbors with which it can create the best clique. This means that nodes can simply follow the protocol from Figure 4, and the efficiency of the clique matching will largely depend on the policy for modifying partial views.

As our algorithm is decentralized we would prefer to implement the partial views maintenance functionality also in a fully decentralized way. For this purpose we use a gossiping/epidemic protocol. Gossiping [28] is a simple, lightweight and robust type of peer-to-peer protocol that found its application in information dissemination, peer sampling, resource management, and most importantly from our perspective, topology construction. The framework of a gossiping protocol used for creation and maintenance of various overlays is summarized in Figure 5. Here, each node keeps a list of nodes of a specific small size c. The partial views are modified when nodes exchange among each other portions (of size b) of their views.

Different rules incorporated into the three functions from the framework will result in different overlays. In this paper, we consider two implementations: *Random* and *Pruning*, described in Figure 6. The goal of the *Random* exchanges is to provide enough variety of the partial view contents for the subsequent executions of clique matching protocol. This enables nodes to discover all nodes in the network and explore all possible neighbor combinations. At the same time, the drawback of this approach is that good candidates for clique members might be discarded too easily and be replaced by other random nodes. Conversely, the idea behind *Pruning* exchanges is that nodes send out portions of their partial views that are

most "promising" from the recipient's perspective. Moreover, nodes keep in their partial view only the "promising" neighbors and we use the pruning measure described in previous subsection to separate "promising" neighbors from the rest. The risk of using *Pruning* lies in the possibility of partitioning the overlay network induced by partial views if pruning turns out to be too greedy. Therefore, we also investigate a third approach which is the combination of the *Random* and *Pruning* approaches, in which separate gossiping protocols implementing the former two approaches are stacked on top of each other (see Figure 7), similarly to the Vicinity protocol described in [5].

Another advantage of using gossiping to implement partial views is that it provides a natural mechanism for tackling changes to the network by disseminating information about newly joined nodes or by gradually removing from partial views nodes that left the system. This is a desirable feature even considering that we are dealing with servers (and not end-user systems) and thus that it is fair to assume that churn will be very low. As further reported in our previous work (see, e.g., [29]), gossiping is ideal for effectively and efficiently handling the adverse effects of churn. Further investigations about effects of churn on our k-clique matching protocol with partial views is left for future research.

5.4 Gossiping updates

The timely convergence of the k-clique matching protocol is contingent on nodes having up-to-date information about the cliques pursued by their neighbors. Therefore, in all versions of the protocol presented so far, each node v after computing a new value of $\mathbf{C}_v$, sends to all its neighbors its new value of $\mathbf{w}_v$, which afterwards is used by v's neighbors to determine if they can conceivably propose a better clique to v. However, this means that in each round the number of messages sent through the network can reach the order of $|V|^2$.

Instead of such an expensive broadcast mechanism, we can use a gossiping protocol for this purpose. In the previous section we have shown how a gossiping algorithm can be used to maintain and modify partial views of nodes. The same mechanism can be also used to spread the values of clique weights pursued by each node. To this end, a separate gossiping protocol can run in the background.

This protocol follows the same framework from Figure 5 but instead of exchanging only the contact information to nodes in the network, each item, stored in the view and exchanged between nodes, consists of an *id* of some node v, its contact information, the value of $\mathbf{w}_v$ and a counter indicating the *age* of this information. These age counters are increased at the beginning of each loop iteration in the active thread of the gossiping protocol, as well as upon an exchange of information between nodes. If node v finds itself to have two items of the same node id (e.g., as a result

---

Active thread loop:

1: $u \leftarrow$ `selectNode()`
2: *buffer*$_{out} \leftarrow$ `selectItemsToSend()`
3: **send** *buffer*$_{out}$ **to** u
4: **receive** *buffer*$_{in}$ **from** u
5: `selectItemsToKeep()`

Passive thread loop:

1: **receive** *buffer*$_{in}$ **from** v
2: *buffer*$_{out} \leftarrow$ `selectItemsToSend()`
3: **send** *buffer*$_{out}$ **to** v
4: `selectItemsToKeep()`

Figure 5 Gossiping protocol framework.

Random
`selectItemsToSend()`
active thread: randomly select $b - 1$ nodes from the protocol's view and add yourself
passive thread: randomly select b nodes from the protocol's view
`selectItemsToKeep()`
keep all b received nodes, removing (if necessary) the nodes selected to send (and in case of *active thread*, the node returned by selectRandomNode())

Pruning
`selectItemsToSend()`
select b nodes whose weights are best from the point of the receiving node
`selectItemsToKeep()`
keep c best out of all nodes from the received buffer and current view

Figure 6 Implementation details of *Random* and *Pruning* protocols.

of a gossip exchange) it keeps the item with the smaller age. This way, older information about the clique weights is seamlessly discarded.

The efficiency of the clique matching protocol will largely depend on the speed at which the gossiping protocol propagates current information on clique weights through the network. In Figure 8 we present details of possible rules to incorporate into the three core functions of the gossiping protocol. In Section 6, we will compare the impact of various combinations of these rules on the convergence of the clique matching protocol. We will also examine other factors, such as the gossiping communication frequency.

Although we have mentioned that this protocol can run in parallel, completely independently from other protocols, there is also a potential for consolidating the dissemination of $\mathbf{w}_v$ values with the dissemination of contact information and the maintenance of partial views. We leave the evaluation of these dissemination ideas to future research.

6 Performance evaluation

6.1 Simulation setup

In the following simulations, we examine the efficiency of the presented protocols in partitioning the network into k-cliques. We focus on measuring convergence of various versions of our k-clique matching algorithm. Note that measuring the quality of created k-clique matchings as compared to the optimal solution is not possible as it is computationally infeasible to derive the latter.

The execution of simulations is based on the notion of rounds. In each round, every node executes the entire loop body exactly once. The ordering in which the nodes execute their protocols in each round is entirely random.

The number of elapsed rounds is not always the best time metric as it does not reflect the computational costs incurred by nodes during a single round when different versions of the protocol are used or even when comparing the same protocol for different values of k. Therefore, when needed we adopt the average number of cliques considered by nodes since simulation start. This metric

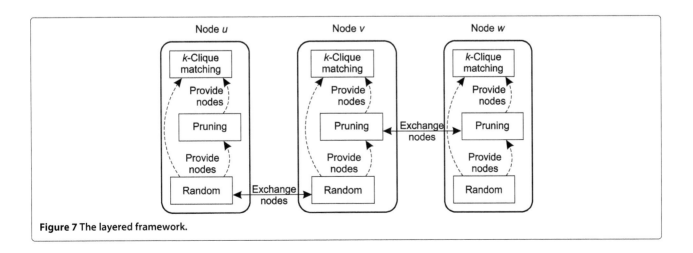

Figure 7 The layered framework.

```
selectNode()
```
random: randomly select node from the view
oldest: select node whose item has the highest age
youngest: select node whose item has the lowest age

```
selectItemsToSend()
```
create an item with node's own clique weight info and fill the remaining $b - 1$ places in the buffer with:
random: randomly selected items from the view
oldest: oldest items from the view
youngest: youngest items from the view

```
selectItemsToKeep()
```
if a received item has its counterpart (item with the same node's id) in the view, keep the item with the smaller age, otherwise simply add the received item to the view

---

Figure 8 Implementation details of gossiping protocol for clique weights dissemination.

reflects more closely the differences between the computational complexities of the protocols.

All of our simulations are conducted on complete graphs, which means that for each node v the neighbor set $N(v)$ is equal to $V - \{v\}$. As a result, any k nodes can potentially form a clique. This guarantees that, irrespectively of the distribution of edge weights, it is always possible to find a k-clique matching that consists of $\lfloor n/k \rfloor$ cliques.

Each edge is assigned a weight drawn uniformly at random from the interval $(0, 1)$. The weight of a clique is computed as the arithmetic mean of the respective edge weights in the clique. The objective of the nodes in a network is then to maximize the weight of the clique they are going to be part of.

All simulations presented here were conducted using PeerSim [30], an open-source simulator for peer-to-peer protocols. Each presented curve is an average of 5 simulations executed with the same parameters but different random number generator seeds. In each simulation, all nodes start without any clique chosen.

6.2   Performance of k-clique matching protocol

First, let us focus on the convergence speed of the basic k-clique matching protocol from Figure 3. Figure 9(a) depicts the percentage of nodes in cliques against the number of elapsed rounds. In a network of 300 nodes, the number of rounds necessary for all nodes to form disjoint cliques increases with the size of the cliques. Nonetheless, even for a clique size of $k = 5$, the time needed for full convergence does not exceed 20 rounds.

Although the clique size, k, does not have a dramatic effect on the protocol performance in terms of convergence rounds, it does affect it with respect to the amount of computation required by each node. This is depicted in Figure 9(b), which plots the same metric (percentage of nodes in cliques) as a function of the number of cliques considered on average by each node. Here, the

discrepancies of the computational load under different values of k become clearly pronounced (notice the logarithmic scale of the horizontal axis). In fact, the exponential increase in computational load comes as no surprise, as each node has to evaluate all $\binom{|N(v)|}{k-1}$ possible cliques in each round, as specified by the basic protocol from Figure 3.

The next pair of graphs shows the differences in the convergence speed of the basic protocol for different sizes of networks. In Figure 10(a) we do not observe significant discrepancies in the number of rounds needed by all nodes to find their cliques. Yet again, as we take into account the average number of cliques evaluated by each node, we can observe that with each twofold increase in the size of the network, the convergence time grows by a factor of 2^{k-1}. Again, this is the direct consequence of the fact that in the basic algorithm every node evaluates $\binom{|N(v)|}{k-1}$ possible cliques.

Note here that in case of a sparse graph the computational cost (as well as the communication one) of the basic protocol would be much lower. For example, if the size of each node's neighborhood was in the order of the logarithm of the network size, $O(log|V|)$, the computational cost of a single round would be only in the order of $O(|V|)$ instead of $O(|V|^k)$ (and each node would send only $O(log|V|)$ messages per round). For such graphs, our basic protocol would be really efficient and would scale gracefully with increase in clique and/or network size. Yet, for graphs where neighborhoods of nodes are much larger, we need other strategies to lower the costs and preserve the performance.

6.3   Performance with heuristics

To assess the performance of the k-clique matching protocol that uses heuristics, we compare it against the basic version of the protocol. Figure 11 shows the convergence (explained below) as a function of the average number of

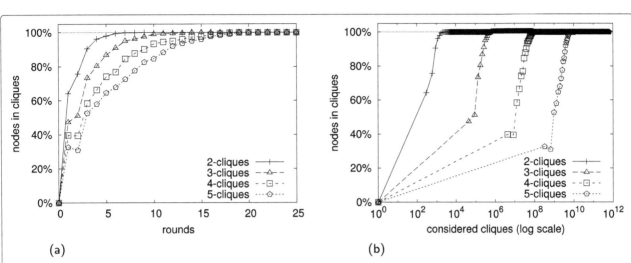

Figure 9 Performance of the basic *k*-clique matching protocol; percentages of nodes matched into cliques for various values of *k* plotted against: (a) number of rounds, (b) average number of cliques evaluated by a single node since the beginning of a simulation.

cliques considered per node, for 5 different versions of the *k*-clique matching protocol: (1) the basic one, (2) using the VNS heuristic, (3) using pruning and the VNS heuristic, (4) using the random subset heuristic (RS), (5) using pruning in combination with RS. The convergence of the protocols is not expressed by the percentage of nodes in cliques at a given point, but by the percentage of nodes in cliques that has been reached at a given point and remains above this level till the end of experiment. This results in curves being monotonically increasing and is done only for the sake of legibility. The size of the network is 300 nodes and $k = 4$. The size of the random subset is set to 40. The halting condition of the VNS protocol is based on the number of cliques considered by a node. This number is chosen in such a way that it provides a fair comparison

between VNS and random subset heuristics. Given that with the random subset heuristic a node will consider in a single round not more than $\binom{40+k-1}{k-1}$ cliques, the number of cliques that a node using the VNS heuristic can check in a single round is also set to $\binom{40+k-1}{k-1}$.

In Figure 11, we see that both the VNS and the RS heuristics outperform the basic *k*-clique matching protocol. This can be attributed to the fact that nodes make much better use of the cliques formed by other nodes. Moreover, adding pruning mechanisms speeds up the convergence of each of the heuristics further. We see that the difference between using VNS and the RS heuristics is minimal, which means that we can often use the simpler and cheaper RS heuristics to achieve the same results. Apparently, having only a relatively small subset of

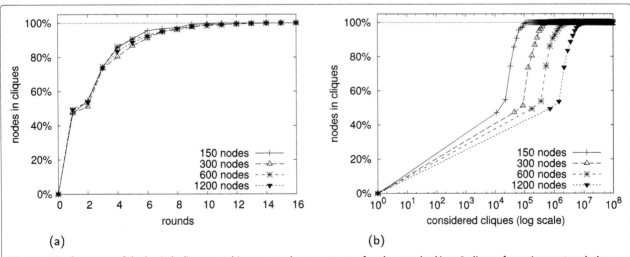

Figure 10 Performance of the basic *k*-clique matching protocol; percentages of nodes matched into 3-cliques for various network sizes plotted against: (a) number of rounds, (b) average number of cliques evaluated by a single node since the beginning of a simulation.

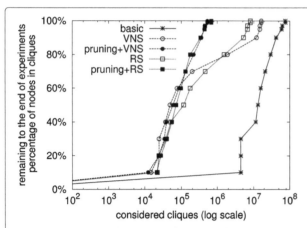

Figure 11 Comparison between performance of the basic *k*-clique matching protocol and the *k*-clique matching protocol employing heuristics and pruning; plotted against the average number of cliques evaluated by a single node since the beginning of an experiment.

neighbors already achieves the major effect also attained by VNS. A more comprehensive comparison between the basic protocol, VNS with various halting conditions and RS with various random subset sizes is presented in [24].

Figure 12 focuses on the performance of the VNS heuristic for clique size 2, 3, and 4, and for networks of 300, 600, 1200, and 2400 nodes. The halting condition for "VNS (M)" is set to $\binom{M+k-1}{k-1}$ considered cliques. This means that "VNS (40)" ("VNS (60)") considers almost 2^{k-1} (3^{k-1}) cliques more in each round compared to "VNS (20)". Firstly, we can observe that pruning significantly speeds up the convergence of the protocol. Further, we can observe that the convergence times get slightly longer when the size of the network increases, but the increase in the size of the clique has a much bigger negative impact. This can be attributed to the increase in the solution space of the best clique for a given node, which is equal to $\binom{N-1}{k-1}$. When the size of the network grows by a factor of two, the solution space increases by a factor of circa 2^{k-1}; when the size of the clique increases by just 1, the solution space increases by a factor of N/k. For small values of k, the latter will be significantly larger than the former. The increasing differences between results for "VNS (20)", "VNS (40)", "VNS (60)" with pruning can be explained in a similar manner.

We see a similar regularity in performance of the RS heuristic (see Figure 13). Moreover, when compared to VNS, the random subset heuristic seems to converge slightly faster. This is especially encouraging in light of our next simulations regarding partial views.

6.4   Performance with partial views

Interesting results have been obtained for the performance of the *k*-clique matching protocol that uses partial

views. In Figure 14 we can see the comparison between the partial views implementing *Random*, *Pruning*, and layered *Random+Pruning* approaches. We can observe that layered *Random+Pruning* outperforms *Random* implementation for all clique and network sizes investigated, which suggests that using pruning in combination with some randomness to maintain partial views does help in the convergence of our *k*-clique matching protocol.

At the same time, we can see curious results for the *Pruning* implementation. For $k = 2$ it performs worse than both *Random* and *Random+Pruning*; for $k = 3$ it starts to perform better than *Random* across all network sizes but is still worse than *Random+Pruning*; finally, for $k = 4$ it starts to outperform also *Random+Pruning*. The explanation lies in the close dependency between the size of the clique and the strength of pruning, as hinted already in Section 5.2. For $k = 2$, pruning is very efficient but this is exactly the source of the problem. At the beginning of a simulation, the situation in the network is very unstable and many cliques are created and broken from round to round. Pruning acts then over-zealously, discarding from partial views nodes that are potentially very attractive but for this brief moment are unavailable or uninteresting. With the increase of the clique size, pruning becomes more and more relaxed and its performance improves. Nonetheless, to prevent hyperactivity of pruning, one might consider disabling it in the early stages of algorithm execution and enable it only once the system starts to settle down. We leave for future research investigation of how nodes could recognize the right moment to switch on pruning.

When we compare the convergence times of the simulations with partial views with *Random* implementation (see Figure 14) and the simulations of random subset heuristic *without* pruning, we do not observe any major discrepancies. To the contrary, the results for partial views with *Pruning* differ highly from the results for random subset heuristic *with* pruning. In all setups, adding pruning to random subset heuristic improved the convergence of the protocol significantly. This was not the case for partial views with *Pruning*. This differences can be explained by the fact that in case of the random subset heuristic nodes have the knowledge of all other nodes in the network and apply pruning to the full list of nodes anew at the beginning of each round, thus removing from a consideration a node has the effect only for duration of a single round. Conversely, if node decides to replace in its partial view one node with another, it must reckon that it might take some time before it will stumble upon this node again.

6.5   Performance when gossiping clique weights

We start our evaluation of the gossiping protocol for clique-weight dissemination by comparing the effectiveness of various implementations of the two core methods

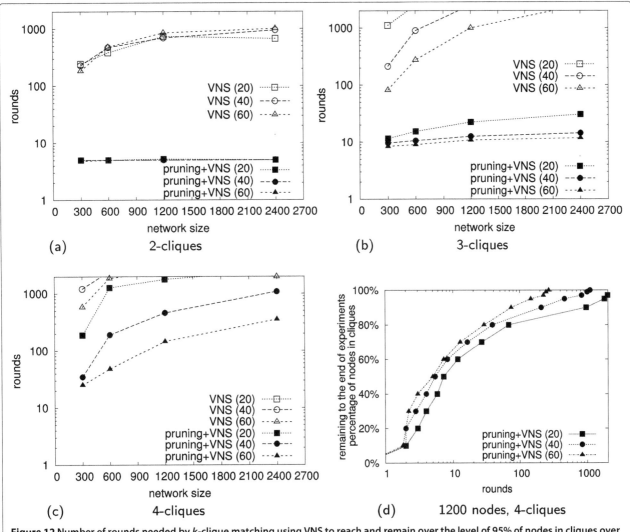

Figure 12 Number of rounds needed by *k*-clique matching using VNS to reach and remain over the level of 95% of nodes in cliques over different network sizes (a)–(c) and an example of convergence (d).

selectNode() and selectItemsToSend. In Figure 15 we can see simulation results of the basic *k*-clique matching protocol that, instead of broadcasting new clique weight values, uses a gossiping protocol to disseminate this information. Each iteration of the *k*-clique matching protocol loop is followed by a single execution of the active thread loop of the gossiping protocol. The simulations have been performed on a network of 300 nodes and for *k* = 3. The size of the buffer for the gossiping protocol has been set to 10. Each curve corresponds to a different combination of selectNode() and selectItemsToSend implementations, as detailed in Section 5.4.

In Figure 15 we can distinguish four different groups of curves. The fastest convergence times have been achieved, when selectItemsToSend() chooses the *youngest* items from the view, and selectNode() returns either the oldest or a random node. For the

same two implementations of selectNode() but with selectItemsToSend() returning *random* items, the convergence of our *k*-clique matching protocol slows down almost twofold. Moreover, when selectItemsToSend() returns the oldest items, the protocol converges even more slowly and does not manage to achieve 100% in the first 1000 rounds. Yet, the worst results have been obtained for selectNode() that returns the node from the youngest item, for any of the implementations of selectItemsToSend(); the *k*-clique matching protocol gets stuck at 30%.

These results can be explained by considering the role of the age counter attached to every item. This counter coincides with the freshness of the clique weight information. Therefore, when nodes choose the youngest items in selectItemsToSend(), they contribute to the dissemination of the most up-to-date information about other nodes' clique weights. On the other hand, when a

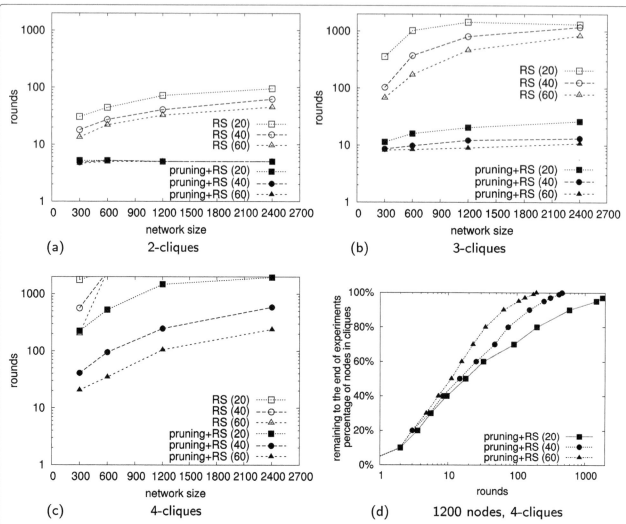

Figure 13 Number of rounds needed by *k*-clique matching using random subset heuristic to reach and remain over the level of 95% of nodes in cliques over different network sizes (a)–(c) and and example of convergence (d).

node selects the node from the youngest item as the next node to communicate with (via `selectNode()`) it falls in to the trap of exchanging information with the same node over and over again; when a node selects items to send, it always adds an item with its own clique weight; this item is going to become the youngest item in the view of the recipient.

Even with the most efficient combination of `selectNode()` and `selectItemsToSend()` implementations, *k*-clique matching using gossiping to disseminate clique weight information is significantly (over 30 times) slower than its counterpart that uses broadcast. Nonetheless, the convergence can be improved by increasing the number of items exchanged by nodes between any two executions of *k*-clique matching protocol loop. This can be done by either increasing the number of items exchanged in every gossiping communication or

by increasing the frequency of the gossiping protocol relatively to the *k*-clique matching protocol. Here we present the results for the latter.

First, note that when broadcast is used, a node has to send out $N - 1$ messages with its new clique weight in every round. At the same time, when gossiping is used in every round each node initiates only one exchange and, thus, on average it is also contacted by one other node. As a result, each node sends out the number of items equal to twice the size of the gossiping buffer. If the frequency of gossiping relatively to the *k*-clique matching protocol is increased, the average number of items sent out will also increase linearly to the frequency increase. The differences between the message load of broadcast and gossiping with different frequencies is depicted in Figure 16(a): the network size equals 300 and the size of the gossiping buffer is set to 10. Furthermore, in

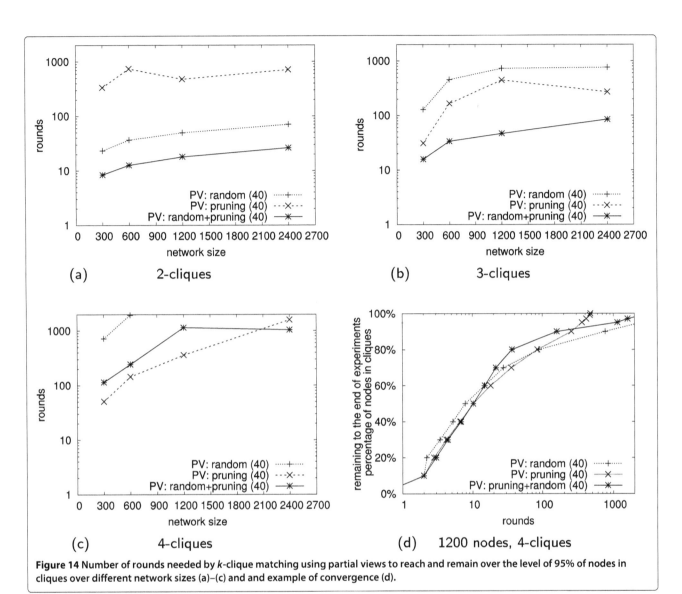

Figure 14 Number of rounds needed by *k*-clique matching using partial views to reach and remain over the level of 95% of nodes in cliques over different network sizes (a)–(c) and and example of convergence (d).

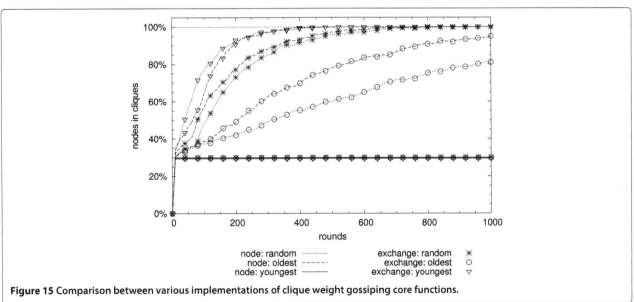

Figure 15 Comparison between various implementations of clique weight gossiping core functions.

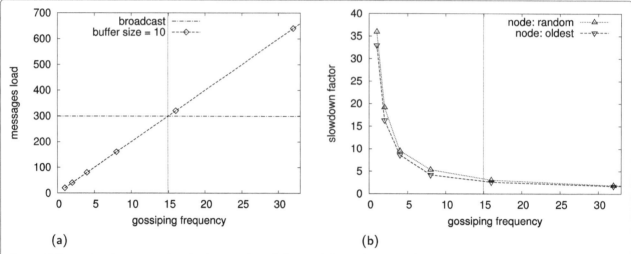

Figure 16 Comparison between various implementations of clique weight gossiping core functions: message load (a) and slowdown factor (b) versus gossiping frequency.

Figure 16(b) we can see that the convergence speed of the k-clique matching protocol with gossiping of clique weights improves exponentially. This shows that gossiping is a viable alternative to the brute force broadcast of clique weights.

7 Conclusions

In this paper we presented a protocol that finds an approximation of a k-clique matching in the network. The protocol can be used to divide entities in the network into fixed size groups, based on the pairwise assessments between nodes. The final partitioning emerges from nodes' local decision on which neighbors to link to.

Although the convergence of the protocol in its basic form in terms of rounds looks very attractive, there are hidden costs of the protocol imposed on each of the nodes in terms of computational complexity related to the evaluation of all possible combinations of neighbors performed in each round. To elevate these costs we proposed that nodes use a heuristic to compute their new choice of $k - 1$ neighbors instead of performing a full search over the solution space. The two heuristics that we used were (1) variable neighborhood search heuristic that was reported to outperform other heuristics for finding heaviest k-clique and (2) a simple random subset heuristic. As our simulations show, the protocol using any of these two heuristics achieves a converged state faster than the original protocol. We attribute these results to the fact that the nodes share their best clique with its other members, which significantly speeds up the search for the best clique by implicit parallelization of computations. In contrast, in the basic version on the protocol, nodes perform their computations fully on their own and than only agree on the clique's weight.

To further improve the performance of the protocol, we employed a pruning mechanism that temporarily (for the period of a single round) removes from consideration those neighbors that have no prospects for participating in a clique better than the current one. We validated by simulations that combining heuristics with pruning performs better than applying heuristics alone.

The fact that the random sample heuristic performed equally well as a more elaborate variable neighborhood search heuristic, led us to exploring a variation of the protocol where each node keeps only a subset of all its neighbors in its local memory (creating a partial view of the full neighbor set). To discover new neighbors nodes periodically exchange parts of their partial views. Thus in each round, similarly to the random subset heuristic case, they consider a different subset of neighboring nodes. This approach is especially attractive for the scenarios in which the set of neighbors is equivalent with the set of nodes in the network and the assumption that nodes know all their neighbors would be too strict. The simulations confirmed that the partial views approach provides performance indistinguishable from the random subset heuristic.

Independently from these improvements, we have also investigated to what extent the broadcast communication between the nodes in the protocol can be replaced by other methods of information dissemination through the network. The initial results of the use of gossiping protocol instead of broadcast show the viability of this approach and its tradeoff in terms of slower convergence times.

In our future work we plan to focus on extending the protocol to support formation of cliques of different sizes and relaxing the constraint that each node can be part of only one clique, by allowing nodes to set their own limits on the number of cliques they are interested to participate in.

Endnote

[a]We adopted the terminology of the k-clique matching from [12] where Kann uses the term H-matching to describe a set of disjoint subgraphs in a given graph where each of these subgraphs is isomorphic to H. This term is also used by Crescenzi and Kann in the highly cited [13]. After a more thorough search of related work we observe that the term H-packing is more widely used to describe this notion. Nonetheless, to stay consistent with our previous paper, we keep our terminology of k-clique matching.

Competing interests
The authors declare that they have no competing interests.

Authors' contributions
AC is the main contributor of this work, which was undertaken as part of her Ph.D. studies. She is also the author of a first version of this paper. SV has been daily supervisor for AC, with main contributions to the design of the algorithms, notably concerning extensions including gossiping. MvS has been supervisor for AC, contributing to all work reported in this paper. He is the main author of the revised version of this paper when submitting it to JISA. All authors have read and approved the final manuscript.

References
1. Foster I, Berry D, Djaoui A, Grimshaw A, Horn B, Kishimoto H, Maciel F, Savva A, Siebenlist F, Subramaniam R, Treadwell J, Von Reich J (2006) The Open Grid Services Architecture, Version 1.5. GGF Informational Document GFD-I.080
2. Chmielowiec A, van Steen M (2010) Optimal decentralized formation of k-member partnerships. In: SASO 2010 proceedings of the 4th, IEEE international conference on self-adaptive and self-organizing systems. IEEE Computer Society, Washington DC. pp 154–163. doi:10.1109/SASO.2010.14
3. Chmielowiec A, Pierre G, Gordijn J, van Steen M (2008) Technical challenges in market-driven automated service provisioning. In: MW4SOC '08: proceedings of the 3rd workshop on middleware for service oriented computing. ACM, New York. pp 25–30. doi:10.1145/1462802.1462807
4. Jelasity M, Montresor A, Babaoglu O (2009) T-man: gossip-based fast overlay topology construction. Comput Netw 53(13):2321–2339. doi:10.1016/j.comnet.2009.03.013
5. Voulgaris S (2006) Epidemic-based self-organization in peer-to-peer systems. PhD thesis. Vrije Universiteit, Amsterdam, The Netherlands
6. Micali S, Vazirani VV (1980) An $o(\sqrt{(|v|)}|e|)$ algorithm for finding maximum matching in general graphs. In: SFCS '80: proceedings of the 21st annual symposium on foundations of computer science. IEEE Computer Society, Washington, DC. pp 17–27. doi:10.1109/SFCS.1980.12
7. Blum N (1990) A new approach to maximum matching in general graphs. Automata Languages Program 443:586–597. doi:10.1007/BFb0032060
8. Gabow HN, Tarjan RE (1991) Faster scaling algorithms for general graph matching problems. J ACM 38(4):815–853. doi:10.1145/115234.115366
9. Hell P, Klein S, Nogueira LT, Protti F (2005) Packing r-cliques in weighted chordal graphs. Ann Oper Res 138:179–187
10. Czygrinow A, Hańćkowiak M (2007) Distributed approximations for packing in unit-disk graphs. Distr Comput 4731:152–164. doi:10.1007/978-3-540-75142-7_14
11. Czygrinow A, Hańćkowiak M, Wawrzyniak W (2008) Distributed packing in planar graphs. In: Proceedings of the twentieth annual symposium on parallelism in algorithms and architectures. SPAA '08. ACM, New York. pp 55–61. doi:10.1145/1378533.1378541
12. Kann V (1994) Maximum bounded h-matching is max snp-complete. Inform Process Lett 49(6):309–318. doi:10.1016/0020-0190(94)90105-8
13. Crescenzi P, Kann V (1998) A compedium of NP optimization problems. http://www.nada.kth.se/~viggo/problemlist/compendium.html
14. Kirkpatrick DG, Hell P (1978) On the completeness of a generalized matching problem. In: STOC '78 proceedings of the tenth annual ACM symposium on theory of computing. pp 240–245
15. Gabow HN (1990) Data structures for weighted matching and nearest common ancestors with linking. In: SODA '90: proceedings of the first annual, ACM-SIAM symposium on discrete algorithms. Society for Industrial and Applied Mathematics, Philadelphia. pp 434–443
16. Hoepman J-H (2004) Simple Distributed Weighted Matchings. http://arxiv.org/abs/cs/0410047
17. Lotker Z, Patt-Shamir B, Pettie S (2008) Improved distributed approximate matching. In: SPAA '08: proceedings of the twentieth annual symposium on parallelism in algorithms and architectures. ACM, New York. pp 129–136. doi:10.1145/1378533.1378558
18. Nieberg T (2008) Local, distributed weighted matching on general and wireless topologies. ACM, New York. doi:10.1145/1400863.1400880
19. Manne F, Mjelde M (2007) A self-stabilizing weighted matching algorithm. In: Stabilization, safety, and security of distributed systems. LNCS, vol 4838/2007. pp 383–393. doi:10.1007/978-3-540-76627-8_29
20. Hassin R, Rubinstein S (2006) An approximation algorithm for maximum triangle packing. Discrete Appl Math 154(6):971–979
21. Chen Z-Z, Tanahashi R, Wang L (2009) An improved randomized approximation algorithm for maximum triangle packing. Discrete Appl Math 157(7):1640–1646. doi:10.1016/j.dam.2008.11.009
22. Preis R (1999) Linear time 1/2-approximation algorithm for maximum weighted matching in general graphs. In: In STACS 99: proceedings symposium on theoretical aspects of computer science. Springer, Berlin. pp 259–269. doi:10.1007/3-540-49116-3_24
23. Avis D (1983) A survey of heuristics for the weighted matching problem. Networks 13:475–493. doi:10.1002/net.3230130404
24. Chmielowiec A (2014) Decentralized k-clique matching. PhD thesis. Vrije Universiteit Amsterdam
25. Brimberg J, Mladenovic N, Urosevic D, Ngai E (2009) Variable neighborhood search for the heaviest k-subgraph. Comput Oper Res 36(11):2885–2891. doi:10.1016/j.cor.2008.12.020
26. Gendreau M, Potvin J-Y(eds.) (2010) Handbook of metaheuristicsInternational, Series in Operations Research & Management Science, vol. 146. Springer, New York. doi:10.1007/978-1-4419-1665-5
27. Hansen P, Mladenović N, Moreno Pérez JA (2010) Variable neighbourhood search: methods and applications. Ann Oper Res 175(1):367–407. doi:10.1007/s10479-009-0657-6
28. Kermarrec A-M, van Steen M (2007) Gossiping in distributed systems. SIGOPS Oper Syst Rev 41(5):2–7. doi:10.1145/1317379.1317381
29. Jelasity M, Voulgaris S, Guerraoui R, Kermarrec A-M, van Steen M (2007) Gossip-based peer sampling. ACM Trans Comput Syst 25(3):8. doi:10.1145/1275517.1275520
30. Jelasity M, Montresor A, Jesi GP, Voulgaris S The Peersim Simulator. http://peersim.sourceforge.net/

15

Using popular social network sites to support requirements elicitation, prioritization and negotiation

Norbert Seyff[1,2]*, Irina Todoran[2], Kevin Caluser[2], Leif Singer[3] and Martin Glinz[2]

Abstract

Social networks have changed our daily life and they have the potential to significantly influence and support Requirements Engineering (RE) activities. Social network-based RE approaches will allow us to overcome limitations of traditional approaches and allow end users to play a more prominent role in RE. They are key stakeholders in many software projects. However, involving end users is challenging, particularly when they are not within organizational reach. The goal of our work is to increase end user involvement in RE. In this paper we present an approach where we harness a social network to perform RE activities such as elicitation, prioritization and negotiation. Our approach was applied in three studies where students used Facebook to actively participate in RE activities of different projects. Although there are limitations, the results show that a popular social network site can support distributed RE.

Keywords: Requirements engineering; Social network sites; End user involvement

1 Introduction

The involvement of stakeholders such as future system end users is a key success factor for Software Engineering (SE) in general, and for Requirements Engineering (RE) in particular [1].

Several process models are available to describe RE activities [2]. Key activities include requirements elicitation, prioritization and negotiation. *Requirements elicitation* is the process of seeking, capturing and consolidating requirements from available requirements sources (e.g. stakeholders) [3]. The requirements gathered should be prioritized. The *priority* of a requirement shows its importance in comparison to others; it also helps decide which requirements to include in a project [3,4]. Furthermore, prioritization supports *requirements negotiation* which focuses on conflict resolution by finding a settlement that mostly satisfies all stakeholders [5].

Some approaches foster the involvement of success-critical stakeholders (e.g. end users) in requirements elicitation, prioritization and negotiation [6]. However, these approaches do not sufficiently support non-traditional contexts such as mobile computing [7], cloud computing [8] or software ecosystems [9]. This is due to the fact that in these contexts, we need to involve a large number of heterogeneous, globally distributed and potentially anonymous stakeholders [10]. Although the underlying idea of involving success-critical stakeholders is still valid in those settings, there is a lack of suitable elicitation techniques [8] and novel RE approaches and methods are needed to give end users their own voice [11].

In order to be successful and to cope with short time-to-market periods, the methods used need to be fast, easy and inexpensive. However, most state-of-the-art RE approaches and tools are built from an RE perspective and require end users to get familiar with a particular system and procedure. We therefore envision that novel RE approaches will focus on the end user perspective.

For this, we have investigated the potential of popular social network sites (SNS) for requirements elicitation, prioritization and negotiation. Considering the number of registered users and regional popularity, we selected four candidates for our studies: Facebook, Twitter, LinkedIn

*Correspondence: norbert.seyff@fhnw.ch

[1]University of Applied Sciences and Arts Northwestern Switzerland, Bahnhofstrasse 6, Windisch, Switzerland

[2]University of Zurich, Binzmühlestrasse 14, Zurich, Switzerland

Full list of author information is available at the end of the article

and Google+. From these, Facebook [12] was chosen as the support for this research. Today, many end users are familiar with social network sites in general and Facebook in particular. By using a platform that is part of end users' daily lives, we aim to overcome current limitations of RE tools in terms of end user acceptance and involvement.

However, from an RE perspective, this strategy can cause new problems. Popular social network sites have not been designed for RE and might therefore not support RE activities adequately. Therefore, our aim is to investigate whether and how existing functionalities of a current social network site can support RE activities. To our knowledge, these are the first exploratory studies that research the possibility of using social network sites for meeting RE needs. Our exploratory studies with students and their Facebook friends lead to qualitative data showing that Facebook provides basic capabilities to support RE activities. Moreover, our findings show the advantages and limitations of an SNS-based approach for the RE activities mentioned.

Following the EasyWinWin methodology [6], we foresee that our lightweight and end user focused RE approach has many potential applications. We particularly see its relevance within novel software paradigms such as mobile and cloud computing and software ecosystems, where end users are not within immediate reach and where the support provided by traditional methods is insufficient. For example, smartphone application developers or cloud service providers could use our approach to elicit, prioritize and negotiate stakeholder needs. In software ecosystems, our approach provides a new channel for eliciting ideas and needs as well as receiving feedback from stakeholders who are not directly reachable by product owners or development teams. Moreover, we also see its application within traditional software projects as an additional means for involving end users.

The remainder of the paper is structured as follows: In Section 2, we discuss the research goal and questions. Section 3 gives an overview on how current social software is being used within the field of RE. In Section 4, we present a generic SNS-based RE approach. Section 5 introduces candidate SNS suitable for implementing our approach. In Sections 6 to 9 we report on three exploratory studies where students and their friends applied our approach with Facebook. After revisiting the research questions and discussing threats to validity in Section 10, we conclude the paper and present potential future research directions in Section 11.

2 Research goal and questions

The goal of our research is to investigate whether and how popular social network sites have the potential to support RE activities. We identified three research questions (RQ) to define the focus of our research:

RQ 1: Can a social network site support requirements elicitation, prioritization and negotiation? If so, how can existing features be used to elicit, prioritize and negotiate end users' requirements?

Firstly, we are interested in finding out whether existing features exhibited by a social network site such as Facebook can help gathering, prioritizing and negotiating users' requirements. To answer this question, we set up three exploratory studies and analyse their results. Moreover, we investigate how the existing features can be utilized, i.e. how an RE activity should be designed to make good use of the SNS features.

RQ 2: What are the benefits of using a social network site approach compared to existing elicitation, prioritization and negotiation techniques?

Secondly, we identify in what ways and under which circumstance such an SNS approach is better suited than traditional RE methods. Additionally, we investigate how this approach could potentially complement existing techniques.

RQ 3: What are the challenges and limitations of using a social network site for requirements elicitation, prioritization and negotiation?

Thirdly, we analyse potential issues associated with using an SNS approach to support RE activities, including their limitations. Relying on our findings, we elaborate preliminary guidelines that can be followed when utilizing SNS for RE activities.

3 Related work: RE and social software

Requirements Engineering is a multidisciplinary field [13] that requires active communication and interaction between different stakeholders. Depending on the project, its activities may be interleaved, iterative and span across the entire software life cycle [14]. Although various RE reference process models exist [15,16], it is generally agreed upon that early RE activities include (1) requirements elicitation and (2) requirements analysis and negotiation [14]. For each of these activities, there are several sub-activities that vary between projects – e.g. identifying key stakeholders, brainstorming stakeholder interests, prioritizing ideas and negotiating them [17]. Several RE approaches and tools follow these high level models and provide step-by-step guidance and support (e.g. EasyWinWin [6,17]). However, it might be hard for an end user to understand the sequence of activities, sub-activities and their respective purpose. Our work is inspired by EasyWinWin which focuses on providing support for requirements elicitation, prioritization and negotiation.

Social network sites are an example of social software and used for connecting and communicating with others – anytime and anywhere. Boyd and Ellison [18] describe social network sites as web-based services that allow individuals to (1) maintain a public or semi-public profile within a particular system, (2) maintain a list of connected users (e.g. *friends*), people with whom they share a connection and (3) view and follow connections made by themselves and by other users. Social network sites usually either target a specific user group (e.g. private people, business people or even specific groups such as photographers) or support a specific task (e.g. StakeSource [19] as an example for a social network site supporting RE activities).

The idea of using social software for supporting such RE activities has been explored by both researchers and practitioners throughout the recent years. This section presents related work focusing on strengthening end user involvement in RE with the help of social software. While conducting the analysis, we identified three categories of tool support. The first represents *work on dedicated RE tools that include concepts of social software.*

The idea of using social tools for RE and software design is not new - it was already discussed by Conklin and Begeman in their 1988 paper on gIBIS: a hypertext tool for exploratory policy discussion. This was also meant to be used in early RE activities such as design deliberations. The tool implements the IBIS method, which was designed to solve complex design problems by taking the perspectives of the stakeholders involved [20].

More recent research focuses on identifying and prioritizing stakeholders. This is supported by StakeSource which is a lightweight web-based tool implementing the StakeNet method [19]. The work by Lim et al. is based on social network analysis as well as collaborative filtering and provides requirements engineers with a list of the key stakeholders. The method requires an initial set of already identified stakeholders who themselves identify and suggest new stakeholders (snowballing effect). In addition, StakeSource provides basic capabilities to identify, negotiate and prioritize requirements [19]. Although this approach is rather straightforward, stakeholders need to make themselves familiar with the forms that allow entering and rating requirements.

According to the authors, SoftWiki is well suited for end users not familiar with RE practices. It is a dedicated web-based tool that allows stakeholders to enter and manage requirements themselves [21]. To make the processing by requirements engineers easier later on, the tool incorporates semantic web technologies [22]. However, end users would still have to learn how to use the tool. Letting end users structure and annotate requirements with semantics can bring further challenges and create a barrier for end users participation.

In their work on WinBook, Kukreja and Boehm [23,24] explore social network functionalities to develop a new avatar of the WinWin framework [6]. Early evaluation results suggest that the toolset supports non-technical stakeholders in negotiating requirements. However, no more in depth evaluation studies have been conducted yet.

The second category we identified is *work that describes the use of existing social software to support RE and also SE activities.*

Early work in this field focused on comparing asynchronous text chats to face-to-face meetings for requirements negotiation [25]. The study conducted with geographically distributed students revealed that face-to-face meetings become more effective if they are preceded by text-based, asynchronous discussions. This resolved several conflicts and reduced the workload in the following physical meetings. However, the use of chats was only complementary to the physical meetings and therefore not sufficient on its own.

Researchers such as Maalej et al. [26,27] highlight the importance of end user involvement in today's software development projects. They promote a conceptual framework which combines several existing techniques for better handling continuous user input during the elicitation phase.

A particular approach supporting elicitation and product development is presented by Hess et al. [28] who report on participatory product development in and with online communities. Their work represents an example of user-centered, community-based requirements elicitation as part of participatory design. They targeted a large population of heterogeneous and globally distributed users and facilitated the interaction by using online tools. Moreover, they demonstrate that the role of user representatives is vital when managing heterogeneity in an online community.

Apart from research, companies have started to include social media in their software development processes. Bajic and Lyons present a study on social media used by different software development companies [29]. They figured out that, in an early stage, especially small companies use social media to gather feedback from their customers. It is unclear, however, how far companies integrate these initiatives into their development processes and whether they use traditional RE approaches at all.

Companies such as UserVoice.com [30] have started to reduce barriers for involving end users in the software development process by providing a service that allows software companies to gather feedback from their customers. Other organizations already use existing social media tools, such as Facebook and Twitter [31]. It is however unclear whether the use of these tools goes beyond the purposes of marketing and public relations.

A third category of relevant research we have identified is the *work that focuses on the analysis of data documented within SNS.*

Currently, there are attempts to utilize users' reviews that can be found in app stores for mobile platforms to mine requirements or extract features. For instance,

Harman et al. use data mining techniques to extract feature information which is then used to analyse technical, business and customer aspects of the apps. Such approaches target large-scale, unknown and heterogeneous audiences [32].

In their research, Guzman and Maalej [33] also focus on analysing user reviews in app stores. They have developed an automated approach that supports developers in filtering, aggregating and analysing user reviews in order to conduct a fine-grained sentiment analysis.

Apart from research including or focusing on the end user perspective, there is research focusing on developers. For example, Singer et al. have investigated how developers stay current using Twitter [34]. Furthermore, researchers are starting to mine information stored in GitHub [35] to better understand how developers collaborate [36]. This research also focuses on open source software development. However, we would like to highlight that in our work we are focusing on the end user perspective, investigating how end user involvement can be strengthened in RE activities.

We conclude that there are manifold ways of using social software for RE. Dedicated RE tools based on social software allow the involvement of end users in the RE process. However, these tools might still require end user training and other additional effort (e.g. registration) before RE activities can take place. Apart from dedicated RE methods and tools, researchers and practitioners are using existing social software to support RE and SE activities. This means that instead of providing methods and tools which are fully based on using the functionality of an SNS, those functionalities are only used in part to complement existing processes. We conclude that current attempts to use existing social software tools in an RE context are still in an early stage.

4 Designing a social network site-supported RE approach for requirements elicitation, prioritization and negotiation

Following our research goal to investigate whether and how popular SNS can support RE activities, we aimed at providing a generic RE approach based on well-known social network functionalities. This approach should present RE activities from an end user perspective and require neither lengthy process guidance nor support documents. It should be usable ad hoc, anytime and anywhere to allow distributed requirements elicitation, prioritization and negotiation in an iterative manner.

Inspired by EasyWinWin, our approach is driven by a moderator, a person who has an interest in the system to be, and whose aim is to gather requirements for that system. Our solution is designed to also require minimal training for the moderator (e.g. a mobile app developer

who would like to gather requirements from potential end users).

We distinguish three high-level activities and detailed steps which require the participation of the moderator, stakeholders (e.g. end users) or both. Those activities and steps can also be interpreted as requirements an SNS has to satisfy so that it is possible to apply the approach we propose.

The first activity contains *required preparation activities (1)*. The moderator undertakes the following steps:

1.1 Set up a space for discussion: As a first step, the moderator creates a discussion space (e.g. a group) with an appropriate title for the project at hand. The moderator can decide to create an open or a private discussion space.

1.2 Provide key information about the project: The moderator provides the initial information (such as a vision statement for the project). This information should be structured and it should be possible to discuss several topics - e.g. information about the project, instructions for the participants.

The second high-level activity implements *requirements elicitation, prioritization and negotiation activities (2)*. The following tasks are mainly performed by the participating stakeholders (e.g. end users), guided by the moderator. It should be noted that steps 2.1 through 2.4 are running simultaneously and in an iterative manner. They will not necessarily follow a strict sequence.

2.1 Invitation of participants: The moderator invites stakeholders to the group. The invitation itself might include key information about the project and purpose of the group. Depending on the project, the moderator can ask invitees to support the stakeholder identification by inviting more participants.

2.2 Participants brainstorm ideas: The moderator invites stakeholders to begin posting their ideas, needs, and concerns that can later be turned into well-defined requirements for the project.

2.3 Participants discuss ideas: As soon as ideas are posted, stakeholders can start a discussion. They can ask questions for clarification and post issues they identify regarding a certain idea. This allows the inclusion of several different stakeholder perspectives. The moderator should now engage with the participants in order to stimulate and steer the negotiation – e.g. by asking questions for further clarification.

2.4 Participants approve and prioritize ideas: Participants communicate their approval of ideas and comments in this step. It can help to guide the direction of a discussion. Furthermore, the number of approvals given for an idea or comment can highlight its importance.

The third high-level activity implements *requirements analysis and follow-up (3)*, and is performed by the moderator:

3.1 Transcribe ideas into prioritized requirements: Stakeholder (e.g. end user) contributions may vary in quantity, quality and content. Although the moderator is available during discussions, we do not expect the process output to provide high quality requirements descriptions. As a last step, he can transcribe initial user needs into well-defined requirements. By analyzing the number of approvals per idea, the moderator can also define the priority of requirements. For this analysis we do not request explicit support from an SNS. It strongly depends on the skills and expertise of the moderator.

We conclude that in order to support the approach depicted, an SNS has to fulfill the following key requirements:

R1: The SNS must enable users to communicate ideas.

R2: The SNS must enable users to comment on ideas.

R3: The SNS must enable users to express approval for ideas and comments.

R4: The SNS must enable users to control content distribution.

R5: The SNS must provide a dedicated space for group discussions.

R6: The SNS must enable users to control group access.

5   Analyzing social network sites for RE support

Facebook, Twitter, LinkedIn [37] and Google+ [38] are prominent examples of SNS that have millions of registered users. We choose them to become our candidates for an implementation of our generic RE approach since all of them have a high number of registered and active users - according to the statistics provided by Alexa [39]. Another criterion was regional popularity – the selected SNS are popular in central Europe where we performed our exploratory studies. In order to identify the most suitable SNS, two of the authors performed an initial comparison after we had defined the key requirements for our generic SNS-supported RE approach.

We investigated which of their features would allow us to support the predefined key requirements (Table 1).

Our analysis revealed that all would allow an individual end user to express an idea – i.e. a requirement, a need (R1). Apart from Twitter, all platforms would allow users to post comments (R2). Except Twitter, all social networks allow people connected to publicly express their approval of an idea (R3). This, for example, includes *like* in Facebook or *+1* in Google+. Twitter contains similar mechanisms (retweet, favorite), but only notifies the owner of a post. Facebook, Twitter and Google+ users are even able to restrict the access to their ideas and can therefore control the distribution of the content (R4). In LinkedIn, however, an idea is automatically shared with all connected people.

Although people could discuss an idea on a user profile, we consider a single, protected (private) and dedicated space for group discussions to be more adequate (R5). Facebook, LinkedIn and Google+ allow their users to create such a space. Those *groups* represent a dedicated space for discussing and communicating ideas and allow the moderator to invite stakeholders and manage user settings – e.g. define whether group members may invite additional contacts (R6).

After an initial comparison of the four social network sites, we concluded that three out of four would allow us to instantiate and apply our generic SNS-supported RE approach. Although all three candidates (i.e. Facebook, LinkedIn and Google+) would have fulfilled our initial requirements, we selected Facebook to become the platform for further investigation. Our main reasons were: (1) Facebook has over a billion users worldwide and is currently the leading social network site; and (2) the target group for our experimental studies (students and their friends) would be more likely to already have an account and be accustomed to Facebook.

6   SNS as an RE tool - exploratory studies

We performed three exploratory studies with a popular SNS (i.e. Facebook) to evaluate our SNS-supported RE approach. Our aim was to apply it in settings where moderators have limited RE knowledge and where potential end users for the systems under discussion are available to participate. We targeted projects with real-world character but which would still allow some level of control regarding the participants and the topics discussed. While designing our studies, we had in mind the metaphor of a mobile app developer who would set up a group on Facebook and act as moderator; this in order to gather

Table 1 Initial comparison of social network sites

Requirements	Facebook	Twitter	LinkedIn	Google+
R1: Users communicate ideas	✓	✓	✓	✓
R2: Users comment on ideas	✓	✓	✓	✓
R3: Users express approval	✓	✗	✓	✓
R4: Control content distribution	✓	✓	✗	✓
R5: Dedicated space for group disc.	✓	✗	✓	✓
R6: Control group access	✓	✗	✓	✓

requirements for a new app he is planning to realize or to elicit requirements for the evolution of an existing app. The developer could then, for example, invite existing end users of his app(s) for a discussion. Based on this metaphor we decided to perform evaluation studies within RE lectures in Switzerland and Austria, where students basically have some, but limited, RE knowledge. Those students acted as moderators and invited potential end users (other students and friends) to requirements discussions on Facebook. In Study I and Study II the evaluation was presented as an exercise to train the students' moderation skills and to also highlight the dynamics of distributed RE for those students who were participating as end users. In Study III the evaluation was conducted to gather requirements for real-world projects the students were involved in.

All studies followed an approach where we first had a briefing session. This for example included the presentation of a description of the RE approach as depicted in Section 4. However, students were not told that they were using a novel RE approach. The briefing session was followed by the actual evaluation. In all three studies students were given a timeframe of two weeks to conduct their requirements engineering activities. However, in Study I, students would have had the option to prolong the given period. We did not interact with the students during this period. The evaluation was followed by a debriefing either directly with the students or using a questionnaire. The debriefing meetings were held to understand the benefits and limitations of the process. Facebook friends, who were invited to the discussion in some studies, were not involved in the debriefing activities. This means that in those studies the debriefing focused on the moderator who always was a student.

The studies were performed in sequential order. Therefore, the output of a preceding study supported us in defining the scope of the following study in more detail. The results of each study were analyzed by at least two authors of the paper as soon as the study was finished. One of the authors performed a qualitative analysis as described below and the first author reviewed those results for all three studies. He also checked the validity of the requirements gathered (i.e. are they relevant and useful for the implementation of the system under discussion and will they satisfy user needs?).

The third author acted as the main analyst and performed the analysis for two of the three studies. The remaining study was analyzed by the second author of the paper and results were reviewed and approved by the third author before the first author conducted a final review.

As a first step the author conducting the analysis exported all the data from Facebook to Microsoft Excel. This was done by copying and pasting the data. The following content analysis of the data gathered included the task of identifying the type of the content posted. We distinguished *elicitation, negotiation, moderation* and *other* posts. In this context, *elicitation posts* refer to statements communicating a new idea; *negotiation posts* discuss an idea; *moderation posts* represent statements from the moderator or other participants to facilitate the discussion; *other posts* refer to any other statements identified in the discussions. To better understand the nature of the posts, we applied a goal-design level metrics for categorization [40]. We distinguished the following categories: *goal-level, domain- and product-level* and *design-level* posts. We extracted the total number of distinct requirements from the end users' posts and differentiated between functional and non-functional requirements. The non-functional were classified according to Volere [41,42].

The following sections present the three studies in detail. We discuss the different settings, the methods used, the results and the findings. For the quantitative analysis, we report on key numbers (e.g. invited stakeholders, participating stakeholders, active days, generated posts, distinct requirements). For calculating some of these numbers, we had to define metrics. For example, we defined *active days* as days where some group interaction took place, (e.g. stakeholders being added, ideas being posted, comments added to discussions).

7   Evaluation study I

The first study was conducted at FHNW University of Applied Sciences in Switzerland. Participants were second term iCompetence Bachelor students. The iCompetence curriculum includes design and management oriented subjects in addition to computer science courses. In their first term, the students get an overview on software engineering and programming. At this time they are typically in their early twenties. In contrast to other computer science studies, the students of iCompetence include a large number of female students (typically more than 50%).

7.1   Method

The study was presented as an exercise within the RE course (taught by the first author). This course gives an introduction to Requirements Engineering and discusses topics similar to the content requested by the IREB CPRE certification schema [43]. The goal of the exercise from the students' perspective was to train their moderation skills and to give them the chance to experience distributed RE with stakeholders. We made clear that the exercise would not be graded. In general, students were familiar with Facebook and also used it to stay in touch with their friends and colleagues.

The evaluation was in three parts: briefing, evaluation and debriefing. During the briefing, the students were informed of the purpose of the exercise and the task they were about to perform. We presented the process depicted in Section 4 and asked the students to think of a software-intensive system that they would like to gather requirements for (e.g. the fridge of the future, a personal finance manager). For each group a moderator was chosen; he invited Facebook friends (people who could be potential end users or who have a general interest in the topic) to discuss the topic in a Facebook group. During the evaluation, we did not contact students to give advice. In this first study we suggested a timeframe of two weeks to conduct the experiment but, as we were not aware of the dynamics of our RE approach, we did not strictly limit this timeframe. We told them to start immediately and to inform us when the group discussions had stopped, which in all the cases was within the two weeks timeframe we suggested. In the debriefing, we discussed the results with the students and asked them to fill out an online questionnaire on how they experienced requirements elicitation, prioritization and negotiation using Facebook. After the debriefing meetings, we accessed the group discussions and started to analyze the students' contributions.

7.2 Results

In total, 17 students and 74 external persons were involved in this study discussing requirements within 8 different Facebook groups (see Table 2). The students came up with innovative ideas for potential software systems. Those ideas were focusing on novel systems and also on the evolution of existing systems.

Group 1, for example, discussed requirements for a mobile app which supports healthy cooking by providing adequate recipes. Students discussed requirements such as that the app should know about the allergies of its user. Group 2 investigated how the agenda planner of the future should look like. They envisioned a ubiquitous system and requested, for example, an agenda available also when driving a car and that the car should present the agenda on the windscreen. Group 3 focused on the fridge of the future and discussed requirements such as the automatic generation of shopping lists. Group 4 elaborated how media could be consumed in the future and were, for example, requesting to replace remote controls with alternative solutions. Group 5 investigated the functionality of future SNS such as Facebook. For example, they suggested the SNS should be able to provide more information on the character of a person by analysing available content. Group 6 was looking for requirements for an app which should support their studies. For example, they discussed the option to get information about students in the same courses. Group 7 caused quite some discussion as the goal was to provide an app which would support someone who would like to become a dropout (i.e. a hermit). Requirements included guidelines for building shelters and huts, also a function which would warn the hermit of poisonous food (e.g. mushrooms). Group 8 discussed requirements for a personal finance manager app. Requirements included that the app automatically tracks the money spent on certain goods (e.g. clothes).

As some students participated in several groups, the eight Facebook groups considered in this analysis contained a total of 184 stakeholders. However, on average only 31% responded positively – meaning that 57 stakeholders joined the groups and actively contributed to the Facebook discussions (e.g. by posting comments and using likes). Therefore, the average of Facebook friends involved in each group was about seven members, with a minimum of four and a maximum of 11.

Table 2 Study I - Results

	Gr 1	Gr 2	Gr 3	Gr 4	Gr 5	Gr 6	Gr 7	Gr 8	Avg
Invited people	37	17	27	17	24	18	23	21	23
Contributing people	12	4	11	4	7	5	6	8	7.1
Active days	4	4	4	2	4	5	7	4	4.3
Total posts	39	10	28	10	24	12	33	18	21.8
% Elicitation posts	54	90	79	40	75	100	76	61	71.9
% Negotiation posts	31	10	21	60	25	0	24	39	26.3
% Moderation posts	13	0	0	0	0	0	0	0	1.6
% Other posts	3	0	0	0	0	0	0	0	0.4
Distinct requirements	22	10	22	8	21	13	23	16	16.9
% Functional req.	82	90	73	75	90	69	83	100	82.9
% Non-functional req.	18	10	27	25	10	31	17	0	17.1
Likes	12	4	33	4	42	5	9	10	14.9

On average, the groups were active for 4.3 days. While the shortest discussion lasted only for two days, the maximum was seven days. Figure 1 aggregates the eight different groups of Study I and highlights the distribution of the different kinds of posts over time.

The 57 contributing stakeholders created 174 posts, thus generating an average of 3.1 posts per participant. There were no major differences among the eight groups (Table 2).

For the qualitative analysis, we categorized posts by the type of content they represented (Table 2). A very high number (71.9%) were elicitation posts discussing new ideas. 26.3% were negotiation posts whereas the moderation and other posts were rather rare (1.6% and 0.4% respectively).

We also analyzed the elicitation posts regarding the level of abstraction of needs posted [40]. The most numerous posts could be aligned with the domain and product-level requirements category (96%), with only 1.9% discussing goals and 2.4% implementation details.

We analyzed the number of *likes* in order to get an idea on the priority of the needs posted. On average, a participant used the *like* functionality 2.1 times. However, the use of *likes* varied significantly between the groups (see Table 2).

An analysis of the posts allowed us to extract 135 distinct requirements. We identified duplicates and overlaps which revealed that, on average, each of the eight groups gathered 16.9 requirements resulting in 2.4 distinct requirements per active participant. The majority of the participants posted ideas that led to functional requirements (82.9%). The 23 non-functional requirements collected referred mostly to look and feel needs (56.5%), followed by usability requirements (17.4%), performance (8.7%), environmental (8.7%), security (4.4%) and cultural requirements (4.3%).

7.3 Findings

This study investigated whether and how end users were able to participate in an SNS-supported RE approach and whether students with limited RE knowledge were able to facilitate the approach. The main findings of this study are highlighted below:

1.1 End users were able to follow the process and communicated their needs: As shown by the results, following the approach proposed and without training, end users were able to express their needs and discuss ideas on Facebook. By analyzing the ideas and needs communicated by end users, we were able to identify a high number of requirements. For example, the group discussing needs for the Fridge of the Future mentioned: *"The fridge suggests recipes that take into account the current content of the fridge".*

1.2 Moderation was insufficient: Although moderators were present, they did not fully play their role. They also got involved in elicitation and negotiation activities (e.g. posted new ideas). We could only identify dedicated moderation posts in one group (see Table 2). One main reason might be the students' limited RE knowledge and moderation experience.

1.3 Most of the content was created within the first days: In this study, all moderators mostly invited stakeholders only at the beginning of the discussion. An analysis of the group discussions revealed that most content was created after participants were invited. This suggests that participants are only active in the group discussion for a limited amount of time.

1.4 Prioritization results were insufficient: Some groups hardly used the like functionality (see Table 2). The *likes* provided by the participants were not sufficient to build a prioritized list of requirements. However, we were able to identify some favorites in most groups.

1.5 No snowball effect: We had expected some *"friends of friends"* to join the discussion. In half the groups, none of the friends invited took part in the stakeholder identification. In the other groups, some participants invited friends. However, there was no real snowball effect, especially as the contribution of *"friends of friends"* did not even result in one single requirement.

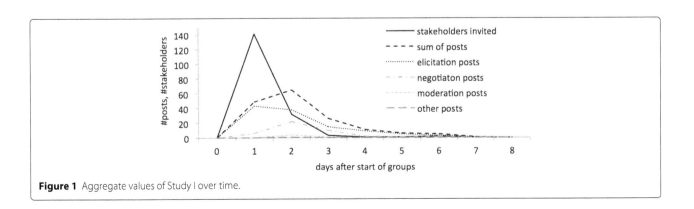

Figure 1 Aggregate values of Study I over time.

8 Evaluation study II

The second study was conducted at the University of Zurich in Switzerland. The participants were seven computer science graduate students. All of them had successfully completed an undergraduate course on RE and some of them already had industrial experience.

8.1 Method

The study was presented as an exercise in an advanced course on RE (taught by the fifth author) where selected RE topics are discussed with students. Again, this exercise had no impact on the students' grades. As in the first study, the evaluation was structured into briefing, evaluation and debriefing phases. In the briefing session, the students were advised to work with Facebook and invite friends – but not fellow students – in order to train their moderation skills and experience requirements elicitation and negotiation with stakeholders. We further told them not to invite all friends at once and to ask their friends to additionally invite other friends who might be interested in the topic. Furthermore, we asked them to explicitly invite the participants to use the *like* functionality as soon as the discussion had produced stable needs. This time, we defined upfront two discussion topics we knew all participants would be familiar with – the *Fridge of the Future (FoF)* and the *Smartphone of the Future (SoF)*. While four student moderators chose the first topic, the remaining three wanted to discuss needs regarding the SoF.

As several groups were discussing the same topic, we asked the students to consolidate and aggregate their results after the individual discussions. Furthermore, they were advised to invite all participating discussants for a final prioritization using likes. As the group of students

also included one of the authors of this paper, we chose to exclude his group when we presented the analysis of the results. During the exercise, we had no contact with the students and no access to their groups. We limited the timeframe of the exercise to two weeks and told the students to start immediately. We conducted a debriefing meeting to explore the students' experiences after the exercise and requested access to their groups for further analysis of the results.

8.2 Results

The six moderators invited a total of 73 friends, 38.4% became active members of the groups (28 friends). In the smallest group, there were two active participants while the largest group had seven contributors. On average, the participation was 4.7 friends per group. Groups were active for an average of four days – the longest discussion lasted six days while the shortest took two days (Table 3). The six groups generated a total of 131 posts with 78 posts originating from the FoF groups and 53 from the SoF groups. The result is an average 6.5 and 3.3 posts respectively per contributor. 18.7% of the posts in the three FoF groups were elicitation posts. 29.7% of the posts focused on negotiation, 46% on moderation and 5.6% were other posts. In the SoF groups we identified 48.7% elicitation, 20.7% negotiation, 26.6% moderation and 4% other posts. For example, in their posts, participants were asking for longer battery run times (elicitation post). The moderator requested a more detailed discussion (moderation post) and other participants started a negotiation. One participant requested that the battery of the smartphone of the future should at least last for 16 hours, while another participant's vision included a smartphone which

Table 3 Study II - Results

	SoF1	SoF2	SoF3	Avg SoF	FoF1	FoF2	FoF3	Avg FoF	Author
Invited people	8	6	13	9.0	32	9	5	15.3	19
Contributing people	6	5	5	5.3	7	2	3	4.0	11.0
Active days	5	4	4	4.3	6	2	3	3.7	8.0
Total posts	17	12	24	17.7	47	18	13	26.0	168.0
% Elicitation posts	70	42	34	48.7	19	6	31	18.7	26.0
% Negotiation posts	12	17	33	20.7	28	38	23	29.7	44.0
% Moderation posts	18	33	29	26.6	36	56	46	46.0	8.0
% Other posts	0	8	4	4.0	17	0	0	5.6	21.0
Distinct Requirements	13	7	14	11.3	34	14	15	21.0	80.0
Consolidated req. SoF: 26					**Consolidated req. FoF: 48**				
% Functional req.	46	29	36	36.8	74	79	80	77.4	90.0
% Non-functional req.	54	71	64	63.2	26	21	20	22.6	10.0
Likes individual groups	8	2	8	6.0	2	6	0	2.7	38.0
Likes consolidated	38	29	22	29.7	13	26	24	21.0	98.0

would not run out of battery at all by using novel energy sources such as solar energy.

We analyzed the posts' abstraction level. Regarding the FoF, most posts referred to domain- and product-level details (77.3%). The remainder discussed design-level details (21%) and goals (1.7%). For the SoF, 17.6% of the posts discussed goals, 55% domain- and product-level requirements and 27.4% design-level details. These posts led to a total of 63 (FoF) and 34 (SoF) requirements. While the FoF groups mainly gathered functional requirements (77.4%), the SoF groups found more non-functional requirements (63.2%). The 35 non-functional requirements (NFR) mostly referred to needs regarding look and feel (40% FoF, 50% SoF) and usability (40% FoF, 30% SoF), but also performance (13.3% FoF, 20% SoF) and environmental issues (6.7% FoF, 0% SoF). For example, participants requested that the SoF should be no thicker than 5.0 mm.

After the individual group discussions, we consolidated the requirements gathered. The moderators identified overlaps regarding requirements among the different groups. 11 duplicates could be found within the FoF topic and 3 within the SoF topic. For example, all groups discussing the FoF highlighted the need to be informed when the food is approaching its expiration date. After the moderators entered the transcribed requirements in a new Facebook group, participants were invited to prioritize. 88% of the participants who had contributed to the individual group discussions also participated in this phase. They used the *like* functionality 152 times (63 for FoF, 89 for SoF) giving an average of 5.6 *likes* per contributing participant and 2.1 *likes* per requirement. The highest rated requirements were *liked* eight times while the lowest rated requirements received no *likes* at all.

We also analyzed the results of the author's group (see Table 3). This group managed to gather 80 requirements, 13 of which could also be found in the other FoF groups. The number of requirements per contributing participant was considerably higher than the average of the other groups in Study II (7.3 compared to 3.5).

8.3 Findings

2.1 No prerequisites required for participants: The result of Study II shows that it is not necessary for a participant to have RE knowledge in order to take part in the proposed SNS-based RE approach. We discussed who students invited to the discussions in debriefing meetings. This revealed that the friends invited had various backgrounds, mostly unrelated to computer science. All of them were familiar with the topic under discussion and had a Facebook account and Facebook experience prior to the discussion. However, we did not request any more demographic data on the friends invited, this was for privacy reasons.

2.2 Factors improving success: The group of the author and FoF1 produced better results in terms of distinct requirements gathered. Analyzing the groups in more detail, we could identify three possible reasons: (1) High motivation of the moderators resulting in intensive care of the participants, (2) using friendly, lauding, and some-times funny posts to engage people in discussions and stimulate creativity and, (3) continuously inviting new participants to keep the discussions alive over a longer period of time.

2.3 Consolidation and prioritization: Although participants were not explicitly asked to use *likes* within the individual group discussions, several *likes* were generated (see Table 3). In Study II, the moderators provided consolidated requirements for each topic and invited participants to like them. This resulted in a prioritized list of requirements.

2.4 Again, no snowball effect: Although in several groups the moderators actively asked participants to invite their friends, no snowball effect occurred. One single friend of a friend joined the group, which cannot be seen as a snowball effect.

2.5 Friendship and interests made friends participate: Debriefing meetings revealed that many friends participated in order to support their friend – the moderator. Furthermore, the friends who contributed, because they were generally interested in the topic, had a sudden brilliant idea they wanted to share or they participated out of curiosity.

2.6 Knowledge and skills: Although the students adopted the role of moderator more strictly than in the first study – in terms of more moderation posts – this did not result in more requirements (16.9 in Study I vs. 16.2 in Study II on average). However, the number of requirements per contributing participant increased from 2.4 in the first study to 3.5 in the second study.

9 Evaluation study III

The third study was conducted at FH Hagenberg, a University of Applied Sciences in Austria. Second term mobile computing students who were involved in projects with industrial partners had to identify needs for their projects. We wanted to investigate whether the fact that participants have to build the systems under discussion had an effect on the outcome. The students had basic software engineering skills but had not attended an RE course before.

9.1 Method

The study was presented as an exercise within their RE course (taught by the first author). This course gives an introduction to RE and is aligned with the content requested by the IREB CPRE certification schema. In the briefing meeting, we discussed the SNS-supported

RE process with the students and advised them to invite stakeholders – friends or fellow students – who were potential end users and likely to provide requirements for their projects. Furthermore, we gave the same instructions as in Study II: ask friends to invite friends, consolidate the results of group discussions and then explicitly ask for *likes* for requirements prioritization. After the evaluation, we requested that the students answer an online questionnaire and we accessed their Facebook groups for further analysis.

9.2   Results

In total, 18 students and 81 external persons (*friends*) were involved in this study. In our study we had nine groups gathering requirements for software systems (mostly apps) they were about to develop. The customer for those apps was either from industry or an internal customer (e.g. professor) of the applied university. One additional group, where students were not involved in a particular project, was asked to gather requirements for the Smartphone of the Future (SoF). The results of this group were not considered in the later evaluation because of this different setting.

The nine groups working on real-world software projects had to gather requirements for different systems that did not exist. This means no group was discussing requirements regarding the evolution of an existing system. For example, Group 1 had to develop an app which would allow its users to control personal expenses. Group 2 had a more technical topic and was focusing on programmers as end users. Their goal was to develop an OpenGL image shader. The aim of group 3 was to build an app capable of counting the user's steps while Group 4 was working on an app which would provide the optimal push-up training for its users. Group 5 was to provide an app supporting a yearly soccer tournament. In contrast, Group 6 with their "City Detective" app had the idea to develop an app for tourists where they would play the role of detectives in order to visit important sights of a city. Group 7 was working on an app supporting the local paramedic group. Group 8 had to provide an app to manage a user's sticker collection and Group 9 was working on a friends finder app.

As some students participated in several groups, the nine Facebook groups considered in this analysis contained a total of 134 stakeholders. In total, 59 became active group members (41.2%). While 64% of the participants were fellow students, 36% were usually other Facebook friends. The smallest group had two active participants while the largest had 11. On average, 6.6 participants were engaged in a group discussion.

The groups were active for an average of 7.2 days. While the shortest discussion lasted three days, the longest took ten days. In total, the 59 participants created 290 posts. An average of 4.9 posts was generated per contributing participant (see Table 4).

Again, we categorized the posts by type of content represented. We identified an average of 41.7% elicitation posts, 35.7% negotiation posts, 21.4% moderation and 1.2% other posts. Only 2.2% of the posts reflected end user goals. Around 85.6% were assigned to the domain- and product-level category. Around 12.2% discussed design-level issues.

We were able to define 203 distinct requirements. On average, each of the nine groups gathered 22.6 requirements resulting in 3.44 distinct requirements per active

Table 4 Study III - Results

	Gr1	Gr2	Gr3	Gr4	Gr5	Gr6	Gr7	Gr8	Gr9	Avg	SoF
Invited people	33	7	21	12	28	19	8	8	7	15.9	6
Contributing people	10	5	4	7	11	7	7	2	6	6.6	3
Active days	5	5	8	9	10	9	10	6	3	7.2	6
Total posts	23	34	28	39	43	44	32	22	25	32.2	16
% Elicitation posts	35	53	21	23	76	34	41	36	56	41.7	25
% Negotiation posts	22	29	50	56	19	50	31	32	32	35.7	19
% Moderation posts	43	18	21	21	5	16	25	32	12	21.4	50
% Other posts	0	0	8	0	0	0	3	0	0	1.2	6
Distinct requirements	14	24	24	22	31	36	25	12	15	22.6	11
% Functional req.	79	63	50	73	77	86	72	92	87	75.3	45
% Non-functional req.	21	38	50	27	23	14	28	8	13	24.7	55
Likes individual groups	39	36	3	10	34	4	0	14	5	16.1	1
Likes consolidated	-	29	78	47	-	83	37	27	22	46.1	20

participant. The majority of the requirements was functional (75.3%). The 52 NFR included requirements regarding usability (19.2%), look and feel (28.9%), performance (13.5%), operation and environment (34.6%), security (1.9%) and legal (1.9%).

After the moderators consolidated the group discussions, they explicitly asked participants for *likes*. Without considering Group 1 and Group 5 who did not perform this task (see Table 4), the number of *likes* was 323 in total. On average, a participant used the *like* functionality seven times.

9.3 Findings

3.1 A motivated moderator is a success factor: The fact that students had to realize the system under discussion might have been a key motivational factor. Although the students in this study had limited RE skills (similar to the students in Study I), they were engaged moderators. This is reflected in the high number of moderation posts and the high quality of the posts. The data suggests that the students really wanted to know what end users would expect from the system to be built. This might also be reflected by the high percentage of posts referring to the design-level and the high number of moderators' posts asking for clarification. The students' high motivation might have caused the high number of requirements identified. In particular, the average number of distinct requirements gathered for industrial projects in Study III (22.6) was significantly higher than the number of requirements describing the *Smartphone of the Future* in Study III (11).

3.2 Students were satisfied with the results: Besides our analysis, we asked for their opinion on the results. For 81% of them, the results were satisfying. Furthermore, 68% stated that the use of Facebook to support requirements elicitation and negotiation was a good idea. However, the students also mentioned the limitations of Facebook, e.g. using *like* for prioritization is not precise enough and it is hard to keep sight of the overview in Facebook discussions.

3.3 Sense of duty and interest made students participate: The questionnaire revealed several reasons given by students for participating in the discussions. One main reason was that it was an exercise within a lecture and their participation was expected. Another reason was their interest in the topic and they wanted to be part of the discussion.

3.4 Minor differences between friends and fellow students: Analyzing the results, again, we could not identify any difference in the results they produced. However, we did identify issues related to the opportunity to participate. While 58.9% of the fellow students invited actually participated, on average only 27.2% of the *friends* invited joined the discussions.

3.5 Requirements prioritization worked: Moderators did not explicitly ask participants for likes before they consolidated the needs. Nevertheless, three groups gathered more than 30 likes each. This allowed for a prioritized list of requirements. Participants from other groups completely ignored this opportunity (Table 4). However, asking for likes on the consolidated requirements led to a sufficient number of *likes* for all the groups to come up with a prioritized list of requirements.

3.6 The discrepancy of the Smartphone group: In Study III, one group was not involved in an industrial project and discussed the topic *Smartphone of the Future*. Analyzing the requirements, we identified more non-functional requirements (55%). This pattern also appears in the Study II Smartphone Groups but it is different from all the other groups in our three studies. We cannot give a clear explanation but we have a hypothesis: identifying requirements for the *Smartphone of the Future* is hard for the average person. The features of smartphones were extended significantly in the last years. People are overwhelmed by new functionalities and might already be satisfied with the current capabilities of their smartphones. However, they might want an improved quality as shown by the high number of non-functional requirements.

10 Research questions revisited and threats to validity

We sought to answer the three research questions from the standpoint of our conceptual solution and the findings of the studies conducted. The empirical evidence we collected allows us to clearly identify trends. However, given the exploratory nature of the studies, we cannot present any statistically significant results.

10.1 RQ 1: Can a social network site support requirements elicitation, prioritization and negotiation? If so, how can existing features be used to elicit, prioritize and negotiate end users' requirements?

The findings of all three studies reveal that existing features of Facebook, e.g. the possibility to build dedicated groups, comment on or like posts, support RE activities such as requirements elicitation, prioritization and negotiation. Generally, end users were able to follow the process, express their needs, provide input to ongoing discussions (Finding 1.1) and prioritize requirements (Finding 3.5). They used the commenting functionality to mention what they would want the system or product to be, and the liking feature for prioritizing their needs. For these tasks, no prerequisites were required of the participants (Finding 2.1) since they were already familiar with Facebook, the chosen social network site. Moreover, the students participating in Study III, who also had to develop the system themselves, were satisfied with the needs elicited (Finding 3.2) and considered them to be valid requirements (i.e. relevant and useful for their future implementation). For all studies the first author of this paper investigated the validity of the requirements and came to the conclusion that the involvement of several stakeholders discussing their needs leads to requirements that are agreed and useful for the implementation of the system under discussion. However, as in Study I and II the output of the discussion was not used for actual system development, we do not know which of them would have actually been implemented. Also for Study III we do not know which of the requirements discussed were actually implemented.

Using an SNS-based RE approach in real-world settings could increase end user involvement in RE and support projects with a list of end user needs. This should be seen as an initial vision and not as an exhaustive list of validated requirements. As expected, the approach did not provide well-defined requirements but rather end user needs which could then be turned into requirements. The output obtained with our approach does not in any way exclude the usage of other existing elicitation and prioritization methods but rather complements them.

10.2   RQ 2: What are the benefits of using a social network site approach compared to existing elicitation, prioritization and negotiation techniques?

With the emergence of cloud systems and the growing development and popularity of smartphone and tablet applications, understanding the needs coming from geographically distributed, heterogeneous and often unknown potential users becomes increasingly challenging [8]. Therefore, there seems to be a need for RE methods that can be used in these contexts. Our social network site approach supports the gathering of needs from such audiences without adding any learning overhead to users, i.e. no prerequisites are required from the participants (Finding 2.1), given the assumption that the large majority is used to the Facebook platform. Moreover, according to our findings, the consolidation and prioritization of needs can be supported on a large scale (Finding 2.3) and the social aspect plays an important role: friendship and common interests are significant incentives for people to participate in elicitation activities (Finding 2.5). These features of our approach differ from traditional RE methods such as interviews or workshops and stem from its distinct nature: it is based on an SNS end users are already familiar with. Therefore, it can be integrated in the overall RE process to supplement existing techniques when working in contexts like the ones mentioned above. Furthermore, applying our approach within a social network adds a unique side to the RE process: new stakeholders get involved because their friends are already taking part thus embedding the participation in their relationship. This

characteristic is virtually never supported by traditional methods.

10.3   RQ 3: What are the challenges and limitations of using a social network site for requirements elicitation, prioritization and negotiation?

Naturally, there is no single general purpose RE technique. As explained under RQ2, our approach is best suited for particular contexts and should generally be used in conjunction with other existing methods. One of its limitations is that the number of needs elicited, prioritized and negotiated can overly depend on moderator's abilities and motivation (Finding 1.2). As a result, in Study I, the prioritization results were insufficient (Finding 1.4). Therefore, special care should be taken when choosing and potentially training the moderator. For instance, when the Study III moderator was highly motivated, the results obtained were satisfactory for the participants questioned (Finding 3.2). Additionally, generating a snowball effect can be challenging (Findings 1.5 and 2.4). We did hope to see this effect, which could have led to more stakeholders discussing the system under investigation, but we do not consider its occurrence to be a prerequisite for successful SNS-based RE.

The approach we propose is inspired by the EasyWinWin methodology [6]. As recommended by EasyWinWin, it uses brainstorming to elicit requirements. Brainstorming is a widely recognized requirements elicitation technique and is described in e.g. [44]. Our approach uses Facebook posts to bring brainstorming about. Facebook likes allow the communication of approval and support requirements prioritization. Although stakeholders can prioritize requirements, this approach does not allow them to communicate a certain degree of approval which is supported by state-of-the-art prioritization approaches [4]. Comments to posts support requirements negotiation. By using comments, stakeholders can discuss issues regarding a requirement posted in a way similar to the one proposed by EasyWinWin. However, the content of a Facebook comment cannot be defined in more detail. This means it is not possible for the stakeholders to immediately grasp the purpose of the post (e.g. to see whether it is an issue or an option). Stakeholders have to keep in mind the structure of a discussion while more elaborate negotiation tools provide this kind of support (e.g. by highlighting the WinWin tree) [45].

As far as the guidelines that can be followed when utilizing SNS for early RE activities are concerned, the main lessons (L) we learned are the following:

L1: Moderators play an important role in steering discussions and should be carefully chosen. Evidence: Findings 2.2, 2.6 and 3.1.

L2: High inner motivation of participants leads to high numbers of generated and prioritized needs. Evidence: Findings 3.1 and 3.3.

L3: The social aspect is a factor contributing to success: friendships, personal relations and interests increase the participation rate. Evidence: Finding 2.5.

L4: The moderator should, on a regular basis, invite participants to have continuous contributions. Evidence: Findings 1.3 and 2.2.

L5: Friendly and funny posts stimulate discussions and creativity and should therefore be encouraged. Evidence: Finding 2.2.

These findings and lessons learned hold for Facebook, the SNS we used as support for our study. We expect that similar results could be obtained when using other social network sites, as long as the necessary features for our approach are present (see Section 4). However, when replicating this study in other contexts, users' interaction with the SNS should also be considered. For example, whereas LinkedIn may provide rather similar features that could support the method introduced here, LinkedIn users tend to log-in and check their network activity more rarely than Facebook users. This could potentially lead to less input from users or to longer periods of waiting for gathering needs and requirements. We cannot draw any objective conclusions in this direction and further studies are needed to find out to what extent and how other SNS can be used successfully to support our approach.

10.4   Threats to validity

In our studies, we asked RE students to become the moderators of Facebook groups. In two of the three studies the students might have had a limited interest in the exercise. Only in Study III did the students have a stake in the outcome of the Facebook discussion as the results would contribute to their projects.

The studies heavily relied on the participation of RE students and friends of moderators. Although debriefing meetings suggest that participating friends had diverse backgrounds, we consider the lack of a broader audience in our studies a threat to construct validity.

We focused on a setup that would reflect real-world settings in an uncontrolled environment such as the one provided by Facebook. For example, the moderator students in Study III can be compared to real-world app developers asking their customers – who might include their friends – for new ideas and comments on a planned app. However, several contextual issues – e.g. presenting the study in the form of an (ungraded) exercise and assigning predefined topics – might have had an influence on the results. These issues are threats to the internal validity.

The results of the three studies do not allow us to make statistically significant claims, which is a threat to conclusion validity. However, students and friends were able to identify relevant requirements in all the three studies. This allows us to draw conclusions on the feasibility of the approach we presented.

In the three studies the authors focused on a setting where stakeholders were students and therefore motivated to participate. In real-world settings we need to identify other ways to motivate potential contributors. Only one popular social network was considered within our initial studies. The profile, background, motivation and behaviour of users might be different in other social networks. This can be seen as a threat to external validity.

11   Contribution and future work

The work presented in this paper investigates whether and how popular social network sites (i.e. Facebook) can support and allow end users to participate in RE activities such as elicitation, prioritization and negotiation. Inspired by EasyWinWin we have developed a generic SNS-based RE approach. We foresee that such approaches will increase end user participation in RE and allow geographically distributed end users to communicate their needs in an asynchronous way. Our three exploratory studies reveal that potential end users and moderators with limited RE knowledge are able to identify needs for the system under investigation.

We would like to stress that the approach presented does not necessarily provide well-specified requirements but rather reveals end user needs. However, we envision that SNS-supported RE approaches will become additional channels for RE. Therefore, they will complement traditional RE methods and tools and could potentially also support projects with limited RE budgets (e.g. mobile app development). Instead of highly skilled requirements engineers being trained to apply complex RE approaches and tools, the moderator within the SNS-supported RE approach presented could be a person who only has limited RE knowledge.

Further work is needed to answer open questions and outline the scope, capabilities and limitations of such a lightweight approach.

Better understanding risks and issues: This work focused on feasibility. However, future work will also need to clearly identify issues regarding SNS-supported approaches. This, for example, includes issues regarding participation (e.g. privacy issues) and tool-support (e.g. limited prioritization capabilities).

Evaluation of other suitable SNS: As discussed in Section 5, we know that SNS other than Facebook would allow researchers and practitioners to instantiate our generic SNS-based RE approach. Although our exploratory studies have shown that the approach works with Facebook, we cannot be certain if and how the approach would actually work with other SNS. For example, in LinkedIn, members maintain contacts on a more professional level which might have an influence on the results. Further studies are needed to investigate this issue. Moreover, our main aim was to investigate how an SNS-based RE approach could be used in practice and we see the chosen SNS as a support for leveraging our idea.

Evaluation in real-world projects: Apart from Study III, the studies presented focus on exercise projects rather than real-word industrial projects. Further evaluations will target the application of our approach in industrial settings. We are currently discussing the option to use our approach within a company developing mobile apps.

Exploring the motivation of end users: We would like to better understand the motivation of end users and have therefore started collaborating with the Department of Psychology at the University of Zurich. The degree of end user commitment may vary within projects. In some projects, it might be the duty of end users to participate in requirements elicitation, prioritization and negotiation activities. Other end users might draw motivation from different sources (e.g. interest in the topic, supporting a friend, curiosity). Better understanding the motivation of end users will support us in defining more stable and predictable approaches.

Competing interests
The authors declare that they have no competing interests.

Authors' contributions
NS, IT and KC are the main authors of the article. They have jointly conducted the studies, analyzed the results and worked on the manuscript. LS contributed to a first version of the manuscript. MG was involved in writing the manuscript and gave continuous feedback. All authors read and approved the final manuscript.

Acknowledgements
This research is partly funded by the Swiss National Science Foundation (project number 200021_150142). We are grateful to all participants contributing to the presented research. Furthermore, we would like to thank Simone Schoch, Anne Koziolek, Olga Liskin, Dustin Wüest and Noële Renard for feedback and input.

Author details
[1] University of Applied Sciences and Arts Northwestern Switzerland, Bahnhofstrasse 6, Windisch, Switzerland. [2] University of Zurich, Binzmühlestrasse 14, Zurich, Switzerland. [3] University of Victoria, 3800 Finnerty Rd, Victoria, Canada.

References
1. Kujala S, Kauppinen M, Lehtola L, Kojo T (2005) The role of user involvement in requirements quality and project success. In: Proceedings of the International Requirements Engineering Conference. IEEE, Piscataway, NJ, USA. pp 75–84
2. Aurum A, Wohlin C (2005) Requirements engineering: Setting the context. In: Aurum A, Wohlin C (eds). Engineering and Managing Software Requirements. Springer, Secaucus, NJ, USA. pp 1–15
3. Glinz M (2014) A Glossary of Requirements Engineering Terminology. Version 1.6. http://www.ireb.org/fileadmin/IREB/Download/Homepage%20Downloads/IREB_CPRE_Glossary_16.pdf. Accessed 2014-12-23
4. Berander P, Andrews A (2005) Requirements prioritization. In: Aurum A, Wohlin C (eds). Engineering and Managing Software Requirements. Springer, Secaucus, NJ, USA. pp 69–94
5. Easterbrook S (1991) Handling conflict between domain descriptions with computer-supported negotiation. Knowl Acquis 3:255–289
6. Boehm B, Gruenbacher P, Briggs R (2001) Developing groupware for requirements negotiation: Lessons learned. IEEE Soft 18(3):46–55
7. Seyff N, Ollmann G, Bortenschlager M (2014) Appecho: A user-driven, in situ feedback approach for mobile platforms and applications. In: Proceedings of the 1st International Conference on Mobile Software Engineering and Systems. MOBILESoft 2014. ACM, New York, NY, USA. pp 99–108
8. Todoran I, Seyff N, Glinz M (2013) How cloud providers elicit consumer requirements: An exploratory study of nineteen companies. In: Proceedings IEEE International Requirements Engineering Conference (RE). IEEE, Piscataway, NJ, USA. pp 105–114
9. Dittrich Y (2014) Software engineering beyond the project – sustaining software ecosystems. Inf Softw Technol 56(11):1436–1456
10. Lloyd WJ, Rosson MB, Arthur JD (2002) Effectiveness of elicitation techniques in distributed requirements engineering. In: Proceedings IEEE Joint International Conference on Requirements Engineering. IEEE, Piscataway, NJ, USA. pp 311–318
11. Seyff N, Graf F, Maiden N (2010) Using mobile RE tools to give end-users their own voice. In: Proceedings IEEE International Requirements Engineering Conference (RE). IEEE, Piscataway, NJ, USA. pp 37–46
12. Facebook. https://www.facebook.com. Accessed Dec 2014
13. Nuseibeh B, Easterbrook S (2000) Requirements engineering: a roadmap. In: Proceedings of the Conference on The Future of Software Engineering. ACM, New York, NY, USA. pp 35–46
14. Kotonya G, Sommerville I (1998) Requirements engineering - processes and techniques. John Wiley & Sons, New York, NY, USA
15. Zowghi D (2000) A requirements engineering process model based on defaults and revisions. In: DEXA Workshop. IEEE, Piscataway, NJ, USA. pp 966–972
16. Rolland C (1994) Modeling the requirements engineering process. In: Information Modelling and Knowledge Bases, IOS B.V., Amsterdam, Netherlands. pp 85–96
17. Grünbacher P (2000) Collaborative requirements negotiation with EasyWinWin. In: DEXA Workshop. IEEE, Piscataway, NJ, USA. pp 954–960
18. Boyd D, Ellison NB (2007) Social network sites: Definition, history, and scholarship. J Computer-Mediated Commun 13(1):210–230
19. Lim SL, Quercia D, Finkelstein A (2010) Stakesource: harnessing the power of crowdsourcing and social networks in stakeholder analysis. In: Proceedings of the 32Nd ACM/IEEE International Conference on Software Engineering - Volume 2. ACM, New York, NY, USA. pp 239–242
20. Conklin J, Begeman ML (1988) gibis: A hypertext tool for exploratory policy discussion. ACM Trans Inf Syst (TOIS) 6(4):303–331
21. Lohmann S, Dietzold S, Heim P, Heino N (2009) A web platform for social requirements engineering. In: Münch J, Liggesmeyer P (eds). Software Engineering (Workshops). LNI. Köllen Druck Verlag GmbH, Bonn, Germany Vol. 150. pp 309–315
22. Lohmann S, Riechert T (2010) Bringing semantics into social software engineering: Applying ontologies to a community-oriented requirements engineering environment. In: 3rd International Workshop on Social Software Engineering. Köllen Druck Verlag GmbH, Bonn, Germany
23. Kukreja N, Boehm B (2012) Process implications of social networking-based requirements negotiation tools. In: Proceedings of the 2012 International Conference on Software and System Process. ICSSP 2013. IEEE, Piscataway, NJ, USA. pp 68–72
24. Kukreja N, Boehm B (2013) Integrating collaborative requirements negotiation and prioritization processes: A match made in heaven. In: Proceedings of the 2013 International Conference on Software and System Process. ICSSP 2013. ACM, New York, NY, USA. pp 141–145
25. Damian D. E, Lanubile F, Mallardo T (2006) The role of asynchronous discussions in increasing the effectiveness of remote synchronous requirements negotiations. In: Osterweil LJ, Rombach HD, Soffa ML (eds). ICSE, ACM, New York, NY, USA. pp 917–920
26. Maalej W, Happel H-J, Rashid A (2009) When users become collaborators: towards continuous and context-aware user input. In: Arora S, Leavens GT (eds). OOPSLA Companion. ACM, New York, NY, USA. pp 981–990
27. Maalej W, Pagano D (2011) On the socialness of software. In: Proceedings of the IEEE Ninth International Conference on Dependable, Autonomic and Secure Computing. IEEE, Piscataway, NJ, USA. pp 864–871
28. Hess J, Randall D, Pipek V, Wulf V (2013) Involving users in the wild—participatory product development in and with online communities. Int J Human-Computer Stud 71(5):570–589

29. Bajic D, Lyons K (2011) Leveraging social media to gather user feedback for software development. In: Proceedings of the 2nd International Workshop on Web 2.0 for Software Engineering. Web2SE '11. ACM, New York, NY, USA. pp 1–6

30. UserVoice. https://www.uservoice.com. Accessed April 2015

31. Twitter. https://twitter.com. Accessed April 2015

32. Harman M, Jia Y, Zhang Y (2012) App store mining and analysis: MSR for app stores. In: IEEE Working Conference on Mining Software Repositories (MSR). ACM, New York, NY, USA. pp 108–111

33. Guzman E, Maalej W (2014) How do users like this feature? A fine grained sentiment analysis of app reviews. In: Proceedings IEEE 22nd International Requirements Engineering Conference (RE). IEEE, Piscataway, NJ, USA. pp 153–162

34. Singer L, Figueira Filho F, Storey M-A (2014) Software engineering at the speed of light: How developers stay current using twitter. In: Proceedings of the 36th International Conference on Software Engineering. ICSE 2014. ACM, New York, NY, USA. pp 211–221

35. GitHub. https://github.com. Accessed April 2015

36. Kalliamvakou E, Gousios G, Blincoe K, Singer L, German DM, Damian D (2014) The promises and perils of mining GitHub. In: Proceedings of the 11th Working Conference on Mining Software Repositories. MSR 2014. ACM, New York, NY, USA. pp 92–101

37. LinkedIn. https://www.linkedin.com. Accessed April 2015

38. Google+. https://plus.google.com. Accessed April 2015

39. Alexa. http://www.alexa.com. Accessed April 2015

40. Lauesen S (2002) Software Requirements: Styles and Techniques. Addison-Wesley, Glasgow, UK

41. Volere Requirements Resources. http://www.volere.co.uk. Accessed April 2015

42. Robertson S, Robertson J (1999) ACM Press/Addison-Wesley Publishing Co.

43. International Requirements Engineering Board (IREB). http://www.ireb.org/en/home.html. Accessed April 2015

44. Zowghi D, Coulin C (2005) Engineering and Managing Software Requirements. In: Aurum A, Wohlin C (eds). Springer, Secaucus, NJ, USA. pp 19–46

45. Grünbacher P, Seyff N (2005) Engineering and Managing Software Requirements. In: Aurum A, Wohlin C (eds). Springer, Secaucus, NJ, USA. pp 143–162

16

An analysis of security issues for cloud computing

Keiko Hashizume[1*], David G Rosado[2], Eduardo Fernández-Medina[2] and Eduardo B Fernandez[1]

Abstract

Cloud Computing is a flexible, cost-effective, and proven delivery platform for providing business or consumer IT services over the Internet. However, cloud Computing presents an added level of risk because essential services are often outsourced to a third party, which makes it harder to maintain data security and privacy, support data and service availability, and demonstrate compliance. Cloud Computing leverages many technologies (SOA, virtualization, Web 2.0); it also inherits their security issues, which we discuss here, identifying the main vulnerabilities in this kind of systems and the most important threats found in the literature related to Cloud Computing and its environment as well as to identify and relate vulnerabilities and threats with possible solutions.

Keywords: Cloud computing, Security, SPI model, Vulnerabilities, Threats, Countermeasures

1. Introduction

The importance of Cloud Computing is increasing and it is receiving a growing attention in the scientific and industrial communities. A study by Gartner [1] considered Cloud Computing as the first among the top 10 most important technologies and with a better prospect in successive years by companies and organizations.

Cloud Computing enables ubiquitous, convenient, on-demand network access to a shared pool of configurable computing resources (e.g., networks, servers, storage, applications, and services) that can be rapidly provisioned and released with minimal management effort or service provider interaction.

Cloud Computing appears as a computational paradigm as well as a distribution architecture and its main objective is to provide secure, quick, convenient data storage and net computing service, with all computing resources visualized as services and delivered over the Internet [2,3]. The cloud enhances collaboration, agility, scalability, availability, ability to adapt to fluctuations according to demand, accelerate development work, and provides potential for cost reduction through optimized and efficient computing [4-7].

Cloud Computing combines a number of computing concepts and technologies such as Service Oriented Architecture (SOA), Web 2.0, virtualization and other technologies with reliance on the Internet, providing common business applications online through web browsers to satisfy the computing needs of users, while their software and data are stored on the servers [5]. In some respects, Cloud Computing represents the maturing of these technologies and is a marketing term to represent that maturity and the services they provide [6].

Although there are many benefits to adopting Cloud Computing, there are also some significant barriers to adoption. One of the most significant barriers to adoption is security, followed by issues regarding compliance, privacy and legal matters [8]. Because Cloud Computing represents a relatively new computing model, there is a great deal of uncertainty about how security at all levels (e.g., network, host, application, and data levels) can be achieved and how applications security is moved to Cloud Computing [9]. That uncertainty has consistently led information executives to state that security is their number one concern with Cloud Computing [10].

Security concerns relate to risk areas such as external data storage, dependency on the "public" internet, lack of control, multi-tenancy and integration with internal security. Compared to traditional technologies, the cloud has many specific features, such as its large scale and the fact that resources belonging to cloud providers are completely distributed, heterogeneous and totally virtualized. Traditional security mechanisms such as identity, authentication, and authorization are no longer enough for clouds in their current form [11]. Security controls in Cloud Computing are, for the most part, no

* Correspondence: ahashizu@fau.edu
[1]Department of Computer Science and Engineering, Florida Atlantic University, Boca Raton, USA
Full list of author information is available at the end of the article

different than security controls in any IT environment. However, because of the cloud service models employed, the operational models, and the technologies used to enable cloud services, Cloud Computing may present different risks to an organization than traditional IT solutions. Unfortunately, integrating security into these solutions is often perceived as making them more rigid [4].

Moving critical applications and sensitive data to public cloud environments is of great concern for those corporations that are moving beyond their data center's network under their control. To alleviate these concerns, a cloud solution provider must ensure that customers will continue to have the same security and privacy controls over their applications and services, provide evidence to customers that their organization are secure and they can meet their service-level agreements, and that they can prove compliance to auditors [12].

We present here a categorization of security issues for Cloud Computing focused in the so-called SPI model (SaaS, PaaS and IaaS), identifying the main vulnerabilities in this kind of systems and the most important threats found in the literature related to Cloud Computing and its environment. A *threat* is a potential attack that may lead to a misuse of information or resources, and the term *vulnerability* refers to the flaws in a system that allows an attack to be successful. There are some surveys where they focus on one service model, or they focus on listing cloud security issues in general without distinguishing among vulnerabilities and threats. Here, we present a list of vulnerabilities and threats, and we also indicate what cloud service models can be affected by them. Furthermore, we describe the relationship between these vulnerabilities and threats; how these vulnerabilities can be exploited in order to perform an attack, and also present some countermeasures related to these threats which try to solve or improve the identified problems.

The remainder of the paper is organized as follows: Section 2 presents the results obtained from our systematic review. Next, in Section 3 we define in depth the most important security aspects for each layer of the Cloud model. Later, we will analyze the security issues in Cloud Computing identifying the main vulnerabilities for clouds, the most important threats in clouds, and all available countermeasures for these threats and vulnerabilities. Finally, we provide some conclusions.

1.1 Systematic review of security issues for cloud computing

We have carried out a systematic review [13-15] of the existing literature regarding security in Cloud Computing, not only in order to summarize the existing vulnerabilities and threats concerning this topic but also to identify and analyze the current state and the most important security issues for Cloud Computing.

1.2 Question formalization

The question focus was to identify the most relevant issues in Cloud Computing which consider vulnerabilities, threats, risks, requirements and solutions of security for Cloud Computing. This question had to be related with the aim of this work; that is to identify and relate vulnerabilities and threats with possible solutions. Therefore, the research question addressed by our research was the following: What security vulnerabilities and threats are the most important in Cloud Computing which have to be studied in depth with the purpose of handling them? The keywords and related concepts that make up this question and that were used during the review execution are: secure Cloud systems, Cloud security, delivery models security, SPI security, SaaS security, Paas security, IaaS security, Cloud threats, Cloud vulnerabilities, Cloud recommendations, best practices in Cloud.

1.3 Selection of sources

The selection criteria through which we evaluated study sources was based on the research experience of the authors of this work, and in order to select these sources we have considered certain constraints: studies included in the selected sources must be written in English and these sources must be web-available. The following list of sources has been considered: ScienceDirect, ACM digital library, IEEE digital library, Scholar Google and DBLP. Later, the experts will refine the results and will include important works that had not been recovered in these sources and will update these work taking into account other constraints such as impact factor, received cites, important journals, renowned authors, etc.

Once the sources had been defined, it was necessary to describe the process and the criteria for study selection and evaluation. The inclusion and exclusion criteria of this study were based on the research question. We therefore established that the studies must contain issues and topics which consider security on Cloud Computing, and that these studies must describe threats, vulnerabilities, countermeasures, and risks.

1.4 Review execution

During this phase, the search in the defined sources must be executed and the obtained studies must be evaluated according to the established criteria. After executing the search chain on the selected sources we obtained a set of about 120 results which were filtered with the inclusion criteria to give a set of about 40 relevant studies. This set of relevant studies was again filtered with the exclusion criteria to give a set of studies which corresponds with 15 primary proposals [4,6,10,16-27].

2. Results and discussion

The results of the systematic review are summarized in Table 1 which shows a summary of the topics and concepts considered for each approach.

As it is shown in Table 1, most of the approaches discussed identify, classify, analyze, and list a number of vulnerabilities and threats focused on Cloud Computing. The studies analyze the risks and threats, often give recommendations on how they can be avoided or covered, resulting in a direct relationship between vulnerability or threats and possible solutions and mechanisms to solve them. In addition, we can see that in our search, many of the approaches, in addition to speaking about threats and vulnerabilities, also discuss other issues related to security in the Cloud such as the data security, trust, or security recommendations and mechanisms for any of the problems encountered in these environments.

2.1 Security in the SPI model

The cloud model provides three types of services [21,28,29]:

- Software as a Service (SaaS). The capability provided to the consumer is to use the provider's applications running on a cloud infrastructure. The applications are accessible from various client devices through a thin client interface such as a web browser (e.g., web-based email).
- Platform as a Service (PaaS). The capability provided to the consumer is to deploy onto the cloud infrastructure his own applications without installing any platform or tools on their local machines. PaaS refers to providing platform layer resources, including operating system support and software development frameworks that can be used to build higher-level services.
- Infrastructure as a Service (IaaS). The capability provided to the consumer is to provision processing, storage, networks, and other fundamental computing resources where the consumer is able to

deploy and run arbitrary software, which can include operating systems and applications.

With SaaS, the burden of security lies with the cloud provider. In part, this is because of the degree of abstraction, the SaaS model is based on a high degree of integrated functionality with minimal customer control or extensibility. By contrast, the PaaS model offers greater extensibility and greater customer control. Largely because of the relatively lower degree of abstraction, IaaS offers greater tenant or customer control over security than do PaaS or SaaS [10].

Before analyzing security challenges in Cloud Computing, we need to understand the relationships and dependencies between these cloud service models [4]. PaaS as well as SaaS are hosted on top of IaaS; thus, any breach in IaaS will impact the security of both PaaS and SaaS services, but also it may be true on the other way around. However, we have to take into account that PaaS offers a platform to build and deploy SaaS applications, which increases the security dependency between them. As a consequence of these deep dependencies, any attack to any cloud service layer can compromise the upper layers. Each cloud service model comprises its own inherent security flaws; however, they also share some challenges that affect all of them. These relationships and dependencies between cloud models may also be a source of security risks. A SaaS provider may rent a development environment from a PaaS provider, which might also rent an infrastructure from an IaaS provider. Each provider is responsible for securing his own services, which may result in an inconsistent combination of security models. It also creates confusion over which service provider is responsible once an attack happens.

2.2 Software-as-a-service (SaaS) security issues

SaaS provides application services on demand such as email, conferencing software, and business applications such as ERP, CRM, and SCM [30]. SaaS users have less control over security among the three fundamental

Table 1 Summary of the topics considered in each approach

Topics/References	[4]	[6]	[10]	[16]	[17]	[18]	[19]	[20]	[21]	[22]	[23]	[24]	[25]	[26]	[27]
Vulnerabilities		X	X	X	X	X	X	X	X			X			X
Threats		X	X	X	X	X	X	X	X	X	X	X	X	X	X
Mechanisms/Recommendations	X		X			X		X				X	X	X	X
Security Standards							X			X					
Data Security	X		X				X		X		X		X		X
Trust			X								X		X	X	X
Security Requirements	X		X						X		X			X	X
SaaS, PaaS, IaaS Security					X				X			X			

delivery models in the cloud. The adoption of SaaS applications may raise some security concerns.

2.3 Application security

These applications are typically delivered via the Internet through a Web browser [12,22]. However, flaws in web applications may create vulnerabilities for the SaaS applications. Attackers have been using the web to compromise user's computers and perform malicious activities such as steal sensitive data [31]. Security challenges in SaaS applications are not different from any web application technology, but traditional security solutions do not effectively protect it from attacks, so new approaches are necessary [21]. The Open Web Application Security Project (OWASP) has identified the ten most critical web applications security threats [32]. There are more security issues, but it is a good start for securing web applications.

2.4 Multi-tenancy

SaaS applications can be grouped into maturity models that are determined by the following characteristics: scalability, configurability via metadata, and multi-tenancy [30,33]. In the first maturity model, each customer has his own customized instance of the software. This model has drawbacks, but security issues are not so bad compared with the other models. In the second model, the vendor also provides different instances of the applications for each customer, but all instances use the same application code. In this model, customers can change some configuration options to meet their needs. In the third maturity model multi-tenancy is added, so a single instance serves all customers [34]. This approach enables more efficient use of the resources but scalability is limited. Since data from multiple tenants is likely to be stored in the same database, the risk of data leakage between these tenants is high. Security policies are needed to ensure that customer's data are kept separate from other customers [35]. For the final model, applications can be scaled up by moving the application to a more powerful server if needed.

2.5 Data security

Data security is a common concern for any technology, but it becomes a major challenge when SaaS users have to rely on their providers for proper security [12,21,36]. In SaaS, organizational data is often processed in plaintext and stored in the cloud. The SaaS provider is the one responsible for the security of the data while is being processed and stored [30]. Also, data backup is a critical aspect in order to facilitate recovery in case of disaster, but it introduces security concerns as well [21]. Also cloud providers can subcontract other services such as backup from third-party service providers, which may raise concerns. Moreover, most compliance standards do not envision compliance with regulations in a world of Cloud Computing [12]. In the world of SaaS, the process of compliance is complex because data is located in the provider's datacenters, which may introduce regulatory compliance issues such as data privacy, segregation, and security, that must be enforced by the provider.

2.6 Accessibility

Accessing applications over the internet via web browser makes access from any network device easier, including public computers and mobile devices. However, it also exposes the service to additional security risks. The Cloud Security Alliance [37] has released a document that describes the current state of mobile computing and the top threats in this area such as information stealing mobile malware, insecure networks (WiFi), vulnerabilities found in the device OS and official applications, insecure marketplaces, and proximity-based hacking.

2.7 Platform-as-a-service (PaaS) security issues

PaaS facilitates deployment of cloud-based applications without the cost of buying and maintaining the underlying hardware and software layers [21]. As with SaaS and IaaS, PaaS depends on a secure and reliable network and secure web browser. PaaS application security comprises two software layers: Security of the PaaS platform itself (i.e., runtime engine), and Security of customer applications deployed on a PaaS platform [10]. PaaS providers are responsible for securing the platform software stack that includes the runtime engine that runs the customer applications. Same as SaaS, PaaS also brings data security issues and other challenges that are described as follows:

2.7.1 Third-party relationships

Moreover, PaaS does not only provide traditional programming languages, but also does it offer third-party web services components such as mashups [10,38]. Mashups combine more than one source element into a single integrated unit. Thus, PaaS models also inherit security issues related to mashups such as data and network security [39]. Also, PaaS users have to depend on both the security of web-hosted development tools and third-party services.

2.7.2 Development Life Cycle

From the perspective of the application development, developers face the complexity of building secure applications that may be hosted in the cloud. The speed at which applications will change in the cloud will affect both the System Development Life Cycle (SDLC) and security [12,24]. Developers have to keep in mind that PaaS applications should be upgraded frequently, so they have to ensure that their application development processes are flexible enough to keep up with changes [19]. However, developers also have to understand that any changes in PaaS components can compromise the security of their applications. Besides secure development techniques, developers need to be educated about data legal issues as well, so that data is not stored in inappropriate locations. Data may be stored on different places with different legal regimes that can compromise its privacy and security.

2.7.3 Underlying infrastructure security

In PaaS, developers do not usually have access to the underlying layers, so providers are responsible for securing the underlying infrastructure as well as the applications services [40]. Even when developers are in control of the security of their applications, they do not have the assurance that the development environment tools provided by a PaaS provider are secure.

In conclusion, there is less material in the literature about security issues in PaaS. SaaS provides software delivered over the web while PaaS offers development tools to create SaaS applications. However, both of them may use multi-tenant architecture so multiple concurrent users utilize the same software. Also, PaaS applications and user's data are also stored in cloud servers which can be a security concern as discussed on the previous section. In both SaaS and PaaS, data is associated with an application running in the cloud. The security of this data while it is being processed, transferred, and stored depends on the provider.

2.8 Infrastructure-as-a-service (IaaS) security issues

IaaS provides a pool of resources such as servers, storage, networks, and other computing resources in the form of virtualized systems, which are accessed through the Internet [24]. Users are entitled to run any software with full control and management on the resources allocated to them [18]. With IaaS, cloud users have better control over the security compared to the other models as long there is no security hole in the virtual machine monitor [21]. They control the software running in their virtual machines, and they are responsible to configure security policies correctly [41]. However, the underlying compute, network, and storage infrastructure is controlled by cloud providers. IaaS providers must undertake a substantial effort to secure their systems in order to minimize these threats that result from creation, communication, monitoring, modification, and mobility [42]. Here are some of the security issues associated to IaaS.

2.9 Virtualization

Virtualization allows users to create, copy, share, migrate, and roll back virtual machines, which may allow them to run a variety of applications [43,44]. However, it also introduces new opportunities for attackers because of the extra layer that must be secured [31]. Virtual machine security becomes as important as physical machine security, and any flaw in either one may affect the other [19]. Virtualized environments are vulnerable to all types of attacks for normal infrastructures; however, security is a greater challenge as virtualization adds more points of entry and more interconnection complexity [45]. Unlike physical servers, VMs have two boundaries: physical and virtual [24].

2.10 Virtual machine monitor

The Virtual Machine Monitor (VMM) or hypervisor is responsible for virtual machines isolation; therefore, if the VMM is compromised, its virtual machines may potentially be compromised as well. The VMM is a low-level software that controls and monitors its virtual machines, so as any traditional software it entails security flaws [45]. Keeping the VMM as simple and small as possible reduces the risk of security vulnerabilities, since it will be easier to find and fix any vulnerability.

Moreover, virtualization introduces the ability to migrate virtual machines between physical servers for fault tolerance, load balancing or maintenance [16,46]. This useful feature can also raise security problems [42,43,47]. An attacker can compromise the migration module in the VMM and transfer a victim virtual machine to a malicious server. Also, it is clear that VM migration exposes the content of the VM to the network, which can compromise its data integrity and confidentiality. A malicious virtual machine can be migrated to another host (with another VMM) compromising it.

2.11 Shared resource

VMs located on the same server can share CPU, memory, I/O, and others. Sharing resources between VMs may decrease the security of each VM. For example, a malicious VM can infer some information about other VMs through shared memory or other shared resources without need of compromising the hypervisor [46]. Using covert channels, two VMs can communicate bypassing all the rules defined by the security module of the VMM [48]. Thus, a malicious Virtual Machine can monitor shared resources without being noticed by its VMM, so the attacker can infer some information about other virtual machines.

2.12 Public VM image repository

In IaaS environments, a VM image is a prepackaged software template containing the configurations files that are used to create VMs. Thus, these images are fundamental for the the overall security of the cloud [46,49]. One can either create her own VM image from scratch, or one can use any image stored in the provider's repository. For example, Amazon offers a public image repository where legitimate users can download or upload a VM image. Malicious users can store images containing malicious code into public repositories compromising other users or even the cloud system [20,24,25]. For example, an attacker with a valid account can create an image containing malicious code such as a Trojan horse. If another customer uses this image, the virtual machine that this customer creates will be infected with the hidden malware. Moreover, unintentionally data leakage can be introduced by VM replication [20]. Some confidential information such as passwords or cryptographic keys can be recorded while an image is being created. If the image is not "cleaned", this sensitive information can be exposed to other users. VM images are dormant artifacts that are hard to patch while they are offline [50].

2.13 Virtual machine rollback

Furthermore, virtual machines are able to be rolled back to their previous states if an error happens. But rolling back virtual machines can re-expose them to security vulnerabilities that were patched or re-enable previously disabled accounts or passwords. In order to provide rollbacks, we need to make a "copy" (snapshot) of the virtual machine, which can result in the propagation of configuration errors and other vulnerabilities [12,44].

2.14 Virtual machine life cycle

Additionally, it is important to understand the lifecycle of the VMs and their changes in states as they move through the environment. VMs can be on, off, or suspended which makes it harder to detect malware. Also, even when virtual machines are offline, they can be vulnerable [24]; that is, a virtual machine can be instantiated using an image that may contain malicious code. These malicious images can be the starting point of the proliferation of malware by injecting malicious code within other virtual machines in the creation process.

2.15 Virtual networks

Network components are shared by different tenants due to resource pooling. As mentioned before, sharing resources allows attackers to launch cross-tenant attacks [20]. Virtual Networks increase the VMs interconnectivity, an important security challenge in Cloud Computing [51]. The most secure way is to hook each VM with its host by using dedicated physical channels. However, most hypervisors use virtual networks to link VMs to communicate more directly and efficiently. For instance, most virtualization platforms such as Xen provide two ways to configure virtual networks: bridged and routed, but these techniques increase the possibility to perform some attacks such as sniffing and spoofing virtual network [45,52].

2.16 Analysis of security issues in cloud computing

We systematically analyze now existing security vulnerabilities and threats of Cloud Computing. For each vulnerability and threat, we identify what cloud service model or models are affected by these security problems.

Table 2 presents an analysis of vulnerabilities in Cloud Computing. This analysis offers a brief description of the vulnerabilities, and indicates what cloud service models (SPI) can be affected by them. For this analysis, we focus mainly on technology-based vulnerabilities; however, there are other vulnerabilities that are common to any organization, but they have to be taken in consideration since they can negatively impact the security of the cloud and its underlying platform. Some of these vulnerabilities are the following:

- Lack of employee screening and poor hiring practices [16] – some cloud providers may not perform background screening of their employees or providers. Privileged users such as cloud administrators usually have unlimited access to the cloud data.
- Lack of customer background checks – most cloud providers do not check their customer's background, and almost anyone can open an account with a valid credit card and email. Apocryphal accounts can let attackers perform any malicious activity without being identified [16].
- Lack of security education – people continue to be a weak point in information security [53]. This is true in any type of organization; however, in the cloud, it has a bigger impact because there are more people that interact with the cloud: cloud providers, third-party providers, suppliers, organizational customers, and end-users.

Cloud Computing leverages many existing technologies such as web services, web browsers, and virtualization, which contributes to the evolution of cloud environments. Therefore, any vulnerability associated to these technologies also affects the cloud, and it can even have a significant impact.

From Table 2, we can conclude that data storage and virtualization are the most critical and an attack to them can do the most harm. Attacks to lower layers have more impact to the other layers. Table 3 presents an overview of threats in Cloud Computing. Like Table 2 it also describes the threats that are related to the technology used in cloud environments, and it indicates what cloud service models are exposed to these threats. We put more emphasis on threats that are associated with data being stored and processed remotely, sharing resources and the usage of virtualization.

Table 2 Vulnerabilities in cloud computing

ID	Vulnerabilities	Description	Layer
V01	Insecure interfaces and APIs	Cloud providers offer services that can be accessed through APIs (SOAP, REST, or HTTP with XML/JSON) [42]. The security of the cloud depends upon the security of these interfaces [16]. Some problems are: a) Weak credential b) Insufficient authorization checks c) Insufficient input-data validation Also, cloud APIs are still immature which means that are frequently updated. A fixed bug can introduce another security hole in the application [54].	SPI
V02	Unlimited allocation of resources	Inaccurate modeling of resource usage can lead to overbooking or over-provisioning [17].	SPI
V03	Data-related vulnerabilities	a) Data can be colocated with the data of unknown owners (competitors, or intruders) with a weak separation [36] b) Data may be located in different jurisdictions which have different laws [19,54,55] c) Incomplete data deletion – data cannot be completely removed [19,20,25,56] d) Data backup done by untrusted third-party providers [56,57] e) Information about the location of the data usually is unavailable or not disclosed to users [25] f) Data is often stored, processed, and transferred in clear plain text	SPI
V04	Vulnerabilities in Virtual Machines	a) Possible covert channels in the colocation of VMs [48,58,59] b) Unrestricted allocation and deallocation of resources with VMs [57] c) Uncontrolled Migration - VMs can be migrated from one server to another server due to fault tolerance, load balance, or hardware maintenance [42,44] d) Uncontrolled snapshots – VMs can be copied in order to provide flexibility [12], which may lead to data leakage e) Uncontrolled rollback could lead to reset vulnerabilities - VMs can be backed up to a previous state for restoration [44], but patches applied after the previous state disappear f) VMs have IP addresses that are visible to anyone within the cloud - attackers can map where the target VM is located within the cloud (Cloud cartography [58])	I
V05	Vulnerabilities in Virtual Machine Images	a) Uncontrolled placement of VM images in public repositories [24] b) VM images are not able to be patched since they are dormant artifacts [44]	I
V06	Vulnerabilities in Hypervisors	a) Complex hypervisor code [60] b) Flexible configuration of VMs or hypervisors to meet organization needs can be exploited	I
V07	Vulnerabilities in Virtual Networks	Sharing of virtual bridges by several virtual machines [51]	I

The relationship between threats and vulnerabilities is illustrated in Table 4, which describes how a threat can take advantage of some vulnerability to compromise the system. The goal of this analysis is also to identify some existing defenses that can defeat these threats. This information can be expressed in a more detailed way using misuse patterns [62]. Misuse patterns describe how a misuse is performed from the point of view of the attacker. For instance, in threat T10, an attacker can read or tamper with the contents of the VM state files during live migration. This can be possible because VM migration transfer the data over network channels that are often insecure, such as the Internet. Insecure VM migration can be mitigated by the following proposed techniques: TCCP [63] provides confidential execution of VMs and secure migration operations as well. PALM [64] proposes a secure migration system that provides VM live migration capabilities under the condition

that a VMM-protected system is present and active. Threat 11 is another cloud threat where an attacker creates malicious VM image containing any type of virus or malware. This threat is feasible because any legitimate user can create a VM image and publish it on the provider's repository where other users can retrieve them. If the malicious VM image contains malware, it will infect other VMs instantiated with this malicious VM image. In order to overcome this threat, an image management system was proposed, Mirage [49]. It provides the following security management features: access control framework, image filters, provenance tracking system, and repository maintenance services.

2.17 Countermeasures

In this section, we provide a brief description of each countermeasure mentioned before, except for threats T02 and T07.

Table 3 Threats in cloud computing

ID	Threats	Description	Layer
T01	Account or service hijacking	An account theft can be performed by different ways such as social engineering and weak credentials. If an attacker gains access to a user's credential, he can perform malicious activities such as access sensitive data, manipulate data, and redirect any transaction [16].	SPI
T02	Data scavenging	Since data cannot be completely removed from unless the device is destroyed, attackers may be able to recover this data [10,17,25].	SPI
T03	Data leakage	Data leakage happens when the data gets into the wrong hands while it is being transferred, stored, audited or processed [16,17,20,58].	SPI
T04	Denial of Service	It is possible that a malicious user will take all the possible resources. Thus, the system cannot satisfy any request from other legitimate users due to resources being unavailable.	SPI
T05	Customer-data manipulation	Users attack web applications by manipulating data sent from their application component to the server's application [20,32]. For example, SQL injection, command injection, insecure direct object references, and cross-site scripting.	S
T06	VM escape	It is designed to exploit the hypervisor in order to take control of the underlying infrastructure [24,61].	I
T07	VM hopping	It happens when a VM is able to gain access to another VM (i.e. by exploting some hypervisor vulnerability) [17,43]	I
T08	Malicious VM creation	An attacker who creates a valid account can create a VM image containing malicious code such as a Trojan horse and store it in the provider repository [20].	I
T09	Insecure VM migration	Live migration of virtual machines exposes the contents of the VM state files to the network. An attacker can do the following actions: a) Access data illegally during migration [42] b) Transfer a VM to an untrusted host [44] c) Create and migrate several VM causing disruptions or DoS	I
T10	Sniffing/Spoofing virtual networks	A malicious VM can listen to the virtual network or even use ARP spoofing to redirect packets from/to other VMs [45,51].	I

2.17.1 Countermeasures for T01: account or service hijacking

2.17.1.1 Identity and access management guidance
Cloud Security Alliance (CSA) is a non-profit organization that promotes the use of best practices in order to provide security in cloud environments. CSA has issued an Identity and Access Management Guidance [65] which provides a list of recommended best practiced to assure identities and secure access management. This report includes centralized directory, access management, identity management, role-based access control, user access certifications, privileged user and access management, separation of duties, and identity and access reporting.

2.17.1.2 Dynamic credentials
[66] presents an algorithm to create dynamic credentials for mobile cloud computing systems. The dynamic credential changes its value once a user changes its location or when he has exchanged a certain number of data packets.

2.17.2 Countermeasures for T03: data leakage

2.17.2.1 Fragmentation-redundancy-scattering (FRS) technique
[67] this technique aims to provide intrusion tolerance and, in consequence, secure storage. This technique consists in first breaking down sensitive data into insignificant fragments, so any fragment does not have any significant information by itself. Then, fragments are scattered in a redundant fashion across different sites of the distributed system.

2.17.2.2 Digital signatures
[68] proposes to secure data using digital signature with RSA algorithm while data is being transferred over the Internet. They claimed that RSA is the most recognizable algorithm, and it can be used to protect data in cloud environments.

2.17.2.3 Homomorphic encryption
The three basic operations for cloud data are transfer, store, and process. Encryption techniques can be used to secure data while it is being transferred in and out of the cloud or stored in the provider's premises. Cloud providers have to decrypt cipher data in order to process it, which raises privacy concerns. In [70], they propose a method based on the application of fully homomorphic encryption to the security of clouds. Fully homomorphic encryption allows performing arbitrary computation on ciphertexts without being decrypted. Current homomorphic encryption schemes support limited number of homomorphic operations such as addition and multiplication. The authors in [77] provided some real-world cloud applications where some basic homomorphic operations are needed. However, it requires a huge processing power which may impact on user response time and power consumption.

Table 4 Relationships between threats, vulnerabilities, and countermeasures

Threat	Vulnerabilities	Incidents	Countermeasures
T01	V01	An attacker can use the victim's account to get access to the target's resources.	Identity and Access Management Guidance [65]
			Dynamic credential [66]
T02	V03a, V03c	Data from hard drives that are shared by several customers cannot be completely removed.	Specify destruction strategies on Service-level Agreements (SLAs)
T03	V03a, V03c, V03d, V03f, V04a-f, V05a, V07	Authors in [58] illustrated the steps necessary to gain confidential information from other VMs co-located in the same server as the attacker.	FRS techniques [67]
			Digital Signatures [68]
		Side channel [69]	Encryption [69]
			Homomorphic encryption [70]
T04	V01, V02	An attacker can request more computational resources, so other legal users are not able to get additional capacity.	Cloud providers can force policies to offer limited computational resources
T05	V01	Some examples are described in [32] such as SQL, command injection, and cross-site scripting	Web application scanners [71]
T06	V06a, V06b	A zero-day exploit in the HyperVM virtualization application that destroyed about 100,000 websites [72]	HyperSafe [60]
			TCCP (Trusted Cloud Computing Platform) [63]
			TVDc (Trusted Virtual Datacenter) [73,74]
T07	V04b, V06b	[75] presents a study that demonstrates security flaws in most virtual machines monitors	
T08	V05a, V05b	An attacker can create a VM image containing malware and publish it in a public repository.	Mirage [49]
T09	V04d	[76] has empirically showed attacks against the migration functionality of the latest version of the Xen and VMware virtualization products.	PALM [64]
			TCCP [63]
			VNSS [52]
T10	V07	Sniffing and spoofing virtual networks [51]	Virtual network framework based on Xen network modes: "bridged" and "routed" [51]

2.17.2.4 Encryption Encryption techniques have been used for long time to secure sensitive data. Sending or storing encrypted data in the cloud will ensure that data is secure. However, it is true assuming that the encryption algorithms are strong. There are some well-known encryption schemes such as AES (Advanced Encryption Standard). Also, SSL technology can be used to protect data while it is in transit. Moreover, [69] describes that encryption can be used to stop side channel attacks on cloud storage de-duplication, but it may lead to offline dictionary attacks reveling personal keys.

2.17.3 Countermeasures for T05: customer data manipulation
2.17.3.1 Web application scanners Web applications can be an easy target because they are exposed to the public including potential attackers. Web application scanners [71] is a program which scans web applications through the web front-end in order to identify security vulnerabilities. There are also other web application security tools such as web application firewall. Web application firewall routes all web traffic through the web application firewall which inspects specific threats.

2.17.4 Countermeasures for T06: VM escape
2.17.4.1 HyperSafe [60] It is an approach that provides hypervisor control-flow integrity. HyperSafe's goal is to protect type I hypervisors using two techniques: non-bypassable memory lockdown which protects write-protected memory pages from being modified, and restricted pointed indexing that converts control data into pointer indexes. In order to evaluate the effectiveness of this approach, they have conducted four types of attacks such as modify the hypervisor code, execute the injected code, modify the page table, and tamper from a return table. They concluded that HyperSafe successfully prevented all these attacks, and that the performance overhead is low.

2.17.4.2 Trusted cloud computing platform TCCP [63] enables providers to offer closed box execution environments, and allows users to determine if the environment is secure before launching their VMs. The TCCP adds two fundamental elements: a trusted virtual machine monitor (TVMM) and a trusted coordinator (TC). The TC manages a set of trusted nodes that run TVMMs, and

it is maintained but a trusted third party. The TC partici-
pates in the process of launching or migrating a VM,
which verifies that a VM is running in a trusted platform.
The authors in [78] claimed that TCCP has a significant
downside due to the fact that all the transactions have to
verify with the TC which creates an overload. They proposed to use Direct Anonymous Attestation (DAA) and
Privacy CA scheme to tackle this issue.

2.17.4.3 Trusted virtual datacenter TVDc [73,74] in-
sures isolation and integrity in cloud environments. It
groups virtual machines that have common objectives into
workloads named Trusted Virtual Domains (TVDs).
TVDc provides isolation between workloads by enforcing
mandatory access control, hypervisor-based isolation, and
protected communication channels such as VLANs.
TVDc provides integrity by employing load-time attestation mechanism to verify the integrity of the system.

2.17.5 Countermeasures for T08: malicious virtual machine creation

2.17.5.1 Mirage In [49], the authors propose a virtual
machine image management system in a cloud computing
environments. This approach includes the following security features: access control framework, image filters, a
provenance tracking, and repository maintenance services.
However, one limitation of this approach is that filters
may not be able to scan all malware or remove all the sensitive data from the images. Also, running these filters
may raise privacy concerns because they have access to
the content of the images which can contain customer's
confidential data.

2.17.6 Countermeasures for T09: insecure virtual machine migration

**2.17.6.1 Protection aegis for live migration of VMs
(PALM)** [64] proposes a secure live migration framework
that preserves integrity and privacy protection during and
after migration. The prototype of the system was
implemented based on Xen and GNU Linux, and the
results of the evaluation showed that this scheme only
adds slight downtime and migration time due to encryption and decryption.

2.17.6.2 VNSS [52] proposes a security framework that
customizes security policies for each virtual machine,
and it provides continuous protection thorough virtual
machine live migration. They implemented a prototype
system based on Xen hypervisors using stateful firewall
technologies and userspace tools such as iptables, xm
commands program and conntrack-tools. The authors
conducted some experiments to evaluate their framework, and the results revealed that the security policies
are in place throughout live migration.

2.17.7 Countermeasures for T010: sniffing/spoofing virtual networks

2.17.7.1 Virtual network security Wu and et al. [51]
presents a virtual network framework that secures the communication among virtual machines. This framework is
based on Xen which offers two configuration modes for virtual networks: "bridged" and "routed". The virtual network
model is composed of three layers: routing layers, firewall,
and shared networks, which can prevent VMs from sniffing
and spoofing. An evaluation of this approach was not
performed when this publication was published.

Furthermore, web services are the largest implementation technology in cloud environments. However, web services also lead to several challenges that need to be
addressed. Security web services standards describe how
to secure communication between applications through
integrity, confidentiality, authentication and authorization.
There are several security standard specifications [79] such
as Security Assertion Markup Language (SAML), WS-
Security, Extensible Access Control Markup (XACML),
XML Digital Signature, XML Encryption, Key Management
Specification (XKMS), WS-Federation, WS-Secure Conver-
sation, WS-Security Policy and WS-Trust. The NIST Cloud
Computing Standards Roadmap Working Group has gath-
ered high level standards that are relevant for Cloud
Computing.

3 Conclusions

Cloud Computing is a relatively new concept that presents
a good number of benefits for its users; however, it also
raises some security problems which may slow down its
use. Understanding what vulnerabilities exist in Cloud
Computing will help organizations to make the shift towards the Cloud. Since Cloud Computing leverages many
technologies, it also inherits their security issues. Traditional web applications, data hosting, and virtualization
have been looked over, but some of the solutions offered
are immature or inexistent. We have presented security
issues for cloud models: IaaS, PaaS, and IaaS, which vary
depending on the model. As described in this paper, storage, virtualization, and networks are the biggest security
concerns in Cloud Computing. Virtualization which allows multiple users to share a physical server is one of the
major concerns for cloud users. Also, another challenge is
that there are different types of virtualization technologies,
and each type may approach security mechanisms in different ways. Virtual networks are also target for some attacks especially when communicating with remote virtual
machines.

Some surveys have discussed security issues about
clouds without making any difference between vulnerabilities and threats. We have focused on this distinction,
where we consider important to understand these issues.
Enumerating these security issues was not enough; that

is why we made a relationship between threats and vulnerabilities, so we can identify what vulnerabilities contribute to the execution of these threats and make the system more robust. Also, some current solutions were listed in order to mitigate these threats. However, new security techniques are needed as well as redesigned traditional solutions that can work with cloud architectures. Traditional security mechanisms may not work well in cloud environments because it is a complex architecture that is composed of a combination of different technologies.

We have expressed three of the items in Table 4 as misuse patterns [46]. We intend to complete all the others in the future.

Competing Interests

The authors declare that they have no competing interests.

Authors' contributions

KH, DGR, EFM and EBF made a substantial contribution to the systematic review, security analysis of Cloud Computing, and revised the final manuscript version. They all approved the final version to be published.

Acknowledgments

This work was supported in part by the NSF (grants OISE-0730065). Any opinions, findings, and conclusions or recommendations expressed in this material are those of the author(s) and do not necessarily reflect those of the NSF. We also want to thank the GSyA Research Group at the University of Castilla-La Mancha, in Ciudad Real, Spain for collaborating with us in this project.

Author details

[1]Department of Computer Science and Engineering, Florida Atlantic University, Boca Raton, USA. [2]Department of Information Systems and Technologies GSyA Research Group, University of Castilla-La Mancha, Ciudad Real, Spain.

References

1. Gartner Inc Gartner identifies the Top 10 strategic technologies for 2011. Online. Available: http://www.gartner.com/it/page.jsp?id=1454221. Accessed: 15-Jul-2011
2. Zhao G, Liu J, Tang Y, Sun W, Zhang F, Ye X, Tang N (2009) Cloud Computing: A Statistics Aspect of Users. In: First International Conference on Cloud Computing (CloudCom), Beijing, China. Springer Berlin, Heidelberg, pp 347–358
3. Zhang S, Zhang S, Chen X, Huo X (2010) Cloud Computing Research and Development Trend. In: Second International Conference on Future Networks (ICFN'10), Sanya, Hainan, China. IEEE Computer Society, Washington, DC, USA, pp 93–97
4. Cloud Security Alliance (2011) Security guidance for critical areas of focus in Cloud Computing V3.0.. Available: https://cloudsecurityalliance.org/guidance/csaguide.v3.0.pdf
5. Marinos A, Briscoe G (2009) Community Cloud Computing. In: *1st International Conference on Cloud Computing (CloudCom)*, Beijing, China. Springer-Verlag Berlin, Heidelberg
6. Centre for the Protection of National Infrastructure (2010) Information Security Briefing 01/2010 Cloud Computing. Available: http://www.cpni.gov.uk/Documents/Publications/2010/2010007-ISB_cloud_computing.pdf
7. Khalid A (2010) Cloud Computing: applying issues in Small Business. In: International Conference on Signal Acquisition and Processing (ICSAP'10), pp 278–281
8. KPMG (2010) From hype to future: KPMG's 2010 Cloud Computing survey.. Available: http://www.techrepublic.com/whitepapers/from-hype-to-future-kpmgs-2010-cloud-computing-survey/2384291

9. Rosado DG, Gómez R, Mellado D, Fernández-Medina E (2012) Security analysis in the migration to cloud environments. Future Internet 4(2):469–487
10. Mather T, Kumaraswamy S, Latif S (2009) Cloud Security and Privacy. O'Reilly Media, Inc., Sebastopol, CA
11. Li W, Ping L (2009) Trust model to enhance Security and interoperability of Cloud environment. In: Proceedings of the 1st International conference on Cloud Computing. Springer Berlin Heidelberg, Beijing, China, pp 69–79
12. Rittinghouse JW, Ransome JF (2009) Security in the Cloud. In: Cloud Computing. Implementation, Management, and Security, CRC Press
13. Kitchenham B (2004) Procedures for performing systematic review, software engineering group. Department of Computer Scinece Keele University, United Kingdom and Empirical Software Engineering, National ICT Australia Ltd, Australia. TR/SE-0401
14. Kitchenham B, Charters S (2007) Guidelines for performing systematic literature reviews in software engineering. Version 2.3 University of keele (software engineering group, school of computer science and mathematics) and Durham. Department of Computer Science, UK
15. Brereton P, Kitchenham BA, Budgen D, Turner M, Khalil M (2007) Lessons from applying the systematic literature review process within the software engineering domain. J Syst Softw 80(4):571–583
16. Cloud Security Alliance (2010) Top Threats to Cloud Computing V1.0. Available: https://cloudsecurityalliance.org/research/top-threats
17. ENISA (2009) Cloud Computing: benefits, risks and recommendations for information Security. Available: http://www.enisa.europa.eu/activities/risk-management/files/deliverables/cloud-computing-risk-assessment
18. Dahbur K, Mohammad B, Tarakji AB (2011) A survey of risks, threats and vulnerabilities in Cloud Computing. In: Proceedings of the 2011 International conference on intelligent semantic Web-services and applications. Amman, Jordan, pp 1–6
19. Ertaul L, Singhal S, Gökay S (2010) Security challenges in Cloud Computing. In: Proceedings of the 2010 International conference on Security and Management SAM'10. CSREA Press, Las Vegas, US, pp 36–42
20. Grobauer B, Walloschek T, Stocker E (2011) Understanding Cloud Computing vulnerabilities. IEEE Security Privacy 9(2):50–57
21. Subashini S, Kavitha V (2011) A survey on Security issues in service delivery models of Cloud Computing. J Netw Comput Appl 34(1):1–11
22. Jensen M, Schwenk J, Gruschka N, Iacono LL (2009) On technical Security issues in Cloud Computing. In: IEEE International conference on Cloud Computing (CLOUD'09). 116, 116, pp 109–116
23. Onwubiko C (2010) Security issues to Cloud Computing. In: Antonopoulos N, Gillam L (ed) Cloud Computing: principles, systems & applications. 2010, Springer-Verlag
24. Morsy MA, Grundy J, Müller I (2010) An analysis of the Cloud Computing Security problem. In: Proceedings of APSEC 2010 Cloud Workshop. APSEC, Sydney, Australia
25. Jansen WA (2011) Cloud Hooks: Security and Privacy Issues in Cloud Computing. In: *Proceedings of the 44th Hawaii International Conference on System Sciences*, Koloa, Kauai, HI. IEEE Computer Society, Washington, DC, USA, pp 1–10
26. Zissis D, Lekkas D (2012) Addressing Cloud Computing Security issues. Futur Gener Comput Syst 28(3):583–592
27. Jansen W, Grance T (2011) Guidelines on Security and privacy in public Cloud Computing. NIST, Special Publication 800–144, Gaithersburg, MD
28. Mell P, Grance T (2011) The NIST definition of Cloud Computing. NIST, Special Publication 800–145, Gaithersburg, MD
29. Zhang Q, Cheng L, Boutaba R (2010) Cloud Computing: state-of-the-art and research challenges. Journal of Internet Services Applications 1(1):7–18
30. Ju J, Wang Y, Fu J, Wu J, Lin Z (2010) Research on Key Technology in SaaS. In: International Conference on Intelligent Computing and Cognitive Informatics (ICICCI), Hangzhou, China. IEEE Computer Society, Washington, DC, USA, pp 384–387
31. Owens D (2010) Securing elasticity in the Cloud. Commun ACM 53(6):46–51
32. OWASP (2010) The Ten most critical Web application Security risks. Available: https://www.owasp.org/index.php/Category: OWASP_Top_Ten_Project
33. Zhang Y, Liu S, Meng X (2009) Towards high level SaaS maturity model: methods and case study. In: Services Computing conference. APSCC, IEEE Asia-Pacific, pp 273–278
34. Chong F, Carraro G, Wolter R (2006) Multi-tenant data architecture. Online. Available: http://msdn.microsoft.com/en-us/library/aa479086.aspx. Accessed: 05-Jun-2011

35. Bezemer C-P, Zaidman A (2010) Multi-tenant SaaS applications: maintenance dream or nightmare? In: *Proceedings of the Joint ERCIM Workshop on Software Evolution (EVOL) and International Workshop on Principles of Software Evolution (IWPSE)*, Antwerp, Belgium. ACM New York, NY, USA, pp 88–92

36. Viega J (2009) Cloud Computing and the common Man. Computer 42 (8):106–108

37. Cloud Security Alliance (2012) Security guidance for critical areas of Mobile Computing. Available: https://downloads.cloudsecurityalliance.org/initiatives/mobile/Mobile_Guidance_v1.pdf

38. Keene C (2009) The Keene View on Cloud Computing. Online. Available: http://www.keeneview.com/2009/03/what-is-platform-as-service-paas.html. Accessed: 16-Jul-2011

39. Xu K, Zhang X, Song M, Song J (2009) Mobile Mashup: Architecture, Challenges and Suggestions. In: *International Conference on Management and Service Science. MASS'09*. IEEE Computer Society, Washington, DC, USA, pp 1–4

40. Chandramouli R, Mell P (2010) State of Security readiness. Crossroads 16 (3):23–25

41. Jaeger T, Schiffman J (2010) Outlook: cloudy with a chance of Security challenges and improvements. IEEE Security Privacy 8(1):77–80

42. Dawoud W, Takouna I, Meinel C (2010) Infrastructure as a service security: Challenges and solutions. In: the 7th International Conference on Informatics and Systems (INFOS), Potsdam, Germany. IEEE Computer Society, Washington, DC, USA, pp 1–8

43. Jasti A, Shah P, Nagaraj R, Pendse R (2010) Security in multi-tenancy cloud. In: *IEEE International Carnahan Conference on Security Technology (ICCST)*, KS, USA. IEEE Computer Society, Washington, DC, USA, pp 35–41

44. Garfinkel T, Rosenblum M (2005) When virtual is harder than real: Security challenges in virtual machine based computing environments. In: *Proceedings of the 10th conference on Hot Topics in Operating Systems*, Santa Fe, NM. volume 10. USENIX Association Berkeley, CA, USA, pp 227–229

45. Reuben JS (2007) A survey on virtual machine Security. Seminar on Network Security. http://www.tml.tkk.fi/Publications/C/25/papers/Reuben_final.pdf. Technical report, Helsinki University of Technology, October 2007

46. Hashizume K, Yoshioka N, Fernandez EB (2013) Three misuse patterns for Cloud Computing. In: Rosado DG, Mellado D, Fernandez-Medina E, Piattini M (ed) Security engineering for Cloud Computing: approaches and Tools. IGI Global, Pennsylvania, United States, pp 36–53

47. Venkatesha S, Sadhu S, Kintali S (2009) Survey of virtual machine migration techniques., Technical report, Dept. of Computer Science, University of California, Santa Barbara. http://www.academia.edu/760613/Survey_of_Virtual_Machine_Migration_Techniques

48. Ranjith P, Chandran P, Kaleeswaran S (2012) On covert channels between virtual machines. Journal in Computer Virology Springer 8:85–97

49. Wei J, Zhang X, Ammons G, Bala V, Ning P (2009) Managing Security of virtual machine images in a Cloud environment. In: Proceedings of the 2009 ACM workshop on Cloud Computing Security. ACM New York, NY, USA, pp 91–96

50. Owens K Securing virtual compute infrastructure in the Cloud. SAVVIS. Available: http://www.savvis.com/en-us/info_center/documents/hos-whitepaper-securingvirutalcomputeinfrastructureinthecloud.pdf

51. Wu H, Ding Y, Winer C, Yao L (2010) Network Security for virtual machine in Cloud Computing. In: 5th International conference on computer sciences and convergence information technology (ICCIT). IEEE Computer Society Washington, DC, USA, pp 18–21

52. Xiaopeng G, Sumei W, Xianqin C (2010) VNSS: a Network Security sandbox for virtual Computing environment. In: IEEE youth conference on information Computing and telecommunications (YC-ICT). IEEE Computer Society, Washington DC, USA, pp 395–398

53. Popovic K, Hocenski Z (2010) Cloud Computing Security issues and challenges. In: Proceedings of the 33rd International convention MIPRO. IEEE Computer Society Washington DC, USA, pp 344–349

54. Carlin S, Curran K (2011) Cloud Computing Security. International Journal of Ambient Computing and Intelligence 3(1):38–46

55. Bisong A, Rahman S (2011) An overview of the Security concerns in Enterprise Cloud Computing. International Journal of Network Security & Its Applications (IJNSA) 3(1):30–45

56. Townsend M (2009) Managing a security program in a cloud computing environment. In: Information Security Curriculum Development Conference, Kennesaw, Georgia. ACM New York, NY, USA, pp 128–133

57. Winkler V (2011) Securing the Cloud: Cloud computer Security techniques and tactics. Elsevier Inc, Waltham, MA

58. Ristenpart T, Tromer E, Shacham H, Savage S (2009) Hey, you, get off of my cloud: exploring information leakage in third-party compute clouds. In: Proceedings of the 16th ACM conference on Computer and communications security, Chicago, Illinois, USA. ACM New York, NY, USA, pp 199–212

59. Zhang Y, Juels A, Reiter MK, Ristenpart T (2012) Cross-VM side channels and their use to extract private keys. In: *Proceedings of the 2012 ACM conference on Computer and communications security*, New York, NY, USA. ACM New York, NY, USA, pp 305–316

60. Wang Z, Jiang X (2010) HyperSafe: a lightweight approach to provide lifetime hypervisor control-flow integrity. In: Proceedings of the IEEE symposium on Security and privacy. IEEE Computer Society, Washington, DC, USA, pp 380–395

61. Wang C, Wang Q, Ren K, Lou W (2009) Ensuring data Storage Security in Cloud Computing. In: The 17th International workshop on quality of service. IEEE Computer Society, Washington, DC, USA, pp 1–9

62. Fernandez EB, Yoshioka N, Washizaki H (2009) Modeling Misuse Patterns. In: *Proceedings of the 4th Int. Workshop on Dependability Aspects of Data Warehousing and Mining Applications (DAWAM 2009), in conjunction with the 4th Int.Conf. on Availability, Reliability, and Security (ARES 2009)*, Fukuoka, Japan. IEEE Computer Society, Washington, DC, USA, pp 566–571

63. Santos N, Gummadi KP, Rodrigues R (2009) Towards Trusted Cloud Computing. In: *Proceedings of the 2009 conference on Hot topics in cloud computing*, San Diego, California. USENIX Association Berkeley, CA, USA

64. Zhang F, Huang Y, Wang H, Chen H, Zang B (2008) PALM: Security Preserving VM Live Migration for Systems with VMM-enforced Protection. In: Trusted Infrastructure Technologies Conference, 2008. APTC'08, Third Asia-Pacific. IEEE Computer Society, Washington, DC, USA, pp 9–18

65. Cloud Security Alliance (2012) SecaaS implementation guidance, category 1: identity and Access managament. Available: https://downloads.cloudsecurityalliance.org/initiatives/secaas/SecaaS_Cat_1_IAM_Implementation_Guidance.pdf

66. Xiao S, Gong W (2010) Mobility Can help: protect user identity with dynamic credential. In: Eleventh International conference on Mobile data Management (MDM). IEEE Computer Society, Washington, DC, USA, pp 378–380

67. Wylie J, Bakkaloglu M, Pandurangan V, Bigrigg M, Oguz S, Tew K, Williams C, Ganger G, Khosla P (2001) Selecting the right data distribution scheme for a survivable Storage system. CMU-CS-01-120, Pittsburgh, PA

68. Somani U, Lakhani K, Mundra M (2010) Implementing digital signature with RSA encryption algorithm to enhance the data Security of Cloud in Cloud Computing. In: 1st International conference on parallel distributed and grid Computing (PDGC). IEEE Computer Society Washington, DC, USA, pp 211–216

69. Harnik D, Pinkas B, Shulman-Peleg A (2010) Side channels in Cloud services: deduplication in Cloud Storage. IEEE Security Privacy 8(6):40–47

70. Tebaa M, El Hajji S, El Ghazi A (2012) Homomorphic encryption method applied to Cloud Computing. In: *National Days of Network Security and Systems (JNS2)*. IEEE Computer Society, Washington, DC, USA, pp 86–89

71. Fong E, Okun V (2007) Web application scanners: definitions and functions. In: Proceedings of the 40th annual Hawaii International conference on system sciences. IEEE Computer Society, Washington, DC, USA

72. Goodin D (2009) Webhost hack wipes out data for 100,000 sites. *The Register*, 08-Jun-2009. [Online]. Available: http://www.theregister.co.uk/2009/06/08/webhost_attack/. Accessed: 02-Aug-2011

73. Berger S, Cáceres R, Pendarakis D, Sailer R, Valdez E, Perez R, Schildhauer W, Srinivasan D (2008) TVDc: managing Security in the trusted virtual datacenter. SIGOPS Oper. Syst. Rev. 42(1):40–47

74. Berger S, Cáceres R, Goldman K, Pendarakis D, Perez R, Rao JR, Rom E, Sailer R, Schildhauer W, Srinivasan D, Tal S, Valdez E (2009) Security for the Cloud infrastructure: trusted virtual data center implementation. IBM J Res Dev 53 (4):560–571

75. Ormandy T (2007) An empirical study into the Security exposure to hosts of hostile virtualized environments. In: CanSecWest applied Security conference., Vancouver. http://taviso.decsystem.org/virtsec.pdf

76. Oberheide J, Cooke E, Jahanian F (2008) Empirical exploitation of Live virtual machine migration. In: Proceedings of Black Hat Security Conference, Washington, DC. http://www.eecs.umich.edu/fjgroup/pubs/blackhat08-migration.pdf

77. Naehrig M, Lauter K, Vaikuntanathan V (2011) Can homomorphic encryption be practical? In: Proceedings of the 3rd ACM workshop on Cloud Computing Security workshop. ACM New York, NY, USA, pp 113–124

78. Han-zhang W, Liu-sheng H (2010) An improved trusted cloud computing platform model based on DAA and privacy CA scheme. In: International Conference on Computer Application and System Modeling (ICCASM), vol. 13, V13–39. IEEE Computer, Society, Washington, DC, USA, pp V13–33

79. Fernandez EB, Ajaj O, Buckley I, Delessy-Gassant N, Hashizume K, Larrondo-Petrie MM (2012) A survey of patterns for Web services Security and reliability standards. Future Internet 4(2):430–450

Permissions

The contributors of this book come from diverse backgrounds, making this book a truly international effort. This book will bring forth new frontiers with its revolutionizing research information and detailed analysis of the nascent developments around the world.

We would like to thank all the contributing authors for lending their expertise to make the book truly unique. They have played a crucial role in the development of this book. Without their invaluable contributions this book wouldn't have been possible. They have made vital efforts to compile up to date information on the varied aspects of this subject to make this book a valuable addition to the collection of many professionals and students.

This book was conceptualized with the vision of imparting up-to-date information and advanced data in this field. To ensure the same, a matchless editorial board was set up. Every individual on the board went through rigorous rounds of assessment to prove their worth. After which they invested a large part of their time researching and compiling the most relevant data for our readers.

The editorial board has been involved in producing this book since its inception. They have spent rigorous hours researching and exploring the diverse topics which have resulted in the successful publishing of this book. They have passed on their knowledge of decades through this book. To expedite this challenging task, the publisher supported the team at every step. A small team of assistant editors was also appointed to further simplify the editing procedure and attain best results for the readers.

Apart from the editorial board, the designing team has also invested a significant amount of their time in understanding the subject and creating the most relevant covers. They scrutinized every image to scout for the most suitable representation of the subject and create an appropriate cover for the book.

The publishing team has been an ardent support to the editorial, designing and production team. Their endless efforts to recruit the best for this project, has resulted in the accomplishment of this book. They are a veteran in the field of academics and their pool of knowledge is as vast as their experience in printing. Their expertise and guidance has proved useful at every step. Their uncompromising quality standards have made this book an exceptional effort. Their encouragement from time to time has been an inspiration for everyone.

The publisher and the editorial board hope that this book will prove to be a valuable piece of knowledge for researchers, students, practitioners and scholars across the globe.

List of Contributors

Meirong Liu
Media Team Oulu research group, Department of Computer Science and Engineering, University of Oulu, Oulu, Finland

Erkki Harjula
Media Team Oulu research group, Department of Computer Science and Engineering, University of Oulu, Oulu, Finland

Mika Ylianttila
Media Team Oulu research group, Department of Computer Science and Engineering, University of Oulu, Oulu, Finland

Milad Daivandy
Julich Supercomputing Centre, Forschungszentrum Jülich, 52428 Julich, Germany

Denis Hünich
Center for Information Services and High Performance Computing (ZIH), 01062 Dresden, Germany

René Jäkel
Center for Information Services and High Performance Computing (ZIH), 01062 Dresden, Germany

Steffen Metzger
Max-Planck-Institut for Informatics, 66123 Saarbrücken, Germany

RalphMüller-Pfefferkorn
Center for Information Services and High Performance Computing (ZIH), 01062 Dresden, Germany

Bernd Schuller
Julich Supercomputing Centre, Forschungszentrum Jülich, 52428 Julich, Germany

Paul Rabinovich
Security Software Development, Exostar, Herndon, USA

Kleber Stroeh
Icaro Technologies, Campinas, SP, Brazil

Edmundo Roberto Mauro Madeira
IC - Institute of Computing UNICAMP, University of Campinas, Campinas, SP, Brazil

Siome Klein Goldenstein
IC - Institute of Computing UNICAMP, University of Campinas, Campinas, SP, Brazil

Yongning Tang
School of Information Technology, Illinois State University, Normal, IL 61790, USA

Guang Cheng
School of Computer Science and Engineering, Southeast University, Nanjing, P.R. China
National Computer Network Key Laboratory, Southeast University, Nanjing, P.R. China

James T Yu
School of Computing, DePaul University, Chicago, IL 60604, USA

Bin Zhang
School of Computing, DePaul University, Chicago, IL 60604, USA

Fernando Costa
Distributed Systems Group, INESC-ID, Universidade de Lisboa, R. Alves Redol, 9, 1000-029 Lisboa, Portugal

Luís Veiga
Distributed Systems Group, INESC-ID, Universidade de Lisboa, R. Alves Redol, 9, 1000-029 Lisboa, Portugal

Paulo Ferreira
Distributed Systems Group, INESC-ID, Universidade de Lisboa, R. Alves Redol, 9, 1000-029 Lisboa, Portugal

Malik Loudini
Ecole Nationale Supérieure d'Informatique (ESI), Laboratoire de Communication dans les Systèmes Informatiques (LCSI), B.P 68M, 16270 Oued Smar, El Harrach, Algiers, Algeria

Sawsen Rezig
Ecole Nationale Supérieure d'Informatique (ESI), Laboratoire de Communication dans les Systèmes Informatiques (LCSI), B.P 68M, 16270 Oued Smar, El Harrach, Algiers, Algeria

Yahia Salhi
Ecole Nationale Supérieure d'Informatique (ESI), Laboratoire de Communication dans les Systèmes Informatiques (LCSI), B.P 68M, 16270 Oued Smar, El Harrach, Algiers, Algeria

Vincent Wing-Hei Luk
Department of Electronic and Computer Engineering, Hong Kong University of Science and Technology, Hong Kong, Hong Kong

Albert Kai-Sun Wong
Department of Electronic and Computer Engineering, Hong Kong University of Science and Technology, Hong Kong, Hong Kong

Chin-Tau Lea
Department of Electronic and Computer Engineering, Hong Kong University of Science and Technology, Hong Kong, Hong Kong

Robin Wentao Ouyang
Department of Electronic and Computer Engineering, Hong Kong University of Science and Technology, Hong Kong, Hong Kong

Alexandru Tatar
LIP6/CNRS – UPMC Sorbonne Universités, 4 Place Jussieu, 75005 Paris, France

Marcelo Dias de Amorim
LIP6/CNRS – UPMC Sorbonne Universités, 4 Place Jussieu, 75005 Paris, France

Serge Fdida
LIP6/CNRS – UPMC Sorbonne Universités, 4 Place Jussieu, 75005 Paris, France

Panayotis Antoniadis
Communication System Group – ETH Zurich, 35 Gloriastrasse, 8092 Zurich, Switzerland

Yanik Ngoko
Laboratoire d'Informatique de Paris Nord, Villetaneuse, France

Alfredo Goldman
IME-USP, São Paulo, Brasil

Dejan Milojicic
HP Labs, Palo Alto, USA

Christian Senk
University of Regensburg, Regensburg, Germany

Nikos Fotiou
Mobile Multimedia Laboratory, Department of Informatics, School of Information Sciences and Technology, Athens University of Economics and Business, Evelpidon 47A, 113 62 Athens, Greece

Apostolis Machas
Mobile Multimedia Laboratory, Department of Informatics, School of Information Sciences and Technology, Athens University of Economics and Business, Evelpidon 47A, 113 62 Athens, Greece

George C Polyzos
Mobile Multimedia Laboratory, Department of Informatics, School of Information Sciences and Technology, Athens University of Economics and Business, Evelpidon 47A, 113 62 Athens, Greece

George Xylomenos
Mobile Multimedia Laboratory, Department of Informatics, School of Information Sciences and Technology, Athens University of Economics and Business, Evelpidon 47A, 113 62 Athens, Greece

André Pessoa Negrão
Instituto Superior Técnico, Universidade de Lisboa, Rua Alves Redol 9, Lisboa, Portugal
Distributed Systems Group, INESC-ID, Rua Alves Redol 9, Lisboa, Portugal

Carlos Roque
Instituto Superior Técnico, Universidade de Lisboa, Rua Alves Redol 9, Lisboa, Portugal
Distributed Systems Group, INESC-ID, Rua Alves Redol 9, Lisboa, Portugal

Paulo Ferreira
Instituto Superior Técnico, Universidade de Lisboa, Rua Alves Redol 9, Lisboa, Portugal
Distributed Systems Group, INESC-ID, Rua Alves Redol 9, Lisboa, Portugal

Luís Veiga
Instituto Superior Técnico, Universidade de Lisboa, Rua Alves Redol 9, Lisboa, Portugal
Distributed Systems Group, INESC-ID, Rua Alves Redol 9, Lisboa, Portugal

Anna Chmielowiec
Department of Computer Sciences and The Network Institute, VU University, De Boelelaan 1081A, 1081HV Amsterdam, The Netherlands

Spyros Voulgaris
Department of Computer Sciences and The Network Institute, VU University, De Boelelaan 1081A, 1081HV Amsterdam, The Netherlands

Maarten van Steen
Department of Computer Sciences and The Network Institute, VU University, De Boelelaan 1081A, 1081HV Amsterdam, The Netherlands

Norbert Seyff
University of Applied Sciences and Arts Northwestern Switzerland, Bahnhofstrasse 6, Windisch, Switzerland
University of Zurich, Binzmühlestrasse 14, Zurich, Switzerland

Irina Todoran
University of Zurich, Binzmühlestrasse 14, Zurich, Switzerland

Kevin Caluser
University of Zurich, Binzmühlestrasse 14, Zurich, Switzerland

Leif Singer
University of Victoria, 3800 Finnerty Rd, Victoria, Canada

Martin Glinz
University of Zurich, Binzmühlestrasse 14, Zurich, Switzerland

Keiko Hashizume
Department of Computer Science and Engineering, Florida Atlantic University, Boca Raton, USA

David G Rosado
Department of Information Systems and Technologies GSyA Research Group, University of Castilla-La Mancha, Ciudad Real, Spain

Eduardo Fernández-Medina
Department of Information Systems and Technologies GSyA Research Group, University of Castilla-La Mancha, Ciudad Real, Spain

Eduardo B Fernandez
Department of Computer Science and Engineering, Florida Atlantic University, Boca Raton, USA

Printed in the USA
CPSIA information can be obtained
at www.ICGtesting.com
JSHW051431221024
72173JS00006B/1431

9 781682 851876